The Republic
of Letters

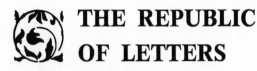 # THE REPUBLIC
OF LETTERS

A History of Postwar American Literary Opinion

Grant Webster

THE JOHNS HOPKINS UNIVERSITY
PRESS   BALTIMORE AND LONDON

This book has been brought to publication with the generous assistance of the Andrew W. Mellon Foundation and the State University of New York at Binghamton.

The section entitled "T. S. Eliot as Critic: The Man behind the Masks" is reprinted from *Criticism* 8, no. 4 (1966): 336–48, by permission of the Wayne State University Press. The section entitled "Allen Tate: The Conservative Critic" is reprinted from *South Atlantic Quarterly* 66 (1967): 591–605, copyright 1967 by Duke University Press.

The Johns Hopkins University Press, Baltimore, Maryland 21218
The Johns Hopkins University Press Ltd., London
Library of Congress Catalog Card Number 79-4951
ISBN 0-8018-2175-4

Library of Congress Cataloging in Publication data will be found on the last printed page of this book.

For Mary

Contents

Preface

This book originated in a quirk of academic fate when, in 1963, as a new Ph.D. specializing in eighteenth-century literature, I was given the choice of teaching either literary criticism or the history of the English language as my first advanced course. I chose criticism, and perforce began to try to figure out for myself the rules of the discipline. Several characteristics of the world of criticism required explanation. First, various views of literature and schools of critics seemed to be mutually exclusive; at least, adherents of a given view mentioned other critics, if at all, only with condemnation, and no real debate between views ever occurred. Second, despite some professions to the contrary, critics' views of literature were not objective or derived from the literature itself, but seemed to reflect values or ideologies brought to literature from life. As I continued my study and teaching of criticism, a third salient fact appeared: that the critical scene is one where new ideas and prophets appear and disappear with bewildering rapidity; where the academic half-life of an idea is a couple of years; where each generation, each year, brings new, previously unknown prophets who are touted as major intellectual forces.

The discipline of the history of criticism seemed to lack the intellectual capacity to even recognize, much less confront and make sense of, these facts. Its classic text is the Edwardian connoisseur George Saintsbury's *History of Modern Criticism*, and its only subsequent resource has been the reduction of all critical schools to Formalism by such "New Critics" as W. K. Wimsatt and Cleanth Brooks in their *Literary Criticism: A Short History* and René Wellek in his *History of Modern Criticism*; or the reduction of literary study to other disciplines like psychoanalysis, myth, or Marxism by such historians as Stanley Edgar Hyman in *The Armed Vision*.

My search for an idea that would meaningfully organize the facts of the critical scene led to a decade of groping through various disciplines. I began by studying the psychology and biography of critics, as well as the "prosopography" or collective biography of critical schools, with the aim of seeing criticism in terms consistent with the personal history of each critic. The quest for a method to analyze disparate critical positions led me through intellectual history to the history and sociology of science, and finally to Thomas S. Kuhn's *The Structure of Scientific Revolutions*, which asked a sensible sequence of questions about the relationships and rise and fall of intellectual paradigms and movements. From this model one gets not the objective truth, the final answer to questions about criticism, but a way of coping with and organizing historical changes in criticism.

Though this is a relativistic position, it is what one might call an agnostic rather than an atheistic relativism. I do not deny the possibility of finding the true values of literature and criticism around which all might unite, but I do deny that any such values have been found, and in any case I prefer to concentrate on questions about the historical value and influence of critics which can be answered factually. As one of John Barth's characters says at the end of *The Floating Opera*:

> I now all at once found myself confronted with a new and unsuspected world. This . . . was the essence of it: if there are no absolutes, then a value is no less authentic, no less genuine, no less compelling, no less "real" for its being relative! It is one thing to say "Values are *only* relative"; quite another, and more thrilling, to remove the pejorative adverb and assert "There *are* relative values!" These, at least, we have, and if they are all we have, then *in no way whatsoever* are they inferior. A corner for you, there! But God, this needed thinking about!

My judgments about the merits of various literary ideologies or paradigms, which I call "charters," are therefore historical ones, based on an estimate of the originality and influence of the charter, and my judgments of individual critics are made in relation to a particular charter, as they exemplify or go beyond it. In analyzing critics, I have followed Dr. Johnson's opinion, expressed in *Rambler* #93, that "he that writes may be considered as a kind of general challenger, whom every one has a right to attack; since he quits the common rank of life, steps forward beyond the lists, and offers his merit to the public judgment. To commence author is to claim praise, and no man can justly aspire to honour, but at the hazard of disgrace." Though I write about critics living or recently deceased, my observations are a response to prose, not personalities; I have heard many of these critics lecture and have lunched with one or two, but I belong to none of the groups I discuss, and therefore hope to avoid both special pleading and insider gossip.

In this volume I discuss the charters of the Formalists and New York Intellectuals, the dominant critical schools of the forties and fifties. In a later volume I will continue the history by examining the charters of such critical schools as psychological and myth criticism, Structuralism and hermeneutics, the American Studies movement, and the counterculture of the sixties. The scope of the present volume is confined to American criticism; although some mention of English critics like William Empson and I. A. Richards is inevitable, I discuss British and Continental critics only peripherally because I find them informed by cultural values very different from our own, and because their influence on American criticism in this period is not great. I omit all comment on criticism of the drama and film, for it is based on performances that are no longer generally available.

If successful, the view of a new historical science of criticism presented here will generate other detailed studies of the relationship of literary schools, institutions, ideas, and critics to literary charters, and this new science will replace the currently dominant theories of the history of criticism. Only an extended demonstration of how the world of criticism can be seen in a new way is capable of overturning established academic views, of causing a revolution in the history of criticism. I hope that the ideas expressed in this book will cause such a revolution.

Acknowledgments

This seems to me the place to acknowledge the educational debts of a lifetime, the greatest of which is to my parents, Grant C. and Mabel T. Webster, for the care and attention they devoted to bringing me up. I am also grateful to Carleton College, where I received a true liberal arts education, and to the English Department of The Ohio State University for my training as a scholar, particularly to my adviser there, Andrew H. Wright. A number of my colleagues at the State University of New York at Binghamton have read sections of the manuscript in draft; I wish to thank them all, particularly my chairman, Bernard Rosenthal, whose intellectual and administrative support aided me in completing the book, and my friend Philip Rogers, who read and commented on the entire manuscript. I am also indebted to the SUNY Research Foundation for two summer fellowships. I am dedicating the book to my wife, who has had very little to do with the book itself but has been central to my life while I was writing it.

Abbreviations and a Select Bibliography

AC	*Anatomy of Criticism*, Northrop Frye (Princeton: Princeton University Press, 1957)
AG	*The Theory of the Avant-Garde*, Renato Poggioli (Cambridge: Harvard University Press, 1968)
ASG	*After Strange Gods*, T. S. Eliot (London: Faber & Faber, 1934)
AV	*The Armed Vision*, Stanley Edgar Hyman (New York: Vintage Books, 1955)
Ax	*Axel's Castle*, Edmund Wilson (New York: Scribner's, 1931)
BC	*Beyond Culture*, Lionel Trilling (New York: Viking Press, 1965)
BT	*The Bit Between My Teeth*, Edmund Wilson (New York: Farrar, 1965)
C	*Contemporaries*, Alfred Kazin (Boston: Little, Brown, 1962)
CC	*Concepts of Criticism*, René Wellek (New Haven: Yale University Press, 1963)
CCo	*Classics and Commercials*, Edmund Wilson (New York: Farrar, 1950)
C&C	*Critics and Criticism*, ed. R. S. Crane (Chicago: University of Chicago Press, 1952)
CE	*Collected Essays*, Allen Tate (Denver: Swallow Press, 1959)
CV	*The Classic Vision*, Murray Krieger (Baltimore: Johns Hopkins Press, 1971)
D	*Discriminations*, René Wellek (New Haven: Yale University Press, 1970)
DN	*Decline of the New*, Irving Howe (New York: Harcourt, 1970)
DR	*In Defense of Reason*, Yvor Winters, 3rd ed. (Denver: Swallow Press, 1947)
DU	*Doings and Undoings*, Norman Podhoretz (New York: Farrar, 1964)
EE	*Eleven Essays in the European Novel*, R. P. Blackmur (New York: Harbinger Books, 1964)
FC	*The Function of Criticism*, Yvor Winters (Denver: Swallow Press, 1957)
FD	*Forms of Discovery*, Yvor Winters (Chicago: Swallow Press, 1967)
FV	*Form and Value in Modern Poetry*, R. P. Blackmur (Garden City, N.Y.: Anchor Books, 1957)
GF	*A Gathering of Fugitives*, Lionel Trilling (Boston: Beacon Press, 1956)
HC	*A History of Modern Criticism*, René Wellek, 4 vols. to date (New Haven: Yale University Press, 1955–)

HCo   *Hateful Contraries*, W. K. Wimsatt (Lexington: University of Kentucky Press, 1966)

HR   *Hudson Review*

II   *Image and Idea*, Philip Rahv, rev. ed. (orig. pub. 1947; New York: New Directions, 1957)

KR   *Kenyon Review*

LC   *Literary Criticism: A Short History*, W. K. Wimsatt and Cleanth Brooks (New York: Knopf, 1957)

Letters   *Letters on Literature and Politics, 1912–1972*, Edmund Wilson (New York: Farrar, 1977)

LH   *The Lion and the Honeycomb*, R. P. Blackmur (New York: Harcourt, 1955)

LI   *The Liberal Imagination*, Lionel Trilling (orig. pub. 1950; Garden City, N.Y.: Anchor Books, 1957)

MI   *Making It*, Norman Podhoretz (New York: Bantam Books, 1969)

MP   *The Myth and the Powerhouse*, Philip Rahv (New York: Farrar, 1965)

MPT   *Modern Poetry and the Tradition*, Cleanth Brooks (Chapel Hill: University of North Carolina Press, 1939)

NAP   *The New Apologists for Poetry*, Murray Krieger (Minneapolis: University of Minnesota Press, 1956)

NC   *The New Criticism*, John Crowe Ransom (Norfolk, Conn.: New Directions, 1941)

NCUS   *New Criticism in the United States*, R. P. Blackmur (Tokyo: Kenkyusha, 1959)

NYR   *New York Review of Books*

NYTBR   *New York Times Book Review*

ONG   *On Native Grounds*, Alfred Kazin (New York: Harcourt, 1942)

OPP   *On Poetry and Poets*, T. S. Eliot (New York: Farrar, 1957)

OS   *The Opposing Self*, Lionel Trilling (New York: Viking Press, 1955)

PG   *Patriotic Gore*, Edmund Wilson (New York: Oxford University Press, 1962)

PI   *A Primer of Ignorance*, R. P. Blackmur (New York: Harcourt, 1967)

PM   *A Piece of My Mind*, Edmund Wilson (Garden City, N.Y.: Anchor Books, 1958)

PP   *The Play and Place of Criticism*, Murray Krieger (Baltimore: Johns Hopkins Press, 1967)

PR   *Partisan Review*

SE   *Selected Essays*, T. S. Eliot (New York: Harcourt, 1950)

SL   *The Shores of Light*, Edmund Wilson (New York: Farrar, 1952)

SO   *Starting Out in the Thirties*, Alfred Kazin (Boston: Little, Brown, 1965)

SoR   *Southern Review*

SR   *Sewanee Review*

SSR   *The Structure of Scientific Revolutions*, Thomas S. Kuhn, 2nd ed. enl. (Chicago: University of Chicago Press, 1970)

SWood   *The Sacred Wood*, T. S. Eliot, 7th ed. (orig. pub. 1920; London: Methuen, 1950)

TC   *Theory of Criticism*, Murray Krieger (Baltimore: Johns Hopkins University Press, 1976)

TCC   *To Criticize the Critic*, T. S. Eliot (New York: Farrar, 1965)

TL   *Theory of Literature*, René Wellek and Austin Warren, 3rd ed. (New York: Harvest Books, 1962)

TN   *The Tradition of the New*, Harold Rosenberg (New York: Grove Press, 1961)

TT   *The Triple Thinkers*, Edmund Wilson, rev. ed. (orig. pub. 1938; New York: Galaxy Books, 1963)

TV   *The Tragic Vision*, Murray Krieger (New York: Holt, 1960)

UP   *The Use of Poetry and the Use of Criticism*, T. S. Eliot (London: Faber & Faber, 1933)

VI   *The Verbal Icon*, W. K. Wimsatt (Lexington: University of Kentucky Press, 1954)

YIT   "Young in the Thirties," Lionel Trilling, *Commentary*, May 1966, pp. 43–51.

WB   *The World's Body*, John Crowe Ransom (New York: Scribner's, 1938)

WBow *The Wound and the Bow*, Edmund Wilson, rev. ed. (orig. pub. 1941; New York: Galaxy Books, 1965)

WWU *The Well Wrought Urn*, Cleanth Brooks (New York: Harvest Books, 1947)

Part I
The New Science of Criticism:
A Historical Model

1. The Development
of Literary Charters

If one considers the statements of its most eminent practitioners, criticism, and consequently the history of criticism, seems to exist now and perpetually in a state of warring sects. René Wellek, the dean of historians of criticism, says that "today the New Criticism is considered not only superseded, obsolete, and dead but somehow mistaken and wrong" because it is a "revival of art for art's sake," unhistorical, scientific, and "a mere pedagogical device"; in Wellek's view "all these accusations are baseless."[1] In contrast Geoffrey Hartman asserts that we are, at this very moment, in the midst of the most significant critical revolution since the Renaissance: "The humanists of the sixteenth and seventeenth centuries created the institutions of criticism as we know it: the recovery and analysis of works of art. ... We are now nearing the end of this Renaissance humanism. ... The notion of unique works of art, certified by the personal name of the author, or located only in their place or origin ... fades away into nostalgia." Criticism now should be creative, hermeneutic, willful; "Writing is a labyrinth, a topological puzzle and textual crossword; the reader, for his part, must lose himself for a while in a hermeneutic 'infinitizing' that makes all rules of closure appear arbitrary."[2] Jonathan Culler, in much the same vein, says: "The lesson of contemporary European criticism, in its most vital moments, is this: that the New Criticism's dream of a fresh and unprejudiced approach to each autonomous artifact is not only impossible but fundamentally misconceived, even as an ideal. To read a work as literature is inevitably and necessarily to read it in relation to other texts, past and present. ... It is a tenuous intertextual construct, and the critical task is to disperse it, to move through it toward an understanding of the systems and semiotic processes which make it possible."[3] When one pauses to ask how these contradictory statements, and the many that have gone before and will follow after, can be reconciled, and to reflect that these fashions will become obsolete as have so many others in the history of criticism, it becomes apparent that what is needed is not more new arguments and prophecies, but a theory of critical history which will enable the reader to organize the inevitable changes in schools and theories of criticism within an intellectual framework, and hence give him the power to master not only the changes in criticism but his own relation to them as he changes his own literary values. We need, in short, a model of critical history which will account for the rise, flourishing, and fall of various schools of criticism, for it is only as we can see criticism as part of a historical process, as a manifestation of the culture and language of which it is a part, and of the personal and social values of the men who express it, that we can understand the values of various critical schools and the literary traditions they create and support.

Such a model can be found in the approach to intellectual history currently employed to understand the rise and fall of ideas in the history of science, particularly in the work of Thomas S. Kuhn, whose *The Structure of Scientific Revolutions* [4] has generated wide discussion in both scientific and humanistic disciplines. [5] In broadening the meaning of science from that of the positivist, who defines knowledge narrowly by laboratory methods and possesses exact and certain knowledge, to that of the historian, who systematically observes the rise, flourishing, and fall of scientific ideas (or paradigms, as he puts it), Kuhn removes one of the principal whipping boys of literary critics and makes available a new and compelling historical version of science. Kuhn's theory is based on a model of how a paradigm— simplistically, a scientific theory such as Newton's laws—explains a certain area of nature well enough to draw adherents to it, is used as the basis for a kind of normal science occupied with solving the puzzles the paradigm poses, confronts a period of crisis when anomalies of observation crop up that it cannot account for, and is finally replaced in a "critical revolution," when a new theory emerges to explain the relevant phenomena in a new way and causes us to see the world differently, as we did after Einstein replaced Newton.

Kuhn's conception of the development of a paradigm in science seems useful to humanists not as a model to be slavishly followed but as a theory that poses the right sequence of questions about the rise and fall of intellectual ideas and groups. It is the task of the historian of criticism not only to bring out the parallels that will establish Kuhn's view as a useful model for criticism but also to make the necessary changes in terminology, emphasis, and value that will make a description of the literary world as accurate as his description of the scientific one. Kuhn's work becomes, then, both a guide and a foil for the historian of literary criticism.

To adapt Kuhn's sequence of development to literary criticism, one must focus clearly on a single paradigm and avoid the confusions (which will be discussed in detail later) between the point of view of a single scientific speciality and science as a whole. If one looks at criticism in terms of a single critical paradigm, one finds the following stages of development:

Stages in the Development of a Critical Paradigm or Charter

The Ideological Period
    Rise of new writers
    Change in intellectual fashions; importing of new ideas from other disciplines or countries

The Critical Revolution
    Rise of new authority figure; necessity of originality, choice
    Creation of a new "charter"
    Gestalt shift: Redefinition of critical value

Normal Criticism
    Formation of critical communities around critical quarterlies
    Practice of normal criticism
        Rewriting of literary tradition; necessity of influence
        Elaboration of normal theory
        Development of the critical voice
    Making of Critical Careers
        Apprenticeship
        Journeyman: Mastery of genres, productivity, making one's name
        Man of Letters: Recognition, shift to judgment
        Superannuation

Crisis in Criticism
    Lack of definite standard of truth leads to pluralism
    Historical change as cause of crisis
        New writers, new questions, cultural shifts in taste
    Result: A strata of critics

Obsolescence
    Goal of critic to become part of history: Eponymous criticism

The Ideological Period

The first stage in the development of a critical school is essentially precritical in that it involves the choice of values from which criticism later springs. In a discussion of the progress of scientific knowledge, Kuhn says that "the explanation must, in the final analysis, be psychological or sociological. It must, that is, be a description of a value system, an ideology, together with an analysis of the institutions through which that system is transmitted and enforced. Knowing what scientists value, we may hope to understand what problems they will undertake and what choices they will make in particular circumstances of conflict."[6] It is similar knowledge of ideology, in the sense of general value systems, which provides the basic explanation of critics and criticism. As the sociological critic Philip Rahv says:

Criticism appears to be inextricably bound up with issues of value, of belief and ideological conflict; and if we are not deluded by purely theoretical models of criticism but look to its actual practice in the past as in the present, we realize soon enough that the greater part of the criticism of consequence that we know is shot through and through with ideological motives and postulations that remain for the most part unanalyzed and unacknowledged. [*MP* 69]

Seen in retrospect, all past critical judgments seem clearly formed and limited by coeval cultural and intellectual situations and by the personal interests of the critic, and there is no reason to believe that contemporary critics reach an objectivity of understanding denied their ancestors. George Boas points out that

the total culture must influence one's taste. . . . the value of the work of art is not embedded in the work of art itself but is partly contributed to it by the culture in which critics live. . . . The interpretation made by the reader is not a function of a man divorced from the society in which he has grown up. Hence whatever goodness or badness he finds in the work is projected into the work as a function of the psychological organism known as a critic, plus all the principles of good and bad that he has absorbed through his education. . . . Relativistic statements are simply more accurate than absolutistic ones. [7]

Seen in a negative way, ideology equals the limitations of the critical view, but regarded positively such limitations equal the particular values the critical view offers.

Perhaps the most potent "ideology" motivating critics who also happen to be writers of fiction or poetry is the set of literary values implicit in the literature they themselves write. In a 1961 essay T. S. Eliot reflects that "in my earlier criticism, both in my general affirmations about poetry and in writing about authors who had influenced me, I was implicitly defending the sort of poetry that I and my friends wrote. . . . I was in reaction, not only against Georgian poetry, but against Georgian criticism; I was writing in a context which the reader of today has either forgotten, or has never experienced" (*TCC* 16). One may compare the statement by William Carlos Williams: "It is principally about the poem that I have written critically in my life. All the emotion that is involved in the making and defining of a poem is brought out. It shows how much I am involved and how my judgment has been twisted in the defense of what I have wanted to defend."[8] W. K. Wimsatt and Cleanth Brooks observe in *Literary Criticism: A Short History:* "So much literary criticism and theory and so much of the best has been written by the men of letters. Often, whether consciously or not, they have written their general theories as a comment on their own best performances in poetry, and on the *kinds* of poetry which were most dear to them" (*LC* ix).

The manner in which various extraliterary ideologies are metamorphosed into literary criticism and applied to literature varies with each particular school of critics, as do the sources of literary value. Among the most common sources of critical ideologies in the post-World War II period have been terms and values drawn from the contexts of other disciplines and applied to literature. These sources of literary charters are usually referred to as "approaches" to literature or "perspectives" on it, and the most common approaches were first expressed in John Crowe Ranson's *The New Criticism* (1941), where, despite his title, he classifies Richards as a psychological critic, Eliot as a historical critic, and Winters as a logical critic, and titles his last chapter "Wanted: An Ontological [or new] Critic." This formula was extended in precision and influence by Stanley Edgar Hyman in *The Armed Vision* (1948), in which twelve critics are discussed as representatives of possible approaches to criticism on the thesis that "what modern criticism is could be defined crudely and somewhat inaccurately as *the organized use of non-literary techniques and bodies of knowledge to obtain insights into literature*" (*AV* 3). Thus Yvor Winters represents evaluative criticism, Constance Rourke folk criticism, Kenneth Burke the criticism of symbolic action, Caudwell Marxist criticism, and so on. By centering on a single person and showing how he represents a kind of criticism (the past history and current use of each approach is traced explicitly) Hyman takes into account both the individual accomplishment and its representative nature (see *AV* 390).

These various approaches were also considered by Wellek and Warren in *Theory of Literature* under the heading "The Extrinsic Approach," where the relation of literature to biography, psychology, society, ideas, and the other arts is treated fully with the purpose of showing the limitation of these approaches compared with the (to these authors) central study of the work itself (the "intrinsic approach"). In a 1961 essay, Wellek reclassifies the tendencies of modern criticism as Marxist, psychoanalytical, linguistic and stylistic, organistic formalism, mythic, and existentialist, but reaffirms his continuing belief that "formalist, organistic, symbolistic aesthetics ... has a firmer grasp on the nature of poetry and art [than existential or mythic criticism]" (*CC* 363-64).

Roughly the same division of the subject was used by William Van O'Connor in *An Age of Criticism, 1900-1950,*[9] which isolates as principal modern critical movements the New Humanism and social, analytical, psychological, and myth criticism. Walter Sutton's *Modern American Criticism*[10] likewise has chapters on New Criticism, Early (Freudian) Psychological Criticism, Psychological (Jungian) and Myth Criticism, Liberal and Marxist Criticism, as well as the Neo-Aristotelians and the

New Humanists. An academic codification of the various contexts of criticism is found in *Relations of Literary Study: Essays on Interdisciplinary Contributions,* edited by James Thorpe. [11] This pamphlet contains essays by noted critics on "literature and" history, myth, biography, pschology, sociology, religion, and music. The extensive bibliographies found in each section attest to the solidity of each of these divisions of literary study and to their usefulness to many critics and readers. [12]

The most recent ideological trend in American criticism is the attempt to see literature in terms of theories of various continental philosophers, linguists, and anthropologists. J. Hillis Miller announces as early as 1966 that, at least among advanced critics at Yale, "part of the impetus for the next advances in literary study will come from one form or another of European criticism. Assimilating the best recent continental criticism, American scholars may come to develop new forms of criticism growing out of American culture as well as out of the encounter with European thought." [13] Since Miller's assessment, movements such as Structuralism, existential phenomenology, and the criticism of consciousness, and thinkers such as Roland Barthes, Jacques Derrida, Ferdinand de Saussure, and Martin Heidegger, have gained wide currency on the American critical scene, have generated a new group of anthologies, [14] and have influenced such American critics as Geoffrey Hartman, Edward W. Said, and Jonathan Culler, as well as Miller himself. In all these cases, an extracritical standard of value or ideology—a new kind of poetry or fiction, another discipline, the work of a "seminal" thinker—is transmuted into a new critical charter at the point when critics begin seeing literature in its terms.

The general question that arises is why critics choose to emphasize some values over others at different periods in the history of criticism. It will be suggested below that the Formalist charter is essentially a displacement of Tory Protestant views from society onto literature, and that the New York Intellectuals' concern with the avant-garde involves the reenactment of the revolutionary political expectations of their youth in a literary sphere. In even more recent times (which will be investigated in a subsequent volume) larger political, social, racial, and sexual issues have often seemed to influence criticism. For example, the rise of literary interest in Marxism can be traced to the revolutionary politics of the sixties; the character of investigations in comparative literature can be traced to the immigration to America of refugee intellectuals in the thirties; and the social influence of the black studies movement, women's literature, and gay literature is obvious. At this point in the development of the history of criticism, these must all be studied as individual cases; no general law has even been proposed to unite them or to predict what new influences will appear in the decades ahead. However, it is equally clear that matters of critical theory which have almost universally been seen as part of the internal history of an autonomous literary discipline can also fruitfully be seen in the context of their historical causes, the problems the theory is designed to solve, and the values it expresses.

The Critical Revolution

Literary criticism proper begins only with the statement of a paradigm that organizes the critic's view of literature according to its values. As Kuhn says, "Nature is vastly too complex to be explored even approximately at random. Something must tell the scientist where to look and what to look for, and that something, though it may not last beyond his generation, is the paradigm with which his education as a scientist has supplied him." [15] A paradigm is a conception that mediates between the observer and what he observes, or, more accurately, the informing conceptions of the observer that determine what he chooses to observe and the nature of what he observes.

A shift of Kuhn's terminology to the vocabulary of law seems appropriate to make it more closely applicable to the world of literary criticism. This modification is necessary because Kuhn has appropriated the most useful terms from the history of grammar—paradigm and exemplar—and made them his own in a way that is now both irrevocable and confusing; Margaret Masterman, for example, isolates twenty-one senses in which Kuhn uses the word *paradigm*. [16] Moreover, one of Kuhn's own definitions of *paradigm* shifts his context from that of grammar to that of law. He says, after conjugating a Latin verb, "In this standard application, the paradigm functions by permitting the replication of examples any one of which could in principle serve to replace it. In a science, on the other hand, a paradigm is rarely an object for replication. Instead, like an accepted judicial decision in the common law, it is an object for further articulation and specification under new or more stringent conditions" (*SSR* 23). David A. Hollinger develops the legal comparison historically, suggesting that Oliver Wendell Holmes, Jr.'s "belief that the law was made by judges, that its life was 'experience' instead of logic, that there was no 'natural law' waiting to be discovered and declared, placed him in opposition to the brittle formalism of his generation's jurisprudence. ... Kuhn's view of science is remarkably like the conventional view of law. ... Law (science) is part of culture, but culture brings great rational and moral resources to the improvement of law (science), and the lack of a transcendent standard does not endanger society's loyalty to law (science)." [17]

One may carry this process of redefinition a step further by using as the equivalent of paradigm for criticism the term *charter*. The advantage of this term is that it is free of confusing associations and seems to imply some of the salient features of literary reality. First among these features is the implication that a charter is a grant from an authority, a sovereign, which parallels critics' general acceptance of theoretical authority. It is social, not logical.

Second, a charter is also a document, like a classic critical text, and as such codifies social values and intentions in words and serves as the licensing authority under which organizations are set up and activities carried out. Charters, then, are identifiable in the citations, footnotes, and allusions of critical articles, which show the authority on which the critic rests his practical literary judgment. Formalists frequently cite T. S. Eliot, New York Intellectuals Lionel Trilling, myth critics Frazer or Jane Harrison, and psychoanalytical critics Freud or Jung, with the implication that if one can trace one's opinion back to a charter text, this in itself is enough to establish its authority. Edward W. Said describes the latest manifestation of this kind of use of authority figures: "A maddening new critical shorthand is to be observed. Instead of arguing a point, there tends often to be a lackluster reference to Nietzsche, or Freud, or Artaud, or Benjamin—as if the name alone carried just enough value to override any objection or to settle any quarrel." [18]

Third, a charter contains the intellectual authority under which a critical school or community defines and organizes itself, as does a chartered colony or lodge. Those operating within such a critical school look to the charter as the definition of value and source of authority for their normal activities, and for an individual critic the school becomes the world within which he works at producing "normal criticism" and the means by which he expresses his own values and makes them influential in society.

Fourth, the historical context of a charter implies that there is a temporal dimension to its authority, which is also true of critical theories. A "charter" implies a limited conception of literary criticism. In a legal context a charter is a grant of authority to pursue a specified and otherwise forbidden activity within a specific historical context that is limited spatially and socially. Usually a charter grants authority for an unlimited time, but as social conditions change it eventually becomes obsolete and is formally revoked or simply forgotten. Since a charter is limited in function, a society can support many incompatible or contradictory charters simultaneously; philosophically speaking, the idea of charters is pluralistic. A charter, then, is a set of literary values which relies on a grant of intellectual authority, is embodied in a document, organizes a critical community, and is limited in time and function, with the corollary that society as a whole can support a variety of critical charters.

The use of the term *charter* instead of *paradigm* emphasizes one important fact about criticism: that it relies on authority, not on theory. Though critics and scholars are often referred to as authorities in a field, very little explicit attention has been given to this idea in the context of the literary world.

It is obvious that the authority of a critic is not a political authority, for the critic has no power to compel anyone to accept his beliefs; he has only the power of persuasion, of opinion. In a survey of the idea of authority, Leonard Krieger isolates a contrast between moral and rational authority which has some parallels to criticism. In the Romans' use of the term, he says, "The three basic forms of . . . authority were: authority as guarantee; authority as origin or creation; and authority as personal prestige. Sources of authority appropriate to it as guarantee were trustees who by declaration confirmed the acts of their wards and elders who by experience confirmed the acts of their people. Sources of authority appropriate to it as origin or creation were planners whose designs were carried out by others and initiators whose proposals were enacted by others. Sources of authority appropriate to it as personal prestige were nature's noblemen—that is, men of recognized moral or intellectual pre-eminence."[19] In a literary context the authority of the trustee seems to be possessed by the scholar, who demonstrates his command of the past and of tradition through monograph, book, and learned note, and gains recognition as a Man of Letters as he accumulates personal authority. The authority of the planner, of one who originates something new, belongs in literature to the poet or novelist, or more specifically to the poet-critic, who defends in critical essays what he creates as literature. When one notes the preeminent place in the history of criticism of poet-critics like Jonson, Dryden, Pope, Dr. Johnson, Coleridge, Arnold, and Eliot, the authority of creation is evident. For the ordinary critic the authority of the creator and that of the trustee seem to combine in the scholar-critic.

M. D. King notes that the question of authority in science is interconnected with that of priority of discovery. King suggests that in the case of revolutionary scientists, "recognition of priority is recognition of *intellectual authority*—of the right of the discoverer or his epigoni to set out research strategies for the new field of inquiry. . . . To confer upon someone the title of 'Father of this or that science' . . . is to concede that he (and perhaps more often his intellectual heirs) [has] earned the parents' right to be heard on questions concerning its future development. What is at stake is not simply the prestige of a 'father' but his authority. . . . To concede priority to a discoverer is to acknowledge as authoritative his interpretation of the discovery or, in Kuhn's terms, to treat his work as paradigmatic."[20] In a literary context, priority of discovery is usually called "originality," and originality is as necessary to a great critic, and confers as much status, as it is to a scientist or a poet. Kuhn says on this point: "In the arts, in particular, the work of men who do not succeed in innovation is described as 'derivative', a term of derogation significantly absent from scientific discourse which does, on the other hand, repeatedly refer to 'fads.' In none of these fields, whether arts or philosophy, does the practitioner who fails to alter traditional practice have significant impact on the discipline's development." [21]

Jerome Ravetz discusses the rise of the idea of originality as scientific property in a way that offers interesting parallels to the social organization of literature. He notes why an original research report is a scientist's property: "As a certification of the scientist's accomplishment, it can bring immediate rewards. And as an implicit guarantee of the quality of his future work, it brings in interest for some time after its production." [22] Like the scientist, the critic accumulates saleable prestige through publication ("publish or perish"), and this prestige is acknowledged in his influence on others. In science "the citation thus represents a payment for use of the material; the author of the original paper derives continuing credit from this evidence of the quality of his work." [23] From both scholarship and creativity, learning and literature, come the authority of personal prestige, of nature's noblemen among critics, who will be discussed below as "Men of Letters." Looking at the development of this authority, the old may take comfort from the fact that once one is an authority, one (almost) always continues to be one, or is at worst an authority about the literary past when one was an authority. One may refer to T. S. Eliot's reflections on his career in "To Criticize the Critic" (*TCC* 11–26) and to Alfred Kazin's *New York Jew* (1978) as examples. The young, or the would-be authority of whatever age, may reflect that, in criticism, charters are always becoming obsolete and new ones are rising to fashion and power, and that energy and luck may bring one in with the next change of fashion: perseverance wins! One may cite Allen Ginsberg's transformation from adolescent delinquent to cultural guru and Susan Sontag's rise from *enfant terrible* to winner of the National Book Award as examples.

The importance of originality in both the scientific and literary worlds implies that at the basis of new literary charters, and hence at the basis of the creative theorizing which lies behind all normal critical practice, is the element of human choice. At the end of *Practical Criticism* I. A. Richards affirms that such a choice underlies all the "scientific" apparatus of his system. He says:

All critical doctrines are attempts to convert choice into what may seem a safer activity—the reading evidence [*sic*] and the application of rules and principles. They are an invasion into an inappropriate sphere of that modern transformation, the displacement of the will by observation and judgment. Instead of *deciding* that we are too cold or too warm we hang up a thermometer. ... When we have the poem in all its minute particulars as intimately and as fully present to our minds as we can contrive—no general description of it but the very experience itself present as a living pulse in our biographies—then our acceptance or rejection of it must be *direct*. There comes a point in all criticism where a sheer choice has to be made without the support of any arguments, principles, or general rules. All that arguments or principles can do is to protect us from irrelevancies, red-herrings and disturbing preconceptions. [24]

One assumes that a critic's choices are the product of a conscious will. Since it involves the exercise of free will on the part of the critic, criticism of a literary work is essentially an act of morality. Indeed, part of the appeal of criticism is that it is one of the few areas left where one can choose in a reasoned fashion between the good and the bad with the confidence that one is distinguishing real qualities of real objects. H. Stuart Hughes describes the assumptions implicit in critical practice at the beginning of *Consciousness and Society*: "The essence of history is *change*—and change must be at least partially the result of conscious mental activity. Somewhere at some time someone must have decided to do something. ... In a metaphysical sense most of us are convinced that each individual choice is free." [25] M. H. Abrams says of his book *Natural Supernaturalism*: "A book of humanistic inquiry is written not only from a particular conceptual perspective, but also from within the temporal perspective, the climate of values and opinions, of the age in which it is composed. Rather than try ineffectually to extricate myself from this perspective in order to achieve a viewpoint *sub specie aeternitatis, I decided* [italics added] to end *Natural Supernaturalism* by identifying, in my *chosen* [italics added] authors, those Romantic positives which deliberately reaffirmed the elementary values of the Western past." [26] Given his decision on message and his choice of texts—he says that another equally good history of the period could be written using Byron as the hero and emphasizing "Romantic irony"—it is not clear why Abrams is chagrined that critics found his assertations "a product of the author's own optimism." Choice is at the heart of the matter and ought to be.

What new charters do for individual critics is to metamorphose their views by bringing about what Kuhn, in his more scientific lexicon, calls a "gestalt-shift." As he says, "At times of revolution, when the normal-scientific tradition changes, the scientist's perception of his environment must be re-educated—in some familiar situations he must learn to see a new gestalt" (*SSR* 112). [27] He goes on to explain in more detail: "One central aspect of any revolution is, then, that some of the similarity relations change. Objects that were grouped in the same set before are grouped in different ones afterward and vice versa. Think of the sun, moon, Mars, and earth before and after Copernicus" (*SSR* 200). Kuhn sometimes even refers to such switches in perception in religious terms; he says, for example, that "the transfer of allegiance from paradigm to paradigm is a conversion experience that cannot be forced" (*SSR* 151). Such gestalt switches are usually considered in a critical context under the heading of changes in taste or fashion, and such changes show how the authority of charters is limited in duration. With an astronomical metaphor that seems almost prescient of Kuhn's discussion, T. S. Eliot reveals how criticism changes:

From time to time, every hundred years or so, it is desirable that some critic shall appear to review the past of our literature, and set the poets and the poems in a new order. This task is not one of revolution but of readjustment. What we observe is partly the same scene, but in a different and more distant perspective; there are new and strange objects in the foreground, to be drawn accurately in proportion to the more familiar ones which now approach the horizon, where all but the most eminent become invisible to the naked eye. ... Dryden, Johnson, and Arnold have each performed the task as well as human frailty will allow. [*UP* 108]

M. H. Abrams describes in detail a similar gestalt shift performed by Eliot himself:

Sometimes a shift in the theoretical vantage effects a spectacular transformation in the description as well as the interpretation and evaluation of works of art. As an example, for centuries it was entirely obvious to all critics of Shakespeare ... that the salient features of his plays were the kind that Aristotle had identified—that is, characters who perform the actions and speak the language constituting the text. Then less than a half-century ago a number of able critics took the theoretical stand that a poetic drama, like all genuine literature, is essentially a mode of language ... is inherently figurative or symbolic, ambiguous in its meaning, ironic paradoxical, and in other ways "counterlogical" in its method, and organized so as to explore a "theme" rather than to assert a truth. In the criticism of writers such as Wilson Knight, Philip Wheelwright, Cleanth Brooks, and Robert Heilman, the salient features of Shakespeare's plays, when examined from this perspective, were not characters, but patterns of words and images, and the central action turned out to be an ironic and paradoxical "symbolic action," of which the dynamic element is an evolving theme. The evaluation of Shakespeare from this point of view equaled the earlier high estimation of his artistic standing, although on very different grounds and criteria. The same perspective, however, when applied to writers such as Donne, Blake, Wordsworth, Shelley, Tennyson, resulted in a drastic reordering of their traditional rankings in the hierarchy of the English poets.[28]

In the accounts of Eliot and Abrams we see in theory and in practice the salient features of critical revolutions: the announcement of a new and original critical authority, the gestalt shift that reorders the values of the literary past according to the new standard of value, the obsolescence of the previously reigning view, and the creation of a new tradition.

The Period of Normal Criticism

The Critical Quarterly as a Community Center

The gestalt or world view of a charter is an intellectual reality, but it is also the cause of a social reality. A charter seems to act on critics much like anthropological myths of origin, in that it confers the authority of the past on the practice of the present and validates current social realities. In describing how various clans among the Trobriand Islanders trace their origin, Bronislaw Malinowski observes: "What really matters about such a story is its social function. It conveys, expresses, and strengthens the fundamental fact of the local unity and of the kinship unity of the group of people descendent from a common ancestress. Combined with the conviction that only common descent and emergence from the soil give full rights to it, the story of origin literally contains the legal charter of the community." In much the same way, a school of critics traces its origin to an authoritative and fertile idea and derives its authority from this source. As with the Trobriand Islanders, "immediate history, semi-historic legend, and unmixed myth flow into one another, form a continuous sequence, and fulfill really the same sociological function."[29] The basic way in which a charter influences society is that it causes the formation of a new community, colony, cabal, or chapter dedicated to the propagation of the values implicit in the charter. Such a community is in a sense an evangelical enterprise, in that it is devoted to the conversion of literary opinion to the new standard of values.

Critical communities are often cohesive social groups, which is to say groups of friends. Allen Tate discusses the meaning of the New Criticism, which was carried on largely by people who originally grouped themsleves around the magazine *The Fugitive,* in terms of such a social community:

I think there is another way of going about this [defining the New Criticism], but it would scarcely look impressive to the public eye. The New Criticism began some twenty-five years ago [in 1925] in this country. Well, what was literary criticism like in the quarterlies then? We had the *Dial* and a few little magazines, and I think these people got together out of a kind of mutual respect. They were seriously *engaged* with literature, and out of that serious engagement certain personal friendships were formed. We all got to know one another. It was inevitable that we became personal friends, with resulting interactions of influence. That's about all the New Criticism comes to.[30]

Such a community of values is much like the community of scientists Thomas Kuhn describes: "A paradigm is what the members of a scientific community, and they alone, share. Conversely, it is their possession of a common paradigm that constitutes a scientific community of a group of otherwise disparate men."[31] Kuhn goes on to describe a scientific community as "the practitioners of a scientific speciality. Bound together by common elements in their education and apprenticeship, they see themselves and are seen by others as the men responsible for the pursuit of a set of shared goals, including the training of their successors. Such communities are characterized by the relative fullness of communication within the group and by the relative unanimity of the group's judgment in professional matters."[32] Such a group also seems similar to the schools of Renaissance artists who learned a particular set of skills and modes of painting in a master painter's studio, or to groups of avant-garde poets, or to the communities of scholars in the various disciplines. Such groups, of course, can be defined at different levels of inclusiveness, ranging from an entire discipline (English literature), to pervasive movements (the New Criticism), to the smaller communities of concretist poets or Freudian critics. Following this model, Kuhn notes that the major groups in science can be readily identified as academic communities, professional societies, subscribers to professional journals, and members of professional societies, while the smaller ones, with perhaps a hundred members, can be isolated by "attendance at summer institutes and special conferences, to preprint distribution lists, and above all to formal and informal communication networks, including the linkages among citations."[33] The parallel with MLA sections and seminars, and with the little magazine whose audience equals its writers, needs only be mentioned to be apparent.

The first impulse of a chartered literary community is to start a magazine to make its values known to the world, and from the advent of T. S. Eliot and his magazine, *The Criterion,* in 1922 to about 1955 the character of critical communities was dominated by the critical quarterly as the locus of critical action. The function of a critical quarterly is described most vividly by W. H. Auden in his poem "Under Which Lyre":

> Lone scholars, sniping from the walls
> Of learned periodicals,
>   Our facts defend,
> Our Intellectual marines,
> Landing in little magazines,
>   Capture a trend.[34]

Howard Nemerov recalls the actual historical situation in the forties:

When I was growing up criticism was a very serious industry, big time for such a little thing as literature. At 18 I thought the *Kenyon Review* was, well, eternity, and that John Crowe Ransom, who edited it, must have been there years and years and years. Only 20 years later, when John asked me if I wanted to succeed him as editor, I went back and looked at the files and found *Kenyon Review* had started only the year before I went to college, and had that imposing appearance of permanence and the imposing tone of authority, shared by the *Partisan Review* and the *Sewanee Review,* and one or two others in those days. Then one wrote because one felt that there was a literary community, life seemed to be a little smaller and more compact. I know I am talking like an elder, but I feel like an elder. About 1955 when Allen Ginsberg emerged from somebody's head, the whole thing exploded and it all got redefined.[35]

The quarterlies, then, were the institution which created literary communities from otherwise disparate groups of people separated widely by geography by articulating a set of critical values by which their contributors and subscribers could define themselves. Publishing in quarterlies was the way in which critical careers were made, and by admitting people whose style and values they admired and excluding others, editors held a great deal of power as the gatekeepers to criticism. Editors of quarterlies also determined the form of criticism, and since they preferred short, elegant, allusive, and unfootnoted essays, this became the accepted mode of criticism in the forties and fifties.

In science, as in literature, specialized journals serve as the institution that authenticates originality, creates influence, and hence establishes the importance of critics. As Jerome Ravetz says: "For a result to be authenticated as a contribution to an established field, it had to be submitted for scrutiny by one of the leaders of the field or by his chosen referees; otherwise it would tend to be ignored by the community which constituted the field. Through the system of recognized journals, the leaders of a field could effectively control the creation of intellectual property by those who aspired to, or claimed membership in the field. Such a dictatorial system is clearly open to abuse."[36] In literature, publication is likewise the certification of merit, but since literary fields are less sharply defined than scientific ones, and since what constitutes knowledge in literature is more vague, literary types tend to turn this requirement on its logical head and claim authority by founding a magazine in the hope that the magazine will make them an authority, rather than rely on their intellectual authority to make the magazine. As Ravetz notes, with the decline of this kind of control by a dominant figure, "through informal contacts and through the proliferation of uncontrolled journals, the mechanism for quality control is inevitably weakened."[37]

Since critical quarterlies are the natural home for critics, it is desirable to define in some detail what they are ideally, and to show how magazines actually embody the ideal.[38] "Critical quarterlies" are by definition separate from other related kinds of periodicals. They are distinguished from "little magazines," the category under which most literary magazines are lumped, chiefly by the fact that their primary aim is to publish essays and reviews, not fiction and poetry. They usually do publish *some* fiction and poetry, but the bulk of their pages are filled with essays. Critical quarterlies are also distinguishable from "reviews" (e.g., *Saturday Review, New York Times Book Review,* or *New York Review of Books*) by their freedom from the demand to review new books, their circulation, and the length of their essays. Writing in reviews is generally limited to two pages or less. Essays in quarterlies are from ten to thirty pages long (though book reviews are often as short as those in the "reviews"). The circulation of a critical quarterly ranges between 500 and 10,000; the circulation of a "review" like the *Saturday Review* is numbered in the hundreds of thousands. Critical quarterlies can also be distinguished from "scholarly quarterlies" like *Studies in Philology* or *Journal of English and Germanic Philology* by the fact that the latter publish "research" not criticism. Scholarly quarterlies publish "objective" articles on historical or textual or linguistic problems, not interpretations and evaluations of literary works, and are marked by the prolific use of footnotes, whereas critical quarterlies often prohibit footnotes altogether.

Formally, then, a "critical quarterly" is a magazine of about 150 pages, with a circulation of 500–10,000, a regular group of contributors, perhaps some poetry and fiction, but with several long, unfootnoted critical essays and many shorter reviews. The magazines that fit this description are *The Criterion* (1922-39), the *Hound and Horn* (1927-34), *Scrutiny* (1932-53), the *Southern Review* (1935-42, 1965-), the *Partisan Review* (1937-), the *Kenyon Review* (1939-71), *Horizon* (1940-49), *Accent* (1940-60), the *Sewanee Review* (1892-), the *Chicago Review* (1946-), the *Western Review* (1931-59), the *Hudson Review* (1948-), the *Massachusetts Review* (1959-), *Critical Quarterly* (1949-), *TriQuarterly* (1964-), *Salmagundi* (1965-), the *Denver Quarterly* (1967-), and *Boundary 2* (1973-). By going to these quarterlies, one can see what the American literary intelligentsia was reading at any given time in recent history, and that the institution itself seems to be of continuing interest, since new quarterlies continue to be founded as old ones die.

Critical quarterlies can also be distinguished, in terms of their relation to society, from both commercial magazines and avant-garde magazines. It is quite clear that the critical quarterlies are not commercial magazines, since no quarterly sells more than 10,000 copies an issue and all need support from private benefaction or public largess. In contrast, commercial magazines such as *Harpers* or *The New Yorker* sell hundreds of thousands of copies and make money. The social question is whether the critical quarterly *should* be commercial or, to put it in some roughly comparable way, should be part of the establishment, should be inside rather than outside.

It is usually the Formalists who express this need, for they feel displaced from the centers of power and believe that their ideas should rule culturally. Monroe K. Spears, editor of *Sewanee Review*, says that the quarterlies "will have to continue with their serious make-believe: trying to operate as if their contributors were professional men of letters and their audience mostly intelligent general readers, and they themselves part of the commercial world. Thus they will try to keep alive the ideal of a profession of letters operating with dignity and integrity at the center of a unified culture. This is an ideal and not a reality; it is grotesquely at variance with the facts.''[39] Similarly, R. P. Blackmur traces what he sees as the failure of the American writer to the fact that "there has never been a dominant class in our society which has set a high value on the aesthetic mode of understanding or expressing human life" (*LH* 52). Add to this the fact that, until 1900, America did not have an intellectual capital in which to concentrate intellectual energy; "intellect and art in the United States tended to operate on a kind of average or low level of potential" (*LH* 53). Hence, according to Blackmur, the writer had to become an entertainer (like Twain) or do without prestige (like Melville); had either to become a part of an important avant-garde group or reduce his standards, fall silent, become eccentric, or go abroad. "Their work had neither a center where it could gain strength and by concentration penetrate the mass, nor was it congruous to any purpose of which the mass was conscious" (*LH* 54).

Very much the same desire to put the writer and the quarterly at the center of culture is expressed much more tentatively, but with more hope, by Reed Whittemore, who says in 1965, in the course of criticizing poets for withdrawing from society: "The alternative to drawing gravy and grub from the culture is so archaic and absurd—like setting up shop at Walden Pond again now that Walden Pond is a nasty little state park. ... I cannot grant that total denial of the social entity is a substantive conclusion of consequence in our world. ... You see before you an old-fashioned, if partly disillusioned, advocate of engagement. I would fill our artists with social consciences and then infiltrate our bureaucracy with artists."[40] An even more recent variant of the engaged view is the "revolutionary" of the sixties, who wants to take over society. As Richard Schechner says, "The newer writers are revolutionary in the sense that they don't want so much to ignore the establishment as to capture it, become it, and reconstruct it."[41]

In all these statements one detects both a yearning for cultural power, or for culture to have power, and a desire to return to the now-irrelevant model of the Victorian *Edinburgh* or *Quarterly Review,* which attempted to have power and sometimes did.[42] Despite the feeling of nostalgia or displacement, however, it is quite clear from the circulation figures that the quarterly is not a commercial magazine and in the present state of society never will be.

A closer model for the position of the critical quarterly in society is the avant-garde, or "little" magazine, which is marked by its opposition to the bourgeois establishment. There have been, in twentieth-century America, two varieties of avant-garde magazine, the eclectic and the doctrinaire. The "eclectic" quarterly is avant-garde, as is the doctrinaire, because it accepts only the contemporary and tries to search out the emerging form of the present, but it differs from the doctrinaire in that it does not pretend to know what this form ought to be.

The classic example of the eclectic type of magazine for poetry and

fiction is the *New Directions* annual, which prints whatever is new and
original, whatever the value. Many critical magazines are of this type.
Charles Newman, editor of *TriQuarterly,* says: "It is no secret that we
assume the eclectic view. We would rather surprise our readers than have
them trust us for a particular viewpoint. If we are doing our job, our own
taste should be expanded with—perhaps even diverted by—each issue. We
stress the discontinuities, the disparities of our culture, its plurality of
style." [43] And John Williams, editor of *Denver Quarterly,* likewise says:
"But manifestoes ... [are] more appropriately the instrument of the
historical 'modern' than of the problematic 'new'. ... The *Denver Quarterly* has no editorial position; that is, it does not exist to defend or exemplify
a particular school, system, or tendency of criticism." [44] The authority of
the eclectic quarterly, then, comes from identification with the avant-garde
and with the cultural status of avant-gardes.

The doctrinaire is the purer and more successful type of avant-garde
quarterly, for it exhibits the habit of all avant-garde movements to issue a
manifesto, form a coterie, and explicate a set of principles (*AG* 20–21). As
John Crowe Ransom says: "The editorial impulse of the little magazine
arises from its location at some center—whether geographical or intellectual
—where there is a cluster of creative ideas to radiate outwards; the magazine
becomes the medium of this radiation. ... It is the quality of these pieces
that they come straight from the new insights and are radical, that is to say
original rather than conventional. ... When the editorial impulse is spent
it seems altogether a mistaken piety to try to 'keep the magazine alive,' as
if there were a virtue in the business." [45] Or as Allen Tate puts it more
grandly and dogmatically: "The critical review stands for ... the intelligence trying to think into the moving world a rational order of value. ...
The critical program must, then, supply its readers with coherent standards
of taste and examples of taste in operation" (*CE* 63, 65). The writer for the
doctrinaire quarterly develops a point of view, or more probably is chosen to
write for the quarterly by the editor, who agrees with his point of view.
The doctrinaire quarterly thus helps to develop critical values and has the
advantage of intensity of feeling and firmness of conviction, but it suffers
from rigidity, narrowness, and a tendency to truculence in defense of its
charter, and eventually becomes obsolete as its charter falls out of fashion.
From 1920 to 1950 most critical quarterlies were of the doctrinaire variety
because most of them existed to defend the practice of the poet-critics who
operated them (e.g., *The Criterion,* or the *Sewanee Review* after Tate's
editorship) or the social values of the editors (e.g., *Partisan Review, Scrutiny*). But several were also eclectic, in that they had no ideological scheme
to enforce (*Hound and Horn, Accent, Hudson Review*). The critical quarterlies thus did not stand at the center of cultural power but defined small

literary communities—either doctrinaire or avant-garde—within the culture. It was expected that the reader, though he would be implicitly defined by the charter of the magazine, its tone, or its taste, would be willing be read about a broad range of English and American literature. In the immediate post-World War II period, the model of general intelligence implicit in the critical quarterlies was the norm within the Republic of Letters.

An academic age began in about 1957, however, which had quite different characteristics. The large historical cause of the shift was the enormous expansion of the American university system that took place after the launching of Sputnik. This expansion, which provided jobs and unaccustomedly large salaries, drew both quarterlies and quarterly critics into the scholarly system and hence made academic standards dominant. Concomitantly, a move toward greater academic specialization occurred, and both critical and scholarly periodicals tended to become more specialized. Magazines appeared that were devoted to charters defined in terms of approach or subject (*Comparative Literature* [1949], *American Quarterly* [1949], *Literature and Psychology* [1951]), to specific genres of literature (*Modern Fiction Studies* [1955], *The Drama Review* [1955], *Poet and Critic* [1964]), and to specific periods of scholarship (*Renaissance Quarterly* [1948], *Victorian Studies* [1957], *Early American Literature* [1966]). The result of this shift was the rise of a new type of periodical, the academic quarterly.

Academic quarterlies differ from the critical quarterlies in that they limit themselves to a field, publish little creative work, often promote literary theory, and have some footnotes; but they differ too from scholarly quarterlies, in that they publish criticism and literary theory, not historical scholarship, and are largely about contemporary, not past, literature. In this group are *Criticism* (1959-), *Contemporary Literature* (1960-), *Twentieth Century Literature* (1955-), *Journal of Modern Literature* (1969-), *New Literary History* (1970-), and *Critical Inquiry* (1975-). In such a world, the Ph.D. becomes the apprenticeship for criticism, and the kind of criticism written is consequently marked by an increase in dull soundness as well as learning. Finally, the end of such criticism becomes the book rather than the essay, and eventually the theoretical book rather than the book of commentary. As Weldon Kefauver notes during a discussion of scholarly publishing and university presses, the book "remains the fundamental academic credential and principal scholarly artifact."[46] Just as the community home for the writer-critic is the critical quarterly, the academic's home is the English department and the accompanying scholarly institutions like the Modern Language Association and various lectureships, summer institutes, seminars, and specialized associations, all of which will be discussed in a subsequent volume.

Normal Criticism: The Making of a Tradition

Once critical values have been articulated into a charter and a critical community has formed, what occurs is "normal criticism." In science, as Kuhn observes, a paradigm is a promise of success in explaining nature and "normal science consists in the actualization of that promise, an actualization achieved by extending the knowledge of those facts that the paradigm displays as particularly revealing, by increasing the extent of the match between those facts and the paradigm's predictions, and by further articulation of the paradigm itself" (*SSR* 24). In science this process assumes the character of puzzle solving. Since the larger questions of theory are determined by the paradigm, the scientist does not have to worry about them and can concentrate with a free mind on a detailed examination of the problem before him. "By focusing attention upon a small range of relatively esoteric problems, the paradigm forces scientists to investigate some part of nature in a detail and depth that would otherwise be unimaginable" (*SSR* 24).

A very similar puzzle-solving process occurs in criticism, except that in this field the critic's attention is devoted to a detailed rewriting of the past according to the standards of the new charter, a process which involves not only the interpretation of texts but also the choice of texts to interpret. The process is circular: the texts that critics choose to interpret lead them to use certain models of interpretation; or the models of interpretation that critics choose lead them to certain texts to interpret; or both occur at the same time. Either way, the critic arrives at a distinguishable way of looking at literature and a distinguishable tradition of literature to look at. Normal criticism involves most critics most of the time in the detailed study of authors of the past who are fashionable in terms of the reigning charter; the construction of definitions of genre and convention; and the reviewing and judging of new books in terms of the charter; and the surveying of forgotten literature of the past for works that will assume new value when seen afresh through the new charter's values. Such a process can consume an almost infinite amount of labor, since the canon of western literature must be revalued in detail according to the new standards, and the study of just one major author can occupy a critical lifetime. In fact the task is never finished, for new charters are forever appearing with new standards of values to apply. Normal criticism, then, is the ongoing rewriting of literary tradition in terms of the values of a new charter. [47]

The result of normal criticism in any given period is a new tradition, a set of classics the critic can read and reread and look upon as a standard of value for his literary judgment. In fact such traditions become quite exclusive, and established traditions take a form which is so fixed that certain authors can serve as touchstones to one's total literary taste.

In an ironic comment on the fifties, Randall Jarrell asks, after remarking on academic specialization:

Aren't many intellectuals almost as great specialists in Important—that is to say, currently fashionable—books? ... It troubled me to remember the conversation at the literary parties at which he and I had occasionally met. Here people talked about few books, perhaps, but the books they talked about were the same: it was like the Middle Ages. ... If, at such parties, you wanted to talk about *Ulysses* or *The Castle* or *The Brothers Karamazov* or *The Great Gatsby* or Graham Greene's last novel—Important books—you were at the right place. ... But if you wanted to talk about Turgenev's novelettes, or *The House of the Dead*, or *Lavengro*, or *Life on the Mississippi*, or *The Old Wive's Tale* [etc. etc.] ... or any of a thousand good or interesting but Unimportant books, you couldn't expect a very ready knowledge or sympathy from most of the readers there. [48]

Likewise, in a review of the year's poetry for *The New Republic*, Harold Bloom remarks: "A critic like Hugh Kenner probably would find this year's significant volumes of verse to include books by George Oppen, Louis Zukofsky and the late Charles Olson. That would reflect a vision that saw Pound, Eliot, and Williams as the central American poets of this century. I myself prefer E. A. Robinson, Frost, Stevens, and Hart Crane, who seem to me the rightful inheritors of Emerson, Whitman, and Dickinson and therefore *my* choices among this year's books are sure to be affected by my own view of tradition. Doubtless, this is a limitation, but no critic is or can be free of such limitation." [49] A critic's preference for Donne or Shelley, Lawrence or James, Bellow or Mailer, Spenser or Webster, thus implies a charter by which the critic ultimately justifies his practical literary judgment.

One should note that the elaboration of the traditions of normal criticism, like normal science, is relatively unoriginal and relies on a faith similar to that of scientists that such puzzle solving is meaningful. Clear examples of this kind of critical activity are the repeated explications of the same poem done according to the Formalist charter, the solving of the puzzles of Joyce, or the uncovering of the mythic structures of Faulkner and Melville. Perhaps because the value given to originality is greater in literature than in science, such critical work is often decried as unoriginal and worthless. Nevertheless, it cannot be denied that many critics gain a great deal of influence by merely reworking the insights of others into a form that is widely applicable to literature. As Cleanth Brooks says, for example, in his preface to *Modern Poetry and the Tradition*: "Readers acquainted with modern criticism will find obvious the extent to which I have borrowed from Eliot, Tate, Empson, Yeats, Ransom, Blackmur, Richards, and other critics. ... Such credit as I may legitimately claim, I must claim primarily on the grounds of having possibly made a successful synthesis of other men's ideas rather than on the originality of my own" (*MPT* xxxi). This derivative character is true of all Brooks's criticism, yet he has had more cultural influence than any American critic, particularly with the textbook *Understanding Poetry*, which revolutionized the classroom teaching of literature.

A different kind of derivative yet influential contribution is made by Northrop Frye, who borrows most of his ideas and terms from "Cambridge anthropologists" like Frazer and Jane Harrison, yet reworks them into a simplistic pattern of myth and genre which influenced a decade of critics. Another case in point is Lionel Trilling, whose criticism is derived from the dialectic form of Freud and Marx, yet is rephrased as the debate between reality and intellect, thereby becoming the model for a generation of New York Intellectuals whose own moral position he embodied and expressed. Such critics are influential as "representative critics" by virtue of their capacity for popularization and their communicability. It is unclear whether such contributions fall within the limits of innovation for scientists, but a parallel might be drawn between the representative critic and the creator of new techniques of experimentation, the inventor rather than the conceptual scientist.

In the historical view, then, normal criticism has value not only as the fleshing out of a tradition but also as a process of educating critics in a tradition. The result of developing a critical tradition is a list of great books that serve to educate the young in a charter's view of literature, just as scientists are educated by scientific exemplars. Seen in this context, the academic reality of "publish or perish" is justified, for publication testifies to the apprentice's mastery of an acceptable critical technique. Reading lists, exam requirements, and "great books" courses assume a similar reality as culture's understanding of particular literary traditions.

One can evaluate charters, and distinguish the good from the bad on pragmatic grounds, by measuring the capacity of the charter to generate practical criticism that will reevaluate the literary tradition in terms of the gestalt of the new charter; or, to put it in another way, by measuring the capacity of the charter to become influential. As M. H. Abrams says: "Once an assertation is adopted as the premise of a critical theory, 'its origin and truth-claim cease to matter,' for its validity is to be measured by its demonstrated power to yield valuable critical insights."[50]

Critical history also provides clear examples of what might be called "normal theory," the articulation of the theoretical implications of a charter within its initial set of values. When one examines the work of Murray Krieger, one finds the repetition and increasing elaboration and refinement of a set of concepts taken from the Formalist charter. In the course of reviewing Krieger's *A Window to Criticism* (1964), W. K. Wimsatt says that there are two possible reactions to the history of modern criticism:

(1) "spontaneity and innocence"; (2) the response of Krieger, "the master dialectician who would prove himself superior to the preceding poetic conversation by virtue of his intimate, even finicky, knowledge of every phase through which the conversation has evolved, and his hairsplitting capacity to show the impossibilities and paradoxes in which the conversation has got itself involved."[51] As has been suggested, literary theory is not necessary for critical practice, nor does it determine critical practice. It is, instead, a systematic elaboration of the values of a charter. As such, it performs much the same function of fleshing out and fortifying a charter as does the making of a new literary tradition through normal criticism.

The Critical Voice

Functioning as it does as the intellectual world within which the critic operates, the critical charter defines the questions an individual critic can ask and hence limits the literature he can talk about effectively. The critic, however, is not as dependent upon his charter as the scientist is upon his paradigm, because the puzzles of normal science are totally defined by the relevant theory. Thus the relationship of scientist to theory is one of acceptance and use of the theory, while the relationship of the critic to his theoretical charter is one of mastering and developing the charter into an expression of individual critical authority; the latter requires that the critic be able to transform the critical charter into an element of his unique literary sensibility and apply it to literature effectively. Much more than the scientist, the critic thus tends to become creative as he develops what is commonly called his critical "voice" and becomes in a sense like the artist.[52]

Because of this element of creativity in the critic's job, it is sometimes claimed that criticism is at best (or should become) a kind of literature, and critics sometimes strain mightily to give their criticism a literary look; one could cite Ihab Hassan's "paracriticism" or the alogical connectives of J. Hillis Miller's prose in this regard. This effort mistakes the nature of critical creativity, which is not a matter of the creation or use of new stylistic or generic forms, but rather involves the creation of new critical values through the extension of a critical charter into new areas of application or its transformation into a compelling individual response to literature. The critic, then, aims to make himself into an authority, not an artist, and the progress of his career can be seen in relation to this goal.

The concept of a critical voice appears in several guises in critical theory, such as the *cogito* of the French critics of consciousness, the form a writer's mind takes in all his works; or the "signature" that Leslie Fiedler opposes to the "archetype" and defines as the "sum total of individuating factors in a work, the sign of the Persona or Personality through which an Archetype is rendered."[53] "Voice" is used here to refer to the combination of choice of values and development of style which render a critic's work recognizable and unique. The development of such a voice marks the mature critic, the Man of Letters.

The formation of a critic's true voice usually takes him through his twenties, and sometimes his thirties as well, as he goes through a process of actualization, of discovering his identity as a critic, the charter he wishes to defend, and the style he wishes to use in the process of writing essays. Criticism is not a young man's game. Forming a critical voice is usually not an act of conversion, like St. Paul's on the road to Damascus; rather, it is a process of self-education. Literary essays are the historically true self of the critic, and many critics testify that the public personality is not different from the private one. During a symposium on the Fugitive critics, Allen Tate commented: "I can't agree it [the Agrarians' mind] was a different sort of mind [from the Fugitives] given the particular cultural situation that we find ourselves in since the end of the 18th century. You know the literary critic doesn't turn on a different mind; it is a different mode that he is operating in."[54] The New York Intellectual Philip Rahv says in very similar terms: "May we not say that subjectively the critic cannot help but regard his work as an end in itself, for in reacting to art he is expressing his own ideas, elaborating his own meanings, and in fact projecting a vision of life ... by actively absorbing and pronouncing upon the visions of the artists that engage him?" (*MP* 75). And the scholar Bernard Weinberg also testifies that "criticism of whatever brand is a completely personal affair; no self-respecting critic would want anybody else to teach his theory, nor would he consent to apply another's aesthetics in his own study of works. In this area, the individual professor will have to be both theorist and practitioner."[55]

It is important to recognize, however, that once the critic makes his choice, he is formed in a way which for practical purposes seems irrevocable; at least, most critics in fact use the voice and defend the charter that they form in their twenties throughout their careers. Critics from various schools testify to the truth of this generalization. René Wellek observes that F. R. Leavis "clings, as I suppose we all do, to the discoveries of his youth: Conrad, Lawrence, Hopkins, the early Eliot";[56] or that Kant "could not change or enlarge his taste, as time went on, just as most of us cling to the artistic experiences of our youth" (*D* 123). The New York Intellectual Norman Podhoretz says of Edmund Wilson, one of his idols: "Wilson is a very stubborn man, so stubborn that no writer has ever really been able to shake any of the attitudes or prejudices with which he began his career as critic more than forty years ago" (*DU* 53). Likewise, F. J. Hoffman notes in a scholarly work on the twenties that H. L. Mencken "began his investigation with a few simple principles or prejudices, many of them borrowed from his reading of Nietzsche. His survey of American culture was motivated entirely by an urgent necessity to prove himself right in these original assumptions."[57] Because critics form a constant vision of things in early maturity, their work can be accurately understood only by placing it in this context, as well as the context in which an essay is written, which may be fifty years later.

It is therefore necessary to undertake the task which René Wellek isolates only to reject when he says in the beginning of his *History of Modern Criticism*: "The individual critic himself will be motivated by his personal history: his education, the demands of his calling, the requirements of his audience. To investigate such psychological causes would lead us into biography and the whole variety of personal histories. Only now and then will we be able to refer to such possible motives of critical positions" (*HC* 1: 8).[58] One may emulate the historian Lewis Namier, who in *The Structure of Politics at the Accession of George III* (1929) revolutionized the study of English parliamentary history by interpreting political abstractions like "Whig" and "Tory" in terms of the politicians who used them. According to one account, "when asked what the phrase 'Namierizing history' really meant, Namier would laugh and reply, 'It means finding out who the guys were.'"[59] Namier's conclusion that political concepts are to be understood only in terms of the men who use them is applicable to critics and critical terms as well, and an essential part of the history of criticism should be the biography of the critic. The limit of this kind of reasearch is, for practical reasons, that which is in print, but in practice this is not a constraint, for critics (like other writers) are only too eager to confess and propound what they believe.

To analyze the individual voices of critics therefore leads to a kind of career analysis in which abstractions about choice and free will are metamorphosed into the historical reality of publication, position, preferment, and reputation; the profiles of critics found at the end of this book give the facts with which such an analysis must begin. One then moves back and forth between charter and voice, between the historical and intellectual forces which form and limit a critic and his individual style, his uniqueness as a writer. While a charter is implicit in all criticism, the greatness of an individual critic lies in the creation of a distinct voice, a new model of response to literature. The influence of a charter is necessary, but only originality of voice is sufficient to create the great critic; the best critics use a new charter of criticism in a voice that is their very own.

Stages in the Career of a Modern American Critic

The careers of modern American critics develop in a fairly uniform pattern through four stages: apprenticeship, Journeyman, Man of Letters, and superannuation. In broader terms the pattern is characterized by three phases or rites of passage: the period of formation, when the critic defines his charter and finds his own style; the time of naming, when the critic breaks into literary society, makes it, achieves a reputation, and people become interested in reading his work because of his personal authority; and superannuation, the point at which culture and/or time pass the critic by, leaving him without an audience or without a cause.

Apprenticeship.   Post-World War II America has witnessed the development of two dominant types of critic: the writer-critic and the scholar-critic. The writer-critic's apprenticeship is an extension of the traditional Grub Street or newspaper city-room route to criticism. Beginning by writing and publishing poems, novels, stories, and essays in little magazines or the underground press, he progresses to criticism to defend a new literary charter of a rising generation, or to make his reputation. Hence the writer-critic tends to begin by writing reviews. In contrast, the scholar-critic serves his apprenticeship by going to graduate school and getting a Ph.D. in English, and his progress to criticism represents an escape from the factual world of the historical scholar to a discipline where he can assert his literary values directly and explicitly in critical essays. Of the two the writer-critic has an easier time of it intellectually, since his values are contained in the literature he writes and defends or in the clique he is trying to advance. The scholar-critic has the more difficult task of freeing himself from the impersonality of the academic charter in order to develop his own voice, but has the advantage of belonging to the dominant intellectual class of post-World War II America, the academicians. As the poet W. D. Snodgrass somewhat resentfully writes:

> And one by one the solid scholars,
> Get the degrees, the jobs, the dollars,
> And smile above their starchy collars. [60]

In both cases the apprenticeship begins with a search for the literary value a charter contains and ends when the critic finds a consistent, satisfying, and successful critical voice that permits him to produce critical essays. As with the adolescent novelist, the "critic of adolescence" does not develop but can express only the outrage of youth at the real world. The more mature critic becomes a worker, a professional. He is the one who has chosen, and he is the one who can judge.

The Journeyman Critic.   The Journeyman period begins when the critic decides what he is going to say and learns how to say it. Although such "stages" should not be regarded as absolutes, since some critics conduct their education in public and discover who they are by publishing their thoughts, the distinction between the private formulation of value and the public accretion of influence is clear, and the Journeyman is occupied with production, breaking in, "making it," getting his essays published. He is hence concerned with mastering the genres of normal criticism.

Someone once said that Cervantes managed to build into *Don Quixote* all the possibilities that other novelists spent the next four centuries exploring. Similarly, Dr. Samuel Johnson used practically all the genres that later critics and scholars were to employ: the book review, the essay, the preface or introduction, the biographical-critical life of an author and judgment of his works, the edition, and the learned footnote. The only critical genre in which the good doctor did not excel was the lecture on literature, which was first practiced by Dr. Hugh Blair in *Lectures on Rhetoric and Belles Lettres* (1783) and later exploited by Coleridge, Hazlitt, and others. These bottles have, of course, been filled with very different wines since the eighteenth century, but the genres themselves remain much the same. These genres are all marked by that mixture of values and facts which characterizes writing about literature, with values predominating at the beginning of the list and facts at the end. Inasmuch as the facts of literature are the province of the scholar, and values are the concern of the critic, one may say that the *normal* critical genres are the review, the preface, the essay, and the lecture, since these afford the best modes in which to assert literary values directly. In the period dominated by the critical quarterlies, the form that the critic has to master is the essay, the essential genre of the writer-critic, since it is in essays that personal values can be expressed most clearly. In his autobiographical account of his career, Austin Warren describes how, after writing four scholarly books, "I found that the book was less the form, or the length, for me than the essay. My 'genius' in writing . . . was for compactness. My characteristic revision excised. I wanted my critical essays to be the equivalent of a book, —so to speak its concluding chapter."[61] The primacy of the essay in this period is worth insisting on, and can be seen in the most ambitious books of criticism, each the product of a decade or more of essay writing: Brooks's *Modern Poetry and the Tradition,* Wilson's *The Wound and the Bow,* Eliot's *Selected Essays,* Frye's *Anatomy of Criticism.* In each an attempt is made to state a coherent critical position by giving theoretical essays pride of place and title or by shaping earlier theoretical essays into the structure of a complete book, but even the most systematic of them retains something of its original fragmentary form.

A critic breaks in by having his reviews or essays published in critical quarterlies, where after a time he makes a name for himself. The American critic advances from little magazines and scholarly journals to the major academic and critical quarterlies; the difficulty of breaking in is illustrated by the ratio of manuscripts accepted to those submitted. The *Hudson Review,* for example, had 5,000 manuscripts submitted to it in 1965 and accepted 100 (2 percent). The *Partisan Review* accepted 100 of 1,200 submissions; *Contemporary Literature,* 25 of 150 submissions; and *Criticism,* 14 out of 225.[62] One may conclude that it is difficult to break into any "big-time" quarterly, nearly impossible to do so in New York magazines, and only a little easier in academic quarterlies. In all cases, however, social propinquity to the editors, which is to say membership in a critical community, is the key to success. Because the critical quarterlies select from numerous bright and hopeful contributors largely on the basis of friendship or personal recommendation, a certain entrée to intellectual circles or the acquaintance of established friends is helpful.

The accounts of how Susan Sontag, Norman Podhoretz, and Seymour Krim establish themselves as reviewers illustrate this point. William Phillips, editor of *PR*, says of Miss Sontag: "My own view of Susan Sontag ... is a biased one, in her favor. I must also admit to some personal satisfaction in her development into one of our most intelligent and exciting writers. I remember the first time I met her, ten years ago, at one of those brawls known as a cocktail party. I remember her shyness, taking the form of self-assurance, as she asked me how one gets to write a review for *PR*. Fumbling for a quick and clever reply, as one does desperately on these occasions, I said, 'One asks.' 'O.K.,' she said, 'I'm asking.' "[63] Similarly, it is Podhoretz's position as a student of F. R. Leavis that wins him entry into the quarterlies; he describes his successful imitation of Leavis's style and values and says: "The whole thing reached so rapid and thorough a consummation that before the end of my first year at Cambridge, the master's ultimate accolade was bestowed upon me: he invited me to write for *Scrutiny*. Thus it was that at the age of twenty-one and in the notoriously hardest to crack of all magazines of its kind in the world, I made my first appearance as a literary critic" (*MI* 60). Describing his somewhat less successful encounter with the *Hudson Review*, Seymour Krim reminisces that after publishing a few short stories "I graduated to *The Hudson Review,* the very latest and coolest and technicalest of the swank highbrow quarterlies. My editor was Frederick Morgan, Park Avenue and Princeton. ... I punished myself to produce a couple of critiques that whatever their merit had no relationship in the pain of composition to what I could have said given the encouragement to loosen up. ... I succeeded and became one of *The Hudson's* secondstring boys until I lost favor."[64] These examples of writer-critics can be paralleled by the advancement of Ph.D. students by their advisers among scholar-critics in the well-known "old boy" network.

One of the main qualifications for success as a Journeyman is productivity, which is a testimony to the critic's energy. One essay, or even one book, does not make a career; as with Mozart, da Vinci, Picasso, Stravinsky, the great men of letters are those who produce, and without exception our great critics have written many essays. For example, Donald Gallup lists 681 "contributions to periodicals" for T. S. Eliot from 1905 to 1965.[65]

Robert K. Merton notes the importance of even unoriginal or "normal" scientific publication and its symbolic relationship to really revolutionary work: "The large majority of scientists, like the large majority of artists, writers, doctors, bankers and bookkeepers, have little prospect of great and decisive originality. For most of us artisans of research, getting things into print becomes a symbolic equivalent to making a significant discovery. Nor could science advance without the great unending flow of papers reporting careful investigations, even if these are routine rather than distinctly original."[66]

The importance of at least seeming productive is testified to by the habit of critics of recycling essays; what was originally an introduction to a book will reappear as a book review, an essay, a lecture, a chapter of a book, and reappear in numerous further "Collected Essays." Edmund Wilson describes this development: "My own strategy ... has usually been, first to get books for review or reporting assignments to cover on subjects in which I happened to be interested; then, later, to use the scattered articles for writing general studies of these subjects; then, finally to bring out a book in which groups of these essays were revised and combined" (*CCo* 113). As formidable in quantity as modern criticism is, it is not quite as formidable as it seems, because of the mileage critics get out of a single piece of writing. For example, Ralph Ellison, in the course of a literary quarrel with Irving Howe, notes of Howe's essay "Black Boys and Native Sons": "I gave in to my ear's suggestion that I had read certain of his phrases somewhere before, and I went to the library, where I discovered that much of his essay was taken verbatim from a review in the *Nation* of May 10, 1952, and that another section was published verbatim in the *New Republic* of February 13, 1962. ... Howe spliced these materials together with phrases from an old speech of mine, swipes at the critics of the *Sewanee* and *Kenyon* reviews ... and the Baldwin-Wright quarrel."[67]

In addition to being a stage in all critics' development, the Journeyman period can also be perpetual. Some critics never progress beyond this stage because they fail either to choose a critical charter or to develop their own critical voice. For the critic the choice of a charter is a difficult one; Renato Poggioli explains that followers of the avant-garde have the choice of joining one avant-garde movement—for instance, Structuralism or Marxism—and making it their own, or of embracing each successive movement as it comes along and remaining perpetually avant-gardist (*AG* 84-85).The choice is to adopt a charter, with the productivity, influence, and possibility of obsolescence it implies; or not to commit oneself fully to any particular charter, but to rely instead on one's sensitivity as a writer to embrace each change in literary culture while accepting the implicit lack of time to develop any particular position or to spread one's influence through a particular literary group. The choice of the critic, then, is to become at sixty a passé cultural heavyweight, a Man of Letters; or a perpetual reviewer, a dapperwit Journeyman whose voice lacks the cultural clout a charter provides. Between the extremes of Journalistic triviality and obsolescent ideas lies the dialectic of critical careers.

Writer-critics generally fail to become Men of Letters because they fail to develop a charter. Mainly because they limit themselves to the genre of the review, it is difficult for them to work out a consistent intellectual position in the space allowed. Such critics lack the authority of a charter, which can be argued with and which would provide them with consequent historical influence. Instead, they are known for their voice, their style, their personality, their obsession, rather than their position. Such critics include John W. Aldridge, Malcolm Cowley, Benjamin DeMott, F. W. Dupee, George P. Elliott, Elizabeth Hardwick, Granville Hicks, Randall Jarrell, Seymour Krim, Mary McCarthy, Dwight Macdonald, Marvin Mudrick, Howard Numerov, Kenneth Rexroth, Roger Sale, Delmore Schwartz, Karl Shapiro, Wilfrid Sheed, Diana Trilling, William Troy, and Reed Whittemore. They have the authority of sensibility, not the authority of thought.

In contrast, Journeyman scholar-critics work within the research charter of scholarship and within these limits are conceptual to a fault, but they lack the voice, the personality, the style, necessary for the expression of critical value. Such critics submerge themselves in their subject and become "the Pater man" or "the Poe man," doing a great deal of useful interpretative work without developing their own voice. Journeyman critics lack charter *or* voice, intellectual position *or* personal style, and thus fail to attain the highest level of importance to which critics aspire. Journeymen are, however, the workers in the vineyard, and most "normal criticism" is done by them.

The Man of Letters. When a critic succeeds in making his charter influential and achieves a personal voice, he ascends to the dignity of a "Man of Letters," a title which marks not a stage of life but a successful career. One may think of this term in a slightly more favorable way than does John Gross when he defines it as meaning, in nineteenth-century England, "a writer of the second rank, a critic, someone who aimed higher than journalism but made no pretence of being primarily an artist."[68] Speaking of America after 1935, the term should be applied to a critic who is widely enough known for the writing of essays and books about literature that his opinion has personal authority and carries weight because it is *by him*. Thus the term is honorific, since these are the men who are doing better what so many Journeymen are doing well. The importance of achieving an authoritative name and a reputation is illustrated by F. W. Bateson's remarks about the practice of printing anonymous reviews in the

Times Literary Supplement:

A reviewer, by the nature of his trade, can only present the reader with part of the evidence from which he has reached his conclusions. In TLS, where most of the reviews are comparatively short, the reader does not really expect much more than the reviewer's considered opinion. But the worth of an opinion varies with the degree of respect we have for the holder of the opinion—which in its turn depends upon our knowledge and approval or disapproval of whatever other opinions he or she may have already expressed. ... In other words, *the reviewer's name is an essential part of the meaning of the review.* [69]

The mark of the Man of Letters is that because his opinion is accepted as being worth something in itself, he is asked to do things he once appealed to do as an apprentice. Hence his dominant mode of critical activity changes from developing his charter, working out his values, to punditry, laying down the law. The easiest way to describe the activities of the Man of Letters is to reproduce Edmund Wilson's famous list of the things he would not do:

READ MANUSCRIPTS,
WRITE ARTICLES OR BOOKS TO ORDER,
WRITE FOREWORDS OR INTRODUCTIONS,
MAKE STATEMENTS FOR PUBLICITY
  PURPOSES,
DO ANY KIND OF EDITORIAL WORK,
JUDGE LITERARY CONTESTS,
GIVE INTERVIEWS,
CONDUCT EDUCATIONAL COURSES,
DELIVER LECTURES,
GIVE TALKS OR MAKE SPEECHES,
BROADCAST OR APPEAR ON TELEVISION,
TAKE PART IN WRITERS' CONGRESSES,
ANSWER QUESTIONNAIRES,

CONTRIBUTE TO OR TAKE PART IN
  SYMPOSIUMS OR "PANELS" OF
  ANY KIND,
CONTRIBUTE MANUSCRIPTS FOR SALES,
DONATE COPIES OF HIS BOOKS TO
  LIBRARIES,
AUTOGRAPH BOOKS FOR STRANGERS,
ALLOW HIS NAME TO BE USED ON
  LETTERHEADS,
SUPPLY PERSONAL INFORMATION ABOUT
  HIMSELF,
SUPPLY PHOTOGRAPHS OF HIMSELF,
SUPPLY OPINIONS ON LITERARY OR OTHER
  SUBJECTS. [*Letters* 690]

The normal genre for the Man of Letters is the lecture he is asked and paid to give rather than the essay he is trying to get published. The Man of Letters is also asked to edit texts, write introductions, accept fellowships and fill distinguished chairs. Hence he has access to whatever money there is in criticism, and deserves it, since he has developed his talent and done the work.

Robert K. Merton describes the similar kinds of activities that occupy senior scientists when "the prestige they have gained in the research role often leads them to be sought out for alternative roles as advisors, sages, and statesmen, both within the domain of science and in the larger society. ... They become more receptive to the opportunities for taking up other roles: administering research organizations, serving as elder statesmen to provide liaison between science and other institutional spheres, or, occasionally, leaving the field of science altogether for ranking positions in university administration or international diplomacy."[70] All these activities have parallels among critics, who move into the academic world as "Distinguished Professors"; rise in the ranks of the Modern Language Association as leaders of symposia, or even as in the case of Northrop Frye, president of MLA; become the organizers of centers for the humanities funded by the National Endowment for the Humanities; become cultural attachés in the American Embassy in London, as did Cleanth Brooks; or begin schools of criticism and theory supported by universities, as did Murray Krieger at the University of California at Irvine.

Politically and socially the Republic of Letters has an almost medieval structure. Each of the senior Journeymen and Men of Letters has his own set of friends, allies, and enemies, his own magazines or preferred outlets, his own publisher and editor, usually his own professorship and power base in an English department, his own disciples and students, his own contacts with foundations, institutes, lectureships. Critics combine in groups united by friendship and allegiance to the values of a charter and relate to each other in a network of reviews and citations. In a 1928 essay, Edmund Wilson describes the principal authorities and groups of the time (Eliot, Mencken, the Neo-Romantics, the social revolutionary writers, the psychological and sociological critics) and concludes that in general "they do not communicate with one another; their opinions do not really circulate. It is astonishing to observe, in America ... to what extent the literary atmosphere is a non-conductor of criticism. What actually happens, in our literary world, is that each leader or group of leaders is allowed to intimidate his disciples, either ignoring all the other leaders or taking cognizance of their existence only by distant and contemptuous sneers" (*SL* 369). When these two *groups* of critics retreat to the allegiances of their origins, the scholars accuse the writers of being superficial, unsound, ignorant, ill-formed journalists, while the writers accuse the scholars of being hidebound, stuffy, imperceptive, constipated, unread scholars. Thus the general political situation is controlled by a number of rural barons or war lords whose beliefs, allegiances, and political arrangements shift in time. These shifting alignments will be traced in detail in subsequent chapters.

The Man of Letters combines an authoritative voice with the conceptual power that comes from using a critical charter. He has a position that can be argued with; he takes a stand and develops it, or through the force of his voice develops the voice itself into a charter which is a historical presence. At his best the Man of Letters combines style and position, voice and charter, in a synthesis which adds a new possibility of response to the history of criticism. As Shakespeare says in Sonnet 58:

Be where you list; your charter is so strong
That you yourself may privilege your time
To what you will.

Because of the difference in conditions of apprenticeship, one can distinguish two distinct groups of modern American Men of Letters: the writer-critics and the scholar-critics. The Formalist writer-critics include R. P. Blackmur, Kenneth Burke, T. S. Eliot, John Crowe Ransom, and Allen Tate; the New York Intellectual writer-critics are Irving Howe, Alfred Kazin, Philip Rahv, and Edmund Wilson. The Formalist scholar-critics (and their opponents) include Cleanth Brooks, R. S. Crane, Murray Krieger, Austin Warren, W. K. Wimsatt, René Wellek, and Yvor Winters; the Intellectual scholar-critics are Richard Chase and Lionel Trilling. These are the critics who seem, from the present historical perspective, to combine originality, productivity, voice, and influence in a way that gives them an honorific historical status among the Formalists and New York Intellectuals treated in this volume. In a subsequent volume equally close attention will be given to the myth critics like Northrop Frye, Leslie Fiedler, and Norman Holland; continentally influenced critics like Jonathan Culler, Geoffrey Hartman, J. Hillis Miller, Paul de Man, Frederic Jameson, George Steiner, and Edward W. Said; theorists like M. H. Abrams and E. D. Hirsch, Jr.; counter-cultural critics of the sixties like Susan Sontag, Ihab Hassan, and N. O. Brown; and a number of academic critics whose work will come to seem important in terms of new charters as they develop.

Superannuation. The superannuation of a critic is caused by age or a change in critical fashion, when the critic who created or applied the values of a single charter or school dies or is made obsolete by the rise of a new generation with different interests. Charters and critics are historical, not eternal, and the period from manifesto to obsolescence is never more than fifty years, the working life of a precocious critic who finds his voice at twenty. The reason for the superannuation of scientists (and critics) is partly disciplinary; as a person applies the original ideas of his youth in the kind of research characteristic of normal science, he tends to lose sight of new ideas that are appearing. Robert K. Merton suggests that "young scientists are more apt than their expert teachers to be abreast of the range of knowledge in their field. Since advanced research in science demands concentration on a narrow range of problems at hand, the established specialist experts, intent on moving ahead with their own research, tend to fall behind on what others are doing outside their own special fields." Scientists also become superannuated because they choose to do things outside their discipline, to fill other roles in society. Bernard Barber says that "as a scientist gets older he is more likely to be restricted in his response to innovation by his substantive and methodological preconceptions and by his other cultural accumulations; he is more likely to have high professional standing, to have specialized interests, to be a member or official of an established organization, and to be associated with a 'school.'"[71] The result, as Thomas Kuhn points out, is that "when, in the development of a natural science, an individual or group first produces a synthesis able to attract most of the next generation's practitioners, the older schools gradually disappear. In part their disappearance is caused by their members' conversion to the new paradigm. But there are always some men who cling to one or another of the older views, and they are simply read out of the profession, which thereafter ignores their work" (*SSR* 18–19). Or as Max Planck puts it more trenchantly: "A new scientific truth does not triumph by convincing its opponents and making them see the light, but rather because its opponents eventually die, and a new generation grows up that is familiar with it."[72] The situation is the same in literature, as Dr. Johnson observed to Oliver Goldsmith in 1773:

"Why, sir, Mallet had talents enough to keep his literary reputation alive as long as he himself lived; and that, let me tell you, is a good deal!

In a normal career, superannuation usually occurs at about the age of fifty, when the critic realizes that a new generation, with new values and enthusiasms, has replaced him and his friends as the avant-garde. As Alfred Kazin notes, this realization can be painful: "The lead review in the *New Republic,* a single page usually written by [Malcolm] Cowley himself, brought the week to focus for people to whom this page . . . represented the most dramatically satisfying confrontation of a new book by a gifted, uncompromising critical intelligence. A time would come, in the early Forties, when Cowley could report with astonishment that a famous Broadway designer he had met on the train no longer kept up with these lead reviews; an era had passed" (*SO* 18–19).

The drama here, of course, lies in the fact that a critic's voice is in large part a response to the time and society he grows up in, becomes the essential form, the public being, of the critic himself; eventually, however, that voice will be perceived as irrelevant by a new audience with new problems. The reaction to the problem of changing times is one of the true tests of critic, scientist, and tragic hero. Robert K. Merton says that even scientists

are ready to pass invidious judgments upon the behavior of those in "the other" age stratum. Older scientists then describe younger ones as parochial if not downright barbarian in outlook, little-concerned to read and ponder the classical work of some years back and even less concerned to learn about the historical evolution of their field (the judges forgetting all the while that the new youth in science are only reproducing the attitudes and behavior they had exhibited in their own youth).

In turn, younger scientists deride the orientation of older ones to the past as mere antiquarianism, as a sign that they are unable to "keep up" and so are condemned to repeat the obsolete if not downright archaic stuff they learned long ago. [73]

In the Republic of Letters critics also avoid or deny the problem of their aging by pretending that the old vision is still relevant (as have Krieger and Howe); by recognizing that things have changed while clinging resolutely to the old values (as has Tate); or by realizing that things have changed and coming to terms with the new and one's own aging (as did Ransom and Eliot). In 1940 Eliot says of his own poetic career: "The generations of poetry in our age seem to cover a span of about twenty years. I do not mean that the best work of any poet is limited to twenty years; I mean that it is about that length of time before a new school or style of poetry appears. By the time, that is to say, that a man is fifty he has behind him a kind of poetry written by men of seventy, and before him another kind written by men of thirty. This is my position at present" (*OPP* 295).

One of the most pathetic refusals to accept change is seen in the disciple who refuses to accept his master's change of heart and tries instead to refute the older man with arguments borrowed from the younger man. For example, W. K. Wimsatt says of the later Eliot: "What, then, does the present collection [*To Criticize the Critic*] ... do to the image of Eliot the poet-critic in the eye of an academic reader who found the Eliot of the *Selected Essays*, 1932, so potently instructive an authority? What should it do? In my opinion absolutely nothing. Let us pay the old possum, the aged eagle, the self-depreciatory and recantatory elder statesman, the tribute in 1966 of asserting that he himself has not had the right or the power to subvert his own image." [74]

The most productive reaction of the critic to the realization that time has passed him by is his acceptance of this state and his turning to the past via memoirs and reminiscences to call it up again and make it live in the present. In this kind of writing the critic functions as historian of himself, and his recollections are uniquely valuable as a record of a time that is gone by one who was there. Reminiscence thus serves not as criticism of literature but as the means to understand that criticism, in that it illuminates not only the values of the critic who wrote it but also the values of the time in which he lived.

In a sense, recognition of obsolescence is a pessimistic view of the meaning of intellectual effort, for it involves a critic's acceptance of his own failure. But it is in such recognition and acceptance that a critic (or any man) discovers the limitations of human understanding and the transitoriness of human effort. As I. A. Richards says of an arrogant critic: "With him are many Professors to prove that years of endeavor may lead to nothing very remarkable in the end." [75] This recognition, I believe, is akin to that of the tragic hero, but it is a recognition not of the evil deed but of the "evil" of the finitude of man, of oneself. It is this kind of recognition of personal and human failure that R. P. Blackmur found in Henry Adams, who to him exhibited "the failure of the human mind, pushed to one of its limits, to solve the problem of the meaning, the use, or the value of its own energy: in short the failure to find God or unity" (*LH* 86). What Blackmur asserts as the greatness of Adams is the greatness of all critics: the effort to find truth along the way, not the truth found; the struggle, not the result.

> The greatness is in the effort itself, in variety of response deliberately made to every possible level of experience. It is in the acceptance, with all piety, of ignorance as the humbled form of knowledge; in the pursuit of divers shapes of knowledge— the scientific, the religious, the political, the social and trivial—to the point where they add to ignorance. ... As it is a condition of life to die, it is a condition of thought, in the end, to fail. Death is the expense of life and failure is the expense of greatness. (*LH* 95)

Historical Change as Crisis in Criticism

The causes of change in criticism seem to differ sharply from those in science. According to Kuhn, the cause of crisis in the sciences is a largely technical anomaly in normal problem-solving activity caused "by the persistent failure of the puzzles of normal science to come out as they should" (*SSR* 68). The standards of truth a paradigm provides for a single subdiscipline are much more rigid in the scientific world than in criticism, and hence departures from an established paradigm are more readily perceivable in the sciences. After the gross failure of a test, "because the test arose from a puzzle and thus carried settled criteria of solution, it proves both more severe and harder to evade than the tests available within a tradition whose normal mode is critical discourse rather than puzzle solving." [76] The standard of truth and falsity in normal science, then, is rigid and unambiguous.

In contrast, criticism is marked by semantic ambiguity and shifting meanings for elements of its disciplinary matrix. Critics often begin to do different things under a traditional rubric such as *explication de texte,* as, for example, the Formalists did when they changed the meaning of that process from the French historical explication to an ahistorical procedure. Conversely, critics sometimes seem to carry on much the same kind of critical activity under different names—the Chicago Critics or myth critics do very much the same kind of explication as do Eliot and the Formalists— while making much of their originality.

Science and criticism also differ in that critical communities are much looser, less institutionalized, less collective, than those of scientists, who generally do collective work in a laboratory. Because adherents of a charter are often defined as contributors or subscribers to a literary quarterly, they are not necessarily acquainted. One result of this lack of a cohesive community and of an unambiguous truth is that in criticism there is no equivalent of the enforcement power of a paradigm, or the reading out of the discipline of a critic who does not follow the other adherents of his charter. There is no such thing as a maverick scientist, but maverick critics like Yvor Winters, Robert Graves, and others continue as members of the critical community. Speaking of the reaction to his *Natural Supernaturalism,* M. H. Abrams says: "A humanistic demonstration, unlike a scientific demonstration, is rarely such as to enforce the consent of all qualified observers. For it to carry the reader through its exposition to its conclusions requires some grounds for imaginative consent, some comparative ordering of values, some readiness of emotional response to the matters shown forth, which the reader must share with the author even before he begins to read; and these common grounds are no doubt in part temperamental, hence variable from reader to reader. If this assertion constitutes relativism, then we simply have to live with the relativism it asserts." [77]

Another result of the lack of accepted standards of truth and the lack of enforcement powers in criticism is that individual critics and groups of critics tend not to become aware of crises in criticism, but continue to do their own thing without regard for challenging views. For example, in the 755 pages of their *Literary Criticism: A Short History* (1957), W. K. Wimsatt and Cleanth Brooks scarcely mention the principal theoretical alternative to their Christian dualism, the "methods" approach developed by Stanley Hyman in *The Armed Vision* (1948).

Criticism may be much like science, however, if the context of discussion is science as a whole rather than a single science like physics, where a reigning paradigm quells alternative views and creates "normal science." There seems to be some confusion among Kuhn and his commentators on this point. Kuhn remarks that "what has been said so far may have seemed to imply that normal science is a single monolithic and unified enterprise that must stand or fall with any one of its paradigms as well as with all of them together. But science is obviously seldom or never like that. Often, viewing all fields together, it seems instead a rather ramshackle structure with little coherence among its various parts" (*SSR* 49). Later he expands this view to note that "though scientists are much more nearly unanimous in their commitments than practitioners of, say, philosophy and the arts, there are such things as schools in science, communities which approach the same subject from very different points of view." [78]

Looking at science in this synchronic way, one sees a world which seems much like that of criticism, a world where there are competing views of the same subject as well as different subspecialties with views that are not ultimately reconcilable. For example, if one considers the practice of *explication de texte* as a single subspecialty, like electromagnetics, one finds that the New Critics' and the Chicago Critics' views of how to do it are separable but relatively similar, and that both groups oppose each other as well as the dissimilar kind of explication carried on by philologists. This state of affairs seems to parallel Kuhn's view of the relation of different scientific communities to one another: "Because the attention of different communities is focused on different matters, professional communication across group lines is likely to be arduous, often gives rise to misunderstanding, and may, if pursued, isolate significant disagreement."[79]

This kind of confusion afflicts even so astute a critic as M. H. Abrams, who in the course of defending the unique virtues of critical knowledge says: "The physicist tacitly shares with other physicists a perspective which sharply limits what shall count as facts; ... on the other hand, a critic employs one of many available perspectives to conduct a fluid and largely uncodified discourse. ..." Thus, "this progress [in criticism] consists in part in the accumulation of alternative and complementary critical theories and procedures, in a fashion very different from the progress of the science of physics toward ever-greater generality."[80] If one takes as the proper parallel "physicist/Freudian critic" or "scientist/critic," then determining the relationship of scientist to critic is about the same as asking whether knowledge is to be gained by approaching nature as physicist or biologist, or literature as Formalist or Myth Critic; the relationship between the various kinds of science and criticism is about the same.

Kuhn's book, then, could more accurately be called "The Structure of Revolution in Scientific Subspecialties." This revision of Kuhn's thought leads to two conclusions. First, the sequence of historical change should be focused firmly within a critical school, since this is the equivalent of the disciplinary subspecialty to which Kuhn's theory mainly applies. Second, the implication for critical theory, the theory of the whole of criticism, is to see it as Kuhn sees the whole of science, as a ramshackle conglomeration of various disciplines that are as yet not reconcilable under a single theory. The aim of critical history in this view is not to see all literary criticism in terms of a single conception that the historian thinks for one reason or another is preferable. Rather, it is to explain the methods, traditions, institutions, careers, judgments, and values of critics—the community and disciplinary matrix of criticism—in terms of the organizing conception, the charter, which gives the activity of any group of critics meaning. Without the universal truth of an "objective" science, it is only in terms of such historically defined organizing principles that the history of criticism or science can have meaning.

In criticism the equivalent of the scientific anomaly that leads to a new paradigm is basically a historical shift in taste which gives rise to needs that cannot be met by the original charter, questions that the charter cannot answer, and literature that it cannot explain. The rise of new writers is the most easily demonstrable of these "anomalies"; T. S. Eliot provides a clear example of creative change when he reevaluates poetry in the twenties in order to praise the Metaphysicals and French Symbolists, whose works resemble his own, and to criticize Milton and the Romantics, whose poetry he had to replace so that he might be heard. When Allen Ginsberg first published his "Howl," in the *Evergreen Review* in 1956, it did not fit either the standards of paradox, ambiguity, and tragic complexity of the Formalists or the moral realism of the New York Intellectuals, and since neither group could explicate it or make it meaningful as part of its avant-garde dynamic, the only alternative was to call it bad, which both groups did. The continuing difficulty creativity poses for criticism is seen in the yet unsolved problems that, say, the new novelists of the sixties—Thomas Pynchon, John Barth, Kurt Vonnegut, Thomas Berger, and others—pose for critics, who have tried unsuccessfully to organize them under a number of charters, such as the literature of the absurd, wasteland literature, black humor, etc.

A second cause of change in criticism is the new question that critics learn to ask, usually by importing it from a thinker in another intellectual discipline. The parallel in science is described by Kuhn: "No natural history can be interpreted in the absence of at least some body of inter-twined theoretical and methodological belief that permits selection, evaluation, and criticism. If that body of belief is not already implicit in the collection of facts ... it must be externally supplied, perhaps by a current metaphysic, by another science, or by personal and historical accident" (*SSR* 16-17). As has been demonstrated above, similar ideologies influence criticism under the guise of "perspectives" or "approaches" to literature, and as new ideologies cause the formation of critical charters and schools, so a change in ideologies causes the obsolescence of those same schools.

The third way in which anomalies occur in criticism is through large shifts in cultural taste, which make the assumptions of a decade or generation seem suddenly dated in the light of new social and cultural needs and values. Such a shift occurred among Neo-Marxists in the thirties, when the rise of Nazism made the need to revolutionize America seem unimportant compared to the need to help the war effort and be patriotic. In 1976 Hilton Kramer speculates in the *New York Times:*

Less than a decade after the campus revolts, the colleges are quiet, Woodstock and the "love generation" a distant memory, and economic security the overriding priority. ... Broadway abounds in revivals of the well-made play and the romantic musical. Museums are mounting expensive revivals of academic painting, and the beauty of Beaux-Arts architecture is enthusiastically rediscovered by champions of the modern movement. Realist painting has made significant inroads in a market formerly dominated by abstraction. ... The [avant-garde] appetite for outrage and innovation, for shock and squalor, for assaults on the audience and on the medium, has clearly diminished where it has not completely disappeared. The taste now is for clarity and coherence, for the beautiful and the recognizable, for narrative, melody, pathos, glamour, romance, and the instantly comprehensible.[81]

There is no accounting for such a shift of taste, but there is no escaping it either, and the result in criticism is that the kinds of "anomalies" mentioned, the result of time and change, cause critical charters to become obsolete.

The success of a critic's career is thus partly determined by the relation of his career to the charter he chooses; if he comes of age at the beginning of a charter's development, the effectiveness of the charter may last as long as his own active career; if he embraces a charter as it is about to become obsolete, his own career may be thwarted by cultural change—who will be the last living New Critic? Much of the dynamics of criticism lies in the relationship between "charter time" and what might be called the "career time" of the critic. One can estimate a fruitful critical life span by comparing the date of the formation of a critic's voice with the "birth" date of the charter of his movement. T. S. Eliot expresses most of the essential doctrines of Formalism in *The Sacred Wood*, published in 1920 when he is thirty-two. As early as 1940, and decisively in 1956, when he is sixty-eight, Eliot observes that the movement is finished and accepts the fact gracefully (*OPP* 295). Eliot's active career thus coincides with his movement, as do the careers of Ransom, Tate, Blackmur, Winters, and Brooks, all of whom were born around the turn of the century. Murray Krieger publishes his book on the aesthetics of Formalism, *The New Apologists for Poetry*, in 1956, but he is only thirty-three at the time, and the charter he uses to form his opinion of the literary world becomes obsolete just as he finds his own voice; thus he becomes superannuated just as his career is beginning. A similar pattern is observable among the New York Intellectuals. Lionel Trilling begins publishing essays about 1940, when he is thirty-three; in 1950 his *Liberal Imagination* formulates the Intellectuals' charter. Norman Podhoretz, a student of Trilling's, publishes his first book, *Doings and Undoings*, in 1964, when he is thirty-four, but the tension of the Intellectual's charter has collapsed. Thus Krieger and Podhoretz are superannuated almost as they are born as critics, because their career times and cultural or charter times do not coincide, and hence they are deprived of cultural influence.

As mentioned earlier, a critic seldom changes his charter once he has worked it out, while cultural movements change more rapidly than critics retire or die. Thus, given the ordinary career pattern—that a critic adopts his charter at the age of thirty and retires at sixty-five—one can allow a thirty-five-year life span for critical opinions. For example, as John E. Jordan says in "Literary History at Berkeley": "Much of the Germanic philology hung on until after the retirement of Professor Arthur Brodeur in 1955. Then only Old and Middle English were required, then only Middle English, and now no such language requirements remain."[82]

Looked at synchronically, then, the history of criticism resembles a geological time table, with the critics of the older schools about to retire and the younger ones piled on top of them, doing normal criticism according to the values of their charters. At present, things look much like this:

Year of Fashion	Charter
1975	Hermeneutics
1970	Lévi-Strauss and Structualism
1965	Phenomenology and Existentialism
1960–	Northrop Frye and Myth Criticism
1940–	Formalist "New" Criticism
1940	Semantics, History of Ideas
1930–40	Marxist and Parringtonian Criticism
1930	New Humanism
1920–40–	Historical Scholarship, Philology, Psychological Criticism
1910	Impressionism

The more recent theories in this list are, of course, what might be called candidates for charterdom, in that they have been presented as ideologies their supporters think ought to be important charters. Such presentations include the 1966 Johns Hopkins conference on Structuralism and the special issue of *Yale French Studies* on Jacques Lacan and literature (1977); to date, however, these candidates have not demonstrated that they can generate normal criticism or the rewriting of literary tradition in a way which will be generally influential.

The Obsolescence of Charters: The Eponymous Critic

Returning to the theoretical discussion of the development of charters, one sees that the parallel to superannuation on the individual level is obsolescence on the intellectual level. The sequence of development in scientific fields is noted by Jerome Ravetz: "With the state of immaturity corresponding to the infancy of a field, from which only the hardy survive, we can see the phase of maturity giving way, in its turn, to one of senescence. The lasting achievements of the phase of immaturity will be a few aphoristic insights of a philosophical character, and perhaps some tools and techniques; those of the phase of maturity will be a mass of positive knowledge. But when the basic insights are exhausted and the leading problems shift elsewhere, the field enters senescence, useful only for its standardized information and tools purveyed through teachers."[83]

The fate of past truths in the humanities is different, however, in that, as Kuhn remarks, "though contemporaries address them with an altered sensibility, the past products of artistic activity are still vital parts of the artistic scene. Picasso's success has not relegated Rembrandt's paintings to the storage vaults of art museums. Masterpieces from the near and distant past still play a vital part in the formation of public taste and in the initiation of many artists to their craft. ... Unlike art, science destroys its past."[84] Looked at from the point of view of individual critics and schools, superannuation and obsolescence undoubtedly occur, and critical schools, like artistic ones, rise and fall with amazing rapidity.[85] But criticism regarded as a whole is much like art in that the best statements, those which endure, become part of academic history. Robert M. Adams observes (somewhat over-pessimistically) of the process of obsolescence in criticism: "As it [a critical thesis] proves itself against resistance, every newly proposed critical pattern thus takes its place in the sluggish, unceasing stream of accepted opinion—is adopted into a structure, drained of its vitality, fossilized into a formula, repeated by rote for a while, renewed perhaps for a fresh function, and finally cast aside to become a specimen in the 'history of criticism' courses. ... Criticism is always changing yet never 'gets anywhere,' never 'settles anything.' Hence critical systems inevitably become obsolete without formal refutation."[86]

Thus, the only possible goal of a critic is to become part of history, since historical survival is the immortality of criticism. Eventually, successful critical documents attain academic recognition and work their way into the history of criticism, where they take their place alongside Aristotle's *Poetics*, Horace's *Art of Poetry*, Longinus's *The Sublime*, Sidney's *Defense of Poetry*, Dryden's *Essays*, Pope's *Essay on Criticism*, Johnson's *Lives of the Poets*, Coleridge's *Biographia Literaria*, etc., as the equivalents of scientific classics like Aristotle's *Physica*, Ptolemy's *Almagest*, Newton's *Principia* and *Opticks*, Franklin's *Electricity*, Lavoisier's *Chemistry*, and Lyell's *Geology*. Kuhn notes of such scientific works that they "served for a time implicitly to define the legitimate problems and methods of a research field for succeeding generations of practitioners ... [because] their achievement was sufficiently unprecedented to attract an enduring group of adherents away from competing modes of scientific activity. Simultaneously, it was sufficiently open-ended to leave all sorts of problems for the redefined group of practitioners to resolve" (*SSR* 10). Critical charters that survive become the classics of criticism; they serve as our culture's legacy of critical understanding of our literature.

The purpose of studying the history of criticism, in the absence of a total truth toward which one can progress, is to inform oneself of the possible vocabularies and values, the human responses, that critics of the past have used to interpret literature. Bernard Weinberg says sensibly that "we might well regard the great theoretical statements [of literary criticism], from Plato to Maritain, not merely as museum pieces or as historical monuments, but as exemplars of the many ways in which man has conceived of the art of poetry and of the possibilities for reading, understanding, and judging the work of art."[87] In this view one school of critics does not displace another, as in science, but contributes to the richness of possible responses, as in the history of art. As M. H. Abrams says: "Critical definitions and theories may be discrepant without conflict, and mutually supplementary instead of mutually exclusive, since each delimits and structures its field in its own way. The test of the validity of a theory is what it proves capable of doing when it is put to work."[88] Thomas Kuhn observes that "just because the success of one artistic tradition does not render another wrong or mistaken, art can support, far more readily than science, a number of simultaneous incompatible traditions or schools."[89] And T. S. Eliot proposes that we study the history of criticism "not merely as a catalogue of successive notions about poetry, but as a process of readjustment between poetry and the world in and for which it is produced. ... By investigating the problems of what has seemed to one age and another to matter, by examining differences and identities, we may somewhat hope to extend our own limitations and liberate ourselves from some of our prejudices" (*UP* 27, 28).

As one looks over the history of critics and schools of criticism and tries to place them in their time, one can isolate one highest state beyond the flux of time to which a critic may aspire; I call this state *eponymous criticism*. This, the historical equivalent of the aesthetic absolute, is the kind which seems in the eye of history to incarnate the essential literary value of an age. In a discussion of the reward system in science Robert K. Merton says:

Heading the list of the immensely varied forms of recognition long in use is eponymy, the practice of affixing the name of the scientist to all or part of what he has found, as with the Copernican system, Hooke's law, Planck's constant, or Halley's comet. In this way scientists leave their signatures indelibly in history; their names enter into all the scientific languages of the world. At the rugged and thinly populated peak of this system of eponymy are the men who have put their stamp upon the science and thought of their age. Such men are naturally in very short supply, and these few sometimes have an entire epoch named after them, as when we speak of the Newtonian epoch, the Darwinian era, or the Freudian age.[90]

Similarly in criticism, as Joseph Strelka points out, "in each age certain critics produce interpretations which, despite their entirely subjective origins, turn out to be far more than merely subjective; they become valid for the whole age and sometimes even for those to come. The lack of an absolute norm thus does not necessarily indicate the opposite extreme of a purely subjective dead-end and chaotic anarchy."[91] As one casts an eye back over the history of Anglo-American criticism, eponymic status seems to have been attained only by poet-critics who expressed their time creatively and analyzed it critically. Our highest plane of criticism seems to be the most personal, the kind in which reason articulates in prose what genius has expressed in verse. So far, to the roster of great names, to the eponymic ages of Dryden, Johnson, Coleridge, and Arnold, one can add only T. S. Eliot, the eponymous figure of our age.

2. A Preliminary Theory of Literary Charters

The basic philosophical question that charters pose is, What is the ultimate reality of the values which they formulate? There are three possibilities: (1) the values of a charter may be an objective description of the texts of literature; (2) they may be projected into literature by an individual critic; or (3) they may be defined and validated by the consensus of a culture or community—that is, they may be social.

Such questions have provided the focus of much discussion about Kuhn's *The Structure of Scientific Revolutions,* and the clarity with which the arguments are presented is helpful in focusing on similar questions in literary criticism. One main line of attack against Kuhn has been mounted by philosophers of science, the most eminent of whom is Sir Karl Popper, who are concerned to defend science as providing a rational, objective, true description of nature. In a simplistic formulation of this alternative, science describes what is out there, the reality of nature, in an objective, value-free way. Statements are true or false insofar as they can be tested by empirical reality. The critical equivalent of the objectivist view is held by the Formalists, or "New Critics," who believe that a reader can be objective and that the standard or test of his reading is conducted by referring to the text itself. To cite only one example, Cleanth Brooks says in *The Well Wrought Urn* that his judgments on poems are rendered "not in terms of some former historical period and not merely in terms of our own: the judgments are very frankly treated as if they were universal judgments" (*WWU* 217). Likewise, Northrop Frye defends his system as objective on the explicit model of science. He says: "Literary criticism is now in such a state of naive induction as we find in a primitive science" (*AC* 15). Critics must find the true conceptual principle, the hypothesis, the paradigm, the charter, which, "like the theory of evolution in biology, will make us see the phenomena it deals with as parts of a whole," see criticism as "a totally intelligible body of knowledge" (*AC* 16).

One corollary of the objectivist position is that science, since it accumulates objective truths, progresses toward an ideal of total truth, of what Herminio Martins calls "philosophical *logotopias*: visions of complete, perfect, and final knowledge and the criteria and procedures involved in the search for it. Baconian inductivism, Cartesian rationalism, Platonic geometricism are good examples of influential and fertile logotopias."[1] Speculating on the effect of such a logotopia in criticism, M. H. Abrams says: "If, however, instead of holding up such certainty as an abstract ideal, we realize in imagination the form of life in which such critical discourse would be standard, we find it inhuman and repulsive; for it is an ideal that could be achieved only in a form of political, social, and artistic life like that which Aldous Huxley direly foreboded in *Brave New World* or George Orwell in *1984*."[2] For Kuhn, objective knowledge in science is confined to normal science, where progress consists in working out the puzzles a paradigm poses. Kuhn observes that while textbooks written from the point of view of present paradigms and the limited projects of normal science seem to support the idea of progress, science as a whole does not progress. "The developmental process described in this essay has been a process of evolution *from* primitive beginnings— a process whose successive stages are characterized by an increasingly detailed and refined understanding of nature. But nothing that has been said or will be said makes it a process of evolution *toward* anything" (*SSR* 170-71). Thus, successive stages in scientific development are marked by "an increase in articulation and specialization," but "without benefit of a set goal, a permanent fixed scientific truth, of which each stage in the development of scientific knowledge is a better exemplar" (*SSR* 172, 173). Kuhn's theory is thus antiteleological. David Hollinger says that "Kuhn's theory of science dispenses with the idea of a fixed, permanent natural order that can function both as a standard for truth in the case of particular theories and as a goal for the progress of science. Kuhn also rejects the a priori methodological unity of science." In Hollinger's interpretation, Kuhn thinks that we can survive the tension of looking for truth without assuming that it can be known, and that his work "can be read as an invitation to forsake at last the fictional absolutes of natural theology."[3] Kuhn asserts that "to say with pride, as both artists and scientists do, that science is cumulative, art not, is to mistake the developmental pattern in both fields."[4]

With the introduction of Einstein's theory, the view that science can provide objective truth about nature was destroyed in the collapse of the Newtonian world order. According to Imre Lakatos: "Now very few philosophers or scientists still think that scientific knowledge is, or can be, proven knowledge. But few realize that with this the whole classical structure of intellectual values falls in ruins and has to be replaced: one cannot simply water down the idea of proven truth—as some logical empiricists do—to the ideal of 'probable truth' or—as some sociologists of knowledge do—to truth by changing consensus."[5] If this is a fair summary of the course of science, the ideal of science as an objective description of nature is a false goal for criticism.

One may, however, claim that the charter theory of criticism is as scientific as Kuhn's theory of paradigms, in that criticism can be judged as good or bad in the same terms that Kuhn proposes for evaluating science: "accuracy, consistency, scope, simplicity, and fruitfulness."[6] Taking these terms in reverse order, *fruitfulness* is for the critic productivity: a good critic is productive; the good charter is one that leads to a wide revaluation and reinterpretation of the literary tradition, and this process leads to the fulfillment of the requirement of broad *scope*. By *simplicity* Kuhn means that a scientific theory functions to bring "order to phenomena that in its absence would be individually isolated and, as a set, confused" (p. 322). This is what a new charter does for literature; it enables critics to see literature in a new orderly way. By *consistency* Kuhn means that a "theory should be consistent, not only internally or with itself, but also with other currently accepted theories applicable to related aspects of nature" (pp. 321-22). The widespread application of Kuhn's theory to humanistic disciplines serves to authenticate his theory in this way. Not only does the theory of charters applied to the literary world provide further proof of Kuhn's theory, but its relation to similar theories in other disciplines serves to establish it as more credible, and on this point more scientific, than other theories unrelated to larger intellectual movements. The greatest variation between scientific and literary worlds occurs in the definition of Kuhn's first term, *accuracy*. The lack of clear, unambiguous, and generally accepted standards of truth makes the demonstration of error in criticism impossible and leads to its replacement by historical criteria of influence and obsolescence. Kuhn argues against philosophers of science, who believe that the choice of theories in science can be made in terms of an objective theory that would be able to "dictate rational, unanimous choice"; but his sense that "the criteria of choice with which I began [accuracy, etc.] function not as rules, which determine choice, but as values which influence it" (p. 331), is exactly congruent with my sense of the way literary charters work.

A number of thinkers in various fields express similar arguments against the possibility of an objective understanding of cultural life: E. H. Gombrich studies the limits that conventions impose on artistic perception; Benjamin Whorf analyzes the limits language places on our understanding;[7] Freud isolates projection, sublimation, and rationalization as psychological distortions of objectivity; and functionalist anthropologists show how specific cultures limit meaning. Quentin Skinner analyzes philosophical distortions of the history of ideas, concluding that "there are no perennial problems in philosophy. ... Whenever it is claimed that the point of the historical study of such questions is that we may learn directly from the *answers*, it will be found that what *counts* as an answer will usually look, in a different culture or period, so different in itself that it can hardly be in the least useful even to go on thinking of the relevant question as being 'the same'. ... The classic texts, especially in social, ethical, and political thought, help to reveal—if we let them—not the essential sameness but rather the essential variety of viable moral assumptions and political commitments."[8] In criticism, Claudio Guillén rejects the concept of history as "the discovery of underlying designs, polarities, or 'deep structures' beneath the actual tale of events and processes of which history is made"; as the study of the individual event or object, the literary masterpiece; and as "the abstracting from history [of] a final cause or concept, such as progress, ultimate redemption and judgment, or inevitable revolution"; instead, he favors the kind of study that "seeks to recognize enduring constructions and meaningful relations in history itself, actual structures and systems in the agelong career of existing civilizations."[9]

The central point at issue is whether critical judgments can be objective; whether there is a value-free, universal knowledge of literature which one may oppose to the value judgments of the "public critic" of Northrop Frye (*AC* 8-11) or to the judgmental reviewer who has been the traditional model of the Man of Letters. The thesis of this book is that criticism is essentially valuational, and that the theorist's choice of categories of analysis and of a tradition to study are inherently as valuational as more explicitly judgmental criticism. Such a view commands some support. The Formalist theoreticians René Wellek and W. K. Wimsatt essentially agree with the valuational view, though they hold their own values to be more equal than others. Wimsatt says that criticism is "antecedent to knowing the true text and an instrument for knowing it. The same principle, applied in a wider theater, argues that there can be no literary history independent of criticism,—that such is unimaginable—because even the selection of works for inclusion in a history is an act which implies evaluation" (*VI* 260; for Wellek's view, *CC* 5, 52, 68). Similarly, historian Russell B. Nye says that "the historian is not a camera; he cannot include all the facts for he cannot know them all. [*sic*] and even those that he knows are not all of equal value. The facts that the historian uses do not choose themselves; he selects them, orders them within some context."[10] E. D. Hirsch, Jr., takes the further step of saying that criticism is not only valuational but pluralistic: "In the modern world no single hierarchy of values is privileged. We lack the institutionalized authority or the genuinely widespread cultural consensus which could sponsor truly preferential criteria in literary criticism. Absolute evaluation requires an absolute; it requires a universal church. But the actual world of literary evaluation has been for some time now a protestant world where preferential criteria are in fact only the preferences of a sect. To hope for more absolute sanction is to pursue a will-o-the-wisp."[11]

One may say, then, that criticism as a whole provides not the truth about literature but several incompatible and unrelated views of it. Put negatively, this means that there is no truth by which critical views can be judged to be mistaken; one can say that any individual piece of criticism is a good or bad application of its charter, a good or bad Formalist, Marxist, Structuralist article, but one cannot say that the charters themselves are true or false. As in Kuhn's view of science, "at most one may wish to say that a theory which was not previously a mistake has become one or that a scientist has made the mistake of clinging to a theory for too long. ... [In Sir Karl Popper's theories] 'mistake' has been borrowed from normal science, where its use is reasonably clear, and applied to revolutionary episodes, where its application is at best problematic."[12]

When one regards the way critics actually behave in terms of a pluralistic theory of critical truth, the theory appears to be compatible with the practice. This is seen most clearly in the failure of critics to reconcile common critical charters or approaches except by the very strained and shaky application of metaphor, most common of which is the "perspectives" metaphor drawn from art history. For example, Wellek and Warren claim that "the unsound thesis of absolutism and the equally unsound antithesis of relativism must be superseded and harmonized in a new synthesis which makes the scale of values itself dynamic, but does not surrender it as such. 'Perspectivism' . . . [means] a process of getting to know the object from different points of view which may be defined and criticized in their turn. Structure, sign, and value form three aspects of the very same problem and cannot be artifically isolated" (*TL* 156). Likewise, James Thorpe tries to reconcile the various approaches in *Relations of Literary Study* by elaborating on the same metaphor:

This is a book about some new perspectives for the study of literature. Our first hope is that literary students will be able to extend their vision by looking at literature from a series of vantage points. If we try them out, one after another, in a certain sequence, it is possible that a stereoscopic view will result which can lead to a truer understanding of the nature of literature. That is one form of vision, the vision of some of the infinite complexity and some of the beautiful integration which is the work of art. Another form of vision is perception into depth, into the beautiful mystery which is also the work of art. [P. ix]

Stanley Hyman turns to the stage for his metaphor of reconciliation. "A collective or symposium criticism would have the virtue not only of establishing a multiplicity of readings and meanings, but also of giving them all a hearing, and in the last analysis of establishing some true and valid ones. It would be not only plural, but in a very real sense dialectic or dramatistic. From the interplay of many minds, even many errors, truth arises, as our wise men have known since Plato's dialogues. This synthesis of critical method is not simple multiplicity or plurality or anarchy, but a genuine dialectic contest or *agon*. From it, too, truth will arise" (*AV* 401). It is obvious from the unsatisfactory nature of these metaphoric attempts at unity that the various common approaches of criticism exist as separate charters to be developed and applied rather than as parts of a comprehensive critical scheme.

E. D. Hirsch, Jr., analyzes the philosophic implications of the "approach" metaphor: "The perspectival implications of the word 'approach' lead us logically to the sceptical conclusion that scholars and critics who use different approaches are just not perceiving or talking about the same reality. ... Implicitly it [perspectivism] rejects the possibility of an interpretation that is independent of the interpreter's own values and preconceptions; ultimately it repudiates correctness of interpretation as a possible goal. ... [for] critical validity is entirely a function of the encounter between a text and one's inescapable cultural self. ... Perspectivism is a version of the Kantian insight that man's experience is pre-accommodated to his categories of experience." Hirsch, of course, is trying to point out the weakness of the perspectival view to one for whom "meaning is an object that exists *only* by virtue of a single, privileged, pre-critical approach," which for Hirsch is the discovery of the author's intention. Nevertheless, his essay is also useful in that it explicates the relativistic implications of the metaphor, particularly the idea that "verbal meaning exists only by virtue of the perspective which gives it existence" and that hence such criticism "is not interpretation but authorship."[13]

M. H. Abrams discusses the implications of affirming evaluative criticism within the larger perspective of the history of criticism:

Whatever analogue we adopt needs to bring out the fact that critical definitions and theories may be discrepant without conflict, and mutually supplementary instead of mutually exclusive, since each delimits and structures its field in its own way. The test of the validity of a theory is what it proves capable of doing when it is put to work. And each good (that is, serviceable) theory, as the history of critical theory amply demonstrates, is capable of providing insights into hitherto overlooked or neglected features and structural relations of works of art, of grouping works of art in new and interesting ways, and also of revealing new distinctions and relations between things that (from its special point of view) are art and things that are not art. One way to estimate their diverse contributions is to imagine the impoverishment to criticism if we did not possess the theoretical writings of, say, Aristotle,

Horace, Longinus, Kant, Coleridge, Eliot—or Clive Bell. No theory is adequate to tell the whole story, for each one has limits correlative with its powers.[14]

If one proceeds in this pluralistic fashion, one searches for the kind of historical understanding advocated by Robert Marsh, who says: "We need a kind of inquiry that involves no special thesis or argument and that will indeed yield the fullest possible diversity of artistic principles and concepts in terms of which we may formulate our working hypotheses about the natures of particular works. ... It must be an inquiry into differences of basic 'philosophic' principles and of methods of reasoning, an inquiry based on the idea that by attempting to grasp a man's fundamental assumptions and his mode of thought ... we are in a better position than we might be otherwise to determine the precise meanings of his terms and his various statements about the subject." For Marsh the history of criticism thus provides a selection of alternative interpretations for the critic as he goes about his task, a means by which "to consider and eliminate, for a 'given' work, all reasonable interpretive possibilities but the one historically most probable."[15]

If criticism is valuational, not objective, and if several sources of value exist in literary culture, then the only kind of theory that can explain this set of conditions must be a pluralistic one, in the sense defined by Maurice Mandelbaum in a discussion of the problems of writing specialized histories: "If the pluralistic approach were espoused, we should not have to write the history of the discipline with which we were dealing in terms of the history of some larger social or cultural unit of which it was a facet or part. On the contrary, our task would be that of tracing influences between specific events, regardless of the field of their provenance."[16] One may also concur with the position of Claudio Guillén, who says that "a section of historical time—the goal, that is, of the concept of period—should not be monistically understood as an undivided entity, a bloc, a unit, but as a plural number or cluster of temporal processes, 'currents,' 'durations,' rhythms or sequences."[17]

The idea of literary charters is thus useful to the historian of criticism because it permits him to describe the complex social and intellectual realities behind criticism and to relate them to practical literary judgments in a relativistic way that does not suppress or distort opposing literary schools in the interests of theoretical uniformity. Implicitly the theory of charters provides for a relativistic conception of the history of criticism, including, of course, the relativity of the idea of critical charters; the theory admits that future generations will look at criticism quite differently, by standards as alien as neoclassical order and Victorian morality are to us now. Explicitly the theory of charters allows for the coexistence of contradictory schools in the present and for their decline and fall.

Kuhn's solution to the collapse of an objective standard of truth and progress for science is to make the judgment of truth the standard of the critical community. He says: "Confronted with the problem of theory-choice, the structure of my response runs roughly as follows: take a *group* of the ablest available people with the most appropriate motivation; train them in some science and in the specialties relevant to the choice at hand; imbue them with the value system, the ideology, current in their discipline ...; and, finally, *let them make the choice.* If that technique does not account for scientific development as we know it, then no other will. ... That position is intrinsically sociological."[18] Though such a standard has been criticized by one of his more vehement critics as making the standard of truth "mob psychology,"[19] M. D. King says that Kuhn's limitation of authority for judgment to a specialists' group relies on "the collective psychology of a group of men whose very activity engenders a respect for order, a group more akin to a body of lawyers than to a revolutionary mob."[20]

A similar reliance on group judgment as a standard of truth is expressed in literary criticism. Edmund Wilson says of such a critical elite: "But how, you may ask, can we identify this elite who know what they are talking about? Well, it can only be said of them that they are self-appointed and self-perpetuating, and that they will compel you to accept their authority. Impostors may try to put themselves over, but these quacks will not last. ... [Elite critics] know what they know, and ... are determined to impose their opinions by main force of eloquence or assertion on the people who do not know" (*TT* 268).

In a scholarly context M. H. Abrams asserts that *"expert readers* of history and of literary criticism possess and apply criteria—which under challenge can be made explicit—for deciding between principled or unprincipled, controlled or arbitrary, sound or unsound, penetrating or silly, interpretations, be they in the Marxist, Freudian, archetypal, Auerbachian, Abramsian, or any other interpretative mode [italics added]."[21] Abrams also insists on the social nature of such standards. Faced with attack from deconstructionist critics, he says:

The reason our confidence is vulnerable is that when our interpretations are so challenged, there is no way to "prove" that our interpretation is right, in the ordinary logical or scientific sense of demonstrating that it must be accepted by all reasonable people. ... We are, in the last analysis, reduced to the claim that we are competent in the language we interpret. From this point of view, deconstruction can be characterized as the systematic deployment ... of a variety of strategems for destroying our confidence in the interpretative skills that we in fact manifest, whose results are largely confirmed by other interpreters who share our condition of undeconstructed innocence."[22]

A similar group standard is found in the famous "we" that New York Intellectuals use to buttress their authority and, in a more intellectually developed form, in the consensus of scholarly opinion represented by MLA bibliographies, surveys of scholarly opinion, and the like.

In his article "The Republic of Science," Michael Polanyi stresses the collective nature of scientific authority. In his view, "scientific opinion is an opinion not held by any single human mind, but one which, split into thousands of fragments, is held by a multitude of individuals, each of whom endorses the other's opinion at second hand, by relying on the consensual chains which link him to all the others through a sequence of overlapping neighborhoods. ... The authority of scientific opinion remains essentially mutual; it is established *between* scientists, not above them. Scientists exercise their authority over each other." Polyani goes on to show how this collective authority is exercised to grant appointments in universities, how referees determine what is published in scientific journals, how textbooks standarize scientific orthodoxy and the teaching of science in schools, and how "the whole outlook of man on the universe is conditioned by an implicit recognition of the authority of scientific opinion."[23] Parallel authorities in related activities govern the social structure of the Republic of Letters.

The most important and identifiable role in which the critic exerts the authority which makes him part of a group of "expert readers," part of the critical elite, is that of referee for a journal or press, accepting and certifying as worthy of publication new critical articles and books or works of poetry and fiction. Though a critic's authority is personal, it is exercised in a social context, as part of a matrix of editors, editorial boards, other referees, and financial sources. In an account of the origins of the scientific journal in the *Transactions* of the Royal Society, it is suggested that the journal attained authority because almost all prominent scientists supported it, and that "this authority based on demonstrated competence provided mutually reinforcing consequences for scientists in their triple roles as members of the Royal Society, as contributors to the *Transactions* and as readers of it."[24] As producers of science, members wished to have their work recognized and competently assessed by other scientists and to have their priority of discovery certified. The knowledge that a paper would be judged by referees led to the more careful preparation of papers and to the internalization of higher standards of competence. As consumers of science, members wished to have the work of other scientists tested so they could rely on its authenticity. As readers of the journal, members served as a check on editors and referees through "letters to the editor": "In providing the organisational machinery to meet these concerns, the Royal Society was concerned with having its authoritative status sustained by arranging for reliable and competent assessments. ... Through the emergence of the role of editor and the incipient arrangements for having manuscripts assessed by others in addition to the editor, the journal gave a more institutionalised form for the application of standards of scientific work."[25]

In the literary world, however, the critical elite enforces its standards differently. A principal point of difference is that the standards of knowledge among humanists are much more various, and less commonly accepted, than those of science, so that the judging of a work as good or bad, which can be done with some certainty in the mathematical or experimental context, is much more open to question in literature. In a symposium on scholarly publishing, Willard A. Lockwood says: "Scholarly standards are a very elusive set of qualities. While we can identify a number of component aspects, most of us would be at a loss to codify the absolutes that we—much less our colleagues in scholarship or scholarly publishing—would defend as *the* scholarly standards by which we measure all scholarly things. As in any value system, scholarly standards are objective, as distinct from absolute or subjective; they tend to be dynamic rather than static; and they reflect to a large degree the intellectual climate and cultural attitudes of their time and place."[26]

One comparative study of journals in the sciences and humanities notes that the rejection rate for manuscripts in the humanities ranges from 69 to 90 percent (in language and literature it is 88 percent), while in the hard sciences the rate is between 20 and 31 percent. The authors of this study conclude that "these fields of learning [the humanities] are not greatly institutionalised in the reasonably precise sense that editors and referees on the one side and would-be contributors on the other almost always share norms of what constitutes adequate scholarship."[27]

Though the decision as to what constitutes good and bad, competent and amateurish, perceptive and dull, scholarship and criticism is marked by uncertainty, the process of judging becomes even more uncertain because critics (often covertly) confuse standards of good and bad with the values of their charters, much as a chemist might judge an article on physics as bad chemistry, or more to the point, a critic might judge a farce as bad comedy. A Formalist *explication de texte* submitted to a mythically oriented magazine, a Marxist study submitted to a scholarly magazine, a source study submitted to a journal of psychoanalytic criticism—all will be rejected, not because they are not good works of their kind, but because they are the wrong kind. Even more narrowly, they will be rejected because the author does not belong to the clique of the editor.

Looked at in terms of a group standard of truth, some of the practices of magazine editors become more comprehensible. Despite the sobriquet "little magazine," the aim of every editor is to expand his magazine in size and eminence as much as possible. This explains the practice of luring famous names to the magazine to add authority to the editor and other contributors, as well as the publishing of lists of famous past contributors.

The editor's aim, then, is to make himself an authority because his position as the judge of other authorities and the gatekeeper to publication demands it. The difference between literature and science is that one has to have knowledge to be a scientific authority, but one may be a proponent of literary values with nothing more than enthusiasm and opinion. If successful, an editor and his clique may form a new critical community and create a new "mob psychology," to put the worst face on it. Scientific knowledge must be discovered, but a literary charter can be created, and becomes good by the process of convincing others that it is good and by changing the relative rank of charters in literary society to make the newcomer influential.

The social standard of value is seen even more clearly in the world of book publishing, in the contrast between the vanity press and commercial and university presses. In a vanity press the decision to publish is made solely by one person, the author who is willing to pay, and such books are not regarded as meaningful academic credentials. In university presses, where most critical books are published, manuscripts go through an elaborate process of editorial scrutiny and submission to readers chosen for their objectivity. As one editor describes it: "The editor tries to avoid readers who might bring to the manuscript considerations that are irrelevant, such as friendship, animosity, competition, political bias, and so forth. Readers from the same institutions (past and present) as the author and those who have engaged in open disputes with the author should be avoided. The editor must be alert as well to second-generation disputes—scholars who cleave to the grudges of their mentors."[28] Finally, these manuscripts are submitted to a faculty board or a committee for institutional or corporate approval, such approval taking the social form of money. In all these stages, the social or group standard of value is apparent, and the greatest prestige and authority is given to presses and institutions that follow these procedures. A prime example of the union of scholarly merit and institutional support is the *Oxford English Dictionary*.

If one takes the critical community as the standard of judgment and tries to measure truth historically, the implication is that the theory that is (has been) true is the theory that is (has been) influential. According to Kuhn, the difference between science and other professional communities in this regard is that the scientist is concerned solely with the approval of his peers in his paradigm community, while "the most esoteric of poets or the most abstract of theologians is far more concerned than the scientist with lay approbation of his creative work" (*SSR* 164). Yet this distinction may be overdrawn if the essential characteristic of a critical magazine is, as was asserted above, the avant-gardist one of separating itself from the surrounding bourgeois society and addressing only others like itself. Thus "influence" for critics is not broad social influence, but influence within the relevant sections of the professional literary community, and the importance of a critical charter is by this standard easily measured by the number of further references, discussions, and essays it generates, by its efficacy in producing "normal criticism" and theory. By placing the standard of value in the judgments of critical communities (elite groups whose standards are separate from the mass audience), one escapes the identification of critical value with the judgment of the mass audience, whose taste is usually antithetical to that of the elite, and one assumes the historical task of defining such critical elites. I have said that one of the criteria of important criticism is that it is original, and such a quality effectively separates it from the platitudes of mass culture. Positing historical influence as a standard for criticism also separates good criticism from merely subjective interpretations, since nothing can please many and please long that is merely individual.

Defending himself against the relativist and subjective objections to his position, M. H. Abrams asserts that the several different views of a subject validated by the relativist critic are valuable because "the resulting vision in depth is a characteristic feature of humanistic truth, as distinguished from mathematical or scientific truths," and that, though critical judgments are subjective, valid criteria for distinguishing good and bad judgments are found in the judgments of expert critics. Though he does not say so explicitly, his position seems to come down to that of Kuhn's, if his approval of Wittgenstein represents his own view. Abrams summarizes Wittgenstein's position as follows: "On the whole, better judgments will be made by those who are expert, but ... this expertise is not acquired through a course of systematic instruction but only 'through "experience"', and can only be described by a vague expression such as having a 'better knowledge of mankind.'"[29]

If criticism is viewed as both essentially a matter of value and determined by personal and historical forces that are relative in nature, then the relative value of various critical statements also must be determined historically. The ultimate assumption and charter of this book is that the historical explanations of critics and critical charters and schools are more exact, more real, more compelling, than alternative kinds of explanations. By examining a critic's *influence* and the *originality* of his vision, one can judge critical statements historically. Such investigations fall under the familiar scholarly classifications of reputation study and biography, both of which judge the critic in relation to his time.[30] Such a standard of value produces not agreement as to the truth about critical method but the definition of various critical charters and the schools clustered around them. If *meaning* is defined as a synoptic vision, a universal truth, a unified interpretation of the Republic of Letters, the reader will be disappointed. What is offered here is a charting of the territory, a critical

Baedeker, as it were. The chapters that follow—on the Formalists and New York Intellectuals—are discrete and disparate interpretations of separate historical schools. These schools are important because they are influential historically, which in turn may be taken as evidence that they organize the values of literature in a way that pleases a few for at least a little while.

At this point one could speculate about the result if critics, or the critical world in general, were to adopt the position outlined here—that is, if they were to see themselves and their ideas as having a limited usefulness and life time. The first consequence would surely be a lowering of the ideological temperature, so that critics would no longer conceive of their remarks in an implicitly metaphysical or theological context, which sees literary criticism as leading to Truth or Salvation. Critics would then perhaps cultivate the virtue of humility. Second, the relative relationship between criticism and literature would be changed; criticism would again become a dependent art, and would be justified as it contributed to the illumination of literary works or literary culture. Emphasis on the usefulness of criticism in creating literary tradition would also alter the present balance between literary theory and practical criticism; the ultimate standard would become practical application in reinterpreting the literary tradition rather than theoretical interest and complexity. Third, an emphasis on seeing American critics in their historical contexts would, perhaps, reveal the fact that they are (almost) all middle-class, tenured, respectable, scholarly, elite, sub- or ex-urbanites, and family men; such a view might shift attention from a world of abstraction—fantasies of revolution, apocalypse, silence, and the polymorphous perverse—to the actual historical realities of the situation. Seeing their values and charters as defined by the actual world in which they live, one might come to understand the historical men and women who go about their business as critics of literature.

It is in this historical and empirical sense that the adoption of the theory of charters would create a new science of criticism. It would not be a science in the traditional sense of giving a view of the subject which is true, objective, and unquestioned, what Kuhn calls "textbook science." The new science of criticism would seek out the variety in criticism rather than suppress it in the interests of a single "truth" and it would find the meaning in this variety by discussing critics in the social and ideological contexts that give their critical work value, as well as in terms of the relationship of their values to larger cultural contexts.

**Part II
The New Critics as
Tory Formalists**

3. T. S. Eliot
and the Tory Charter

The American New Criticism has been discussed more than any other critical movement in recent history and has spawned a large number of books and essays on its message and doctrines, but, to date, an adequate history of this phenomenon, or of the stages of its development has not been written. [1] The history of the phrase itself is simple. Joel Spingarn used it as the title of a lecture given at Columbia in 1910 where it referred to the beliefs of Croce. This lecture later became the title essay of an anthology of criticism published by Edwin Berry Burgum in 1930. The present sense of the phrase dates from John Crowe Ransom's use of it as the title of a book, published in 1941, on Eliot, Richards, Winters, and Empson. Unfortunately Ransom does not define what the New Criticism is exactly, except to indicate in passing that it has "depth and precision" and centers on the "structural properties of poetry." Ransom's main definition is ostensive; he quotes at length and says: "Writings as acute and at the same time as patient and consecutive as this have not existed in English criticism, I think, before Richards and Empson. They become frequent now; Richards and Empson have spread quickly. That is a principal reason why I think it is time to identify a powerful intellectual movement that deserves to be called a new criticism" (*NC* 111).

As a collective noun, however, "New Criticism" is both confusing and unenlightening, and half a century after the beginning of the movement it seems time to substitute a name which indicates the nature of what is basically a unified movement. I propose "Tory Formalism" as the term which best characterizes the charter of a group of men who believe in or wish for a social and intellectual world and a literature that express belief in tradition, order, hierarchy, the fallen nature of man, the war of good and evil, and the ultimate union of warring dualisms in the Word of God and the metaphors of poetry. [2] As critics, the Formalists (as I shall call them) practice a method of explication, chiefly of poetry, that is marked by a sense of discipline, a concern with the past as found in the allusions and form of the poem, and an intensive study of the text itself as the embodiment of a paradoxical but ultimately meaningful truth.

Formalism develops in three stages: first, the making of the Tory charter in the twenties, principally by T. S. Eliot, but also by the poet-critics Allen Tate and John Crowe Ransom; second, the Age of Explication, from 1938 to 1948, when Cleanth Brooks, R. P. Blackmur, Yvor Winters, R. P. Warren, and their disciples Robert Heilman, Arthur Mizener, William Van O'Connor, R. W. Stallman, and others displace Tory doctrines into Formalist practice through the explication of individual poems in an academic setting, most notably in Brooks and Warren's *Understanding Poetry* (1938); and third, the Age of Theory, when Formalist doctrines are developed theoretically by René Wellek, W. K. Wimsatt, Cleanth Brooks, Murray Krieger, and by their collaborators Austin Warren and Monroe Beardsley, in works like Krieger's *The New Apologists for Poetry* (1956), Wimsatt and Brooks's *Literary Criticism: A Short History* (1957), and René Wellek's *A History of Modern Criticism* (1955-).

The greatest of the masters of Formalism, the Ur-Formalist, is T. S. Eliot, whose influence cannot be overestimated. For all practical purposes Eliot states the essential doctrines of the Formalist charter in the early twenties in *The Sacred Wood* and "The Metaphysical Poets." To be sure, Eliot had no apparent intention of proclaiming a new aesthetic, but he caused a critical revolution because of the immense use others made of his opinions, despite their occasional and disparate origins. In Eliot we have the startling case of a critical voice so authoritative that what were originally the random pronouncements of a youngish American reviewer between 1917 and 1927 formed a critical charter according to which an entire generation of critics was content to live. The influence of Eliot's criticism was felt first in the new English School of Cambridge University, where he gained wide recognition for the doctrines of the "impersonal theory of poetry," the "objective correlative," the "dissociation of sensibility," and for his conception of tradition, as expressed through his books and the Clark lectures on Donne in 1926. In 1958 E. M. W. Tillyard reminisces of this period: "Reflecting now on these sentences of Eliot, I conclude that he was the man really responsible for introducing into Cambridge a set of ideas that both shocked and satisfied. I cannot think of anyone else who counted in this way." [3]

Eliot's influence was also recognized by another Cambridge don, Basil Willey, at about the same time, and Willey describes in detail the shift in sensibility Eliot caused:

Well, I noticed it more and more in supervisions. Old and familiar intellectual clothes were being discarded, and new styles coming into fashion. Old literary luminaries were sinking below the horizon, and others rising into the sky. It was now to be down with Milton, and up with Donne. Milton, we learnt to our amaze-ment, was a Chinese Wall blocking the onward course of English poetry; or in the other metaphor, he had applied to it surgery so drastic that it had never really recovered. Donne, on the other hand, was everything that a poet should be; he was witty, subtle, argumentative, ironical, had his intellect at the tips of his senses, could think passionately and feel intellectually, had a unified sensibility, and so forth. ... Other divinities of the romantic century were ignored, or treated to passing lip-service. Shelley became a reproach and a hissing; and Arnold, though respectfully saluted, was found to be a muddled thinker after all. [4]

Willey here describes the gestalt shift which marks the coming of a revolu-tionary authority whose dicta become a new charter that changes the way the literary tradition of the past is viewed.

An important source of critical influence for Eliot was his editorship of *The Criterion,* issues of which adorned the coffee tables of the intelligentsia of the twenties and thirties. [5] It is difficult to measure the influence of a literary quarterly, but Allen Tate called it "the best critical quarterly of our time" (*CE* 70), and the impact of both Eliot and his magazine in England can be judged by some lines written by a young English poet, W. H. Auden, in "Letter to Lord Byron":

A raw provincial, my good taste was tardy,
    And Edward Thomas I as yet preferred;
I was still listening to Thomas Hardy
    Putting divinity about a bird;
    But Eliot spoke the still unspoken word;
For gasworks and dried tubers I forsook
The clock at Grantchester, the English rook.

All youth's intolerant certainty was mine as
    I faced life in a double-breasted suit;
I bought and praised but did not read Aquinas,
    At the *Criterion's* verdict I was mute,
    Though Arnold's I was ready to refute;
And through the quads dogmatic words rang clear,
"Good poetry is classic and austere." [6]

Eliot's critical authority rests ultimately on his preeminence as a poet, as author of *The Waste Land,* which Ransom called "the most famous poem of our age" (*NC* 136). It is really Eliot's poetry that caused him to become an "International Hero," a "Literary Dictator." [7] Moreover, his influence was not confined to England but reached almost instantaneously to America, largely through *The Dial.* As George Watson notes: "Eliot's success [as both poet and critic] was not only profoundly merited, but was total and instantaneous within the terms it had set itself: the capture of young intellectuals of creative energy in England and the United States in the

1920's. That capture involved, in a very few years, the capture of the seats of literary power, of the London literary journals and of influential younger teachers of literature in the universities."[8] Eliot's essays become influential on the Formalists in America through the early essays by R. P. Blackmur in *Hound and Horn,* and through Allen Tate, who uses Eliot's doctrines in his own criticism.[9] In *Modern Poetry and the Tradition,* Cleanth Brooks cites Eliot as a source of his work, as Eliot's poetry was subject of it, and John Crowe Ransom recognizes his preeminent authority in *The New Criticism* in 1941.

Eliot's great achievement was to propel his literary generation in the direction of Toryism, by which one means not the Toryism of Churchill and Heath, but Dr. Johnson's definition: "One who adheres to the ancient constitution of the state, and the apostolical hierarchy of the church of England, opposed to a whig or more generally a conservative." Eliot's avowal that his general point of view is "classicist in literature, royalist in politics, and anglo-catholic in religion" came only in 1928, but it was the result of a decade spent in working out a consistent Tory position. Although in his early poetry Eliot expressed many typical avant-garde positions—the antagonism toward bourgeois culture, the alienation of an artistic elite based on sensibility, the agonism of modern society with its complexity and tension, and the nihilism of modern life—which led avant-garde critics to praise his poetry, in about 1928 he became and remained opposed in his prose writings to the avant-garde on Tory grounds, and his poetry became religious in its message. In 1934 Eliot speaks of the "apparent incoherence between my verse and my critical prose" and explains that "in one's prose reflexions one may be legitimately occupied with ideals, whereas in the writing of verse one can only deal with actuality" (*ASG* 28).

Both Eliot and the Formalists oppose the desire for permanent values and a stable society to the avant-garde cult of fashion; they stress their belief in original sin, not alienation; they have a cult of maturity, not of youth; they oppose to the urban setting of the avant-gardist the virtues of Agrarianism; they oppose organic virtues and concepts to avant-garde technology; and they oppose the old and permanent to the avant-garde cry to "make it new," which is seen most clearly in their defense of "tradition" against the nihilistic experimentalism and futurism of the avant-garde. It is this opposition to the dominant avant-garde ethos which gives the Formalists much of their importance as the "alternative culture" to the modernism of the twenties or the Marxism of the thirties. As both Eliot and Ransom admit, they are fighting against the tide in what is basically a romantic and avant-garde age. Renato Poggioli says: "In modern poetry and art, classicism can operate only as a retrospective utopia, as a logical counterbalance to the futuristic utopia" (*AG* 222). Nevertheless they do oppose their age with all their hearts, and in this opposition one finds the

Tory essence of their value as critics. According to Russell Kirk, the true Tory (or conservative) opposes science and modernism and (1) has "affection for the proliferating variety and mystery of traditional life, as distinguished from the narrowing uniformity and equalitarianism and utilitarian aims of most radical systems"; (2) has the "conviction that civilized society requires orders and classes"; (3) has a sense of man's evil nature and hence a belief that "man must put a control upon his will and his appetite. . . . Tradition and sound prejudice provide checks upon man's anarchic impulse"; (4) has a "belief that a divine intent rules society as well as conscience," [10] and it is these doctrines that become the Formalist literary values.

These ethical and political principles are familiar to literary students as organic unity and ambiguity, levels of meaning, tradition, and the problems of meaning, which when applied create the traditions of the regionalist and Metaphysical writers discussed below, and establish these traditions by constructing a world organized on a principle of hierarchy, the "conviction that civilized society requires orders and classes." This sense of the hierarchical order of things found particular historical expression for the Formalists in the myth of the Old South. As Wallace Douglas expresses it: "Southerners still believe that the 'natural order of things' warrants the social hierarchy"; and, somewhat more specifically, "it is sometimes hard to keep from thinking that the Agrarians just wanted to make the whole world take on the ineluctable and subtly graded social distinctions of the [Southern] small town." [11] Both social hierarchy, as embodied in Eliot's cathedral and the Fugitives' plantation, and the medieval intellectual hierarchy of the great chain of being and the Elizabethan world picture seem permanent characteristics of the Tory mind. And in the literary context, according to Brooks, "the characteristic unity of a poem . . . lies in the unification of attitudes into a hierarchy subordinated to a total and governing attitude" (*WWU* 207). The Formalists find hierarchies both in the poem and in their response to it, both formally and affectively, and their highest ideal for the reader is that he become an ordered critic, by seeing the poem as a hierarchy (usually called "levels of meaning") and by ordering his response to it. It is not clear whether the Formalists believe that this hierarchy is projected into the poem by the ordered mind of the critic, or exists innately in the poem for the critic to discover, but whether Aristotelian or Platonic, the effect on the process of criticism is the same. Thus in chapter 16 of *Principles of Literary Criticism,* Richards isolates six levels of response to a poem, and in *Practical Criticism* analyzes sense, feeling, tone, and intention as the four aspects of the meaning of a poem. Empson's seven types of ambiguity are, in this context, seven ways to respond more completely to the levels of language of a poem. In "Allen Tate as a Teacher," Warren Kliewer shows how Tate applies the doctrine of levels in the classroom through "a method of analysis based on medieval biblical exegesis, which resulted in four levels of meaning." [12]

The hierarchical organization of poems is described most clearly by Wellek and Warren in *Theory of Literature,* where they assert that "the real poem must be conceived as a structure of norms ... not merely one system of norms but rather of a system which is made up of several strata, each implying its own subordinate group" (*TL* 150, 151). They elaborate this insight in the rest of the book by taking each norm in sequence (meter, image, sound, etc.) and investigating it in detail. In a later essay, Wellek traces this idea philosophically to the Polish phenomenologist Roman Ingarden, according to whom "the work of art is a totality but a totality composed of different heterogeneous strata." For Wellek, "such a concept of the literary work of art avoids two pitfalls: the extreme of organicism which leads to a lumpish totality in which discrimination becomes impossible, and the opposite danger of atomistic fragmentation" (*CC* 68). Similarly, Yvor Winters criticizes R. S. Crane for lacking a sense of hierarchy, and points to the final cause implicit in such an order: "Yet there seems to be no consistent awareness in his remarks that the most important end of such study would be the establishment of some kind of hierarchy of potentialities among the various forms, their subdivisions, and their elements; nor that the establishment of any such hierarchy would be impossible unless we had a clear idea of what the final cause of literature should be, so that we could evaluate the different forms in relationship to this cause" (*FC* 20).

The Formalists conceive of the role of the critic as a literary, moral, and spiritual leader atop the hierarchy—that is, as an elite. The most articulated social definition of Eliot's elitism is his *Notes Towards the Definition of Culture* (1949), in which he expresses the belief that culture is created by talented individuals, but is preserved and transmitted by cultural elites composed of both single individuals and families. As John J. Soldo shows, Eliot's ideas of elitism thus arise naturally from his conception of his own place as part of a superior family in American society.[13] In his first essay on Milton, Eliot writes: "Of what I have to say I consider that the only jury of judgment is that of the ablest poetical practitioners of my own time" (*OPP* 157). When he confronts critics who rely on their own judgment, on what Eliot calls the "inner voice" rather than on public tradition and order, his conception of his own authority and his contempt for the unenlightened become apparent: "The possessors of the inner voice ride ten in a compartment to a football match at Swansea, listening to the inner voice, which breathes the eternal message of vanity, fear, and lust" (*SE* 16); Lawrence and the inner light give "the most untrustworthy and deceitful guide that ever offered itself to wandering humanity" (ASG 59).

In the course of defending Formalism against the attacks of Eric Bentley, Robert Heilman claims that an elite is necessary to a sound society, points out the existence of a technocratic elite and the elite status enjoyed by artists and intellectuals, and concludes: "The real debate, it would seem, would have to center in the consideration of whether a stable, responsible, organic core of society can, by exemplifying at their purest the cultural affirmations of that society, be a tonic and sustaining influence without which the society must become retrograde, or whether such an elite must from the start act as a brake upon the aspirations of the good society." [14] For Heilman, an elite is desirable; following Matthew Arnold, he assumes the necessity of the critical faculty in society as the saving remnant.

The assumption that justifies and makes necessary a critical elite is the theological belief in the evil nature of mankind. As Eliot says, speaking of Baudelaire: "Baudelaire perceived that what really matters is Sin and Redemption ... the recognition of the reality of Sin is a New Life; and the possibility of damnation is so immense a relief in a world of electoral reform, plebiscites, sex reform and dress reform, that damnation itself is an immediate form of salvation—of salvation from the ennui of modern life because it at last gives some significance to living" (*SE* 378-79). [15] Since mankind is fallen, it can be saved from its own evil nature only by external order and tradition, and the critic who articulates them. In theoretical terms, the Formalists argue that since a good work of literature must express a struggle between dialectical opposites, one must have evil to have opposition; literature which ignores evil does not have tension, is not complex or mature. Wimsatt and Brooks say:

We recognize the fact of material concreteness in human experience, and though matter itself be not evil (as in the Persian scheme), yet it does seem the plausible enough ground for some kind of dualism, division, tension, and conflict, the clash of desires, and evil and pain. ... Of course the reflective and responsible theorist will say that he doesn't call evil itself, or division, or conflict, desirable things. He is sure, however, that facing up to them, facing up to the human predicament, is a desirable and mature state of soul and the right model and source of a mature poetic art. ... Anybody will have to admit that there could never be any drama or story, either comic or tragic, without tension, without conflict, without evil. [*LC* 743; see also *HCo* 32]

Because man is evil, the critic must have a sense of reading as a discipline in order to belong to the critical elite, and this demand is a refrain among the Formalists; for them, reading literature is a high calling, done for truth, not for pleasure, and it is not to be trusted to the immature, the unserious, the "amateur" critic. Indeed, for Formalists this sense of exclusiveness, of participating in an arduous, disciplined experience, gives the method of explication much of its attractiveness in a permissive age. Literature, the Formalists assure us, is an experience one cannot have for the asking, but must suffer and sweat for. It is discipline which marks the elite. Robert Heilman says: "Surely the soundest democracy must insist upon the qualifications, the necessary discipline, of the *demos*. But that exercise belongs to the few." [16] In the course of a debate with H. J. Muller, Cleanth Brooks says: "Now tolerance, amiability, and breadth are always virtues. But they cannot replace, and need not exclude other virtues: clear definitions, reference to first principles, critical discipline." [17]

The evil nature of man also begets a concern with literary form as a means of controlling passion and anarchy. Allen Guttman points out: "Conservatism is almost always politically formalistic because institutional structures, without which Conservatism is impossible, are by definition forms of behavior transmissible from generation to generation. . . . There is a profound insight in T. S. Eliot's witticism, 'The spirit killeth, but the letter giveth life.' " [18] Actually, the study of the past and the study of forms have much the same cultural value. Herbert Howarth says of the Fugitives: "In them and in Eliot alike form was a pre-occupation, because form is a repository of tradition and the sensory projection of a passion for tradition. Out of the horror of the present they and Eliot alike nourished a special love for the past, enabling a sympathetic entry into the past, the reliving of it in sharp reality, the recovery of energy from it." [19]

The way in which Tory values can be translated into structural terms and made a standard of poetic value is shown clearly by Cleanth Brooks in his comment on Eliot's statement that a good poem should be "coherent, mature, and founded on the facts of experience" (*UP* 96). Brooks observes that the good critic "will regard as acceptable any poem whose unifying attitude is one which really achieves unity ('coherence'), but which unifies not by ignoring but by taking into account the complexities and apparent contradictions of the situation concerned ('mature', and 'founded on the facts of experience')" (*WWU* 255). The critic, then, "would be able to find a criterion [of value] in the organization of the poem itself by assessing the relative complexity of the unifying attitude—the power of the tensions involved in it, the scope of the reconciliation which it is able to make" (*WWU* 255-56). Poetic value for the Formalist is thus identified with poetry that is complex: "Semantic analysis such as that associated with Richards and Empson does seem to imply a value in complexity itself. The great poems reveal an organic structure of parts intricately related to each other, and the totality of meaning in such a poem is rich and perhaps operative on several levels. In terms of this view of poetic excellence, a principal task of criticism—perhaps *the* task of criticism—is to make explicit to the reader the implicit manifold of meanings" (*LC* 652). By applying this standard of value, Brooks is able to arrive at the practical judgment that sentimental poetry is bad, and that the highest kind of poetry is tragedy, the genre which reconciles the true evil nature of the world and the complexities of the past in an ordered, artistic unity. The method of *explication de texte* must be regarded, then, as essentially Tory in its confrontation with tragedy and evil, its mastery (through disciplined study) of forms and of the past, and in its end in interpretation of the Word of literature.

In brief, the Formalists assume the validity of the Tory view of reality, fail to find these values in existing society, and so internalize Tory values as a psychological response around which they then organize the world of literature. According to this view, their criticism depends on a prior judgment of value and act of allegiance which, because they are willed, not logical, are irrefutable by rational argument. Such a critical charter is comprehensible only historically, as one comes to understand the experience that led the Formalists to adopt Tory values and express them through Formalist literary doctrines. This etiology includes five stages: (1) *defeat,* a sense of the loss of value in society caused by the collapse of traditional values after World War I; (2) *contemptus mundi,* a strategy of exclusion which separates the literary world from the real world, author, or audience; (3) *the word as world,* the creation of a new world of poetry—constructed around the Tory struggle between good and evil—which functions as a spiritual home; (4) *tradition,* the rewriting of literary history to make that literature good which expresses Tory principles; and (5) *the sacred word,* the assumption of God or an aesthetic absolute as justification for the whole complex Tory critical charter (see chart on pp. 72-73).

Stage One: Defeat

Eliot's poetry and his life provide the best clues to the first stage of twentieth-century Toryism, the sense of the defeat of conservative values in society. One should not forget the effect of the incredible bloodletting of World War I on postwar England; the titles and imagery of Eliot's *The Waste Land,* Pound's "Hugh Selwyn Mauberley," and Robert Graves's *Good-bye to All That* are testimony enough to the collapse of the temporal values of Western civilization. Eliot's crisis of belief in the twenties seems to have been largely a personal matter. He said while defending tradition and the impersonal theory of poetry: "But, of course, only those who have personality and emotions know what it means to want to escape from these things" (*SE* 10-11). When one recalls his situation in the early twenties as an émigré in a foreign country with an underpaid job in Lloyds bank and a neurotic wife, his nervous collapse in 1921 and his subsequent embrac-

T. S. Eliot as Authority Figure

Formalism

The Sacred Wood (1920)/"The Metaphysical Poets" (1921)

Dial Award for *The Waste Land* (1922)/Editor of *The Criterion* (1922–1939)/Clark Lectures at Cambridge (1926)

Richards, *Practical Criticism* (1929)/ Empson, *Seven Types of Ambiguity* (1930)

Development of Tory Formalism in America, 1922-1938

Fugitives' analysis of their own poetry, 1922–1925

Toryism

Love of tradition/Sense of hierarchy, orders, classes/ Man's nature evil: need for discipline/Critical elite/ Belief in divine order

Scopes trial; Southern Fundamentalism/Agrarianism and Regionalism/*I'll Take My Stand* (1930)/Ransom, *God without Thunder* (1930)/Eliot, *After Strange Gods* (1934)/Tate, *Reactionary Essays* (1936)

1936-1939: Defeat of political hopes

Rejection of Audience
Eliot's problem of belief/Wimsatt's affective fallacy/Conception of Ideal Reader

Rejection of World
Poetry as pseudostatement/Heresy of paraphrase/ "A poem should not mean/But be"

Creation of Formalist Charter

Word of Poem as New World
Dissociation of sensibility/Poem as objective correlative of fallen world, dualistic in nature/ Metaphor unites thought and feeling, texture and structure, in the Ideal Poem/Standard of organic unity, holism

Rejection of Author
Impersonal poet of Eliot/Intentional fallacy of Wimsatt

Creation of New Literary Tradition
Aesthetic of regionalism; the mind of Europe/
Poetry of Metaphysicals and moderns/Good
literature mature, tragic, coherent

The Age of the Explicators, 1938–1948

Development of Normal Criticism: *Explication de texte*
Blackmur, *The Double Agent* (1935), *The Expense of Greatness* (1940)/Ransom, *The World's Body* (1938)/Brooks, *The Well Wrought Urn* (1947)
Analysis of paradox, tension, ambiguity; the poem as a drama/Source in Fundamentalist exegesis of Bible

Creation of Critical Communities
Influence spread by *Sewanee Review*, *Southern Review*, *Kenyon Review*/Beginning of Kenyon School of English (1948)

Revolution in the Teaching of English
Brooks and Warren, *Understanding Poetry* (1938)/Spreading of Formalist influence in universities/Opposition of old scholars (Chicago Aristotelians, Lovejoy's history of ideas)

Triumph: Eliot's Nobel Prize (1948)

The Age of the Theorists, 1949–1978

Wellek and Warren, *Theory of Literature* (1949)/Wimsatt, *The Verbal Icon* (1954)/Krieger, *The New Apologists for Poetry* (1956)/Wimsatt and Brooks, *Literary Criticism: A Short History* (1957)/Wellek, *A History of Modern Criticism* (1955–)

Obsolescence of Formalism

Rise of Myth Criticism; Frye's *Anatomy of Criticism* (1957)/Rise of "beat" poetry; Ginsberg's *Howl* (1956)/Rise of counterculture, New Left, anti-Vietnam revolution/New fashion for Continental criticism, Structuralism, Phenomenology

ing of the most high Tory versions of social and intellectual order seem natural psychological responses to a chaotic personal and social situation. [20]

Eliot repeats his pattern of despair in the late thirties when his feeling of defeat is caused by the rejection by society of the Christian alternative he had spent the years 1928-38 arguing for, and the consequent anomie he felt facing the rise of Nazism. When he gives up editing *The Criterion* in 1939, he says: "In the present state of public affairs—which has induced in myself a depression of spirits so different from any other experience of fifty years as to be a new emotion—I no longer feel the enthusiasm necessary to make a literary review what it should be." [21]

A similar need for tradition, and the consciousness of its defeat, was present in the American South from the Civil War to World War I, and this feeling is central to the Southern consciousness of all the Formalists. In about 1928, after absorbing Eliot's doctrines about poetry, the American Formalists turned, as he had, to conservative social and cultural movements. Alfred Kazin writes of the period: "Everywhere in criticism as the twenties drifted to their end in panic, there had been . . . a desperate search for some primary and inclusive article of faith. . . . criticism now significantly proclaimed itself a central moral activity. . . . both the Marxists and the Formalists were united in their contempt for the whole existing order and their confidence that they could help make another" (*ONG* 403-6). As the titles of their books suggest, the Marxists represent the left wing of this struggle for culture, while the Formalists represent the right. Eliot writes *For Lancelot Andrewes* in 1928, *After Strange Gods: A Primer of Modern Heresy* in 1934, and *Murder in the Cathedral* in 1936; Ransom publishes *God without Thunder: An Unorthodox Defense of Orthodoxy* in 1930 and "The Aesthetics of Regionalism" in 1932; Winters's *Primitivism and Decadence* and *Maule's Curse* appear in 1937 and 1938; Tate's biographies *Stonewall Jackson: The Good Soldier* and *Jefferson Davis: His Rise and Fall* are published in 1928 and 1929, and his *Reactionary Essays on Poetry and Ideas* appears in 1936; Robert Penn Warren writes *John Brown's Body: The Making of a Martyr* in 1929; and Ransom, Warren, and Tate all contribute to the two Agrarian symposia of that period, *I'll Take My Stand: The South and the Agrarian Tradition* (1930) and *Who Owns America?* (1936).

But the real consciousness of the defeat of all that they held valuable occurs for Eliot and the Fugitives and Agrarians in the late thirties. As Alexander Karanikas says: "By 1936 it was clear that the Agrarian leaders were generals without an army. No significant section of the people, North or South, had been convinced to abandon their money-based industrial economy, nor could the Agrarians seem to find new and compelling arguments to make further debate profitable." [22] Using Tate as his exemplary figure, R. W. Stallman sums up the feeling produced by this defeat of the Formalists' ideals by the realities of the modern world: "There is one basic theme in both the criticism and the poetry of the Southern poet-critics. . . . It is the dislocation of modern sensibility. . . . [The theme] operates thus through these thematic variations: *the loss of a tradition, the loss of a culture, the loss of a fixed convention, the loss of a world order.*"[23]

What is lost for both Eliot and the American Formalists is the traditional, hierarchical, ordered, religious society they thought had been embodied in Old England and the Old South, and this society is replaced by a world dominated in everyday life by vulgar businessmen and soulless scientists, in philosophy by crass positivists, and in politics by Yankee liberals. Their defeat and rejection by this twentieth-century world leads almost to a feeling of *contemptus mundi,* somewhat similar to the Existentialists' rejection of bourgeois social values and customs after World War II.

Stage Two: Contemptus Mundi

The basic effect of defeat and loss on the Formalists is to make them adopt a strategy of exclusion to rid themselves of the world. That the Formalists almost totally exclude political life from poetry after the defeat of their Neo-Christian and Agrarian political program becomes apparent in about 1938. As Malcolm Cowley says of them in 1950: "I will tell you one way in which the New Critics are reactionary. . . . They are reactionary in the sense that they are pleading for a lack of interest in politics, either objectively pleading for it or else substantively pleading for it by never mentioning politics. Therefore, they are helping, in a sense, to separate an intelligent sector of the American public from political interest."[24] The position they arrive at in the forties is a diversion of political energy to the taking over of the universities, which is expressed in attacks on scholars, historicists, and Neo-Aristotelians (see below), and in a defense of the purity of language and letters as the only part of the public sphere over which they had any control. According to Reed Whittemore: "The political problem, then [c. 1940] as they saw it, was first to find an area over which they might exert a measure of control, and *then* try to be responsible for and about it. The area they chose was language; their responsibility, as Allen Tate put it, was to preserve the vitality of language."[25] As their political energy became focused on language, they adapted their strategy of exclusion to rid criticism of all uncontrollable extralinguistic realities, specifically the modern world as represented by science, the romantic author, and the audience.

The case against conceiving of poetry as giving knowledge of the real world is made by I. A. Richards in *Science and Poetry* (1926) in his now-famous distinction between scientific "statements" about physical reality and the "pseudo-statements" of poetry, which have no referential reality but only the reality of poetic effect on the audience.[26] Science is, however, only the general name the Formalists give to the aspects of the world they wish to exclude,[27] and one should not confuse the object of their attack with real science or scientists, since Formalists refer to social, not physical, scientists and there is no evidence that they have any exact idea of what scientists do, of the processes of the scientific mind, or of the intellectual operations of scientific or mathematical work, to say nothing of "Positivism." The only "scientific" book they ever refer to is *The International Encyclopedia of Unified Science* (*CE* 21; *NC* 281), which contains a section on "semiosis" by Charles W. Morris. This ignorance of science seems to characterize the Formalists from the twenties to the present. John L. Stewart analyzes Ransom's misconceptions of science at some length,[28] and F. R. Leavis demonstrates his for the world to see in his conflict with C. P. Snow.

The "scientist" the Formalists talk about most is I. A. Richards, who graduated with first-class honors in the *Moral* Science Tripos at Cambridge and taught in the Cambridge English School. They probably talk about him because he gave a "scientific" (i.e., psychological) explanation of the process of communication in his work of the twenties, and they had the satisfaction of seeing him converted to the Formalists' belief in the cognitive properties of poetry in *Coleridge on Imagination* (*CE 43-47; WB* 156, 163-65).[29] It should be remembered in this context that it was ridicule of the South for its unscientific attitude at the Scopes trial which first propelled the Formalists into their Agrarian phase.[30]

The Formalists' application of their antiscientific view to criticism can be seen in their essays on the problem of science, even though their references are more often cracks against scientists than sustained arguments. For example, in *The New Criticism*, John Crowe Ransom develops the theory that science uses abstract language while poetry uses concrete language, with such assertions as: "A pure science is one in which the terms of discourse are entirely functional. ... And by this technical device of bounding the meanings of its terms, science immunizes itself against the wandering or diffusion of interest. ... Poetical discourse does not deny its logical structure as a whole, but it continually takes little departures from it by virtue of the logical impurity of its terms" (*NC* 41-42). Ransom also uses a (loaded) metaphor to contrast poetry and science: "A poem is a democratic state ... that restrains itself faithfully from a really imperious degree of organization. It wants its citizens to retain their personalities and enjoy their natural interests. But a scientific discourse is a totalitarian state" (*NC* 43-44).[31] Allen Tate's position is similar to Ransom's in that he criticizes science for reducing the spiritual realm to "positivist procedure" (*CE* 4), and opposes to it a poetics which, like Ransom's, makes poetic language more complete than scientific language, thereby offering "the only complete, and thus the most responsible versions of our experience" (*CE* 4; cf. *CE* 20-21; *WWU* 9). When estimating the worth of the Formalists' aesthetic, however, it is a mistake to take this antiscientific bias as substantive argument, since it is grounded on ignorance and on the Formalists' rhetorical need to establish their own views of poetics and of the world. It should be understood as a prejudice necessary to justify a place for poets and the kind of knowledge poetry embodies in a world the Formalists believe is dominated by scientists and positivists.

The exclusion of the world from criticism is expressed in a specifically literary context in one of the most famous Formalist phrases, "the heresy of paraphrase." In the final essay of *The Well Wrought Urn*, Cleanth Brooks concludes: "It ought to be readily apparent that the common goodness which the poems share will have to be stated, not in terms of 'content' or 'subject matter' in the usual sense in which we use these terms, but rather in terms of structure" (*WWU* 193).[32] This doctrine is expressed in Archibald MacLeish's most famous line, from "Ars Poetica," "A poem should not mean / But be" (see *VI* 81). In practical terms this radically antimimetic position leads to a rejection of the subject matter of literature as a relevant topic of critical consideration.

The strategy of exclusion is applied to the author in Eliot's "impersonal theory of poetry," which refutes the romantic assumption that the author is the key to the interpretation of poetry, and that hence the best criticism is biography. The *locus classicus* is the statement in "Tradition and the Individual Talent" that "the more perfect the artist, the more completely separate in him will be the man who suffers and the mind which creates; the more perfectly will the mind digest and transmute the passions which are its material" (*SE* 7-8). Eliot later explains that

in one sense, but a very limited one, he [the poet] knows better what his poems "mean" than can anyone else; he may know the history of their composition, the material which has gone in and come out in an unrecognisable form, and he knows what he was trying to do and what he was meaning to mean. But what a poem means is as much what it means to others as what it means to the author; and indeed, in the course of time a poet may become merely a reader in respect to his own words, forgetting his original meaning—or without forgetting, merely changing. [*UP* 130]

This "impersonal theory" about the nature of the relationship between poet and poem is part of Eliot's anti-romanticism of the twenties and thirties and is argued at length in a debate between C. S. Lewis and E.M.W. Tillyard in *The Personal Heresy*,[33] but for the Formalists the position is stated definitively by W. K. Wimsatt and Monroe Beardsley in "The Intentional Fallacy" in 1946. According to this essay, the art of judging poetry is different from the art of inspiring poets to write it, and in judging poetry it is better to rely on the public, internal evidence of the words of the poem itself than to accept the private, external evidence found in diaries, letters, and the like, which describe the author's process of composition. The poem "is detached from the author at birth and goes about the world beyond his power to intend about it or control it. The poem belongs to the public. It is embodied in language" (*VI* 5). It seems historically accurate to say that no article in recent critical history has aroused more sustained interest. In "Genesis: A Fallacy Revisited" (1968), Wimsatt reviews twenty years of argumentation (including some thirty articles) and adheres to his original view.[34]

The process of exclusion is extended to the audience by Eliot (after Richards) under the heading of the problem of belief; he argues that the actual beliefs of an audience are irrelevant to the understanding of poetry, thus separating poetry from the ideas of its readers and consequently from the historical world. In his pamphlet *Dante* (1929) he says:

> My point is that you [the reader of poetry] cannot afford to *ignore* Dante's philosophical and theological beliefs, or to skip the passages which express them most clearly; but that on the other hand you are not called upon to believe them yourself. . . . your belief will not give you a groat's worth more of understanding and appreciation; but you are called upon more and more to understand it [what Dante believed]. If you can read poetry as poetry, you will "believe" in Dante's theology exactly as you believe in the physical reality of his journey; that is, you will suspend both belief and disbelief. . . . That is the advantage of a coherent traditional system of dogma and morals like the Catholic; it stands apart, for understanding and assent even without belief. [*SE* 218-19; cf. *SE* 229-31. See also Ransom, *NC* 193-208; and Brooks, *MPT* 47-50 and *WWU* 151ff., on Keats's "Ode to a Grecian Urn"]

Eliot later develops this opinion to introduce a specifically Tory criterion of value for beliefs. He says of Shelley: "The ideas of Shelley seem to me always to be ideas of adolescence. . . . I find his ideas repellent; and the difficulty of separating Shelley from his ideas and beliefs is still greater than with Wordsworth. . . . Some of Shelley's views I positively dislike, and that hampers my enjoyment of the poems in which they occur; and others seem to be so puerile that I cannot enjoy the poems in which they occur" (*UP* 89, 91; cf. his criticism of Yeats, *UP* 140). Eliot goes on to give a standard for beliefs which substitutes an ethical for a historical response to literature: "When the doctrine, theory, belief, or 'view of life' presented in a poem is one which the mind of the reader can accept as coherent, mature, and founded on the facts of experience, it interposes no obstacle to the reader's enjoyment, whether it be one that he accept or deny, approve or deprecate" (*UP* 96).

The problem of belief is also the object of much theoretical discussion,[35] chiefly by Wimsatt and Beardsley in "The Affective Fallacy," where they argue against confusing the poem with its results, its effect on the audience, largely because this method of reading "ends in impressionism and relativism," and because "the poem itself, as an object of specifically critical judgment, tends to disappear" (*VI* 21). Thus the aim of the Formalists is to avoid the multiplicity of readings of a poem implicit in impressionism and to adopt instead a single "objective" interpretation of its formal structure.

Because Formalists eliminate the actual audience from criticism, they are obliged to posit a hypothetical audience as an absolute standard for judging a poem, and they personify this audience as the Ideal Reader. As Brooks says: 'The formalist critic assumes an ideal reader: that is, instead of focusing on the varying spectrum of possible readings, he attempts to find a central point of reference from which he can focus upon the structure of the poem or novel." The Ideal Reader is, of course, what all these critics hope (and implicitly claim) to be. Although Brooks admits that "there is no ideal reader, of course," he goes on to maintain, in a circular argument, that "for the purpose of focusing upon the poem rather than upon his own reactions, it is a defensible strategy" for the practicing critic. Brooks argues from the (false) dichotomy that "the alternatives are desperate: either we say that one person's reading is as good as another's and equate those readings on a basis of absolute equality and thus deny the possibility of any standard reading. Or else we take a lowest common denominator of the various readings that have been made."[36] The elimination of interest in the psychology of existing readers thus leads not to objectivity but to idealized, hypothetical readers.

W. K. Wimsatt projects the doctrine of the Ideal Reader onto the public at large by positing a kind of preestablished harmony between the nature of poetry and the nature of man:

Criticism of structure and of value is an objective criticism. It rests on facts of human psychology (as that a man may love a woman so well as to give up empires), facts, which though psychological, yet are so well acknowledged as to lie in the realm of what may be called public psychology—a realm which one should distinguish from the private realm of the author's psychology and from the equally private realm of the individual reader's psychology. ... Such a criticism, again, is objective and absolute, as distinguished from the relative criticism of idiom and period. [*VI* 82][37]

Here one sees the Ideal Reader abstracted from time and projected as a quality of mankind ("public psychology"), not abstracted or idealized from a number of existing readers. Cleanth Brooks describes the assumptions on which the doctrine of the Ideal Reader is based: "What the author and the various readers of a work do need to hold in common, I would suggest, is not so much the same set of beliefs about the universe as the same set of general human responses."[38] And in their *Literary Criticism: A Short History*, Wimsatt and Brooks broaden the concept still further, resting their critical theories on the explicit assumption of the universality of man's nature: "The assumption that man exists and that his fundamental oneness transcends the innumerable differences that set apart individual men and set apart men of various cultures and periods of history seems implicit here [in Eliot and Tate]. Perhaps it should be brought to light and stated quite flatly. For it may be the necessary assumption if we are to undertake to talk about poetry at all. Unless we can assume it, we necessarily abandon any concept of an aesthetics of poetry in favor of a tabulation of various kinds of social and personal expressions" (*LC* 678; see also *LC* 546-47, 731-32).

The most effective argument against the doctrine of the Ideal Reader lies in the results the application of the Formalist method has had. As Mark Spilka cogently points out:

What are we to say, for instance, when sensitive, intelligent formalists reveal the co-existence, in "After Apple Picking," of nightmares with contemplative delights? ... One is reminded here of Randall Jarrell's complaint of 1952, that "Criticism will soon have reached the state of scholarship, and the most obviously absurd theory—if it is maintained intensively, exhaustively, and professionally—will do the theorist no harm in the eyes of his colleagues." Apparently that state has come to pass. ... Confronted by such readings, we cannot merely explicate the same details more sensibly and rest our case. Inclusiveness and coherence, those touchstones of objective certainty, will not avail us: ... Objective readings, equally exhaustive and consistent, merely cancel out when diametrically opposed, and objectivity itself reverts to armed impressionism.[39]

The advantage of accepting the Formalists' strategy of exclusion is that one is free to detach the work of literature from its origins in the author and the historical context, and to use each individual poem and novel as a building block to construct an autonomous realm of literature, or a "tradition." That is to say, one can construct a revised history of the past, as does Leavis in *New Bearings in English Poetry* or Brooks in *Modern Poetry and the Tradition*, because by accepting the separation of the poem and poet from their origins one is freed from the interference of the actual past in this construction. However, acceptance of the arguments to eliminate the world, author, and audience from critical consideration has been, as M. H. Abrams points out, "comparatively rare in literary criticism." Abrams cites Aristotle's *Poetics*, the Idealist (Kantian) tradition in aesthetics, and the "art for art's sake" school at the end of the nineteenth century as the only historical analogues to this objective approach and says (in 1953): "In America, at least, some form of the objective point of view has already gone far to displace its rivals as the reigning mode of literary criticism."[40] Only when one sees Formalism as a flight from the war, the science, the urbanism, the condition of modern man, does such a rejection make any cultural sense. The psychological purpose of the intentional and affective fallacies, and of poetry as pseudostatement, is to make irrelevant the kinds of reality that are uncontrollable and to concentrate on what can be ordered and known. As Allen Guttmann points out, "Artistic autonomy is the literary equivalent of the conservative's call for an end to 'politics' and an acceptance of society as the Conservative wants it."[41] For Richards, Eliot, Ransom, and the other Formalists, the function of literature is to order experience in a satisfying way, a way that cannot be achieved in the real world.

Stage Three: The Word as World

The creation of a brave new world of poetry to live in is the third stage of the Tory progress; as Cleanth Brooks says, in the Formalist view "the verbal construct that is the poem is then at some level a simulacrum of the world of reality—necessarily so since it is formed out of words and in accordance with the laws of the mind. It is a portion of reality as viewed and valued by a human being. It is rendered coherent through a perspective of valuing."[42] Like the poet, the critic forms his own view of poetic reality and organizes the world of poetry as the poet orders nature, in terms made coherent by his own "perspective of valuation," or literary charter. The English Marxist Alick West analyzes the way in which the world of literature can function as a satisfactory replacement for the social world that has been left behind, the sense in which one can become a fulltime and committed citizen of the Republic of Letters:

Just as the conflict around social solidarity interferes with the enjoyment of poetry, so, on the other hand, the enjoyment of poetry can offer a substitute satisfaction for the impulses of social solidarity which find no other recognized activity. ... If he [the critic] can enjoy the [poetic] utterance as a fact of mind, irrespective of the utterance to be tested in practice about the state of affairs, then he can identify himself with society through its past cultural activity without having to think or make up his mind about the practical activity of society and his own share in it now.[43]

The Formalists' perspective of valuation, the result of their strategy of elimination, makes the poem, in Eliot's phrase, an "objective correlative" for the world.[44] As Eliot writes in "Hamlet and His Problems," "the only way of expressing emotion in the form of art is by finding an 'objective correlative'; in other words, a set of objects, a situation, a chain of events which shall be the formula of that *particular* emotion; such that when the external facts, which must terminate in sensory experience, are given, the emotion is immediately evoked" (*SE* 124–25). The term *objective correlative* is important because it hypostatizes a conception of the poem free from external encumbrances and is invoked by other Formalists to justify (with Eliot's authority) considering the text of the poem without any further knowledge of its background or relationship to audience, author, or subject.

What exists for the critic, then, is an Ideal Poem. If a poem gives knowledge, has ontological status, it must of course be perfect, in the sense that there are no "mistakes" of thought or ultimately unresolvable incoherencies of feeling in it. As Formalists are fond of pointing out, one must assume that a poem "means what it says." Hence, all the meanings that analysis can get out of the words on the page are justifiable. Murray Krieger explains the theoretical implications of this doctrine:

I am of course assuming an ideal poem, that is, the perfection of the poetic context in its workings—a perfection that in fact rarely if ever occurs. To the extent that it does not occur, the critic's judgmental function requires him to point out as deficiencies in the poem those places where its unique language system fails, where it opens too easily and immediately to his common language, and ours. To the extent that the critic must struggle—as, in this essay, I have him struggling—with a unique language system in the totality of its operations, using only his own inadequate language, he is acknowledging the aesthetic perfection of the poem, so that his struggles carry an implied evaluation of the highest sort. [*PP* 9]

In the definition of the nature of their new poetic world, the Formalists' essential distinction is again made by Eliot, who in his remarks on "dissociation of sensibility" makes it clear that his poetic world is a fallen one, and hence organized dualistically around the struggle between good and evil. In his 1921 essay "The Metaphysical Poets," Eliot asserts that in these poets "there is a direct apprehension of thought, or a recreation of thought into feeling, which is exactly what we find in Donne" (*SE* 246; see also *SWood* 23). He notes, however, that in the seventeenth century "a dissociation of sensibility set in, from which we have never recovered. . . . While the language became more refined, the feeling became more crude. . . . The poets revolted against the ratiocinative, the descriptive; they thought and felt by fits, unbalanced; they reflected" (*SE* 247–48). Thus, for Eliot, the history of English poetry is divided into a golden age, when poets had a unified sensibility, and a fallen age, when thought and feeling were separate and poetry was hence partial and limited.

What is important here is not whether Eliot manages to describe the course of poetry in the seventeenth century accurately—Ransom says of the dissociation of sensibility, "having worked to the best of my ability to find the thing Eliot refers to in the 17th Century poets, and failed, I incline to think there was nothing of the kind there" (*NC* 183)—but the fact that by this distinction Eliot establishes the present age as postlapsarian. Such a view of literature is Tory in its construction, for it assumes that the form of literature parallels the conservative view of the form of life— good and evil locked in struggle. As Ransom says," "The kind of poetry which interests us is not the act of a child, or of that eternal youth which is in some women, but the act of an adult mind; and I will add, the act of a fallen mind, since ours too are fallen" (*WB* viii).

The assumption of the reality of evil even in Ideal Poems leads to a compulsive concern with a dualistic view of the literary object, a dualism which is expressed by the Formalist critics in a variety of terminologies. One may cite Ransom's distinction in "Poetry: A Note on Ontology" be- tween physical or imagistic poetry and Platonic or idea poetry, which he finds are united in metaphysical poetry; or his later statement that "a poem is a *logical structure* having a *local texture.*" [45] The same dialectic of opposites is seen in Allen Tate's assertion that poetry contains extension (or denotation) and intension (or connotation), both of which punningly and substantively create tension; "the meaning of poetry is its 'tension,' the full organized body of all the extension and intension that we can find in it" (*CE* 83; see also *WWU* 18 and *VI* 147-49). Tate says that his "in- tension [*sic*] is connotation, or Ransom's texture; extension, denotation— or Ransom's structure. ... May we say that Winters's concept is Ransom's structure, and his emotion, Ransom's texture? All these correspondences are only proximate, but they witness a remarkably similar critical impulse in men of different ages and backgrounds." [46] The "later" Richards also finds that poetry combines subjective and objective, idealistic and real, views of the world, and thus is man's "completest mode of utterance." [47] In a Hegelian phrase which both Ransom and Wimsatt use as an essay title, poetry unites the particular and the general in "the Concrete Universal."

It follows from the dualistic theory of the poem that the language of poetry has a special "ontological" status compared to the language of science or prose, since it contains both the concrete image and abstract thought—in Ransom's terms "a loose logical structure with an irrelevant local texture" (*NC* 280). Implicit in this conception of poetry is the defense of poetic language as offering a unique knowledge to mankind. The Formalists thus progress from dualism to a reunification of the halves of their reality in a new unity of form and content which re-creates poetically a coherent and orderly world that is yet faithful to the full richness of experience. As Brooks says, the poet's task "is finally to unify experience" (*WWU* 212), which he does through paradoxes.

On the level of literary theory, this concern to find the unity of a work of art is usually called "holism." Wimsatt summarizes the holistic position in an article defending the linguistic unity of the Formalist conception of the poem against the unities of plot and genre emphasized by the Chicago Critics:

The holism of such modern critics as Eliot, Richards, and Brooks (as, earlier, of Coleridge and the Germans) has been something not so much determined by size, titles, and genre definitions as by the value principle of variety in unity or the reconciliation of opposites; and hence it has been something related quite practically to technical principles of ambiguity, polysemy, paradox, and irony. Wholeness is not just a form, but a form arising out of a certain kind of matter; wholeness is a certain organization of meaning in words; it supposes a certain grade and intensity of meaning. [*VI* 51] [48]

The Formalist version of the reunion of opposites ends in theory in the concept of the Incarnation (*LC* 746) and in practice is expressed in the organic unity of the poem; the Formalists believe that literary form is organic, "that in a successful work, form and content cannot be separated." [49] The doctrine of the organic unity of poetry was first expressed in English by Coleridge, and the most influential modern statement is I. A. Richards's chapter on the imagination in *Principles of Literary Criticism* (see *MPT* 41). From the doctrine of organic unity it follows that the chief practical concern of criticism is with the relation of the parts of the work—conceived linguistically in terms of sound, rhythm, style, image, symbol, myth, and genre—to the whole. The standard of good poetry, then, is the formal one of coherence (*LC* 748); a good poem is one in which the greatest richness of meaning is organized logically into one unified whole. As Cleanth Brooks says, "One way in which to put the implications of a contextual theory of poetry is to say that it shifts the emphasis from truth of correspondence to truth of coherence." [50]

It follows from the belief in organic unity that the central reality of a poem lies in its metaphors, for metaphor is how conflicting realms of being are united in poetic language (*VI* 79). [51] According to Wimsatt and Brooks: "The *discordia concors* of the metaphysical metaphor or simile has seemed to some critics of our generation the very type and acme of the poetic structure ... metaphor combines the element of necessity of universality (the prime poetic quality which Aristotle noticed) with that other element of concreteness or specificity which was implicit in Aristotle's requirement of the mimetic object. Metaphor is the union of history and philosophy which was the main premise of Sidney's *Defence*. And metaphor would seem to be the only verbal structure which will accomplish this feat" (*LC* 749; see also *VI* 133–51). Since metaphor is so central a concept, there is a tendency to reduce other common critical terms to it. Ransom's "texture" becomes an imagistic variety of metaphor;[52] and as he says, "myths are conceits, born of metaphors" (*WB* 140).

The explication of metaphors is thus the usual occupation of practical Formalist critics because it is in metaphor that the cognitive truth of the poem lies. Cleanth Brooks argues that "poetry is not merely emotive, therefore, but cognitive. It gives us truth, and characteristically gives its truth through its metaphors" (*WWU* 259). And further: "If metaphor is the necessary and inevitable means for saying what the poet has to say, the implications for poetry are considerable. The poet becomes no rhetorician glozing the truth found in some process external to poetry. His truth— which I grant is not scientific truth—is arrived at through his own instruments, and his essential instrument, metaphor, becomes itself a mode of apprehension and a method of discovery."[53]

The practical justification for the Formalists' emphasis on metaphor is that the modern poetry which they write and study embodies what Renato Poggioli calls "the metaphysics of the metaphor." Poggioli says the characteristic tendency of modern poets is to abandon the reality to which the metaphor has traditionally referred and to make it hermetic, self-enclosed, a monad: "The image often aims at making itself an emblem or hieroglyphic, cipher or seal. . . . The modern metaphor tends to divorce the idea and the figure, to annul in the last-mentioned any reference to a reality other than its own self. . . . Poetry and language aspire to transcend the world of the senses, to attain a superreality which is at once a sublimation and a negation of human and terrestrial reality" (*AG* 197). Around the metaphor the Formalists organize a poetic world which is perfectly adequate intellectually to replace the real world they reject, is constructed on proper principles, embodies the evil of reality and the good of form, and unifies them in a coherent way in the Ideal Poem.

Stage Four: The Tradition

Writing of Matthew Arnold, Eliot remarks: "For Arnold, as for everyone else, 'poetry' meant a particular selection and order of poets. It meant, as for everyone else, the poetry that he liked, that he re-read" (*UP* 113). Like Arnold, the Formalists express their Tory charter in practical literary judgments and try to rewrite literary history to illustrate their principles. It is, of course, Eliot who, in "Tradition and the Individual Talent," makes "tradition" a central rubric of Formalist discourse: "The historical sense compels a man to write not merely with his own generation in his bones, but with a feeling that the whole of the literature of Europe from Homer and within it the whole of the literature of his own country has a simultaneous existence and composes a simultaneous order. This historical sense . . . is what makes a writer traditional" (*SE* 4; see also *ASG* 18-30). Eliot's definition of "history" here is the opposite of the usual sense of the term, in that it does not imply a sequence of events in time but implies that temporal events should be seen from an ideal, timeless perspective: "The existing monuments form an ideal order among themselves, which is modified by the new (the really new) work of art among them" (*SE* 5). [54] One sees here writ large the relation between the parts of a work and the whole which the Formalists discuss in an individual poem; as a part of a poem finds its meaning only in relation to the whole poem, so the whole poem functions and finds its meaning as part of the western cultural tradition. Macrocosm equals microcosm.

Eliot identifies tradition with the ordered Latin culture of Europe, the culture stemming from Virgil and embodying French principles of order and decorum. Thus, in *After Strange Gods,* he devotes a chapter to "the crippling effect upon men of letters [Lawrence, Babbitt] of not having been born and brought up in the environment of a living and central tradition" (*ASG* 49). In practice this means that "with the disappearance of the idea of intense moral struggle, the human beings presented to us both in poetry and in prose fiction today, and more patently among the serious writers than in the underworld of letters, tend to become less and less real" (*ASG* 42). In his essay on Blake, Eliot says: "What his genius required, and what it sadly lacked, was a framework of accepted and traditional ideas which would have prevented him from indulging in a philosophy of his own, and concentrated his attention upon the problems of the poet" (*SE* 279-80; see also *UP* 99).

The positive contrast to Blake in Eliot's tradition is his love for Dante, which is expressed in *The Sacred Wood,* in his long 1929 essay, in "What Dante Means to Me" (*TCC* 125-35), and in "A Talk on Dante" (1952). [55] Eliot's praise of Dante rests on three foundations: his preference as a poet for the clear visual images of Dante (*SE* 204) as opposed to Milton's rhetoric of sound (*OPP* 139); his own personal need for an articulated religious system like Dante's, "the most comprehensive, and the most *ordered* presentation of emotions that has ever been made" (*SWood* 168); and his belief in the literary traditions and ideals of the "Great Europeans." This last idea, which seems a projection onto history of Eliot's ideal of himself, is one of the most recurrent of his concerns; his relative ranking changes occasionally over the years, but the debate always involves Sophocles, Dante, Racine, Goethe, and Shakespeare. In varying contexts, Eliot proposes criteria by which one may recognize the Great Europeans: universality, permanence, abundance, amplitude, and unity (*SE* 200, 219; *OPP* 240-50). Very closely related to his idea of the Great Europeans is his idea of the classic writer; the classic writer has universality and maturity, "maturity of mind, maturity of manners, maturity of language and perfection of the common style" (*OPP* 60). The classic writer, like Pope and Dr. Johnson, writes in a mature period which has a settled history behind it. Beyond the classic writers, Eliot distinguishes "the perfect classic," in which "the whole genius of a people will be latent, if not all revealed"; the perfect classic must also have "comprehensiveness" (*OPP* 69). Eliot's unique example of the perfect classic is Virgil: "he is at the centre of European civilization, in a position which no other poet can share or usurp" (*OPP* 70). Here Eliot expresses the heart of his literary and social ideals, the perfect poet in the perfect culture, the kind of mature achievement he himself longed to embody but sensed he could not since the age was hostile to the universality, the comprehensiveness, the common style, he felt was necessary for greatness.

In his analysis of the Great Europeans, Eliot brings up one of the concepts which is at the philosophical heart of his system, the paradox of regionalism. He consistently assumes that the most universal meanings have a kind of incarnation in particular places and times. He notes of the Great Europeans specifically: "They are local because of their concreteness: to be human is to belong to a particular region of the earth, and men of such genius are more conscious than other human beings" (*OPP* 251). "In short we take these men as representative only to find them unrepresentative. For a man can be unrepresentative not only by being behind or ahead of his age, but by being above it" (*OPP* 253). Although he relates regionalism to the needs of good poetry, saying "the music of poetry, then, must be a music latent in the common speech of its time. And that means ... of the poet's *place*" (*OPP* 24), the basic source of his paradox of regionalism is his conception of culture. In *Notes Towards the Definition of Culture*, he defines culture as "the way of life of a particular people living together in one place," and he goes on to note that national cultures based on language are transcended by regional cultures united by religion: "It is in Christianity that our arts have developed; it is in Christianity that the laws of Europe have—until recently—been rooted. It is against a background of Christianity that all our thought has significance."[56] Eliot's defense of the Great Europeans, and of Dante as a Great European, ultimately leads to his defense of Christianity as a cultural home for his own religious sensibilities, and to his application of the principle of incarnation to poetry. Thus his criticism progresses from a system of purely literary values to one based on his own historical, social, and ethical values as well. His "tradition" is finally that of Christian European civilization.

Other Formalists seem to organize many of the same ideals Eliot finds in the Great Europeans in what may be called, from the title of an essay by Ransom, the aesthetic of regionalism. [57] Brooks says that "our most authentic literature has been coming from the provinces and not from the great metropolitan centers. Whether it be Thomas Hardy's Wessex, or W. B. Yeats's Ireland, or Dylan Thomas's Wales, or Robert Frost's New Hampshire, a literature rooted in a regional culture stands out in sharp contrast to the rootless urban civilization." [58] It is notable that the famous special issues of the *Southern Review* were on Yeats and Hardy. Though the Formalists praise both English and American regionalists, the *concept* of regionalism seems peculiarly American: *E Pluribus Unum*. Donald Davie notes that "when Eliot welcomes 'regionalism' in *Notes Towards the Definition of Culture,* this is not going to satisfy people who define themselves as Scottish or Welsh, let alone Irish." [59] American Formalists value regional writing because it fulfills their demand that literature be "tragic," that it exhibit the complexity which knowledge of evil brings. In *Modern Poetry and the Tradition* Brooks says: "In tragedy a conflict is set up within the mind of the auditor himself—conflict between the impulse to condemn the protagonist as he breaks the moral laws in which the audience believes, and the impulse to sympathize with him in his struggle. The tragic attitude is complex" (*MPT* 205). For Brooks, Elizabethan tragedy displays "the same structure as is found in the poetry of wit: specifically, the unity of both is a complex unity, founded on the resolution of the incongruous and the discordant" (*MPT* 212).

Brooks identifies the tragic sense specifically with his own region: "In the Southern experience there is a sense of the tragic. Evil possesses an immediacy and a reality that cannot be evaded or explained away. . . . The literature of the South, then, has characteristically moved in reaction to the utopian tendencies. It has criticized the dominant urban culture from the point of view of a conservative minority culture. This, as I have hinted earlier, has been the essential role of the provincial literatures everywhere in the English-speaking world." [60] In a lecture delivered in Georgia, Brooks gives a more complete list of the elements in the life of the South which are important for its literature:

(1) the concreteness of human relationships including the concreteness of moral problems; (2) the conflict and tension which everywhere confront one in the Southern scene and which, because they are conflict and tension, make for drama; (3) the

pervading sense of community; (4) the sense of religious wholeness—I dare say that the South is the last part of the country which still believes instinctively in the supernatural; (5) the belief that human nature is mysterious and relatively intractable, and that it is not a kind of social putty which can be shaped as the politician or the social scientist may be tempted to shape it; and (6) a sense of the tragic dimension of life.[61]

He then goes on to record how he had taken his old Oxford professor on a tour of Louisiana plantations: "What I had shown him was not merely the confident future but also the past with its sense of loss and defeat. Nowhere else in America, he told me, had he seen any such thing, and the very fact of its existence had reassured him. The South in this regard was closer to the older European tradition, for it had some access to a more profound vision of human life."

The Formalists have been as assiduous in puffing Southerners as the New York Intellectuals have been with Jewish novelists. A host of writers have benefited from this regionalist predilection—Eudora Welty, Flannery O'Connor, Caroline Gordon, Peter Taylor, Andrew Lytle—as well as the major figure of William Faulkner. It is interesting to note, however, that the Formalists paid little attention to Faulkner until after he was rediscovered in 1946 by the New York Critic Malcolm Cowley, perhaps because they felt *Sanctuary* did not present the proper image of the Old South. It was not until Cleanth Brooks's *William Faulkner* was published in 1963 that Faulkner was discussed at any length by a Formalist (see below).

One should also note in connection with the Formalists' defense of regionalism that only Tory regions qualify. The Formalists are consistent in their attack on the regionalism of the North and Midwest as expressed in the poetry of Carl Sandburg, Vachel Lindsay, and others in the Whitman tradition.

The relation between the aesthetics of regionalism and the poetry of the Formalists is found in their joint allegiance to form. Thomas Daniel Young remarks in re Ransom's years in England: "Convictions were forming in his mind that would not be fully articulated for almost a quarter of a century: ritual and ceremony, form and pageantry are ingredients essential to the development of a formal tradition, and the proper function of such a tradition is, as he would later describe it, 'to instruct its members how to transform instinctive experience into aesthetic experience.'"[62]

The tradition of the Metaphysicals is what the Formalists are identified with most prominently, and it is an essential and continuing part of their critical culture. The essential distinction is made by Eliot in "The Metaphysical Poets": "The poets of the seventeenth century, the successors of the dramatists of the sixteenth, possessed a mechanism of sensibility which could devour any kind of experience," and thereby unite thought and feeling; these poets "are in the direct current of English poetry" (*SE* 247, 250). Eliot says, more specifically, of Elizabethan literature: "My point is this: that the Elizabethan drama did tend to approach that *unity of feeling* which Sidney desires" (*UP* 42), by uniting tragedy with comic relief. "For me the violence of contrast between the tragic and the comic, the sublime and the pathetic, in the plays of Shakespeare, disappears in his maturing work" (*UP* 44). Eliot continues: "What I see, in the history of English poetry, is not so much demoniac possession as the splitting up of personality." A partial personality had developed in the national mind between Dryden and Johnson, and in Eliot's view, "surely the great poet is . . . one who not merely restores a tradition which has been in abeyance but one who in his poetry re-twines as many straying strands of tradition as possible" (*UP* 84–85).

The permanent importance of Eliot's championing of the Metaphysicals— the most famous doctrine of his tradition—is a complex question. It was long accepted that because of Eliot's essay "The Metaphysical Poets" the school of Donne was rescued from obscurity to become an important part of our literature. Moreover, the whole of New Criticism is sometimes seen as an effort to explicate fully the metaphors and conceits of this kind of poetry. As fashion changed, however, a reaction set in; Frank Kermode argues that Eliot's concept of "dissociation of sensibility" is not tenable as a description of the seventeenth century but is "the projection onto an historical scale of a developed Romantic-Symbolist view of the Image," [63] an opinion which parallels Eliot's concept of himself as a poet-critic. Kermode continues: "There can be no doubt that the success of Mr. Eliot's formula, which happens not to be a very good way of putting something that had been put many times, is due in part to the fact that he was the first symbolist poet in England to achieve wide recognition as distinctively 'modern.'"

But Eliot denied his own originality in 1923, noting that "Donne's popularity is neither recent nor limited," [64] and he repeats this denial in 1961 (*TCC* 21–22). If some have been deceived by Eliot's persona of the critic as lawgiver, they have only themselves to blame. Eliot's hostility toward the Romantics and Victorians is the reverse of his fondness for the Metaphysicals, and likewise it stems from his own needs as a poet. He says in 1920: "There may be a good deal to be said for Romanticism in life, there is no place for it in letters" (*SWood* 32). Speaking retrospectively in 1955, he explains the reason for his opposition: "I had, over the years, found myself alienated from the major English poets of the nineteenth century . . . their philosophy of life came to seem to me flimsy, their religious foundations insecure. But I had had the experience of living through that poetry in my boyhood: that remained to me. I had been, for a time, very much moved by these poets" (*OPP* 243; see also *UP* 33–34). Thus Eliot's doctrinal rejection of the Romantics and Victorians is only a part of his attitude toward them. After dismissing them in theory, freeing himself from their influence so that he could write his own kind of poetry, he qualified this dismissal in practice, writing appreciatively of Kipling and Shelley, among others. [65] It was neither Romanticism nor Classicism, but theorizing about them, that he finally came to dislike. In an interview in 1962, Eliot admits: "I'm not so much interested in the classical-romantic distinction as I once was. You can find the romantic wherever you look for it and the classical in the best of the romantic. To tell the truth, the discussion rather bores me now." [66]

The significance of the redefinition of tradition for Formalists like Cleanth Brooks is that both "the metaphysical poets and the modernists stand opposed to both the neo-classical and Romantic poets on the issue of metaphor" (*MPT* 11). Having accepted the Metaphysical tradition as central, Brooks undertakes the more ambitious task in *The Well Wrought Urn* of showing that the same paradoxical language is found in Shakespeare, Milton, Herrick, Pope, Gray, Wordsworth, Keats, Tennyson, and Yeats—that all poets are, in a sense, Metaphysical: "The discipline gained from reading Donne may allow us to see more clearly the survival of such qualities in the later style of Shakespeare" (*WWU* 28). As he points out in the appendix, "The preceding chapters obviously look forward to a new history of English poetry" (*WWU* 215).

The importance of Eliot's championing of the Metaphysicals is, for him, that supporting this tradition permitted him to get his own poetry written. Its importance for the history of criticism lies in the fact that it led a generation of critics to value Metaphysical poetry above other kinds and to explicate all poetry as if it were Metaphysical poetry. Thus a new tradition of poetry and of normal criticism was created on the basis of the implicit standard of the complexity of the Metaphysical poem.

The reverse of this view, of course, is that Romantic poetry is bad, and this view had an equally great effect on the shape of literary history. Edmund Wilson comments in *Axel's Castle* (1931): "It is as much as one's life is worth nowadays, among young people, to say an approving word for Shelley or a dubious one about Donne" (*Ax* 116–17). Such a judgment governed the critical world until the mid-1950s, when the rise of the Neo-Romantic poetry of the "beats" and critical interest in Romantics like Blake, Wordsworth, and Shelley expressed by critics like Northrop Frye, Geoffrey Hartman, and Harold Bloom led to the obsolescence of Eliot's tradition and the creation of yet another critical revolution. [67]

Stage Five: The Sacred Word

The fifth and last stage of the Tory progress is belief in God and in divine order in the world. The stages of Tory psychology which I have traced all point toward and rest on belief in God. T. S. Eliot says in 1934: "The chief clue to the understanding of most contemporary Anglo-Saxon literature is to be found in the decay of Protestantism. . . . Individual writers can be understood and classified according to the type of Protestantism which surrounded their infancy and the precise state of decay which it had reached" (ASG 38). In "Metaphor and the Function of Criticism," Cleanth Brooks comes as close as he ever will to a real credo when he states that it is no "accident that so many of the modern [Formalist] critics who have . . . taken a position sympathetic to Hulme in making metaphor the essence of poetry, have gone on, either to avow an orthodox religious position, or else to affirm the possibility and necessity for metaphysics as a science." [68] Allen Tate says further: "I might even say that my writings have influenced my religious beliefs. That is to say that the whole effort of the literary imagination is toward a kind of incarnation of reality in language." [69]

Implicit in the conception of an ordered metaphorical world, then, is a spiritual power which justifies it; at the end of his essay "Poetry and Morals," Wimsatt says that "even a great poem . . . may fall short of being moral," but that "poems as empirically discovered and tested do tend . . . to point toward the higher integration of dogma" (VI 100). For Wimsatt, the Christian critic finds that "Christian dogma will aid the artist [and the critic] not by giving him a privileged and special subject-matter but rather by defining for him a perspective from which 'full light' can be had on all subject matters" (VI 100). Richard Weaver says likewise: "If poetry is this system of universal analogy, and if the analogy mounts up toward that which most resembles everything else, or that which has the most universal being, it is true that all poetry is a form of worship. Poetry and religion have been too often conjoined in cultural history for the union to be fortuitous." [70] For a Formalist, critical concepts are not only ontological but eschatological. There is at least a penumbra of holiness in the Formalists' many heresies, and in their tendency to use religious phrases like Wimsatt's verbal icon, Tate's angelic imagination, or Ransom's arbitrarily calling metaphor a miracle: "It must be insisted that the miraculism which produces the humblest conceit is the same miraculism which supplies to religions their substantive content" (WB 140). As Yvor Winters says: "I am aware that my absolutism implies a theistic position. . . . My theism is derived from my critical and moral notions" (DR 14).

In life the Formalists have been notable for converting or reverting to orthodox Christian principles. Eliot, Ransom, Brooks, and Tate are all the sons or grandsons of Protestant ministers. Eliot and Tate announced their dramatic conversions to Anglo-Catholicism and Catholicism in 1928 and 1950. Ransom, Wimsatt, and Brooks never left the faith of their fathers, and Brooks especially, after a period in the thirties and forties when he said little about it, began in the fifties to offer an overtly Christian reading of literature (in *The Hidden God*). It would be a great oversimplification, however, to say that the Formalists are Christian critics. As Brooks says, "It is no accident that many of these critics are communicants of the church, or sympathetic with orthodox religion," but consequently "it is precisely those critics who, by and large, manifest a deep concern for religion, who are also concerned to maintain the independence of literature and its distinction from religion" because "they are men who, in their devotion to literature, refuse to make literature support a burden which it cannot support." [71]

But certainly these Formalists are religious critics if we accept Brooks's statement that "religion may be roughly defined—one aspect of it at least—as that system of basic values which underlies a civilization." [72] René Wellek says of him: "Though Brooks holds fast to the distinction between poetry, politics, and religion, poetry is for him ultimately a way to truth, a way to religion." [73] As Wimsatt puts it, "There is a certain sense in which religion is the only theme of important poetry" (*HCo* 39). It is a mistake in emphasis to insist that to be a Formalist one must believe in God; but one must have at least a fideistic or willed belief in a spiritual power to support the Formalists' Tory literary world and hierarchial response to it. Wimsatt says flatly: "The religious mind would seem, in the end, to be more hospitable to the tensional and metaphysical view of poetry than the naturalistic mind is able to be" (*HCo* 48). Their need is for an ultimate principle of order, a need which can be satisfied philosophically as well in a belief in the Kantian view of the absolute nature of the aesthetic experience as in the theory of Wellek; or poetically in the avant-garde notion of the mystical purity of art, as in Imagist poetics.

However, the religious and philosophical implications of Formalism can also be ignored altogether if one is not of a bent to worry about ultimate principles. It is this option which has accounted for Formalism's appeal for the millions of teachers and students who have embraced it. Although choosing to ignore metaphysical implications does not make them go away, it is a psychologically rewarding tactic, since in literary Formalism one can have all the comforts of Tory psychology without having to worry about God. The fact is that the literary world of the Formalists is so well constructed, so satisfying, so autonomous, that one need not ask ultimate questions but may simply live in a way Brooks suggests when he says that the little town on Keats's Grecian urn, properly interpreted, "comes to have a richer and more important history than that of actual cities" (*WWU* 162). In terms of poetic tradition, one has here what Renato Poggioli calls "the poetics of the Word," where "it is not God who is made Word, but Word made God. ... For modern poetry the word is not sound-sense, but idea-thing; in its vision the Word is not spirit which became flesh, but flesh which became spirit" (*AG* 199). The grail that one ultimately finds in the depths of *The Sacred Wood* is the sacred word.

4. The Age
of the Explicators,
1938-1948

In his survey of the Agrarian movement, Alexander Karanikas notes that "by the end of the thirties, when the economics of Agrarianism had obviously crumbled, Ransom, Tate, Brooks, and Warren turned to a new task: the reformation of college English studies, and the revamping of literary criticism."[1] The instrument of this reformation is the method of *explication de texte*, which is demonstrated by Brooks in *Modern Poetry and the Tradition* (1939), *Understanding Poetry* (with R. P. Warren) (1938), and *The Well Wrought Urn* (1947); by Ransom in *The World's Body* (1938); and by Blackmur in *The Double Agent* (1935) and *The Expense of Greatness* (1940). At the end of the period the method is developed theoretically in Wellek and Austin Warren's *Theory of Literature* (1949). The development of Formalism from 1938 to 1948 goes from practice to theory, as techniques for reading poetry are developed into general speculation about the aesthetic position implicit in Formalist practice. This combination of practical utility and theoretical force is in a worldly sense successful, in that the Formalists conquer the university world by the end of the period, and as Karanikas notes, gain access to whatever big money is around in the literary world.[2]

Close Reading as Normal Criticism: Cleanth Brooks

Scholars propose sources for the method of close reading in various obscure corners of literary history; in a 1950 symposium "New Criticism," Malcom Cowley states that it "developed out of a pedagogy first in France. ... The New Criticism is a very old criticism. I had a brain-and-bellyful of it at the University of Montpellier in 1921. There it was called *explication du* [sic] *texte*."[3] The similarity here seems more superficial than real, however, since the French *explication* is more historically oriented than its American counterpart, and more concerned with etymology, philology, and historical scholarship.[4]

The first historically verifiable model for the Formalist method of reading is the practice of self-criticism of the Fugitive poets of the twenties (and perhaps the kind of criticism Pound gave Eliot). The Fugitives, who met weekly at Vanderbilt University in Nashville from 1919 to 1925 to criticize one another's poetry, included Ransom, Allen Tate, Robert Penn Warren, Donald Davidson, among others. The criticism which they did of poetry in conversation later became the New Critical practice in essays. Donald Davidson describes their ideal in these words: "A poem had to prove its strength, if possible its perfection, in all its parts. The better the poem, the greater the need for a perfect finish. An inequality in technical performance was sure to be detected. It was not enough for a poem to be impressive in a general way." Davidson goes on to describe the effect of this kind of criticism on poetry: "In its cumulative effect this severe discipline made us self-conscious craftsmen, abhorring looseness of expression, perfectly aware that a somewhat cold-blooded process of revision, after the first ardor of creation had subsided, would do no harm to art. It also led to what we called a 'packed' line. The poet, anxious to fortify his verses against criticism, strove to weed out anything 'loose.'"[5] Throughout Formalist criticism one finds the claim that it is a "technical" criticism, the kind of criticism that one writer gives to the details of another's work to improve it; it is essentially a writer's criticism of other writers. Cleanth Brooks claims that a "'well-schooled' literary mind is perhaps the kind of mind closest to the poet's own. It approaches the poem by emphasizing the total context, and since each context is a unique whole, each poem becomes a special case, to be read in the light of its own nature."[6] Paradoxically, this authorial perspective is in a way the most "Romantic" aspect of Formalism, since it brings back not the study of the author but the point of view of the author as the central perspective from which to view a work of literature.

The Fugitives' influence is also apparent upon the initial event in the history of English *explication de texte,* the publication in 1930 of *Seven Types of Ambiguity,* by William Empson, then a twenty-four-year-old student of I. A. Richards at Cambridge. The link between the Fugitives' talk and Empson's writing may be Laura Riding, who published in *The Fugitive* and was familiar with the kind of criticism the Fugitives practiced, and who in 1926 left Kentucky for England and a collaboration with Robert Graves on *A Survey of Modernist Poetry* (1927).[7] Richards (Empson's thesis adviser) describes the effect on Empson of the kind of technical analysis Graves and Riding did. "At about his third visit he brought up the games of interpretation which Laura Riding and Robert Graves had been playing with the unpunctuated form of 'The expense of spirit in a waste of shame.' Taking the sonnet as a conjurer takes his hat, he produced an endless swarm of lively rabbits from it and ended by 'You could do that with any poetry, couldn't you?' This was a Godsend to a Director of Studies, so I said, 'You'd better go off and do it, hadn't you?" (*AV* 263). The result is the model for New Critical textual analysis, the exhaustive analysis of all possible meanings of the words in a poem, with an emphasis on the linguistic categories—ambiguity, paradox, tension—with which this semantic richness could be confronted.

The most active and argumentative explicator, the Fugitives' champion in a chivalric sense, is Cleanth Brooks. Brooks admits that he "borrowed from Eliot, Tate, Empson, Yeats, Ransom, Blackmur, [and] Richards" and claims credit himself only for having "made a successful synthesis of other men's ideas rather than on the originality of my own" (*MPT* xxxi). His collaborator on *The Poems of Mr. John Milton,* John Hardy, says of him, "there is a remarkable adaptability in Brooks's style, an apparent capacity of his mind for anonymity, indicated in the fact that he has been able to collaborate with several people of vastly different interests and training and bent of thought."[8] M. K. Spears observes that Brooks's virtues are "not primarily those of the pioneering theorist, but those of the teacher, whose main function is to systematize, extend, and apply doctrines originated by others. Mr. Brooks is, in the most praiseworthy sense of the word, a popularizer, expounding with missionary ardor and defending with great polemical skill ideas derived from others but believed in so passionately that they have become his own."[9] He is representative, not original. Unlike Eliot, Tate, Blackmur, or Winters, he does not express a personal response which transcends the collective identity of his group, and consequently his worth lies in his spirited development and defense of the Formalist charter in a way which made it historically influential. He is not original, but he is the most influential of the explicators, as a glance at Joseph M. Kuntz's *Poetry Explication: A Checklist of Interpretations since 1925* ... (1962) will show; and the history of Formalism from 1938 to 1948 is largely a history of his career and opinions. Simply because he has influenced many other critics, however, one should not saddle him with all the sins of his disciples, the "fanatical fringe adherents of the formalist movement—a sort of part-time, night- or correspondence- course students who have taken up, from haphazard reading, the doctrines merely as shields to hide their incompetence in any other kind of scholarship."[10] Brooks's own opinions have been firmly expressed and amazingly consistent over forty-five years, and are rooted in the reality of his background and life.

In terms of the Tory charter sketched above, Brooks assumes the necessity to exclude the real world, and concentrates his efforts on the definition of the properties of a new world of poetry. His original contribution is that he expresses the doctrines of his masters practically, in a neutral manner which the reader can imitate without confusion. It may be an advantage for Brooks that he is a mere critic, not a famous poet like Eliot or Ransom, since the average reader is not distracted by the peculiarities of genius, but feels that Brooks's method of explication is only common sense, well within his own reach.

Anyone reading through Brooks's essays will be struck by the consistency of his view, or to put it another way, his preoccupation with the repeated expression and refinement of a few central terms and concepts. His view is thus best summarized by showing the meaning he gives to his central terms: *irony, the poem as drama, ambiguity,* and *paradox.*

The result of the Tory sense of evil is the development in modern poets of a sense of cosmic irony, and the Fugitives express the same standard in the context of poetic structure. Writing in 1949, Brooks observes: "The poem which meets Eliot's test [of coherence, maturity, and fidelity to experience] comes to the same thing as I. A. Richards' 'poetry of synthesis'—that is, a poetry which does not leave out what is apparently hostile to its dominant tone, and which, because it is able to fuse the irrelevant and discordant, has come to terms with itself and is invulnerable to irony."[11] This ironic ideal is realized in the poetry of the teacher and leader of the group, John Crowe Ransom, as well as in other modernist poets like Eliot, Hart Crane, Yeats, and Tate, and the same ideal established as critical orthodoxy governs the practice of the "academic" poets of the forties and fifties. As Brooks argues: "Irony . . . is to be found in poetry of every period and even in simple lyrical poetry. But in the poetry of our own time, this pressure reveals itself strikingly. A great deal of modern poetry does use irony as its special and perhaps its characteristic strategy."[12] Rephrased in terms of practical criticism, the irony of the poem leads the critic to consider it as a dramatic structure. "The poem is like a little drama. The total effect proceeds from all the elements in the drama, and in a good poem, as in a good drama, there is no waste motion and there are no superfluous parts. . . . Poems never contain abstract statements. That is, any 'statement' made in the poem bears the pressure of the context and has its meaning modified by the context. In other words, the statements made—including those which appear to be philosophical generalizations— are to be read as if they were speeches in a drama."[13] In practical terms, Brooks here expresses the doctrine that a poem is to be judged in terms of the relationship of its parts to the whole, by its coherence. In fact, however, this doctrine does not lead to the judging of a poem as a drama, by its imitation of life and by the pleasure, use, and catharsis it gives, but reverses the process and judges dramas as lyric poems.

What irony is to the larger structures of poetry, ambiguity is to language, and Brooks's concern with language is to unravel its hierarchical levels of meaning. Ambiguity is of course Empson's term, but Brooks's use of it is similar, though he disavows any influence of Empson on his work, claiming that "I read Empson's *Seven Types of Ambiguity* for the first time in 1938." [14] Brooks notes in 1952 that "the values of Empson's *Seven Types* lay not at all in the provision of seven pigeonholes into which puzzles could be thrust, but rather in the powerful documentation of the fact that words are many-sided and in the often brilliant discussion of individual poems." [15] For Brooks, "the term ambiguity, even in its present worn and battered state, still retains some sense of a tension between meanings. It ought to mean ... the accommodation to each other of rival meanings, the pressure of one upon the other that results in a third and more precise meaning." [16]

The more precise concept which Brooks is searching for, which will give him the exact meaning of the poem, often comes to him as a paradox: "There is a sense in which paradox is the language appropriate and inevitable to poetry" (*WWU* 3). He never clarifies the difference between paradox and metaphor exactly, but paradox seems to be the more specific term applicable to the individual poem, while metaphor is the theoretical and general term which refers to poetry as a whole (see *LC* 747). In one general discussion of metaphor Brooks says that paradox is characteristic of all poetry and that it lies at the heart of metaphor, but he seems to mean by this only that, since the two terms of a metaphor are not exactly equivalent, there is an element of absurdity in all comparisons. [17] For him, both paradox and metaphor are terms under which opposites are united in an interpretation of the poem which is as invulnerable to irony as the poem itself. In sum, Brooks defines his tradition and his method as follows: "Our age rejoices in having recovered Donne; but in doing so we have recovered not just Donne's poetry, but poetry. This is so generally true that for many of us the quality of poetry—as distinguished from that of the more empty rhetorics—is bound up with functional metaphor, with dramatic tension, and with the fusion of thought and emotion—qualities which we associate with the poetry of Donne. Small wonder then if we try to find these qualities, or comparable qualities, in the work of anyone to whom we give the name of poet." [18]

Brooks has the courage to apply his positive standard negatively. In practice a poem either realizes his ideals or he refuses to admit that it has any poetic quality. He says of William Carlos Williams's poetry, for example: "His 'Red Wheelbarrow'—to cite a famous short 'objective' poem—remains for some of us quite inert. I see the white chickens and the raindrops glazing the red paint, but I have to take on faith the author's statement that 'so much depends' on this scene."[19] In point of fact, for Brooks there has been no poetry since modernism; his sympathies are (like Leavis's) fixated in the literature of the twenties, and he has found no new enthusiasm since he wrote *Modern Poetry and the Tradition* in 1938, except for some Formalist protégés like Randall Jarrell and Robert Lowell.

Some idea of how Brooks's method of explication works in practice can be gained by examining his interpretation of a passage in *Paradise Lost* (IX, 445–69) which culminates with the words

> That space the Evil one abstracted stood
> From his own evil, and for the time remained
> Stupidly good. . . .

Brooks says:

"Stupidly good" constitutes the pivot for the whole passage. What does it mean? "To stupify" originally is to astound, to stun. Satan is momentarily "good" from bewilderment. But "stupify" suggests too a kind of torpor, a numbness or Stupor. . . . But when the Evil one is abstracted from his own evil, he is not only good (as separated from evil), but stupidly so, for he has so thoroughly given himself up to evil that he is now abtracted from part of himself, and can be "good" only in a dazed and stupid manner, having lost his wits, his directing purpose. If, on the other hand, we remember the pleasant rural scene, with its smell of grain and tedded hay, "stupidly good" acknowledges the rural setting, and accommodates Satan to the rustic scene. . . . I do not believe that I have exhausted the meanings of the phrase—certainly not all the shadings of meaning. But all that I have been able to think of are relevant.[20]

It is passages like this, so typical of Brooks, that give substance to John Hardy's remark that Brooks's "essays sometimes give the impression that he has never read a book for pleasure."[21] They also lend substance to the charge that the Formalist method of explication, which began as a revolt against science, has itself become scientific in the sense of being methodological, industrious, humorless. Hardy says of Brooks that he is "probably at his most serene when he appears at his grubbiest—a kind of monk devoutly spading the abbey garden."[22] This image is more revealing of the essential Brooks than the scientific one; his labors seem to be sustained by a simple faith that the process of explication is inherently meaningful because it in some ways reveals the Word.

Southern Tory influence on *explication de texte* is apparent when one notes the parallel between this explicatory method and the Fundamentalist heritage of many Formalists. This heritage is a dominant one, since Eliot, Ransom, Brooks, and Tate grew up around the parsonages of the Protestant church. Ransom describes Brooks's method as concentrating on the metaphors of the poem, trying to see their paradoxes and irony, and finding the central metaphor, what in this context might be called the old rugged crux. Ransom says: "Then he [Brooks] proceeds to wrestle as much of the poem as possible under it [the crux] as the dominating figure; it is likely to have philosophical or religious implications; and there is his sense of the poem." He goes on to point out the source of Brooks's procedure and the historical context which gives it its meaning:

Brooks's method, however, is a homiletic one if I am not mistaken. In my boyhood I heard many a sermon preached where the preacher unpacked the whole burden of his theology from a single figurative phrase of Scripture taken out of context. Brooks heard them too. The fact is that Brooks and I were about as like as two peas from the same pod in respect to our native region, our stock (we were sons of ministers of the same [Methodist] faith, and equally had theology in our blood), the kind of homes we lived in, the kind of small towns; and perhaps we were most like in the unusual parallel of our formal education. So we have more in common than we can have acquired separately. If we have diverged a little for the moment, perhaps it is only because now our habitations are far apart. Brooks's particular theologism resembles that of Scotus, who preached as all critics know the individuality or *haecceitas* of the well-regarded object.[23]

Brooks's method is a specifically Fundamentalist one in that he assumes the essential unity of the Ideal Poem as the Fundamentalist assumes the unified and divine origin of the Bible. Austin Warren testifies in his "In Search of a Vocation" that "Biblical exegesis also interested me (hermeneutics, the science of the interpretation of texts, which plays so important a part in the 'new critical' study of literature, owes much to its fount)."[24] One may contrast this method of explication with the "higher criticism," which assumes that the Bible is essentially a disunified document composed of various historical "layers" by various authors which it is the duty of the critic to separate. Like the Fundamentalist with his sacred scripture, the Formalist assumes an Ideal Poem, one in which there are no mistakes, where he subsumes what he must consider to be only apparent ironies and contradictions under one controlling figure or paradox. The Formalist's conception of the poet likewise seems to parallel the Fundamentalist's conception of God, since the work of neither is to be questioned but is accepted as given, and since both work in mysterious ways their wonders to perform.

The end toward which the method of explication is directed is eloquently expressed by Leo Spitzer in a *Southern Review* defense of the Formalists' position: "I feel strongly that the explanation of a poem is strongly akin to the practice of reducing *omnia in majorem Dei gloriam*; in both one refers all observable details and facts to one central force resuming the whole and, by a to-and-fro (or 'tautological') movement between the whole and the parts, one hopes to grasp the ultimately ungraspable (*individuum ineffabile*). A thorough inspection and description of a thing of beauty seems to me the best act of worship towards its 'author.' "[25] E. D. Hirsch, Jr., traces the Formalist method of interpreting a text to this same end in the larger context of literary theory and history: "The renewed impulse to discuss what a text means rather than how, when, or where it was caused is the continuation of a tradition that is far more venerable than the positivism against which modern scholars reacted. Close commentary, particularly on religious texts, goes back further than any recorded interpretations to an ancient tradition of teaching and oral exegesis. Consequently, the interpretive side of the new movement was not what was new in it, for the primary aim of close commentary has always been interpretation, not criticism."[26] This conception of the sacred nature of the poem lies behind the Formalists' emphasis on the Word and justifies the meaning of explication in the same way that the Divine Presence justifies the labors of the theologian. As R. P. Blackmur says: "Consider too . . . the enormous mass of exegetical criticism it has seemed necessary and desirable to apply to Eliot's poetry and indeed to the whole school of Donne. This criticism neither compares, nor judges; it elucidates scripture" (*LH* 202).

Extension of Influence in the Quarterlies

From 1935 on, the Formalists extend their literary influence through their control of literary quarterlies: the *Southern Review,* edited by Brooks and Warren from 1935 to 1942; the *Kenyon Review,* edited by Ransom from 1939 to 1959; and the *Sewanee Review,* edited by Allen Tate and other Fugitives after 1944. Tate describes the situation candidly in a letter to Brooks when upon taking over the *Sewanee* he removes Brooks as associate editor. "There is a very specific reason for this . . . and I am sure that you will understand and approve it. It is simply that most of our crowd have been on most of the magazines for the past ten or fifteen years, virtually taking in one another's washing, and I think it advisable to make our influence more effective by concealing it."[27]

The list of regular contributors to the *Southern Review* at that time includes most of the Fugitives, as well as Kenneth Burke, Morton Zabel, Francis Fergusson, L. C. Knights, Delmore Schwartz, Philip Rahv, and a number of less prominent Southerners. The practice of using their magazines as instruments of propaganda as well as self-promotion is defended theoretically by Tate in 1936 in his article in the *Southern Review,* "The Function of a Critical Quarterly." There he describes the necessity for a quarterly to get a group of like-minded writers together and for the editor to keep his program in focus; as Tate puts it, the editor "owes his first duty to his critical principles, his sense of the moral and intellectual order upon which society ought to rest" (*CE* 71). "A sound critical program has at least this one feature: *it allows to the reader no choice in the standards*

of judgment. It asks the reader to take a post of observation, and to occupy it long enough to examine closely the field before him. . . . This,
one supposes, is dogmatism . . . [but] dogma is coherent thought in the
pursuit of principles" (*CE* 65-66).

In its seven-year history the *Southern Review* reflects faithfully, or perhaps in some sense creates, the shift in interests of the Formalists as a
whole. From 1936 to 1940 Brooks and Warren devote a good deal of
space to political writers like Herbert Agar and to Southern history,
Agrarianism, and regional interests, as well as to attacks on Fascism,
Communism, and New York writers; but in 1940 they turn to the con-
quest of the academic world by publishing articles like L. C. Knights's
"University Teaching of English and History: A Plea for Correlation,"
Leo Spitzer's "History of Ideas versus Reading of Poetry,"[28] and most
notably the symposium "Literature and the Professors," published jointly
with the *Kenyon Review.* The cause they defend is, of course, that of the
Formalists versus the historical scholars, and the modernist tradition versus
the historical study of literature of the past.

In its literary interests the *Southern Review* also embodies the progress
of the Formalist group as a whole from 1936 to 1948. The beginning is in
critical practice; it is the time when Brooks works out the earlier remarks
of Eliot and others on "wit," the dissociation of sensibility, and the Metaphysical tradition, and applies them to poetry.[29] This interest in establishing their tradition continues throughout the life of the magazine, from
the publication of Brooks's articles on Eliot and Yeats to Tate's "Tension
in Poetry" in 1938, the special issues on Hardy and Yeats in 1940-42, and
publication of a number of favorable reviews of one another's critical
books. The Formalists' progress from practice to theory is completed in
the last issue, with the publication of Wellek and Warren's "The Mode
of Existence of a Literary Work of Art," which becomes the central chapter
of *Theory of Literature* (1949). The Formalists' characteristic support of
traditionalism, attack on scholars, the practice of close criticism, and
interest in theory are thus first established in the *Southern Review.*

In the *Kenyon Review,* however, all interest in Agrarianism, or regionalism, is dropped, and a shift in emphasis occurs which Ransom's move
from Vanderbilt to Kenyon College in Ohio in 1937 symbolizes in life.
In the *Kenyon Review,* we see the Formalist movement at its best, not
stiffened by the defensiveness of the rejected Agrarians of the thirties, but
under Ransom's editorship, tolerant, open to new literature, and leading
the way toward a new literary meaning for life. Its effect at the time may
be judged by John L. Stewart's testimonial. "It is not easy to say how it
happened. There had been other great reviews. . . . But it was *The
Kenyon Review* that made the difference. To many of us its members
made up our Bible, and Ransom was sometimes Jeremiah, sometimes

Ecclesiastes, sometimes even the second Isaiah, but mostly he was Moses leading us through the deserts to the promised land of poetry."[30]

Ransom's effect on the literary world of the forties was due in part to his authority as a poet; like Eliot, he could practice what he preached. It seems also to have been due to his lingering authority as a teacher over his ex-students—Robert Penn Warren, Allen Tate, and Randall Jarrell at Vanderbilt; and Robert Lowell, Peter Taylor, and Robie Macauley at Kenyon—as they became influential Men of Letters themselves. Even allowing for testimonial rhetoric, many seem to have been influenced by Ransom's unfailing personal kindness and Southern courtesy, as Arthur Mizener, R. S. Crane, and others witness. But in the end it was not who he was but what he did that was most influential, and what he did was to edit a quarterly which, in its taste and in what Ransom brought out in his contributors, served as a model for its time. As R. P. Blackmur says, "There never was a better editor to work for."[31]

One cause of Ransom's excellence as an editor is his tendency to become increasingly inclusive and appreciative. As he says at the end of *The New Criticism:* "Eliot is one of the foci of a distinguished group of literary men [including Tate] with whose sentiments I have always had complete sympathy; I am convinced of their rightness, but not of what I should call their righteousness; for they do not propose to have commerce with the world. ... increasingly now I find such a policy is too luxurious for my blood" (*NC* 200–201). Ransom's inclusiveness is seen in the *Kenyon Review's* boards of advisory editors; the first included Blackmur, Tate, Mark Van Doren, Paul Rosenfeld, Philip Timberlake, Roberta Teale Swartz (wife of the president of Kenyon College and a supporter of the magazine), and Eliseo Vivas, who with the managing editor, Philip Blair Rice, was a professional philosopher. This presence of philosophers led to the early symposia "New Encyclopediasts" (the theory of signs of Charles Morris), "The Legacy of Sigmund Freud," and "New Naturalism" in 1939, 1940, and 1941. As G. A. M. Janssens points out, during these years the *Kenyon Review* is "almost exclusively concerned with the opposition between poetry and science, and John Crowe Ransom kept up a running battle against what he considered to be presumptions and intrusions of science."[32]

In 1942, however, Ransom turned to a more exclusive interest in literature; when the *Southern Review* folded, he took over its subscription list and named to his own board of editors men who served until after his retirement in 1958: Cleanth Brooks, R. P. Warren, Lionel Trilling, and Eric Bentley (1945–63). Thus, during its great days, the *Kenyon Review* was edited by both ex-Fugitives and New York Intellectuals and thereby united the two most active and often hostile groups of critics under one benevolent aegis.[33]

As far as criticism is concerned, Ransom's editorship was marked by a high general level of essays and reviewing; like the editors of *The Dial*, he picked what seems from a historical view an all-star cast: Tate, Blackmur, Burke, Mizener, Delmore Schwartz, Philip Wheelwright, William Empson, and Bentley. Ransom also published new promising critics as they appeared; Alfred Kazin, Isaac Rosenfeld, Robert Warshow, Richard Chase, Leslie Fiedler, Irving Howe, and Richard Ellmann all began to write for the magazine in the late 1940s. Robie Macauley, Ransom's successor as editor, points out that Ransom published many of the best poets of the forties and fifties, including W. H. Auden, Dylan Thomas, James Dickey, John Berryman, Wallace Stevens, Robert Graves, and Ransom's students Robert Lowell and Randall Jarrell. Macauley also notes that the magazine "had its shortcomings and omissions. T. S. Eliot did not appear. . . . Saul Bellow was given a cold shoulder. The French existentialists were ignored. The remarkable group of Italian fiction writers who appeared just after World War II went almost unnoticed. Lorca was there, but Neruda was not. There was one story by John Wain, but the 'angry young men' in postwar England—Braine, Osborne, and Amis among them—were never represented nor was Graham Greene or Frank O'Connor. Fiction was always one of John Ransom's blind spots."[34] As one reviews his twenty years of editing, Ransom's central achievements seem to be his special issues on Henry James (Autumn 1943), Gerard Manley Hopkins (Summer 1944), Dante (Spring 1952), and "English Verse and What It Sounds Like" (Summer 1956).

From the particular point of view of a historian of criticism, the climax of the magazine comes in the three-part series in 1950 and 1951 entitled "My Credo: A Symposium of Critics," in which Leslie Fiedler, Herbert Read, Richard Chase, William Empson, Cleanth Brooks, Douglas Bush, Northrop Frye, Stephen Spender, Arthur Mizener, and Austin Warren state their personal critical views.[35] In retrospect, this symposium seems historically pivotal, since Brooks's essay sums up the Formalist position, Bush's the opposition of the scholars to it, and Chase's the liberal/avant-garde approach of the New York Intellectuals, while Fiedler's essay "Toward an Amateur Criticism" and Frye's essay on myth criticism serve as points of departure for the critical movements of the fifties.

The institutional manifestation of the conflicts and values this "credo" sets forth theoretically came in the summers of 1948, 1949, and 1950, during the meetings of the Kenyon School of English. Made possible by a grant from The Rockefeller Foundation, the school was founded by Ransom, Lionel Trilling, and F. O. Matthiessen. The interest of the Fellows was in forming responsible literary judgments and in training students to make critical evaluations to supplement the historical and factual knowledge they learned in graduate school. For the most part, the teachers during these first three sessions were Formalists, both English and American, but the groups were leavened by several New York Intellectuals. The staffs were as follows:

Fellows of the Kenyon School of English, 1948

Austin Warren	William Empson
Eric Bentley	Cleanth Brooks
Allen Tate	John Crowe Ransom
Richard Chase	F. O. Matthiessen

Fellows of the Kenyon School of English, 1949

Philip Rahv	Eric Bentley
René Wellek	John Crowe Ransom
Allen Tate	Herbert Read
Mark Schorer	Yvor Winters

Fellows of the Kenyon School of English, 1950

Arthur Mizener	William Empson
Robert Lowell	John Crowe Ransom
Kenneth Burke	L. C. Knights
Delmore Schwartz	C. M. Coffin
P. B. Rice	

The gathering of this galaxy of critics was important because it gave Formalist criticism a kind of institutional and public identity it had not had before. In a way, in the Kenyon School, Ransom managed to reconcile in life those tensions between opposing positions which he worried over perpetually in his criticism. Here the Fugitives and the New York Intellectuals came together—Southern regionalist and urban Jew, Agrarian and Marxist—in a way that seemed impossible when criticism was at the poles only a few years before.

The fate of the Kenyon School of English also serves to mark the movement of critics generally to the universities. When the Rockefeller grant ran out in 1950, the school was taken over by Indiana University, where it flourished until 1972. The Fellows of the Kenyon School, however, continued to be the main contributors to the *Kenyon Review* during the rest of Ransom's editorship and maintained the influence of Formalism during the fifties.

Ransom's part in the history of Formalism is thus defined by his editorial role and by his entrepreneurship of the Kenyon School in the forties. As John L. Stewart says in 1962: "Inevitably his reputation in criticism will decline. The theories are too insubstantial and the criticism (of which there is surprisingly little, considering how much he wrote about it) is too occasional."[36] This is just; there is no piece of Ransom's practical criticism to which one can now turn for illumination, as one can still turn to Brooks's readings of Eliot, Auden, or Yeats in *Modern Poetry and the*

Tradition. Ransom's obsession with the structure-texture distinction and the concrete universal seem neither poetic nor philosophical, neither imaginative nor rigorous. Ransom is the master of the ad hoc distinction, but these distinctions seem more decorative than substantive in the long run, as when Ransom repudiates his long-held belief that a poem has structure and texture and says that a poem is an organism which (in a chain of reasoning which relies on the pun) has organs, and should be considered under the categories of "the head, the heart, the feet."[37] As Morgan Blum says, "What he constantly does is approach each critic through his own dialectic ..., and consequently through a terminology and a set of questions that may not always have the most immediate relevance."[38] Ransom's work as editor, however, was graceful beyond reach of philosophy. As poet, teacher, and friend he had a personal talent which made the *Kenyon Review* the model, the embodiment of the best in the Formalist spirit of the forties.

The relationship of the third Formalist magazine, the *Sewanee Review,* to the movement as a whole is somewhat more complicated than that of the *Southern* and *Kenyon Reviews.* Like the others, it is supported by a college, the University of the South, a small Episcopalian men's school in Sewanee, Tennessee, and hence shares a similar interest in regional issues and in the propounding of a Christian view of culture. Unlike them, it is much older, having been founded in 1892 and edited successively by William Peterfield Trent (1892-1900), John Henneman (1900-1908), John McBryde (1909-19), George Clark (1919-25), and William S. Knickerbocker (1925-42). Because the magazine was not founded by Formalists in its early years it took a more objective attitude toward their specific political and literary interests, as seen in the statements of Knickerbocker, its editor in the twenties and thirties, and in what he chose to publish.[39] In 1932 the magazine's historian Alice L. Turner concludes that "apparently Mr. Knickerbocker is interested particularly in having the *Sewanee Review* advance the study of Victorian literature and the significant literary movements and schools of the day. ... [chiefly] the humanist movement and the re-interpretation of the South's role in American culture."[40] Thus, though Knickerbocker published articles by Ransom, Tate, and others in the thirties, the *Sewanee Review* was not a Formalist or Agrarian organ in his time.

By the forties, however, change was in the wind. From the Formalists' point of view, the crucial events in the magazine's history were the displacement of Knickerbocker in 1943 and the assumption of the editorship by Allen Tate in 1944. In his initial editorial, Tate aims to mediate between "good writing which has not yet got on the New York Market" and "an audience which is not only small but scattered and, without high-pressure advertising, hard to reach." By creating this provincial center

of culture, Tate hoped to separate himself from the mindless literary
nationalism of Bernard De Voto, Archibald MacLeish, Van Wyck Brooks,
and Carl Sandburg, as well as from the "once-powerful school of Marxist
critics" now turned liberals, in favor of a defense of the Neo-Symbolist
movement of 1900-1925, chiefly Henry James, Stephen Crane, T. S. Eliot,
James Joyce, and Proust. He also hoped to publish whatever new literature
was to come after World War II.[41] Tate's immediate contribution to the
magazine was to quadruple its circulation (from 512 in the summer of
1944 to over 2,000 in the spring of 1945) and to publish the work of his
friends in the magazine. By 1945 the old order had been almost completely replaced, and contributions by essayists Bentley, Brooks, R. P.
Warren, Ransom, Maritain, O'Connor, Weaver, Blackmur, Heilman,
Burke, Mizener; poets Lowell, Jarrell, William Meredith, Berryman; and
fiction writers Andrew Lytle, Peter Taylor, Caroline Gordon (Tate's wife),
and Katherine Anne Porter all had appeared.

A special project of the *Review* during this period involved Tate's friend
John Peale Bishop, who died in 1944. A memorial prize honoring Bishop
was announced in 1944 in cooperation with Prentice-Hall, but it does not
seem to have been awarded. Some of the enduring quality of what was
published can be gathered from the contents of the 1945 volume, which
includes Tate's "Techniques of Fiction," Eliot's "The Man of Letters and
the Future of Europe," Cowley's "William Faulkner's Legend of the South,"
Blackmur's "The Economy of the American Writer," and Joseph Frank's
"Spatial Form in Modern Literature."

More important, even though Tate was editor of the *Review* only until
1946, he set the magazine on the path it has followed to the present day
as a defender of the Formalist tradition in literature, the Christian tradition in education, and the development of this view through an interest
in critical theory. The editors since Tate have been the former managing
editor of the *Southern Review* J. E. Palmer (1946-52), Monroe K. Spears
(1952-61), Andrew Lytle (1961-73), William Ralston for a time in 1967,
and George Core (1974-). All are increasingly obscure members or students
of the original Fugitive group, and in their editorial statements all pay
tribute to the tradition Tate established. Palmer says in 1946: "Honesty
and maturity in criticism leading to just evaluation—such it was the basic
objective of this magazine under Mr. Tate's editorship to provide, and
such it will continue to be. ... Above all we shall hope to retain the
principle of objectivity in judgment." Like Tate, Palmer is consciously
anti–New York and rejects "all that happens to be dominating for the
moment the conversations of the metropolis, or all that is full of the right
sort of social consciousness, or all that is *avant-garde,* or new, or—most
obtrusive of all—'American.'"[42] Monroe Spears makes a similar re-
dedication to the faith in 1952: "Since I think that *The Sewanee Review,*

as edited by Allen Tate and then John Palmer, has been the best literary quarterly in the world, I intend to do my best to preserve the character of the magazine as they formed it." Spears emphasizes the relationship of the traditional South to the international community of letters, as well as the relationship of religion to education, and he makes an appeal, typical of Formalism at that time, to broaden the *Review*'s audience to include more professional academics and the clergy. Spears appeals to religious and philosophical values to supplement Formalism and supports an "impure criticism," and his values are the typical ones of "disciplined awareness," "coherent evaluation," and the conception of literature as "a unifying center."[43]

As the *Sewanee Review* moves into the sixties, its editors seem aware of their increasing estrangement from the currents of contemporary literary thought, but their invitation to new and unpublished writers is extended only to unpublished writers who write to traditional specifications. In his initial "State of Letters" in 1961, Andrew Lytle says: "This [editorial] policy is not hard to state; it is an allegiance to the human tradition in learning and letters. If it had one figure out of the past who could best define this attitude, it would be Sir Thomas More. He saw no reason why the new learning should contradict the old faith. ... His sense was of a Christendom forever alive. ... Judgment comes out of a basic religious belief, and with us this must be Christianity."[44] In 1967 William Ralston is even more pessimistic about the times: "In dark days people have always drawn a circle around the citadel, within which, if it were a monastery, the service of God and the study of the Word could continue. ... Unless someone, somewhere is taking some care about tradition, about words continuing to 'mean what they say,' our language will deteriorate into a technology of communication and persuasion, a sophistical device, rather than remain an instrument for the articulation of truth, a paedeutic rhetoric. ... When the language is in danger of drowning in its own words, you build an ark."[45] Likewise, George Core notes: "The Roman Empire endured for three centuries by drawing in its overextended frontiers: this may have emblematic significance for a quarterly such as *SR*."[46] The progress of the *Sewanee Review* from 1944 to 1976 thus seems to be an opening out into a consideration of the central Symbolist tradition under Tate and a gradual return to Southern and Christian roots as the general current of literary discussion moves in other directions. One must say of the magazine, however, that at least until 1974 it had rather a geriatric air about it. The long-time editors and members of the editorial board— Tate, Lytle, Francis Fergusson, and Spears—were born respectively in 1899, 1902, 1904, and 1916, which makes their average editorial age about that of members of a Senate committee.

In the period when Formalism flourished, however, the *Sewanee Review* serves as an important outlet for Formalist critics, and is particularly receptive to discussion of the theory of criticism; both "The Intentional Fallacy" and "The Affective Fallacy" first appear there in 1946 and 1949. Reviews, which comprise between one-third and one-half of the magazine (at least 250 pages a year) also are important in that the editors are able to review seriously all the books that fall within their definition of the significant. In terms of sheer quantity, the *Sewanee Review* surpasses all other literary quarterlies in the number of pages devoted to reviews. In general, the editors defend the tradition of Formalism and the Symbolism of the twenties. Though occasional attention is given to other fields, the usual emphasis is on Shakespeare, Milton, and the Metaphysicals; on the modern poets Eliot, Pound, Auden, Stevens, H. Crane, and Yeats; on novelists Joyce, Lawrence, James, Flaubert, Hemingway, Faulkner, Conrad, and Fitzgerald; and on the work of Formalist and Southern writers.

Following the advice of Tate in "The Function of a Critical Quarterly," the editors enlisted the services of a number of "constant contributors," who can be broken down into several classes. One strong chorus was provided by Englishmen, including Eliot, Empson, Leavis, Herbert Read, Bonamy Dobrée (who wrote a "London Letter" for many years), Geoffrey Tillotson, and in the sixties the poet and essayist Kathleen Raine. Other groups included the conservatives Russell Kirk, Hugh Kenner, and Richard Weaver; philosophers Eliseo Vivas and Philip Wheelwright; and academicians Arnold Stein, F. Cudworth Flint, Brewster Ghiselin, Joseph Frank, Austin Warren, Richard Ellmann, Marius Bewley, John Edward Hardy, John Henry Raleigh, Louis D. Rubin, and Wallace Fowlie. During an ecumenical period in the early fifties, the magazine even published reviews by such New York Intellectuals as Richard Chase, Irving Howe, and Lionel Trilling.

The editorial policy of the *Sewanee Review* today favors those who came to be called the "academic" poets of the fifties (as opposed to the "beats"); in addition to the Formalist critic-poets, others like Daniel Hoffman, James Dickey, Charles Tomlinson, Katherine Hoskins, James Wright, Richard Eberhart, Howard Nemerov, Reed Whittemore, and John Frederick Nims appear with some frequency. The emphasis in fiction is more parochial and Southern, marked by the frequent publication of the fiction of Peter Taylor, Eleanor Ross Taylor, Caroline Gordon, Flannery O'Connor, Robert Penn Warren, Harry Brewster, Brainerd Cheney, and Alicia Ostriker. Though the magazine was also receptive to such avant-garde figures of the sixties as Sylvia Plath, Theodore Roethke, and Anne Sexton, its main loyalty remains with the Formalists and the South. To a critic, the *Review*'s greatest contributions have been its three special issues of homage: to John Crowe Ransom in 1948 on his sixtieth birthday, to Allen Tate in 1959 on his sixtieth birthday, and to T. S. Eliot in 1966 as a memorial.

Each of these special issues gathers analysis, reminiscence, and biography which provide a valuable picture of both the subject and his times. The other projects of the editors—the special issues on Christian civilization in 1957 and on Italian criticism of American literature in 1960, or the *Sewanee Review* fellowships given in the fifties (usually to aspiring young Southern writers)—do not seem to have made as much of an impact.

In sum, one must judge the *Sewanee Review* as one judges the work of Tate. Since 1944 the magazine has kept the faith, has tried far more consistently than any other magazine to provide a unifying center for culture. But what its editors consider to be the center has in terms of the general culture become a dead center, a graveyard of issues of the past. As such, it stands as most faithful and most forlorn of the Formalist magazines, with the irony of the criticism it expresses being itself judged by the irony of history.

Formalism Conquers the Universities

The first Formalist organization of an English curriculum centered on the reading and explication of the texts themselves was put into effect in the twenties during the liberalization of the Cambridge English School. E.M.W. Tillyard says of that era: "We felt rather as some of the first Protestants had felt about Scripture. This had been so overlaid with gloss and comment that the pure text had been hidden. So they reversed the process and cut away scholastic accretion, that the Christian might have direct access to the huge riches, the 'enormous bliss', of God's unadulterated word. In the same spirit we told our pupils to go to the texts first and to the text-books afterwards."[47] This emphasis on the text itself led to the experiments in reading carried on at Cambridge by I. A. Richards and published in *Practical Criticism* (1929). Richards's greatest contribution to the establishment of explication was his demonstration that a new method of analyzing literature was desperately needed.[48] When he gave unidentified poems to his honors students in English at Cambridge, he found that they were incapable of telling what a poetic text meant or of evaluating it without information about the author. He proposed a way to arrive at an exemplary reading of a poem by eliminating the difficulties in reading he found in his students (stock response, sentimentality, doctrinal interference, insensitivity to imagery, etc.) and by analyzing the sense, feeling, tone, and intention of the work. Though American Formalists did not follow Richards's recipe for analyzing a poem exactly, his demonstration of the need for a new method of reading poetry which concentrates on poetic language established the basis for the academic acceptance of *explication* as a solution to a demonstrably unsatisfactory situation. The result, as Douglas Bush puts it, is an advanced course in remedial reading.[49]

Explication was extended to the teaching of English in American universities and gained its widest influence via one of the few important textbooks in literary history, *Understanding Poetry*, by Cleanth Brooks and Robert Penn Warren. Ransom praises the book as "easily the best manual for the study of poetry which the new criticism has furnished" (*NC* 63), and John A. Meyers, Jr., testifies to its usefulness for a generation of teachers:

> For us, the real revolution in critical theory . . . was heralded by the publication, in 1938, of *Understanding Poetry*. . . . The real effects of this book, of course, were not felt until the years immediately following World War II; but for many of us who were preparing ourselves to *teach* English in those years . . . this book . . . came as a kind of revelation. It made *sense* because it opened up for us a way of talking about an actual poem in an actual classroom, and because the technique of focusing upon a poem as *language*, rather than as history or biography or morality, gave a whole new meaning to and justification for the teaching of poetry.[50]

The Formalists' development of a viable teaching method, and the continuing exposure of their ideas about literature and education in the quarterlies, led, in the late forties, to their advance from the academic hinterland of regional universities and marginal appointments to the influence and security of tenured positions at major universities, to the "big time." In 1943, while refuting Kazin's charge in *On Native Grounds* that the New Formalists are "infecting" the universities, Brooks says: "[He] has taken far too seriously the alarm of a few orthodox professors fearful of being disturbed at their footnotes. I can assure him personally that the new formalists have next to no influence in the universities."[51] This claim can be illustrated by an autobiographical anecdote by Arthur Mizener, who was fired from Yale in 1940 for being "not good enough." Mizener says: "I began writing as what I suppose would now be called a 'New Critic' with articles in the old *Southern Review*, the *Sewanee* and the *Partisan*. It didn't do me any good: 'Do you,' said an elderly Yale professor, more hurt than angry, 'think that a scholar, who is committed to the ideal of objectivity, ought to write for something called *The Partisan Review*?'"[52] And yet, in 1947, Cleanth Brooks was brought from Louisiana State to Yale as a full professor.

Following the careers of the other Formalists in their moves out of obscurity is something like regarding an elaborate game of professorial musical chairs; Robert Penn Warren left Louisiana State (and Brooks) in 1942 to become a professor of English at the University of Minnesota, but rejoined Brooks at Yale in 1950. Allen Tate replaced Warren at Minnesota, where he remained until his retirement. Robert Heilman left Louisiana State in 1948 to become chairman of the English Department at the University of Washington. Yvor Winters was given his professorship at Stanford in 1949, Austin Warren his at Michigan in 1948, and Mizener himself became a professor of English at Cornell in 1951. The conclusion one may draw from these facts is that by 1950, Tory Formalism was firmly established in the centers of academic power and influence. The replacement of the old by the new did not come without a fight, however; or more accurately, without three ongoing feuds between the Formalists and (1) the old scholars, (2) the historicist students of A. O. Lovejoy and George Boas at Johns Hopkins, and (3) R. S. Crane and the Neo-Aristotelians at the University of Chicago.

The quarrel between scholarship and criticism is centuries old and is itself a fit subject for the scholar to trace, but the particular phase of the quarrel which is relevant to this study of the Formalists begins in the late thirties with the publication of R. S. Crane's "History versus Criticism in the University Study of Literature" in 1935 in the *English Journal* and John Crowe Ransom's "Criticism Inc." in the *Virginia Quarterly Review* in 1937.[53] What unites these two men with the rest of the Formalists is an attack on "scholarship" and on such scholarly champions as Howard Mumford Jones, Frederick Pottle, and Douglas Bush. Since the main function of the scholar for the Formalists is to be the "enemy," they transfer to him much of the automatic odium with which they had previously regarded industrialists, liberals, urbanites, and other enemies of Toryism. Because the Formalists' dislikes vary somewhat, it is difficult to define exactly what a "scholar" is to them, but essentially they agree that he is a product of rigorous training leading to the Ph.D., is in control of the universities and hence of establishment study of literature, and that he must be deprived of this power because of his evil nature and effects. From the Formalist viewpoint, scholars are interested in seeing the past as the past saw itself, and are therefore trained in historical disciplines, in *The Art of Literary Research* to quote the title of Richard Altick's defense of scholarship. The scholar is interested in facts about the past; in analytical bibliographies of literary texts; in philology and the study of the development and meaning of forgotten words and past languages; in problems of authorship and the biographies of authors; in tracing the sources, reputation, and influence of books and authors. This is the world of Pollard and Redgrave's *Short-Title Catalogue*; of Grimm's law and John Livingston Lowes's *A Road to Xanadu*; of E. K. Chambers's *The Medieval Stage*; of the *DNB, OED, NCBEL,* and the Public Records Office. Yvor Winters recalls the depth of hostility between scholars and Formalists at Stanford: "The late Professor A. G. Kennedy ... told me that criticism and scholarship do not mix, that if I wanted to become a serious scholar I should give up criticism. He told me likewise that poetry and scholarship do not mix, and that he had given up writing poetry at the age of twenty-five. And he added that my publications were a disgrace to the department" (*FC* 13). Likewise, René Wellek says that at Iowa in about 1939 "Austin Warren and I met a highly respected member of the [English] department, a good historical scholar, and tried to suggest to him that, in writing about Milton and the English essay in the seventeenth century, he had also written some criticism. He turned red in the face and told us it was the worst insult anybody had ever given him" (*D* 40). Wellek goes on to note that "present-day students seem completely unable to realize the situation of the early decades of the century in most English departments. Criticism was taboo, contemporary and even American literature was not taught at all, foreign literatures were largely ignored, texts were studied only as philological documents, in short, nineteenth century positivism reigned unchallenged and supreme" (*D* 42).

To get a sense of the terms in which the Formalists expressed their dislike of this scholarly world, the tone and substance of the specific charges they made, one can turn to the symposium published jointly by the *Kenyon Review* and the *Southern Review* in 1940/41 under the title "Literature and the Professors."[54] Some of the attacks make rather ironic reading thirty years later, when viewed in the light of the unprecedented flourishing of present-day literary scholarship. Ransom says that scholars "have done so well, in fact, that the job is about finished, and they must look for another job, like the victims of technological unemployment. . . . The professor is not needed; the handbooks are there" (pp. 226, 227). He asserts that the history of criticism is not enough, and criticizes a symposium on Romanticism in the March 1940 *PMLA* on the grounds that scholars lack value judgments and cannot use "modern equipment in semantics and psychology" because of their commitment to seeing the past as it was. What is needed, Ransom says, is a critical attitude that is "tough, scientific, and aloof from the literary 'illusion' which it examines" (p. 235). Tate, on the other hand, criticizes historical scholarship for being too scientific, and for ignoring man's religious values, saying it is "but a step from the crude sociologism of the normal school to the cloistered historical scholarship of the graduate school. . . . The historical scholars, once the carriers of the humane tradition, have now merely the genteel tradition. . . . [The scholar's] substitution of 'method' for intelligence takes its definite place in the positivistic movement which, from my point of view, has been clearing the way for the slave state" (pp. 229, 240). In his essay, Cleanth Brooks uses Edwin Greenlaw's *Province of Literary History* as a stalking horse and asserts that the scholar "has little or no knowledge of the inner structure of a poem or a drama . . . he is ignorant of its architecture; in short, he often does not know how to *read*" (p. 405). And so they wrote, damning present and future colleagues alike.

Needless to say, the scholars of this time were not mute, and the most vocal defenders of the value of the historical disciplines were Douglas Bush, the great Renaissance scholar from Harvard; Frederick A. Pottle, editor of the Boswell Papers at Yale; and Rosemond Tuve, who quarrels with the Formalists' reading of seventeenth-century poetry in *Elizabethan and Metaphysical Imagery* (1947), *A Reading of George Herbert* (1952), and *Images and Themes in Five Poems by Milton* (1957). Bush's attack on the Formalists' ignorance and cavalier generalizations, "The New Criticism: Some Old-Fashioned Queries," is a masterpiece of witty critical demolition which should be read in its entirety (see note 49 above). A more sustained argument is carried on by Frederick Pottle, Cleanth Brooks's colleague at Yale. Pottle first states his views in 1941 in the Messenger Lectures at Cornell (later published as *The Idiom of Poetry*).[55] He takes the position, based on the relativism of physics and linguistics, that aesthetic judgments are relative to the critic and to the historical period in which they are made (though moral judgments are not), and he opposes not Formalism but absolutism: "The view I am propounding is that an absolute basis of feeling has no more existence than an absolute frame of space. All original criticism is subjective, being a report of the impact of the work upon the critic's sensibility; all criticism is relative to the critic's sensibility" (pp. 17-18). Pottle thus refutes the Formalists' assumption of the Ideal Reader and goes on to oppose their view that there is a timeless "tradition" from which we can judge literature as good or bad; his view is that "*the poetry of an age never goes wrong*" (p. 22), and that hence "poetic language is language that expresses the qualities of experience *in terms of a given* [individual and historical] *sensibility*" (p. 72). "Good taste in literature is, like good taste in language, the expression of sensibility in accordance with the accepted usage of the time"; thus "the chief function of the critic of contemporary literature is to recognize and to define the emergent idiom: to detach it from the background of the moribund but highly respectable idiom which obscures it" (p. 46).

In a 1953 essay, "The New Critics and the Historical Method,"[56] Pottle modifies this critique somewhat by admitting the rigidity of the scholars of the twenties and saying: "I am now convinced that to make contemporary literature the main reference for the study of the literature of the past is the right orientation, and it was a great thing for the New Critics to have made us see it" (p. 20). He goes on to describe the New Critics as a "militant movement to establish the autonomy of modern literature" (p. 16), a movement based on an attempt to substitute a normative conception of history like Toynbee's for the positivistic and genetic conception that had been dominant for the past century; he suggests that "because of their unwillingness to grant that the present is part of history, they [the New Critics] themselves are subscribing to the doctrine of historical limitation in an inverted form" (p. 22). In this essay Pottle also explicates the Tory assumptions of the Formalists, noting that they discover "with somewhat monotonous regularity . . . in all the modern literature that they are

willing to call good: Original Sin and the Collapse of Modern Civilization"
(pp. 19-20). In all these arguments, Pottle describes the Formalist position
accurately, but he does not sufficiently stress that the value of the Formalists lies in their articulated absolutism, and that the proper way to
appreciate the virtues of the Formalists is to regard them as having added
a new absolutist and Tory charter to the history of critical responses.

In the late fifties the quarrel between scholars and Formalists seems to
quiet down somewhat as they become colleagues in the same English
departments and get a little older; each group seems more inclined to
admit the other's worth. In the journal *New Literary History,* begun in
1969, Robert Weimann surveys the history of the Formalist-historicist
quarrel and concludes that the literary historian must be aware of both the
genesis and the function, both the mimetic and the affective dimensions,
both the past and the present meanings, of a work of art.[57]

Proponents of the study of the "history of ideas" also serve as constant
antagonists of the Formalists in the early forties.[58] The center for such
studies was The Johns Hopkins University, and the *magister* of the school
was A. O. Lovejoy, whose *The Great Chain of Being* (1936) demonstrates
the possibilities of this historical approach. The distinction between the
history of ideas and usual historical scholarship is that while the latter
deals with events which happened in a particular time and place, the
former studies "unit ideas," "implicit or incompletely explicit *assumptions,*
or more or less *unconscious mental habits,* operating in the thought of
an individual or a generation." Some of the possibilities the history of
ideas suggests to Lovejoy are the study of "dialectical motives," "suscepti-
bility to various kinds of metaphysical pathos," "the sacred words and
phrases of a period or a movement"—all those intellectual habits which
seem to be immutable to the thinking of an age but which are really historically conditioned.

The study of the history of ideas is thus cross-disciplinary, since "ideas
are the most migratory things in the world." Proponents of this view are
not concerned with the aesthetic value of the literature they study; they are
interested in "the manifestation of specific unit-ideas in the collective
thought of large groups of persons, not merely in the doctrines or opinions
of a small group of profound thinkers or eminent writers."[59]

The effect of the clash between the Formalists and the historians of ideas
in the early forties is described by Gerrit H. Roelofs, then a graduate
student at Johns Hopkins and later a professor of English at Kenyon
College:

After the war, in 1946, I went to The Johns Hopkins University, the supposed
stronghold of Bright's *Anglo-Saxon Grammar,* Lovejoy's *The Great Chain of Being,*
and the old line Germanic pedagogy. It was here of all places that I began to

realize—and this under the ghastly portrait of Greenlaw in the English seminar room—that there was something else besides words, sources, biography, and historical ideas. That year also I met Mr. Ransom for the first time, not at Hopkins, but at a Rhodes Scholarship interview where I lost and was mercifully sent back to the JHU stacks. His courteous surprise at my strangled responses, my own dreadful embarrassment, as well as torpedoing questions by my graduate instructors as I pawed at a few poems, woke me up. It is devilishly easy to be satisfied with information "about . . .," cultural and historical ideas, the dull *et cetera* which protect you from the poem if you are terrified or embarrassed in its presence. Mr. Ransom, without my knowing it was he, took the curse off graduate studies in that old stronghold of *Primitivism and Related Ideas in Antiquity*, philological lore, and the learned note, without denying the possibility of the fruitfulness of such labors if rightly applied. When I came to write my thesis on Spenser and natural law, Professor Don Cameron Allen, who Northrop Frye once told me is the "most formidably learned scholar" he has ever known, repeatedly cautioned me against drowning *The Faerie Queene* in a stew of sweaty proof-text quotations. The tradition of natural law is useful only if it helps explicate the poem. *The Faerie Queene* is what counts, not the tradition. To hear D. C. Allen renounce learning for poetry destroyed forever whatever faith I had in the religion of Greenlaw and Havens, the latter a grand but pathetic man who responded magnificently but only accidentally to poetry. He never knew what hit him. For Raymond Havens, Mr. Ransom's roses bloomed too late. If John Crowe Ransom could harrow the Hopkins stacks, freeing poetry from the rigors of scientific scholarship, giving hope to anxious graduate students, what did he do elsewhere?[60]

The *Journal of the History of Ideas* was founded in 1940 to spread Lovejoy's ideas; on its board of editors were such eminent philosophers, historians, and literary scholars as George Boas, Crane Brinton, Richard McKeon, Perry Miller, Marjorie Nicolson, and John Herman Randall. In his introductory essay to the first issue, Lovejoy argues specifically against the Formalist view of literature:

The very notion, then, of a work of art as a self-contained kind of thing is a psychological absurdity. It *functions* as art through what it does for the experiencer of it; nothing in it has aesthetic efficacy except through its power to evoke certain responses in him; so that one may say that, except in a physical sense, its content is as much in him as in itself. And this general consideration alone, even apart from the citation of particular examples, seems to establish a sufficient presumption against the doctrine, now somewhat fashionable in various quarters, that, in the reading of literature, ignorance is always bliss, that the best reader is the one who has least in his mind, and that, consequently, the sort of knowledge which may result from the historical study of literature is never serviceable to the aesthetic purposes of that art.[61]

A reply was immediately published by Leo Spitzer in Brooks and Warren's *Southern Review*. Spitzer here argues for concentrating on the language of poetry, for a kind of reading which "has for its goal the admiration of the ever-possible miracle of timeless beauty"; he argues against emphasizing biographical information, which "prevents the appreciation of the tone-contents of the poem"; against source study, which causes a deflection of the "eye of the observer away from the existent whole of an artistic organism toward certain parts of it which have been artificially detached and recombined with extraneous elements"; against genre study, which he considers to be an abstraction of the reality of the poem itself; and against the relationship of art to life, for "art is not life, but a new architecture, built of fancy and the poetic will, apart from life and beyond life." [62] Spitzer's essay eloquently anticipates much of the argument of the next decade and reveals the idealistic aesthetics behind the Formalists, the contemplation of beauty itself.

Despite this initial joust, historians of ideas have not aroused much specifically literary interest, [63] and in practice have not shown much interest in literary criticism in the intervening years. The exception is Roy Harvey Pearce, who was trained at Johns Hopkins and has written, among other works, *The Continuity of American Poetry* (1961) and *Historicism Once More* (1969). In "'Pure' Criticism and the History of Ideas," [64] Pearce argues that historical understanding is a necessary supplement of Formalism by showing how Brooks's analysis of Herrick's "Corinna's Going a-Maying" in *The Well Wrought Urn* is only partial. Pearce formulates his most elaborate defense of the usefulness of the history of ideas for criticism in his 1958 essay "Historicism Once More." [65] In this essay he contends that we must try "not only to see literature in history, but to see history in literature" (p. 557), and he defends his view by pointing to the historical nature of language and style. In so doing he attacks specifically the Christian Eliot, "for whom the problem of history and thus the problem of language, is resolved in the dogma of the Word" (pp. 558–59); Wellek and Warren's inaccurate assumption that historical study is reductionist; and Murray Krieger's failure to deal with the role of language in the creative process. The basis of Pearce's defense is, however, his own absolute: "the writer's primal intuition . . . that man, the self, is at the center of all literature and that literary works are necessarily created in terms of a fixed, unchanging and unchangeable sense of what it is to be aware of oneself as a man, whatever one's situation in historical time" (pp. 573–74). It is this sense of *humanitas* that the "wholeness" of the literary work embodies; and the end of literature is "the objectification of such historical data as . . . may be formed into ideally possible wholes" (p. 575).

This attempt to reconcile the Formalists' sense of the absolute meaning of the wholeness of literature with the relativism of George Boas and other historians of ideas did not satisfy either camp. René Wellek says of it, in an unusual display of irritation: "Pearce's historicism is a confused mixture of existentialism and historicism, a string of bombastic assertions about humanity, the possibility of literature, and so on, with the constant polemical refrain that 'criticism is a form of historical study.' . . . It is not worth trying to disentangle the hopeless muddles of Pearce's amazing stew of existence, eschatology, history, the 'creative ground of all values,' the whole weird mixture of Rudolph Bultmann, Américo Castro, Kenneth Burke, and Walter J. Ong, S.J., all quoted on one page" (*CC* 10-11). One notes in this exchange the development, on a theoretical level, of the battle between the scholars and the "New Critics" in the forties. But interest in this theoretical struggle also waned; aside from an essay by Mark Spilka, who cites Pearce as an authority and argues that "style" is the concept that links the work itself with the author and period, and defenses of the Formalist position by Wimsatt (*VI* 11-13) and Krieger,[66] the literary battle between Formalists and historians of ideas appears to have come to an end.

Further theoretical objections to the history of ideas have been made, however, by theoreticians of history. Maurice Mandelbaum says that "it would frequently lead us away from those features of an author's work which were most likely to be central to his motivation, and which might also be most important for his historical influence; it might also lead us to minimize the independence of an author's thought, suggesting lines of historical connection where such connections have not been established and may not have existed."[67] Similarly, René Wellek says: "Pure 'history of ideas' does not encourage any synoptic understanding of sometimes loosely put together and even self-contradictory systems of individual theorists, any development of the individuality and personality, the peculiar attitude and sensibility of the great critic" (*HC* 1: 11). These objections seem compelling because of the way critics function in practice; the novels and poems they praise or condemn, the articles they as editors accept or reject, and their formulation of a historical tradition depend much more on their charter and circumstances than on any set of abstract ideas. Critical ideas come together only in the critic, and only a study of the man, his charter, and his times will reveal their true historical identities.

The third center of opposition to the Formalists was the "Chicago School," led by Ronald S. Crane and including among its proponents Elder Olson, W. R. Keast, Richard McKeon, Bernard Weinberg, Norman Maclean, and many graduates of the English Department of the University of Chicago, where Crane was chairman from 1935 to 1947.[68] The writings of this group appear mostly in *Modern Philology* (published at Chicago), which Crane edited from 1930 to 1952. It was Crane, in fact, who first issued the call (in 1935) to reform the study of English by replacing historical scholarship with criticism.[69] His enthusiasm is that of the convert, since in the twenties and early thirties he was a follower of A. O. Lovejoy and the history of ideas method and was one of four general editors of the *Documentary*

History of Primitivism. According to Hoyt Trowbridge, "The most important turning point in Crane's intellectual and professional life came in 1934, with the arrival of Richard McKeon [the Aristotelian philosopher], under whose influence Crane and others developed the concepts and methods of the 'Chicago School.'"[70] The change in the curriculum at Chicago to the "Great Books" program of Robert Hutchins and Mortimer Adler also may have had some influence on Crane.

Like the Formalists, the "Chicago Critics" eliminate the author, the audience, and all other external or extrinsic factors that bear on a literary work so that they can study "the internal causes which account for the peculiar construction and effect of any poem qua artistic whole" (*C&C* 20). The essential argument between the two schools is that the Formalists approach literary works largely in terms of linguistic categories (paradox, tension, ambiguity, metaphor) while the Chicago School stresses the authority of Aristotle (they are often called the Neo-Aristotelians). According to the Chicago Critics, "It is the merit of Aristotle, uniquely among systematic critics, that he grasped the distinctive nature of poetic works as *synola,* or concrete artistic wholes" (*C&C* 17). From Aristotle the Chicago Critics derive their emphasis on the formal categories of plot, character, and genre, and they criticize the Formalists chiefly for ignoring these structural elements: "Most of the 'new critics,' under the still powerful influence of the assumption that poetry is best considered as a kind of discourse, continue to read all poems as if their authors had constructed them on identical principles, confusing, for instance, mimetic forms with didactic, and treating lyrics and novels, tragedies and essays, by means of the same distinctions" (*C&C* 15).

From the first, the intent of the Chicago Critics is polemical. Of the essays gathered in their central work, *Critics and Criticism,* which Crane edited in 1952, those on modern criticism attack the Formalists directly: Keast's "The 'New Criticism' and *King Lear*" is a reply to Robert Heilman's *This Great Stage: Image and Structure in "King Lear*; Olson's "A Symbolic Reading of the *Ancient Mariner*" responds to Robert Penn Warren's essay on the poem, and his "William Empson, Contemporary Criticism, and Poetic Diction" examines critically *Seven Types of Ambiguity*; while Crane's "The Critical Monism of Cleanth Brooks" is a reply to *The Well Wrought Urn.*

The Formalists' replies have been equally vigorous. W. K. Wimsatt speaks of the "pattern of retracted pluralism" (*VI* 47) of McKeon and Crane, who claim to be pluralistic and hence less dogmatic than their Formalist opponents, but who also claim that their Aristotelian theory is better than the Formalists'. Wellek says that "in practice Crane's 'method of multiple hypotheses' is constantly abandoned by the Chicago critics in favor of a dogmatic scheme which serves as a polemical instrument against the New Criticism and the propounders of symbolist and mythic interpretations of literature. Plot, character, genre are the central concepts, while language is relegated to the lowly position of a mere material cause or occasion of poetry" (*CC* 321). And Yvor Winters says of Crane: "As a critic, he is a scholarly amateur; he knows no more about criticism than Tate, Ransom, and their agrarian friends of twenty years ago knew about farming. He exhibits no knowledge of the structure or history of lyric poetry in English, and his few remarks on the subject make one suspect that he would write badly if he tried to write of it. He seems in brief to have come to poetry through an interest in criticism, rather than to criticism through an interest in poetry" (*FC* 22).

Crane renews his attack on both Formalists and "Myth Critics" in *The Languages of Criticism and the Structure of Poetry* (1953). Here too his intent is to establish the Aristotelian approach as more adequate to the criticism of literature than any alternative method, and to characterize the Formalists as "reductionist." Repeating a charge made in *Critics and Criticism*, he says: "For Brooks, there are no other points. Irony, or paradox, is poetry, *tout simplement*, its form no less than its matter. ... The same tendency toward a monistic reduction of critical concepts is manifest in Allen Tate's doctrine of 'tension,' in John Crowe Ransom's principle of 'texture,' in Robert Penn Warren's obsession with symbols, above all in I. A. Richards' Pavlovian mythology concerning the 'behavior' of words. The doubts which Brooks inspires thus become doubts about the general state of critical learning" (*C&C* 84).

E. D. Hirsch, Jr., says of all these battles: "The most vigorous polemics in recent critical theory arose between the Chicago critics and the New Haven critics who shared the same revolutionary goal of deposing extrinsic scholarship in favor of intrinsic criticism; the Trotskyites were embattled against the Leninists over the true method of the revolution, and only the vigor of their conflict sufficed to mask the structural identity of their aim." [71]

One may conclude that ultimately the Chicago School failed because it did not produce any practical criticism of note on which to establish its own "tradition" (Elder Olson's "Sailing to Byzantium" and *The Poetry of Dylan Thomas* [1954] and Crane's article "The Concept of Plot and the Plot of *Tom Jones*" are practically the only examples). Nor did it produce a method of "normal criticism." As Northrop Frye notes in his review of *The Languages of Criticism*: "The principles, as well as the sparse examples from *Macbeth* and Gray's *Elegy*, remain very general in formulation. With the best will in the world it is difficult to see the practical application of, for instance, 'the shaping principle of form and emotional "power" without which no poem could come into existence as a beautiful and effective whole of a determinate kind.' "[72] And Walter Sutton observes:

"The active movement that the leaders hoped for never developed, although their work undoubtedly encouraged a renewal of interest in genre criticism, shared by critics like Kenneth Burke and Northrop Frye in modified forms and by many other scholar critics within the universities."[73]

Another reason for the lack of influence of the Chicago School is that it was an "old man's" movement. Its effort to be an avant-garde in the universities was compromised by the fact that all the members of the group had already risen through the ranks and were *emeriti* of the inflexible university world (Crane was sixty-six when *Critics and Criticism* was published in 1952). Ransom clearly distinguishes the Chicago Critics from the Formalists on this basis. "The professional [i.e., Formalist] critic is always *avant garde*, occupying himself with poetic effects that are strange, and eventful for the development of poetic practice. Consequently he occupies himself preferably with recent and contemporary poetry."[74]

A third reason for the Chicago Critics' lack of influence is the turgidity of their writing. It is regrettably almost impossible to read their prose and make any sense out of it, not because they are too learned, but because they wear their learning so heavily and display it in what Northrop Frye calls a "pythonic sentence structure." Both Vivas and Wimsatt analyze the opaqueness of McKeon's writing in some detail.[75] Richard Foster says of Elder Olson: "When he turns to criticism he stops being a man of letters and begins pulling the levers and pushing the buttons of the Neo-Aristotelian tabulator, and the writing comes out like something from the olden tyme translated by Butcher. Most of the time this officialese is just pedantic camouflage for the most simple-minded banalities."[76]

The great contribution of the Chicago School, as might be expected from the scholarly training and philosophical interests of its members, is to the history and theory of criticism. McKeon has edited and written on Aristotle's *Poetics*; Olson has written *Tragedy and the Theory of Drama* (1961) and *The Theory of Comedy* (1968); and Bernard Weinberg has published *History of Literary Criticism in the Italian Renaissance* (1961). In addition, the school has produced or influenced such theoretical works as Paul Goodman's *The Structure of Literature* (1954); Wayne Booth's *The Rhetoric of Fiction* (1961), *A Rhetoric of Irony* (1974), and *Modern Dogma and the Rhetoric of Assent* (1974); and Elder Olson's *On Value Judgments in the Arts and Other Essays* (1976). Nevertheless, as Crane himself acknowledges, "though commitment to method in this [pluralistic] sense is inescapable, not even the soundest or most completely developed theory can compensate, in practical criticism, for the critic's want of sensibility and knowledge; these by themselves are not, as is often supposed, sufficient conditions of good criticism, but their absence is enough to make criticism bad" (*C&C* 9). Crane is one of the best at close scholarly analysis of other people's confusions of premise or failures of coherence, but the usefulness of Neo-Aristotelianism as a way of responding to literature would seem to be almost nil; the insights and distinctions of the Chicago Critics have had the effect of burying Aristotle, not resurrecting him as a part of a usable past. Though Wellek's arguments may be influenced by his scholarly disagreements with Crane (*CC* 156, 199), his conclusion that the Chicago School's Aristotelianism "seems an ultra-academic exercise destined to wither on the vine" (*CC* 360) seems about right. Olson in particular continues to develop the Aristotelian theory on such occasions as the Texas "Symposium on Formalist Criticism,"[77] and Booth's *The Rhetoric of Fiction* (1961) has had considerable influence,[78] but the theoretical issues raised by the Aristotelians have become obsolete even before the death of their defenders, *de mortuis nil nisi bonum.*

Given this conclusion, it is only appropriate that the phoenix is the symbol of the University of Chicago Press, which in 1974 began publishing a new magazine, *Critical Inquiry,* edited by second-generation Aristotelians Sheldon Sacks, Arthur Heiserman, Robert L. Streeter, and Wayne C. Booth. In its first four years, this magazine has stressed the relationship of literature to art history, cinema, and music and has shown a particular interest in problems of narrative structure in the novel. Specific discussions of the work of Kenneth Burke, Northrop Frye, and M. H. Abrams have evoked spirited responses in their "Critical Forum," but as yet the editors have issued no critical manifesto or charter defining their critical position. They are most interested in British literature of the modernist period, particularly novelists like Woolf, Forster, Joyce, Lawrence, James, and have published a number of statements on art by such eminent figures as Saul Bellow, Joyce Carol Oates, and John Gardner. They seem, in short, to have a better claim to be truly pluralistic than were the Aristotelian "pluralists" of the first generation, but they support a pluralism focused on problems of the modern novel.

Eliot's Triumph and the Reaction

As one looks back, then, on the Formalists from 1938 to 1948, their period of explication and polemics seems to be marked by conspicuous success in that they were able to express their position convincingly and defend it against the opposition of redoutable scholars, historians, and Aristotelians. This is the age when it became fashionable to refer to T. S. Eliot as a literary dictator, and indeed, his winning of the Nobel Prize in 1948 is a kind of objective correlative of his suzerainty. The strength of the Formalists' position can be gauged best by the incident which closed that decade, the awarding of the Bollingen Prize to Ezra Pound by the Fellows of the Library of Congress in American Letters, a group supposedly dominated by Eliot, Warren, and Tate.[79] The award was important not because it was given to Pound, then escaping trial for treason for his World War II pro-Mussolini broadcasts by being incarcerated for madness in St. Elizabeth's Hospital in Washington; nor because of the nature of the defense the Fellows made of the choice, which was based on the Formalist separation of the literary excellence of the work from its anti-Semitic content. Its importance for criticism lies in the fact that it was attacked viciously by Robert Hillyer, an old-time pastoral poet and ironically a colleague of Ransom's at Kenyon College, in two articles, "Treason's Strange Fruit: The Case of Ezra Pound and the Bollingen Award" and "Poetry's New Priesthood," published in the *Saturday Review of Literature* on June 11 and 18, 1949. As Robert A. Corrigan points out, "Perhaps the most intriguing aspect [of this attack] is how quickly Pound himself was pushed into the background and the emphasis shifted to T. S. Eliot, the new poetry, and the Higher Criticism."[80] Hillyer claims that "both Pound and Eliot, and Eliot especially, have a stranglehold on American poetry through the so-called "new criticism."[81] Continuing his attack, he notes:

The party line of Eliot and the new esthetes (including the self-styled "new critics") is merely the old doctrine of art-for-art's sake titivated [sic] with plumes of voodoo jargon to overawe the young. . . . Their current pre-occupation is a new vocabulary that has no purpose but its own creation. . . . Their power is enormous, especially in the colleges and even the preparatory schools. A large proportion of funds for cultural purposes from the great charitable foundations is earmarked for their use. . . . What I have been leading up to in this sketch of the new estheticism is that its sterile pedantry, based on a sense of personal inadequacy, and its failure to command our common English, result in a blurring of judgment both esthetic and moral. I have said that in the Bollingen award to Pound the clouds of an intellectual neo-Fascism [Toryism] and the new estheticism [Formalism] have perceptibily met.[82]

In defending Hillyer in the June 11 issue, the *Saturday Review*'s editors note that one of their purposes is "to call attention to the incredible and dangerous intellectual snobbery that is a dominant strain of the 'new criticism.'"

Historically speaking, this controversy seems to indicate that Eliot, who had captured the best minds of Cambridge in the twenties, had at last reached the center of bourgeois critical circles in the person of Hillyer (identified as receiving an award from the Lyric Association Foundation [sic] for Traditional Poetry); the members of the Poetry Society of Texas and the Poetry Society of America, who wrote letters supporting him; and the editorial board of the *Saturday Review of Literature*. The fact that those who in 1938 were a defeated minority as Tories had as Formalists become influential on everyone who came of age intellectually between 1940 and 1955 (and through them had reached millions of teachers and pupils)—the fact that a revolution in taste had occurred—finally penetrated even the densest popular minds.

Because the *Saturday Review* would not publish a rebuttal, the answer to Hillyer's unfactual attack appeared in *The Case against the "Saturday Review,"* a pamphlet published by *Poetry* magazine. The Fellows of the Library of Congress in American Letters argued that beyond the grant of the money, the Bollingen Foundation had no connection with fascism or the award given to Pound; Eliot did not propose Pound for the award or speak in his behalf; the jury felt that the *Cantos* was, judged by purely literary criteria, the best book of the year; the Fellows were not members of a single critical school, and especially not of the "New Critical" school. Hillyer's attempt to become the Joe McCarthy of the literary world, which was similar to Archibald MacLeish's effort a decade earlier to judge writers by their Americanism, did cause the Library of Congress to withdraw the Bollingen Prize, but Hillyer did not cow the literary world as he wished, nor did he turn back the clock to the fashion of poetry he embodied. The best answer to Hillyer's attack was Eliot's triumphant lecture tour in 1956, when, in the University of Minnesota field house, he attracted what was perhaps the largest audience to listen to a lecture on literary criticism in the history of the world.

Hillyer's polemic did, however, signal a reaction against academic Formalism, which in the fifties went through a stage of being attacked as the natural enemy of poetry by Randall Jarrell in "An Age of Criticism" (ironically, a lecture first delivered at the Indiana School of Letters); by Karl Shapiro in a number of essays collected in *In Defense of Ignorance* (1960); by Leslie Fiedler in "Toward an Amateur Criticism";[83] and most notably by T. S. Eliot himself in "The Frontiers of Criticism." Some of the tone of these objections can be gathered from the following excerpts:

The false dualisms set up by Eliot between art and social action are symptomatic of the insanity of much modern criticism. In any case, it was Eliot's attractive formulation of these dualisms that neutralized so many critics and led Criticism itself into a squirrel cage where it performs so brilliantly for its own amusement.— Karl Shapiro[84]

Some of this criticism is as good as anyone could wish. ... But a great deal of this criticism might just as well as have been written by a syndicate of encyclopedias for an audience of International Business Machines. It is not only bad or mediocre, it is *dull*; it is often ... an astonishingly graceless, joyless, humorless, long-winded, niggling, blinkered, methodical, self-important, cliché-ridden, prestige-obsessed, almost autonomous criticism.—Randall Jarrell[85]

We are in danger even of pursuing criticism as if it was a science, which it never can be. ... Thirty-three years ago, it seems to have been the latter type of criticism, the impressionistic, that had caused the annoyance I felt when I wrote on "the function of criticism." Today it seems to me that we need to be more on guard against the purely explanatory.—T. S. Eliot[86]

Return to the Past

As a result or concomitant of this attack, the Formalists in the fifties retreat from polemics, settle back, and return to their Tory roots. The most conspicuous conversion is that of Allen Tate, who, perhaps under the influence of the French Neo-Thomist Jacques Maritain, embraced Catholicism in 1950. The formative influence of religious training on Cleanth Brooks's method of explication is sketched above; in *The Hidden God* (1963) he expresses his Tory beliefs directly by defending the essentially Christian pattern and meaning of Hemingway, Yeats, Eliot, Warren, and Faulkner. Except for Hemingway, all are traditionalists and regionalists of the Tory school, and Brooks defends them on the basis of their Tory values, of which belief in God, or defense of the Christian virtues, is central.

In *William Faulkner*, Brooks returns to the study of the Christian South by giving a close and detailed reading of Faulkner's fourteen novels about Yoknapatawpha County.[87] Operating under the typical Formalist assumption of the nature of his task, Brooks discusses the relationship of the parts of a work to the whole, taking due account of its complexity. He says, for example, that *"Go Down, Moses* has a great deal more over-all unity than a superficial glance might suggest" (p. 244), and he goes on to demonstrate it. The values which Brooks sees in Faulkner are the Tory ones of belief in God and the Agrarian culture of the South. As Brooks asserts, "There is a Christian framework within which his [Faulkner's] sensibility operates but against which at any particular time it may—and does—rebel" (p. 41). From this initial assumption of God's existence, the rest of the Tory cluster of doctrines follow: the fallen nature of man, the sense of sin and evil, the organic community. In an early chapter of his book, Brooks is especially concerned to refute the view that Faulkner is a kind of romantic: "I find nowhere in Faulkner the notion that man, if he would only know his true nature, could be at home and happy in the world. . . . Faulkner's men are not innocent in this sense. They are already fallen and alienated. In effect, then, Faulkner seems to accept the Christian doctrine of original sin" (p. 37).

The social order that is concomitant with Brooks's Christian conception of man is the agrarian South, the only kind of society which in his view produces a true sense of community.[88] For Brooks, "community" is the social equivalent of organic unity in the poem, and serves as the concept which both describes and evaluates societies. This sense of community applies to all social classes in the South: "The great majority of Faulkner's poor whites are members of a community and, according to their own lights, law-abiding. . . . [Even the Gowries in *Intruder in the Dust*] have their code of values, their sense of community, and their religion—embodied physically in the little frame church back in the hills" (p. 23). The importance of this idea of community for Brooks's reading of Faulkner can be seen in his abstract definition of it in his peroration:

Taken together, the Yoknapatawpha novels and stories create for us an amazingly rich and intricate world, and one that embodies its own principles of order. . . . It bears a special and significant relation to history. It has a sort of collective memory. Because it does, it can see itself in a dramatic role. It embodies a style of life. Most of all, this society is bound together by unspoken assumptions—that is to say, it is a true community. . . . The fact that it is provincial does not prevent its serving as an excellent mirror of the perennial triumphs and defeats of the human spirit. [P. 368]

Thus, Brooks places Faulkner's South in the context of the Tory regionalist tradition he asserted in the thirties, comparing it to Yeats's Ireland and Frost's New England, and makes a major effort in *A Shaping Joy* (1971) to interpret Yeats and Auden in terms of the same Tory regionalist tradition. Brooks devotes chapters to Yeats's poetry in both *Modern Poetry and the Tradition* and *The Well Wrought Urn*. In addition to categorizing Yeats as a Formalist poet, Brooks finds Formalist values in Yeats's criticism. In "William Butler Yeats as a Literary Critic," Brooks traces all the stages of the Tory charter.[89] In Brooks's view, Yeats rejects the world: "Like Wilde, Yeats too was out of tune with his own age, but he took another course. He eschewed rhetoric. He sought solitude" (p. 36). For Yeats, art is impersonal. He is conscious of the evil in the world: "The genuine poet will be truthful in recording the defect, the ugliness, the evil that is to be found in reality" (p. 23). The result is a poetry of the tension of dialectical opposites: "The dialectic through which the poem is produced gives its own impress to the poem. The tension developed in the play between opposites is built into the poem" (p. 20). Or as Yeats said, "We make out of the quarrel with others, rhetoric, but of the quarrel with ourselves, poetry" (quoted on p. 22). According to Brooks, Yeats believes in tradition: "Yeats wrote himself down as a man for whom unity of being was of supreme importance. The great ages for him were those in which a high degree of cultural unity was attained. The burden of his various accounts of literary history is the inevitable falling away from these periods of great and rich unity—the descent into mechanization, division, and abstraction. . . . English literature since the Middle Ages is described as essentially a movement from unity of culture to the isolation of the individual" (p. 27). And finally, "Authentic poetry is a form of knowledge, and yet one can truly know only what one has himself made" (p. 33)—that is, Brooks interprets

Yeats as saying that now that man has lost his faith, he must spin his tradition spider-like out of his own guts and make a new religion out of art. Brooks also sees Auden's view of literature as Formalist. In "W. H. Auden as a Critic," after noting Auden's interest in generic, cultural, archetypal, and Christian criticism, Brooks claims that Auden's "most fully matured" statement (in "Nature, History, and Poetry" [1950]) reveals a Formalist position. Auden's definition of a poem as "a community of feelings truly embodied in a verbal society" leads, in Brooks's interpretation, to making the problem of poetic value one "of discovering whether the poem is truly unified or chaotic, whether its parts are related or unrelated." How, asks Brooks, does the poet transform words and feelings into a verbal community? His answer is the Formalist dualism, through tension and dialectic. Brooks goes on to draw other parallels between Auden's work and Formalist theory and concludes: "That Auden, the poet of civilization, the student of cultural history, the serious moralist, should hold what amounts to a formalist conception of poetry may come as a shock. Yet it is plainly a fact."[90]

Brooks's comparison of authors so radically disparate in nationality, genre, and world view as Yeats, Auden, and Faulkner, and his assessment of their writing in terms of the same values—"community," tension, dialectic, etc.—reveal the projective nature of his criticism. The danger, of course, lies not in finding Formalist values in these authors, not in adding a new dimension to our reading of their works, but in reducing them to Formalists when in fact these values form only a part, and often only a small part, of their statements.

The later expression of John Crowe Ransom's Christian beliefs involves, as seems temperamentally natural to him, no great shifts of allegiance, no leavings and no conversions. Essentially he is at the end what he was at the beginning. In 1930, in *God without Thunder,* he writes: "I am the son of a theologian, and the grandson of another one, but the gift did not come down to me."[91] Nevertheless, he gives to modern man and presumably to himself this commandment: "With whatever religious institution a modern man may be connected, let him try to turn it back towards orthodoxy. Let him insist on a virile and concrete God, and accept no Principle as a substitute. Let him restore to God the Thunder" (pp. 327–28). Perhaps the best way to think of this as a *moderate* view for Ransom is to recall the fanaticism of the Southern Fundamentalist in the world of the Scopes trial and William Jennings Bryan. Thirty-five years later, at the age of seventy-seven, Ransom reaffirms his religious beliefs and describes their relationship to his criticism. Talking of the morality of a poem, he says: "When we dwell upon the poet's system of ideas about good and evil, we shall be philosophizing; ... if it is not criticism in the usual sense, it is metacriticism; about the metaphysic of the poet. I find myself turning easily to Scriptural terms, being neither capable nor desirous of abandoning the instruction I received in my own father's parsonage; beginning always with the idea of the God who created out of chaos a slowly evolving universe, coming to its highest climax in the mind and brain of man. What better hypothesis can I find to explain the fact?"[92] More interesting as an insight into the whole body of Ransom's practical criticism is his remark later in the same essay (made in response to a question asked during a lecture on Renaissance prosody in which he proposed considering "rhythms as perhaps a sort of ritual"): "I was asked by a distinguished professor if the continuity of the new rhythms did not rise at the same time as the general breakdown of the Faith and might not have acted as a sort of substitute which had the advantage of seeming secular rather than religious, felt dimly but not sworn to. I had to agree."[93] If one thinks of Ransom's long preoccupation with metrics as a kind of listening to the service at the far end of the great cathedral of modern poetry, the essential religiosity of his practical criticism becomes apparent.

5. The Formalist
Men of Letters

If one stops here and reviews the permanent achievement of practical Formalist criticism, the essential record is in. Perhaps the most influential of the group was Cleanth Brooks, whose method of explication and adherence to a narrowly methodological and hence teachable position gave him great currency in academic circles. However, the list of other critics who rose above the movement of which they were a part to attain the individual and permanent status of Men of Letters must include as pre-eminent T. S. Eliot, the founding father of Formalist criticism, who went on to transcend his own movement through his late anagnorisis and meditation on his early self. Allen Tate, whose actual *oeuvre* of poems and essays is astonishingly slight, nevertheless has a permanent place as the gladiator of American Formalism, as the archetypal conservative who proves that perseverance wins. R. P. Blackmur's early essays on Eliot, Yeats, Stevens, Cummings, and others define and explain the modernist tradition in the thirties in a way that is superior to the volumes of explication which followed him. And Austin Warren developed the writing of essays into a fine art. In addition to these masters, Formalism produced two notable maverick Men of Letters, Yvor Winters and Kenneth Burke, whose considerable presence on the literary scene is vitiated by narrowness and autodidacticism.

T. S. Eliot as Critic: The Man behind the Masks

The problem of separating Eliot from his influence in order to discover his true identity involves a return to narrow considerations of history and culture, and to an examination of the personality of this most elusive person.[1] Despite his poetic modernity, Eliot belongs to the old school of the impressionistic gentleman-critic that he was so hard on when he was a young man; his criticism is expressive, not impersonal. It can be said of him, as he said of his friend Charles Whibley, that "it is the unity of a personality which gives an indissoluble unity to his variety of subject" (*SE* 446). Although Eliot became influential as the father figure of Formalism, and his casual utterances in reviews became the sacred writ that chartered a generation of normal criticism, understanding Eliot as a critic, as distinguished from the influence of his criticism, demands a study of the voice of one of the most learned, ironic, and complex literary personalities of our time. Summarizing a talk he made in 1955, the *Times Literary Supplement* notes Eliot's own observation that "writers discussing his critical essays . . . have been too much inclined to treat these as if they were a single systematic treatise, written at one time; and have reproached him with inconsistencies where they should merely have noted that, over the years, like the rest of us, he has often changed his mind."[2] In 1961 Eliot writes: "I find myself constantly irritated by having my words, perhaps written thirty or forty years ago, quoted as if I had uttered them yesterday" (*TCC* 14). The important point is that Eliot's criticism, like that of Dr. Johnson, is valuable not only because of the subject, and not because what he says is right or wrong, but because we can experience in his writings a first-class mind in action, and can learn another valuable response to literature and life. The primary context in which Formalist doctrines like "impersonality" and "tradition" must be seen is Eliot's personality; and we must consider his criticism not as a body of doctrines, a philosophical system, but as the record of a man thinking.

　　It is well to stress here that when one speaks of Eliot's personality, one can talk only of his public and literary personality—his persona—not his private, inner self. But a persona such as Eliot's, maintained constantly for fifty years, is an expressive extension of his private self, not a fictional character, and must be thought of ultimately as being real and embodying Eliot's own reaction to the literary world. One can distinguish Eliot's voices chronologically, since his career is clearly divisible into three phases.[3] From 1916 to 1927 Eliot was learning his trade, and his voice here is marked by a convincing illusion of authority. Largely through the art of obscure allusion and recondite comparison,[4] he manages to sound like the Aged Eagle of criticism while still in his twenties; he was only thirty-two when his first volume of collected essays, *The Sacred Wood*, was published in 1920.[5] Edmund Wilson has parodied the voice of this phase:

He is very much given, for example, to becoming involved in literary Houses-that-Jack-Built: "We find this quality occasionally in Wordsworth," he will write, "but it is a quality which Wordsworth shares with Shenstone rather than with Collins and Gray. And for the right sort of enjoyment of Shenstone, we must read his prose as well as his verse. The 'Essays on Men and Manners' are in the tradition of the great French aphorists of the seventeenth century, and should be read with the full sense of their relation to Vauvenargues, La Rochefoucauld and (with his wider range) La Bruyère. We shall do well to read enough of Theophrastus to understand the kind of effect at which La Bruyère aimed. (Professor Somebody-or-other's book on 'Theophrastus and the Peripatetics' gives us the clew to the intellectual atmosphere in which Theophrastus wrote and enables us to gauge the influences on his work—very different from each other—of Plato and Aristotle.)" At this rate (though I have parodied Eliot), we should have to read the whole of literature in order to appreciate a single book, and Eliot fails to supply us with a reason why we should go to the trouble of doing so. [*Ax* 124]

Eliot's phase as a social and religious critic began in about 1928, with his famous declaration in the preface to *For Lancelot Andrewes* that his "general point of view may be described as classicist in literature, royalist in politics, and anglo-catholic in religion." In this period, which continues through *Thoughts After Lambeth* (1931), *After Strange Gods* (1934), *The Idea of a Christian Society* (1939), and *Notes Towards the Definition of Culture* (1948), Eliot's voice in this phase is somewhat unpleasant, hectoring the world for its lack of morality and a little grumpy because the world refuses to respond properly. In Eliot's third phase (from 1948 until his death), his voice, under the softening influences of his increasing fame and affluence and his happy, late remarriage, becomes increasingly genial, self-deprecatory, mock modest, and authoritative. In this period his essays are all written as lectures, the genre of the established Man of Letters, and are all on literary subjects.

Despite these historical differences in emphasis, however, Eliot's personality is essentially unified after 1920, and can be studied synchronically. W. H. Auden speculates about Eliot's constant personae in these words:

Eliot is a household with at least three permanent residents. ... The Archdeacon, who believes in and practices order, discipline, and good manners, social and intellectual, with a thoroughly Anglican distaste for evangelical excess ... a violent and passionate old peasant grandmother, who has witnessed murder, rape, pogroms, famine, flood, fire, everything; who has looked into the abyss and, unless restrained, would scream the house down ... [and] a young boy who likes to play slightly malicious jokes. [6]

Eliot's persona is uniquely interesting to Americans, since it is that of a boy from St. Louis who was better and went farther than most, but who still exemplifies the flight from the provinces and the natural Puritan character of the typical American. If we keep in mind that Eliot was an American making his way by his wits, his somewhat defensive assertions about Classicism and Royalism become humanly understandable as the actions of an émigré trying on new faces. Moreover, Eliot's belated confessions of arrogance become humanly appealing—for example, when the 1928 Eliot says of the 1920 Eliot: "Especially I detect [in *The Sacred Wood*] frequently a stiffness and an assumption of pontifical solemnity which may be tiresome to many readers" (*SWood* vii). Sometimes he states explicitly that his persona is a self-conscious one, as when he says in a late appreciation of Wyndham Lewis: "You may have noticed that [this article] is not quite in my *Times-Literary-Supplement*-leading-article manner."[7] Eliot's style is, of course, an important part of his persona, and Hugh Kenner's description of his early style is apt: "Eliot extended and generalized his *Egoist* manner into what was to be, until fame overtook him, his fundamental critical strategy: a close and knowing mimicry of the respectable. ... The rhetorical layout of essay after essay can best be described as a parody of official British literary discussion; its asperities, its pontification, its distinctions that do not distinguish, its vacuous ritual of familiar quotations and bathetic solemnities."[8] As we read Eliot we should remember that the Old Possum may, at any point, be having his little joke. To ignore this pervasive expression of Eliot's personality—he was a notorious practical joker in real life—only insures that the joke will be on us.

R. P. Blackmur uses Auden's words to support his own belief that "it is the order of his [Eliot's] personality that gives force to his thought about literature," but he asserts that Eliot's personality is the antithesis of his concept of tradition. Tradition, Blackmur says, "is what is impersonal in the personality, and it is the materials of which we make the form—the mask—of personality. ... The word tradition should always be associated with the idea of the individual and with the idea of personality. ... As order is what we do with disorder, impersonality is what we do with personality" (*LH* 165, 169–70). In saying this, and in affirming Eliot's continued belief in tradition, the impersonal poet, and the objective correlative, Blackmur distorts the conception of Eliot's personality he proposed early in his essay; he shifts the context of his discussion from an expressive to a formal one, and rather than consider Eliot's criticism in the context of his personal world, relegates Eliot's personality to a subordinate role in a literary universe.

The point which must be affirmed clearly is that Eliot-the-critic is expressive of and subordinate to Eliot-the-man. Eliot-the-critic discusses his opinion of the poetic process, of tradition, of what poetry is; but Eliot-the-man comes to regard all such discussions as tentative—a perspective expressed largely in his later essays, which were unavailable to Blackmur—and finally emphasizes that they are to be regarded as dependent upon his personality and life. Eliot must be studied as a critic talking about poetry, and as a man talking about his critical theories; it is the latter voice, that of the Elder Statesman, which needs emphasis, for it serves to qualify considerably his early critical statements and thus puts them in a new perspective. For example, he says:

The poet writing for the theater may, as I have found, make two mistakes. [*OPP* 101]

When you read *new* poetry, poetry by someone whose name is not yet widely known . . .
you are exercising, or should be exercising, your *own* taste. There is nothing else to
go by. [*OPP* 50]

In the development of taste and critical judgment in literature . . . there are, according to my own experience, three important phases. . . . the third stage of
development—of maturation so far as that process can be represented by the history of our reading and study—is that at which we begin to enquire into the reasons
for our failure to enjoy what has been found delightful by men, perhaps many
generations of men, as well qualified or better qualified for appreciation than
ourselves. In trying to understand why one has failed to appreciate rightly a particular author, one is seeking for light, not only about that author, but about oneself.
[*OPP* 241–42; cf. *UP* 19, 33–34]

In these passages Eliot indicates specifically the dependence of his critical
doctrines on his personal response and needs; although tradition itself may
be part of the impersonal mind of Europe, Eliot's tradition is part of his
own mind, part of the historical process.

   This awareness of change in his opinions about poetry and criticism
came to Eliot gradually, but one of the first fully self-conscious statements
appears in his 1940 essay on Yeats, which he wrote at the age of fifty-two.
"The generations of poetry in our age seem to cover a span of about twenty
years. . . . By the time, that is to say, that a man is fifty, he has behind
him a kind of poetry written by men of seventy, and before him another
kind written by men of thirty. That is my position at present" (*OPP* 295).
Such expressions of the elder statesman are found, as they say, *et passim*,
but his 1956 essay "The Frontiers of Criticism" is devoted almost entirely
to a revision of his earlier opinions, and to the placing of his criticism
within the context of his own personality. The most amusing way he does
this is through a pretense of amnesia, when he says in effect that although
he may have written something in the past, he is now unable to recall
it, or cannot bear to reread it, and since it has vanished from his memory
it cannot be objectively present. For example, he says: "In 1923 I wrote
an article entitled *The Function of Criticism*. . . . On re-reading this essay
recently, I was rather bewildered, wondering what all the fuss had been
about. . . . I cannot recall a single book or essay, or the name of a single
critic, as representative of the kind of impressionistic criticism which
aroused my ire thirty-three years ago."[9] He then goes on to acknowledge
that it is now teachers, not journalists, who write criticism; that criticism
has been transformed by the ancillary studies of psychology, sociology, and
aesthetics; that source study is not very valuable—one *Road to Xanadu*
is enough; that while thirty-three years ago the world needed to guard
against Impressionism, "today it seems to me that we need to be more
on guard against the purely explanatory" (*OPP* 131). Recognizing these
changes, he repudiates system-building and rests the case for the value of

his own criticism on his own thinking about poetry, calling it a kind of "workshop criticism."

The best of my literary criticism . . . consists of essays on poets and poetic dramatists who had influenced me. It was a by-product of my private poetry-workshop; or a prolongation of the thinking that went into the formation of my own verse. In retrospect, I see that I wrote best about poets whose work had influenced my own, and with whose poetry I had become thoroughly familiar, long before I desired to write about them or had found the occasion to do so. My criticism has this in common with that of Ezra Pound, that its merits and its limitations can be fully appreciated only when it is considered in relation to the poetry I have written myself." [*OPP* 117]

Eliot reiterates his conception of himself as a poet-critic in his 1961 lecture "To Criticize the Critic," and states more absolutely than before the inevitability of a personal element in all literary judgment: "My particular reason for referring to my response to the work of Lawrence is that it is well to remind ourselves, in discussing the subject of literary criticism, that we cannot escape personal bias "(*TCC* 25). In two sentences near the end of his essay Eliot reverts to the moral didacticism of his middle period and identifies his personal standards with an objective moral system, saying that "it is impossible to fence off *literary* criticism from criticism on other grounds, and that moral, religious, and social judgments cannot be wholly excluded" (*TCC* 25). But he goes on to affirm the poet-critic as the purest of critics, and to place his judgments in that class.

To support the view that Eliot's criticism is best seen in the context of his personality, we must come to terms with his tradition—his specific judgments about literature—and looking at the whole of Eliot's critical work, one must regard his personal "tradition" as a historical study in qualification rather than a Platonic set of forms. Eliot took back or modified almost every categorical judgment he ever made about literature, and even rephrased his Royalist-Classicist-Anglican tradition in the context of his own personality, confessing in his 1955 address "Goethe and the Sage" the difficulty Goethe poses "for anyone like myself, who combines a Catholic cast of mind, a Calvinistic heritage, and a Puritanical temperament" (*OPP* 243). To relate Eliot's tradition to his personality is essentially only to relate it to change, which he insists on after, say, 1925. Although Eliot desires the permanent, the unchanging, it is only a desire; he recognizes change in the way we see literature: "It is not he [Pascal] who changes, but we who change" (*SE* 355). And he insists on the need for literature to keep in touch with contemporary speech: "There is one law of nature more powerful than any of these varying currents, or influences from abroad or from the past: the law that poetry must not stray too far from the ordinary everyday language which we use and hear" (*OPP* 21).

As we place Eliot's criticism against the background of his life and times, rather than in the context of the ultimate truth, one of its chief interests becomes an antiquarian one. In his extensive periodical writings and in *The Criterion*, which he edited from 1922 to 1939, one can see the literary life between the two wars in a way that is otherwise impossible. Eliot points out that in his early essays "I was in reaction, not only against Georgian poetry, but against Georgian criticism; I was writing in a context which the reader of today [1961] has either forgotten, or has never experienced" (*TCC* 16). He is uniquely interesting in this respect because it is only through the reactions of a person of such eminence, who was himself involved, that one can truly see the strange literary contours of that time, when the great literary figures of the day were Hilaire Belloc, H. G. Wells, Shaw, Kipling, Chesterton, and Ford Madox Ford; when the great difference was between Eliot's generation of 1925 "which accepts moral problems," and that of the last generation, "which accepted only aesthetic or economic or psychological problems."[10] Eliot has prophesied that "if my phrases are given consideration, a century hence, it will be only in their historical context, by scholars interested in the mind of my generation" (*TCC* 19), and he is probably right.

To say that Eliot's criticism is interesting because it is antiquarian is disturbing, since it implies to the "modernist" generation that its own youthful enthusiasms are dated, its avant-garde sensibilities old hat. That Eliot's battles for Joyce, Pound, Donne, and Baudelaire have already been won, and that these authors have been supplanted by new fashions, are facts which were recognized by no one more clearly than Eliot himself. Our problem of perception is to place him securely in his time as one of the great teachers of his generation, a role that at the end he claimed for himself, saying of his most famous phrases: "I think they have been useful in their time. They have been accepted, they have been rejected, they may soon go out of fashion completely: but they have served their turn as stimuli to the critical thinking of others" (*TCC* 19).

In almost all his writings, Eliot passes his own test for a critic; he does not "lapse from his own standards of taste" (*OPP* 195). To appreciate the worth of Eliot's criticism is not to say that Eliot is always right or that one must like him; he is the quintessence of the Puritan, the WASP, and this is not everyone's cup of tea. But one may insist that critics not distort Eliot's doctrines to serve their own ends, and that they not confuse his literary beliefs with his religious ones. What is needed in Eliot's critics is a clear and constant recognition of Eliot as a man writing, with all the faults and virtues implicit in the word *human*. By studying his complex and personal response to literature in all its fullness, we may learn how to be better readers ourselves. We must try to sense the humility and humor, the literary sensitivity, of the man behind the masks.

It is true that in some ways it is harder to perceive the true voice of

Eliot in the seventies than it was before his death in 1965, since he was then the reigning literary figure in the English-speaking world. The personal Eliot receives less attention today than before partly because the chief new interest in Eliot in the sixties is in the explication of his relationship to the Idealist philospher F. H. Bradley, which occurred because Eliot's dissertation on Bradley was published (as *Knowledge and Experience in the Philosophy of F. H. Bradley*, edited by Anne C. Bolgan) only in 1964. Thus Eliot's early philosophical work began to be studied only after he himself had almost forgotten it.[11] Interest has also waned because of the law of diminishing returns; the distinctions that Eliot proposed and the judgments he made have been masticated too much, and articles like "Dissociation of Sensibility Once More" or "The Objective Correlative Revisited" have become obsolete rather than productive of further insights. Eliot says of I. A. Richards in 1927: "Such questions as Mr. Richards raises are usually not answered; usually they are merely superseded. But it will be a long time before the questions of Mr. Richards will be obsolete: in fact, Mr. Richards has a peculiar gift for anticipating the questions which the next generations will be putting to themselves."[12] Prescience is a gift Eliot shares with Richards, but the next generation has come and gone, and with it has gone the fashion for his theory.

But the main reason Eliot is less available to us now than he was is that the revolutionary fervor of the sixties in America, with its renewed interest in the occult, the counterculture, Marxism, rock music, the black revolution, the third world, and the like, seems antithetical to the Puritan restraint and Anglo-European tradition of Eliot. The particularly literary focus of this critical revolution has been a renewed interest in the work of Ezra Pound. It is not now fashionable to say so, but one must agree with K. L. Goodwin that "Pound's direct influence on the content and technique of criticism in the present century has been neither extensive nor significant," and that "Pound has had a wider and more permanent influence on English criticism through his influence on Eliot than through his own writings."[13] Nevertheless, Pound's stock rose rapidly in the sixties, in part because of the interest in his revisions of *The Waste Land* generated by the 1971 publication of the original manuscript as edited by Valerie Eliot. Hugh Kenner is perhaps the most prominent academic Poundian, and his *The Pound Era* (1971) attempts to replace Eliot's eponymic authority with that of Pound. In poetic circles, Charles Olson found in Pound a poetic father, and set him up, with William Carlos Williams, as a generative figure against Eliot, Brooks, and the Metaphysicals in a way which appealed to a number of "Black Mountain" and "San Francisco" poets.[14] But such shifts in taste and rewritings of history cannot abolish the historical record, where it is clear that from 1920 to 1950 Eliot was the leading American poet *and* critic, the eponymous authority of that age.

It is biography that provides hope for a better understanding of Eliot the man, and hence for a better understanding of the nuances of the voice of Eliot the critic. The case is hopeful because, even though Eliot forbade the writing of any official biography, the many reminiscences from his acquaintances, as well as the forthcoming publication of his letters, provide a context in which the humor, dignity, and authority of Eliot become increasingly apparent.[15] For example, Lawrence Durrell reminisces of Eliot, his publisher, that when he arranged a meeting between Eliot and Henry Miller, "I think Eliot himself was a little intimidated by the thought of meeting the renegade hero of *Tropic of Cancer* in the flesh, while Miller was still half convinced that Eliot would be dressed like a Swiss pastor. At any rate, the relief on both sides was very apparent, and I remember a great deal of laughter. They got on famously." Durrell concludes that Eliot

differed very greatly from others I have known, in the qualities of self-abnegation and a sense of responsibility to the culture of this time. He was a responsible man, who felt that his words were acting as a formative influence on the age, and that it was necessary to use them creatively, to further insight. He could not stand displays of temperament and talent devoted to inferior ends like glory. ... But I was lucky that the hazards of chance enabled me to catch sight of the human being, who is often hidden in his work. The sober and cautious and humble man could also laugh; and it is his laughter that I best remember.[16]

Allen Tate: The Conservative Critic

At times all men are victims of paranoia and nostalgia, but Allen Tate is defined by the enemies he keeps in a more consistent way than most. A connoisseur of lost causes, Tate has faced his enemies for a period of fifty years, struggling like Cuchulain against the invulnerable tide of progress and Positivism, and showing us a criticism whose energies are the energies of opposition. The Agrarian movement and Tate's relationship to it have been ably traced.[17] What I wish to do here is to describe Tate's persona, show its usefulness as a critical stance, explicate the doctrines which support his public face and project it into larger intellectual and social contexts, and judge the worth of the literary criticism which depends on his response to literature.

Tate says of Faulkner after his death: "But for one meeting in Rome about 10 years ago he seemed to me arrogant and ill-mannered in a way that I felt qualified to distinguish as peculiarly 'Southern'."[18] Tate strikes many in the same way, and whether true or not in life, the persona of Tate's writings is that of the intellectual snob—contemptuous of others' opinions and certain of his own, asserting instead of proving, setting himself above his audience as a tutor addressing a none-too-bright pupil.

Throughout his career as a critic, one feels that Tate's real effort has been to arouse his enemies—enemies whose crime is not that they oppose Tate but that they ignore him. Tate was most contentious when young, from the time of his controversy with Ransom about *The Waste Land*[19] until the end of the Agrarian movement (c. 1938).

Tate's persona, then, had a consistently irritating effect on people, especially those of a liberal persuasion. As an example, one may cite Sidney Hook's reply to "The Present Function of Criticism" in 1941: "Unfortunately he [Tate] has the bad manners of all belated reactionaries. And by bad manners I do not mean merely arrogance but intellectual bad manners—gross distortion and misstatement, evasion of fundamental issues, and blithe fabrication of facts whenever it seems convenient for his purposes. ... I have less fear of the effects of positivism [on the American tradition] than of the intellectual manners of Mr. Tate in discussing positivism."[20] In the preface to his *Collected Essays* Tate makes a specific apology: "Another source of regret is the toplofty tone of some of these essays and reviews. Minorities cringe or become snobs. ... Snobbishness, of which the explanation is not the excuse, was the unredeemed course open to me" (*CE* x). But while apologizing to Ransom in 1963 for his insufferable manners when young, he says: "[Ransom's] poetry can scarcely be read by a young, coarse, and ignorant generation."[21] Even at his best, one must occasionally exercise magnanimity to read Tate.[22]

The basis of Tate's approach to criticism is, in a phrase taken from a 1929 essay, "the irresistible need of the mind for absolute experience."[23] Or, as he projects the same need in a social context: "The literary artist is seldom successful as a colonial; he should be able to enjoy the *normal belief* that he is at the center of the world" (*CE* 280, italics added). Tate objectifies his need for absolute experience in three ways—in the tradition of the South, in poetry, and in the Catholic church—but his situation in life is always such that he feels himself deserted by his gods. It is this combination of his absolutist demands and his lack of social fulfillment which seems to account for his arrogant persona, at once despised and superior, the noble scapegoat.

Tate's first objectification of the absolute, which sustains him from the beginning to about 1938, is the historical tradition of the South. The *Times Literary Supplement* summarizes as well as anyone what the South means to Tate: "He has made the old South, in his criticism and in his poety, bear the weight of a lust for tradition that is partly pastoral but is partly Yeats's dream of unity of being, Mr. Eliot's belief that there was some period or place in history where 'a certain dissociation of sensibility' had not set in."[24] Tate says in a letter in 1953, in re a review of Eliot's poems by Ransom: "He [Ransom] alluded to our old views of the late twenties when we were rebelling against modernism, and pointed out that we never got much further than Nostalgia because no historic faith came into consideration. I think there's a great deal in that. We were trying to find a religion in the secular, historical experience as such, particularly in the Old South. I would now go further than John and say we were idolaters. But it is better to be an idolater than to worship nothing, and as far as our old religion went I still believe in it."[25] The specifics of Tate's belief in Southern Agrarianism, as expressed in *I'll Take My Stand* (1930), *Who Owns America?* (1936), and elsewhere, have been discussed at length. What is important is the character of his belief as wish-fulfillment, or as a moral absolute that "ought" to be true. When asked in 1961 if he still thinks of himself as a Southern Agrarian, he says: "Yes, I do. That doesn't mean I think Southern Agrarianism will prevail. ... I think that the point of view expressed in that symposium ... represents the permanent values of Western society."[26] Tate's need to believe in the South is sometimes so strong as to cause him to ignore contemporary reality in favor of history. As Robert Lowell says of his visit with the Tates in 1937: "I began to discover what I had never known. I, too, was part of a legend. I was Northern, disembodied, a Platonist, a puritan, an abolitionist. ... I realized that the old deadweight of poor J. R. Lowell was now an asset. Here, like the battered Confederacy, he still lived and was history."[27] Sometimes Tate believes in the past, sometimes in what he wants to believe of the present: "Of the social sciences I know little, and I am not entitled to suspect that they do not really exist; I believe this in the long run because I want to believe it, the actuality of a science of human societies being repellent to me" (*CE* 473). John Stewart suggests a reason for Tate's escapism from the present to an absolute past: "Good, for Tate, is the security and serenity that comes of escape from the self—the vortex of Quality—through community with others, a community so desperately needed that it cannot be taken for granted as it is in Ransom's prose. ... The final function of society is to enable the individual to cope with himself."[28]

Tate projects his need for the absolute onto society, but the beginning and end of his search is his poetry, and by extension the "modern" poetry of the early part of this century, that written by Eliot, Hart Crane, Pound, and others. As a critic, Tate expresses the common doctrine of Aesthetic Formalism, that poetry is the way to know truth here on earth. In Tate's words, "Literature is the complete knowledge of man's experience, and by knowledge I mean that unique and formed intelligence of the world of which man alone is capable" (*CE* 15; see also *CE* 48). Bradbury cogently sums up the difficulties of this position: "The argument here ... is tautological. Literature has been defined as 'the complete knowledge of man's experience,' and this knowledge is expressed in terms of the 'completeness ... of the experienced order,' which is 'mythical,' which in turn is an expression of the 'hard realities' of experience. The circularity of the argument results ... from Tate's failure to supply any external referent for his knowledge.' To place his knowledge '*in* the poem,' rather than in the object or in the knowing mind, is to deny it any verification outside itself, and furthermore to allow no criteria for distinguishing true from false knowledge."[29]

Tate's search for unity in poetry is also expressed as an attack on his enemies, whom he thinks of as the enemies of poetry. In 1934 they are science and Romanticism (*CE* 99). In 1938 he attacks "the fallacy of communication in poetry" (*CE* 77). In 1940, he notes: "I am not attacking the study or the writing of history for use in the criticism of literature. I am attacking the historical method" (*CE* 58). And in 1959 he concludes: "I am saying in this book [*On the Limits of Poetry*] with very little systematic argument, that it [poetry] is neither religion nor social engineering" (*CE* xi).

Tate's conception of the importance of literature to man does lead, however, to one of his more viable critical doctrines, the need for the Man of Letters to defend the language. As he said when he defended his vote to give Ezra Pound the Bollingen Prize in 1951, "The specific task of the man of letters is to attend to the health of society *not at large* but through literature—that is, he must be constantly aware of the condition of language in his age" (*CE* 535; cf. *CE* 379, 390). In this narrowing of the earlier Agrarian attempt to reform society to the concept of the Man of Letters reforming the language, one must see Tate's recognition of an almost total rejection of his social beliefs by the modern world, and his attempt to seize the kind of power which is open to him. Although the later Tate speaks of Agrarianism as only an intellectual movement for him,[30] his early essays seem to be the statements of a man who wanted to prevail. The irony with which the later Tate regards Agrarianism was not expressed at the time, but is the irony of history. Tate's slow move to the Catholic church may be regarded as an embracing of a higher truth, but it must also be regarded as the defeat of the lower "truth" of the Old South. Between these two alternatives, between 1938 and 1951, Tate joined other New Critics in advocating Aesthetic Formalism.[31]

Tate's need for a better objectification of absolute experience than either the Old South or poetry could provide led in 1950 to his unsurprising conversion to Catholicism.[32] The decision seemed inevitable; as explained by John Crowe Ransom in the *Sewanee Review*'s issue "Homage to Allen Tate": "Allen accepts the old order and the unified life, but the historic instance which he first cited was only the nearest one; the Southern tradition in these United States. That had its defects, and from a world view it was too local or provincial. He found a world order more to his purpose in a Church which has an imperial name [and Scholastic theology]."[33] Or as Tate himself puts it in a 1952 symposium: "What I had in mind twenty years ago, not too distinctly, I think I see more clearly now; that is, the possibility of the humane life presupposes, with us, a prior order, the order of a unified Christendom."[34] When Tate became fully committed to Catholicism, he did not transcend his earlier interest in social doctrine but, like Eliot, made culture depend on religion. In a 1954 address to a conference in Florence, he says: "There can be no culture for us, in the true sense, without our unique Revelation."[35] He thus moved from motherland to mother church, and despite Richard Foster's hope that "soon, probably, they will be speaking of the work of the fifties as the beginning of his third [creative] period,"[36] Tate never did much more than reminisce pleasantly and unpleasantly after his conversion. One should stress, however, that the relationship between poetry and the search for unity in religion has always been organic for Tate. As he says during the Fugitives' reunion, "You know, the literary critic doesn't turn on a different sort of mind [than the moral critic], it's a different mode that he's operating in."[37]

Tate always comes to his ultimate unity by resolving a tension between two opposing forces, as both R. K. Meiners and Monroe Spears note. Spears comes closest to an accurate description of the form of Tate's thought when he observes: "There is a strong Aristotelian element in Mr. Tate's whole philosophy: the highest good is the contemplation of absolute truth. ... Mr. Tate's mind seems to work in terms of extremes vs. the mean."[38] The dichotomies of Tate's social thought are first formulated in *I'll Take My Stand*, where he opposes the short view of things, in which history is seen as a series of concrete events in time, with the long view, in which all particular events are observed as part of a logical series *sub specie aeternitatis*, and in which tradition is destroyed. Here he also opposes, in a not very clearly related distinction, the half-horse of Abstract Positivism to the half-horse of the mystical uniqueness of things, and says they are united in the whole horse of religion. Tate becomes somewhat clearer in "What is a Traditional Society?" (1936), when he shows how man's way of life and his livelihood are split in modern society, resulting in the "week-end traditionalist" who works at Bethlehem Steel and lives in a Jeffersonian mansion in the country. Tate thought that these two halves of life would be united in the traditional society where men make their living off the land, and this formulation occupied the center of his social thought during his Agrarian period.

Tate makes his most interesting social distinction—between a regional and a provincial society—in 1945: "Regionalism is that consciousness or that habit of men in a given locality which influences them to certain patterns of thought and conduct handed to them by their ancestors. Regionalism is thus limited in space but not in time. The provincial attitude is limited in time but not in space" (*CE* 286). He projects these two extremes of time and space onto history in "Johnson on the Metaphysical Poets," in which he claims that "the neo-classical age was an interlude between modernisms, that it had by-passed the Renaissance Nature of *depth* and restored the classical Nature of *surface.* But the *Prelude* brought us back: to the breakup of the solid object in the dynamic stream of time. . . . The neo-classical age died because it could not move; we may be dying because we cannot stop moving. Our poetry has become process" (*CE* 505). As a solution to this opposition, he offers the Aristotelian view that "into that space time entered not as process but as myth" (*CE* 506). In short, Tate structures the choice so that one must choose between a (preferred) regional society and a (hated, Positivist) provincial society, or the union of the two in the unified traditional society of the past.

The dichotomies of Tate's literary criticism take much the same form as T. S. Eliot's famous "dissociation of sensibility," the split between thought and feeling which he analyzed in "The Metaphysical Poets" (1921). Eliot's general influence on Tate is acknowledged, and Tate follows his master in defending Donne in particular and Metaphysical poetry in general. In 1934 he talks about poetry of the practical will and Romantic poetry united in poetry of the "concrete whole" (*CE* 91). Tate's most famous critical distinction is that of "tension," which unites the extremes of extension (denotation) and intension (connotation). Metaphysical poets are "at or near the extensive or denoting end of the line; the romantic or Symbolist poet at the other, intensive end" (*CE* 86). "The meaning of poetry is its 'tension,' the full organized body of all the extension and intension that we can find in it" (*CE* 83).

Tate rephrases his conception of poetry after his conversion to Catholicism; the two poles to be united are now the knowledge of things, of sense perception, and "the angelic imagination" exemplified by Edgar Allan Poe. The angelic imagination "suffers none of the limitations of sense; it has immediate knowledge of essences; and this knowledge moves through the perfect will to divine love, with which it is at one. . . . I call that human imagination angelic which tries to disintegrate or to circumvent the image in the illusory pursuit of essence" (*CE* 413). The two extremes of sense and essence are united in the "symbolic imagination" of Dante. The symbolic imagination, which is "the poetic way" and is restated in Baudelaire's *Correspondances*, "conducts an action through analogy, of the human to the divine, of the natural to the supernatural, of the low to the high, of time to eternity" (*CE* 412). In short, it unites all the extremes Tate can think of in that unity which he prizes so highly.

Tate also uses the concept of tension in his practical criticism; he says of his own poetry in "Narcissus as Narcissus": "Serious poetry deals with the fundamental conflicts that cannot be logically resolved: we can state the conflicts rationally, but reason does not relieve us of them" (*CE* 252).

Thus Tate finds the "tension between abstraction and sensation" in Emily Dickinson and in all great poetry (*CE* 204). He sees Hart Crane as the Romantic pole of the struggle pushed to its suicidal limit (*CE* 236–37). "Yeats's doctrine of the conflict of opposites says nothing about the fundamental nature of reality: it is rather a dramatic framework through which is made visible the perpetual oscillation of man between extreme introspection and extreme loss of the self in the world of action" (*CE* 222). Donne uses the problem of body and soul as "the dramatic framework for his individual emotion. This is the center of Donne" (*CE* 327). And it is the center of Tate's criticism as well. Indeed, Tate's situation seems much like that of Donne and Dickinson, and his most productive years as both poet and critic were those when he was actively debating within himself the tension between North and South, industrial and Agrarian, progressive and traditional. Tate, in short, seems to seek the support of an absolute against the strife of life, but paradoxically flourishes under tension. In a reminiscence in *Memoirs and Opinions* he says: "I could not know that August 5, 1914, was the end of the nineteenth century, and that four years later, when I entered college, I would be in a new world so different from the old that I would never quite understand it, but would be both of it and opposed to it the rest of my life."[39] The dualism of Tate, like that of Eliot and Ransom, may simply be that of a man trying to reconcile the Edwardian assumptions of his childhood with the modern world, or his Southern values with his choice of life in the North. Tate at his best can live with and reconcile tension, but too often he withdraws into an affirmation of his absolutes and ignores much of the world he should consider.

The most important of Tate's sins of omission is the world of science and technology, which he ignores as beneath contempt. John Stewart has spoken at some length of Ransom's misunderstanding of science, and most of the same criticisms apply to Tate: he takes as his model scientist a mythical mechanistic grub in a laboratory and ignores the complexity of physics, engineering, and the rest; he refuses to admit that scientists are capable of any human feelings and sees them only in the role of devil he has designed for them; and he maintains that the language in which scientists describe the world is somehow more abstract than poetic language.[40] Tate's attitude carries over to the "mere social sciences"; he tars with the same brush of Positivism Freud, economics, business, politics, sociology, and scholarship. In this, Tate is consistent from beginning to end. In 1927 he says that I. A. Richards "is not a great critic. He is a master of laboratory technique."[41] In 1966 he says: "The servile imitation of scientific method is doubtless to blame [for bad Ph.D. dissertations]; but method can always be institutionalized. Intelligence cannot."[42]

In his practical criticism, Tate's sympathies are among the most exclusive of any major critic; he wrote about the Eliot school when it was most fashionable (Donne, Yeats, Pound, Poe, and somewhat belatedly in 1951, Dante). He has written very well about his friends Hart Crane and John Peale Bishop; and he has briefly reviewed Americans like Emily Dickinson, Archibald MacLeish, and E. A. Robinson. But he is not a critic like Cleanth Brooks, who can provide sound readings of a poem on demand, as it were; in his criticism Tate is much more concerned with his absolutes than with the text. Indeed, the only first-rate close reading he has ever done is of his own "Ode to the Confederate Dead." In 1965 he says: "I am indifferent to most of it [poetry]; and as I get older I am able to read less and less of it. I have wondered why people have been so kind as to describe me as a literary critic, or more narrowly as a critic of poetry; for I have never been able to concentrate on any poetry that could not be useful to me. A literary critic is a person who likes to read books, and even to study them." [43] Although one must make some allowance for rhetorical modesty here, Tate is essentially accurate, since only by considering narrowness of sympathy and narcissism as virtues of the mind can Tate be accounted a major practical critic.

Tate's sins of commission are a carelessness about facts and distinctions and a tendency to leave problems of theory unresolved. One of the most pervasive of Tate's faults of thinking is the false dichotomy through which he moves to the unity he needs. In essence he says that either religion is true and found in poetry or man will lose his humanity. This dichotomy is usually found in the formulation that those who do not believe in poetry and religion have lost their humanity, and Tate, along with other Aesthetic Formalists, has been criticized for his belief in "life for art's sake." [44] The other objection to this defense of poetry is that raised against all kinds of fideistic thought—in brief, that because Tate wants or believes or needs poetry to embody truth does not necessarily make it so. [45]

Another problem Tate has been unable to resolve is the question of determinism. Tate often assumes that society determines men's lives; this assumption underlies his Agrarian argument that society must be changed to permit man to live humanistically and his belief that modern man is condemned to spiritual death; in practice he judges Poe, Crane, and Robinson as exhibiting this sad fate (*CE* 458, 225, 362-63). His view is derived from Eliot's 1920 essay "William Blake," in which Eliot asserts that "what his [Blake's] genius required, and what it sadly lacked, was a framework of accepted and traditional ideas which would have prevented him from indulging in a philosophy of his own" (*SE* 279).

Tate's assumption that a good (traditional) society is needed to produce good literature quickly founders on the fact that the Old South never produced any literature worthy of the name. [46] Moreover, Tate confuses the issue by asserting that it is not traditional society but its decline which stimulates the artist. As he says of Emily Dickinson: "In Miss Dickinson, as in Donne, we may detect a singularly morbid concern, not for religious truth, but for personal revelation. . . . In religion, it is blasphemy; in society it means usually that culture is not self-contained and sufficient, that the spiritual community is breaking up. This is . . . the perfect literary situation" (*CE* 208).

Bradbury is probably correct in saying that Tate gave up determinism in its naive form in the late thirties in favor of a renewed interest in art.[47] But the evidence is confusing. In 1965 Tate says: "We must not fall into the historical trap where, immobilized, we apply a doctrine of historical determinism to poets, and pretend that after a certain date a certain kind of poetry could not be written. I fell into the trap thirty-five years ago when I said that after Emerson had done his work, the tragic vision was henceforth impossible in America."[48] Here he throws out determinism in order to praise Robert Lowell. But at the Fugitives' reunion he says, while defending *I'll Take My Stand*: "We all assume that a kind of religious humanism is the moral and spiritual condition which is favorable to poetry."[49] Here determinism is back, but on the intellectual, not the social, plane. One suspects that Tate's failure to resolve this question reflects his own ambivalence; he would like to be (or to have been) part of a determined, safe, traditional culture, but he knows that if he is determined by any society, it is the evil one of the North. This is to say only that Tate claims free will and the strength of character to resist society for himself and his favorites but thinks of all others as determined by society; *or,* he fudges the question altogether and takes whatever view is most convenient. Whatever judgment one ultimately makes, Tate's failure to resolve this fundamental issue adds to the confusion of his critical theory.

Tate's contempt for the facts has given him trouble from the time of his humiliation by the Southern Historical Association to the present,[50] and is one of the most disturbing of his intellectual manners. An amusing example brings profession and practice together. In "The Unliteral Imagination" he says of his unscholarly temperament: "It is difficult for me to acquire information at the source. If I wanted to know just where John Dryden was when the Dutch fleet was sailing up the Thames, I would telephone my friend Samuel H. Monk; but since I seldom need to know this sort of thing, I telephone him often for less frivolous reasons, such as the prospect of some Jack Daniel at half-past five."[51] A Kentuckian who is inaccurate about the name of his whiskey might well make even Tate's sympathizers uneasy.

With a critic as poetic in his intellectual discipline as Tate, it is a mistake to try to fit him too closely into any well-formulated philosophical or theological system, since he does not use technical philosophical terms to mean what they ordinarily mean and is not consistent in his usage.[52] It is one of the ironies of the study of Formalist criticism that men who claim to be so concerned with the exact word in poetry should be so indifferent to the meanings of philosophical definitions and terms. In "A Southern Mode of the Imagination" Tate says: "Our [the Fugitives'] initiation into the knowledge of good and evil, like everybody else's, must have been at birth; our later improvement in this field of knowledge, haphazard and extra-curricular. John Ransom taught us—Robert Penn Warren, Cleanth Brooks, Andrew Lytle and myself—Kantian aesthetics and a philosophical dualism, tinged with Christian theology, but ultimately derived from the Nicomachian ethics" (*CE* 556-57). Perhaps the best way to judge Tate's criticism as intellectual history is to think of it as the remnants of a classical undergraduate education.

The solution to objections to Tate's intellectual bad manners is to transcend both the compulsion to be aestheticians and logical habits of mind; it is to consider him not as a systematic thinker but as an example of a particular response to literature and life. Instead of worrying about the truth value of Tate's work, we should regard it as he does himself. As he says, "I have tried to remember, from the time I began to write essays, that I was writing, in the end, opinion, and neither aesthetics nor poetry in prose" (*CE* x). For although Tate himself has not analyzed other critics or done much analysis of his own criticism, he has given some of the best advice there is about how to regard criticism in general. In "Reflections on American Poetry, 1900-1950" he surveys New Criticism and says: "We have of late turned to fiction and examined its cannier techniques; so that one wonders why we have not considered critically the relation of our points of view to what we are looking at. In writing criticism we forget that we occupy 'posts of observation,' that we ourselves are 'trapped spectators.'"[53] Consistent with this is his earlier opinion that the critical quarterly should represent a definite point of view. "A sound critical program has at least this one feature: *it allows to the reader no choice in the standards of judgment.* It asks the reader to take a post of observation, and to occupy it long enough to examine closely the field before him. ... This, one supposes, is dogmatism, but it is arguable still that dogma in criticism is a permanent necessity: the value of the dogma will be determined by the quality of the mind engaged in constructing it" (*CE* 65). Tate's distrust of system, his lack of respect for the disciples who apply the methods of New Criticism, and his emphasis on and trust in individual intelligence (especially his own) are constant features of his conception of criticism (see *CE* 147-53, 483-87).

Perhaps the best way to judge Tate finally is to compare the quality of his mind with that of his teachers and peers T. S. Eliot and John Crowe Ransom. Like both of them he is a poet-critic, and like them he has been actively engaged during his lifetime as a Man of Letters, doing all the tasks this phrase implies—editing, writing introductions, teaching, reviewing, making poems and novels, lecturing, serving as a member of symposiums. Despite the fact that he is more intimately and personally associated with Ransom, his debt to Eliot is the greater.[54] He of course borrows many of his early critical distinctions from Eliot—his idea of the necessity of social tradition, dissociation of sensibility, his literary tradition of Donne, Dante, and the rest. But more significantly, he seems in a way to have lived Eliot's life in his search for a usable past, in his conversion to Catholicism and his late remarriage, in his relative decline as a lyric poet, and in his late attention to a long religious poem like the *Four Quartets* ("Seasons of the Soul"). In his searching, Tate has seemingly been less successful than Eliot in finding a goal satisfactory to himself. While Eliot in "The Frontiers of Criticism," delivered at Tate's own University of Minnesota in 1956, radically revised his earlier allegiances and came to a kind of acceptance of himself and the world as it is, Tate has not made such a statement, and he never reached the mood of acceptance of Eliot's final years.

If Eliot is Tate's model, Ransom is his teacher. Although it is impossible to say what anyone—even a Tate in a class of Ransom's—learns in freshman composition, Tate and Ransom's association as Fugitives, their discussions about poetics and free verse in the twenties, their Agrarian projects, and their later association with the *Kenyon* and *Sewanee Reviews* and the Kenyon School of Letters were unquestionably beneficial to both. The poles of Tate's dualism are in some ways parallel to Ransom's "structure-texture" distinction, but the two men are quite different in spirit. Ransom is skeptical, self-contained, rational, gently ironic; Tate is fideistic, arrogant, mystical, despairing, polemical. Like Eliot, Ransom seems to have made his peace with life. Tate says at the Fugitives' 1957 reunion: "I feel very little interest in the literary scene," and this rejection is typical. Ransom says in 1959, explicitly contrasting himself with Tate. "I have had a small persistent hope ... in considering that the new barbarians are of our own breed and country, our friends, perhaps even our children, and surely must be destined to erect a new culture."[55] One feels from statements like these that Ransom is the better man, or has come to a more mature understanding of his situation in life. Tate, however, is the better critic, not only because his output is greater, but because his value *is* his intransigence. In an age which values objectivity, humility, science, scholarship, realism, the liberal imagination, Tate's refusal to give up makes him one of the exemplary critics of our time. As Reed Whitemore says: "His influence here, particularly on my generation, has been great ... to my generation Mr. Tate's name led all the rest on the anti-positivist roles."[56] Tate's strength in clinging to the old values, the old absolutes, however escapist, however pathetic, gives us something we would otherwise lack—the living model, with the will intact, of the conservative critic, the keeper of the faith, like the statue of General Lee in Richmond, which Henry James describes in *The American Scene* (1907):

So long as one stands there the high figure, which ends for all the world by suggesting to the admirer a quite conscious, subjective, even a quite sublime, effort to ignore, to sit, as it were, superior and indifferent, enjoys the fact of company and thereby, in a manner, of sympathy—so that the vast association of the futile for the moment drops away from it. But to turn one's back, one feels, is to leave it again alone. ... I recognized something more than the melancholy of a lost cause. The whole infelicity speaks of a cause that could never have been gained. [Pp. 393-94]

R. P. Blackmur: The Critic Almost Prophetic

It is part of conventional academic wisdom to regard R. P. Blackmur as a good technical critic, an able practitioner of *explication de texte,* who is spoiled in mid-career by his devotion to an excessively convoluted, gnomic style. René Wellek says that "the deterioration seems to set in about the year 1950," when "on occasion one cannot avoid the suspicion that he is engaging in deliberate obfuscation, in verbal jugglery and even charlatanry."[57] It is true, as Wellek says, that in his early essays (from 1928 to 1940) Blackmur is an able and orthodox Formalist critic whose achievement as author of the first and best explications of Eliot, Yeats, Pound, Stevens, and other modernists will endure as long as the poets. But Blackmur's development is more complicated than Wellek's reduction of him to a valuable Formalist and an "imposter or Confidence Man" will allow.[58] The complete Blackmur has three voices, all of which are present throughout his career, though they tend to dominate sequentially: the techical critic, like his first hero T. S. Eliot; the failure, like Henry Adams; and the aphorist, like Dr. Faustus.

In "A Critic's Job of Work" (1935), Blackmur, following Eliot,[59] describes his approach as a "technical" one which "treats of nothing in literature except in its capacity of reduction to literary fact. ... Aristotle, curiously, is here the type and master; as the *Poetics* is nothing but a collection and explanation of the facts of Greek poetry" (*FV* 365-66; see also *FV* 271). Technical description is not sufficient, however; "for the arts, *mere* technical scrutiny of any order is not enough without the direct apprehension—which may come first or last—to which all scrutinies that show facts contribute" (*FV* 366). Blackmur's technical criticism thus becomes judgment, as at the end of "The Masks of Ezra Pound": "The judgment that flows from this essay needs hardly to be stated; it is judgment by description" (*FV* 109). In these early essays the criterion of judgment is the standard Formalist one of the coherence of the poem as demonstrated by its technical crafts-manship (see *FV* 255): "The work of Shakespeare, even the Sonnets, is not for us an elongation of the poet's self, but is independent of it because it has a rational structure which controls, orders, and composes in external or objective form the material of which it is made; and for that effect it is dependent only upon the craft and conventions of the art of poetry and upon the limits of language. We criticize adversely such work where it fails of objective form or lacks articulated composition, as in the Sonnets or *Hamlet*" (*FV* 254; see also *SE* 124-26). Like the other Formalists, Blackmur eliminates extrinsic realities like the author in order to concentrate on the text.

Using his technical criterion of poetic value, Blackmur establishes the tradition of the new modernist poetry; for him the great poets of the period are Eliot, Yeats, and Pound. They have their limitations: "Magic performs for Yeats the same fructifying function that Christianity does for Eliot, or that ironic fatalism did for Thomas Hardy; it makes a connection between the poem and its subject matter and provides an adequate mechanics of meaning and value. ... The point here is that fatalism, Christianity, and magic are none of them disciplines to which many minds can con-sciously appeal today" (*FV* 33-34). Yet "the work of Yeats, Eliot, and Pound belongs in the full tradition of literature. It is they who stand between the Victorians and Romantics and whatever it is that comes after them" (*FV* 386). Compared to these three, Wallace Stevens, Marianne Moore, and E. E. Cummings are "full of syllables where the others are full of words. Each is a kind of dandy, or connoisseur, a true mountebank of behavior made song" (*FV* 383).

At this stage, poetic technique for Blackmur is equivalent to reason itself. He criticizes E. E. Cummings for lacking mind and for being part of a Surrealist or Dada tradition: "The general dogma of this group is a sentimental denial of the intelligence and the deliberate assertion that the unintelligible is the only object of significant experience" (*FV* 288). "This is the extreme form, in poetry, of romantic egoism: whatever I experience is real and final, and whatever I say represents what I experience. Such a dogma is the natural counterpart of the denial of the intelligence" (*FV* 289). He says of Lawrence, as Eliot said of Blake (*SE* 279): "The piety was tortured—the torture of incomplete affirmation. The great mystics saw no more profoundly than Lawrence through the disorder of life to their ultimate vision, but they saw within the terms of an orderly insight. In them, reason was stretched to include disorder and achieved mystery. In Lawrence, the reader is left to supply the reason and the form" (*FV* 267). In the thirties Blackmur stresses the need for reason. He says in 1935: "The typical great poet is profoundly rational, integrating, and ... a master of ultimate verbal clarity. Light, radiance, and wholeness remain the attributes of serious art. And the fact is disheartening because no time could have greater need than our own for rational art. No time certainly could surrender more than ours does daily, with drums beating, to fanatic politics and despotically construed emotions" (*FV* 269). Thus technique becomes valuable as it serves as a touchstone of rationalism; description, severely technical, of Stevens and others reveals the absence of rational articulated meaning, as the same process reveals greater meaning in Eliot, Yeats, and Pound.

Blackmur's later image of this technical criterion of judgment is "Lord Tennyson's Scissors," what "Tennyson meant when he said he knew the quantity of every English vowel except those in the word scissors" (*FV* 373). On the basis of its bad prosody Blackmur dismisses the "Apocalyptic or Violent school" of Vachel Lindsay, Robinson Jeffers, Carl Sandburg, Kenneth Rexroth, and others: "All of these stem poetically and emotionally from Whitman-Yates: and all are marked by ignorance, good will, solipsism, and evangelism. . . . It is Lord Tennyson's scissors, and not any other instruments of insight, that tell us sadly both Lawrence and [Hart] Crane were outside the tradition they enriched. . . . Prosody as reason is what the central school of the time [that of Donne] has over and above our two anti-intelligence schools" (*FV* 380-81). At the base of this technical criticism is the ultimate value of the Word, "the principle that the reality of language, which is a formal medium of knowledge, is superior and anterior to the reality of the uses to which it is put, and the operative principle, that the chaos of private experience cannot be known or understood until it is projected and ordered in a form external to the consciousness that entertained it in flux" (*FV* 262). Poetry written in the Donne tradition is "a poetry which depends on the reality of words to carry all other reality" (*LH* 189).

With the possible exception of his opinion of Stevens, Blackmur's judgments of the weaknesses and strengths of modernist poets have proved to be permanent revisions of the tradition. It is a measure of the importance of Blackmur's criticism that it is also original—made in the early thirties when most of the critical world was concerned with fringe political movements of the Left or the Right. To elevate Formalism to a standard of value in those charged political times and to pursue it undistractedly to a successful conclusion—that is originality indeed.[60] Blackmur's application of the Formalist charter to the novel also endures, especially his classification and praise of the technical artistry of Henry James (*LH* 240-88). His judgment that Melville failed as a novelist "because of his radical inability to master a technique—that of the novel—radically foreign to his sensibility" (*LH* 144) has been drastically altered, not by a refutation of Blackmur's accuracy of observation, but by a shift in charters which changes the definition of a good novel from a work exhibiting dramatic form to one exhibiting mythic reality.

In his early technical criticism, then, Blackmur applies the standard Formalist charter, with its strategy of elimination of author and historical reality to concentrate on the Word of the text, and its conception of the poem as an objective correlative exhibiting a standard of coherence and organic unity. He differs from other Formalists, however, in his ultimate secularity, in his belief that modern literature and culture can be mastered by the critic through reason, as modern artists like Joyce, Mann, or Gide master the world through symbol. He says that "in the world as it is, there is no way to get a mastery of the subject except in the aesthetic experience" (*LH* 208). "It is through the aesthetic experience of it that we discover, and discover again, what life is, and that at present, if our account of it is correct, we also discover what our culture is" (*LH* 211). It is up to the critic to show the meaning of present culture, which only the artist has been able to master. Blackmur's ideal is again rational: "What I mean by judgment is what Aristotle would have meant by the fullest possible declaratory proposition of identity. Again, the ideal of judgment . . . is theological: as a soul is judged finally, quite apart from its history, for what it really is at the moment of judgment. . . . What I want to evangelize in the arts is rational intent, rational statement, and rational technique; and I want to do it through technical judgment, clarifying judgment, and the judgment of discovery, which together I call rational judgment" (*LH* 212).

Blackmur develops his second voice through the same circumstance that drove the Agrarians to explication, a sense of defeat; but what is lost for him is not the Tory vision of the Old South or the established church, but the more natural vision for a Bostonian of the loss of a cultural capital and a decline in the authority of the rational layman critic, a vision personified for him in Henry Adams. According to Blackmur, "Failure is the appropriate end to the type of mind of which Adams is a pre-eminent example: the type which attempts through imagination to find the meaning or source of unity aside from the experience which it unites" (*LH* 94). Like Adams, and the other Formalists, Blackmur fails to make his rational and aesthetic solutions prevail. For him, Adams's failure is "the failure which as we feel it is also our own in prospect" (*LH* 81). However, "for Adams, as for everyone, the principle of unity carried to failure showed the most value by the way, and the value was worth the expense" (*LH* 96).

The social concept which embodies Blackmur's lost Utopia is the "cultural capital," which he seems to think disappeared in America after the election of Andrew Jackson in 1828 (*NCUS* 143) and in all of modern Europe:

"Where in 1800 the capitals of economic, political, and cultural power were the same, sometime between 1900 and 1920 they had become different. London, New York, and Paris made a division of human roles ... that has seemed in its present consequence very nearly fatal to human intelligence" (*LH* 63). Blackmur finds a symptom of the defeat of rational unity in America in expatriates like Adams, James, and Eliot: "The expatriate is the man or woman who chooses to live in a country not his own because he cannot do his serious work as well in his own country as he can in another" (*LH* 61). The expatriate is a demonstration of "the disintegration consequent upon the division of function in the social system of the Western world" (*LH* 70). Blackmur's heroes, Adams and James, "were trying to provide the cohesive or attractive force which would allow a cultural capital to emerge. ... John Adams and Jefferson were haunted by the idea of a national university as a necessary cohesive power to our minds. We still don't have such a thing" (*NCUS* 140).

The ideal which animates Blackmur's defense of a cultural capital is the control of social forces by intellectual ones. America's failure to establish a cultural capital "only ratified the general heresy of the late nineteenth and twentieth century that the arts and learning can be divorced from the power and the resources of society without danger to both. The danger involved is social impotence" (*LH* 67). Here Blackmur seems to be trying to broaden his early Formalism to make a plan in which reason may come to be socially influential. In "A Feather-Bed for Critics" he says: "Without the profession of writing behind him the individual writer is reduced to small arms; without society behind it, the profession is impotent and bound to betray itself. A deep collaboration is necessary ... which is marked by the unity they [the writer and society] make together, and by the culture which the individual, by the act of his convicted imagination, brings to light."[61]

Blackmur translates the patrician dominance of Adams into the more personally projective image of the dominant scholar-critic, whose reason could be made to triumph over the illiteracy of modern society. Speaking in the context of the new illiteracy of the Middle East, he expresses his own ideal when he says: "Yet this remnant of the old [bourgeois] elite ... is the only class whose cause can be promoted with any hope of tempering, reducing, and perhaps obviating the dangers of the new illiteracy which flows from universal education. This elite remains, by reason of history and snobbery, an attractive force in society" (*LH* 14). Blackmur sees himself as part of this critical elite, and the elite as part of the old American patrician class, which ought to have the running of society. As he says, "I should remind the reader that I am in political affiliation a species of tory-anarchist, which I suspect was the party which wrote and got ratified the Constitution of the United States" (*PI* 157; see also *NCUS* 142–43). In this hankering for lost aristocracy, Blackmur reminds one of Edmund Wilson, who came from the same WASP patrician class as Adams.

Blackmur's "rational man" is always the amateur, the layman, perhaps because in a world of professional academics he is egregious for having completed his formal education in the Boston public schools and for having educated himself by hanging around the bookstores of Cambridge in the thirties. In philosophical terms the layman is the skeptic. In "A Critic's Job of Work" (1935) Blackmur says: "Imaginative skepticism and dramatic irony—the modes of Montaigne and Plato—keep the mind athletic and the spirit on the stretch" (*FV* 343). *The Tempest, The Magic Mountain,* and Dante have the skepticism built in, but with *Hamlet,* Shelley, or Blake, "we have in reading, in criticizing, to supply the skepticism and the irony, or, as may be, the imagination and the drama" (*FV* 344). Blackmur defines the "complete scholar-critic" as the person who is "the master-layman of as many modes of human understanding as possible in a single act of the mind. ... He will, in short, be a lover of everything that may be done in language conceived as an act of the whole mind" (*LH* 183). Speaking of himself, he says: "I certainly have nothing but a lay mind. . . . [Like Adams,] one wanted to be ideally the layman expert in significance of the new forces [of society] in the hope that we might find the ability of managing them in our own interests rather than committing the energies to the hands of those whose only knowledge was the knowledge of that management" (*NCUS* 93–94).

To understand Blackmur's achievement, one must come to terms with his "layman's" voice, which can best be described as (in his own words) "heuristic" and "saltatory." "Heuristic"—which means "valuable for stimulating or conducting empirical research but unproved or incapable of proof"—appears constantly in Blackmur's criticism. He says of Yeats: "Magic and its burden of symbols may be a major tool of the imagination. A tool has often a double function; it performs feats for which it was designed, and it is heuristic, it discovers and performs new feats which could not have been anticipated without it, which it indeed seems to instigate for itself and in the most unlikely quarters. It is with magic as a tool in its heuristic aspect—as an agent for discovery—that I wish here directly to be concerned" (*FV* 37; see also *FV* 3; *LH* 214). Often for him, "literature is heuristic" (*LH* 214).

The action of the ideal mind for Blackmur is "saltatory"—"jumping, like a frog." As he puts it: "I have a vicious, but I believe a very healthy belief that the mind proceeds by jumps. The mind is essentially saltatory; it leaps or jumps from place to place as best it can, a sign of liveliness, at any rate, that it could jump" (*NCUS* 18; see also *LH* 296, 303). Criticism is, then, a kind of wordplay, not in the narrow sense of punning, but in the sense of the discoveries made by letting words and their attendant concepts play on one another; he calls a dictionary a "palace of saltatory heuristics."[62] Like art, criticism originates in the linguistic imagination: "Words bring meaning to birth and themselves contained the meaning as an imminent possibility before the pangs of junction. To the individual artist the use of words is an adventure in discovery; the imagination is heuristic among the words it manipulates" (*LH* 138).

The form which such instructive jumping takes in Blackmur's criticism is the judgmental comparison of two poets. Blackmur follows Eliot's advice that comparison and analysis are the proper tools of the critic (*SE* 21). For example, his early comparisons of Hardy and Yeats (*FV* 284), or of Pound, Eliot, and Stevens, serve to illuminate essential qualities of the poets which lead to judgments of comparative value: "Both Eliot and Pound condense; their best verse is weighted—Pound's with sensual experience primarily, and Eliot's with beliefs. ... [Stevens's] visual images never condense the matter of his poems; they either accent or elaborate it" (*FV* 197). Or: "Pound's images exist without syntax, Mr. Stevens' depend on it. Pound's images are formally simple, Mr. Stevens' complex. The one contains a mystery, and the other, comparatively, expounds a mystery" (*FV* 199-200). Criticism thus becomes an art: "It is in the arts above all that creation is discovery. Every form of the imagination belongs to the heuristic mode of the mind. Better, the heuristic mode belongs to the polymorph of the imagination" (*EE* 79). Here we see the action of the layman's mind, the tradition of skepticism and change, transformed into the art of criticism.

For Blackmur, the symptom of the defeat of reason in criticism is (again like Wilson) the substitution of specialized, academic, professional, knowledge for the unified mastery of intellect found in the operations of the layman critic. In *Anni mirabiles*, Blackmur remarks that the old literacy must struggle with the "new illiteracy, which is not ignorance but fragmented and specialized knowledge" (*PI* 7). He is, of course, especially concerned with literary criticism, and in 1956 he criticizes the over-specialized way that Formalist criticism actually developed into "art for exegesis' sake" (*NCUS* 157). He says: "It appears to me that what we are very largely up to in practice, and to a considerable extent in theory, is the hardening of the mind into a set of unrelated methodologies without the controlling advantage of a fixed body of knowledge, a fixed faith, or a fixed purpose" (*LH* 178; see also *NCUS* 97). Blackmur wants to broaden the scope of his early Formalism, "to keep the rhetoric but to get rid of its dominance and to put it into living and variable relation to other modes of the mind; I should like to add poetic and dialectic; I should like to build Aristotle on to Coleridge or develop Coleridge out of Aristotle" (*LH* 191).

The result of the new illiteracy for the writer is art for art's sake: "Faced with the dissolution of thought and the isolation of the artist, faced with the new industrialization of intellect and professionalism and methodology, what else could he do but make his declaration of independence and self-sufficient supremacy both as intellectual and artist?" (*NCUS* 153; see also *PI* 5). "Bohemia, remember, is, or was, the practical social experiment which makes the objective correlative to Art for Art's sake" (*NCUS* 152). A further consequence is that "with the rise of symbolism and art for art's sake the heroes of a considerable body of work began to be portrayed as artists. The subject of the artist and the special sensibility of the artist began to be the heroic subject and the heroic sensibility which best expressed society itself" (*LH* 44).

The alienation of the arts from society implies a problem of communication, and here we find the function, or what Blackmur calls the "burden," of criticism: "To make bridges between the society and the arts: to prepare the audience for its art and to prepare the arts for their artists. . . . The audience needs instruction in the lost skill of symbolic thinking. The arts need rather to be shown how their old roles can be played in new conditions" (*LH* 206).

In this complicated development of thought, Blackmur reverses the historical sequence of the other Formalists. Instead of letting the defeat of his social ideals propel him into Formalist explication, as it did the Agrarians, he assumes the centrality of technical criticism from the beginning, and the failure to make this ideal prevail propels him into a position where he sees the arts, both critical and creative, as separate from social reality. In short, Blackmur adopts the avant-garde view of the opposition of the arts and society (the bourgeoisie) which characterized the thinking of the New York Intellectuals in the forties. He says in a review of the *Oxford Anthology of American Literature* that "American literature is scrub oaks from mighty acorns, that the stunting, the lack of virility, the resort to nostalgia, refinement, allegory, and violence in wide assortment, comes from a radical failure in the double knowledge (or awareness) of good *and* evil. It is this most 'moral' race that is morally stunted in its imagination."[63] Blackmur differs from the New York Intellectuals, however, in that he does not revel in the tension between art and society— Lionel Trilling's "moral realism"—but wants to make reason prevail, wants to see the layman critic, who embodies reason—a figure very much like Blackmur himself—at the center of social power. Like the other Formalists and F. R. Leavis, he feels that the critic should be the moral authority of society.

In his third voice, that of Dr. Faustus, Blackmur's concern is to bring to the arts and society a new union. After 1950 Blackmur, like Eliot and Brooks, realizes that Formalism has "completed a certain stage with honor" (*LH* 176), and he turns to the task of creating a new union, or as he calls it, a "modus vivendi": "a means of getting along without loss of vital purpose in a concert of conflicts, not a unison, not a solo, not a harmony, but a concert of the conflicts with which we necessarily find out our problematic relations with others, nations, jobs, or friends" (*LH* 28). After 1950 Blackmur makes numerous attempts to formulate the elements of reality into a duality, and to subordinate them to the dominion of the mind. Speaking of Irving Babbitt, he says: "One would like to be, as a mind, where he thought he was, at the median, focusing, balancing point, at the fulcrum of higher and lower, the one and the many, the intuitive and the rational, the inner and the outer, the expansive and the contractive tendencies of the human imagination at work, yet at once immersed in the imperfection of human nature and having access, within the self, to the will of God" (*LH* 148). Or as he says generally: "When you get maturity of imagination and of intellect, (I did not say perfection, only maturity,) balance without loss of passion or vitality, you get great literature and great criticism, or let us say, criticism that has become a part of literature or literature that has become a part of criticism" (*NCUS* 26). The basic form of Blackmur's mind is thus a classical dualism of passion and intellect mastered by the unifying mind of the critic. As Joseph Frank says, "The dialectic between unity and chaos, or order and disorder, or orthodoxy and heresy, controls the framework of Mr. Blackmur's reflections,"[64] an interpretation that Blackmur specifically approves of (*NCUS* 18).

Blackmur's best-known theoretical formulation of the duality of reality opposes the *Numen* and the *Moha*. *Moha*, a Sanskrit word meaning "cow," is defined by Blackmur as "the basic, irremediable, irreplaceable, characteristic, and contemptuous stupidity of man confronted with choice or purpose," and also man's "tenacity of will" in confronting life (*LH* 294). It is something like the Devil (*LH* 293). It is man without beauty, without "harmony, wholeness, radiance" (*LH* 294). *Numen* is something like the life force; like myth, it is "that power within us greater than and other than ourselves, that moves us, sometimes carrying us away, in the end moving us forward unless we drop out, always overwhelming us" (*LH* 293). When it gets into behavior, the *Numen* becomes the *Moha*, so they seem to be related as the ideal and the actual, or possibility and actuality, or inspiration and behavior (*LH* 302). Blackmur asserts that the ancients saw "both the gods and behavior—the *Numen* and the *Moha*—in something like a single experience and in their poetry made myths which were plots of the relations between the two. Something of the same sort seems to have taken place in the work of Dostoevski, Joyce, and T. S. Eliot" (*LH* 300). It is to literature, and conceptions about it, that Blackmur looks for his embodiment and formulation of unity.

Blackmur's formulation of the concept of union progresses from the standard Formalist conception of "organic unity" to reliance on myth, gesture, and symbol. He says in 1936: "The poet (and, always, the reader) has to combine, to fuse inextricably into something like an organic unity the constructed or derived symbolism of his special insight with the symbolism animating the language itself" (*FV* 36). In 1942, speaking of a musician, he says: "His form and his substance will be united in process as well as at the end; united as gesture."[65] Further, "Gestures are the first step toward the making of symbols,"[66] and a symbol "is what we use to express meaningfulness in a permanent way which cannot be expressed in direct words or formulas of words with any completeness; a symbol is a cumulus of meaning which, once established, attracts further meanings to it until, overloaded, it collapses. The making of symbols is a steady occupation for minds at all aware."[67] The basis for this conception of the symbol seems to be Jungian, for according to Blackmur in 1941, "the man who uses the symbolic imagination [i.e., poet, priest, philosopher] must find the most part of his poetry already written for him out of the live, vast waste of disorder of the actual, out of those myths which as Jung says somewhere we may think of as the dreams of the people—the needful vision of the tribe" (*LH* 153).

In this later criticism Blackmur thus takes a position akin to that of Ernst Cassirer and Susanne Langer in positing for the human mind a basic symbol-making capacity: "The imagination requires images, as vision requires fables and thought requires formulas, before conceptions can be realised; which is to say that the faculties of men are not equal to their needs except by the intervention of symbols which they discover rather than create" (*EE* 123). Though Blackmur differs from the rest of the Formalists in relying on the evidence of psychology and myth to establish symbols as the ground of art, he is like them in making symbols eschatological: "I do insist that it is both necessary and possible that we make a secular equivalent of the religious imagination" (*LH* 152). "It is only the religious imagination which has the advantage of including the traditional standards of life along with a minute knowledge of its immediate experience" (*LH* 151). In a 1948 essay on *Ulysses* he says: "What we come on will be what for us is living in the tradition; which, as it once created the symbols which became the Christian world, will no doubt create the symbols which will become whatever it is that will follow Christianity. Many of the symbols will be the same, though they may seem to have opposed forms, or seem formless and only the story of the experience itself, as there was once only the story of Christ's life" (*EE* 46–47). Consequently "the masterpieces of our time gradually reveal themselves by the uses to which we are forced to put them, as philosophies, religions, politics— and as the therapies and prophecies of these" (*EE* 76). There is, however, none of the crypto-Christianity and concealed apologetics in Blackmur that one finds in Brooks, Tate, Eliot, and Ransom. He is not progressing teleologically to the Word but is coping with its absence; for him, Christianity is testament to a human need and an answer that was satisfying in the past but is not so for the future: "The props are gone, the values remain. There is society itself which has produced state and church from everlasting, and will do so again at the next moment of mastery, when its convictions are made plain. Meanwhile the writer has merely the greater labor to do of seeing with supreme attention not only the actual but also, what had previously been largely given him free of attention by church and state, the values that enlighten the actual as the actual grounds the values. This is critical labour."[68] As formulated here, the concept of the symbol functions as "tradition" does for Eliot and the rest of the Formalists, as the carrier of the permanent values of the past into the present.

Unlike other Formalists, but like the New York Intellectuals, Blackmur turns to the novel rather than poetry as the genre that best portrays the duality of art and society, and he adds to his Formalist greats—Eliot, Yeats, Pound, and James—the novelists Joyce, Gide, Flaubert, Mann, Tolstoi, and Dostoevsky because "it is the novel since at least the eighteenth century which has had the charge of organizing all our disorders into theoretic forms of life" (*LH* 306). Like Trilling, he becomes interested in manners, "for manners are the medium in which the struggle between the institutions of society and the needs of individuals is conducted" (*EE* 8). He says of James and Eliot: "The imbalance between the insider and the outsider, between anarchy and order, which both men felt in their lives, was never settled, but was left, rather, always teetering. ... The struggle for balance, not balance but the struggle for it, preoccupied both, and became the major theme in the work of each" (*LH* 75). Likewise, he says of Tolstoi: "There is thus at work in the novels of Tolstoi a kind of dialectic of incarnation: the bodying forth in aesthetic form by contrasted human spirits of 'the terrible ambiguity of an immediate experience' through their reactions and responses to it. It is this dialectic which gives buoyancy and sanity to Tolstoi's novels" (*EE* 4). Blackmur's essays on the novel, collected in 1964 as *Eleven Essays on the European Novel*, fail, however, to reconcile the duality of art and society, perhaps because, René Wellek suggests,[69] Blackmur can read the novels only in translation and hence is unable to use this technical criticism to deal with the art of language.

For Blackmur, the fictional character who embodies the symbolic unifying power of reason is Dr. Faustus. Blackmur says that in Thomas Mann's version of the character one has "the Faustian spirit, the spirit of imagination, the ultimate irresponsibility as he calls it, the ultimate moral freedom as James would call it, the combination of the dynamo and the virgin as Adams would call it! All these forces fighting against the dictatorship of the scum of the earth" (*NCUS* 150). Faustus is the image of the mind which can unite the *Numen* and the *Moha*; he combines "the two traditions of light and darkness. There is on the one side the tradition of reason and revelation and inspiration, and on the other side the tradition of the daemonic, the chthonic, and the magical. Somehow in the image of Faustus the two traditions are combined" (*EE* 98–99). Faustus is, of course, the man of knowledge, and hence he seems to be a symbolic version of the elite of scholar-critics which Blackmur earlier saw as the embodiment of reason. In this progress from the technique of Eliot to the figure of Henry Adams, Blackmur dramatizes the inadequacy of Eliot's technique in life; and in the progress from Adams to Faustus, Blackmur seems to find new faith in the efficacy of the mind.

It is at this point that the essential judgment of Blackmur's own mind must be made. His later pronouncements come in the voice of an oracle, a prophet, one who has meditated long and deeply on the canon of modernistic literature and is delivering his judgments. In this mode, *Anni mirabiles, 1922-25,* Blackmur's 1956 Library of Congress lectures, is his masterpiece.[70] Here one finds such statements as:

In Whitman you find the sprawl of repetition, in Pound the heap of ideographs; in either case we ourselves make the thought emerge. [*PI* 48]

His [Cumming's] unity is in the substantial unity of emotion in experience. Dryden's unity is in the achieved unity of intellect taken as conviction. [*PI* 51]

Byron has the sneer of position, Williams the cry of sincerity. Byron is the snobbism of conventionality, Williams its primitivism. [*PI* 53]

These judgments are the result of jumps of the saltatory mind; they are in an aphoristic form which requires meditation rather than the assent appropriate to sound technical description. Aphorism is a very different and now-unpracticed mode of response to literature. The question is whether Blackmur's aphorisms are ultimately wise; and if so, is their wisdom, and the wisdom of many other similar statements, enough to sustain a claim to critical greatness? Does Blackmur become a successful Faustus, the secular doctor who can unite the contraries of our world successfully through aphorism? In short, does Blackmur's voice become a charter in itself, a new resource for the history of criticism like that of Dr. Johnson or Arnold or Eliot?

Qualitatively, Blackmur's third voice succeeds; his judgments do have the authority of an intelligence who has pondered long and deeply on literature, of one who says: "As for Gide, I have loved him with aversion, and have fought him with delight, for above a quarter century. . . . As for Joyce, he is a part of my bloodstream since my sixteenth year, and as my blood changed so he changed with it" (*PI* 29–30). Quantitatively, however, Blackmur did not do enough work in this idiom to sustain a major claim. This may be due to the fact that, unlike Dr. Johnson, who found his Boswell, Blackmur never found the proper medium through which to deliver his judgments; or to the fact that the time in which he lived favored gurus of the sensibility over an oracle of reason. Despite their intrinsic authority, Blackmur's later essays have not had wide influence, and he remains in the seventies the forgotten prophet of modernism. But like fragments of Sanskrit in *The Waste Land*, once heard, Blackmur's aphorisms and comparisons remain in the ear, incomplete and peculiar evocations of an intelligence which unites both art and culture in a rational voice better than our time deserves. Of the myriad of American analytical critics, he was the first and the best.

Austin Warren: The Ideal Regionalist

Austin Warren's first role as a critic was as a mediator, between criticism and "scholarship" in the thirties,[71] and then between the American Formalist tradition and the Prague Structuralism and Kantianism of René Wellek in Wellek *and* Warren's famous handbook, *Theory of Literature*. Warren began as a scholar, with his *Alexander Pope as Critic and Humanist* (1929) and *Richard Crashaw: A Study in Baroque Sensibility* (1939). The particular version of the regionalist tradition which serves as Warren's critical charter is a New England version of High Episcopalianism. In a charming memoir Warren recalls how, at the age of twenty-four, he and a friend, Benjamin Bissell, founded a summer school in Hebron, Connecticut: "Our precedents for the school were Little Gidding and Alcott's Concord School of Philosophy; our intention, to give corporate form to Christian humanism, as represented by the powerful influences of Irving Babbitt, my teacher at Harvard, and Albert S. Cook, Ben's at Yale. What we designed was conceived of—and became—an intellectual 'community.' "[72]

The Humanistic movement quickly "went underground" into the history of the careers of its disciples,[73] but Warren's devotion to its Christian-Humanist ideals remained and was transmuted into the study of literature. He says of his first four books: "There was one discernible common denominator between all except the *Pope*: an interest in the interrelations of literature and religion, the theme, never overtly and abstractly exposited (as yet), upon which my life's intellectual work has centered."[74] What this means historically is that Warren, as he developed from a scholar to a critic in the thirties, identified himself with conservative groups like the British Distributists, the French Neo-Scholastics, and the Southern Fugitives and Agrarians and became "a New England regional humanist, Catholic minded."[75] Warren thus resembles another New Humanist, Stuart Sherman, whom he praises: "He carried 'standards' into the Middle West. ... In his best days, he was a Regionalist: he taught that one did not have to live east of Albany to have civilized 'standards'; one did not have to be

a Harvard man. One could live in Iowa, or Nebraska, or Michigan. 'Regionalism' was, in fact, the good old doctrine of Concord, Massachusetts: it
was, paradoxically, Superregionalism.''[76] It is, of course, at Iowa and
Michigan that Warren spent his scholarly career.

It is thus as a regional critic that Austin Warren has functioned for the
last forty years, and his four books of critical essays—*Rage for Order*
(1948), *New England Saints* (1956), *The New England Conscience* (1966),
and *Connections* (1970)—are almost entirely about New Englanders and/or
Anglican clergyman. As he says, "The sense of the past is with every
antiquary, bound up with things, places, local attachments.''[77] Wallace
Fowlie calls him "the living example for me of the Yankee.''[78] In *The
New England Conscience,* Warren says: "As I have been describing—
and prescribing for—the sick conscience, I have been describing what is
called the 'New England conscience' in its pathology. The Puritan conscience
as such is one which gives predominance—and undue predominance—
to self examination and self discipline.''[79] Warren's books seem to embody
an overstressed examination of his own Puritan tradition. What he says of
his sketches in *New England Saints* applies to his other essays as well:
"Like Dr. Sprague [author of *Annals of the American Pulpit* (1857-59)],
I intend not theological history but hagiography; and like him I shall
chiefly limn the portraits and recount the 'sayings' of the divines whose
spiritual father was the neo-Calvinist Reverend Jonathan Edwards.''[80]
By way of personal illustration of the operations of the Puritan spirit,
Warren says: "If I am a professor, my duty—and what centrally matters,
morally, even—is to prepare my lectures and correct my students' essays
and examinations and keep my office hours. ... The 'outer' is my honest
performance of my vocation; the 'inner'—what corresponds, perhaps,
to that subjective of *intentions and motives* which in philosophy from
Kant to Kierkegaard has been made the *all* of ethics—is to be thought
of as *willing* my vocation. ... The morality of work is consciously *willing*
the duties of the profession in which (for whatever biographical circumstances) I find myself engaged.''[81]

If Warren's examination of New Englanders is viewed as self-examination,
the lack of conclusiveness to his essays can be seen as historically determined. Writing of Edwin Arlington Robinson, he says: "New England
once had, in its intellectuals, dogmatic assurance. By the times of Adams
and Robinson, such dogmatic assurance is no longer possible to the let-
tered. But one can keep himself from feigning an assurance he no longer
feels and from uttering dogmas all too plainly subjective.''[82] We are here
far removed from the dogmatism of Babbitt, Tate, or Winters, and the
tentative nature of Warren's essays, which come to no point or conclusion,
can be seen as a moral tolerance forced on him by the decline in dogmatic
certainty of his chosen tradition.

Warren's exposition of the spirit of New England complements the effort of Southern Formalists to defend their own region and boost new Southern writers, but it has received much less general recognition, perhaps because many of his essays are on obscure subjects like Cotton Mather, Michael Wigglesworth, Fénelon, and C. E. Norton. In his essays on modern subjects, Warren explicates and defends his Humanist friends Irving Babbitt, Paul Elmer More, and John Brooks Wheelwright, and develops his views on Hawthorne, Emerson, Thoreau, the Jameses, and T. S. Eliot. He also expresses the Tory love of the past: "Lovers of 'old things' are sad at the way Progress demolishes all the monuments—and the miniatures, too—which call the past, and continuity to our remembrance. For mankind ignorant of its past is like a man without memory, condemned to live in the flux of Now."[83] Sometimes this love descends to mere antiquarianism, as in his appreciation of obscure English dons like the ghost-story writer M. R. James or the garrulous English essayist A. C. Benson, author of *From a College Window* (1906).[84]

In large part the lack of attention to Warren's work seems justified.[85] One may ask of him, as he did of T. S. Eliot in response to "What is a Classic?": "What is he so 'intense' about, and of what use, either to a practicing poet or a practicing teacher of literature, is what he has to say?"[86] At least, it is hard to see who his essays are for, since they are not theology, philosophy, or intellectual history, not scholarly examinations of subjects or close examinations of texts, but seem at best to be popular summaries or testimony designed to convert rather than inform the reader. In consequence, Warren seems ultimately to be the last of the New England prophets, the last of "that long line of New Englanders who have looked back to the glories of the forefathers and the pristine purity of the Idea," as Cotton Mather was the first.[87] For Warren, New England is not the home of John Fitzgerald Kennedy and Route 128: "The real New England is not a geographical area but a Holy State. Now long in the economic and political hands of 'aliens', now long a combination of academic institutions and summer resorts—still, the 'real New England' was always a Platonic Idea, like that of the pre-lapsarian Adam."[88] He also seems like Mather and the ancient prophets in his founding of his ideal community—St. Peter's School—and in his preaching of the gospel of New Humanism in the wilderness of Iowa and Michigan. In his devotion to New England ideals he is the defender of a Formalist region, as are the Fugitives, Yeats, or Hardy. Even more than they, however, he defends a region whose ancient ideals have vanished in fact, and so he becomes an ideal regionalist, an ectype of the old prophets, a keeper of the faith. For Warren, as for Mather, "New England shall yet live like Little Gidding or Brook Farm or Periclean Athens or the Florence of the Medici or any other temporary embodiment of the idealized and transcendent Idea—only with the dif-

ference, of course, that the Theocratic State symbolizes not only the aspirations of a merely humanist culture but God's own Polity."[89]

Yvor Winters: The Critic as Puritan Narcissist

Yvor Winters is a critic who would seem to have the highest claims to
recognition, for he has been a regional correspondent with Allen Tate for
Hound and Horn, a frequent contributor to the leading literary quarterlies
(as critic and as poet), and the subject of chapters in John Crowe Ransom's
The New Criticism and Stanley Hyman's *The Armed Vision.* He lived most
of his life in the West, and was a leader of the American regionalist movement as editor of *Seven Poets of the Pacific* and contributor to West Coast
magazines like *Contact.* At the same time, he has a Ph.D. from Stanford
and was an important academic presence as a professor there, especially
in his own eyes: "It has been a common practice for years for casual
critics to ridicule my students in a parenthesis; this has been an easy way
to ridicule me. . . . But I think the time has come when my faithful reader
may as well face certain facts, no matter how painful the experience; namely,
that I know a great deal about the art of poetry, theoretically, historically,
and practically; that a great many talented people have come to Stanford
to work with me; that I have been an excellent teacher; that six or seven of
my former students are among the best poets of this century" (*FD* 346).
Winters has, however, managed to negate all these advantages by a combination of bad temper and bad judgment, and his fame has suffered a
precipitous decline in recent years. Winters's reputation now seems to rest
on two supports: puffing by his former students, such as Gerald Graff,
author of *Poetic Statement and Critical Dogma* (1970), and Don Stanford,
co-editor of the influential *Southern Review;*[90] and the fact that John Fraser
thinks he resembles F. R. Leavis.[91] He is indeed much like Leavis. Both
derive their tradition from the early writings of Eliot and feel sorry for
themselves because they were not as great a success as Eliot; neither (unlike Eliot) has changed his mind since about 1930; both are provincials
who divide the world into fools and their own friends; Winters's voice is
like Leavis's, hectoring and intemperate in the expression of opinion and
absolutely convinced of his own rectitude, righteousness, and worth; both
suffer from feelings of persecution and neglect while teaching at the most
distinguished universities (see *FD* 346; *FC* 13).

Winters resembles Irving Babbitt more than Leavis, however (see *AV* 45).
Winters recalls that "for the young men of my generation, Babbitt was
the Professor in person: the other professors were an indistinguishable
crowd. And Babbitt had a way of saying stupid things about great poems:
so we looked elsewhere for our enlightenment. We found our enlightenment in Ezra Pound" (*FC* 12). Yet he claims to be using universal stan-

dards of judgment for literature in the manner of Babbitt and the Humanists in whose company he made his critical debut in 1930 (*DR* 568–69). According to Winters, "Historical relativism is philosophically unsound; and what is even worse, it is historically unsound" (*FD* 186). In the preface to his collected works, *In Defense of Reason*, he says:

> The theory of literature which I defend in these essays is absolutist. I believe that the work of literature, in so far as it is valuable, approximates a real apprehension and communication of a particular kind of objective truth. The form of literature with which I am for the most part concerned is the poem. ... The poem is good in so far as it makes a defensible rational statement about a given human experience ... and at the same time communicates the emotion which ought to be motivated by that rational understanding of that experience. ... Finally, I am aware that my absolutism implies a theistic position, unfortunate as this admission may be. [*DR* 11, 14; cf. *DR* 464, 505]

On this general and abstract level, Winters's thinking is certainly consistent with Christian thinking; John Fraser finds it Christian,[92] and Richard J. Sexton makes it out to be even more specifically Thomist.[93] Winters says of himself: "I myself am not a Christian and I fear that I lack permanently the capacity to become one; but Aquinas's examination of the nature of man appears to me acute and extremely usable, and his disposition of theological difficulties perhaps the best disposition possible" (*DR* 408; see also *DR* 370–72).

Whatever his religious position may be, Winters's *literary* theory derives from that of T. S. Eliot and parallels the development of the other Formalists. His rejection of the experimental verse of Pound, Williams, and his own youth in favor of reason and Humanism dates from about the same time as Eliot's (*FD* 315); and *Primitivism and Decadence* (1937) stands with Formalist works of the period like Eliot's *After Strange Gods* (1934) and Tate's *Reactionary Essays* (1936) as an expression of the Tory mentality of the time. Echoes of Eliot's "The Metaphysical Poets" are found in Winters's statement, "I am concerned with literature which may be loosely described as artistic: that is, with literature which communicates not only thought but also emotion" (*DR* 7). In his categorization of primitive and decadent poetry (*DR* 90ff.) he uses the standard Formalist dualism of thought and feeling and accepts this dualism of reason and emotion as a theoretical expression of the truth about the nature of poetry (*FC* 161; *DR* 502) and about Hawthorne and American literature (*DR* 174). His insistence on reason in poetry seems to elaborate this Formalist dualism by adding reason to the romantic emotionalism of modern experimental poetry, as Ransom adds structure to texture or Tate adds extension to intension (see *FD* xiv–xxii). In a way which echoes Brooks he makes the same dualism the form of tragedy: "The great poet judges the tragic subject completely, that is, rationally and emotionally" (*FC* 180). And he develops the same distinction historically in a way which echoes Eliot's "dissociation of sensibility": "There has been a general deterioration of the quality of poetry since the opening of the eighteenth century. . . . Our literary culture (to mention nothing more) appears to me to be breaking up" (*DR* 13; see also *DR* 414). Winters believes that poetry is "a real apprehension and communication of a particular kind of objective truth. . . . The poem is good in so far as it makes a defensible rational statement about a given human experience . . . and at the same time communicates the emotion which ought to be motivated by that rational understanding of the experience" (*DR* 11). This statement likewise echoes the Formalist insistence that poetry is a form of knowledge. The same dualism is again used as a (largely negative) standard of value for poetry. One may compare Eliot's criticism of Blake (*SE* 279) with Winters's remark that W. C. Williams "is wholly incapable of coherent thought and he had not the good fortune to receive a coherent system as his birthright" (*DR* 93). The reader is referred to Winters's criticism of Hart Crane (*DR* 602), Shelley (*DR* 368), or American literature (*DR* 230) for other applications of the same standard. There are other echoes. Winters's approach to ideas in a poem as a kind of "hypothetical acquiescence" (*DR* 273) parallels Eliot's handling of the problem of belief, despite Winters's explicit denial of Eliot's theory (*DR* 475–79). Finally, Winters associates himself with "Ransom, Tate, Brooks and Blackmur" as leaders in the invasion of the universities by criticism (*FC* 13), and increasingly embraces the scholarly world as he becomes more a part of it, though he does not seem to think "objective" scholarship is possible (*DR* 415–16). He says in 1943: "It is only, I believe, in a combination of the talents of the poet with the discipline of scholarship that one can hope to produce a really finished critic" (*DR* 557). "The university is the intellectual and spiritual center of our world" (*DR* 569).

The most perdurable doctrine Winters takes from the Tory Eliot is an intense dislike of Romanticism, which becomes the central preoccupation of his later criticism. For him, the Romantics "offer a fallacious and dangerous view of the nature both of literature and of man. The Romantic theory assumes that literature is mainly or even purely an emotional experience, that man is naturally good, that man's impulses are trustworthy, that the rational faculty is unreliable to the point of being dangerous or possibly evil. . . . Literature thus becomes a form of what is known popularly as self-expression. . . . The ultimate ideal at which such a theory aims is automatism [and automatic writing]. . . . Determinism is Romanticism in a disillusioned mood" (*DR* 8–9). Winters's later criticism is dominated by this ideological preoccupation, and since he writes mainly about American nineteenth- and twentieth-century literature, he is forced to write almost exclusively about literature he does not like. He says that his first book, *Primitivism and Decadence,* is "a study very largely of the forms of unconscious and of conscious obscurantism which are the ultimate development of Romantic aesthetic principles" (*DR* 153). In *Maule's Curse,* he writes: "[Poe's] clinical value resides in the fact that as a specimen of late romantic theory and practice he is at once extreme and typical. To understand the nature of his confusion is to come nearer to an understanding not only of his American contemporaries, but of French Symbolism and of American Experimentalism as well" (*DR* 260-61).

As Stanley Hyman and others show, it is very difficult to decide what doctrines Winters supports; it is, however, very easy to discover what he is against, so he may be justly called a negative absolutist.[94] He classifies eminent poets like Eliot, Pound, Williams, Moore, and Tate as eccentrics and says: "The eccentrics, as such, are all motivated by the same ideas about poetry and human nature which destroyed the poetry of the eighteenth and nineteenth centuries: they are nominalists, relativists, associationists, sentimentalists, and denigrators of the rational mind" (*FD* 323). This will serve as a list of specific modern "errors," and in general, Winters's most pervasive critical categories—primitivism, decadence, obscurantism, eccentricity, nonsense—are negative ones, designed to define the failures of modern thought. The most charitable construction that can be put on his theory comes from R. P. Blackmur, who says that "most of the principles of thought turn out to be foibles of manner and crotchets of personality: touchstones that get in the way of the facts if taken seriously but illuminating enough if taken, as they mostly are, as contributory facets of fact."[95] The problem is that Winters is unrelenting in his seriousness about the objective importance of his own work and exhibits a humorlessness and lack of ironic distance which are historically characteristic of Babbitt and the New Humanism of the thirties.

Insofar as he is a theorist, then, Winters's charter is like that of the other Formalists: a codification of some of Eliot's tactical and disjointed remarks into an absolute standard of judgment. However, Winters avoids Brooks's patient explication of poetry, which was the most influential and productive legacy of Formalism. He rather resembles poet-critics like Tate in his reliance on a personal standard of judgment unsupported by tradition or authority, and he does not have even Tate's Old South or Eliot's church as exterior support for his opinions. His campaign against Romanticism parallels Tate's against Positivism as a development of a particular exclusionary aspect of Formalist theory, and his status as Romanticism's severest critic seems secure.

Ironically, since Winters makes such a fuss about being rational, his practical criticism lacks an intellectual charter altogether, for what he means by "reason" is never clear, and he does not apply in practice the canons of the Formalist charter he echoes in his theory. We are left with

Winters's pure voice, one which *is* original and does have an immediately recognizable style, but one which also strikes most readers as arrogant, petulant, and defensive.

Winters's practical criticism really rests on the concept of an absolutely perfect taste, the Ideal Reader absolutized, and his hallmark as a critic is his fancied ability to select out of reams of bad verse the only poems or lines worthy of saving, a position which assumes an absolute and unerring judgment on his part. As he says, "The taste which enables a reader to recognize a good poem among fifteen hundred or more pages of bad is very rare" (*FD* 324; see also *DR* 188). The end of his exemplary critical process is "the final act of judgment, a unique act, the general nature of which can be indicated, but which cannot be communicated precisely, since it consists in receiving from the poet his own final and unique judgment of his matter, and in judging that judgment" (*DR* 372; see also *DR* 464). His ideal critic is, naturally, Dr. Johnson (*DR* 565), and he praises Gibbon and Macaulay for having this faculty: "The final literary form of the history represents an evaluation, a moral judgment, of the material which he [the historian] has held in his mind" (*DR* 415). In practice Winters's method amounts to a touchstone theory much like the method he attributes to Allen Tate: "Like Arnold before him, he [Tate] gives us a handful of touchstones: passages of poetry which he likes, although he admits that some of them are not the greatest poetry, and which are notable mainly for the reason that they resemble each other in no very obvious way" (*FC* 18-19). Winters gives us his list of classic touchstone poems (*FD* 188) and another list of moderns (*DR* 570-71). The effect of his selective procedure is to eliminate major poems altogether, since they are impure and irrational, and to concentrate on minor poets or minor works of major poets. Winters is always selecting the good poems out of a critic's canon, or the good stanzas, or the good lines, and he presents the reader with these shards of poetry as the product of his own ideal taste, so he is, like his Cooper, "essentially a man of fragments" (*DR* 198). His stated aim in *Forms of Discovery* is "to revaluate certain established reputations; to offer a new historical outline and a new set of critical emphases; and to base my conclusions on poems individually named" (*FD* 2).

When Winters constructs his own literary tradition, his rejections are truly magnificient. He finds that even the best of poetic drama (pace Shakespeare) is inferior to the lyric (*DR* 492). As Jonas A. Barish shows, "Nowhere in his account of the moral life is there room for the idea of play, or play-acting, for childish fantasy or indulged illusion."[96] Winters also dismisses the novel: "For the fact of the matter is . . . that the novel in our time is nearly dead. Unless there is a serious reconsideration of materials and methods, not merely in the interests of what may seem to the uninstructed to be novelty, but in the interests of intelligent achievement, the next generation will see the novel as dead as the drama is now. The most damnable fact about most novelists, I suppose, is their simple lack of intelligence: the fact that they seem to consider themselves professional writers and hence justified in being amateur intellectuals" (*FC* 39). Since his most notorious opinion about the novel is that Edith Wharton is better than Henry James (*DR* 300-343), his lack of attention to this genre may not be much missed. Stanley Edgar Hyman notes a further narrowing of Winters's area of interest: "He seems to be totally unfamiliar with any Continental literature other than the French. ... It is absurd to list the great novelists or poets, as Winters has done endlessly, and make them all English and American" (*AV* 47).

Winters outdoes Eliot in rigor when he says of the genre of poetry that "the two great periods in the poetry of our language are the period from Wyatt to Dryden, inclusive, and the period from Jones Very [1813-80] to the present" (*FD* 358). English poetry receives short shrift; the best sixteenth-century poetry is rational and "reaches its highest development in Fulke Greville and Ben Jonson and in one poem by George Herbert (*Church Monuments*). From there on the tradition begins to deteriorate [into the naïvely pietistic verse of Herbert, Crashaw, Vaughn, Marvell, and Traherne, and the worldly poetry of Sedley and Rochester] ... [and] in Milton the rational structure is decaying toward association" (*FD* 122-23). The "greatest English poem of the eighteenth century" (*FD* 145), because it works by a principle of rationally controlled association, is Charles Churchill's *Dedication* (to Bishop Warburton)! Of the Romantics and Victorians, Winters feels the less said the better, since they are totally corrupted by the sentimentalism of Shaftesbury and the associationism of Locke and Hobbes (*FD* 124 and 149). Of his own survey of them he says: "This essay will be monotonous, for the characteristics repeat themselves, and the poets are bad" (*FD* 149; see also *FD* 315). In the modern period, Winters finds "only a few poets from the British Isles of any importance: Hardy, Bridges, and T. Sturge Moore in particular; and in their various ways Hopkins, Yeats, Elizabeth Daryush, and Thom Gunn" (*FD* 358). Yeats and Hopkins are dismissed as eccentrics or worse. Winters says of Yeats: "His ideas were contemptible. I do not wish to say that I believe Yeats should be discarded, for there are a few minor poems which are successful, or nearly successful. ... [but] in the long run it is impossible to believe that foolishness is greatness, and Yeats was not a great poet [but a romantic bard like] Mussolini, Father Coughlin, and Adolf Hitler" (*FD* 234; see also *FD* 205). Elizabeth Daryush (Robert Bridges's daughter) is hailed as "better than any other poet produced in England between T. Sturge Moore and Thom Gunn. England has not given us much notable poetry in the past two hundred and fifty years" (*FD* 347). So much for the sceptered isle.

In his condemnation of English poetry Winters reminds us of his arch-villain Poe, of whose criticism he says: "In these passages Poe begins that process of systematic exclusion, in the course of which he eliminates from the field of English poetry nearly all of the greatest acknowledged masters, reserving the field very largely to Coleridge, Tennyson, Thomas Moore, himself, and R. H. Horne" (*DR* 238). If one substitutes for these names Churchill, Dickinson, Bridges, Daryush, F. G. Tuckerman, Jones Very, J. V. Cunningham, Mina Loy, N. Scott Momaday, and Adelaide Crapsey, one gets very much the same effect. Winters says: "Every literary critic has a right to a good many errors of judgment; or at least every critic makes a good many. But if we survey Poe's critical opinions we can scarcely fail to be astonished by them" (*DR* 256). Ironically, most analysts have felt this way about Winters.[97]

It is only in his judgments about American literature in *Maule's Curse* that Winters reveals any kind of positive critical standard. As usual, his judgments are eccentric: "F. G. Tuckerman (1821-73) was one of the three most remarkable American poets of the nineteenth century. The others were Jones Very (1813-80) and Emily Dickinson. ... Of Poe (1809-49) and Whitman (1819-92) the less said the better" (*FD* 253-54). Winters seems to praise a Puritanism much like Hawthorne's, and his own critical practice seems reflected in his statements about Puritanism, which he believes separates men as he separates poems, "sharply and certainly into two groups, the saved and the damned, and, technically, at least, ... [is] not concerned with any subtler shadings. This in itself represents a long step toward the allegorization of experience" (*DR* 158). Winters's critical manner seems to partake of Puritan intensity: "The Puritan may be said to have conceived the Manicheistic struggle between Absolute Good and Absolute Evil ... as a kind of preordained or mechanical, yet also holy combat, in which his own part was a part at once intense and holy and yet immutably regulated" (*DR* 162).

Though Winters quotes at length from the authors he criticizes, and gives us detailed analyses especially of metrics, his critical judgments do seem to reflect an allegorical absolutism. For example, his judgment that Emily Dickinson's "I like to see it lap the miles" is "abominable" (*DR* 284), whereas "Farther in summer than the birds" is "one of the most deeply moving and most unforgettable poems in my own experience" (*DR* 293), seems to reflect his feeling of the necessity to make absolute judgments rather than any quality of the poems themselves. Winters appears to believe that Calvinistic Puritanism produced our great nineteenth-century writers. He says that Calvinism, "which, as an historical fact, had enabled Hawthorne to produce *The Scarlet Letter*, existed only in a few rapidly crumbling islands of culture, such as that to which we owe Emily Dickinson [see also *DR* 298], and the mystical Puritanism which had lived in Anne Hutchinson and in Jonathan Edwards existed nowhere that we can determine save in the spirit of Jones Very" (*DR* 269). He says that *Moby Dick* "is not only a great epic; it is profoundly an American epic" (*DR* 220) which reflects both the spiritual and the physical adventuring of New Englanders. Henry James is seen as a late expression of the New England conscience (*DR* 305). In sum, in nineteenth-century America, New England "produced nearly all of the major literary talent" (*DR* 304). Since Winters praises only these authors and in doing so seems to assume that their culture determined their merit, one may assume that he finds the Puritan mentality an artistically healthy one. He relates this Puritan ethos to his moral absolutism by asserting that the Puritan moral sense "was the product of generations of discipline in the ethical systems of the Roman Catholic and Anglo-Catholic churches" (*DR* 302). The problem for the coherence and sincerity of his critical thinking is that he himself does not believe in Puritanism; he says that it is a shame and an anomaly that Jones Very should be left "to the best defense that one, like myself, at every turn unsympathetic with his position, is able to offer" (*DR* 269). Hence his critical judgments become artificial, almost vicarious, for they are made in terms of a tradition which Winters himself does not uphold.[98] This guarded support of Puritanism as the determining form of the best American literature is the only positive ideal Winters expresses in his criticism. Like the Neo-Humanists and Eliot in the thirties, he is condemned, because he lives in a Romantic age, to be *against* almost everything.

When he judges contemporary poets, Winters seems to express a private critical tradition since he praises only his friends and students. He says of his student J. V. Cunningham: "[He] seems to me the most consistently distinguished poet writing in English today, and one of the finest in the language" (*FD* 299).[99] He says that Eliot and Tate, "along with Yeats and Hopkins, and along with Stevens most of the time, might be described as the great eccentrics of the modern period. By this I do not mean that they are great poets, for they are not: the great poets are Bridges, Hardy, Robinson, T. Sturge Moore, Cunningham" (*FD* 323). The six good "post-Symbolist" poets he discusses in chapter 5 of *Forms of Discovery* are F. G. Tuckerman, Dickinson, Stevens, Louise Bogan, and his students Edgar Bowers and N. Scott Momaday. Winters seems to favor these particular poets because they depend on him as teacher or critic. He has long been famous as the only critic who ever heard of Elizabeth Daryush; T. Sturge Moore has elsewhere been ignored; and Cunningham, Momaday, Bowers, and Gunn were students of Winters's at Stanford.[100]

According to Winters, "If Bridges survives, he will have my talent to thank as well as his own, and I might never have been born" (*FD* 324). Especially in his later work (after 1947) Winters devotes himself almost exclusively to his own coterie. When he condemns, he is a Titan, but when he praises he is a miniaturist, almost a portraitist, since he praises mostly his friends. Ultimately, of course, his lack of empathy makes him a narcissist; in the end Winters's criticism, like that of Eliot, Coleridge, and other poet-critics, rests on his own practice. Philip Hobsbaum, an admirer of Winters whose considered judgment is that Winters is "one of the two or three greatest critics ever to have written in the English language," admits that "it can hardly be a coincidence that such themes as those I have mentioned, especially those of mortal vulnerability and distilled wisdom, form the subject-matter of Winters's own finest poems. It can hardly be a coincidence, either, that the form he most strongly advocates in English, the short poem in heroic couplets, is one that he has peculiarly made his own. . . . It will be seen, then, that if Winters is an absolutist, the absolute rests upon his practice in his own poems. Since even his most devoted admirer could hardly rank him among the greatest poets, it would seem that his criterion is indeed a limited one."[101] As Hobsbaum claims, such limits are indeed true of the greatest critics. The difference is that Winters's conception of good poetry is both idiosyncratic and anachronistic, so that when he projects his standards onto poetic history, he discovers mediocre poets in the past and personal dependents in the present.

Despite the claims by John Fraser that Winters's clique is the coming group,[102] this particular tradition gets help *only* from its friends. Though Winters's voice is original, it is so eccentric that it has had little influence beyond his personal disciples, and his reputation as one of the cranks of criticism is just.[103] Stanley Edgar Hyman puts Winters in the tradition of John Dennis and Thomas Rymer, defending him in 1948 because "he has, almost single-handedly, kept an important critical function, evaluation, alive for us" (*AV* 52). So he has, but the necessity for wisdom to illuminate a critical voice, or for an intellectual charter to control it, has never been clearer than with Winters, and it is this that distinguishes him from Dr. Johnson or T. S. Eliot. His historical accomplishment has been to give evaluation in our age a bad name. One may, then, finally judge Winters as he judges Poe: "Poe rests his case for art on taste, and though we may disagree with him, yet we are bound to examine his own taste, for if he has no taste, he has nothing" (*DR* 256).

Kenneth Burke: The Critic as True Believer

Kenneth Burke is among the most durable of those associated with the New Critical movement; he began writing for *The Dial* in 1922 and continues with unabated vigor in the seventies. During this period he has written many books while developing his system of "dramatism," which treats literature as a "symbolic action" or strategy for dealing with various situations. Like Ernst Cassirer and Susanne Langer, he assumes that man is a symbol-using animal and hence that analysis of symbols will illuminate basic human reality. One of the most important of his strategies is what he calls "perspective by incongruity"—the seeing of one reality in terms of a metaphor drawn from another reality. This insight and a number of others, including an addiction to scatological Freudian wordplay, are all subordinated to a systematic compulsion. As one of his best critics and disciples, Stanley Edgar Hyman, says, "The lifelong aim of Burke's criticism has been precisely his synthesis, the unification of every discipline and body of knowledge that could throw light on literature into one consistent critical frame" (*A V* 360). In *The Philosophy of Literary Form* (1941) the components of Burke's system include "the naming of the three ingredients in art as: 'dream,' the symbolic factors; 'prayer,' the rhetorical factors; and 'chart,' the factors of realistic sizing up" (*A V* 334). These components are later developed into a pentad of terms: act, scene, agency, agent, and purpose. Burke sees in these terms the basic relationships of literature and other areas of discourse as well, and his criticism seeks to analyze these relationships (the scene-agent ratio, the act-agency ratio, etc.).

Kenneth Burke's criticism cannot be illuminated, however, by attempting to write a précis of the millions of words he has written; only by examining the attitude Burke demands that the reader take toward his writing can this be accomplished. This conclusion is reinforced by Burke's reactions to a recent essay by René Wellek which gives a conventional academic summary and judgment of Burke's work. Wellek, like many others before him, concludes that "in his [Burke's] theory, literature becomes absorbed into a scheme of linguistic action or rhetoric so all-embracing and all-absorbing that poetry as an art is lost sight of and the work of art is spun into a network of allusions, puns, and clusters of images without any regard for its wholeness or unity. . . . In Burke extremes meet easily. All distinctions fall. The laws of evidence have ceased to function. He moves in a self-created verbal universe where everything may mean everything else." [104] Burke's response to this is that Wellek wrongs him greatly because he refuses to accept Burke's own system of terms and distinctions: "It is doubtless true that the questions I am asking often differ considerably from the ones for which he [Wellek] has been seeking answers. My complaint is that the nature of his approach makes it impossible for him to represent adequately even the tenor of my observation." [105]

Burke's response to Wellek is essentially to answer his objections by rephrasing them within the terms of his own dramatistic system. Burke demands of his readers that they adopt his system of terms and categories, which he has been devising and revising for fifty years, and see the world as he sees it. In short, Burke demands not readers but disciples. The question readers of Burke must answer, then, is whether they wish to see the world as he sees it, for it is impossible to read Burke seriously without succumbing to the demands of the terminology and the system. [106]

The alternative response is to view Burke as a poet, and Burke's disciples tend to use both alternatives as convenient, without much regard for (or perhaps rejoicing in) the logical "perspective by incongruity" of the contrast. For example, in his notes to *Critical Responses to Kenneth Burke,* William H. Rueckert says that Harold Rosenberg "saw in 1936 that *Permanence and Change* was only the beginning of a very long book which Burke is still writing, and the whole endeavor was to be a kind of poem, a creative and visionary work on the grand scale. It was a long time before anyone else saw so clearly what Burke was going to do." [107] Burke's poetic procedure "is really very Emersonian and should be recognized as such" (p. 96), and one who objects to Burke's factual inaccuracy misses the point. "It was not a historian he was reading, but a visionary, a myth maker, and system builder" (p. 97). Yet later Rueckert criticizes George Knox for seeing Burke as Emersonian and as a nonsystematic thinker: "This view is the opposite of the one which can be found in Hugh Duncan, Mrs. Nichols, Malcolm Cowley, Leland Griffin and my own book; and it is a view which now seems to be clearly controverted by the fact of everything Burke has published since 1957. Burke's work is clearly systematic and coherent now. . . . [He] has provided one with a whole usable model of reality" (p. 322). Instead of uniting the insights of poetry with the rigors of demonstration of philosophy, Burke seems to unite the compulsive wordplay of poetry with the compulsive scaffolding of philosophy, combining the vices rather than the virtues of both disciplines.

Perhaps it is best to view Burke as essentially solipsistic, for he transforms nature and literature into a personal reality that unites poetry and philosophy in an original and unparalleled vision. For example, when he analyzes Keats's "Ode to a Grecian Urn" and translates "Beauty is truth, truth beauty," into "Act is scene, scene act," it is clear in this context what is meant, but the meaning is absolutely opaque if one tests Burke's conclusion by referring to the poem. [108] In this, Burke is much like Claude Levi-Strauss, whose transformation of the Oedipus myth involves much the same kind of combination of poetic insight and compulsive demonstration [109] and leads one in amazement along the road by which he reaches his conclusions. If Burke is a poet, then he is a Metaphysical poet in Dr. Johnson's sense of the term: "The most heterogeneous ideas are yoked by violence together. . . . In the mass of materials which ingenious absurdity has thrown together, genuine wit and useful knowledge may be sometimes found buried perhaps in grossness of expression, but useful to those who know their value." [110]

The autodidactic character of Burke's writing has from the beginning limited his influence to the merely suggestive. Hyman notes that in the thirties Burke was read widely and influenced a number of critics, including Harry Slochower, his old friend Malcolm Cowley, and his colleagues at Bennington College Francis Fergusson and Hyman himself (*A V* 354-59). He is at present largely ignored or rejected by the intellectual public, by academicians in particular, by philosophers, and by all Europeans;[111] he seems to be fashionable only among teachers of speech and rhetoric.[112] Most recently, Fredric R. Jameson wants to use Burke's method to teach us history. "to prolong the symbolic inference until it intersects with history itself"; but he too acknowledges that "this immense critical corpus, to which lip service is customarily extended in passing, has—read by virtually everybody—been utterly without influence in its fundamental lessons, has had no following, save perhaps among the social scientists."[113]

Despite the claims of a few disciples, Burke has been widely read, widely criticized, but not productively influential among students of literature, because his method cannot be applied by others and too few have been willing to join him as true believers in his system of dramatism. He seems best regarded, then, as an old-time American crank inventor who might have been Edison except that his work lacks any relation to reality outside his own mind. Dramatism is his system—he invented it and he believes in it—but one must suspend disbelief and become a true believer indeed to see the world and literature as Burke sees them.

6. The Age
of the Theorists,
1949-1978

The major turn taken by the Formalists in the late forties and early fifties was a shift from practical criticism to an academic concern with critical theory. Brooks says in 1948: "The criticism characteristic of our time has come to fruition, or has arrived at a turning point, or, as some writers hint, has now exhausted its energies. For those who would dwell upon this darker note there are further corroborative signs: the increasing tendency to talk about the 'methods' of the new criticism; the growing academic respectability of the new criticism; the attempt to codify the new critics and to establish their sources and derivations."[1] One sign of this exhaustion is the turning of able erstwhile Formalists like Arthur Mizener, Richard Ellmann, and Mark Schorer into the traditional scholarly path of the biographer, in the teeth of the intentional fallacy. The future, Brooks continues, lies in the development of critical theory: "I think that I can point out something that needs to be done ... to discriminate more closely among the various problems with which criticism in the large is concerned." Brooks's prediction here is less a hope than an advertisement for Wellek and Warren's *Theory of Literature* (1949), since Brooks published the central chapter of that work in the *Southern Review* in 1942, and says of it in 1949: "I predict that *Theory of Literature* will constitute nothing less than a new organum for literary studies," and "I am happy to accept the position on this question [of absolutes] which Wellek and Warren assume."[2]

Theory of Literature led to a golden age of Formalist theory by a quartet of critics—René Wellek, W. K. Wimsatt, Cleanth Brooks, and Murray Krieger—who, together with their collaborators Austin Warren and Monroe Beardsley, produced a cluster of substantial theoretical works in the following decades: Wellek's first two volumes of *A History of Modern Criticism* (1955); Wimsatt and Beardsley's *The Verbal Icon* (1954); Krieger's *The New Apologists for Poetry* (1956); Wimsatt and Brooks's *Literary Criticism: A Short History* (1957); Wellek's *Concepts of Criticism* (1963); Wimsatt's *Hateful Contraries* (1965); Krieger's *The Play and Place of Criticism* (1967), *The Classic Vision* (1971), and *Theory of Criticism* (1976); the second two volumes of Wellek's *History of Criticism* (1965) and his *Discriminations: Further Concepts of Criticism* (1970). These critics are sometimes called the "Yale theorists," after the university home of Wellek, Brooks, and Wimsatt.[3]

In the event, then, the process that was going on was more deflection of energies than exhaustion. The Formalists had done all they could to show how their method worked. Brooks, Warren, and Heilman had published their textbooks applying the Formalist method to all the genres; and Brooks published *The Well Wrought Urn* in 1947 to demonstrate that the Formalist method of explication is applicable to poetry of all periods, Neoclassical and Romantic as well as Metaphysical and modern. Having done this, they took up the task of turning *explication de texte* into a normative ideal of criticism, insight into philosophy, epiphany into theology.

Looked at from a sociological point of view, the process seems to mark a withdrawal from the avant-garde literary wars the Formalists fought to establish their taste and procedure in the marketplace to a kind of writing in which they attempt to establish the academic importance of Formalism's place in history by rewriting the history of criticism to make their view central and permanent. Wimsatt says: "In academic criticism you see less genius than in some other kinds, but more deliberacy, self-consciousness, program, literalism, and repetition. When a critical conception arrives at academic status, it is a public fact, an established part of history" (*HCo* 5).

René Wellek: Theorist of the Aesthetic

The achievement of Formalist theory is thus an organizing and classifying of the questions of literary theory in order to make the Formalist view of poetry central. This task is first attempted by Wellek and Warren, who divide criticism into "extrinsic" and "intrinsic" schools and maintain the superiority of the intrinsic in their *Theory of Literature*.[4] Rather than examine this book in detail, however, one must study the critical theory of René Wellek as a whole, as in 6 more volumes and some 225 articles and reviews he attempts to express a consistent and coherent literary theory for all the Western European literary cultures since 1750. Wellek is Czech by birth and education and is fluent in the language and informed in the literature of the Slavic countries, Germany, France, Italy, Spain, England, and America. Thus his defense of literary theory stems from his origins. As he says, "Coming from the Continent to England and the United States, I felt strongly that there is a particular need of theoretical awareness, conceptual clarity and systematic methodology in the English-speaking countries, dominated as they are by the tradition of empiricism."[5]

Roger Sale points out that Wellek has achieved his present eminence as a historian of literary criticism simply by knowing more than anyone else: "Blessed with a prose style no one would describe as better than adequate [in English at least], equipped with a literary sensibility that strikes few as being superior to their own, possessed of an intelligence that reveals no originality and seldom more than judiciousness, he has simply blown competitors from the field with erudition."[6] Be that as it may (Wellek would probably classify Sale's "limitations" as scholarly virtues), one can admit Wellek's commanding erudition without accepting the charter the learning supports. Only by studying his values can we make sense of Wellek's work.

The search for the underlying values of Wellek's theory is consistent with his assumptions that "there are no neutral facts in literature" (*D* 20); that "true literary scholarship is not concerned with inert facts, but with values and qualities" (*CC* 291); and that "the only true objectivity obtainable to man [is not] a neutral scientism, an indifferent relativism and historicism but a confrontation with the [literary] objects in their essence: a dispassionate but intense contemplation which will lead to analysis and finally to judgments of value" (*CC* 295; see also *D* 338). The centrality of value judgments applies to all three of Wellek's carefully distinguished branches of literary study: literary theory, or the study of the principles of literature, its categories and criteria; literary criticism, or the static study of concrete works of art; and literary history, the study of the chronological development of literary works. For Wellek the study of the history of ciriticism is also a study of values, and this assumption underlies the writing of his monumental *History of Modern Criticism*. As he says in the preface to volumes 3 and 4, "I keep, and want to keep, a point of view and am convinced of the truths of several doctrines and the error of others" (*HC* 3:vi–vii; see also *HC* 1:5).

The value in Wellek's axiology on which all else rests is the Kantian one that there exists an autonomous realm of the aesthetic value of the beautiful which parallels the values of the true and the good. Wellek expresses this assumption most forcefully in his late article "Kant's Aesthetics and Criticism":

Only in Kant do we find an elaborate argument that the aesthetic realm differs from the realm of morality, utility, and science because the aesthetic state of mind differs profoundly from our perception of the pleasurable, the moving, the useful, the true, and the good. Kant invented the famous thesis that the aesthetic response consists in "disinterested satisfaction". ... The aesthetic realm is thus that of imagination, not of thought or goodness or utility but of imagination represented, objectified, symbolized, distanced, contemplated. However we rephrase it, it seems to me that Kant has clearly grasped the nature of the aesthetic and the realm of art. [*D* 124-26; cf. his remarks on Leo Spitzer, *D* 201; Jeffrey, *HC* 2:119; and Shelley, *HC* 2:125][7]

Wellek stresses the idea of criticism as contemplation of aesthetic emotion as embodied in the work of art: "All art is 'making' and is a world in itself of illusion and symbolic forms" (*CC* 255). One must also assume that art exists as a qualitatively distinct and morally desirable state of mind for the reader of literature: "All of us *should* respond to great art and distinguish between the good and the bad if we are to be fully human" (*D* 128). From the Kantian autonomy of art Wellek derives the important subsidiary doctrines of his literary theory; the dualism of appearance and reality, subjective and objective, general and particular, imagination and reason; and the reconciliation of these dualisms in the organic nature of the work of art as embodied in the tradition of Romantic and Symbolist art.

A second value related to Wellek's Kantian charter is his defense of the necessity of a "scientific" literary theory. As he says, "[Kant] has put his finger on the central issue of aesthetics. No science is possible which does not have its distinct object" (*D* 125; see also *D* 50-51; *CC* 293). The distinctness of the aesthetic realm seems for him a necessary precondition for true literary scholarship (which for Wellek includes history, criticism, and theory), but the desirability of theory seems to be a separate assumption for Wellek, since it does not follow from the fact that there is an aesthetic realm of literature that there need by literary scholarship to elaborate on it. Physics is not implicit in nature. Assumption of the independence of literary criticism as a discipline also leads Wellek to ignore the relationship of the theory and practice of writing to concrete works of art. He says: "We shall proceed mostly on the assumption that the relation between theory and practice is very indirect and that we can ignore it for our purposes, which after all, are directed mainly toward an understanding of ideas" (*HC* 1: 7). This assumption seems to contradict his own emphasis elsewhere on the primacy of concrete works of art in developing critical values. As he says while arguing with Northrop Frye, "Literary theories, principles, criteria cannot be arrived at *in vacuo*: every critic in history has developed his theory in contact ... with concrete works of art which he has had to select, interpret, analyze, and, after all, to judge" (*CC* 5). In any case, Wellek's ideal of criticism is that it "upholds ideals of correctness of interpretation, observes the laws of evidence, and must aim, ultimately, at a body of knowledge which we hesitate to call 'science' only because the natural scientists have preempted the term in English" (*D* 257-58). Thus, whether inferred or assumed, a central axiom for Wellek is that "criticism is conceptual knowledge, or aims ... at systematic knowledge about literature, at literary theory" (*CC* 4). For Wellek, adequate literary theory transcends barriers of language, is based on an objective concept of taste, and hence offers not relative but absolute knowledge.

Wellek's assumption that literary theory transcends linguistic reality is conveyed, most often negatively, by reference to the myth of the Tower of Babel: "the Babylonian confusion of tongues which characterizes our civilization" (*CC* 54; see also *CC* 2, 341; *D* 53). But positively Wellek describes the ideal of general literature as cross-linguistic: "No grounds of total evaluation can, I conclude, be established by linguistic or stylistic analysis as such" (*D* 341); "what matters is the concept of literary scholarship as a unified discipline unhampered by linguistic restrictions" (*CC* 290; see also *D* 53). Or as he says elsewhere, "The mere fact that great poets and writers—Homer, Virgil, Dante, Shakespeare, Goethe, Tolstoy, and Dostoevsky—have exercised an enormous influence often in poor and loose translations which hardly convey even an inkling of the pecularities [*sic*] of their verbal style should demonstrate the comparative independence of literature from language" (*D* 333). Wellek's theory remains historical, however, not universal like that of Northrop Frye: "An international, supralinguistic poetics or literary theory is, one should emphasize, an empirical science, concerned with a historical manifold" (*D* 335).

Wellek's assertion that literary scholarship should transcend the barriers of linguistic provincialism is disproved by his own observations and practice, in that he is compelled to note that literary critics seem to be consistently bound by their national cultures, as are, in point of fact, the chapters in his *History*, which might as well be grouped as national histories as by chronological period. At the beginning of his *History of Modern Criticism* he says: "The effects of Cartesian rationalism, Lockean empiricism, and Leibnizian idealism are imprinted on the criticism of the three leading nations, and seem to a large extent to account for the differences between French, English, and German criticism" (*HC* 1: 8). In volume 3 he says: "There is also a dark side to literary nationalism . . . in the fragmentation of criticism. We must take into account the astonishingly decreased sense of community (even compared with the Romantic Age) among the European nations in the late 19th century and the increased differences among their developments" (*HC* 3: xv). And in his surveys of the latest critical schools he concludes: "At least one overwhelming impression I carried away from my travels deserves further reflection: the sense of the gulfs yawning between the different national traditions in spite of all the many attempts at building bridges—that is, of the tenacity with which the main European nations cling to their distinct critical traditions" (*D* 345–46; see also *CC* 345). Just as comparative literature originates largely with men who themselves straddle two cultures (*CC* 287), so from a psychological point of view Wellek's attempt to posit a cross-linguistic and

cross-cultural ideal of criticism seems more a projection of his own achievement in learning languages than a description of criticism and critics as
they are, for his adherence to "the great tradition of German aesthetics
from Kant to Hegel" (*CC* 363-64) shows the triumph of a national
intellectual tradition, not a universal one.

Wellek's emphasis on theory is based on the assumption, again Kantian,
of the universality of taste. For Kant, the aesthetic judgment "is subjective, but there is an objectivity in the subjective; in the aesthetic judgment egoism is overcome: we appeal to a general judgment, to a common
sense of mankind, but this is achieved by inner experience, not by accepting the opinions of others or consulting them or counting their opinions. It
is not an appeal to men, but an appeal to humanity, to an ideal totality of
judges" (*D* 127-28). Here we see a philosophical version of the concept of
the Ideal Reader which we have seen in all the Formalists, and again this
authority is assumed as an a priori axiom of faith rather than verified by
any inductive process.

For Wellek, then, the theorist properly grounded in aesthetics and following proper scholarly methods can give us the truth about questions of
literary scholarship: "Men can correct their biases, criticize their pre-
suppositions, rise above their temporal and local limitations, aim at objectivity, arrive at some knowledge and truth" (*CC* 14). For him, "all
relativism is ultimately defeated by the recognition that 'the Absolute is in
the relative, though not finally and fully in it' " (*TL* 156; see also *CC* 20).[8]
In "The Criticism of T. S. Eliot", Wellek praises Eliot for understanding
this.[9] The parallel between absolute and relative and the relationship of
Christ to the world in Wimsatt and Brooks's concept of the Incarnation
should be obvious. Wellek's animus against relativism, which is particularly
noticeable in contrast to his usual restraint, is found throughout his writing
in such statements as "[complete relativism] leads to paralyzing
skepticism, to an anarchy of values, to the acceptance of the old vicious
maxim: *de gustibus non est disputandum*" (*CC* 17; see also *CC* 19-20, 265,
329; *TL* 146; *HC* 1: 26, 124). The particular kind of relativism he views as
most threatening is the German historicism he finds embodied
convincingly in Erich Auerbach (*CC* 11-14) and poorly in Roy Harvey Pearce
(*CC* 10-11). Wellek distinguishes a proper historical sense from historical
relativism on the grounds that "the historical sense should be defined as a
combination of the recognition of individuality [of the poet, period, and
types of art] with a sense of change and development in history" (*HC* 1: 26).

One of the most productive of Wellek's recent activities follows from his
concept of history: the historical definition of central terms of literary
theory like Romanticism, Realism, Symbolism, evolution, Classicism,
Baroque, and form and structure. He says, "The meaning of a word is the
meaning it assumes in its context and which has been imposed on it by its

users" (*CC* 36); "one must conceive of them [period terms] not as arbitrary linguistic labels nor as metaphysical entities, but as names for systems of norms which dominate literature at a specific time of the historical process" (*CC* 129). Wellek is concerned theoretically to defend the use of period terms against Anglo-American Nominalism, which considers them mere linguistic labels, and a German elevation of them into metaphysical entities known only by intuition (*CC* 224); but sometimes he asserts what might be called the Idealistic Nominalism of Croce, "that an idea is not there until it is expressed [and hence] we must ascribe great importance to the question of terminology" (*D* 56). One can, I think, reconcile these partly contradictory statements by noting Wellek's limitation of history to the autonomous internal history of art rather than to the history of events in a temporal sequence. As Wellek says, paralleling Eliot, the history of literature is a question of "monuments," not "documents" (*CC* 15; see also *D* 20), and his effort is the Adamic, or rather Linnean, one of naming the flora and fauna of the intellectual world. What he wants theory to do in practice is quite clear; he wants a theory which "prepares for synthesis, draws our minds away from the mere accumulation of observations and facts, and paves the way for a future history of literature as a fine art" (*CC* 114; see also *D* 121).

The importance of this immense effort to define terms and establish theoretical boundaries depends on another of Wellek's assumptions: that good theory makes good critics. In the chapter "The Study of Literature in the Graduate School" in *Theory of Literature*, and in Wellek's other essays on education, there is a sustained drive for educational reform based on this assumption. In "American Literary Scholarship" he says:

If criticism is to transform American literary scholarship in the universities success-fully, it must face a number of problems. . . . If they [New Critics] abandon the old philology with its definite methods and body of knowledge, they will have to replace it with a new body of doctrines, a new systematic theory, a technique and meth-odology teachable and transmissible and applicable to any and all works of liter-ature. In this respect, much modern American criticism is still deficient. . . . Its vocabulary often differs far too sharply from author to author and even from essay to essay: its assumptions are rarely thought through in their philosophical impli-cations and historical antecedents. Many American critics . . . use a homemade terminology demanding a considerable effort of interpretation. . . . They are thus open to misunderstanding by the wider public. . . . Thus a measure of agreement on basic issues of theory will have to be reached sooner or later. One can defend individual terminology up to a point; but indulgence in idiosyncrasies damages the cumulative effect of criticism. [*CC* 311]

Wellek is also firm in his condemnation of poet-critics like T. S. Eliot as being too impressionistic and biased in favor of their own modes of poetry and hence not necessarily able to evaluate others without "egocentricity and narrowness." "If we are concerned with criticism as organized knowledge, as interpretation and judgment of publicly verifiable objects, we must dismiss poetic criticism as an irrelevancy" (*D* 256). In these statements one sees the idea that corporate criticism is better than individual taste, that theoretically articulated judgment is better than metaphorical or gnomic or theoretically contradictory judgment, that there is an objectivity which is better than subjectivity, that criticism has a "cumulative effect."

The trouble with this complex of assertions is that there is no evidence that it is true, in the sense of accurately describing the way critics perform. Historically, at least in the English-speaking world, Wellek does not (and I believe cannot) point to a single critic whose writing has been improved by literary theory. From this it follows that Wellek's conception of criticism rests on an expression of faith that the aesthetic realm exists and that literary theory is desirable because it produces good critics; if one denies these premises, these values, one denies the objective validity of Wellek's *History*. This is to say only that Wellek's *History* itself is normative, not descriptive, that it rests on value judgments, as he admits.

Wellek's assertion of the universal truth of his value judgments creates some difficulty when it leads to his judging the entire English and American empirical tradition by theoretical values it has not held. In a summary paragraph, he condemns Englishmen of the Victorian era for their "crippling relativism and an anarchy of values," and for losing their grip "on the unity of content and form"; "no poetic theory was produced in England that could claim novelty and systematic coherence" (*HC* 3:xiii–xiv). Faced with the sweeping effects of this statement, however, Wellek reverses himself and defends the period as a "laboratory of criticism"; "happily, concepts, arguments, and doctrines come alive in the work of a great critic in a configuration that is not repeated anywhere else, that is unique and therefore valuable if we value personality and man" (*HC* 3: xiv). Unhappily, Wellek does not usually emphasize the importance of personality and the man in his practical judgments, but consistently judges critics as they approach theoretical excellence. Looking at the chapters of his *History* on English and American criticism, we see that Wellek seems only too eager to hang good Englishmen for being bad Germans, for being insufficiently theoretical. An example of this is Wellek's judgment of the greatest English critics of the early period, Dr. Johnson, Coleridge, and Arnold. Of Dr. Johnson, Wellek says: "He is one of the first great critics who have almost ceased to understand the nature of art, and who, in central passages, treats art as life. He has lost faith in art as the classicists understood it and has not found the romantic faith" (*HC* 1: 79). Johnson's defense of Neoclassicism, particularly his rationalistic conception of metaphor, demonstrates his "incomprehension of the centrally metaphorical character of poetry" (*HC* 1: 99). His didactic criterion of judgment "often becomes a demand for mere moralizing" (*HC* 1: 82). "Johnson does not realize that the requirement of sincere grief in the poet himself . . . does away with three-quarters of the world's literature and introduces the standard of the individual experience of the author, which is both inde-terminable and aesthetically false" (*HC* 1: 80–81). In the light of the trenchancy with which he describes Johnson's failures, it seems somewhat like a civil leer of assent for Wellek to say that "Dr. Johnson's criticism, however, is not defeated by the conflicting theories of realism, moralism, and what is here called abstractionism. The three strands were no doubt reconcilable in his own mind. . . . Johnson wrote valuable analyses of many critical questions" (*HC* 1: 87). If this is true, then Wellek's assumption that critical theory produces good criticism is false; or Wellek simply contradicts himself by labeling Johnson as the worst theorist and best critic of his age.

The most explosive charges Wellek has made against Coleridge are that "most of Coleridge's key terms and distinctions are derived from Germany" (*HC* 2: 156), and that many of his most famous passages are plagiarized directly from Schelling, Schiller, and Schlegel (*HC* 2: 151–55). "His theory of literature is his most impressive achievement," but it suffers from a failure to unify the German Symbolic tradition with the English empirical concern with the pleasure principle and emotionalism, and hence is "fragmentary and derivative" (*HC* 2: 185). "All we have been saying explains why Coleridge is quite disappointing on the level of genre criticism or anywhere in the realm between general theory of poetry and practical criticism" (*HC* 2: 179). Wellek also criticizes Coleridge's practical criticism severely: "Throughout Coleridge's criticism one can find striking formulas and here and there finely phrased poetic appreciations in the manner of Lamb, but the modern reader will again and again be disconcerted by evidences of amazing prudishness, bigotry, and chauvinism" (*HC* 2: 185). So in the end Wellek is reduced to praising Coleridge for his eclecticism, since he helped to transmit German ideas to the obstinately empirical English. Wellek's decision here seems to turn on the choice between bad theory and no theory at all, and he opts ruefully for bad theory: "Coleridge carries enough of the Aristotelian and empirical tradition to make the idealistic elements palatable. His very looseness and incoherence, the wide gaps between his theory and his practice, his suggestiveness, his exploratory mind, his 'inquiring spirit'—these will always appeal to certain apparently permanent features of the Anglo-Saxon tradition" (*HC* 2: 187).

As bad as Coleridge is in his theory, according to Wellek things get worse. In England after 1830, "the idea of a coherent literary theory dis-appears almost completely and with it any technique of analyzing literature and any interest in form. The nature of literature is misunderstood. Literature becomes, for most critics, a purely didactic or emotive activity"

(*HC* 3: 86). "Around 1859 English criticism . . . reached a nadir in its history" (*HC* 4: 141). Though "Arnold, almost singlehandedly, pulled English criticism out of the doldrums" (*HC* 4: 180), and Wellek praises his practical criticism, Arnold fails the theoretical test: "The contradictions in Arnold's concept of poetry and its limitations—the alternatives of mere didacticism or soulful religious seriousness—are connected with Arnold's lack of clarity on such central problems of poetics as the relations between content and form, between totality and local detail. Arnold (like his time in general) has a feeble grasp of the difference between art and reality" (*HC* 4: 167). "The whole theory of the grand style is vitiated by this belief in form apart from meaning" (*HC* 4: 169). Wellek calls Arnold's concept of touchstones "an obvious contradiction of the insight into unity, an atomistic principle that may be used to justify the most willful and erratic prejudices" (*HC* 4: 171), and claims that his "preoccupation with the defence of letters is superfluous and tiresome" (*HC* 4: 156). Moreover, Arnold derives much from the Germans; his defense of culture "is neither novel nor distinctly Arnoldian. One can say that he merely restates the ideal of German *Bildung* as it was formulated by Goethe and Wilhelm von Humboldt" (*HC* 4: 155).

Though these quotations are obviously qualified by some praise and by pages of exposition of doctrine, it seems fair to say that when Wellek makes value judgments, he applies his Kantian standards to English critics and condemns them for being inadequate theorists. It would be tedious to list examples, but Wellek's other chapters on English critics follow the same pattern of exposition and judgment according to such Kantian standards as the aesthetic reality of the literary work, the organic unity of form and content, the avoidance of historicism, relativism, didacticism, and the like. For Wellek, nineteenth-century English criticism is seen as a history of what might be titled "Varieties of Critical Failure"; he remarks with regret that "in England the distrust of the intellect and of any organized knowledge has gone apparently further than in any other country, at least in academic scholarship. Resignation in the face of any more difficult and abstract problem, unlimited skepticism as to the possibilities of a rational approach to poetry, and hence a complete absence of any thinking on fundamental problems of methodology seem to have been characteristic [of the English]" (*CC* 264).

The Kantian standards by which Wellek measures criticism are expressed in history in the criticism of the early German Romantics, particularly the Schlegels. "In the Schlegels and a few critics around them a satisfying theory of poetry was developed which guarded its fences against emotionalism, naturalism, and mysticism and successfully combined symbolism with a profound grasp of literary history. This view seems to me valuable and substantially true even today" (*HC* 2: 3; see also

D 29). In the dark times between the fall of Romanticism and the twentieth century, the great tradition was kept alive by "Taine and Baudelaire in France; De Sanctis in Italy; Nietzsche and Dilthey in Germany; Henry James in the United States. . . . These critics prepared the way for the regeneration that came in the 20th century with Croce, Valery, T. S. Eliot, and many others. . . . Something has been reconstituted in the 20th century that had fallen apart in the 19th: a sense of the unity of content and form, a grasp of the nature of art" (*HC* 3: xiv–xv).

When Wellek gets to T. S. Eliot, whom he calls "by far the most important critic of the twentieth century in the English-speaking world,"[10] his judgment seems almost schizophrenic. On the one hand he maintains his belief in system and asserts that "Eliot has been constantly working at a general theory," that "something very much like a system emerges [from all Eliot's criticism] which defines or describes most central issues of poetic theory" (p. 400). On the other hand he does not demonstrate that Eliot's theory has the theoretical virtue of coherence, but quite correctly says that "in Eliot's theory of criticism there is very little that accounts for what he was engaged in himself so successfully: for his function in changing the taste of the time, in defining and evaluating the usable past, in describing the creative process itself" (p. 405), and that "Eliot has constructed the tradition very selectively; it converges on his own practice as a poet" (p. 442). In these statements Wellek affirms the fact that for Eliot, value is prior to theory, or to put it another way, that Eliot projects his personal and literary values in the realm of literary theory, and that theory as such is not very important in his criticism. As Wellek says, "[Eliot] has buttressed his literary opinions with a theory, which, in spite of its emotionalism, gives a convincing description of the poetic process and a suggestive analysis of the work of art" (pp. 442–43). Wellek's conclusion thus seems to be not that Eliot is a good theorist or a theorist at all, but that Wellek agrees with his opinions and must satisfy his own qualms by calling him theoretical.

Similar difficulties appear in Wellek's treatment of the other major twentieth-century English critics, F. R. Leavis and I. A. Richards.[11] Wellek's differences with Leavis go back to an exchange of views in *Scrutiny* in 1937 (6: 59–70). In "The Literary Criticism of Frank Raymond Leavis," Wellek criticizes Leavis's abrasive personality, the contradiction between his emphasis on linguistic reality and his emphasis on life, the contradiction between his "emphasis on civilized tradition, on [Arnoldian] humanism, and his advocacy of life for life's sake" (p. 189), and says: "I am, I fear, too much of a theorist not to feel strongly the ambiguity, shiftiness, and vagueness of Leavis's ultimate value criterion, Life" (p. 190). He goes on to trace the meanings of "Life" for Leavis as realistic art, English provincial rural tradition, and pedagogical routine, and notes that this accounts for "Leavis's provinciality and insularity" (p. 191). In conclusion he says: "Leavis's gravest failing seems to me his distrust and even hatred for theory: his resolute, complacent, nominalistic empiricism, his worship of the concrete and particular at any price. This allows him to leave his norms unexamined: the standards of life, common speech, centrality, firm grasp of the actual, impersonality, no afflatus, no emotionality" (p. 191). However, when one then compares Wellek's accurate statement that Leavis has "succeeded in defining his taste, identifying the tradition he considers central, and imposing his judgment on his contemporaries" (p. 192), and that he "has succeeded in establishing himself as the most influential English critic of this century after Eliot" (p. 177), the inapplicability and impracticability of Wellek's theoretical standards of judgment again become apparent.

Wellek also criticizes I. A. Richards, not for his lack of interest in theory, but for his erroneous conceptions of it when judged from the Formalist position. He spends most of his essay "On Rereading I. A. Richards" criticizing Richards for violating the intentional and affective fallacies by trying to find the "mode of existence of a work of art in the inaccessible psychic state of its author. . . . [or] in the anarchic variety of any number of readers' responses" (p. 543). He also criticizes Richards for not realizing that literature is a strata of norms (p. 552); for having an overoptimistic Utilitarian view of man which ignores both transcendental realities and tragic experience (p. 538); and for denying the existence of an autonomous aesthetic reality because of his English empirical beliefs (pp. 534–37). According to Wellek, the best thing Richards did was to show (in *Practical Criticism*) the sources of students' misreadings of poetry. Thus, "the stimulus that Richards gave to English and American criticism (particularly Empson and Cleanth Brooks) by turning it resolutely to the question of language, its meaning and function in poetry, will always insure his position in any history of modern criticism" (p. 554).

After the period of domination by the Formalists, Wellek sees a new period of decline. With specific reference to comparative literature, he says in 1965: "The whole enterprise of aesthetics and art is being challenged today; the distinction between the good, the true, the beautiful, and the useful known to the Greeks but most clearly elaborated by Kant, the whole concept of art as one of the distinct activities of man, as the subject matter of our discipline, is on trial" (*D* 48). He ends his survey of "Trends of Twentieth-Century Criticism" with a rejection of the myth criticism and Existentialism that follow Formalism and concludes: "It still seems to me that formalistic, organistic, symbolistic aesthetics, rooted as it is in the great tradition of German aesthetics from Kant to Hegel, restated and justified in French symbolism, in De Sanctis and Croce, has a firmer grasp on the nature of poetry and art. Today it would need a closer collaboration with linguistics and stylistics, a clear analysis of the stratification of the work of poetry to become a coherent literary theory capable of further development and refinement, but it would hardly need a radical revision" (*CC* 363-64; see also *CC* 342). Thus, for Wellek, the good periods of criticism are 1790-1830 and 1935-1955, the periods when Formalist aesthetics were most influential; for him the "New Criticism" is not new at all, but is a restatement of basic German Idealism. His demand for theoretical objectivity seems doubly odd when one recalls his emphasis on criticism as the expression of values and his admission that he expresses in his own work a unique set of values defined by his own personal history, linguistic background, and cultural aspirations. His condemnation of American critics—that "they are open to misunderstanding by the wider public" because of their theoretical inconsistency— contradicts his usual dismissal of the affective criteria of judgment (of Richards and others) and is again refuted by the fact that inconsistent public critics are more widely read than consistent theoretical ones. In the end, it seems that Wellek's theoretical system rests on the assumption that theory is superior in itself in the nature of things, or that literary theory helps to convey the autonomous aesthetic realm at the heart of Wellek's system. For him, literary scholarship, "the confrontation with the objects in their essence," becomes "an act of the imagination, like art itself, and thus a preserver and creator of the highest values of mankind" (*CC* 295). And, as Eliseo Vivas once said about that, "If a man, after learning what is involved [in the aesthetic experience], says to the aesthetician, 'You keep it; I don't want it,' there is no more to be said."[12]

There is enough of the basic Formalist pattern in Wellek to justify regarding him as the leading theoretician of Formalism, "whose basic insights seem to me valid for poetic theory" (*CC* 359). Like other Formalists, he retreats to a world of art; like them, he excludes consideration of artist, audience, or temporal events in his descriptions of the nature of art; like them, he defends a conception of a work of art which reconciles the dualities of form and content in a new organic unity; and like them, the justification for his entire approach is faith, not in God, but in the aesthetic experience as described by Kant. In explicit contrast to them, however, he defends a conception of the universality of literature, at least in the European world, in contrast to the Formalists' defense of regionalism. Moreover, his defense of literature as not essentially a matter of language (*D* 341-42) stands in contrast to the Formalists' emphasis on explication of a unique linguistic structure, and here, of course, his assumptions undermine the greatest practical importance Formalism has had, its method of explication.

Yet there is ambiguity even in this faithful defender of aesthetic reality. In a late essay, "The Fall of Literary History," he says: "I myself have failed in *The History of Modern Criticism* to construct a convincing scheme of [historical] development. I discovered, by experience, that there is no evolution in the history of critical argument, that the history of criticism is rather a series of debates on recurrent concepts. . . . There is no progress, no development, no history of art [or criticism] except a history of writers, institutions and techniques. This is, at least for me, the end of an illusion, the fall of literary history."[13] And when he says further that art "may stand in relation to anything in the past," that the values of art "are created in a free act of the imagination irreducible to limiting conditions in sources, traditions, biographical and social circumstances," not all such choices, presumably, could be based on German idealist aesthetics. If choice is free, if it serves as the basis of the making and hence rewriting of literary history, and of literary criticism, then Wellek has abandoned his standard of the Kantian aesthetic as the measure of the rise and fall in literary criticism in favor of a history of the choices of artists and critics. If so, could the late Wellek—*mirabile dictu*—be coming to a relativistic view of the history of literary opinion similar to that of the history of science of Thomas Kuhn, and to the view of criticism advocated here?

The other massive Formalist contribution to literary theory, W. K. Wimsatt and Cleanth Brooks's *Literary Criticism: A Short History* (1957), represents the extension of the Formalist view of criticism to the entire history of literary criticism and gives a more historical treatment of modern criticism than is provided by the topical arrangement of *Theory of Literature*. The book is not, however, a comprehensive history; rather, it is "a history of ideas about verbal art and about its elucidation and criticism" (*LC* ix). It is not a neutral history but confessedly an argumentative one. Its standard of value is the typical Formalist one that a work of art is best seen as a linguistic object which unites warring dualisms in the new organic unity of the poem. The dominance of this concern with a dualism that is resolved in a work of art is seen in the authors' treatment of the Symbolists; of Yeats's poetry, which has a "real working dualism" (*LC* 606); of Richards's theory that literature causes a synesthesia of opposites in the reader (*LC* 616); of Eliot's transposition of "poetic theory from the axis of pleasure versus pain to that of unity versus multiplicity" (*LC* 665); of Leslie Fiedler's failure to reconcile form and content (*LC* 713); and elsewhere. One also finds in *Literary Criticism* an emphasis on metaphor as the concept which unites the dualistic struggle in a new unity (*LC* 643-46); a defense of complex, ironic poetry (*LC* 646-53); a defense of the organic conception of the poem (*LC* 691); and other typical Formalist concerns. In their summing up, the authors confess the goal toward which they have been pointing: "The kind of literary theory which seems to us to emerge the most plausibly from the long history of the debates is far more difficult to orient within any of the Platonic or Gnostic ideal world views, or within the Manichaean full dualism and strife of principles, than precisely within the vision of suffering, the optimism, the mystery which are embraced in the religious dogma of the Incarnation" (*LC* 746). Thus the end of the theoretical progress of the Formalists is again Christian metaphysics.

From this point of view Wimsatt and Brooks are able to find flaws in every critical position but their own. Occasionally they do this overtly, as when they say of the Realist and Marxist tradition in literary criticism: "In the crudity both of its determination and of its inconsistent propagandism, the socio-realistic tradition of literary criticism has on the whole contributed little to an understanding of the relation which universality bears to individuality in artistic expressions" (*LC* 473). But for the most part, Wimsatt and Brooks qualify the views of their opponents, like the myth critics or the Chicago Critics, or ignore them altogether, as they do Stanley Edgar Hyman and his pluralist approach to criticism and literature.

The fear which all its reviewers express, that the book will be misleading to students who do not know its preconceptions and take it to be "objective," seems to be well founded.[14] But the critical value of the book surely lies in its doing just what its reviewers criticize it for, projecting the literary charter of the present and of the authors onto the past, and making a metaphysical poem of the history of criticism. As Robert Marsh points out, Wimsatt and Brooks find analogies to their position in the most historically unlikely places, and hence they become "Metaphysical" in Dr. Johnson's sense of the word: "nature and art are ransacked for illustrations, comparisons, and allusions; their learning instructs, and their subtlety surprises."[15] Not only does theory become a kind of poetry but it becomes Metaphysical poetry; the wheel of Formalism comes full circle from Eliot to Wimsatt and Brooks, from prophecy to theory, from poem as theory to theory as poem.

Murray Krieger: The Unrevolutionized Critic

The youngest of the Formalist theoreticians, Murray Krieger, is also the most articulate, if by articulate one implies the articulation—the systematic theoretical development—of the precepts he learned in the forties as a student of Eliseo Vivas and John Crowe Ransom. Like them, Krieger is concerned to defend the reality of the poem, but he does so not as a poet who, like Eliot or Tate, implicitly defends the worth of his own poetry, but as an academic theorist whose personal involvement with the subject began in his Ph.D. dissertation. His basic assumption is the philosophical one that poetry is important because it embodies aesthetic experience. "The poem must in one sense, as a special form of discourse, be nonreferential, even as it must be referential to be any form of discourse at all. It must, as organic, be autonomous, even as it illuminates human experience. If it is to be the ground of the integrated, disinterested, even selfless experience I would denominate as aesthetic, the poem must be distinguished by what have been termed [by Eliseo Vivas] 'immanent meanings' " (*NAP* 22). Krieger makes each poem, not poetry as a whole, an aesthetic object with a unique language system. Secure in his faith, he affirms the old Formalist shibboleth of the ideal poem: "The myth of verbal totalization in the poem must assume that every deviation serves a teleological pattern and must be transformed into the indispensable element in it."[16] "As critics we must always expect and hope for the perfection of the work of art."[17] He calls this view "contextualism": "The claim that the poem is a tight, compelling, finally closed context—not reducible to any prior context— leads this theoretical approach to be properly termed 'contextualism' " (*TC* 17). He says that for the contextualist critic "the insistence on closed form, to which his version of unity leads him, dictates that all 'literary openness' be automatically excluded from the realm of the literary valuable (or valid). ... Whenever the critic, after vain efforts at formal synthesis, finds duality between the word and its reference, he charges the work with allegory, a failing that relegates it to crypto-rhetoric ... excluded from the honorific realm of *poesis*. Whenever unformed experience finds its way into the poem in its original, untransformed state, he again sees a violation of the enclosure he requires" (*TC* 20-21).

From Krieger's affirmation of the uniqueness of the language system of particular poems, a nominalistic theory of language follows which denies that words in poetry have meaning as universals, denies that all meaning is found in the language system, because to do so would be to deny the aesthetic uniqueness of the individual poem. "If the poem, as uniquely particular, does give us access to a face of reality to which no other discourse can lead us, then this face of reality, in its particularity, must slip through the universals constructed by our normal propositions" (*CV* 33; see also *TC* 19).

Like Wellek, Krieger finds the source of his aesthetics in the philosophy of Kant, particularly Kant's positing of the realm of the aesthetic (or beautiful) as existing equally with the realms of the good and the true. Krieger thus operates within the long and distinguished tradition of Neo-Kantian philosophical speculation, and the issues and distinctions he finds meaningful are based in this tradition. In *Theory of Criticism* (1976) he says: "It may seem that I am doing little more than, in a retrograde Neo-

Kantian fashion, raising the ghost of Ernst Cassirer" (*TC* 243). In "Literary Analysis and Evaluation—and the Ambidextrous Critic," he begins with Kant's assumption of an aesthetic realm:

Every aspect of the work would contribute to keeping us enclosed within its symbolic world, preventing our escape to the world of reference and action beyond, the world of external relations in which the cognitive and/or the moral tend to preclude the merely aesthetic. We can see how criteria like irony, ambiguity, paradox, tension are given value as means of preventing that escape. From this enclosure of internal relations, at once mutually inhibiting and mutually satisfying, can arise such a series of criteria according to which we can judge the work's efficacy as an *aesthetic* object. [18]

As is apparent here, Krieger values the Formalists' categories of criticism as the ones which make a poem aesthetic. He notes the dependence of the Formalist method on the assumption of the aesthetic reality, but for him "it is enough to let the critic proceed: his circular theoretical assumptions permit him to define what the poem *qua* poem, having a unique and indispensable function, must do insofar as he, as *literary* critic judging its literary (and thus aesthetic) quality, can speak authoritatively about the relative quality of its performance. What he sees and how he judges follow accordingly. Obviously, this is how the contextualist critic has proceeded." [19]

Like the other Formalists, Krieger finds the linguistic basis of a poem's aesthetic uniqueness in its metaphors:

The metaphor, as the formal enabling cause of our vision—its source and its mouth—in the self-enclosure of its extremity, resists all propositional extrapolation. . . . To be metaphor it must insist on the miracle by which things change their nature, become other than themselves, their substance dissolving into other things. So as the metaphor exerts the equal pressure, the unrelenting tightness of a total aesthetic control everywhere within its domain, it creates the vision of the messy center of our experience *becoming* its own purified reduction at the hard edge. [*CV* 29]

Metaphor inevitably leads to religion; like Wimsatt and Brooks, Krieger proceeds to the Incarnation: "As I have argued elsewhere, figuratively (that is, in terms of the *figura*) the Trinitarian paradox is the very model of the poet's farthest claim for metaphor as transubstantiating miracle, with its union-in-duality of tenor and vehicle. . . . *A Window to Criticism* rests almost wholly on an attempt to demonstrate the contextually sustained metaphor as the secular substitute for a theologically sustained transubstantiation" (*CV* 17). In a summarizing note in *Theory of Criticism* he says:

In each of my books I have argued that the metaphor works wholly and miraculously (as a substantive transfer of properties) only while reminding us that, as verbal play, it cannot finally work at all: from the earliest pages of *The New Apologists for Poetry* (Minneapolis, 1956), pp. 17-18, through the treatment of Mann's *Doctor Faustus* in *The Tragic Vision* (New York, 1960), pp. 87-102, until it becomes the informing principle of *A Window to Criticism*. By *The Classic Vision*, pp. 31-32, I concede that 'all poems must covertly contain their anti-poems,' at once committing themselves to their metaphorical reduction and seeing its miracles broken up and dragged to earth. This is, finally, my theme in Chapter 7, above. [*TC* 224, 22]

Echoing Ransom's theological vocabulary and penchant for punning, Krieger finds poetry miraculous: "We indeed accept the poem as present, as the present, and as *a* present, a miraculous gift that seems to exclude all else, . . . [as] that sacramental moment of aesthetic experience, when the entire poem suddenly becomes ours and we are its" (*TC* 209). And he continues to affirm the "the claim to vivid corporeality" of the poem-made-flesh. Without apparent consciousness of the parodic humor of the blasphemy, he says: "But the word-made-form-for-its-fiction's-sake claims neither to find nor to create a world in which to live: it claims no objective teleology, no cosmic purpose, *and* no subjective teleology, no willed purpose [as do "critics of consciousness"]. It claims only the teleology of the word" (*TC* 191). Echoing the seige metaphors of *Sewanee Review* editors, Krieger says: "Fighting to re-create the word as fiction in this last humanistic fastness, the traditional theorist can reclaim for the word, now subverted and reconstituted, the power to make a total form that metaphorically contains a world while it skeptically acknowledges that it contains no more than itself" (*TC* 192). Thus, Formalist theory might be said to have reached its perfection in Krieger, for he has remained true to the same system he learned at the feet of Ransom in the forties and expounded in *The New Apologists for Poetry* in 1956. [20]

Krieger's emphasis on the uniqueness of the poetic object, and its enclosed symbolic world, leads him to the continuing dilemma of whether language and literature are referential or autonomous, correspondent to reality or coherent. This dilemma is expresed in the central conceit of his *A Window to Criticism: Shakespeare's "Sonnets" and Modern Poetics,* where he asks us to consider the poem "(1) as a window to the world, (2) as an enclosed set of endlessly faceted mirrors ever multiplying its maze of reflections but finally shut up within itself, and (3) as this same set of mirrors that miraculously becomes window again after all." [21]

For Krieger, "the poem does not, in the end, turn its back on reality. Instead, it subverts our normal ways of meaning because those ways lead to the dead universals that must also be subverted if we are to break through to the throbbing existence beyond. The poem becomes almost a microcosm of the particularizations that existence offers so profusely" (*TC* 36). Beneath ordinary existence, hidden by universalizing veils of language, lies "the brawling chaos—the jumble of unique instances—that is actually out there (and within us) ready to show its Manichaean face to any who dare thrust the veil aside to look" (*CV* 9).[22] Language is here seen as a veil that hides the true face of reality, since it does not deal with it in all its particularity, and the tragic existent is one who "has pierced the veil and rushes to embrace the consequences of confronting existential extremity" (*CV* 46).

As Krieger's criticism develops, what began as Formalist literary theory becomes a metaphysics when he finds a parallel between the Formalists and existentialists in their hatred of universals. Aesthetic microcosm thus comes to equal social macrocosm. In one discussion, Krieger traces the hatred of universals, the "anti-Platonism" of Ransom and Tate, and their defense of poetry as embodying particularity, the "world's body": "Our very viewing of reality and of language is made to be a moral act. . . . What seems to be the contextualist attack on those who finally allow poems to yield propositional meaning now turns out to be the personalist attack on those who subsume persons and their actions within universal principles of an objective morality."[23] The form of ethical life, then, comes to reflect the tension between universal and particular that the Formalists find in the poem, and linguistic Formalism becomes philosophical Existentialism or Manichaeanism. The concept that linguistic universals obscure reality thus becomes the basis of Krieger's entire ethical system, for if one sees life through universals, one is not seeing it truly, in its true Manichaean character, just as one cannot truly see a poem in terms of other poems.

Krieger develops his aesthetic concerns into "existential" ones most completely in *A Tragic Vision,* where he claims that "this aesthetic, for all its seeming purity, can, through thematic analysis, be pushed back—perhaps where it belongs—into a metaphysic" (*TV* ix). Here, confronting and explicating the duality of tenor and vehicle united in metaphor in the poem becomes the model of response for confronting the Manichaean nature of reality itself. "We can define *thematics* as the study of the experiential tensions which, dramatically entangled in the literary work, become an existential reflection of that work's aesthetic complexity. . . . What is being insisted upon here as Manichaean is not the ultimate nature of metaphysical or noumenal reality so much as the existential nature of that reality which makes itself dramatically available to the poet" (*TV* 243). It should be clear, then, that what Krieger has actually constructed is a cosmology where the microcosm of the poem and the macrocosm of our human existence express the same Manichaean character in a kind of existential, preestablished harmony. He says in *A Tragic Vision*: "I am again reasserting in thematic terms the aesthetic claim that the poetic mode of discourse is extra-propositional. The propositional, then, becomes the discursive equivalent of that 'ethical' substitute for existence, moral philosophy; and the poetic, contextually defined, becomes the discursive equivalent of that existential realization into which the extreme situation propels its victim" (*TV* 246). In criticizing poetry we confront existential reality vicariously. Krieger postulates that "our profoundest literature cannot reach beyond an existential conviction of dualism any more than it can reach to the propositional" (*TV* 260-61). Thus we are led to the study of the same tragic literature which Cleanth Brooks praises for its incorporation of evil because it reflects Manichaean reality: "For I could not see how the tragic is conceivable without the dual vision that lies at its very center" (*TV* viii). For Krieger, the aesthetics of the word leads to the ethics of life; the Formalist charter becomes a new Toryism where one must confront not only the evil of man but the dual face of existence. One must not be a naturalist, one of the "naively optimistic believers in a structured social morality and in social progress"; like Kierkegaard, one must confront "the existential absurdity of the moral life" (*TV* 15), which is "the only authentic attempt at realism" (*TV* 21).

This compulsive dualism, which lacks the final religious unity of the other Formalists, seems to mark most of Krieger's later work; criticism is marked by "play" but also has a "theoretical place." As part of a unique language system poetic language is self-contained, different in kind from prose, but as part of language it is also referential: "There is, on the one hand, then, the unique existential context of cultural forces, and there is, on the other hand, the unique poetic context of the literary work." [24] This facing of the reality of existential conflict is what Krieger sees as the modern tragic vision: "The tragic vision remains what it was, but it can no longer be made through tragedy to yield to an order and a shared religious vision" (*TV* 17).

One possible way to unity is through affirmation of the existential dualism of literature and the positing of an aesthetic unity. As Krieger says of *Moby Dick*, "It leads us to an aesthetic wholeness rather than to a higher Christianity" (*TV* 254). But aesthetic wholeness, which "has forced into a perceptual union the cleavages which, in existence, remain asunder," is "an aesthetic delusion, since the wholeness has not dissolved or resolved or even relaxed the ineluctable tensions that the vision of the work has generated" (*CV* 37). Krieger considers a religious resolution in the final chapter of *A Tragic Vision*, making specific reference to Wimsatt and Brooks's *Short History*, but he draws back from their resolution of the question of whether literature is "closed" or "open" in the moral order of the Incarnation (see also *CV* 40-41).

Krieger finally reconciles the dualism he finds at the heart of literature and life in the "classic vision." Comparing the tragic and the classic vision, he says: "They both turn upon a view of the existential trap *as* trap, of the face of reality as fearfully and maddeningly Manichaean. ... But while the tragic confronts and even embraces extremity, ... [the classic] is enabled, that is, at once to see it as extremity and not to choose it. Knowing what extremity is and means, the classic vision chooses to reject it, to turn, in mature acceptance, away from it toward the wholly compromised human condition" (CV 4).

In The Classic Vision, Krieger sees the classic existent, like Wordsworth's leech gatherer, Dostoevsky's peasant women, or Faulkner's Lena Grove, as one who exists without self-consciousness (CV 44). The classic visionary, like the tragic visionary, faces the extremity of life and reality, but unlike him rejects it in favor of a catholic embrace of the dualities of life as it is. Thus the linguistic veil that conceals reality for the merely ethical person and becomes rent for the tragic visionary is refashioned into a canopy (CV 48)—the artist as tentmaker. Seeing existential reality, the classic visionary embraces the illusion of language, for "it is an illusion he sees as fostered by the bond of our common humanity in our common history" (CV 48).

In this reconciliation of a stubbornly maintained dualism by sleight of hand, word play, and poetic allusion, Krieger is a true student of Ransom's. The classic visionary rejects extremity through "the worship of bloodless abstractions" (Pope and Dr. Johnson); "the embrace of the natural human community" (Wordsworth and George Eliot); "the acceptance of the human barnyard" (Gulliver, Walter Shandy, and All the King's Men); and the "posing of an alternative to sainthood" (Murder in the Cathedral, Light in August). The place of the critic in all this is that of a poet manqué who confronts poetry as the poet confronts existential reality, living a vicarious life through the criticism of literature: "The poet explores his freedom in his affectionate toying, his love play with the world's body. The critic must follow in a similar spirit, disdaining the ideological adaption, the propositional use of poems; he rather must play with them as converted objects of his love that deserve no less than his unwilful, sportive resting among them. ... The contextualist critic ... follows the poet in the free—yet imitative—play that makes his activity creative as well."[25] What all this means for the critic is that he "must create his own dialogue of dialogues fed by the tragic and classic dialogues of our literary visionaries. ... By partaking of the dialogues and standing atop them, thanks to our visionaries who worked through them, the critic pursues his literary discipline of thematics, which becomes another term for dialogistics. ... We ourselves, even less bold than our cautious literary visionaries, dare not give up the ethical as our order of existence; but we are forever newly broadened by our dialogistic visions and the dialogue we conduct among them" (CV 51-52). The reader of criticism thus confronts literary reality only thirdhand in this Plato's cave of criticism.

However, one may object to Krieger's assumption that one can experience literary works directly, without the intervention of categories.

Krieger concedes "the practical impossibility of keeping criticism inductive, of keeping taste out of it, once we first concede—in a post-Kantian manner—the constitutive role of our categories of perception in conditioning all we experience."[26] Yet he believes ultimately in the aesthetic experience as a state that exists "in advance of actual experiences." "So I *can* say, once we have agreed about the defining qualities of this [aesthetic] experience as an *a priori*, analytic type, that certain objects can be seen and described as being so constructed as to produce it in us, provided we are willing, and knowledgeable enough, to submit."[27] The difficulty—which Krieger admits as a possibility (*TC* 21, 32)—is that if one does not admit the existence of an unmediated aesthetic experience, if being "willing, and knowledgeable" implies an elaborate system of moral, linguistic, cultural, philosophical, and intellectual categories of various kinds, then Krieger's system must lose its preferred status and become another possible response among many. Thus Krieger demonstrates with great diligence and articulation what occurs when one takes the aesthetic experience of the word as the charter of one's literary theory. Certainly if one takes the view of Thomas S. Kuhn and others outlined above, one must so regard it.

The point at issue is whether there is a reality, literary or physical, which exists apart from the critic or scientist and can be known directly by him. Krieger often expresses belief in such a reality: "Though the work seems to exist for us only as our categories permit it to be defined, only as our commonplace generic symbols reduce and distort its unique symbolic structure—still there must be something in the work as it must exist (or subsist?), on its own outside our categorical structures and symbols. This something can force our structures and symbols to work radical transformations upon themselves."[28] For Krieger, the critic's charter is ultimately determined by his contact with an objective literary reality. Kuhn, in contrast, emphasizes that the world cannot be known directly, that "paradigm changes do cause scientists to see the world of their research-engagement differently. In so far as their only recourse to that world is through what they see and do, we may want to say that after a revolution scientists are responding to a different world."[29] For Krieger, the change from geocentric cosmology to heliocentric cosmology must be determined by direct observation of the world; for Kuhn, the change from the Shelley of Brooks to that of Bloom is determined by the paradigms of the critic. Only if one believes in unmediated experience does Krieger's theory stand, and it is on this point that the reader must accept or reject his view.

In his latest struggle with the issue of whether the aesthetic quality of objects exists objectively in the objects, Krieger admits that "we are responsible for creating all our experiences, and thus for constituting the object on our horizon" (*TC* 14); therefore we project our aesthetic responses into them. But he then says that "as readers and critics, we must operate as if there were a difference between an object that we are convinced has not within itself the capacity to authorize the aesthetic experience . . . and an object that can exhibit those characteristics which will permit others to respond aesthetically, as we have" (*TC* 15). The aesthetic quality of Krieger's object, which he admits is created out of our experience of it, thus exists only as a function of his desire: "As critics, we must have an object out there for us to talk about, independently of this single experience of it, even if all we can actually do is add other discrete experiences of it to this one. So, out of his experiences of the object, the critic must postulate an object-in-experience. Indeed, he constitutes it as an object-*for*-experience; that is, he constitutes an object made to produce the experience whose ground he can claim to find in *it*" (*TC* 15). This later assumption of the innate aesthetic quality of objects is even less convincing than it was in 1956, considering the history of painting since then and the rise of pop art and Andy Warhol's soup can, which clearly show the transformation of the nonaesthetic object into the aesthetic.

A related ambivalence in Krieger's thought is that sometimes he recognizes that there is only a personal basis for his aesthetic response to poetry, and hence for his assertions about theory, while at other times, like Wellek and Brooks, he wishes to assert his conclusions as objective truth because he believes that an aesthetic quality exists objectively in the poem. Early in *The New Apologists* he discusses the theory he has derived from his own experiences in reading poetry: "Since I have had this kind of poetic experience, . . . I prefer to reject the [referential] theory rather than the most valued and most intimate phases of my psychological history" (*NAP* 20–21; see also *TV* 243). He then says: "If one should ask about the legitimacy of other poetics needed to justify other possible experiences of the poem, I can hardly outlaw them. I prefer, at least tactically, to take refuge in my private interest. . . . Nor will we for a moment insist on the truth-value or even the meaningfulness of the assumptions we use. . . . No one, then, must for a moment suspect that I shall be making a single objective claim" (*NAP* 19–20). In a later chapter, however, he writes: "The theory of the poetic object entered upon in this section presupposes that as aesthetic object, the poem is an independent entity containing aesthetic value. . . . the objectivity of value, hardly a universally accepted view today, has been assumed" (*NAP* 156). Despite occasional *apologia*, Krieger usually maintains the latter position, and claims to be, or to be trying to be, the Ideal Reader, who in Krieger's view considers his personally based theory to be objective truth.

There are also some practical difficulties in applying Krieger's theory to literature. One problem, related to his affirmation that each literary work has a unique language system which gives us unmediated access to aesthetic reality, is that a great deal of his practical criticism is based on translations—that is, on works translated out of the unique language system of the German of Kafka or Mann, the French of Gide, Malraux, or Camus, or the Italian of Silone—into another unique language system, that of the English used by the translator. Thus Krieger is either implicitly confessing that a language system is not unique to a work of literature, if translations are the same as the original, or he is saying that we are dealing with distortions of the unique literary work if translations are not the same.

Another practical objection which must be made is that Krieger always speaks of literature in general as poems or poetry, and of authors as poets. Though he explicitly defines poetry as all aesthetic and imaginative works (*TC* 3), in fact many of his remarks are sensible only when applied to lyric poets. For example, at one point, while distinguishing the poet from the historian, he says that the historian's need for "evidence" "suggests a criterion, a need for support, for empirical relevance, that is foreign to the poet in his freer creativity" (*TC* 155). This is true perhaps for a lyric poet, but it is not true for most novelists, as Ian Watt demonstrates in his *The Rise of the Novel* when he shows how the novelist follows not only historical but the more narrowly legal notions of evidence.

One may also object that though Krieger's theory is based on the uniqueness of each literary object, his own criticism is thesis-bound in the extreme. Unlike Cleanth Brooks, he chooses works which fit his thesis, not representative works, and the thesis sometimes distorts the works. For example, in his treatment of Dr. Johnson's "Vanity of Human Wishes" he says that "Johnson's excellently consistent management of his artificialities and his abstractions is a way of mediating the intensities of experience, of preventing himself from indulging them; that what is so studiously left out of his poem asserts its effect *upon the poet* by the very studiousness of his omission" (*CV* 134, italics added). It is a commonplace of Johnsonian studies that Johnson's formality, and the formality of the period and the period style, are a defense against disorder, or Existential horror as Krieger would put it; but for Johnson, abstract poetic style is a way of expressing, not concealing, experience: "From Marlb'rough's eyes the streams of dotage flow, / And Swift expires, a driv'ler and a show" (ll. 317-18). The conflict in the poem is not between unexpressed horror and linguistic abstractions, but between the expressed, historically inevitable horrors of life and Christianity: " Enquirer, cease, petitions yet remain, / Which heav'n may hear, nor deem religion vain" (ll. 349-50). For Johnson, Latin restraint does not conceal but reveals.

Similarly, Krieger distorts the historical meaning of Jane Austen's *Pride and Prejudice* by importing his Existential standard of reality into this pre-Existential world: "We must wonder how much this society is worth, with its values that she so pervasively satirizes. Are these superficial idols . . . in their turn worth the sacrifice of that interiority—that consciousness of an isolated self—before which they would crumble?" (*CV* 231). For Krieger, Austen's world contains a "hardly impressive set of social values" (*CV* 242) which fail to reach the true classic, in his definition, because she avoids, rather than confronts, the existential reality: "Austen's is a precious world, preserved by the *a priori* exclusion of what she dares not allow to disturb it. It precludes, rather than rejects, extremity" (*CV* 242). But surely it is riding a thesis to judge the English bourgeoisie as petty, superficial, unimpressive, and precious just because Austen does not define "reality" as Kierkegaard did (according to Krieger's view of him). Austen's bourgeoisie is far more historically "real" than any Existentialist, and her novel is an admirable one, since at the end her characters are judged not by the standards of a deficient social structure based on rank, but by intelligence and morality; at the end both the Wickhams and Lady Catherine are excluded, and "the comfort and elegance of their family party at Pemberley" includes the Gardiners as well as the others to the proper moral degree. If this is not the classic vision, where is classicism to be found?

But the most telling historical objection that can be made to Krieger as a theorist in the seventies is that his defense of the Existentialism and New Critical poetics of the forties is now irrelevant to further critical developments. In the sixties, Krieger devotes considerable effort both to admitting that Formalism is dead and to saving the theoretical part of it that concerns him most. In "After the New Criticism" he admits that some Formalists are too anxious to deny the changes time has brought and the decay of Formalism, but he asserts that Formalism "has a serious and continuing claim to our theoretical interest and respect." "The New Critical movement leaves behind it notions that will never allow us to look at poetics again in the old way"; but it will be "a still significant shaping force in what is to come after."[30]

Krieger's assertion of the continuing relevance of Formalism is, however, only a matter of hope, not of evidence, and his awareness of this fact leads him to some rueful *apologia*. He admits in the preface to the paperback edition of *The New Apologists* in 1962 that "when I completed this study in 1955, the living moment I was examining was, perhaps more than I then realized, just about a completed entity. Time was running out on its vitality. . . . My own struggles with it and the frustrating conclusions in theoretical dead ends to which it seemed from every direction to lead may have been indications of the death it had to die" (*NAP* vii). Sometimes he is hopeful: "So long as we also think of it [criticism] as a discipline, we must try to guard whatever normative and sharable element may yet be saved out of the critical procedure."[31] In 1966 he admits defeat: "But the recent defenders of literary openness, romantically embattled and self-consciously undisciplined, have insisted on an alternative kind of voice for literature, the instinctual voice. ... [I assume] the desirability of closedness, of integrity [of the poem] without proving the claim at its foundation. To attempt a justification of what has seemed so obvious for so long, to meet head-on its recently arisen alternative, its restless, chaos-seeking, brawling antagonist, is beyond my interest as it is beyond my daring" (*PP* ix). In 1969 he sees himself as part of the past: "Let me admit that I offer myself as a new offshoot of that contextualist movement, now perhaps deservedly displaced among those doing our most adventurous theoretical probings."[32] And finally, in *Theory of Criticism*, he says: "If postmodernism sees such [aesthetic] claims as quaintly obsolete, swept aside by the deluge of three or four decades of bloody living and dying, then I write this book as the postscript to a dead past" (*TC* 33).

Krieger is, of course, aware of subsequent theorists and attempts to relate his thinking to theirs. In the introduction to *Northrop Frye in Modern Criticism* (1966) he discusses Frye; in "Literary Analysis and Evaluation" he considers the theory of E. D. Hirsch, Jr.; in *The Classic Vision* (pp. 10-16) he discusses Georges Poulet; in "Mediation, Language, and Vision in Literature" he refutes Geoffrey Hartman and Ihab Hassan; and in "Poetics *Re*constructed: The Presence vs. the Absence of the Word" (pp. 352-62) he discusses Structuralism and Derrida. But none of these critics, or Jonathan Culler, Fredric Jameson, J. Hillis Miller, Robert Scholes, or Edward W. Said, among others, ever mention Krieger or confront his theory in their work, since his theories from the past are irrelevant to their developing thought. At issue here is the basic question of the historical relationship of intellectual movements. Krieger's implicit view is that one movement derives logically and historically from another, so that his Formalism can be related to movements that come after it. The view of Kuhn, and the view maintained in this book, is that the change in movements involves a "critical revolution," a shift in paradigms or charters, so that the new movement is not, and *cannot* be, related to the old, since the new movement asks different questions, expresses a different charter, uses different critical procedures.

Krieger's position, then, is that of the man at the height of his powers who is out of fashion and hence largely uninfluential even as he talks about the decline of the movement of which he is the last spokesman. His failure is a reflection not of his ability but of his choice; it is a historical failure. He is a classic case of the man born too late, in 1923, which makes him three years younger than *The Sacred Wood* and brings him to critical maturity and the writing of his widely praised book on Formalism in that movement's final hours. His problem is that of the man who finds no period when his career time and charter time fruitfully coincide, and pending an unlikely conversion, he remains unrevolutionized, our best example of the superannuated critic. Because the standard of truth is more ambiguous in criticism than in science, the fate of the superannuated critic is kinder than that of the superannuated scientist, who is "read out of the profession." But intellectually the two are in much the same position with regard to the ideas of the moment. As one surveys the Formalists, with Eliot, Ransom, Tate, Blackmur, Winters, and Wimsatt all gone, Krieger seems to be in much the situation of Justice Shallow: "Jesu, Jesu, the mad days that I have spent! and to see how many of my old acquaintance are dead" (*2 Hen*. IV, III, ii, 37).

The Obsolescence of Formalism

When one sums up the contributions and qualities of the Formalist theoreticians, the following points seem central: (1) Despite occasional differences, they express consistently the charter we have labeled Tory Formalism. (2) For over two decades they have been in possession of the field of literary theory mostly by default; if one wanted to study the theory of literature or criticism in English, until now one had to go to Wellek, Wimsatt, Brooks, and Krieger. (3) The Formalists take themselves very seriously indeed, as seen in Wellek's scorn for the relativist; Krieger's disdain for "the self-deceptions of our John Dewey's: those of our insistent naturalists who ... are yet naively optimistic believers in a structured social morality and in social progress" (*TV* 14-15); or Wimsatt's contempt for "amateur" critics like Leslie Fiedler: "The only reservation the theorist need have about such critical impressionism, or expressionism, is that, after all, it does not carry us very far in our cogitation about the nature and value of literature. It is not a very mature form of cognitive discourse" (*HCo* xvi-vii; cf. *VI* 28-31). Theirs is a tragic vision, somewhat melodramatically conceived, in which there is very little room for humor, foible, or folly, and as life departs from it, it becomes necessary (but a little tedious) to read it as part of the history of criticism.[33]

And life is departing; in the late fifties the decline of Formalism as an active and vital intellectual force becomes apparent in the gradual decline of interest in its conservative charter, in the distinctions it uses, and in the questions it is prepared to answer. The turning point comes in about 1956 or 1957 (insofar as cultural shifts can be exactly dated), with the publication of Northrop Frye's *Anatomy of Criticism* and Allen Ginsberg's *Howl*. With Frye and Ginsberg, critical interest shifts to "myth criticism" as a better grounding for the need to believe, and poetic interest moves away from the "academic" poets, who write the kind of tightly controlled, ironic verse that the Formalists favor, to the looser, more bardic tradition of Whitman. The contrast can be seen clearly in the mutually exclusive contents of two anthologies of poetry—Hall, Pack, and Simpson's *The New Poets of England and America* (1957) and Donald Allen's *The New American Poetry, 1945-1960* (1960). This is only to assert the principle of obsolescence: critical questions are never refuted but are changed when they are no longer of interest. After the melancholy reflection that readers no longer seem convinced by his arguments, Wimsatt says in 1968 in his retrospective review "Genesis: A Fallacy Revisited": "There is no way to keep the simpler kinds of intention-hunters from jumping on the vehicle of literary inquiry . . . but at the precise level of abstraction and definition at which Mr. Beardsley and I argued the question, I do not see that any notable revision is required, or even any very emphatic repetition."[34] Wimsatt is right, of course, but his observation is beside the point because the movement of criticism is temporal, not logical, and critical values will change whether arguments are right or wrong.

In the literary culture of the sixties and seventies, Formalist values come to seem totally irrelevant to almost everyone except the original Formalists and the converts they made in their heyday. In critical books like Leo Marx's *The Machine in the Garden* (1964), Susan Sontag's *Against Interpretation* (1965), N. O. Brown's *Love's Body* (1968), Ronald Berman's *America in the Sixties: An Intellectual History* (1968), Theodore Roszak's *The Making of a Counter Culture* (1969), and Morris Dickstein's *Gates of Eden: American Culture in the Sixties* (1977), there is no mention of any of the Formalists or any of their concerns. The wheel of fortune has turned so far that Edward W. Said, reviewing Cleanth Brooks's *A Shaping Joy* and Ransom's *Beating the Bushes* in 1972, can say: "It is hard to know what in either contemporary literature or contemporary criticism can prepare the reader adequately for these two books. . . . Perhaps it is that the books somehow lack a context, as if their authors' great fame depended on arguments and audiences not now readily heard or seen. . . . The unfamiliarity, to me at least, of the audience being addressed and the issues being debated gives the central polemic in these essays its frequent air of energetic lostness. . . . The New Critics present today's reader with the muddle of intense amateurism hooked to semiprofessionalism."[35]

The still-active Formalists sturdily resist these new critical forces. In "The Attack on Literature," René Wellek discusses the politicizing of literature by Louis Kampf, the "literature of silence" of Susan Sontag and others, and Marshall McLuhan's fascination with the media and populat art, and defends again distinctions of quality based on aesthetic judgments (though it is unclear how his tracing of the history of the words "literature," "poetry," etc., supports his belief). According to Wellek:

In understanding these lexical distinctions we shall be able to reject the wholesale attack on literature: the political attack, which makes literature a reactionary force although it obviously can be and has been the opposite; the linguistic attack, which despairs of the very possibility of speech; and the antiaesthetic attack, which revolts against quality and form in favor of subliterature or the impersonal permutations of the computer. . . . Predictions of the end of literacy, of the triumph of television, should make us more aware of the need of a literary culture. The new barbarism, the know-nothingism, the mindless repudiation of the past in favor of so-called "relevance"—one trusts that these are only a passing mood of this country and decade of ours.[36]

In "Day of the Leopards," W. K. Wimsatt seems almost to give in to the irrationality of the sixties. After paralleling quotations by critics approving of violence and irrationality with journalistic accounts of such forces being acted out in murders, bombings, and the student takeover at Columbia, he says:

Large portions of our major cities are destroyed of a summer—in fulfillment of prophecies uttered by liberal voices in the spring. Our campuses become places of privilege for a repertory of violence ranging from incivility through hoodlum trespass and vandalism to armed banditry. These are the platitudes of an escalating history of outrage. If the leopards break into the temple often enough, according to the parable by Kafka, in time their violence becomes accepted as part of the rite. . . . At this moment in our history, it may be difficult to say which affects the other more strongly:—on the one hand, the art of negation produced by the advance guard of sophisticates, the end-game drama of absurdity, blackness, cruelty, destruction, the so-called "Living Theater," and the new "young poets" of the "guerilla" school; and on the other hand, the debased folk art of the red-neck Dallas flysheets, the tragic mythopoeist with the Mannlicker-Carcano rifle, the Evergreen poets of the revolver, the brickbat, and the [Molotov] cocktail.[37]

Wimsatt concludes in despair: poetry and the university have become a "sanctuary for the intolerable," Nero fiddles, the best lack all conviction. Though he wrote the essay in 1969, he seems to hold to the same opinion in 1976 in the preface to *The Day of the Leopards*: "When institutions are crumbling, when chaos surges at the gates, art can only record the event it has perhaps helped to bring on—sometimes with an accent of guileless impotence, sometimes pathetically, wringing its hands. Art has no remedies."[38]

Wimsatt is forgivably pessimistic in 1969, but somewhat blindly so in 1976, after five years of quiet in the universities and a large cultural shift away from irrationalism and violence. What actually happens in the seventies is conducted on an academic and theoretical plane, and consists largely in ignoring the terms, concerns, and values of the Formalists and in favoring the newly fashionable Continental movements in criticism—the Phenomenologists, Critics of Consciousness, and Structuralists. The new men ignore Tory Formalism with its invincibly Anglo-American character, seek with Geoffrey Hartman to go "beyond Formalism," or occasionally curtly dismiss a Formalist in passing, as does Jonathan Culler: "Although

Brooks and others have found tension and paradox in poetry of all sorts, the theory fails as an account of the nature of poetry because one can find similar tension in language of any kind."[39] The theories of practical critics like Winters, Blackmur, Tate, and Ransom have dropped beneath theoretical notice, while Eliot is sometimes mentioned for his poetry and Wimsatt is sometimes taken to task by new sympathizers of Romanticism. The gestalt has shifted, a critical revolution has occurred, and Formalism is finished as an active force among contemporary theorists.

Theoretically, Formalism is dead, but on the practical level, particularly in academic classrooms and in journals devoted to discussions of individual works of literature, it flourishes. E. D. Hirsch, Jr., says in 1973 that, despite pleas from social, psychological, and historical critics for greater recognition of their disciplines, "the calls have not been answered on a big scale because so far they have not been followed by counterproposals that can compete with New Criticism in intellectual stature or practical effectiveness. On a practical level, for example, these counterproposals do not imply educational goals sufficiently definite to form the basis of textbooks and teaching guides like *Understanding Poetry*."[40] If one adopts the view that Formalism is basically a displaced Protestantism, then its continuing success may be due to its conformity to the dominant Protestantism of the country. In a sense it is America's first indigenous literary criticism, and as long as it continues to seem natural to study the Word of God and listen to sermons expanding upon a sacred text, treating literature in the same way will probably continue to flourish. The practice of explication is also compatible with the idea of culture which is at the intellectual base of the American university system, and the evangelical tone and emphasis on discipline associated with much Formalist writing also serve to strengthen the use of literature for cultural self-improvement. With such permanent support in the social institutions of the country, it seems unlikely that Formalism will vanish as quickly as the more narrowly based charter of the New York Intellectuals. Formalism's struggle with the forces of irrationality in the sixties seems, then, much like the struggle between anti-Puritans and Puritans in the twenties, a struggle which Puritanism never wins, but in which it is never vanquished.

One can say, generally, that Formalism lives now in the careers of its practitioners, many of whom have outlived the flowering of the movement, and of their students, and that it is likely to be believed in by, or to have been part of the development of, any literary person who came of age intellectually from 1935 to 1955. Despite the demise of the *Kenyon Review* and the Indiana School of Letters, aging Formalists still have outlets for their essays and reminiscences in the *Southern* and *Sewanee Reviews*, and in new magazines run by their disciples, such as Radcliffe Squires's *Michigan Quarterly Review*. And most astonishing of all, Formalism, conveniently divorced from its historical context, is becoming fashionable in England and on the Continent. In an article which seems uninformed of the progress of American criticism, David Pole finds that Formalism "subsists, in a large sense, as the reigning orthodoxy."[41] The French journal *Poetiqué* has published several articles dealing with Formalism, notably Keith Cohen's "Le New Criticism aux États-Unis (1935–50)."[42] Formalism thus assumes a place in the history of responses to literature somewhere between Parrington and Frye, in what will probably come to be called, without irony, the Age of Eliot. The Formalists' easily teachable method of explication and their control of jobs and magazines combined to create a solid literary power structure which dominated the American literary life of their time. As Margot Hentoff recalls, "It is no exaggeration to say that in the late '40's and early '50's, for the hippest of the young (even among those who were beginning to be beat) the best thing in the world to be was T. S. Eliot or Edmund Wilson. Literary criticism was the philosophers' stone."[43]

Part III
New York Intellectuals:
The Bourgeois Avant-Garde

7. The Essential Dialectic: Reality versus Imagination

The only way one can begin to talk sensibly about literary criticism in New York City is to make one's way through *Making It* and other accounts by interested parties to a more basic intellectual reality. The point is not to criticize Norman Podhoretz's book, which has suffered enough,[1] but to point to its essential inaccuracy as literary history, quite apart from its merits as confession or exposé.

The first problem is one of focus, which is closely related to Podhoretz's attempt to categorize the New York Intellectuals as a Jewish family. A minor error is his assumption that there are three "generations" of intellectuals, which leads Podhoretz into a mania of genealogical categorization reminiscent of Vance Packard's *The Status Seekers* or *Esquire*'s July 1963 charts of the "red-hot center" of literary life. All the criticisms Harold Rosenberg made in 1958 of Podhoretz's attempt to distinguish his mature, family-oriented generation from the older, alienated, ex-Red Marxists still apply. Rosenberg says: "When I first encountered this 'Marxist' generation in the mid 'thirties it already had its present character; it was, in its own terms, 'responsible' and 'mature' and opposed to personal radicalism and Bohemian life. . . . Today's younger generation of intellectuals consists of the late arrivals to the generation that made its appearance as American 'Marxists' and which has lived its entire life with Marxism" (*TN* 250). Socially, as ex-Marxists, and as defenders of a single tradition of modern literature, the group which Podhoretz describes has a single character, is a single entity, whatever one may think it is.

The more important misconception is Podhoretz's attempt to categorize the New York Intellectuals as a Jewish family. Other writers echo Podhoretz's claim. In a symposium on "New York and the National Culture," Irving Howe says: "These things are hard to measure objectively. Still, do we not all feel in our bones that for good and/or bad something of the moral fervor, the polemical fury, the passion for idea and ideology that prevailed among the New York writers had its roots in secular and no doubt pre-secular Jewish life?"[2] In his account "The New York Intellectuals," Howe says: "I am working on the premise that in background and style there was something decidedly Jewish about the intellectuals who began to cohere as a group around the *Partisan Review* in the late 30's—and one of the things that was 'decidedly Jewish' was that most were of Jewish birth!" (*DN* 215).

One very important difficulty that neither of these writers mentions is that Jews differ culturally; this fact is important here because (as E. Digby Baltzell shows in *The Protestant Establishment*) the lives, values, and careers of German, Russian, and other Jews vary enormously, as does American reaction to them. Podhoretz himself brings up a second difficulty of his hypothesis: "Of course the metaphor of a Jewish family runs into certain difficulties of its own, for several core members (Dwight Macdonald, Mary McCarthy, F. W. Dupee, William Barrett, Elizabeth Hardwick, John Thompson, James Baldwin, and the late Richard Chase) and a few kissing cousins (Robert Lowell, Ralph Ellison, John Berryman, Kempton himself, Michael Harrington, the late James Agee, and the late William Troy) were not Jewish at all. Nevertheless, the term Jewish can be allowed to stand by clear majority rule and by various peculiarities of temper I shall try to describe" (*MI* 83). Considered genetically, then, the New York Intellectuals are only partly or questionably Jewish, but considered formally, there is nothing identifiably "Jewish" about their work at all, no "peculiarity of temper" which can be related to their existence as Jews, as opposed to their existence as New Yorkers, or educated men, or journalists, or political beings.

Podhoretz nowhere isolates what he considers to be the formal qualities of Jewish writing, but he does mention that because of "the feeling that a book is something special, belonging to a different class of phenomena from articles or lectures," the family's "characteristic form has been the short piece": "Like the Talmudic scholars who were surely numbered among their forefathers, they not only regard books as holy objects but, haunted by what was perhaps the most ferociously tyrannical tradition of scholarship the world has ever seen, they seem to believe that one must have mastered everything before one is entitled to the temerity of saying anything on paper" (*MI* 198). It is unclear here whether Podhoretz is distinguishing between Talmudic books and intellectual articles, in which case the Intellectuals would not be "Jewish" in their essays; or whether, as seems more likely, he is paying a false historical compliment to the Intellectuals' standard of scholarship. In either case, as its history from Addison to Eliot demonstrates, the critical essay is not proved to be a "Jewish" form, nor is New Testament or Formalist explication "Jewish."

Alfred Kazin tries to isolate as the formal quality of Jewish writing its concern with a particular theme: "Just as it was Southern writers, with their knowledge of defeat and their instinctive irony, who in the 40's spoke to the chastened American mind, so it is Jewish writers who now [1966] represent to many Americans the unreality of their prosperity and the anxiety of their condition."[3] However it may apply to fiction, "Jewishness" is irrelevant to criticism, irrelevant to the "key book on Matthew Arnold and to the definitive biographies of Henry Adams, Henry James, James Joyce" which Kazin rightly cites as monuments of scholarship by Jews.

Another claim for a parallel between Jewishness and the Intellectuals' criticism is made by Isaac Rosenfeld in 1944: "But the position of Jewish writers—artists and intellectuals in general—is not entirely an unfortunate one. For the most part the young Jewish writers of today are the children of immigrants, and as such—not completely integrated in society and yet not wholly foreign to it—they enjoy a critical advantage over the life that surrounds them. They are bound to observe much that is hidden to the more accustomed native eyes. The insight available to most Jewish writers is a natural result of their position in American life and culture. Jews are marginal men."[4] But since non-Jews also are immigrants here, and since the exclusion of Jews from parts of Anglo-Saxon society is forced on them, while the alienation of the intellectual from all bourgeois society is voluntary, marginality is not uniquely Jewish, and again the parallel seems forced.[5]

It is more likely that the actual state of affairs for these critics is somewhat like that described by Lionel Trilling, who says that although "it is never possible for a Jew of my generation to 'escape' his Jewish origin," nevertheless "I cannot discover anything in my professional intellectual life which I can specifically trace back to my Jewish birth and rearing. I do not think of myself as a 'Jewish writer.' I do not have it in mind to serve by my writing any Jewish purpose. I should resent it if a critic of my work were to discover in it either faults or virtues which he called Jewish."[6] For Podhoretz and Howe, then, the "Jewish" Intellectual is a product of definition; all the people one wishes to call "Intellectuals" are Jewish or "Jewish by proxy," while the people one does not wish to call Intellectuals are excluded whether or not they are Jewish. Furthermore (as Howe points out [*DN* 217]) the model of all these "Jewish" Intellectuals is Edmund Wilson, whose voice (as Podhoretz points out) "has always been the voice of the old Anglo-Saxon America" (*DU* 34). One must conclude that the attempt to categorize the accomplishment of the New York Intellectuals as "Jewish" is mistaken.

What we do have in the Intellectuals, as one (and only one) part of

New York literary culture, is a group of men and women whose intellectual life is defined in terms of a dialectic or tension between social reality and avant-garde tastes. On the one hand they acknowledge the reality of society, defined in quasi-Marxian terms as the struggle of classes, the importance of economic motives, the existence of institutions, and (as Trilling defined the reality of Dreiser): "material reality, hard, resistant, unformed, impenetrable, and unpleasant" (*LI* 10–11). In this half of their concern, the Intellectuals are essentially bourgeois and realistic in a way which is fully supportive of their own economic interests and the interests of the capitalist state. The literary half of their intellectual life, however, is defined by the idea of the avant-garde, which as Renato Poggioli has shown in his *The Theory of the Avant-Garde,* is marked by its antagonism toward bourgeois culture, its compulsive desire to make cultural fashion, and its defense of the avant-garde, "modernist" tradition in literature and art. Hence, the Intellectuals are essentially cultural middlemen, and the group's charter involves a dialectic or tension between these two forces as they have developed during the last forty years (see chart on pp. 214–15).

This charter is understandable only "genetically," in terms of a historical trauma which marked the Intellectuals for life. In brief, these Intellectuals come of age in Marxist circles in the New York of the thirties and define themselves intellectually in relation to the futuristic and radical politics of that time. As Irving Howe puts it, "The Movement was my home and passion, the Movement as it ranged through the various left-wing anti-Communist groups."[7] However, this political ardor was soon destroyed by the inescapably totalitarian events in Russia, chiefly the Moscow trials from 1936 to 1938, when Stalin killed hundreds of thousands of his countrymen, and by the Nazi-Soviet pact of 1939, which wedded Marxism with the Fascist persecutor of the Jews.[8] The result was the death of Marxism in Intellectual circles in America for thirty years. The important result of this shift for literary criticism is the displacement of what was originally a political radicalism onto literature, which can be seen clearly in the change that takes place in the *Partisan Review* from 1936 to 1937. All the revolutionary expectations of the Intellectuals' early years are sublimated into a defense of "modernist" literature, and their geographical Utopia becomes Bohemia, not Russia. One may characterize the Intellectual in this early period in terms of Edmund Wilson's books, as a person en route from the *Finland Station* to *Axel's Castle.* For literary purposes, then, the Intellectuals' movement into the literary avant-garde in about 1937, rather than their earlier flirtation with Marxism, marks their significant alienation from bourgeois America, and the opposition of bourgeois liberalism to new alienated and aristocratic avant-garde values creates a tension which marks the Intellectuals' thinking during the period of their greatest

achievement and influence, from 1939 to 1952. In this period they establish
the literary authority of their group with the publication of Rahv's *Image
and Idea* (1949), Chase's *Herman Melville* (1949), *Quest for Myth* (1949),
and *Emily Dickinson* (1951), Trilling's *The Liberal Imagination* (1950),
Howe's *Sherwood Anderson* (1951), and Dupee's *Henry James* (1951).

In their prime, the Intellectuals are defined by their allegiance to *both*
bourgeois society *and* the avant-garde. Their ideal charter is the tension
Trilling found in F. Scott Fitzgerald: "As much as to anything else in
Fitzgerald, we respond to the delicate tension he maintained between
his idea of personal free will and his idea of circumstance: we respond to
that moral and intellectual energy. 'The test of a first rate intelligence,' he
said, 'is the ability to hold two opposed ideas in the mind, at the same time,
and still retain the ability to function' " (*LI* 238).[9] As Trilling said even more
clearly of himself: "I think that literature in its relation to life is polemical."[10] This idea of dialectic or tension between society and the imagination serves the Intellectuals as both the ideal form of the mind and their
conception of the "modernist" tradition in literature. As Irving Howe
says, the modern writer "presents dilemmas; he cannot and soon does not
wish to resolve them; he offers his *struggle* with them as the substance of
his testimony; and whatever unity his work possesses, often not very much,
comes from the emotional rhythm, the thrust toward completion, of that
struggle" (*DN* 23; see also *C* 503). More directly important for our purposes, the tension between society and the mind serves the Intellectuals as
the standard of value of their literary criticism. As Alfred Kazin says:
"Conflicts remain at the heart of every achieved work of literature. They
are resolved without being diminished, and in such a way that we gratefully
re-experience the conflict."[11]

The Intellectuals whose work is marked by this dialectic between social
reality and literary imagination include Edmund Wilson, Lionel Trilling,
Diana Trilling, Harold Rosenberg, Dwight Macdonald, F. W. Dupee,
Philip Rahv, Clement Greenberg, Elizabeth Hardwick, Mary McCarthy,
William Phillips, Delmore Schwartz, Richard Chase, Alfred Kazin, the
early Leslie Fiedler, Robert Warshow, Isaac Rosenfeld, Irving Howe, Steven
Marcus, and Norman Podhoretz.[12] One artistic value they defend is that of
Axel's Castle, that is, the avant-garde modernism which becomes fashionable in the twenties and is associated with Picasso, Nietzsche, Stravinsky,
Freud, Valery, Eliot, Dostoevsky, Kafka, Mann, Stendahl, Proust, Lawrence, Henry James, James Joyce, Yeats, Gide, and Rilke. In their realistic
and bourgeois selves they join the American intelligentsia in discussing
"proletarian realism" in the thirties, and after World War II they show
some interest in political novelists like Silone, Malraux, and Moravia; they
also support Jewish writers of the forties and fifties, particularly Saul
Bellow, Bernard Malamud, and Philip Roth. Throughout, their main

The Dual Ideology of the New York Intellectuals

Bourgeois Liberalism	Avant-Garde Radicalism
1934–1939 Ivy league, upper-middle-class background or Jewish immigrant; aspiration to succeed Tradition of realism of Drieser, Steinbeck, Wolfe Liberal political beliefs	Flirtation with Marxism, Trotskyites; Writers' Congresses; the early *PR* Displacement of radical political avant-gardism into avant-garde "modernist" literature; the new *PR* Antagonism to bourgeoisie; alienation

Creation of a New Charter

Trilling's *The Liberal Imagination* (1950)
Dialectic-conflict-tension of reality and mind/imagination = moral realism
Rahv's "redskins" and "palefaces"
Chase's realism and romance

		Normal Criticism
1939–1952	Break with Stalinism; antitotalitarian "cold" warriors; for "liberalism" eventual subsidy by the CIA Defense of literature of experience: Rahv's "redskins" Defense of political literature	Defense of "modernist" tradition in literature, i.e., avant-garde "paleface" writers of the 1920s, who are complex, conservative Opposition to bourgeois professors, mass media Cult of fashion in ideas
↓ Historical Change		→
1952–1964	*PR* symposium "Our Country and Our Culture" Age of conformity; isolation from Eisenhower politics Intellectuals "making it" leave avant-garde for intelligentsia via Kennedy administration, universities, where "modernist" literature becomes new orthodoxy Attempt to establish Jewish writers (Bellow) Rejection of "beats," Mailer, new avant-gardes	Rise of new avant-garde, the "beat" generation, Black Mountain School, etc.
↓ Obsolescence		→
1964–1978	Intellectuals oppose New Left, counterculture as avant-garde, and agonistic and nihilistic qualities of new political avant-garde The new Conservatism	Rise of counterculture, N. O. Brown, Reich, Leary, Mc-Luhan, etc., Weathermen, Panthers, New Left, political avant-garde

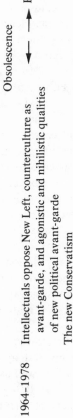

effort is to reinterpret American literature and culture in terms of their dialectic. They have centered their publishing in the *New York Times Book Review,* in *Commentary, The New Republic, The Nation,* and other leftist, anti-Communist, partly political magazines, and most importantly, in the *Partisan Review.* [13]

The Partisan Review *as Community Center*

In 1946 Lionel Trilling says of the *Partisan Review*: "To organize a new union between our political ideas and our imagination—in all our cultural purview there is no work more necessary. It is to this work that *Partisan Review* has devoted itself for more than a decade" (*LI* 95-96). In 1976 S. A. Longstaff says of the magazine: "As the organized center of this expanding circle, *Partisan Review* registered its concerns, spoke up for its accomplishments, regulated entry and standing within its orbit, saw to the recruitment and training of its newest voices, provided its members with a passport to outside centers of power and creativity, and generally served as an emblem of their collective standing in the wider world." [14] The *Partisan Review* has clearly served as a center of community, a forum, a definer of identity for a group of intellectuals, and hence its history must be examined in detail.

The magazine began in February 1934, as "A Bi-Monthly of Revolutionary Literature Published by the John Reed Club of New York," that is to say, as a magazine expressing Marxist views and associated with the Communist party. In the first "Editorial Statement," the editors say: "We propose to concentrate on creative and critical literature, but we shall maintain a definite viewpoint—that of the revolutionary working class. Through our specific literary medium we shall participate in the struggle of the workers and sincere intellectuals against imperialist war, fascism, national and racial oppression, and for the abolition of the system which breeds these evils. The defense of the Soviet Union is one of our principal tasks." [15] The editorial board varies considerably from issue to issue during the *Partisan Review*'s first three years, but always includes Philip Rahv and William Phillips (pseudonym, Wallace Phelps), who is editor of the magazine today. Among the many figures of the literary Left who for reasons of loyalty or prestige appeared on the masthead are Joseph Freeman, Joshua Kunitz, Kenneth Fearing, Edward Dahlberg, Jack Conroy, and Nathan Adler.

During the first three years of its existence, *Partisan Review* published proletarian poems and stories with titles like "Bum's Rush in Manhattan" and "The Scab," as well as essays like "MacLeish and Proletarian Poetry," and "I Came Near Being a Fascist." Of particular historical interest is the first symposium printed in the magazine, "What is a Proletarian

Novel?/Criticism?/Poetry?" (April/May 1935), which is the review's intellectual contribution to the First Writer's Congress, held May 1, 1935, in New
York. In their discussions of criticism in these issues, Rahv and Phillips
warn against Marxist didacticism and narrow-mindedness and opine that
"the Marxian method in criticism cannot be considered a purely sociological one. It is a method of correlating all factors, including the psychological. Yet it is not a haphazard pluralism, but a method which sees
the class factor as the determinant" (p. 22). With volume 3 (February
1936), *Partisan Review* combines with Jack Conroy's *Anvil* and appears
for six issues in a somewhat larger format. Most of the April 1936 issue
is taken up with a second symposium, "Marxism and the American Tradition," where the question of the "relationship between the American
tradition and Marxism as an ideological force in the United States" (p. 3)
elicits replies from Drieser, Newton Arvin, Kenneth Burke, William Troy,
William Carlos Williams, and others. Williams's answer, that the two
ideologies were antithetical, provoked a number of indignant letters.

The interest of the magazine's editors during this period is more political
than literary, and what they publish is part of the history of the Left rather
than the history of criticism, but it is important to understand their psychological position at the time when, as Rahv and Phillips recall, "in our
militant innocence we set out to preach our illusions to the world at large."[16]
This nostalgia for their "revolutionary" youth is shared by all the Intellectuals, but this "radical past," which still in the seventies forms a part
of the self-conception of the Intellectuals, is and was an illusion. Half of
the Intellectuals were from the Ivy League in a day when that meant something for one's class status, and the other half were part of the Jewish
bourgeois community of New York. As Howe says in "A Memoir of the
Thirties": "We did not realize then how sheltering it was to grow up in
this [Jewish] world, just as we did not realize how the 'bourgeois democracy'
at which we railed was the medium making it possible for us to speak
and survive."[17] In their early "radicalism" they were in the same relation
to the bourgeoisie that they later embodied as avant-gardist: antagonistic
but part of the same system, just as "the antinomy between the bourgeois
and the artistic spirit ... implies a relation of interdependence between
the contrasted terms" (*AG* 119-20). Their radical memories thus seem
much like all nostalgic recollections of adolescence and first youth, like
Tom Brown's School Days, and the romance of their lost youth has haunted
them since. As Kazin says: "Though they were fated to make brilliant
careers in the elitist society that was coming, they would not be happy. The
elan of their lives, revolutionary faith in the future, was missing" (*SO* 157).
In recalling their life in the thirties as part of the Communist cultural
apparatus, Rahv and Phillips forecast their future in the fifties as well-paid
academic defenders of modernism; in both cases they were part of a "move-

ment of far-reaching influence and power which knew so well how to maintain the illusion of dissidence and revolutionary idealism within the easy comforts and satisfactions of conformity."[18]

The strain between aesthetic and political standards, as well as the Moscow trials and the disillusioning actions of the American Communist party, began to tell on the editors of the *Partisan Review* in 1936; the magazine suspended publication from October 1936 until December 1937, when it came out with a new board of editors and a new policy. The new editors include Philip Rahv and William Phillips from the old editorial board and F. W. Dupee, Dwight Macdonald, George L. K. Morris, and (briefly) Mary McCarthy, who soon gave up editing to write the "Theater Chronicle." Because there is a tendency to think of the new *Partisan Review* as an integral part of the Marxian, Jewish, New York scene, one should note that its new aesthetic direction has its origin in the Yale background of Dupee and Macdonald and in the little-magazine tradition of *Miscellany*, which they edited in 1930 and 1931. In *The American Literary Review*,[19] Janssens notes the resemblance of the new *Partisan Review* and *Symposium* which has the same urban base, interest in Marxism, and regular contributors. The new editors' first step is to dissociate the magazine from the Communist party: "Formerly associated with the Communist Party, PARTISAN REVIEW strove from the first against its drive to equate the interests of literature with those of factional politics. Our reappearance on an independent basis signifies our conviction that the totalitarian trend is inherent in that movement and that it can no longer be combatted from within."[20] One can still trace the effects of their experiences at this time in the anti-Stalinism and cold-warrior mentality of older New York Intellectuals like Diana Trilling and Irving Howe.

Under the direction of its new editors, the magazine strives to bring about "a rapprochement between the radical tradition on the one hand and the tradition of modern literature on the other,"[21] a feat which they manage with some success by printing works of (and about) the best conservative writers (Eliot, Tate, Stevens, Lowell, Roethke, and others) while preserving something of the polemical tone and enthusiasm of the Left. According to Lionel Trilling, "The political tendency of the Thirties defined the style of the class—from that radicalism came the moral urgency, the sense of crisis, and the concern with personal salvation that mark the existence of American intellectuals" (YIT 47–48). And Irving Howe agrees that "the radicalism of the 30's gave the New York intellectuals their distinctive style: a flair for polemic, a taste for the grand generalization, an impatience with what they regarded (often parochially) as parochial scholarship, an internationalist perspective, and a tacit belief in the unity ... of intellectual work" (DN 220). Although Rahv and Phillips regret that because of the decline in the quality of avant-garde writing, they are unable to discover as much new writing as the little magazines of the twenties, they do discover some, and their taste in choosing among established reputations seems as sure as that of the editors of *The Dial*. *Partisan Review* may also claim prescience for publishing some of the first Myth Criticism—Harold Rosenberg's "Myth and History" (Winter 1939) and William Troy's articles on D. H. Lawrence and Thomas Mann in 1938. Clement Greenberg's "Avant-Garde and Kitsch" (1939) is also one of the first and best studies of this subject.

Specific features of the 1938–43 period reflect the agony of disengagement from Marxism and the facing of the reality of World War II. In a third symposium, "The Situation in American Writing" (*PR*, Summer and Fall 1939), eighteen writers answer such questions as "Are you conscious, in your own writing, of the existence of a 'usable past?' " "Is this mostly American?" "Do you think there is any place in our present economic system for literature as a profession?" "What do you think the responsibilities of writers in general are when and if war comes?" During this period the editors show their new literary tastes by publishing works by and about Kafka, Silone, Gide, Gertrude Stein, Dos Passos, Wallace Stevens, E. E. Cummings, and Edmund Wilson; that is, they belatedly discover the modernist writers of the twenties whom they have supported since.

Internal problems give way to external ones in 1941, however, as the war in Europe becomes more and more of a threat. Lists are printed noting the whereabouts of European artists and writers, George Orwell begins his excellent "London Letter" (March/April 1941), and Macdonald and Clement Greenberg publish "Ten Propositions on the War" (July/August 1941), one of which reads: "To support the Roosevelt-Churchill war regimes clears the road for fascism from within and blocks the organization of an effective war effort against fascism outside." In 1939 the magazine began a long and bitter fight against the philistinism and "patriotism" of Archibald MacLeish and Van Wyck Brooks with F. W. Dupee's "The Americanism of Van Wyck Brooks" (Summer 1939). This continues with Morton Zabel's attack on "The Poet on Capitol Hill" (January/February and March/April 1941), a symposium "On the Brooks-MacLeish Thesis" (January/February 1942), and Rahv's "The Progress of Cultural Bolshevism" (Summer 1944). Yet in the middle of this increased consciousness of *Realpolitik* the review publishes Eliot's "The Dry Salvages," Mary McCarthy's "The Man in the Brooks Brothers Shirt," and criticism by Formalists Allen Tate and R. P. Blackmur. The editors defend their choices with the statement, "Our main task is to preserve cultural values against all types of pressure and coercion" (January/February 1942).

After a quasi-political series of articles entitled "The New Failure of Nerve" (1943), which considers the proposition that rational liberalism is giving way to a search for asceticism, mysticism, revelation, and obscurantism, the magazine turns in a more purely cultural direction when Dwight Macdonald resigns as editor and is succeeded by the poet Delmore Schwartz (September/October 1943). Publication of Eliot's "Notes Towards a Definition of Culture" stimulates a series of opinions entitled "Mr. Eliot and Notions of Culture" (Summer 1944). The cultural emphasis continues into 1945, when the magazine, again anticipating future realities, begins to take account of the literary life of the university in "Notes from the Academy." However, politics returns in the summer of 1946 with a new attack on the "liberals" of *The Nation* and *The New Republic* for wanting to appease Russia and hence being a "Fifth Column," and the main impression left by the war years is that it was a good time for argument but not for literature.

In retrospect, the period 1946–55 appears to be the golden age of the *Partisan Review*, and the magazine's vitality seems to stem from the fact that events allow both the realistic-social-liberal and the imaginative-literary-conservative poles of the Intellectuals' charter to coexist in a productive tension. This creative dialectic results in part from a peculiar combination of editorial talents. During this time, William Phillips and Philip Rahv are the magazine's coeditors, and Rahv writes a number of essays as well, but the unique vitality seems to come from associate editors Delmore Schwartz and William Barrett; at least, it vanishes when they leave in 1955. Of all the Intellectuals, Schwartz is the only one with an imaginative sense of humor, and his regular essays and reviews, written in a variety of styles—poetic, satiric, expansive, morbid—as well as his stories and poems, constitute the spirit of the magazine. The *Partisan Review*'s vitality is also seen in its going from quarterly to bi-monthly publication in September/October 1946, and to monthly publication from 1948 to 1950; by this crude statistical measure, its decline of energy begins in May/June 1950, when it returns to bi-monthly status, and ends when it returns (with some late vacillation) to quarterly publication in 1955. S. A. Longstaff speculates that the cause of the decline may be that "its handling of the McCarthy question divided the *PR* writers and diminished their magazine. The split, in fact, touched the editors themselves, with Phillips supporting the ACCF leadership [in their toleration of Senator McCarthy, and their attack on liberals who were soft on Communism], Rahv doing all he could to distance the magazine from its excesses. But Rahv's efforts were not enough. Many who had once genuflected before *Partisan Review*'s reputation for moral incisiveness, now found in its hemming and hawing over the period's multiple threats to civil liberties something particularly askew—or worse, shabby and inhumane. The magazine was never to recover its old authority."[22]

From 1946 on, the political energies of the *Partisan Review* are spent in a continuing crusade against Stalinism; in protesting the awarding of the Bollingen Prize to Ezra Pound in 1949/50, chiefly on the grounds that he was anti-Semitic; and in quarreling about McCarthyism in the early fifties. But at the heart of the magazine is literary criticism—an "Age of Criticism," according to Randall Jarrell's famous essay published there in 1952. While reviewing Jarrell's *Poetry and the Age,* R. W. Flint remarks: "Criticism has a popular support and an *esprit de corps* which somehow makes it immune from the ravages of summer conferences on the State of Letters."[23]

It is during this period that a rapprochement occurs between the Intellectuals and the Formalists (chiefly John Crowe Ransom and Randall Jarrell) which replaces the situation of the thirties, when critics were split into Marxists and Fascists "at the poles" as Kazin describes it in *On Native Grounds,* by the creative tension of the Intellectuals' charter. As a result, the pages of both the *Kenyon Review* and the *Partisan Review* are opened to writers of both persuasions, and amity is extended to the Kenyon School of Letters as well. Thus, constant features include Mary McCarthy's drama reviews; film reviews by Robert Warshow; art reviews by Clement Greenberg and James Johnson Sweeney; political articles by Hannah Arendt, Sidney Hook, and William Barrett; and literary reviews by Robert Gorham Davis, Alfred Kazin, Richard Chase, and Schwartz. But added to this list are "Fugitives" from the *Kenyon* and *Southern Reviews* like Randall Jarrell, Eleanor Clark, Arthur Mizener, Eric Bentley, Robert Lowell, Peter Taylor, Katherine Anne Porter, and Allen Tate, and Southerners Elizabeth Hardwick and Flannery O'Connor. In addition, the *Partisan Review* shows prescience in publishing the work of rising young critics of the time, chiefly Leslie A. Fiedler, Irving Howe, Isaac Rosenfeld, Steven Marcus, and Hans Meyerhoff, Englishmen like V. S. Pritchett and Stephen Spender, and scholars like Newton Arvin, Wylie Sypher, Erich Auerbach, Joseph Frank, and Francis Fergusson.

The *Partisan Review's* taste in literature also seems foresighted. Although it generally does not publish much by any one poet, it publishes one or two things by the new poets of the time—W. C. Williams, Karl Shapiro, Richard Wilbur, Elizabeth Bishop, John Berryman, Theodore Roethke, Frank O'Hara, W. D. Snodgrass, Daniel Hoffman—so that a reader will at least have heard of them. Its coverage of critical issues is similarly foresighted; essays on French Existentialism, including a "Special French Number" (Spring 1946) with essays by Sartre, Genet, Malraux, Camus, Valéry, and others, are followed later in the year by essays by Simone de Beauvoir and Maurice Merleau-Ponty and by analytical essays by Arendt and Barrett. Interest in French culture continues, with occasional essays and a "Paris

Letter," chiefly by Nicola Chiaromonte. During the late forties, the relationship between literature and "the liberal mind" is much discussed, chiefly
by Trilling, Chase, and Barrett.[24] In 1951 the first black writers—Baldwin
and Ralph Ellison—appear, and in the late forties the *Partisan Review*
begins publishing Jewish novelists (as distinguished from critics) like Saul
Bellow, I. B. Singer, Bernard Malamud, and Wallace Markfeld. In the
fifties it also publishes distinguished essays on major modern writers—for
example, articles by Chase on Melville (May/June 1947), Mizener on
Fitzgerald (January 1950), and Jarrell on Wallace Stevens (September
1949)—and gives some attention to Faulkner when he is resurrected by
Malcolm Cowley in 1949. So far has it strayed from "proletarian realism"
that it even publishes an article by Louis Auchincloss on Edith Wharton
(July/August 1951)! But the *Partisan Review* also manages to remain
faithful to perennial modernists like Kafka, Nietzsche, Mann, James,
Joyce, and Eliot.

In the final view, a magazine like this must be judged by the way in which
it appears in retrospect to have published the best that was being thought or
felt in its time, or at least typical thought or feeling. By this standard, the
Partisan Review from 1946 to 1955 measures up to *The Dial* or *Hound and
Horn,* and essays like Fiedler's "Come Back to the Raft Ag'in Huck Honey"
(June 1948), Rahv's "The Myth and the Powerhouse" (November/December
1953), or Irving Howe's "This Age of Conformity" (January/February 1954),
move from commentary to an existence of their own as representative essays
of a historical period. Rahv and Phillips define their Ideal Reader in terms
which seem to describe the editorial ideals they themselves have realized:

This ideal reader is receptive to new work in fiction, poetry, and art, is aware of
the major tendencies in contemporary criticism, is concerned with the structure and
fate of modern society, in particular with the precise nature and menace of Communism, is informed or wishes to become informed about new currents in psychoanalysis and the other humanistic sciences, is opposed to such "nativist" dema-
gogues as Senator McCarthy and to all other varieties of know-nothingism, and
feels above all that what happens in literature and the arts has a direct effect on the
quality of his own life.[25]

From 1955 to 1960 the *Partisan Review* has an air of marking time—of
déjà vu—about it; occasional essays and reviews by faithful contributors
and symposia on Communism and on Freud appear, but there are few
major essays that would serve to define an era or even cause a stir. The
debate between Stanley Edgar Hyman and Ralph Ellison on "The Negro
Writer in America" (1958), the Intellectuals' encounter with Allen Ginsberg as described by Diana Trilling in "The Other Night at Columbia"

(1959); and Dwight Macdonald's "Masscult and Midcult" (1960) are the only exceptions, and they provide a guarded response indeed to the literary realities that are beginning to peek through the Eisenhower era. Robert Penn Warren is the most frequent contributor of both fiction and poetry, and the editors cast their lot with the academic poetry fashionable at the time. Hall, Pack, and Simpson, editors of the academic anthology *New Poets of England and America* (1957), all appear, as do James Dickey, Richard Wilbur, Louis Simpson, William Meredith, W. S. Merwin, and others. A poem or two by old stalwarts like Lowell, Berryman, and Roethke, and contributions by newcomers like Frank O'Hara, Adrienne Rich, Sylvia Plath, and Anne Sexton also appear. In criticism, R. W. Flint is the winner of a *Partisan Review* fellowship in 1956; Alfred Kazin is the most frequent contributor; A. Alvarez, Richard Wollheim, and Raymond Williams write "London Letters"; and in 1958 Steven Marcus cuts and sharpens his teeth on Hugh Kenner, Maxwell Geismar, and Harry Levin. But the "Age of Criticism" becomes an academic novel as critics (including Rahv, Howe, Kazin, etc.) move from the city to the universities, where the money is. After flirting with the CIA-financed American Committee for Cultural Freedom from 1959 to 1963, the *Partisan Review* institutionalizes its academic leanings by moving in the fall of 1963 to Rutgers University (which appoints Phillips to a professorship) and by appointing Richard Poirier, chairman of the Rutgers English Department, to its editorial board. This editorial staff remains through 1971, with the added services of John Hollander as poetry consultant and Steven Marcus as associate editor after 1960. In 1969 Philip Rahv left the magazine to found his own new magazine, *Modern Occasions,* in Cambridge; it seems odd that after thirty-five years of service his name is dropped from the masthead without so much as a fare-thee-well.

In the sixties the magazine continues to fight the old battles with a flurry of punches but with an inner weariness, as in the symposium "Cold War and the West" in 1962, or in the discussion of Adolph Eichmann in 1963–64. In the early sixties the editors discover a new team of Intellectual social scientists, and articles by David Reisman, Lewis Coser, Daniel Bell, David Bazelon, Dennis Wrong, George Lichtheim, and Michael Harrington appear in 1962–63 alone. This interest is temporary, however, as is the coverage of the art film given in the writings of Penelope Gilliatt, Pauline Kael, and John Simon. The magazine seems to give in to enthusiasms for particular critics, publishing several articles by Lionel Abel in 1962–63 and about as many by Susan Sontag in 1964–65. In 1964 it begins to get in touch with new trends in literary criticism, publishing several reviews of the work of Northrop Frye, reviews by and about Geoffrey Hartman, a review by Paul de Man on continental Structuralist criticism, and some pieces

by Steven Marcus on aspects of pornography. In 1965 it publishes Leslie
Fiedler's survey of "The New Mutants" and Richard Ohmann's review
of Noam Chomsky's generative grammar.

Throughout the decade the *Partisan Review* devotes a good deal of space
and attention to symposia on nonliterary issues like "The New Radicalism"
(1965–66), "What's Happening to America" (1967), "Black Power" (1968),
and the crises at Berkeley, Columbia, CCNY, and other universities; but
in the late sixties literary attention is focused on pornography and Structuralism. Both are traditionally associated with the French, and Susan
Sontag is the most audible spokesman, with her "Notes on Camp" (1966)
and "On Pornography" (1967). The scatological side is expressed fictionally
by Philip Roth in his short story "Whacking Off" (1967), part of *Portnoy's
Complaint.* Increased attention is given to Continental literature as Peter
Weiss reviews Marat/Sade in 1966; Peter Brooks writes on the French
new novel in 1967; Leo Bersani surveys French criticism "from Bachelard
to Barthes" in 1967; and Peter Caws writes on Structuralism in 1968. The
magazine even goes so far as to have brief pieces *by* Structuralists translated,
including one by Levi-Strauss in 1966 and two by Barthes in 1967. In
addition to these new voices, the *Partisan Review* continues to publish old
regulars like Fiedler and McCarthy; a number of substantial articles by
the editor, Richard Poirier, appear; and regular reviewers include Thomas
Edwards, J. H. Raleigh, G. S. Fraser, Richard Gilman, and Morris Dickstein.

In 1969 the magazine publishes a survey, "America I," on Susan Sontag,
the New Left, and the literature of violence, and prints among others
Joyce Carol Oates. "America II," in 1970-71, consists of a symposium
by leading historians and social scientists like Arthur Schlesinger, Jr.,
William Appleman Williams, and Michael Harrington on new conceptions
in American history. Literary essays include Alvarez on suicide and Kate
Millett on feminism in literature, and there is an interview with Allen
Ginsberg. In 1972 the editorial staff is reshuffled, and William Phillips
becomes the sole "editor" in charge of four assistants, five subeditors,
six consultants, and a board of fifteen, like a partridge in a pear tree. This
soon shakes down into a hierarchy with Phillips as editor, Steven Marcus
as associate editor, and Peter Brooks, Morris Dickstein, Richard Gilman,
and Norman Birnbaum as contributing editors who from 1973 on seem to
do most of the writing for the magazine as well. Several articles appear
which analyze the fifties as a decade of historical interest, Richard Poirier
publishes "The Aesthetics of Radicalism" in 1974, Jonathan Baumbach
writes an occasional column on the movies, and Phillips, Marcus, and
Poirier combine to give advice to the academic world in the symposium
"Literature and the Academy." In 1975 a number of painters and other
artists are asked to reminisce about "Then and Now," and several other

articles on the fine arts appear, but it is fair to conclude that no new directions are charted, no new issues discovered.

It is hard, then, to say exactly what summary judgment should be made about the *Partisan Review*. It is an institution, but one which seems to depend on one man, since Phillips, who began editing it in at the age of twenty-six, is still in charge, and when he goes it may splutter and fail, or expire slowly like Ransom's *Kenyon Review*. In its heyday, it was the liveliest of cultural periodicals, though much of its liveliness stemmed from cultural rather than literary issues. Since it is journalistic rather than scholarly, and since its type of criticism is not as useful as Formalist explication for teaching, its avant-garde influence declined as it followed the center of the literary world to the universities. Hilton Kramer says of it in 1977: "*Partisan Review*, though it still speaks in the name of intellectual values, is no longer itself a New York journal, and has not been for some time. It is a Rutgers journal, a journal of academic suburbia ... part of the larger pattern of middle-class life in this country, for the move from New York to Rutgers was exactly parallel to the exodus of the middle class from the problems of city life to the comfort and safety and dullness of the suburbs."[26] If this analysis is correct, and if the New York Intellectuals are "custodians and administrators of the culture of modernism for the rest of the country," then the future of the *Partisan Review* may lie in its relationship to the university and to the almost unexamined culture of the American suburb. In 1978, without public explanation, it moved to Boston.

The Intellectual as Avant-Garde Critic

If the prototypical act of the Intellectual is his flight from his bourgeois home to enlist in the avant-garde, then a systematic study of the nature of the avant-garde ought to illuminate the careers and literary values of the New York Intellectuals. Such a study, Renato Poggioli's *The Theory of the Avant-Garde*,[27] maintains that the "avant-garde" is a modern phenomenon which began in France in about 1870, when "art began to contemplate itself from a historical viewpoint." Avant-garde movements are characterized by a compulsive *activism, antagonism* to bourgeois culture and solidarity within the avant-garde sect, *nihilism,* and *agonism,* a tension and a struggle that will allow art to triumph in the future. According to Poggioli, the avant-garde is an outgrowth of Romanticism, sometimes marked by decadence, and is stylistically pluralistic, subject to changes in fashion, eventual decay, and replacement by a new avant-garde.

Though the Intellectuals have seen themselves as part of the avant-garde for years, and discourse at length on the subject, their discussion is unsatisfactory because they do not have as clear and systematic an understanding of the concept as Poggioli provides, and because they are not self-

aware enough to apply the concept to their own careers, particularly in
the matter of their own obsolescence as avant-gardists.[28] The four ways
in which the concept of the avant-garde illuminates the Intellectuals'
careers are: (1) their antagonism toward the general culture, their consequent alienation, and the solidarity this builds within their group; (2)
the avant-garde nature of the literary tradition they defend; (3) the fashionable nature of their cultural concerns; and (4) their move from an avant-
garde Bohemia to the intelligentsia and their consequent retirement as
avant-gardists.

Antagonism and Alienation

When the Intellectuals' history begins in 1937 with the founding of
the "new" *Partisan Review*, New York Intellectuals put themselves in
the classic avant-garde position of *antagonism* toward the bourgeois culture
on literary grounds. Lionel Trilling describes the antibourgeois character
of their literary tradition: "The author of *The Magic Mountain* once said
that all his work could be understood as an effort to free himself from
the middle class, and this, of course, will serve to describe the chief intention of all modern literature" (*BC* 30). And in 1972 Norman Podhoretz
echoes the same view, saying: "My belief is that Intellectuals have a spiritual
role to play not based on any systematic ideological preconception. Their
role is to be critical of the culture. ... I'm saying something similar to
Trilling in *The Liberal Imagination*. I consider it much the job of the
intellectual periodical to play the adversary role of that community. That
is what I try to do."[29] The important thing about the New York writers'
antagonism toward the bourgeoisie is that it is absolutely typical of avant-
garde movements everywhere. What is to them hard-thought-out and
individual decision-making appears to others to be simply a set of conventional responses. This typicality is seen clearly in the specific points on
which they choose to oppose the general bourgeois culture: their opposition to the professoriate and to the mass media.

The antiacademic bias of the Intellectuals sometimes seems a mere
rhetorical warming-up, a flourish of swords, but the insult to the sterile
professor and to hidebound scholarship remains a favorite trope. In the
forties and fifties the *Partisan Review* runs a feature called "Report from
the Academy," in which the insensitivity of professors and the deadening
effect of hard study are regularly pointed out. For example, Professor
Richard Chase of Columbia begins a discussion of A. O. Lovejoy and the
"history of ideals" by saying that "the chief purpose of the departments
of literature in American graduate schools is to teach prospective teachers
how to avoid discussing literature."[30] Similarly, Professor Newton Arvin of
Smith discusses professors as part of a capitalist "managerial revolution,"
describing them as follows: "None of the definitive characters [*sic*—charac-

teristics?] are missing: the veneration of quantity, the lust of the tangible, the mental ingenuousness, the passion for organizational machinery, the instinct for the immediate and the solidly visible, and (to put it negatively) the contempt for ideas, the hatred of literature and the arts, the fear of criticism, and (singular as it sounds) the distrust of learning itself. Philistinism, obscurantism, anti-intellectualism—these are as truly the stamps of the successful academician as of the successful entrepreneur."[31] One sees here an avant-garde attack on the whole academic enterprise which is clearly distinguishable from proposals for the reform of graduate study like the chapter in Wellek and Warren's *Theory of Literature* (1949 edition only) entitled "The Study of Literature in the Graduate School."

There have been several other feuds with the academy throughout the years, most notably Dwight Macdonald's quarrel with the lexicographers over his *New Yorker* review of *Webster III* and Edmund Wilson's opposition to the Modern Language Association over its editions of American authors.[32] The pedant has, of course, been one of the stock figures of satire since satire was invented, but one must object to this manifestation of prejudice on the grounds of its hypocrisy, unreality, and inhumanity. It is a hypocritical charge on the part of many who make it, since they simultaneously try to sustain the pose of rebel while enjoying the perquisites of academic life and the authority of scholarly opinion. Intellectuals have taken good academic jobs and honorary degrees as soon as they could get them; Rahv, Howe, Fiedler, Kazin, Troy, Trilling, Dupee, and Chase have held tenured professorships for years, and have had their share of fellowships and awards, so it seems like romantic self-indulgence to continue the rhetoric of a vanished independent Bohemia. It is unreal because Intellectuals depend on scholarship for their information and on scholars for their education; indeed, most of the "liberal" part of their thinking seems to derive from the famous "Contemporary Civilization" course at Columbia that Lionel Trilling taught. The rare exception can work systematically and persistently on his own; Alfred Kazin and Stanley Edgar Hyman have spoken with nostalgic affection of the public library readings which led to *On Native Grounds* and *The Armed Vision*. But the best of the critics, like Trilling, Chase, and Fiedler, have Ph.D.'s, and the information provided by scholarship is essential to the making of literary essays. Without it, one has the pathos of Seymour Krim, who confesses: "In simple actuality I didn't have the formal training for this glib seasoned role [as omniscient critic] nor could any of my friends have as much background as they would have needed."[33] Carried into practice, the Intellectuals' ignorance leads to hybristic claims like that of Norman Podhoretz for Dwight Macdonald: "The scholars who have desecrated the King James Version or the lexicographers who are too 'democratic' to discriminate authoritatively between good English usage and bad are worth attacking because they have the power to do great damage, but showing up their weaknesses is child's play for a sophisticated critic [like Macdonald]" (*DU* 96).[34] This is the dumb praising the dumb, as James Sledd has demonstrated. However, the worst thing about the Intellectuals' attack on scholars is their intolerant habit of mind, which categorizes a whole group of men as inferior. This is the kind of thing which Howe bridles at when the category is "Jew" instead of "professor" (*DN* 248); and it is morally unfortunate that this group of critics, all devoting their lives to literature and the fine arts, should indulge in such inhumanity.

The second typically antagonistic position the Intellectuals take is opposition to "mass culture," which begins in about 1940, perhaps as a reaction to their previous espousal of proletarian literature. The Intellectuals' reaction against mass culture should be carefully distinguished from such sympathetic examinations of popular culture as George Orwell's "Boys' Weeklies" (1939), Robert Warshow's movie reviews for the *Partisan Review*, and many later studies.[35] The purpose of the Intellectuals' opposition is to put down mass culture as inferior to the elite modernist art with which they identify; theirs is a polemical position, not an analytical one. Their view is explained clearly by Clement Greenberg in "Avant-Garde and Kitsch,"[36] where he shows how the birth of the avant-garde coincides with the rise of social revolutionary thought and democratic and industrial society, how the avant-gardists use their concept of the bourgeois to define what they are not, and how they "emigrate from the markets of capitalism" to find an absolute (nonobjective) art and a pure poetry, the usual subjects of which are the disciplines and processes of art itself. The tradition the Intellectuals defend is thus in large part negatively defined as "nonkitsch," and the danger to it is not that it is unknown, but that it will become more popular and hence, ipso facto, vulgarized. Dwight Macdonald, the Intellectual who has written most about mass culture, posits that a "Midcult" does this and he notes that "the special threat of Midcult is that it exploits the discoveries of the avant-garde."[37] Ironically, some of Macdonald's best writing is on the movies. Before he became an Intellectual he wrote a series on Hollywood directors for *Symposium* (March–June 1933), and since rejoining the midculture he has reviewed movies for *Esquire;* his movie criticism is collected in *Dwight Macdonald on Movies* (1969). Robert Warshow avoided this stereotyped opposition to the movies in his *The Immediate Experience* (1964), but in general the Intellectuals' attitude is one of haughty disdain. As Philip Rahv says in 1952, "But if under present conditions we cannot stop the ruthless expansion of mass-culture, the least we can do is keep apart and refuse its favors" (*II* 230). The Intellectuals' consistent snobbishness about mass culture is particularly ironic because it is largely the importance of New York City as a center of mass culture, of the publishing, television, and magazine worlds, and as home of the *New York Times,* which gives importance to their views as *New York* Intellectuals, as opposed to San Francisco or Cambridge or Ann Arbor Intellectuals.

This sense of personal antagonism toward the majority culture is expressed in the lives of the Intellectuals as a state of *alienation,* "the feeling of uselessness and isolation of a person who realizes that he is now totally estranged from a society which has lost its sense of the human condition and its own historical mission" (*AG* 109).[38] Lionel Trilling isolates as a cause of this feeling the Intellectuals' divorce from family life. Speaking of his own past, he says: "It is the fact that the intellectuals of the Twenties and Thirties were likely to assume that there was an irreconcilable contradiction between babies and the good life. . . . Intellectual men thought of [children] as 'biological traps,' being quite certain that they must lead to compromise with, or capitulation to, the forces of convention" (YIT 44). And elsewhere, in re Orwell, he says: "The prototypical act of the modern intellectual is his abstracting himself from the life of the family" (*OS* 163). This psychological alienation is given the support of a doctrinaire dogma in the thirties by the Intellectuals' allegiance to Marxism, which cuts them off from this capitalist society while promising them fulfillment in the future, and by their self-identification as Jews, which combines the outcast and the Chosen People in a similar fashion. Kazin's memory of the times seems to combine Marxism and Jewishness:

It seemed to me that we were specially interesting because we were among the dispossessed of history; I saw us as the downtrodden, the lonely, the needy, in a way that fitted my faith in a total redemption. There are times in history when a group feels that it is at the center of events. Poor as we were, anxious, lonely, it seemed to me obvious that everywhere, even in Hitler Germany, to be outside of society and to be Jewish was to be at the heart of things. History was preparing, in its Jewish victims and through them, some tremendous deliverance and revelation. [*SO* 47-48]

As Marxists of the thirties turn into well-paid liberals of the fifties, however, the Intellectuals' alienation becomes not so much a matter of being cast out of society as the fantasy of a loss of identity through the operation of a totalitarian society like that portrayed by Kafka, or by Orwell in *1984.* In "The Orgamerican Phantasy," Harold Rosenberg traces in such sociological fictions of the fifties as Reisman's *The Lonely Crowd,* Whyte's *The Organizational Man,* or Spectorsky's *The Exurbanites* the theme of "the post-radical critic [who] suffers also a nostalgia for himself as an independent individual" (*TN* 280). Rosenberg dismisses the reality of this alienation as being related not to totalitarian tendencies in the society but to the Intellectuals' move to the intelligentsia: "The fear-augury that the Orgman will become everyone in a quiet, unopposable totalitarianism is not a conclusion based on social analysis but a projection of the fate they [the Intellectuals] have chosen for themselves" (*TN* 283). The feeling of alienation is described by Podhoretz as "simply the feeling that this was not *my* country. . . . I was a citizen, and a highly interested one, of a small community in New York which lived by its own laws and had as little commerce as it could manage with a hostile surrounding environment. As an intellectual I was as ghettoized as my ancestors in Eastern Europe had been as Jews" (*MI* 232). Perhaps the best-known summary of the alienation of the Intellectuals in the fifties is Irving Howe's "This Age of Conformity,"[39] which combines the stock themes of the avant-garde: attacks on the traditionalism of professors, the debasing effect of mass culture, the pressure to conform exerted by institutions, and regret for the lost alienation and independence of the avant-garde.

The concomitant of antagonism and alienation, the permanent condition of the avant-garde, is "solidarity *within* a society in the restricted sense of that word—that is to say, solidarity within the community of rebels and libertarians" (*AG* 30–31).[40] This group identity is expressed by Intellectuals in their constant use of "we" to refer to their own opinions, which culminates in Trilling's essay "Our Hawthorne."[41] The origin of the Intellectuals' unique use of "we" may lie in their radical past; Malcolm Cowley reminisces of writers in the thirties that "all the new proletarian writers seemed to gather strength by thinking in terms of 'we,' not 'I', and by merging themselves first with other workers in the arts—provided they were true proletarians under thirty—then with an audience of workers drawn from all the trades and professions; then finally with the entire working class."[42] Harold Rosenberg's remarks on Robert Warshow support and expand this interpretation: "Warshow's entire approach is an 'us' approach, that is to say, a mass-culture approach—though his 'us' is not the masses but the small mass of the intellectuals." Rosenberg's charge is essentially that the Intellectuals are expressing the values of their group, their common experience, and that they are "reluctant to face the mass-culture consequences of their historical self-definition."[43]

The tendency to inflate one's private and fallible opinions into general truths which this "we" leads to is expressed with pride by Leslie Fiedler in the preface to his *End to Innocence*: "I have, as a matter of fact, been pleased to discover how often I have managed to tell what still seems to me the truth about my world and myself as a liberal, intellectual, writer, American, and Jew. I do not mind, as some people apparently do, thinking of myself in such categorical terms; being representative of a class, a generation, a certain temper seems not at all a threat to my individu-ability. . . . I like to think of myself as registering through my particular sensibility the plight of a whole group."[44] The question is not, as Fiedler suggests, the threat to his individuality, but the justness of his claim to speak for multitudes when in fact he may be speaking for only two or three cronies. Irving Howe reveals the compulsive nature of this habit in a footnote to his "The New York Intellectuals": "Is it 'they' or 'we'? To speak of the New York Intellectuals as 'they' might seem coy or disloyal; to speak of 'we' self-assertive or cozy. Well, let it be 'they,' with the proviso that I do not thereby wish, even if I could, to exclude myself from judgment" (*DN* 213). But twenty-three pages later he slips back into the spurious group-identity of "our intellectual life" and says: "In place of the avant-garde we [*sic*] now had the *style of fashion*" (*DN* 236). The latest reincarnation of this durable pronoun is found in Howe's account of *his* immigrant Jewish ancestors in New York City, *The World of Our Fathers* (1976). The compulsion to speak for a group rather than as a private individual only reinforces what Lionel Trilling says in 1942: "The intellectual, the 'freest' of men, consciously the most liberated from class, is actually the most class-marked and class-bound of all men."[45] It seems to be literally impossible for individual Intellectuals to think of themselves as anything but extensions of a group, or to avoid inflating what are essentially personal opinions, or the opinions of a gaggle of twenty or thirty friends, into the representative statements of an age, generation, or some other impressive but fictitious entity. As a group, then, the Intellectuals are avant-gardist, and their preoccupation with mass culture, their antiacademic stance, and their sense of the alienation of their critical community can be understood as the consequences of their original choice of the idea of the avant-garde as the basic concept of their critical charter.

The most influential aspect of the Intellectuals' embrace of the avant-garde is the metamorphosis of the idea of Marxist revolution which they had held in the thirties into the idea of literary revolution carried on by modernist writers. This shift is made easy because "avant-garde" itself has both political and cultural connotations. It is a political term in that it comes from a military context (the lead troops are the avant-garde) which is extended to mean being in the lead of a revolutionary movement, on the barricades, in the vanguard of history. The term is thus easily applied to the new artist who also sees himself as creating a new cultural Utopia. Ironically, in 1940 the Intellectuals were really part of the critical *derrière-garde*, defending what artists had created and critics like Edmund Wilson and R. P. Blackmur had criticized in the twenties. Further irony is provided by the fact that the avant-garde artists the Intellectuals defend— Yeats and Eliot, Pound and Joyce, Lawrence and Gide—are political conservatives, as Lionel Trilling notes (*LI* 291). The originality of their charter, then, lies in the combination of an avant-gardism drawn from leftist revolutionary political expectations but kept exclusively in the area of literary imagination, and liberal ideas also drawn from leftist ideology but transformed in accordance with the bourgeois aspirations of the char-

ter's adherents. Maintaining such a charter is tricky since it involves sup-
pression of the fact that as a liberal, one is also a bourgeois, for by definition an avant-gardist opposes the bourgeois. These are the two ideas the
Intellectuals manage to hold in tension, and they function splendidly for
a time to develop a normal criticism and a new critical tradition.

The Tradition of the New

Having set themselves apart as a literary class alienated from the vulgar
public and from learned professors, much as doctrinaire New Critics isolate
themselves with the poem by using the "intentional" and "affective"
fallacies, the Intellectuals simultaneously develop their own tradition,
which becomes a new kind of aesthetic orthodoxy in which one must believe
in order to be an Intellectual. The primary characteristic of this orthodoxy
distinguishes it sharply from Formalism: it is about the novel, not poetry.
As Norman Podhoretz says: "I do not go to literature for the salvation of
my soul, but only to enlarge or refine my understanding, and I do not
expect it to redeem the age, but only to help the age become less chaotic
and confused. The novel—let me restrict myself to that, since it is the
literary form with which I have been most closely connected . . . plays a
unique, and uniquely valuable, part in the life of our age" (*DU* 3). This
strategy of reducing literature to the novelistic genre is typical; Phillips,
Sontag, Podhoretz, Rahv, Kazin (except for his Blake essay), Dupee,
Rosenfeld, and Macdonald, among others, have not written (or at least
have not collected) a word about the poets of this or any other time, with
the exception of a couple of reviews praising Robert Lowell and attacking
the "beats." The objection is that they reach conclusions about literature
which are presented as universal, but are really generic.

Philip Rahv, echoing in part Irving Howe's "This Age of Conformity,"
carries this tendency into literary theory in "Criticism and the Criticism of
Fiction," where he belittles Formalist critics of novels for being too much
influenced by the techniques drawn from the criticism of poetry. The
three particular points Rahv refers to are (1) "the current obsession with
the search for symbols, allegories, and mythic patterns in the novel,"
as exemplified by R. W. Stallman's reading of Stephen Crane; (2) the
identification of "style as the 'essential activity' of imaginative prose,"
as exemplified by John Crowe Ransom's essay "The Understanding of
Fiction"; and (3) technicism, "the attempt to reduce the complex structure
and content of the novel to its sum of techniques," as in Mark Schorer's
"Technique as Discovery" (*MP* 38). [46]

Another characteristic of the Intellectuals' tradition is that they omit
any consideration of English literature before 1800 and refer to the continent of Europe for their literary authority. The Intellectuals have written
nothing about Chaucer or Shakespeare, much less Webster, Dryden,

Fielding, Sterne, or Dr. Johnson, and they deal with romantic and modern English literature only as it can be seen as part of the modernist dialectic. To Podhoretz, English literature seems "in the nature of an entailed national inheritance carefully fenced around . . . against trespassers from outside the family" (*MI* 68). The Intellectuals' literary criticism is thus in large part a criticism of translations, written in English for English-speaking readers but often referring to another cultural reality expressed in another language. As Howe admits: "No American critic—especially if like myself, he reads Paz through the roughened lens of translation—can engage such a writer without severe risks of misapprehension."[47] This fact, added to their antipoetic bias, may account for the Intellectuals' lack of interest in literary style. As Malcom Cowley has said, "Language is the specifically human gift and the cohesive force that holds each tribe and nation together,"[48] and a great limitation of the Intellectuals is that their heart and their tongue belong to separate cultures.

As the Intellectuals establish their own literary tradition in the forties, they make some attempt to continue their former interest in the "proletarian literature" of the thirties by praising novels written on political subjects or in a naturalistic style—for example, Henry James's *The Bostonians* or the novels of Malraux, Silone, Orwell, and Moravia. The fashion is seen at its narrowest in the subgenre of the ex-Marxist novel (Koestler's *Darkness at Noon* or Trilling's *Middle of the Journey*), where former party members and fellow travelers ruminate on the meaning of it all. Irving Howe is the only Intellectual who applies this political interest to literary criticism to any great extent. In *Politics and the Novel* he defines a political novel as "the kind in which the *idea* of society . . . has penetrated the consciousness of the characters in all of its profoundly problematic aspects, so that there is to be observed in their behavior, and they are themselves often aware of, some coherent political loyalty or ideological identification. They now think in terms of supporting or opposing society as such; they rally to one or another embattled segment of society; and they do so in the name of, and under prompting from, an ideology."[49] Howe finds the tension of a political novel in the struggle between the abstract nature of ideology and the specific nature of human behavior and says that this type of novel must be judged by the amplitude of its moral vision, like any other novel. Though he has returned to naturalists like Hardy and Gissing, even Howe no longer writes about political literature, perhaps because, as Rahv says in 1952, "the rout of the left-wing movement has depoliticized literature" (*II* 228).

A third characteristic of the Intellectuals' tradition is that goodness equals modernism, and the Intellectual critics are fairly well agreed on the qualities of good modern literature and the authors who embody them. The key ideas are "complexity," "difficulty," and "conflict." Thus Philip

Rahv, speaking of James, says: "In modern literature, which bristles with anxieties and ideas of isolation, it is above all the creativity, the depth and quality of the contradictions that a writer unites within himself, that gives us the truest measure of his achievement. And this is not primarily a matter of the solutions, if any, provided by the writer ... but of his force and integrity in reproducing these contradictions as felt experience" (*II* 83; cf. *II* 144, 154). In the forties, Lionel Trilling usually speaks of literature in the context of what it can do for the liberal political mind, and one can infer from such statements what he sees as the value in literature: "The job of criticism would seem to be, then, to recall liberalism to its first essential imagination of variousness and possibility, which implies the awareness of complexity and difficulty. ... Literature is the human activity that takes the fullest and most precise account of variousness, possibility, complexity, and difficulty" (*LI* xii-xiii).

Irving Howe undertakes the most extensive recent discussion of what the Intellectuals mean by modernism in "The Idea of the Modern,"[50] where he describes the avant-garde movement which Poggioli sees more accurately and fully. Howe also defines modernism briefly in his 1961 book, *Thomas Hardy*:

Jude the Obscure is Hardy's most distinctly "modern" work, for it rests upon a cluster of assumptions central to modernist literature: that in our time men wishing to be more than dumb clods must live in permanent doubt and intellectual crisis; that for such men, to whom traditional beliefs are no longer available, life has become inherently problematic; that in the course of their years they must face even more than the usual allotment of loneliness and anguish; that in their cerebral overdevelopment they run the danger of losing those primary appetites for life which keep the human race going; and that courage, if it is to be found at all, consists in a readiness to accept pain while refusing the comforts of certainty.[51]

Looking back on Trilling and the others in 1957, Norman Podhoretz observes: "They all set out to show that liberalism was guilty of a failure to take a sufficiently complicated view of reality. Complexity became a key word in the discourse of the period. ... revisionism came out for the more subtle, skeptical temper with its inhibiting awareness of human limitations and its 'tragic sense of life'. ... the critique of liberalism added up to a defense of wisdom as opposed to rational speculation, to a defense of the qualities of *maturity* against the values of youth" (*DU* 107).

Of the authors the Intellectuals do like—those who constitute their "tradition"—all write after 1800, most are novelists, and most are continental. According to Irving Howe, the Intellectuals "helped bring back the old world to a country that in part had fled from it. ... The theme of return figured significantly in their work—in the dissemination of Russian moods and styles, the explication and advocacy of modernist masters like Kafka, the popularization of Marxist ideas, the insistence that in our time literature can only be international." Marshall Berman also opines that "New York Intellectuals are basically nineteenth century Russian intellectuals, right? . . . They felt that politics, art, everything that might be going on posed some immediate and desperate moral problem. And this sense of life as being desperately problematical and therefore how to live as a moral person evoked endless anguish."[52]

Though nineteenth-century Russian or Russian-Jewish intellectualism has not been studied as, much less demonstrated to be, a source of American literary criticism, it is clear that the New York Intellectuals' origins and interests are neither scholarly nor derived from English traditions; rather, the Intellectuals seem to select their literary favorites not so much for their specifically literary qualities, not on a formal basis, but for their usefulness in illustrating ideological points, in showing "the condition of modern man." Thus Rahv is more interested in Dostoevsky than anyone else, partly because he is an immigrant from Russia, but mostly because Dostoevsky illuminates for him the nihilism of the intellectual betrayed by his movement. Kafka, who is very fashionable in the forties, similarly illuminates the alienation of the Intellectuals and modern man as they are faced with bureaucracy and mass society. Thomas Mann is interesting as a Humanist in exile, an intellectual dispossessed by Hitler. Henry James— everybody's favorite—is the very model of complexity and poised "withdrawal." Edmund Wilson remarks that "a novelist whose typical hero invariably decides not to act, who remains merely an intelligent onlooker, appeals for obvious reasons to a period when many intellectuals, formerly romantic egoists or partisans of the political Left, have been resigning themselves to the role of observer or passive participant in activities which cannot command their whole allegiance. The stock of Henry James has gone up in the same market as that of Kafka" (*TT* 130).[53] The real importance of the Europeans to the Intellectuals is as a standard of value, in the literal sense of a flag to rally 'round. Thus F. W. Dupee says in a review of *On Native Grounds:* "To the critic in fact [alienation] may even apply in a double sense. With Europe's better developed culture as a standard, he sometimes feels estranged not only from America at large but from much of its literature."[54]

European greats do in fact function as genuine touchstones by which to judge American and modern literary works. But more often the standard becomes a club used not only to separate the Intellectuals' literary tradition from the bourgeois culture but also to defend their social position against encroachment from pretenders to authority. Randall Jarrell asks if many Intellectuals are not "specialists in Important—that is to say, currently fashionable—books?" Jarrell describes the Intellectuals as being limited by their tradition: "There are few things more interesting to people of this sort than what a bad critic says of a bad criticism of a fashionable writer. . . . if, at such parties, you wanted to talk about *Ulysses* or *The Castle* or *The Brothers Karamazov* or *The Great Gatsby* or Graham Greene's last novel—Important books—you were at the right place." Jarrell lists some of a "thousand" good or interesting but unimportant books and says: "You couldn't expect a very ready knowledge or sympathy."[55] Seymour Krim describes the exclusionary aspect of this tradition in terms of his unsuccessful attempt to break into Intellectual society, which one did, if he is to be believed, by becoming "a suave masterspeaker (and theoretically thinker) in practically all literary and ideological fields."[56] Thus the European component of the Intellectuals' tradition is that typically avant-garde holy writ which serves to exclude the public.

The Intellectuals' other literary interest is the study of American literature, where they add imagination to realism or experience and attempt to create a new cultural America "after the genteel tradition," which they as Intellectuals can claim. The motivation for their attempt is exactly the same as that of Van Wyck Brooks and Archibald MacLeish, who want to claim America for a nativist New England tradition; and of Tate and the Fugitives, who want to claim it for the tradition of the South and Agrarianism. James Gilbert summarizes the Intellectuals' state of mind in 1936 and 1937: "Within a year Rahv and Phillips had concluded that Marxism had very little to do with the American tradition. In 1937 they wrote that an essential contradiction existed between Marxism and domestic intellectual traditions that could be resolved only through the 'Europeanization of American Literature.' "[57]

The Intellectuals contend that American literature is dominated by the search for experience. According to Rahv, "Poetic technique became the special experience of Ezra Pound, language that of Gertrude Stein, the concrete object was appropriated by W. C. Williams, super-American phenomena by Sandburg and related nationalists, Kenneth Burke experienced ideas (which is by no means the same as thinking them), Archibald MacLeish experienced public attitudes, F. Scott Fitzgerald the glamour and sadness of the very rich, Hemingway death and virile sports, and so on and so forth" (*II* 19). They try to go beyond the "Cult of Experience," which they think dominates American literature in 1940, to add the complexity and consciousness of ideas of their international tradition to the Americans' desire for experience, which, as Philip Rahv says, is at bottom "the theme of the individual transplanted from an old culture taking inventory of himself and of his new surroundings" (*II* 25). Expressing the opposition of mind and experience in "Paleface and Redskin," Rahv contends that "the redskins are in command of the situation and [that] the literary life in America has seldom been so deficient in intellectual power" (*II* 4). His (implicit) solution is to oppose to the redskin the paleface Intellectual, who is "to be credited with most of the rigors and charms of the classic American books" (*II* 6). This dialectic also dominates Trilling's essays of the forties, particularly his attacks on "reality" in American literature from the point of view of "imagination." In the preface to the 1964 edition of his *E. M. Forster,* Trilling says: "I had a quarrel with American literature as at that time [1942] it was established, and against what seemed to me its dullness and its pious social simplicities I enlisted Mr. Forster's vivacity, complexity, and irony."[58] In his essays on Huck Finn, Fitzgerald, Frost, and "our Hawthorne," Trilling's main interest is to make American literature as complex as modernist European literature. But his attempt to make Frost a "terrifying" poet went so against the American grain as to cause a considerable uproar.[59]

The opposition of imagination to the realistic tradition of American literature also provides the formal principle for the first long study of American literature by an Intellectual, Alfred Kazin's *On Native Grounds* (1942). Here Kazin studies "our writers' absorption in every last detail of their American world together with their deep and subtle alienation from it" (*ONG* ix)—that is, he contrasts their realism and the transcendental and idealistic sense which American reality betrays. In this book Kazin merely describes the struggle between the parties of reality and idealism. It is only in the late forties and fifties that this struggle is projected as the ideal form of American culture, particularly by Richard Chase. In his most general book, *The American Novel and Its Tradition* (1957), Chase finds the central form of American fiction to be the romance, which is freed from "the conditions of actuality" and hence embodies virtues of the mind like "rapidity, irony, abstraction, profundity," and he asserts that "the fact seems to be that the history of the American novel is not only the history of the rise of realism but also of the repeated rediscovery of the uses of romance." Chase finds a dialectic not only between conceptions of the genre like realism and romance but also within novels; for him, American literature "pictures human life in a context of unresolved contradictions—contradictions which ... are not absorbed, reconciled, or transcended."[60] Chase thus projects the unresolved dialectic, the tension of the Intellectuals' charter, onto our literary history and presents as historical fact the desire of the Intellectuals to add to the realism of American literature the modernist conception of the mind. As Rahv says, "The Intellectual is the only character missing in the American novel" (*II* 11), and the Intellectuals try to put him there. In the event, however, they get *Herzog* and a reflection of what really happened to them, the college novels which show their move to the intelligentsia.[61]

The Cult of Fashion
According to Poggiolo, the third attribute of the avant-garde is that it

follows the "cult of fashion": "Avant-garde art, because at times its own creation is no more valid or enduring than a fashion, cannot but submit to the influence of fashion" (*AG* 83). For the Intellectuals, fashion is operative chiefly in the area of general cultural ideas, since their literary opinions are consistently modernist. The best way to illustrate the course of the Intellectuals' allegiance to fashion is to recall the various *Partisan Review* symposia and discussions in which the editors solicited opinions from people they considered knowledgeable on topics of current importance. The point of returning to these symposia is to note both their fashionable nature and the compulsion with which the Intellectuals create new issues. It is a fact that basic issues do not change as often as the Intellectuals' interests. Moreover, many basic issues like the atom bomb, the Pentagon, the automobile, the population explosion, or the energy crisis, are not discussed by the Intellectuals at all. Thus, for the avant-garde Intellectual, as for the avant-garde artist, the only error is to be out-of-date; "the only irremediable and absolute aesthetic error is a traditional artistic creation, an art that imitates and repeats itself" (*AG* 82). One notes, too, that the Intellectuals never confront any issue in a practical way, or propose solutions to any of the problems, but simply halt the discussion when they get bored. The only result of the Intellectuals' social theorizing is that he makes up his mind. A "*very* high member of the Kennedy administration" illuminates this point in his reaction to Podhoretz: "I [Podhoretz] asked him whether he disagreed with what I was saying. 'No, no,' he answered, 'what you're saying is all very well, but what should we do about it?' Do? I was not accustomed to thinking in such terms, I was accustomed to making critical analyses whose point was to understand a problem as fully as possible, not to affect or manipulate it" (*MI* 233).

The Superannuation of Intellectuals

The fourth stage in the history of the Intellectuals, which is most important because it is least understood, is the collapse of their dialectic in the fifties as they leave their journalistic Bohemia to "make it," usually in secure positions in universities, and their "modernist" tradition is replaced by new avant-garde movements. Norman Podhoretz, among others, misunderstands the Intellectuals' changing situation: "What the *Partisan Review* symposium ["Art, Culture, and Conservatism," (Summer 1972)] seems to represent is an effort by some of these apologists to fight back by casting the critics of the new sensibility and the counter-culture in the role of the old bourgeois antagonists of an embattled avant-garde. This is so absurd a scenario that only such wildly imaginative apologists as Leslie Fiedler and Susan Sontag might have lent it a touch of plausibility. But they are absent here, and the lesser talents on whom the editors are forced to rely simply do not measure up to the job."[62]

In order to understand the decline and fall of the Intellectuals as avant-gardists, one must apply Poggioli's distinction between two types of avant-garde publics:

One is the group made up of those for whom the valid fashion, in poetry, painting, sculpture, architecture, or theater, is the fashion of one single movement, or of a few movements forming a single series; for them any manifestation alien to that movement, or that series, is not avant-garde art, or is not art at all. The other is the group formed by those individuals who consider the fashions of the various avant-gardes as a whole; . . . they accept every variation of modernism with the same undifferentiated and immoderate enthusiasm, without exception or reservation. [*AG* 84–85]

In these terms, the Intellectuals obviously belong to the former group, which identifies exclusively with the avant-garde "modernism" of the twenties. Thus, since about 1955 they have applied their habits of thought and used their modernist tradition to judge a reality and a literature which have changed dramatically since their charter was first formed. It is not that the Intellectuals have left the avant-garde, but that a new avant-garde has arisen and left them behind, mired in the literary fashion of what is now a past age. The essential tension of the Intellectuals since about 1955 has not been, as it was earlier, a tension between reality and mind, between liberal politics and avant-garde literature, but a tension between their desire to remain the avant-garde and their reluctance to give up the tradition of their youth. As Irving Howe notes: *"Partisan Review* betrays a hopeless clash between its editors' capacity to apply serious [i.e., liberal, modernist] standards and their yearnings to embrace the moment" (*DN* 262).

In part, the cause of the Intellectuals' metamorphosis into a *derrière-garde* is simply the action of time, but looked at in socioeconomic terms they cease to be avant-gardist because they have become part of the "intelligentsia," the group which includes all professionals, "not only the man of letters and the artist, teacher, scholar, the scientist and man of the cloth, the journalist and social worker, but also the engineer and technician, the lawyer and doctor, the veterinarian and midwife, the accountant and surveyor" (*AG* 88). This move is basically a fulfillment of their earlier bourgeois aspirations, and as they move from being marginal journalists to the status of professors and Kennedy intellectuals their economic alienation is cured with a vengeance. By moving to the universities they become cultural functionaries, bureaucrats of the mind, a trend which culminates in the values of *Making It.* After surveying the accomplishments of the Intellectuals in the thirties and forties, Mary McCarthy notes: "Meanwhile, like most American writers, professors, and editors, we were getting richer. And less revolutionary. Not just because

we had more money, but because we are getting older, and because, according to our analysis, it was not 'a revolutionary situation.' "[63]
The dating of the Intellectuals' shift to the intelligentsia is not, of course,
exact, since it involves the careers of many individual men, but it seems to
take place between 1948 and 1953. Philip Rahv speaks of it as a *fait accompli*
in 1952, in the *Partisan Review* symposium "Our Country and Our Culture."
It takes twenty years for their new status as conservatives to sink in, however; not until the 1972 symposium "The New Cultural Conservatism" is it
officially noted that Intellectuals have "a noticeable reluctance to receive
new works, new writers, new forms," and that their conservatism "inflates
established figures, and celebrates old values, old works, old institutions as
though they can never be changed or added to or replaced."[64] This conservatism is basically a projection of the Intellectuals' own worries onto the
culture, in the manner of their earlier symposia "Failure of Nerve" (1943)
or "Religion" (1952). In the 1972 symposium, Morris Dickstein analyzes
the new conservatism correctly as "a noisy campaign by a few well-situated
editors and critics to reverse the cultural direction of the Sixties . . . in
short, backlash."

Evidence of *embourgeoisement* lies in the histories of the institutions
that support criticism; during these years Rahv, Chase, and Schwartz
lectured at the Kenyon School of English and they, as well as Kazin,
Howe, and Fiedler, taught at the Indiana School of Letters. In 1957 Rahv
began teaching at Brandeis, the first American Jewish university, where
Irving Howe was appointed a professor in 1953. Alfred Kazin has been
lecturing at universities since 1944, and took a permanent position as a
Distinguished Professor at SUNY–Stony Brook in 1963. Norman Podhoretz
spent this period as a student at Cambridge on the prestigious Kellett
Fellowship and had a Fulbright as well. F. W. Dupee joined the Columbia
faculty in 1940, and Chase, Trilling, and Fiedler have been in universities
all their lives. In 1951 Dwight Macdonald rejoined the mass media as a
staff writer for *The New Yorker,* Podhoretz joined the staff of *Commentary,*
and Lionel Trilling was seen in an "intellectual" pose (with Jacques Barzun
and W. H. Auden) in ads recommending The Readers' Subscription Book
Club. So the evidence is that the Intellectuals had put the avant-garde
life behind them by about 1953. This career pattern is not atypical; Harold
Rosenberg remarks that "this bent toward careerism of modern Left intellectuals as a social caste is world-wide" (*TN* 252). Irving Howe's statement
that "ideally, the university ought to be a bastion of resistance against
'mass culture,' "[65] seems to rest on the romantic belief that one can transfer
the qualities of Bohemia to institutional life. In reality, after 1953 an
Intellectual is usually a professor without a Ph.D.

The extent of the co-optation of the Intellectuals by the state in America
in the fifties is related to the history of the American Committee for Cultural

Freedom, which supported among much else *Encounter* and was the publisher of the *Partisan Review* from 1959 to 1968.[66] The details of the subsidizing of the ACCF by the Central Intelligence Agency are not yet fully known, but it is clear that, in the words of Christopher Lasch, "intellectuals were unusually sensitive to their interests as a group and that they defined those interests in such a way as to make them fully compatible with the interests of the state."[67] Or as Wilfrid Sheed notes in a review of *Making It*: "Podhoretz has given us some intellectual history here after all—his mind moving, with the rest of the salmon, to pro-Americanism and back, but his tastes moving steadily to individual profit, and winding up somewhere to the right of Horatio Alger. This means that his left-wing opinions are just talk. And talk is cheap."[68]

Similarly, Isaac Rosenfeld speaks of the general publishing situation in 1956, noting that many of the functions of the literary avant-garde in introducing new writers have been taken over by paperback publishers like Anchor Books and that "there is also another so-called little magazine—*Perspectives USA*—which is supported by the funds of a foundation. ... The little magazines at one time were part of the image of garret poverty and obscurity. Now they survive, but survive with a certain opulence, and an opulence that threatens to crush them. Surely the specific idea of the little magazine, just as the specific idea of the *avant-garde*, gets lost in such a translation." Rosenfeld goes on to make a general cultural assessment: "This shrinkage of extremes is, I think, the dominant condition under which we live, and it has had an effect upon the *avant-garde* of practically wiping it out. The *avant-garde* is now replaced by the institutions that can take over their functions, and your Madison Avenue or your Upper Michigan Avenue man, your man in the Ivy League suit, with his paperback books on the shelf and modern furniture on the floor, is the heir of this age."[69]

This progress to the bourgeois section of the publishing industry—what the Intellectuals would earlier have referred to as mass culture—is apparent in their most important magazines. William Phillips writes in the late forties: "For many of its readers who are scattered all over the country it [*Partisan Review*] has served as a focal point in their attempts to orient themselves in the world of modern art and politics. Thus the magazine has come to possess the significance and authority of a stable cultural institution."[70] And at a somewhat more advanced stage of economic assimilation, Podhoretz announces: "*Commentary* was an institution, and as its head I was now entitled to certain of the perquisites of rank" (*MI* 223). The Intellectuals' shift to the intelligentsia makes Howe's plea in 1954 for the return of "the idea of a mind committed yet dispassionate, ready to stand alone, curious, eager, skeptical,"[71] seem like a romanticism, unrelated to the real situation, interests, and ambitions of the Intellectuals in the fifties and sixties. The progress of the Intellectuals as a whole in class terms is described by Norman Podhoretz:

From having carried a faint aura of disreputability, the title "intellectual" all at once became an honorific, and much began to be made in Washington as elsewhere of leading representatives of this particularistic [sic] class. The family did not regard certain of these "leading" representatives who were being honored with invitations to the White House and appointments to government task forces as intellectuals at all—they were, the family said, academics or high-level technicians. ... they may not have regarded others as deserving of the title "intellectual," but no one doubted *their* inalienable right to it. For the first time in their lives, they were in a relation to political power that could not be characterized as hostility reciprocated by indifference. All of us in the family knew and were even friendly with members of the White House staff; they read our magazines and the pieces and books we ourselves wrote, and they cared—it was even said the President himself cared—about what we thought. [*MI* 230-31]

In *Beyond Culture,* particularly in "On the Teaching of Modern Literature" and "The Two Environments: Reflections on the Study of English," Lionel Trilling examines the domestication of the old modernist tradition and its acceptance as orthodoxy in the academy and the cultural world generally. He asks: "Can we not say that, when modern literature is brought into the classroom, the subject being taught is betrayed by the pedagogy of the subject?" (*BC* 10). The fact which is most poignant to him is the deadening effect these books have on his students as compared to the exhilarating effect they had on him in his youth. Alfred Kazin gives similar testimony about the effects of teaching modernist works as part of Establishment culture: "Step by step the great confidence that man could understand his time and build from it, the feeling that provides the energy of modern art, has gone out of us, and we are left teaching such books as if they were models of correctness rather than rare moments of spirit" (*C* 509).

The ambivalence and dismay of the Intellectuals concerning their status as avant-gardists continues. In 1974, in the *Partisan Review* symposium "Literature and the Academy," William Phillips observes that when the magazine was young "everybody assumed we had what Lionel Trilling has called an adversary role in the culture," but today "to put it bluntly, we cannot be an avant-garde." [72] In sum, the historical cause of the Intellectuals' depression is the collapse of their avant-garde tradition into their bourgeois tradition, a collapse which in their case also reflects the progress to middle-age from youth, and to success from Bohemia. From Mother Bloor to George Plimpton, from *New Masses* to *Vogue*, from Williamsburg to the West Side, the Intellectuals have made that immense American journey from the lower to the upper middle class. [73]

The aging of the Intellectuals into respectability in the fifties has three main effects; it brings a shift away from revolutionary politics, an emphasis on the preservation of an old culture, and a rejection of the new avant-garde, with the concomitant attempt to put down a newer generation which is expressing new cultural realities.

The Intellectuals' shift from revolutionary to nostalgic politics is best conveyed by Rahv's 1952 statement that "the idea of socialism, whether in its revolutionary or democratic reference, has virtually ceased to figure in current intellectual discussion" a development he attributes to the *"embourgeoisement* of the American intelligentsia" (II 225). Yet despite its anachronistic character, socialism remains Rahv's position in 1967, as he confesses in the *Commentary* symposium "Liberal Anti-Communism Revisited."[74] Nostalgia for socialism is typical of many Intellectuals, especially Irving Howe, whose magazine, *Dissent*, is a living memorial to his socialist youth. But even Howe sometimes seems ambivalent. In his brief "Memoir of the Thirties" he says: "It is all gone, and we cannot have it back. There is nothing I desire more than a revival of American radicalism, but the past is done with, and I have no wish to recreate it nor any belief in the possibility of doing so."[75] Then, in a 1969 debate with Irving Kristol, he reaffirms his basic position: "I admire Mr. Kristol's rhetorical strategy: in effect, 'Aw come on, Irv, you don't really believe in all that socialist stuff, do you?' But I do. It's lamentable, I know, and a sign of cultural lag. But I really want to see the major segments of the American economy socially-controlled and democratically operated, and I really want a major redistribution of power and wealth in the U.S."[76] Being less nostalgic and thus less ambivalent, William Phillips and Lionel Trilling manage to stick to their conclusions. Phillips says in 1962: "It now looks as though a radical literature and a radical politics must be kept apart."[77] And Trilling says in 1963: "The old connection between literature and politics has been dissolved. For the typical modern literary personality, political life is likely to exist only as it makes an occasion for the disgust and rage which are essential to the state of modern spirituality" (*BC* 83).

Rejection of New Avant-Gardes

An emphasis on the conservation of culture emerges immediately after the disillusionment with Communism which follows the Nazi-Soviet pact. As James Gilbert says of the Intellectuals of 1940: "The war threat to France and its fall to Germany in 1940 took on special meaning aside from any military or political significance. Clement Greenberg . . . expressed the desperate mode of thinking that viewed the avant-garde—socialism even— as a conservative force, capable merely of preserving the culture whose capital had been Paris. 'Today,' he wrote in late 1939, 'we look to socialism *simply* for the preservation of whatever living culture we have right now.' "[78] In a sense the Intellectuals have never been anything but literary conservatives, since they have never defended an absolutely new tradition (as the

New Critics have with their own poetry), but continue to defend the tradition of the twenties established by Edmund Wilson's *Axel's Castle* in 1931, which (because of the literary hiatus in the Marxist thirties) still seems an avant-garde tradition in the forties. As Howe says, "they came late" (*DN* 218).

The Intellectuals' loss of their avant-garde position and the solidification of the tradition of their own group into orthodoxy lead them to reject any cultural reality beyond modernism (except for their concern with their own status as newly powerful Intellectuals). In the forties they totally ignore New Directions writers like Henry Miller, John Hawkes, Kenneth Rexroth, Edward Dahlberg, Gertrude Stein, or William Carlos Williams. In their writing they do not confront the destruction of Europe in World War II and the central fact of the atomic bomb, which makes total destruction of the world possible. William Barrett observes that although Philip Rahv accepted for publication in the *Partisan Review* a piece by Anatole Broyard entitled "The Hipsters," "Broyard represented to him another generation and new things with which he didn't want to cope. His mind was turned backward, rehearsing the sacred canon of the Great Moderns. The other pole of his conservatism was his Marxism." [79]

In a literary context the Intellectuals say little about the Existentialism of Beckett and Sartre or the Theatre of the Absurd, which arose in reaction to the destruction of old values. According to Lionel Trilling: "There is no possible way of responding to Belsen and Buchenwald. The activity of mind fails before the incommunicability of man's suffering" (*LI* 256). Unlike George Steiner or Hannah Arendt, the Intellectuals do not even attempt to come to terms with the new escalation of man's inhumanity to man, though they try to confront Arendt's book on Eichmann. With the exception of Richard Poirier, they ignore or see through the "Marxist" categories of their youth, the rise of the Beatles and rock-and-roll, the "beat" generation and the angry young men, the new interest in drugs and slums and pollution, Che Guevara and the black revolution, women's lib and the occult. Richard Kostelanetz has assembled a telling list of the sins of omission of Irving Howe, and the list applies *a fortiori* to the other Intellectuals, who have almost abandoned social and political speculation:

The frame of political concern expressed in *The Radical Papers* encompasses . . . a number of problems of obvious relevance. However, *The Radical Papers,* as well as Howe's *Steady Work*, conspicuously neglect to confront in any significant way such important dimensions of contemporary social and political existence as the impact and potential of automation and other new technologies, the restructuring of the content of education, . . . the power and influence of all electronic media of communication, the individual's role and ethical responsibility in a bureaucracy, . . . the rapidly increasing rate of population expansion (and the question of eugenics), the administration of a guaranteed annual income, . . . the general awareness of the increasing gap of generational difference, the depletion of natural resources, the pollution of the environment, etc., etc. The point of this list is that the Marxian frame that apparently encases Howe and his fellow dissenters perceives primarily the modern guises of nineteenth century problems, only to neglect the predicaments and possibilities that have developed since Marx's day.[80]

The two test cases which exhibit most clearly the Intellectuals' rejection of the new in literature are the "beats" and Norman Mailer. For Lionel Trilling, the trouble with the beats seems the personal difficulty of a teacher in seeing a student grow beyond his master; Allen Ginsberg was a student of Trilling's, as has been memorably chronicled by Diana Trilling in "The Other Night at Columbia: A Report from the Academy."[81] The only comment of the professor on the student is a veiled reference to "a group of my students who have become excited over their discovery of the old animosity which Ezra Pound and William Carlos Williams bear to the iamb, and have come to feel that could they but break the iambic shackles, the whole of modern culture could find a true expression. The value of form must never be denigrated" (*OS* 96). In Howe's case, the objection is less personal; he seems upset with the beats because they exhibit unfortunate cultural tendencies as "a reflex of the circumstances of mass society." Howe says:

These writers, I would contend, illustrate the painful, though not inevitable, predicament of rebellion in a mass society: they are the other side of the American hollow. In their contempt for mind, they are at one with the middle class suburbia they think they scorn. In their incoherence of feeling and statement, they mirror the incoherent society that clings to them like a mocking shadow. In their yearning to keep "cool," they sing out an eternal fantasy of the shopkeeper. Feeling themselves lonely and estranged, they huddle together in gangs, create a Brook Farm of Know-Nothings, and send back ecstatic reports to the squares: Having a Wonderful Time, Having Wonderful Kicks! But alas, all the while it is clear that they are terribly lost, and what is more pitiable, that they don't even have the capacity for improvising vivid fantasies. As they race meaninglessly back and forth across the continent, veritable mimics of the American tourist, they do not have a Wonderful Time. They do not get happily drunk, many of them preferring milk shakes and tea; and their sexual revelations, particularly in Kerouac's *The Subterraneans,* are as sad as they are unintentional. They can't, that is, dream themselves out of the shapeless nightmare of California.[82]

Alfred Kazin also seems disturbed by the sexual views of Kerouac and Ginsberg, as well as Mailer, Tennessee Williams, and Henry Miller. For Kazin, all of them share an "essential lack of feeling, of direction and point . . . accompanied by the same extreme yet abstract violence of sexual activity and description. I am reminded of the Marquis de Sade" (*C* 363). And Norman Podhoretz, younger than most of the beats, dismisses them grandly in "The Know-Nothing Bohemians," where he displays one of his best rhetorical tricks, an ability to sound like he is fifty and has immense intellectual authority when he is only twenty-eight:

The Bohemianism of the 1950's is another kettle of fish altogether [compared with the twenties]. It is hostile to civilization; it worships primitivism, instinct, energy, "blood." To the extent that it has intellectual interests at all, they run to mystical doctrines, irrationalist philosophies, and left-wing Reichianism. ... Their predilection for bop language is a way of demonstrating solidarity with the primitive vitality and spontaneity they find in jazz and of expressing contempt for coherent, rational discourse which, being a product of the mind, is in their view a form of death. To be articulate is to admit that you have no feelings ... that you can't respond to anything ... and that you are probably impotent. [*DU* 147]

After some further discussion of Kerouac, Ginsberg, and Mailer, Podhoretz concludes: "I think it is legitimate to say, then, that the Beat Generation's worship of primitivism and spontaneity is more than a cover for hostility to intelligence; it arises from a pathetic poverty of feeling as well. ... This is the revolt of the spiritually underprivileged and the crippled of soul" (*DU* 156). Podhoretz's objection here, as in his 1957 essay "The Young Generation," seems grounded intellectually in his adherence to the Intellectuals' idea of ironic complexity and modernism, which he imbibed from Trilling and Leavis. His depth of feeling would, I suppose, be based in his suspicion that he had missed both of the boats in which his generation sailed on its journey, having rejected both academic and hippie life to become a latter-day Philip Rahv. [83]

The other great literary test case is the Intellectuals' judgment of the relative merits of Saul Bellow and Norman Mailer. The comparison is an interesting one because both writers are of the same generation, both are Jewish, and each has been boosted as *the* major novelist of his generation. The problem of judging their relative worth comes to a head in 1964 and 1965, with the publication of *Herzog* and *An American Dream*. Until this time both had been treated, in one of Mailer's favorite metaphors, as contenders for the title; both had been praised but with reservations. William Phillips puts the matter fairly: "Bellow, who started out as a loner, a moral prowler, has reached the ripeness, the mellowness, the confidence of the established man of letters. Mailer, on the other hand, after an assured career, now acts like a young writer, cocky, nervous, and unpredictable. Bellow is admired as a novelist; Mailer has become, particularly for younger people, a messianic underground figure." [84]

The Intellectuals' response to Bellow after *Herzog* (1964) is almost uniformly enthusiastic. Rahv says that with *Herzog* "Bellow emerges not only as the most intelligent novelist of his generation but also as the most consistently interesting in point of growth and development. To my mind, too, he is the finest stylist at present writing fiction in America" (*MP* 218). Elizabeth Hardwick echoes this view: "Saul Bellow is particularly interesting in that he is one of the few fiction writers who used his full intelligence in his fiction. ... He uses every possible aspect of American life; whereas one finds that so many fiction writers are rather afraid of the total thing."[85] In praising Bellow the Intellectuals are of course praising the complexity, difficulty, and alienation of a master of the modernist tradition, as well as the best of the "Jewish-American" novelists.

With *An American Dream* (1965) in front of them, however, the same two critics become hostile and repudiate Mailer for his expression of the excessive and gratuitous sex and violence which seem to be the central qualities of the apocalyptic culture of the late sixties. Rahv says in the *New York Review of Books:* "The trouble with Mailer, to my mind, is that he has let himself become a victim of ideas productive of 'false consciousness'; and these ideas are willful, recklessly simple and too histrionic. He has too many ambition-fed notions and he does not sufficiently value the artistic function. ... Life's cruel and inexorable processes can be arrested neither by the brain nor by the phallus, least of all by the phallus" (*MP* 242-43). Rahv's response here is based on moral, formal, and mimetic standards of literary value traditional to bourgeois thinking. He goes on to criticize the book for being a projection of Mailer's own "desires, power-drives and daydreams," a "hipster's fantasy"; for being inaccurate about the life it describes—"I venture to say that real-life hipsters ... would hardly recognize themselves"; and for imitating an unrepresentative and immoral part of society, the literary swingers. "What they are doing is expressing the fickle moods of a certain sector of American society ... which in every sphere but the political has collapsed into total permissiveness" (*MP* 235-38). The objection to Mailer's violence and perversion is stated even more forcefully by Elizabeth Hardwick: "*An American Dream* by Norman Mailer is a fantasy of vengeful murder, callous copulations and an assortment of dull cruelties. It is an intellectual and literary disaster, poorly written, morally foolish and intellectually empty."[86] Mailer, of course, expresses what seemed quite moral to the young in the sixties, the "White Negro" or hipster philosophy of N. O. Brown, Herbert Marcuse, William Reich, and Marshall McLuhan, whom Irving Howe associates with Mailer in his attack on them in "The New York Intellectuals." In their judgments, then, the Intellectuals consistently repudiate the most contemporary of Mailer's thoughts, those in which he expresses most closely the temper of the "post modernist" era, and this repudiation serves only to date them, not to disestablish the historical reality of the sixties.[87]

The effect of the Intellectuals' coming to literary power is thus a split between the desire to have this power recognized by the young and the desire to remain young themselves; they wish really to abolish the generation coming after them as being unworthy and thus hold on to their youth. In the course of his attack on "the new immoralists" Genet and Burroughs, William Phillips says: "This is not simply a change in sensibility; it amounts to a sensibility of chaos—for it means that every new work has an equal and irresistible claim on us, that it lies outside judgment." In specific reference to Susan Sontag's "Notes on Camp," Phillips continues: "But those [like me] who have stronger roots in another style, one that recognizes that morality has limits but is not ready to abandon morality for any aesthetic stance, are even less prepared to abandon themselves to pure play, or to pure experience, which amounts to the same thing. One finds oneself *judging* as well as experiencing the quality of the new work or the new idea."[88] It would be hard to find a clearer expression of the state which every generation comes to—that of being set in its ways, of preferring the old habits to the new experience. While claiming that *Commentary* was the first magazine of any size to pay attention to the "New Left," Podhoretz says: "I found myself less and less able to go along with the completely apocalyptic sixties notion that American society was hopelessly, incorrigibly corrupt" (*MI* 23); he sees the politics of the sixties as a return of the anti-American clichés of the thirties. In the late sixties and early seventies, Podhoretz makes his opposition to the New Left one of the *idées fixes* of *Commentary*. Philip Rahv criticizes "outright pornography sanctified as a breakthrough to 'new frontiers' " (*MP* viii). In his essay "The Myth and the Powerhouse" he attacks even myth criticism as a "cultism which enables them [myth critics] to evade the hard choice between belief and unbelief" (*MP* 4), and says that this cultism is a revival of romantic neoprimitivism, whose appeal "lies precisely in its archaism, [in its] promises above all to heal the wounds of time" (*MP* 6). While Phillips opposes only his own judgment to the new, Rahv opposes the new with the traditional Marxist philosophical position that accuses the new men of ignoring history ("the powerhouse of change") and time, an ironic position for one who is himself ignoring the changes in fashion which time brings.

Howe is similarly hostile in "New Styles in Leftism," and shows in his analysis a blindness to the avant-garde nature of the new radicals' impatience with the older generation, its style of violence, anarchism, enmity to the Establishment, anti-Americanism, which as a putative avant-gardist he ought to praise. Howe's response to his own anachronism ranges from the pleading to the vindictive. He is worried because "after all these years one may have to face intellectual isolation and perhaps dismissal" (*DN* 261), and in *Steady Work* he pleads for understanding: "I want this book to be read by the younger radicals . . . as a record of intellectual struggle and political commitment . . . so they will understand, for example, why it is that people like myself cannot accept their fashionable 'agnosticism' toward

Communist dictatorship, or why . . . we have come to believe in the primacy of democratic values for any political reconstruction. Then if they wish, they can disagree and if they trouble to write books I promise to read them."[89] This plea for tolerance by Howe rings somewhat hollow when one recalls the series of vituperative attacks he made on older critics when *he* was young.[90] Howe later becomes more belligerent and bitter. In "The New York Intellectuals" he indulges in the wholesale condemnation of "a period of overwhelming cultural sleaziness." The "high priests" of the new "psychology of unobstructed need" are Norman Brown, Herbert Marcuse, and Marshall McLuhan. Howe, like Rahv, finds their position an offshoot of Romanticism, and hence unsound: "The new intellectual style, insofar as it approximates a politics, mixes sentiments of anarchism with apologies for authoritarianism; bubbling hopes for 'participatory democracy' with manipulative elitism; unqualified Populist majoritarianism with the reign of the cadres. . . . [The new sensibility] breathes contempt for rationality, impatience with mind, and a hostility to the artifices and decorums of high culture. It despises liberal values, liberal cautions, liberal virtues. It is bored with the past: for the past is a fink" (*DN* 249, 255).

The nasty streak which is part of the polemics of the thirties comes to the fore in Howe's sniping at Richard Kostelanetz (b. 1940), whose "The Perils and Paucities of Democratic Radicalism" critically analyzes Howe's writing. In "The New York Intellectuals" Howe implies in the text that in the needling questions he gets in "provincial" universities about New York life, "everyone knows what no one says: New York means Jews" (*DN* 248), this despite the fact that Howe and other academics have been talking of the Jewish-American literary renaissance for a decade or more. The purpose of this remark is to allow Howe to accuse Kostelanetz of bigotry in a Bnai-Brith footnote to the above sentence: "Not quite no one. In an attack on the New York writers (*Hudson Review,* Autumn 1965) Richard Kostelanetz speaks about 'Jewish group-aggrandizement' and 'the Jewish-American push.' One appreciates the delicacy of his phrasing" (*DN* 248). After all this, it is amusing to see Howe finish an answer to another critic with the words "But, who is Richard Kostelanetz?" which brings him close, not to polemics or the honest debate he claims to want, but to a loftiness worthy of Edith Sitwell.[91]

This hostility to the new literary avant-garde carries over even to the *New York Review of Books,* despite its flirtation with the political New Left and the Molotov cocktails on its cover. After an exhaustive survey of the magazine, Philip Nobile concludes: "Whatever the 'new sensibility' means, exactly, *New York Review* is insensitive to it. Conservative to the bone, the *New York Review* won't dance with Andy Warhol, the Living Theatre, Kurt Vonnegut, John Hawkes, Jean-Claude van Itallie or Richard Gilman, all of whom have been excoriated between its covers. The *Review*'s roster has been swept clean of known 'swingers' like Susan Sontag, Richard Poirier, Richard Gilman and Albert Goldman. Outsiders like Morris Dickstein and Leslie Fiedler are shunned altogether."[92]

Looked at in Poggioli's terms, what has happened is that the agonistic and nihilistic strains in avant-grade thinking which were subordinated by the modernists' activism, experimentalism, and antagonism toward bourgeois culture have been reborn in the sixties as a new avant-garde movement so strange to the New York Intellectuals that they are unable to recognize it as avant-garde at all.[93] The problem for most of the Intellectuals is thus not only awareness of the death of their avant-garde but self-awareness, the realization that this death applies to them. Lionel Trilling says in 1948: "Surely the great work of our time is the restoration and the reconstitution of the will" (*LI* 258). Irving Howe laments in 1949: "Where, all the while, is the opposition, the rebellious and exuberant *avantgarde?* Nowhere in sight, for it no longer exists."[94] And in 1957, in his long article "The Fate of the Avant-Garde," Richard Chase pronounces more analytically: "There is no service in attacking the avant-garde critics ... [for] their specifically polemical task of the last forty years has expired with the success of the movements they championed. They have not yet clearly formulated what their duties in this interim period are. Meanwhile, they suffer from the well-known maladies of the avant-gardist, especially on the ebb-tide of his influence: sterility, academicism, willful and excessive intellectuality."

That this particular avant-garde movement should be past history is no particular tragedy for most of its members, who have done their bit to defend their tradition and have gone forward into successful academic careers. The only ones who still insist on playing the old adversary role are Macdonald, Irving Howe, and Norman Podhoretz. Macdonald and Howe are given to issuing "unto the breach once more" statements rallying their friends to the good old cause. In his "Masscult and Midcult," Macdonald concludes: "But if we are ever to have more than [accidental culture] it will be because our new public for High Culture becomes conscious of itself and begins to show some *esprit de corps,* insisting on higher standards and setting itself off—joyously, implacably—from most of its fellow citizens."[95] Howe ends "The New York Intellectuals" with the plea: "Yet, precisely at this moment of dispersion, might not some of the New York writers achieve renewed strength if they were to struggle once again for whatever has been salvaged from these last few decades? For the values of liberalism, for the politics of a democratic radicalism, for the norms of rationality and intelligence, for the standards of literary seriousness, for the life of the mind as a humane dedication" (*DN* 264–65). For God, for Irving, and St. George! Howe is quite right in affirming that freedom is essential to the avant-garde Intellectual, [96] but he is less aware that in gaining tenure he has lost his own avant-garde position.

One must then conclude of the Intellectuals that their careers as critics are best understood as parts in an avant-garde play; they have played, and played well for the most part, roles in a drama that is now concluded. The conventional nature of their activity, in later years especially, is revealed by a remark of Podhoretz's: "It is simply that a public existed when she [Susan Sontag] arrived on the scene which was searching for a new Dark Lady [to replace Mary McCarthy], and she was so obviously right that a spontaneous decision was made on all sides to cast her for the role—exactly as I in my time had been chosen for a role I seemed practically born to play" (*MI* 116). Now the drama is ended. "This *is* the inevitable, inexorable destiny of each movement: to rise up against the newly outstripped fashion of an old avant-garde and to die when a new fashion, movement, or avant-garde appears" (*AG* 82). The difficulty is that the actors are still around. The problem, as Poggioli notes, is one of succession: the avant-garde is dead; long live the avant-garde!

8. The Intellectual Men of Letters

The time has then come to estimate the permanent value of the Intellectuals by asking to what extent these critics have managed to express their common charter in a way which would add a new exemplary response to the history of criticism. Have they achieved a voice which is interesting to readers who did not share their youthful infatuation with revolutionary politics and avant-garde literature, and the dialectic that this created with their bourgeois life style?

Lionel Trilling: Critic without a Cause

Of the Intellectual Men of Letters—Rahv, Trilling, Howe—the logical contender for eponymic status, for a permanent place in critical history, is Lionel Trilling. One must regretfully conclude that Trilling does not show us a new way to read and respond to literature, as do Brooks and Empson, or Northrop Frye. Quite apart from his scholarly achievement as the author of *Matthew Arnold*, Trilling's importance as a critic is nevertheless considerable because he is the Intellectuals' Representative Man. Almost every move made by the other members of the group is made by Trilling first and is expressed in his essays. His indispensable role has been to serve as the Intellectuals' consciousness, or as Kazin puts it, as "an Emersonian teacher of the tribe" (*C* 497).

Trilling's first move is to secure his identity as a Jew. He says: "What bound together the group around the *Menorah Journal* [in 1928] . . . was the idea of Jewishness . . . Chiefly, our concern with Jewishness was about what is now called authenticity . . . we had in mind something that probably still goes under the name of a 'sense of identity,' by which is meant . . . that the individual Jewish person recognizes naturally and easily that he *is* a Jew and 'accepts himself' as such" (YIT 46). And Trilling is also the first to move beyond this cause to become part of the avant-garde. When invited to be on the advisory board of *Commentary* (founded in 1945), he declines. As he explains it: "I had had my experience of the intellectual life lived in reference to what Cohen called the Jewish community, and I had no wish to renew it by associating myself with a Jewish magazine. Whatever such an association was for others, and I could understand that it might be anything from a help to a necessity, for me it could now only be a posture and a falsehood."[1] Trilling is thus the first of the Intellectuals to transcend the provincialism of Jewish culture and he never participates in the puffing of Jewish novelists that occupies other Intellectuals in the fifties and sixties. Trilling is also the first Intellectual to make the move from the avant-garde to the intelligentsia; he chose an academic career from the beginning, and though "my appointment to an instructorship in Columbia College was pretty openly regarded as an experiment, and for some time my career in the College was complicated by my being Jewish" (YIT 47), he carries it through successfully and ends his career as a university professor. Thus, at a time when most Intellectuals thought themselves opposed to the general society on literary grounds, Trilling had already begun to discuss the much more complex problem of the tension between avant-garde modernist literature and liberal political thought and action. Since the tension between politics and literature and the effort to reconcile it become the Intellectuals' charter in the forties, Trilling's writing serves the therapeutic and historically important function of bringing the Intellectuals' position to consciousness.[2]

Trilling illuminates the nature of the Intellectuals' struggle with themselves during the course of an analysis of Tess Slesinger's *The Unpossessed*, when he notes that the novel expresses a tension between what is and what might be, the is and the ought, nature and spirit, and continues: "In the radical political culture of the Thirties, the dialectic was to be perceived at work in its fullest ironic force. The doctrine of the politics affirmed freedom; the conduct of the politics was likely to be marked by a dull rigidity. The doctrine was directed toward the richness and fullness that would eventually be given to human life, but a solicitude for mankind in general and in the future had the effect of diminishing the awareness of actual particular persons within the reach of the hand" (YIT 49). In voicing this feeling that liberal politics is not what it ought to be as judged by avant-garde literary standards, Trilling expresses what, as much as the Moscow trials or the anti-Soviet pact, disillusioned American Intellectuals with the Communist party. Trilling's application of literary standards of complexity to the politics of 1940 is his most important act as a critic, for it destroys the naturalistic interpretation of American literature of Parrington and his followers, and paves the way for the movement of the Intellectuals to the intelligentsia and the academy.[3]

Trilling's development of this struggle is expressed in a compulsive attachment to dualistic forms of thought. An examination of Trilling's practical criticism reveals that he is interested almost exclusively in writers who illustrate the tension between reality and imagination, body and intellect, is and ought, that exists within the New York Intellectual community. "Wordsworth, in short, is looking at man in a double way, seeing man both in his ideal nature and in his earthly activity" (*LI* 146). "The dialectic which Keats instituted between passivity and activity presents itself in another form, in the opposition between thought and sensation" (*OS* 29). "It may be said of James ... that virtually all his fiction represents the conflict of two principles, of which one is radical, the other conservative ... energy and inertia; or spirit and matter; or spirit and letter; or force and form; or creation and possession; or Libido and Thanatos" (*OS* 108). "Life and death, good and evil, spirit and flesh, male and female, the all and the one, Anthony and Dionysius—O'Neill's is a world of these antithetical absolutes."[4] Trilling condemns American culture for not recognizing this dualism—that is, for its failure to recognize the spiritual superiority of the avant-garde: "For if the Americans were truly materialistic, they would recognize the necessity of dualism, they would have contrived a life of the spirit apart from and in opposition to the life of material concern" (*GF* 163). As one regards Trilling's practical criticism in toto, it seems clearly projective; as he looks at literature and American culture itself, he sees them as reflections of the struggle between imagination and reality, avant-garde and bourgeois, which is the form of his own mind and of the Intellectuals' charter.

In the context of the history of ideas, Trilling is of course tracing in literature the form of culture held by the great nineteenth-century prophets Marx and Freud: "A culture is not a flow, nor even a confluence; the form of its existence is struggle or at least debate—it is nothing if not a dialectic" (*LI* 7). Trilling usually does not think in Marxist terms of class struggle, however (even between avant-garde and bourgeois); the struggle he is most interested in is the moral struggle between values within the individual. He praises E. M. Forster because Forster knows "class may be truly represented only by struggle and contradiction, not by description, and preferably by moral struggle within in the heart of a single person."[5] The terms of Trilling's polarity are closest to those of Freud; in his last essay on Freud he says that "it is of the essence of both [literature and psychoanalysis] to represent the opposition between two principles, those which Freud called the reality principle and the pleasure principle" (*BC* 96). In "Reality in America" Trilling goes beyond proletarian concern with reality to condemn American literature for not being spiritual enough; his ambiguous use of the term "reality" has been much discussed.[6] For Trilling, Vernon Parrington and Dreiser are representatives of the strong force of reality in our country, and in "Manners, Morals, and the Novel" he defines the term specifically: "Reality, as conceived by us, is whatever is external and hard, gross, unpleasant. Involved in its meaning is the idea of power conceived in a particular way" (*LI* 209). In his essay on Howells he describes reality as "the conditioned," the daily material needs like house-hunting with which the freest spirits have to cope.

In *The Liberal Imagination* he criticizes liberal and democratic social beliefs for being too bureaucratic, too much of the party of reality (*LI* xi, xii, 94–95, 219). In a summary statement he says: "The quarrel with the liberal mind directs itself beyond *PM* and *The New Republic*. I have in view the ideas of our powerful teachers' colleges, the assumptions of our social scientists, the theories of education that are now animating our colleges and universities, the notions of the new schools of psychoanalysis, the formulations of the professors of literature, particularly American literature . . . This is the liberal culture that my own criticism has ultimately, if with insufficient explicitness, been directed against."[7] And in *The Opposing Self* he sees reality as "culture," in the sense of a people's "mere assumptions and unformulated valuations, . . . its habits, its manners, and its superstitions" (*OS* x); he finds this reality in literature in the image of the prison, society's "prisons in the family life, in the professions, in the image of respectability, in the ideas of faith and duty, in (so the poets said) the very language itself" (*OS* x–xi). By reality, then, Trilling means that part of the world which is bourgeois, liberal, physical, scientific, positivistic, Philistine, and evil. And, citing Shakespeare and Keats as examples, he affirms that "the sense of evil is properly managed only when it is not allowed to be preponderant over the sense of self" (*OS* 101).

As one traces Trilling's uses of reality it becomes clear that what is opposed to it is the avant-garde imagination, the idea of the self where true pleasure is to be found. According to Trilling, the chief way in which man expresses and embodies pleasure is in literature, and the reason for this is a Freudian one: literature is the way in which modern civilized man experiences the primitive pleasures of the id (*LI* 283–84; *OS* 99). Thus, naturally enough, the literature-making faculty, the imagination, is the center of the self and of the intellectual life. Trilling thus sees in Freud the basis for a literary tradition that reflects the Intellectuals' avant-garde position and values vis-á-vis their bourgeois liberal politics. For Trilling, the imagination is expressive of what might be called the "Rameau values": "Rameau is lustful and greedy, arrogant yet self-abasing, perceptive yet 'wrong,' like a child" (*LI* 33). These values are "the qualities that are associated with sexuality: high-heartedness, wit, creative innovation, will" (*OS* 136). In a social context they are the qualities of "variousness, possibility, complexity, and difficulty" (*LI* xiii). They are "the life of surprise and elevation, of impulse, pleasure and imagination" associated with Arnold's Scholar Gipsy (OS xiii). They are "the mystery and wildness of spirit which it is still our grace to believe is the mark of full humanness" (LI 220).

The vigor of Trilling's best essays stems from his ability to hold bourgeois reality and avant-garde imagination in his mind at the same time, in a state of tension. Alfred Kazin says: "What raised Trilling above the dull zealots, informants, and false patriots of this agonizing period was the critic's gift for dramatizing his mind on paper. A writer of tremulous carefulness and deliberation, he nevertheless became the master of a dialectical style that expressed his underlying argument with himself. There was an intellectual tension in his essays."[8] This capacity—ambivalence in psychological terms—Trilling explains in moral terms as the idea of "good-and-evil," and it is this complex state of mind which in 1943 he claims is needed to correct the simplistic nature of liberal thinking: "The liberal mind is sure that the order of human affairs owes it a simple logic: good is good and bad is bad ... The mood that is the response to good-and-evil it has not named and cannot understand. Before the idea of good-and-evil its imagination fails; it cannot accept this improbable paradox."[9] Trilling calls the capacity to accept and respond to the paradox of good and evil "moral realism" (LI 213-15).

Trilling also finds this tension, or dialectic, to be the formal principle of the structure of literature. In "The Meaning of a Literary Idea" he says: "Whenever we put two emotions into juxtaposition we have what we can properly call an idea ... Then it can be said that the very form of all literary work ... is in itself an idea. Whether we deal with syllogisms or poems, we deal with dialectic" (LI 274). And more important, Trilling's practical standard of judgment of literature is the maintenance of tension: "No doubt the thing we respond to in great tragedy is the implication of some meaningful relation between free will and necessity, and it is what we respond to in Freud ... His is the Shakespearean vision" (GF 57). It is what Keats called "Negative Capability" (OS 32; LI 298). It is the quality of spirit acting on reality in literature: "We feel that Hemingway and Faulkner are intensely at work upon the recalcitrant stuff of life" (LI 287). And ultimately for Trilling the idea of tension is eschatological; it is found in the tradition of literature which embodies "moral realism," in the great modern works of Proust, Joyce, and Lawrence, James, Eliot, and Yeats, Kafka, Rilke, and Gide, which hold the only hope for the spirit of man. The "dialectic that goes on between spirit and the conditioned" is "man's tragic fate" (OS 93). Ultimately, like Arnold, Trilling believes that "a novel's reconstitutive and regenerating power" will save us from the Philistines (LI 260). "The questions asked by our literature are not about our culture but about ourselves. It asks us if we are content with ourselves, if we are saved or damned—more than with anything else, our literature is concerned with salvation" (*BC* 8). Trilling's importance as a critic lies in the fact that in the 1940s this charter was of great importance to American cultural and intellectual life. In his essays, his novel *The Middle of the Journey*, and in his person, Trilling expresses the intellectual and emotional dialectic of all the Intellectuals.

Like the rest, however, in about 1953 Trilling becomes the victim of his own success and influence. The Intellectuals, helped by his example, move into the academy, and the avant-garde movement in literature he espouses is displaced by new avant-gardes; the group tension he brought to consciousness disappears in reality as the Intellectuals join the bourgeoisie and modernism becomes academic orthodoxy. In *The Liberal Imagination* Trilling is the voice of the forties, a voice which shortly becomes irrelevant to the new professors, myth critics, and "beat" poets, as it had always been irrelevant to the America beyond the Hudson, which did not share the Intellectuals' historical experience of betrayal. Like most other Intellectuals, Trilling refuses to betray his tradition, refuses to respond to the realities of postwar America, and in so doing dates himself. In this connection, Trilling's 1937 remarks on Willa Cather (made when he was thirty-one) seem prophetic: "Miss Cather has gone down to defeat before the actualities of American life. . . . In our literature there are perhaps fewer completely satisfying books and certainly fewer integrated careers than there are interesting canons of work and significant life stories. Something in American life seems to prevent the perfection of success while it produces a fascinating kind of search or struggle, usually unavailing. . . . In this recurrent but heroic defeat, the life of the American writer parallels the life of the American pioneer. . . . The 'spirituality' of Miss Cather's latest books consists chiefly of an irritated exclusion of those elements of modern life with which she will not cope."[10] But in noting that Trilling too ceased to cope, we should not forget that his is also a significant life story.

Trilling's self-awareness is such that he makes several attempts to analyze his retreat from a struggle with contemporary realities and the decline of his avant-garde tradition of literature to a new orthodoxy. His progress is illustrated in the titles of his books. In *The Liberal Imagination* the avant-garde imagination and political reality are locked in a dynamic struggle. The still point of his career is his novel about criticism, *The Middle of the Journey* (1947). In *The Opposing Self* he retreats to the romantic self of the nineteenth century, a retreat which turns into a rout in *A Gathering of Fugitives*. In *Beyond Culture* he has given up the struggle to comprehend contemporary life altogether. In 1951 he says: "Our metaphysical habits lead us to feel the deficiency of what we call literal reality and to prefer what we call essential reality" (*OS* 94). In the mid-fifties he withdraws to scholarship of the past and expresses the desire to withdraw from the struggle, praising the scholarly "quietism" of "Wordsworth and the Rabbis," extolling the "preference for rest over motion" of *Mansfield Park*, and relating the idyllic quality of Mr. Woodhouse in *Emma* to the Christian dream of rest. And in 1964, in the course of showing that modernists should prefer Kafka to Hawthorne because the latter has too close a tie to literal reality, he says wistfully: "The modern consciousness requires that an artist have an imagination which is more intransigent than James could allow, more spontaneous, peremptory, and obligatory, which shall impose itself upon us with such unquestionable authority that 'the actual' can have no power over us but shall seem the creation of some inferior imagination, that of mere convention and habit. Our modern piety is preoccupied by the ideal of the autonomous self, or at least of the self as it seeks autonomy in its tortured dream of metaphysical freedom" (*BC* 205).

In these years Trilling also tries to reconstitute his lost dualism, most notably by proposing the idea of the biological irreducibility of man as a positive ideal which he can oppose to his now-bourgeois imagination and culture. He praises Orwell and the middle class for the "stupidity of things," which he sets up against abstract ideas (*OS* 166); and in "Wordsworth and the Rabbis" he affirms that "every tragic literature owes its power to the high esteem in which it holds the common routine, and the sentiment of being which arises from it, the elemental *given* of biology" (*OS* 148). In re *Ethan Frome* he says that "moral inertia [morality of habit, morality of biology], the *not* making of moral decisions, constitutes a large part of the moral life of humanity" (*GF* 37; see also *LI* 270). And in 1955 he praises Freud: "We must stop to consider whether this emphasis on biology, correct or incorrect, is not so far from being a reactionary idea that it is actually a liberating idea. It proposes to us that culture is not all-powerful. It suggests that there is a residue of human quality beyond the reach of cultural control, and that this residue of human quality, elemental as it may be, serves to bring culture itself under criticism and keeps it from being absolute" (*BC* 113). In the summation of "Young in the Thirties" Trilling says:

It is a characteristic of the modern age that an ever-increasing number of people suppose that they must be involved in the spiritual intellect's great work. Whoever can recall the Twenties and Thirties might well have a clear notion of how constant has been the augmentation of their number. The modern person who has reached a certain not uncommon point of intellectual development lives in relation to *terms*, that is to say, to ideas, principles, pasts, futures, the awareness of the dirty slate and the duty of cleaning it. Some stand closer to the actvity of the spiritual intellect than others, but all are obedient to its imperative, and proud of their obedience. Yet over this necessity there hovers the recollection, or the imagination, of a mode of existence ... that, to use Yeats's language, is of "the body and its stupidity," the blessed stupidity of nature and instinct. [YIT 51]

But biology does not prove a satisfactory opponent for imagination, and

Trilling's final attempt to reestablish the dualistic situation in which imagination is set up against culture involves opposing reason itself to the now-bourgeois avant-garde (*BC* xviii). This attempt, like the others, is never developed at any length. As Alfred Kazin remarks in 1970: "Who can doubt ... that so imaginative a writer as Lionel Trilling has often silenced himself in these last few years because it is impossible to work oneself out of the post-radical dilemma by critical argument alone?"[11]

Thus the later Trilling settles permanently into the respectability of the intelligentsia. Two of the five 1960s essays collected in *Beyond Culture* deal with the problems of the pedagogue at Columbia, and a third chides Dr. Leavis for bad manners and Sir Charles Snow for neglecting Arnold's arguments about literature and science. To justify his own retreat from struggle, Trilling goes so far as to find a *principle* of good in the attenuated independence of the literary literati: "This second [literary] environment must always have some ethical and spiritual advantage over the first [the general culture of reality], if only because, even though its influence and its personnel do indeed grow apace, it will never have the actual rule of the world" (*BC* 227). Unlike Podhoretz, who never knew the independent avant-garde in its heyday, Trilling seems to feel sad and bought off by its progress into the intelligentsia. His pathos is that he failed to change with the times and thus destroyed the dualism which is the essence of his mind; *his* time, the time when he expressed an important social tension, has passed him by and left him, with all his infinite subtlety, a critic without a cause.

In his retirement, nevertheless, Trilling is the beneficiary of what might be called Dilsey's law of cultural reward; thirty-five years after his book on Arnold, twenty-five years after *The Liberal Imagination*, honors are showered on him because he has endured. In 1972 he is chosen to give the first annual Thomas Jefferson Lecture in the Humanities, in which he laments that with the abandonment of the attempt to educate the whole man, the glorification of madness and anti-rationality over objectivity, the replacing of intellectual standards with "affirmative action" in the hiring of faculty and equality of opportunity in the admission of students, the mind itself has come to be thought evil; and that, with the election of the radical Louis Kampf to the presidency of the MLA, "in our time the mind of a significant part of a once proud profession has come to the end of its tether."[12] At the end of this threnody, Trilling reaffirms the importance of the mind as the model of the state, but offers only self-consciousness as a means to avoid despair. In this he is more genteel and less hopeful than Howe and Macdonald, but no more convincing about how the Intellectuals' ideal vision is to be recovered.

Trilling's other late honor is his appointment as Charles Eliot Norton Lecturer at Harvard in 1970. In his lectures, published in 1972 as *Sincerity and Authenticity,* Trilling rings the changes on the idea of sincerity and its twin, insincerity, and the idea of authenticity or facing reality, tracing their development in Western culture from Shakespeare through Diderot, Hegel, Wilde, Austen, and the rest of his heroes to Freud, whose *Civilization and Its Discontents* defends a "firm acceptance of life, of death, and of the developed mode of existence which is yielded by the unremitting dialectic between them."[13] Though this long meditation on intellectual history has a certain interest for those fascinated with the development of Trilling's thought, it is painful reading because it is otherwise pointless, for it neither illuminates the figures he is talking about nor helps the contemporary audience understand how it should look at intellectual history. It is Trilling's swan song, but it now seems more dated than the Norton Lectures given by a literary man in 1933, T. S. Eliot's *The Use of Poetry and the Use of Criticism.*

Howe, Rahv, Kazin

As Trilling was earlier the teacher of the Intellectuals, so his later career is a model for the collapse of their charter into obsolescence. A similar adherence to a tensional dialectic between some version of "realism" and "imagination," as well as the difficulty in maintaining that dialectic, is characteristic of the later careers of the other Intellectual critics.

Irving Howe, twenty years younger than the rest of the Intellectuals (b. 1920), adopts and uses the standard Intellectual charter and because of his comparative youth is the only one to carry the standard into America's third century. In a bicentennial survey of American literature, Howe echoes Trilling: "He [Fitzgerald] said once that the mark of a first-rate mind is the ability to hold two ideas at the same time [and still function (see *LI* 238)]. What makes him central to the course of our literature is that he seems, more than any contemporary, to write with a rich awareness of the Emerson-Whitman tradition and an equally rich awareness of all those forces of social and moral disaster which Eliot dramatized in 'The Wasteland' [*sic*]." After a brief account of the encounter of American romance, idealism, and imagination with history, reality, and tragedy, Howe concludes: "I have sketched a scheme, no more than that, for looking at American literature."[14] Howe's particular version of the Intellectuals' standard dialectic between avant-garde and mass culture, realism and imagination, involves the equation of realism with his democratic or Fabian socialism, which he describes as "the closest we can come to political realism."[15] But Howe has two voices. In *The Critical Point* the realistic Howe, the noblest Howe of them all, is given to seeing himself as the last of an embattled race of decent, civilized (yet radical) Socialists confronting a new race of barbarians: "The obligation to defend and extend freedom . . .

is the sacred task of the intellectual ... even when it means standing alone against fashionable shibboleths like Revolution and the Third World" (pp. 37–38). "Writers like Robinson survive in their work, appreciated by readers who aren't afraid to be left alone with an old book" (p. 96). When he is not indulging in this kind of romantic pretense of isolation and neglect, the noble Howe is given to Jeremiah-like condemnations of the same contemporary world. This voice is characterized stylistically by a list of abstract evils and goods that seem to prove a point until examined closely. For example, see his description of the "beat" writers cited above, or his account of the youth of today: "Impatience with the sluggish masses, burning convictions of righteousness, the suffocation of technological society, the boredom of overcrowded cities, the yearning for transcendent ends beyond the petty limits of group interest, romantic-sinister illusions about the charismatic virtues of dictatorship in under-developed countries—all these tempt young people into apolitical politics ... [where they share] an amorphous revulsion from civilization itself" (p. 30).

The noble Howe acts according to the principles of democratic Socialism which *he* considers to be realistic, and one of the reasons for the frenetic and hysterical note of this voice is the palpable unreality of the ideals he defends, ideals which exist not in reality, not in politics, but in nostalgia for his adolescence. In his adherence to these *fin de siècle* ideals Howe seems something like a Beerbohm cartoon of Oscar Wilde: "Irving Addressing the Burghers of America on the Failures of Their Way of Thought." Indeed, ideology triumphs over reality in Howe so much that when something like higher education for all comes about in the United States, it is "a project which, we socialists would like to think, might better have coincided with the growth of a democratic socialist order" (p. 26). There is no pleasing some people.

Happily, Howe also has a good voice, the voice of the writer of literary appreciations, that of the responsible journalist, the bourgeois critic, and it is this voice which saves him. It is the voice of turn-of-the-century bookmen like Edmund Gosse or George Saintsbury, who offer the reader an informed appraisal of a current enthusiasm, and in point of fact Howe's literary heart seems to lie in the Edwardian period, as his studies of Hardy and E. A. Robinson suggest. In the dialectic between Socialism and nostalgia, the literary Howe seems to be winning; at least he seems to be mellowing, perhaps due to the success of his best-seller, *World of our Fathers,* and to his generally having "made it" in the world of letters. According to Roger Sale: "Howe seems to be trusting his human and literary instincts more than he once did, and that trust is repaying him handsomely. Perhaps his own world has indeed and finally grown more attractive."[16] Though Howe's imagination seldom rises above the journalistic level, he is a first-rate literary journalist, and he has shown an endurance which gives him a kind of institutional status, like someone who has run the Boston Marathon for fifty years. Philip Nobile has aptly called him "The Lou Gehrig of the Old Left."[17]

Philip Rahv, longtime editor of the *Partisan Review* and one of the personally dominant figures among Intellectuals, shows how the charter of the Intellectuals can serve as the basis for a full critical career. The dialectic between politics and literature was, of course, the charter of the *Partisan Review* in its better years. The particular form this dialectic took in Rahv's mind is described by Mary McCarthy in "Philip Rahv, 1908–1973": "All his life he was sternly faithful to Marxism, for him both a tool of analysis and a wondrous cosmogony; but he loved Henry James and every kind of rich, shimmery, soft texture in literature and in the stuff of experience. . . . There were two persons in Rahv, but solidly married to each other in a long-standing union—no quarrels. It would be simplifying to say that one was political, masculine and aggressive, one feminine, artistic and dreamy, but those contrasts were part of it."[18] For Rahv, the "realistic" pole of the dichotomy is his belief in Marxist politics, in history; the "imaginative" pole is his love of writers like Henry James and F. Scott Fitzgerald. In Rahv's hands this dialectic leads to the most memorable critical distinction carved by an Intellectual, the division of American writers into "palefaces" like Henry James and "redskins" like Whitman, although this was but a rephrasing of Van Wyck Brooks's earlier distinction between "highbrows" and "lowbrows."

Rahv projects this dialectic into American literature, examining Melville, Hawthorne, James, Hemingway, Fitzgerald, and Eliot in its terms: "To my mind, the principal theme of this [modern American] novel, from Dreiser and Anderson to Fitzgerald and Faulkner, has been the discrepancy between the high promise of the American dream and what history has made of it" (*MP* 96)—that is, between imagination and reality. Rahv develops his realistic pole in "The Cult of Experience in American Writing" and "The Myth and the Powerhouse," where he argues for historical reality against the spatializing, eternal past of myth and ritual. In the sixties he recasts the familiar dialectic in yet another context, the relationship between the "New Left" in politics and the "new sensibility" in art. In his magazine, *Modern Occasions,* he tries to keep the two separate, supporting the New Left and opposing the new sensibility. Thus he criticizes Daniel Bell's article "Sensibility in the 60's" as "no more than a clever amalgam tactically designed to stigmatize the New Left as being of a piece with the excesses of the counter culture. . . . Sorry, Mr. Bell, the Woodstock nation . . . was not begotten by the New Left. The amalgam simply won't stick."[19] Finally, in one late essay,[20] Rahv seems to be repudiating modernism in an attempt to rejoin the radical and literary halves of his charter again in a new Popular Front, an event which his death aborts.

In the end, then, Rahv seems very much the ordinary Intellectual. Never an original, his importance is limited by the paucity of his output (he wrote only about forty essays during his career) and by the narrowness of his interests. Mary McCarthy says of him: "It was as though he came into being with the steam engine: for him, literature began with Dostoevsky and stopped with Joyce, Proust and Eliot; politics began with Marx and Engels and stopped with Lenin. He was not interested in Shakespeare, the classics, Greek city states; and he despised most contemporary writing and contemporary political groups."[21] Within his limits, however, his presence was forceful, and as an editor enforcing them he was himself a powerhouse.

The obsolescence of the Intellectuals' dialectic exposes the temporal limitation of the ideas they all depend on. Comparatively, the historical situation which led them to try to be both bourgeois and avant-garde at the same time is necessarily limited in both space and time to those who happened to embrace revolutionary Marxism and displace it into literature, and this situation seems much less important in our culture than the displaced protestantism of the Formalists or the myth critics' search for universal archetypes. The truth of the matter is that the "Intellectuals" are dependent on the ideas of others; it is unfair to compare them with original and creative thinkers like Marx or Freud, Frazer or Darwin; and they are much less original, systematic, and useful than scholars who have mastered a field of study and reordered it in a new compelling way. The difference between a scholar and an intellectual has been wittily put by Harry Gideonse, chancellor of the New School for Social Research in New York: "[An intellectual is] a person living articulately in abstractions beyond his intellectual means—if he lives within his intellectual means he's a scholar."[22] Put more positively, the Intellectuals are journalists, and should be seen not as failed scholars but as the most learned and thoughtful members of the Fifth Estate. While it is true that they have brought this misapprehension on themselves by laying claim to the intellectual authority of scholars, perhaps because most of them have found themselves earning their living in university posts, one should free them from this erroneous miscasting.

As journalists, the forms the Intellectuals use most often are the book review and the essay. Howe says that "the essay, a form both flexible and economical, remains the 'natural mode for literary criticism.' "[23] Though the use of this form keeps them from developing an argument systematically or fully, it has the advantages of readability and communicability. As Irving Howe notes in his introduction to the essays collected in *The Critical Point:* "They do not have, nor try to have, the kind of unity we expect in a book that claims a continuous argument from start to finish. Which is to say: this is a *different kind* of book, it is a collection of essays. This, or any other such collection, may be judged a distinguished work, a mediocre work, or a mixture; but let it be judged for what it is."[24] As middlemen, honest brokers between the scholars whose ideas they adopt, simplify, and popularize, and the middle-class audience, they serve a useful social role, and should be honored for what they are. The Intellectual who best exemplifies this journalistic virtue is, in my estimation, Alfred Kazin, whose criticism after *On Native Grounds* consists largely of introductions and brief reviews of current books. Robert Alter agrees—"if Kazin is a one-book critic, he is in many respects an ideal reviewer"—and suggests that "the limits of his own achievement as a critic, . . . after the large and compelling literary-historical narrative he fashioned in *On Native Grounds*, are determined by the fact that he has had no adequate analytic vantage point for getting into those texts to be commented on."[25] Having explicated American literature in terms of the Intellectuals' dialectic, Kazin finds no critical principle to substitute for it when it collapses, and thus retires to be autobiographer and memoirist of the Intellectual milieu in *A Walker in the City* (1951), *Starting Out in the Thirties* (1965), and *New York Jew* (1978).

Steven Marcus, Trilling's most publicly devoted disciple, successfully carries the Intellectuals' dialectic into the new age by developing it academically and projecting it onto Victorian England. He begins with the conclusion that the other Intellectuals resist: "that the modernist movements in literature and art and thought seem to have been the final phases of bourgeois or high culture. And they were never more so than when they were most adversary, critical, apparently subversive and elitist—obscure, hieratic, mystagogical, outrageous. They were the positive fruits of that culture, even when and especially when they were negating it."[26]

In his *Dickens from Pickwick to Dombey* he analyzes the early novels of Dickens in terms of the Intellectuals' dialectic, which defines for Marcus, as for Howe, the conception of the "modern":

It is already possible to discern in *Pickwick Papers* the elements of an original style or technique for representing the complex life of modern society. . . . It is a style in which Dickens's ideas about people and about society are brought to bear upon each other both analogically and by means of dialectical opposition. This is an essentially poetic and modern mode of conception and as a novelistic method it undoubtedly has its first full expression in Dickens. But it had already been prepared for by Jane Austen; in both *Emma* and *Persuasion*, for instance, the issues of society similarly introduce themselves through the issues of personal life.[27]

Marcus traces the dialectic of imagination and reality, purity and sexuality, melodrama and sentimentality, Evangelical and Utilitarian, life and death, through Dickens's early novels in a way which shows an awareness of both the historical circumstances into which the dialectic is transformed and the mythic ways in which Dickens projects it. Like all criticism, Marcus's is projective of his charter, but it shows an awareness of the historical context of the novels in Victorian England and in the history of the novel and acknowledges alternative critical views. As he goes through the novels,

Marcus uses the dialectic not as a Procustean bed but as a tool to reveal the conflicts he sees at the heart of Dickens. Thus he says: *"Oliver Twist* is a more distinguishably Victorian novel than its predecessor [*Pickwick Papers*]. The two major orders of existence—innocence and experience—which were in Dickens's first novel held together by the marvelous intelligence of Sam Weller, are now split apart" (p. 91). In *The Old Curiosity Shop,* however, "the relation of Nell and Quilp reveals the irreconcilability of the crisis of feeling which the novel so precariously represents. Nell is the spirit moving toward the peace of death, detached in her immaculateness from the source out of which spirit springs. Quilp, however, is that source; he is the flesh gone wild, and in a novel whose overpowering movement is toward death, he personifies the energy of life" (p. 152). In *Dombey and Son,* finally, Dickens confronts conflicts both between the individual and society and within the individual:

But as Dickens began to find conflict and division emerging in himself, he began to find them in society as well. Carker and Dombey are two sides of himself, but they are two sides of modern humanity as well, two kinds of men, two aberrations in nineteenth-century society. Carker represents what has been repressed in Dombey, but not as a vision of liberated impulse, spontaneity and fellow-feeling. Dombey is hard and unbending; Carker is supple and feline; Dombey is arid and impotent; Carker is lubricious and seductive. [Pp. 348-49]

In *Dombey and Son* we see how deeply divided Dickens has become. On the one hand he is affirming the changing world symbolized by the railroad, and on the other condemning the society which produced it. That society has in every way grown more uncongenial to the life of feeling and moral decency. More than ever before, these two orders of value . . . are for Dickens incompatible. His insight into the nature of society and the people who represented it was outstripping and working at cross-purposes to his beliefs more relentlessly than ever before. [P. 355]

For Marcus, literature is both formal and mimetic, has its own structure and corresponds to something in the real world, but for him only literature that is about the real world has cognitive status. Like the other Intellectuals he is most interested in the novel, but he is also interested in the way historians, social scientists, and psychologists represent or imagine society in their writings, and thus denies the privileged status of traditional aesthetic structures or genres. For him both novelists and social scientists "imagine through the language of writing a social world or worlds; in another sense, however, they also act as the imaginations of the actual societies in which they live." By studying both kinds of writers, one "may hope to discover something about how society imagines itself, which is to say, how societies represent their realities, their own existence—to themselves."[28] Marcus's prescription is to illuminate literary criticism by importing other cognitive disciplines to it, and by applying the instruments of literary analysis to nonliterary texts. If we take literature seriously, we have to regard it "in ways that are comparable to the ways we regard any of the essential and fundamental human activities, such as language, sexuality or economics."[29]

In his later career Marcus produces interesting studies of each pole of the Intellectuals' dialectic in separate books; in *The Other Victorians* he studies the social meaning of a debased version of what Trilling called "the Rameau values" of imaginative sexuality by examining Victorian pornography. In *Engels, Manchester, and the Working Class* he studies society by examining the literary structure of Friedrich Engels's *The Condition of the Working Class in England in 1844.*

In *The Other Victorians,* Marcus sees the pornography of the period as reflective of the public values of Victorian morality and culture; both the official view of sex, as seen in the works of Dr. William Acton, and the pornographic view completely sexualize reality, but with opposite valuations of sex. Acton tells of "a world hedged in with difficulty and pain, a world of harsh efforts and iron consequences. In such a world reality is conceived of as identical with pain, and negative conscience is the ruling principle. It is a vision of life which is in every way the exact opposite of the vision of life in pornography, and is therefore its counterpart as well."[30] Thus the study of Victorian sexuality provides a new context for the study of Victorian culture and the novel, and Marcus relates many of the scenes in Dickens which were thought fanciful to real incidents found in the central work he examines, an eleven-volume memoir of a man of the period called *My Secret Life.* This work, however, is different in intention from the period's great novelists, since its author accepts the superiority of his own upper class, while the Victorian novelists fought to make the lower classes more human, and this concern for the humanity of the lower classes seems to be Marcus's central moral concern in *The Other Victorians.*

For Marcus, imaginative reality is ultimately eschatological, ultimately becomes an ideal by which one must judge reality. For him a "revolutionary critic may be defined as someone whose project in life is to dramatize the extent to which society does not fulfill its ideals, who demands that the discrepancy between ideals and reality be abolished, and who develops a theory that both accounts for that discrepancy—for how it came about— and as a result sets a direction for possible change."[31] Only literature related to social reality can be knowledge; only social reality informed by the imaginative ideal can be human. By projecting the Intellectuals' dialectic onto Victorian England, Marcus has been able to reconstitute it as a useful instrument of analysis and a productive state of mind in a way none of the other Intellectuals has managed. Though the pornography and industrialization Marcus studies are quite clearly part of the modern world, it is, however, not quite clear how the present reality that Marcus wishes to change is defined, nor is it as evident what ideals are to save that reality as it was when Lionel Trilling wanted to save liberalism by means of imaginative literature. Like the rest of the Intellectuals, Marcus seems baffled by the failure of his dialectic to apply to the present: "The situation at present [1974], therefore, is even more naked and mystifying—if not mystified—than a present cultural situation usually is. With modernism over, the era of high culture seems to have come to an end. Nothing of similar weight or structure has replaced it, and nothing seems in the near future likely to. This puts the humanists in the university in a position that is even more vulnerable and exposed than their ordinary one."[32]

It is only as one comes to the Intellectual Journeymen that one begins to see the real journalistic virtues of the Intellectuals, which are stylistic, not substantive. The Intellectuals like to present as an artillery barrage what is really Fourth of July (or May Day) fireworks. Thus style, panache, the famous wit of Mary McCarthy or Dwight Macdonald, serve as their real achievements, and wit, after all, is the most attractive substitute for a convincing charter. In *Against the American Grain* Macdonald is at his best puncturing the pretensions of Cozzen's *By Love Possessed* and Colin Wilson's *The Outsider.* "Masscult and Midcult" defends a high culture embodied in the standards of the Intellectuals and the artistic achievements of the 1870–1930 avant-garde (i.e., Macdonald, Picasso, Stravinsky, Eliot, Joyce) against the impersonality, lack of taste, and subjugation to the mass market of Masscult (i.e., *Life*, Byron, Farrell, Rockwell, Barrymore) and Midcult, which is also cliched and written for the mass market, but which exploits avant-garde culture and pretends to respect it while vulgarizing it (i.e., Horizon, Book of the Month Club, *Webster's Third International Dictionary,* the Revised Standard Version of the Bible, *Our Town, J.B., John Brown's Body,* and *The Old Man and the Sea*). Macdonald's animus toward Masscult seems to reflect his disenchantment with his employment in the Luce empire; his solution to cultural decay is to keep high and low cultures separate and to rally the *esprit* and snobbery of the avant-garde. His difficulty is that he is himself a Midcult critic. Publishing in mass magazines, he is caught between the high culture of scholars, who know much more than he does and who provide him with his cultural insights, and the folk culture of artists, who are indifferent to his brand of high culture, which seems to consist of the fashionable values of a small group of New York writers and the style sheet of *Fortune,* where he learned his trade. Macdonald stands, then, as more of a journalist than a serious critic; he has a convincing wit and is effective in exposing others' stylistic gaffes, but simply is not learned enough to be a serious voice in making judgments about large cultural questions, particularly those which involve a knowledge of the past.

The Intellectuals' collective accomplishment as stylists was diminished by the untimely deaths of three of the most promising and original writers of the group, Robert Warshow, Isaac Rosenfeld, and Delmore Schwartz.

Though the actual accomplishments of Warshow and Rosenfeld are over-rated by their friends,[33] Schwartz is often underrated, perhaps because he offended so many in his later madness, and because he, uniquely in the group, had a sense of humor.[34] This lack of humor, and the inflated estimate of the importance of one's opinions which constant seriousness implies, is a great weakness of the Intellectuals. Another loss for the world of literature was the shift of two of its best critics, Harold Rosenberg and Clement Greenberg, to the world of art criticism, which has occupied them fully since the early forties.

The other thing which must be pointed out about the Intellectuals' achievement as stylists is that their strongest writers are women, who write brilliant reviews that are personal in nature rather than informed by the Intellectuals' charter. Though Rahv and Kazin can be depended on for common sense, with McCarthy, Elizabeth Hardwick, and Susan Sontag one has a fair chance of brilliance, and Diana Trilling can be counted on for a forcefulness of logic which exceeds anything the men can do.[35] Their total achievement is slight, but in their display of the power of the imagination these women seem to follow a belief of the twenties that, as Lionel Trilling describes it, "women stood in a special and privileged relation to 'nature.' . . . The masculine mind, dulled by preoccupation, was to be joined and quickened by the Woman-principle. . . . Implicit in the *mystique* was a handsome promise made to women—they were to be free, brilliant, and in their own way, powerful, and, like men, they were to have destinies, yet at the same time they would be delightful, and they would be loved because they were women" (YIT 50). In this respect the Intellectuals provide the senior officers of the Women's Liberation movement.

One must conclude, then, that the tension between avant-garde literature and bourgeois liberal politics which marks the New York Intellectuals is historically interesting but not available as a model for others, not perma-nently relevant. Their truth lies not in society but in the life of the avant-garde imagination, and this truth has been best preserved by their women, who stayed at home to defend it, and by the despised scholars of the acad-emy. To the eye of history, then, the "major critics" among the Intellectuals are not men whose charter has failed but men who have mistaken their true calling to be servants of the imagination, men who would have done the good thing had they but recognized it.

Edmund Wilson: The Journalist as Man of Letters

At the end of a study of the New York Intellectuals, one comes full circle to the beginning in the thought of the most eminent Man of Letters of the group, Edmund Wilson, who functions as the authority figure of the Intellectuals in the same way that Eliot does for the Formalists. Wilson (b.

1895) is a generation older than most of the other Intellectuals. Arriving at a position of literary prominence in the twenties, he establishes his authority as a defender of the avant-garde of modernism decisively with the publication of *Axel's Castle* in 1931. Thus, like Eliot, he breaks trail for his group, has the authority of the pioneer, the originator of positions others later adopt. It is therefore important to understand both the intellectual and emotional background from which Wilson comes and the charter he arrived at in the twenties and thirties, since it is only in this historical context that one can fully understand the positions the other Intellectuals took in the forties and fifties.

Again paralleling Eliot, Wilson posits a fall from a formerly unified world into a dualism. However, Wilson's "dissociation of sensibility" occurs not in the seventeenth century but in post-Civil War America; and the elements into which the prelapsarian unity is broken are not Eliot's thought and feeling but the dualism which becomes central to the Intellectuals: commercial reality and idealism, or naturalism and symbolism, or historical and social reality versus artistic reality, or the bourgeoisie and the avant-garde, or liberalism and the imagination. Wilson says in a letter to Allen Tate in 1931:

Symbolism was the atmospheric or arty side of art and naturalism the factual side, which got divorced from each other during the nineteenth century and, in my opinion, ought to be wedded again. What is at the bottom of my own attitude about this, in contrast to yours, is the fact that I am enough older than you to have been brought up on a literature which did mix these two elements in better proportions than the literature of after the war, which was what you were reading when you were in college and which still seems to you the normal thing. It seems abnormal to me and that is the reason I take the point of view I do in *Axel's Castle*; I'm looking back to Shaw, Wells, Bennett, France, Flaubert, Dostoevsky, Ibsen, Renan, et al. [*Letters* 212]

In America before the Civil War, facing the realities of life was combined with a moral idealism which gave to those same realities a spiritual dimension. Then even the businessmen were idealists: "The enterprising breed of New England, with their shipping and banking and mills, had still remained in quite close touch with what Mather called 'the Wonders of the Invisible World' " (*PG* 70). For Wilson, the fall comes with the death of Lincoln: "The intellectual and moral slump that followed the assassination, the slackening from the strain of the war, brought down with them the whole idealistic edifice that the nobler Union supporters had built" (*PG* 159). In Wilson's analysis, "the war left a lasting trauma, and resulted in, not an apocalypse, but, on the one hand, a rather gross period of industrial and commercial development and, on the other, a severe disillusionment for the idealists who had been hoping for something better" (*PG* 125).

The post-Civil War period appeared, then, to be

—perhaps the most provincial and uninspired moment in the history of American society. ... In the seventies, men were still living on the culture and believing in the social ideal which had survived from the founding of the Republic. The doctors, the professors, the lawyers and the churchmen who were graduated from college in the seventies had at once a certain all-around humanism and a serious and dignified attitude toward life; they were carrying on an integrity of moral ideal. But by the eighties Business was flooding in and ideals were in confusion: the old-fashioned lawyer was on his way to becoming a corporation lawyer whose principal function was to keep Business from going to jail; the doctor was on his way to becoming a modern "specialist" and sending Business to a sanitarium; and the church and the university were beginning to be abandoned by first-rate men altogether. ... Humanism went by the board; moral scruples were put to rout; and seriousness about man and his problems was abrogated entirely in favor of the seriousness of Business about things that were not serious. The State became identified with Business; ideas were shot on sight. [*SL* 110-11; see also *SL* 337]

In specifically literary terms, the whole turn of the century belongs to the Philistines: "Between our generation and the Civil War there had extended a kind of weedy or arid waste where people with an appreciation of literature had hardly hoped to find anything of value growing and where they had tended to be suspicious of anything that did manage to bloom" (*CCo* 74). In his criticism Wilson finds the authors of this era to be failures for not having confronted the historical reality of the business world and transformed it. He says of Eliot: "He is distinguished by that combination of practical prudence with moral idealism which shows itself in its later developments as an excessive fastidiousness and scrupulousness. One of the principal subjects of Eliot's poetry is really that regret at situations unexplored, that dark rankling of passions inhibited, which has figured so conspicuously in the work of American writers of New England and New York, from Hawthorne to Edith Wharton. T. S. Eliot, in this respect, has much in common with Henry James. ... The fear of life, in Henry James, is closely bound up with the fear of vulgarity" (*Ax* 102; on James see also *TT* 101; on Wharton see *CCo* 417). As a literary critic, much of Wilson's attention is focused on neurotic or crippled literary men of this period; he has written long studies of Dickens, Swinburne, Housman, Oscar Wilde, John Jay Chapman, Woodrow Wilson, Proust, and others, all of whom could not cope with some aspect of their world and became neurotic because of it.

His praise for the person who has "got through with honor that period from 1880-1920!—even at the expense of the felt-muted door, the lack of first-class companionship, the retreats into sanitariums" (*PM* 228) refers not to Proust but to Wilson's father. If one were to do a Wilsonian analysis of Wilson, one would find that his interest in the ill stems on the personal level from his father, a brilliant lawyer of old New York stock and one-time attorney general of New Jersey, who became neurotic facing the new commercial civilization of the 1880s and had periodic collapses and retirements to spas and sanitariums, leaving young Edmund with his mother, who had been driven neurotically deaf by her husband's behavior. Speaking of his father and uncles, Wilson says: "They had been educated at Exeter and Andover and at eighteenth-century Princeton, and had afterwards been trained, like their fathers, for what had once been called the learned professions; but they had then had to deal with a world in which this kind of education and the kind of ideals it served no longer really counted for much. Such people, from the moment they left their schools, were subjected to dizzying temptations, overpowering pressures, insidious diversions of purpose, and the casualties among them were terrible" (*PM* 207-8). Thus, as an only child, young Wilson is left more or less isolated to construct a new and better world out of his only social world, the gatherings of cousins at his old stone house in Talcottville, New York, and out of books. Wilson speaks of this past, uses it as a point of reference continually in his writing, and (as we shall see) comes back to it in the end.[36]

In contrast, Wilson praises Teddy Roosevelt as a uniquely heroic figure of this period: "In the United States of that era, one sees, among the noble spirits, so many embittered critics, so many neurotic cranks, that it is cheerful to look on at the spectacle of a well-educated and public-spirited man, not merely attempting to formulate an ideal of Americanism that will discredit the pawnbroker and the huckster but punching it out on their own ground with the sordid political boss, the arrogant millionaire, the bought senator, the exploiter of tenements, the Spanish War profiteer—all those types from whom so many of his stratum shrank, with whom they refused to contend" (*BT* 74). And Roosevelt's ideals and analysis of the period seem close to Wilson's own (see *BT* 67-74). Wilson's defense of Socialism and Marxism in the thirties thus takes on meaning as that formulation of the ideal which will save America from the big-business civilization that has plagued it since the Civil War. Wilson as an Intellectual of action seems to be modelling himself on Roosevelt even as he remains fascinated by the paralyzed Intellectual.

It is no wonder, then, that when this business world collapses in 1929, Wilson says: "To the writers and artists of my generation who had grown up in the Big Business era and had always resented its barbarism, its crowding-out of everything they cared about, these years [of the Crash] were not depressing but stimulating. One couldn't help being exhilarated at the sudden unexpected collapse of that stupid gigantic fraud. It gave us a new sense of freedom; and it gave us a new sense of power to find ourselves still carrying on while the bankers, for a change, were taking a beating" (*SL* 498-99). For Wilson, "a reaction against the materialism of the era of unscrupulous millionaires was to bring in time another revival of the traditional American idealism, to express itself in the several varieties of the struggle for a secular 'better world' " (*BT* 98). Wilson's basic effort in the twenties and thirties is thus a struggle to reestablish the balance between the forces of the ideal and the real which was lost after the Civil War. As he says, "The Republic has thus had to be saved over and over again, and it continues to have to be saved" (*PM* 23; see also *BT* 290).

In the literary world in which Wilson made his way—the world of the journalist for weekly or biweekly New York magazines like *Vanity Fair*, *The New Republic, Nation,* and *The New Yorker*—the review is the normal critical genre, and most of Wilson's writing is in this mode. Indeed, he confesses that he begins even his longer essays and books as reviews and works them up (*CCo* 113). In "The Literary Worker's Polonius" Wilson describes the duties of the Journeyman reviewer: "The reader should be given a chance to judge whether or not he would be interested in the book, irrespective of what the reviewer may think of it; and it is an indispensable discipline for the reviewer, or any critic, to give the gist of the book in his own words" (*SL* 606). Matthew Josephson describes Wilson's essays as conventional in form: "They usually established the historical period of the authors studied, provided biographical notes, described and even synopsized their principal works in detail, and gave an appraisal of them."[37] Stanley Edgar Hyman characterizes this aspect of Wilson's work as "criticism by translation," thereby attaching the implication of simple-mindedness to this kind of summary.[38] The commitment to popularization, and/or the economic necessity of writing for popular magazines, is habitual with Wilson; his essays and reviews are perfectly consistent in form, tone, and intention from the beginning of his career to the end.

This "criticism by translation" has both its strengths and its limitations. Though Wilson is often described as a critical leader, this is true only in the sense that he is the first to reach a popular audience; his long essays are always derivative of the work being done by scholars. For example, well over 250 studies of Eliot had appeared before Wilson's treatment in *Axel's Castle*,[39] and his treatment of Joyce relies heavily on that of Stuart Gilbert and others, as Hyman points out. Indeed, Wilson's use of the work of others has sometimes been done without giving proper credit and has evoked charges of plagiarism.[40] Even at his best, Wilson cannot claim to be a startlingly original critic, yet his essays remain useful introductions, particularly to books one has not read and is never likely to read; and because of his common-sense approach even to the new, obscure, or difficult, such books are introduced into the world of critical discourse in a very useful way. Wilson is somewhat like the hostess in one of the books of etiquette he reviews: "She recommends, in a chapter on *The Nature and Meaning of Culture,* that one 'read more than one kind of literature: not mystery stories alone, nor light fiction alone. . . . The whole tone is non-invidious. She makes social life sound easy and jolly" (*CCo* 373). Some of Wilson's reviewing has this same effect, that of culture easily acquired.

In this first phase of his career, Wilson is very much a man of the twenties, attacking in the style of the early Van Wyck Brooks and H. L. Mencken the stupidities of American civilization and hoping to substitute a more enlightened view. In "Thoughts on Being Bibliographed" he speaks of Mencken and Shaw as "prophets of new eras in their national cultures to which they were also important contributors." Continuing, he says: " 'Though their conceptions of their social aims differed, both were carrying on that work of 'Enlightenment' of which the flame had been so fanned by Voltaire. I suppose that I, too, wanted to prove myself a 'soldier in the Liberation War of humanity' and to speak for the 'younger generation' who were 'knocking on the door' " (*CCo* 114). Mencken and others had already established American writing, but "there remained for the young journalist, however, two roads that had still to be broken: the road to the understanding of the most recent literary events in the larger international world—Joyce, Eliot, Proust, etc. . . . and to bring home to the 'bourgeois' intellectual world the most recent developments of Marxism" (*CCo* 114). These tasks Wilson addressed in *Axel's Castle* (1931) and *To the Finland Station* (1940).

In this fight for Enlightenment, which implies the combining of the real and the ideal, Wilson places himself in the classic position of the avant-gardist opposing the bourgeois, Philistine culture. He says, in an essay welcoming Auden to America:

For this feeling oneself a member of a determined resistant minority has been now for nearly a hundred years a typical situation in America. Such people in the later nineteenth century were likely to be defeated or embittered. In our own, they have felt the backing of a partly inarticulate public who are not satisfied with the bilge that the popular media feed them in their movies and magazines, and who are grateful to anyone who will make a stand for that right to think for themselves which is supposed to be guaranteed us by the Bill of Rights and that right to a high level of culture which the framers of the Constitution—taking it so much for granted— would never have thought to include. These American writers of which I speak do not constitute a group, they do not frequent an official café; and on this account, the visitor from Europe is likely to come to the conclusion that, except in the universities, we have no intellectual life. He cannot conceive that the American writers are functioning in the crevices of cities, on the faculties of provincial colleges or scattered all over the country in the solitude of ranches and farms. This kind of life was now to be Auden's lot. [*BT* 359-60]

The Wilson of the twenties hopes that change can be effected, that intelligence can be made to prevail, that progress will come. In a letter to Allen Tate in 1931 he says: "I've never been able to see how anyone who is not a sincere Christian or a believer in some other religious faith can escape

assuming that humanity builds better and makes more sense as it gets
along. . . . What about the cave men?—don't you think our society with all
its faults is an improvement on theirs? . . . that is the faith on which my
own ideas are based" (*Letters* 213). It is this faith in progress which leads
to Wilson's evangelical tone about modern literature. He says of the authors
treated in *Axel's Castle*: "I want to give popular accounts of them which
will convince people of their importance and persuade people to read them"
(*Letters* 150). He recalls of the twenties: "The shadow of Big Business that
had oppressed American culture in our childhood seemed finally to be
passing away" (*CCo* 106). And in 1932, when capitalism seems to have
collapsed, he says: "I still believe in progress as the eighteenth century
people did"; he believes that progress will come through Communism and
Russia. As for theorists and artists, "their true solidarity lies with those
elements who will remodel society by the powers of imagination and thought—
by acting on life to make something new."[41] Wilson in the twenties and
thirties is still the avant-gardist with the traditional cry of "making it new"
on his lips.

For Wilson, being a soldier of the Enlightenment is a profession, and he
sees the good critic as part of a professional group, a member of the intelligentsia, a competent worker. He says of himself: "What is strange [to the
younger generation] is that he [Wilson himself] should seem to belong to a
kind of professional group, now becoming extinct and a legend, in which
the practice of letters was a common craft and the belief in its value a
common motivation. . . . The young men of our earlier classes saw in
literature a sphere of activity in which they hoped themselves to play a
part" (*CCo* 109–10). On these professional grounds he praises not only his
heroes De Quincey, Poe, and Shaw (*CCo* 112), but minor figures of the last
generation like Irving Babbitt, W. C. Brownell, and P. E. More: "Though
their ideas were less 'emancipated,' they possessed a sounder culture than
we; and that, though less lively, they were better craftsmen. They were
professional men of letters, and they had thoroughly learned their trade"
(*SL* 245).

In the literary sphere, Wilson's theory in 1928 is that "European literature has been vibrating for two or three centuries now between what we
ordinarily describe as scientific ideas and what we may roughly call poetry"
(*Letters* 149). The Romantics reacted against poetry based on the mechanistic physics of the seventeenth century, and in the nineteenth century,

mechanistic ideas were given a new impetus from biology, evolution, etc.: the
pendulum swung in the other direction and, in highly developed naturalistic artists
like Flaubert and Ibsen, you got something that really corresponded to the neo-
classicism of Pope. Naturalism (what we loosely call "realism") eventually became,
however, what eighteenth-century neo-classicism had been, a menace to literature:
by its ideal of scientific documentation, it was tending to banish the imagination.

Symbolism was a second swing of the pendulum in the same direction as Romanticism: we have now arrived with this second movement just about where they were with Romanticism a hundred years ago. [*Letters* 149]

Complete withdrawal from society into a world of visions is the furthest extent to which Symbolism can be carried, and Wilson sees this withdrawal embodied in the figure of Rimbaud, the exile, the criminal, the author of "Une Saison en Enfer" [A Season in Hell], and in Axel, the hero of the poem by Villiers de L'Isle-Adam, the visionary, the recluse, the aesthete, the liver of the imaginative life. These are the choices of modern writers, and if one chooses Axel, "one shuts oneself up in one's own private world, cultivating one's private fantasies, encouraging one's private manias, ultimately preferring one's absurdest chimeras to the most astonishing contemporary realities, ultimately mistaking one's chimeras for realities" (*Ax* 287). Axel, then, is the modernist imagination carried to its extreme. For Wilson, the cause of this withdrawl from society is "the fact that in the utilitarian society which had been produced by the industrial revolution and the rise of the middle class, the poet seemed to have no place" (*Ax* 268).

For the poet the turn of the century bourgeois is the enemy, but by 1930 Wilson concludes that escape is no longer enough: "The time is at hand when these writers, who have largely dominated the literary world of the decade 1920–30, though we shall continue to admire them as masters, will no longer serve us as guides. Axel's world of the private imagination in isolation from the life of society seems to have been exploited and explored as far as for the present is possible" (*Ax* 292). For Wilson, the ideal life— the spiritual life alone—must be combined with the real, the historical, in order to make good literature or, for that matter, a good life. Thus Wilson praises Henry James for his "classical equanimity in dealing with diverse forces, on his combination, equally classical, of hard realism with formal harmony" (*TT* 123). And he praises Joyce because "he has, in 'Ulysses,' exploited together, as no writer had thought to do before, the resources both of Symbolism and Naturalism" (*Ax* 204). In isolating, describing, and popularizing the Symbolist pole of culture, Wilson interprets the idealism lost after the Civil War for a new generation, and recreates it as one-half of a necessary dialectic.

In 1930 Wilson concludes that symbolic vision must be supplemented by active political revolution: "Americans and Europeans are both becoming more and more conscious of Russia, a country where a central social-political idealism has been able to use and inspire the artist as well as the engineer" (*Ax* 293). He begins his political avant-gardism with "An Appeal to Progressives," published in *The New Republic* on January 14, 1931. This article, which has much the same effect on the intellectuals of that day as Noam Chomsky's "The Responsibility of Intellectuals" has on intellectuals at the time of the Vietnam War, radicalizes them and places them in active political opposition to the American status quo. As his contemporary the Surrealist Matthew Josephson recalls: "He is a paradigm of the generation born around the turn of the century, which experienced the First World War, became *enfants-du-siècle* in the twenties, then went politically left in a sharp turn at the time of the Great Depression. It should not be forgotten that Edmund Wilson was *the* inspiring leader of the left literary movement of that era. He did his utmost to arouse interest among intellectuals in Marxism and Soviet communism—only to become disenchanted with that cause several years later, rejecting it completely. His is a typical experience of his intellectual generation."[42] In "An Appeal to Progressives" Wilson asserts that capitalism has finally failed absolutely, that ideals which once sustained America, like the development of the West or the amassing of fortunes, have vanished, and that "what began as the libertarian adventure of eighteenth-century middle-class democracy seems to have ended in the cul de sac of an antiquated economic system" (*SL* 526). All attempts to transform capitalism by Liberals or Progressives like Woodrow Wilson and Justice Holmes, heterodox professors like Dewey and Beard, editors like Herbert Croly, have failed, and Wilson concludes that only a radical solution will do: American radicals must "take Communism away from the Communists. . . . asserting that their ultimate goal is the ownership by the government of the means of production" (*SL* 532).

Marxism is thus the political avant-garde position of this era; it will transform the sordid realities of commercial capitalism through the ideal of Socialism. One may note here the double use of "Marxism" in Wilson's dialectic; when contrasted with American capitalism, it stands for the avant-garde ideal, but when contrasted with Symbolism, it stands for facing the realities of life that Symbolism avoids. This transformation of Marxism from historical reality to the ideal and back is part of Wilson's progress in the thirties. In 1935, in a letter to John Dos Passos, Wilson says: "The members of the romantic intellectual generation who did not die off with their personal disappointments like Byron, Shelley, Musset, et al., but lived to expand the romantic emotions into something larger, are the most impressive writers of the nineteenth century. Marx belonged to this class. . . . It was Marxism that was the real second blooming of the Enlightenment and it has still great vitality today. What is needed is to see Marx and Lenin as part of the humanistic tradition which they came out of" (*Letters* 258–59).

Unhappily or happily, the Stalinist trials and the Nazi-Soviet pact soon put an end to the ideal of Marxism for most American Leftists, including Wilson. In 1937, in "Marxism and Literature," Wilson notes that though Marx and Engels were cultivated Germans who did not judge literature in "terms of its purely political tendencies," in Lenin "we come to a Marxist who is specialized himself as an organizer and fighter" (*TT* 198, 199), and under Stalin, literature is either censored or propagandized. In this essay Wilson is rather hard on American Marxists like Granville Hicks and maintains that proletarian literature is false in itself and inapplicable to American reality. He concludes: "Marxism by itself can tell us nothing whatever about the goodness or badness of a work of art. A man may be an excellent Marxist, but if he lacks imagination and taste he will be unable to make the choice between a good and an inferior book both of which are ideologically unexceptionable. What Marxism *can* do, however, is throw a great deal of light on the origins and social significance of works of art" (*TT* 204).

In his practical criticism Wilson uses Marxism only in his 1936 essay "Bernard Shaw at Eighty," where he shows how Shaw learned from Marx how "to analyze society in terms of economic motivation or to understand and criticize the profit system" (*TT* 181). Though Wilson uses Marx in this essay, he does so undogmatically, and by the time of the publication of *To the Finland Station* in 1940, he is so disillusioned with Marxism that the ending is undercut in the same way that Marxism undercut the ending of *Axel's Castle*. In his "Summary as of 1940," appended to the paperback edition of the book, Wilson asks: "Is there nothing left of Marxism, then? Are there not basic Marxist ideas that may still be accepted as true?" He concludes that we can still profit from "the technique of analyzing political phenomena in social-economic terms" and that the desire to be rid of class privilege and exploitation of others is good, but that "it is a goal to be worked for in the light of one's own imagination and with the help of common sense."[43] With his long journey to the Finland Station at an end, Wilson gives up on Marxism as a force of the ideal and returns to his own American ideals.

Wilson's status among Intellectuals in the thirties can be gauged by a reminiscence of Lionel Trilling: "I speak of Wilson in a personal way because he had so personal an effect upon me. He seemed in his own person, and young as he was, to propose and to realize the idea of the literary life. . . . He was, of course, not the only good writer of the time, but he seemed to represent the life of letters in an especially cogent way, by reason of the orderliness of his mind and the bold lucidity and simplicity of his prose . . . and because of the catholicity of his interests and the natural-ness with which he dealt with the past as well as with the present. One got from him a whiff of Lessing at Hamburg, of Sainte-Beuve in Paris" (*GF* 50). Through his constant public presence in articles in *The New Republic* and *The Nation,* and through his status as an eminent writer much courted by both the Communist and the non-Communist Left, Wilson became a leader to Intellectuals like Rahv and Trilling, Howe and Kazin, who were just then beginning their careers.[44]

In the forties and fifties the combination of interests in radical politics
and modernist literature that Wilson pioneered became (as we have seen)
the charter of the Intellectuals, most of whom pay their respects to Wilson
in reviews or reminiscences. Richard Chase finds that Wilson's pieces in
Shores of Light show him to be a true imaginative liberal; Wilson's work
"is the best and fullest expression of the American school of critical realism,
which distantly begins in the work of Walt Whitman and which in Wilson's
essays achieves an intellectual discipline and cosmopolitanism and broadens out into a definitive statement of the liberal, experimental, receptive,
curious, skeptical, language-loving democratic mind."[45] Irving Howe
finds Wilson in *Classics and Commercials* "still a radical": "Unlike so
many of his contemporaries, Wilson has retained the classical picture
of the Enemy: Hollywood, Broadway, mass journalism, middlebrow professors."[46] F. W. Dupee says of *The Triple Thinkers:* "Mr. Wilson's
criticism, though it offers no organic alternative [to the tradition of Eliot],
curbs the sins of specialization of that movement and combines its esthetic
maturity with the insights of social history."[47]

The Intellectual who emulates Wilson most closely is Alfred Kazin. In
On Native Grounds he praises him lavishly:" [He is] the conscience of two
intellectual generations. . . . In an age of fanaticisms and special skills, he
stood out as the quiet arbiter, the private reader of patience and wisdom
whose very skill gave him a public importance. . . . He seemed more than
any other critic in America the experimentalist who worked with the whole
tradition of literature in his bones. . . . He was above all the spectator, the
bookman of active humility and detachment, the kind of mind . . . that
seeks not to acquire but 'quietly to understand'" (*ONG* 448–49). Though
Kazin notes that "what one missed in this criticism, of course, was a
positive affirmation, the intensity of a great conception" (*ONG* 451), he
later recognizes that Wilson's center is not conceptual but personal: it is
his disposition "to picture intelligence as a hero struggling against an age
that threatens the humanity of all."[48] And in *New York Jew* Kazin says:
"From the time I first read *Axel's Castle,* I felt altogether related to him.
He was a basic kind of critic who put you directly in touch with any work
he discussed; he was an original, an extraordinary literary artist who wove
his essays out of the most intense involvement with his materials. . . . The
immense historical sense behind Wilson's criticism, architectural in its
passionate sense of detail, would always represent for me personal sensibility rather than political acuteness. This flinty old American trust in his
own opinions was his flair, his style, his enormous charm for me."[49]

The crisis in Wilson's critical career came in the early forties. As Robert
Alter observes, "He had become a sage with many admirers but at the
same time a cultural mentor without real disciples."[50] He had already

become disillusioned with both the literary and the political phases of the avant-garde which the Intellectuals were discovering and taking up, and at the age of forty-six he was without a literary home. As Granville Hicks recalls:

Wilson's isolation became increasingly apparent. Whether he was opposed to America's involvement in the war or merely indifferent, he felt himself detached from the intellectuals who were backing the government and, of course, from the majority of the people. He had no political ties and no way of working against an economic system he detested. Moreover, he ceased writing for the *New Republic* in 1941, after some twenty years of association with it, and there was no magazine that he could look upon as his organ. It was in this period that he wrote some of the stories that were published in *Memoirs of Hecate County*, and he prepared an excellent anthology, *The Shock of Recognition*. With this kind of writing, and with some lecturing at colleges, he kept busy enough, but at the very peak of his reputation he was homeless.[51]

Wilson was also isolated from the "New Critics," who in the early forties were coming into control of principal quarterlies like the *Sewanee, Kenyon,* and *Southern Reviews*, and were gaining positions of prominence in university English departments; he is barely mentioned as a critic in Wimsatt and Brooks's *Literary Criticism: A Short History* (1957). Further, although Wilson had tried teaching (at the University of Chicago Summer School in 1939), he was unprepared for the historical shift in the center of literary power from New York journalism to the universities, and seemed unwilling to adapt himself to university life. While at Chicago he writes to Tate: "I find that I'm a little dismayed—though perhaps unnecessarily—at seeing how many of the literati are taking to teaching as what *Partisan Review* calls a 'crutch'" (*Letters* 321). And despite some other abortive attempts to adapt to academic life, he says in 1953: I really don't fit very well into academic communities—always find it more of a strain than I expected" (*Letters* 509). This antagonism eventually leads to Wilson's attack on scholars and scholarly editors in "The Fruits of the MLA" in 1968, where he is outraged because his plan for a popular edition of American classics has lost out in competition for National Endowment for the Humanities funds to the Center for Editions of American Authors, sponsored by the Modern Language Association. In 1942, at any rate, Wilson confronts the academics directly in "Thoughts on Being Bibliographed," noting that to "the academic profession, with its quite other hierarchies of value and competitions for status, the literary man of the twenties presents himself as the distant inhabitant of another intellectual world" (*CCo* 109). By 1956 he has retired completely from his avant-garde position: "I do not want any more to be bothered with the kind of contemporary conflicts that I used to go out to explore. I make no attempt to keep up with the younger

American writers; and I only hope to have the time to get through some of the classics I have never read. Old fogeyism is comfortably closing in" (*PM* 205).

In the early forties, then, Wilson finds himself out of place and disillusioned with Marxism as an ideal means of transforming American society, just as earlier he had been disillusioned with the Symbolic alternative. It is during this period that he becomes interested in the Philoctetes myth, in *The Wound and the Bow*, which has led some commentators to falsely classify him as a Freudian critic.[52] In point of fact Wilson's knowledge of Freud is the vague kind associated with Greenwich Village intellectuals of the twenties, and he does not seem much interested in him. Only by classifying everyone who mentions dreams, childhood, or the subconscious as Freudian could Wilson be so labeled; even the theory behind *The Wound and the Bow* is more mythic than Freudian, since it lacks the technical vocabulary of Freudian critics.

In his criticism Wilson does not seem to advance from the general understanding he expresses through his alter-ego hero in the 1929 novel *I Thought of Daisy:* "I had had to learn from Rita [Edna St. Vincent Millay] that any great strength or excellence of character must be, by its very nature, incompatible with qualities of other kinds—that it carries with it weaknesses and ignominies inseparable from excellence and strength."[53] In the only long essay in which he uses Freudian terminology, "Morose Ben Jonson," Wilson classifies Jonson quite perceptively as an "anal-erotic" but goes on to say: "I am not qualified to 'analyze' Jonson in the light of this Freudian conception, and I have no interest in trying to fit him into any formulation of it. . . . but I am sure that Freud has here really seized upon a nexus of human traits that are involved with one another and has isolated a recognizable type" (*TT* 219). On many occasions where Freudian analysis would seem almost inevitable, Wilson either subsumes it under broader generalizations or criticizes Freudian formulations. For example, he says of Proust: "The elements here of Proust's dependence on his mother; his unsatisfactory relations with women; and his impulses toward a sterile and infantile perversity, would, no doubt, be explained in somewhat different ways by different schools of modern psychology: Proust is a perfect case for psychoanalysis" (*Ax* 183). But he then returns to general, not Freudian, observations. Similarly, he hints that Jane Austen's heroines have more of a relationship with sisters than with their purported lovers, but says: "I do not mean to suggest for *Emma* any specific Freudian formula" (*CCo* 202). And he says of Joseph Wood Krutch: "His *Poe*, written back in the twenties, was a rather half-baked performance: incomplete, depending too much on a Freudian oversimplification" (*CCo* 245). In other instances Wilson uses Freud to establish the existence of the Oedipus complex in Sophocles (*WBow* 238) and to inform his analysis of sex as the secret of Henry James, or adolescent trauma as the secret of Dickens, and praises Van Wyck Brooks's biography of Mark Twain, which Fraiberg notes makes him a bad Freudian (*TT* 266). In "The Historical Interpretation of Literature" Wilson says that Freudian criticism is basically part of biography, "an extension of something which has already got well started before, which had figured even in Johnson's *Lives of the Poets*, and of which the great exponent had been Sainte-Beuve: the interpretation of works of literature in the light of the personalities behind them" (*TT* 265–66). Though he admits that Freud made this kind of interpretation "more exact and more systematic," he goes on to classify Freud's essay on Leonardo da Vinci as a case history of little critical interest, and to note that Freud cannot explain artistic genius, that "the problems of comparative artistic value still remain after we have given attention to the Freudian psychological factor" (*TT* 267).

Wilson ultimately takes a skeptical view of the use of Freudian theory even in biography: "It is true of the method that it has led to bad results where the critic has built a Freudian mechanism out of very slender evidence, and then given us what is really merely a romance exploiting the supposed working of this mechanism, in place of an actual study that sticks close to the facts and the documents of the writer's life and work" (*TT* 266).

In sum, Wilson is informed in a general way about Freudian formulations and uses them in a general way, but he cannot be classified as a Freudian critic. Indeed, considering the bulk of his writing, it is astonishing how seldom he mentions Freud. What Wilson really does in "The Historical Interpretation of Literature" is to set up a dialectic between the historical or Marxian critic, who deals with physical reality, and the Freudian critic, who deals with psychological reality. He then transcends the dichotomy by suggesting that neither has anything to do with artistic value, which is in the hands of a critical elite who "know what they are talking about . . . are self-appointed and self-perpetuating . . . and will compel you to accept their authority" (*TT* 268)—in short, in the hands of Wilson himself. Wilson here transcends the Intellectuals' tension between real and ideal, or outer and inner reality, and creates a new ideal persona to oppose to the contemporary world of the forties. In this withdrawl from the avant-garde, Wilson abdicates his leadership of the Intellectuals to Lionel Trilling, who had just established his own authority with his *Matthew Arnold* (1939), and was beginning to write the essays collected in *The Liberal Imagination* (1950). Though Wilson was the first student of both modernism and Marxism, it is Trilling who, as both academic and Jew, becomes the immediate model of the Intellectuals.

What *is* interesting about the wound and the bow theory, then, is how the Philoctetes myth illuminates Wilson's situation when he is (having left *The New Republic* over the issue of America's entering the war) without a secure place in literary society and (Marxism having failed him) without an ideal on which to depend to transform society. "One feels in the *Philoctetes* a more general and fundamental idea: the conception of superior strength as inseparable from disability" (*WBow* 235). And further: "The Philoctetes of Gide is, in fact, a literary man: at once a moralist and an artist, whose genius becomes purer and deeper in ratio to his isolation and outlawry" (*WBow* 236). If Wilson can be seen as this historically wounded figure, what he needs at this point in his career is a new bow, and he finds it by withdrawing from involvement with the real society of America almost altogether; by failing to confront the new literature of the forties as he confronted that of the twenties;[54] by distancing himself by means of physical and intellectual travels to Zuni, Haiti, Soviet Russia, and Israel, to cite the countries described in *Red, Black, Blonde, and Olive*; and most significantly by constructing for himself an ideal persona who lives totally in and refers totally to a literary reality. In the early forties, then, Wilson's progress is from the wound to the book, and the interest in his later career is in the nature of his new voice and values.

A practical solution to the crisis in Wilson's career comes when he replaces Clifton Fadiman as book reviewer for *The New Yorker* in 1944 and thus gains the ear of upper-middlebrow America. Paradoxically, however, even as he attains a secure position in the center of Manhattan at the most prestigious and well-paying of American magazines, he begins a process of withdrawal from New York urban Intellectualism to a defense of provincialism and regionalism and an attack on centralism which are very close to the positions of Formalist regionalists like Allen Tate. He begins thinking of himself as middle-aged and "out of it" in 1942, in "Thoughts on Being Bibliographed," and begins "playing the patriarch" then (*CCo* 112). But he becomes concerned with the power of the state only when he is prosecuted in 1960 for not paying his income taxes, a situation he describes in *The Cold War and the Income Tax* (1963). In *Patriotic Gore* (1962) he comes to identify with a number of secessionist heroes like Robert E. Lee and Alexander Stephens: "It is the question of the exercise of power, of the backing up of power by force, the issue of the government, the organization, as against the individual, the family group—for the South that fought the war was a family group. This issue presses hard on our time. There are moments when we may wonder today ... whether it may not be true, as Stephens said, that the cause of the South is the cause of us all" (*PG* 434). Wilson likewise praises Lee for "the manifestation of a regional patriotism" (*PG* 334). He says that Washington "tried to save America from this [anarchy and disorder], but when the structure he had founded broke down, one naturally remained with Virginia. The classical antique virtue, at once aristocratic and republican, had become a national legend, and its late incarnation in Lee was to command a certain awed admiration" (*PG* 335). In his personal secession, Wilson exiles himself to his country homes in Wellfleet, Massachusetts, and Talcottville, New York, which represent for him the reality of a past society and era, and to identification with beleaguered minorities like Southerners and the Iroquois Indians, whom he defends against incursions from the state in the person of Robert Moses (in *Apologies to the Iroquois* (1960).

Wilson in his late criticism also begins to stress as a standard for judging literature the values of the normal, heterosexual bourgeois family. In *A Piece of My Mind* he says: "Our novels, our plays and our poetry are concerned to what may seem an appalling degree ... with people who are shown as feeling in relation to one another a definite biological attraction yet are prevented from experiencing, or are incapable of experiencing, the full cycle of courtship, fruition, relief" (*PM* 193). Much of the anguish of literary lovers arises, in Wilson's view, from "the basic biological bafflement of the failure to produce children" (*PM* 193). Wilson's list of sexual failures included much of the literature that has interested him:

the doomed guilty passion of the British Victorians and the accepted adultery of the French, the long and uncertain engagements and the rejections of irregular relationships of the James and Howells period in the United States, the glorification of intercourse for its own sake as you get it in D. H. Lawrence, the feminine promiscuity of Edna Millay, the homosexuality of Proust that is really a stunted and embittered form of an intense admiration for women, the adolescent sexuality of Gide that does not much transcend masturbation, the homosexual narcissism of Norman Douglas and the dynamic narcissism of Bernard Shaw, who tries to make his women approximate men and who never went to bed with his wife. [*PM* 193-94]

His ethical judgment of all this is clear: "The renunciations of Henry James, the hysterical orgasms of Lawrence, the impotent and obsessive suspicions of Proust are all equally sexual monstrosities, dislocations of the reproductive instinct" (*PM* 196). Though his futuristic solution (" a new technique of breeding"), may not be widely acceptable, Wilson's late bourgeois morality is echoed in all his criticisms. Like Orwell, he finds that experiencing family life is one way in which the ideal unites itself with the real. Wilson criticizes "the monastic order of English university ascetics" like Pater, Lewis Carroll, Edward FitzGerald, Hopkins, Gray, and Housman for the failure to develop emotionally: "Their works are among the jewels of English literature rather than among its great springs of life; and Alice and the Shropshire Lad and Marius the Epicurean are all the beings of a looking-glass world, either sexless or with an unreal sex which turns only toward itself in the mirror of art. ... Housman has managed to grow old without in a sense ever knowing maturity. He has somehow never arrived at the age when the young man decides at last to summon all his resources and try to make something out of this world he has never made" (*TT* 70-71). He criticizes Ben Jonson as an anal-erotic (*TT* 217). Though he once explains Proust's failings as the last gasp of capitalist culture (*Ax* 190), he concentrates on Proust's sexual incapacity (*Ax* 155), and the fact that Joyce has as his hero Bloom, the ordinary sensual man, is one of the things that makes him superior to Proust (*Ax* 223; see also *PM* 195).

Wilson's personal solution to the crisis in his career is more creative, in that he begins to develop his persona—very much like that of Robert Frost— as the sage of Talcottville, the crusty oracle of the old American verities. It is this atavistic voice of the secular hero which dominates Wilson's later criticism and culminates in *Patriotic Gore* (1962), and through it Wilson successfully saves himself from the obsolescence of his charter and becomes a kind of guru to younger Intellectuals. Perhaps the best portrait of him is that by Alfred Kazin, who describes him sitting on the beach at Wellfleet with the Kennedy intellectuals "with immense authority." For Kazin, "the authority derived from his sound education, from his many books and almost 'bewildering' interests, from being *Edmund Wilson*, became as necessary as the articulation of the bones to the movement of the body. This insistence on 'correctness'—as of a judge or minister or national leader in the days when a few solitary geniuses molded American culture— became basic to the sense of his role in American life. Let the young and the newer stocks have their pretentious social science theories and academic careers and ridiculous 'New Criticism'! He was the last American man of letters, the great anachronism."[55] Wilson thus rises above the Journeyman level, to which his perpetual reviewing would otherwise have condemned him, by a dramatic effort rather than an intellectual one, by the creation of a fictional self rather than an articulated charter. In doing this he realizes the aspiration of other Journeymen, and becomes the model of writer-critics; and (with the exception of Eliot) Wilson's is the most famous persona of any contemporary American Man of Letters.

One must stress here that the persona Wilson is creating in the forties and fifties is a public self, and that this is the most valuable part of him. Critics have uniformly agreed through the years that Wilson's attempts at writing imaginative literature are much inferior to his critical prose. Describing a visit to Edna St. Vincent Millay, he says: "I had, on my side, been saving for her a simile and remarked that on one of the lawns I had passed the dandelions had looked like grated egg on spinach. We were neither of us, perhaps, at our best" (*SL* 775). His lack of poetic talent is demonstrated by the kinds of similes and metaphors he writes down in his journals as being worthy of preservation, which are now embarrassingly being published. For example, in *The Twenties* he writes: "The facts of his life filled up his mind like a scaffolding in a New York street"; or "My brain is like a piece of cheese that quivers with a million mites."[56] To save such clichés, much less publish volumes of equally obvious and banal description, shows a late misjudgment of a quite incredible kind, which seems at variance with much Wilson says about others earlier. For example, speaking of the MLA publication of some background material on W. D. Howells's *Their Wedding Journey*, he says: "What on earth is the interest of all this? Every writer knows how diaries and articles are utilized as material for books, and no ordinary reader knows or cares. What is important is the finished work by which the author wishes to stand. All this scholarship squandered on *Their Wedding Journey* is a waste of money and time."[57] Though this may not be true of an important novelist like Howells, it is certainly true of a unaccomplished novelist like Wilson, and it is Wilson's public persona which should occupy the student of criticism.

One way of defining Wilson's late identity is to examine the change in his alter-egos, the variation in the critics with whom he identifies. His earliest models are Shaw in England and H. L. Mencken in America, both of whom take as their task the shocking and reform of the bourgeoisie. Wilson says of Mencken in *The New Republic* (June 21, 1921): "Mencken is the civilized consciousness of modern America, its learning, its intelligence and its taste, realizing the grossness of its manners and mind and crying out in horror and chagrin"; his parallel of Mencken and Shaw has been quoted above (see *CCo* 114). In the thirties Wilson seems to identify with the French historian Jules Michelet, whom he describes in the beginning of *To the Finland Station:*

In his early years he mastered Latin and Greek with a thoroughness which was at that time already rare; and he later acquired English, Italian and German and devoured the literature and learning of those languages. With small means, he succeeded in traveling pretty much all over Western Europe, and those regions such as the Slavic East, to which his actual travels did not penetrate, his insatiable mind invaded. The impression he makes on us is quite different from that of the ordinary modern scholar who has specialized in some narrowly delimited subject and gotten it up in a graduate school: we feel that Michelet has read all the books, been to look at all the monuments and pictures, interviewed personally all the authorities, and explored all the libraries and archives of Europe; and that he has it all under his hat. ... He is simply a man going to the sources and trying to get down on record what can be learned from them; and this role, which claims for itself, on the one hand, no academic sanctions, involves, on the other hand, a more direct responsibility to the reader.[58]

These qualities of the inquiring reporter, the antiacademic cultural middleman, become less valuable to Wilson as the academic replaces the journalist as the central figure of American literary life. As Wilson withdraws from the struggle in the forties and fifties, he seems on occasion to identify with such figures as Saintsbury, the "connoisseur of literature," whom he describes as "the sole English literary critic of the late-nineteenth-early-twentieth centuries, the sole full-length professional critic, who is really of first-rate stature" (*CCo* 306). Saintsbury is antiacademic, his prose is excellent; like Wilson, "what he has done is create an imaginative world composed almost exclusively of books and their makers, with an admixture of foods and wines" (*CCo* 367). As Wilson would eventually do, "in his attitude toward contemporary writing, he practiced a consistent old-fogeyism" (*CCo* 370). But withdrawal becomes a preparation for return as Wilson identifies himself with Oliver Wendell Holmes, Jr., the last figure of *Patriotic Gore*. As Wilson gives up Marxism, Holmes gives up Abolitionism; the war "cured him for life, of apocalyptic social illusions" (*PG* 747). Like Wilson, Holmes is a hard, compulsive worker, of "grim industry" (*PG* 755). He is irreligious. He is loved by liberals, despite his belief that the power of the law rests on force, and despite his opposition to the redistribution of wealth, because of his belief in free speech. And in his old age he becomes a sage: "The old Justice begins to appear—as he has never in his life done before—in the light of an established sage, a god of the national pantheon. His books are reprinted and read; his minor papers collected and published. . . . In the reaction against the gentility, the timidity, the sentimentality of American cultural life, he is seen to have been a humanist, a realist, a bold and independent thinker, who has required of himself from the first to meet the highest intellectual standards and who has even, with a little public encouragement, succeeded in training himself to become also a distinguished writer" (*PG* 779). He has a lucid prose style; he comes from the Brahmin class, who "are all preachers, lawyers, doctors, professors and men of letters" (*PG* 783). "Through his intelligence and his love of learning, his sharpness of mind and his humor, he has obviously more in common with certain of his Jewish colleagues than with most of his Gentile ones" (*PG* 784–85). He is isolated, "unperturbed and lucid" through the period after the Civil War that destroyed so many. He is beloved by the people for "independence and fair-dealing, no doubt; rectitude and courage as a public official; and a conviction that the United States had a special meaning and mission to devote one's whole life to which was a sufficient dedication for the highest gifts" (*PG* 795–96). He is the last Roman. Is it too much to see this as a portrait of the ideal Wilson, and to see Holmes's life as the model that not only would save Wilson from the fate of his father but would also contribute to the salvation of America? In ending his last book with Holmes, does not Wilson wish us to see himself as he sees Holmes?[59]

As a critic, then, Wilson tries to become an eighteenth-century man in the tradition of the founders of the Republic. This he imbibed from his Princeton teacher of romance literature, Christian Gauss. As Wilson says: "[Gauss] gave me the vision of language and literature as something representing the continuous and never-ending flow of man's struggle to think the thoughts which, when put into action, constitute in the aggregate the advance of civilization. Whatever I may be today or may ever hope to be is largely the result of the germination of the seeds he planted" (*SL* 20). The philosophy that Gauss taught was "the eighteenth-century philosophy which assumed that the world was real and that we ourselves may find some sense in it and make ourselves happy in it" (*SL* 22). Wilson is not an eighteenth-century man in the sense that he studies the period, for he writes about it only occasionally; rather, he is a critic who writes about many subjects with the standards of reality and value which are character-istic of the secular Enlightenment. And he applies his eighteenth-century values not only abstractly but also to life. In his memoir "The Author at Sixty" he says: "I have lately been coming to feel that, as an American, I am more or less in the eighteenth century—or, at any rate, not much later than the early nineteenth. I do not drive a car ... I cannot abide the radio ... I have rarely watched a television program, and I almost never go to the movies" (*PM* 205). From Gauss, Wilson learns eighteenth-century standards of literary value: "This non-English, this classical and Latin ideal, became indissolubly associated in our minds with the summits of literature" (*SL* 14). In his appeal to classicism, Wilson is much like Eliot, but he avoids Eliot's religiosity—Wilson's is a secular Dante (*SL* 22).

A defining characteristic of Wilson's neoclassical position is that he is unreligious; he judges authors and works from a secular standard of value and seems incapable of perceiving religious reality. He says in 1951, in a letter to Allen Tate: "You are wrong, and have always been wrong, in thinking that I am in any sense a Christian. Christianity seems to me the worst imposture of any of the religions I know of. Even aside from the question of faith, the morality of the Gospel seems to me absurd" (*Letters* 495; see also *TT* 250-51). Wilson's basic secularity leads him to take a skeptical and sometimes satirical view of Eliot's Christianity (*BT* 398), or Waugh's Catholic novels (*CCo* 298-305), or the quasi-religious aspects of Marxism: "The one advantage, it seems to me, that the doctrine of Sartre has [over Marxism] is that it does away with Dialectical Materialism and its disguised theological content" (*CCo* 397). Wilson carries this suspicion of the ineffable so far as to attack even mythic reality, and he traces the origin of his attack to eighteenth-century America: "We suffer in this connection from the double disability of being Americans and Puritans. That is to say, we not only found no mythology in the place we came to; we brought none with us from Europe. The English Puritans had already demonstrated that their temperaments were of a kind antagonistic to the spirit that makes myths. ... I hope I have now made it clear a priori once and for all that it is absolutely and forever impossible for an American to succeed with a myth" (*Letters* 124-25; but cf. *PG* 491).

Wilson's skepticism about the validity of other-worldly realities and values leads him to the study of history, where he finds a progression from religious ideology to historical analysis to be characteristic of the proper study of Marxism: "The exaltation of the Marxist religion . . . seized the members of the professional classes like a capricious contagion or hurricane. . . . Later the convert, if he were capable of it, would get over his first phase of snow blindness and learn to see real people and conditions, would study the development of Marxism in terms of nations, periods, personalities, instead of logical deductions from abstract propositions or . . . of simple incantatory slogans" (*WBow* 188). Here Wilson again seems to model himself on Justice Holmes. He notes that the experience of the Civil War, of watching the fall of the South, led Holmes to be "distrustful of exalted states of mind connected with moral crusades" and later led him to an unconventional view of the law, which he regarded "not merely as a sacred code, which had simply to be read correctly, but as a complex accretion of rules accumulated through more than a thousand years and representing the needs and demands of definite groups of people existing in particular places at particular periods of history" (*BT* 92). If there is no other world to provide one with values, one turns to analysis of this world and the historical interpretation of literature.

Such analytical and historical analysis must be written clearly, Wilson argues, and he consistently stresses the need for a clear, lucid prose style. This, he confesses, he learned from his father; he recalls that upon rereading his father's speeches he discovered that "his style had, I saw, a purity quite exceptional in a public—or quasi-public—figure in New Jersey in the early nineteen hundreds, and his language was always distinguished by a silvery quality of clearness. . . . I realized now—and again with surprise—that I had been imitating this literary style as well as his penmanship" (*PM* 155). At his prep school, Wilson was drilled in traditional English, "and we were made to take very seriously—as I have never, indeed, ceased to do—the great Trinity: Lucidity, Force and Ease" (*PM* 156). Early in his career he says: "The qualities of a good prose style in English today are likely to be those of a sound intellectual currency, clipped out by a sharp cutter and stamped by a solvent mint; Rudyard Kipling, Bernard Shaw and T. S. Eliot, however else they may differ, have these characteristics in common. . . . With Kipling, Eliot, or Shaw, the style seems to aim at the effect of an inflexible impersonal instrument designed to perform special functions" (*Ax* 45–46). This kind of style is a consistent standard of excellence for Wilson; he praises Mencken for his "most attractive eighteenth-century qualities of lucidity, order and force, for lack of which the youngest of the younger literary generation . . . have proved so far rather ineffective" (*SL* 236), and he praises Ulysses S. Grant for a similar style (*PG* 143). Alfred Kazin says that for Wilson "there was some particular belief that through style everything, even in his disordered country, would yet fall into place."[60] And a clear, lucid style is paralleled by the necessity of a logical relationship of ideas; Wilson criticizes Gilbert Seldes because "he does not seem to realize that the function of his book is primarily one of exposition—the conveying of information, the unfolding of novel ideas—and that in order to do this successfully, you must cultivate patience and order" (*SL* 156). This kind of style and exposition is, of course, characteristic of journalism at its best, and it is a style which Wilson successfully attains in his own writing.

This emphasis on lucidity, force, and logic also causes Wilson to prefer prose to verse. In *Axel's Castle* he suggests that "verse as a technique of literary expression is being abandoned by humanity altogether—perhaps because it is a more primitive, and hence a more barbarous technique than prose" (*Ax* 120), and he argues against the view of Eliot and Valery that poetry is "some sort of pure and rare aesthetic essence with no relation to any of the practical human uses for which ... only the technique of prose is appropriate" (*Ax* 119). He goes on to praise Joyce as "the great poet of a new phase of the human consciousness" (*Ax* 221), reflecting the new relativistic reality of Einstein and Whitehead. And in his later essay "Is Verse A Dying Technique?" he shows how "verse was once made to serve many purposes for which we now use prose" (*TT* 15), how poetry has come to be defined as "primarily lyric verse, and this only at its most poignant or most musical moments" (*TT* 20), and suggests that the term *poetry* now be applied to all imaginative literature, since the technique of prose "is showing itself quite equal to that work of the imagination which caused men to call Homer 'divine': that re-creation, in the harmony and logic of words, of the cruel confusion of life" (*TT* 30). For Wilson, prose seems to be better fitted to express both the practical reference to life and history and the imaginative power which transforms history into art. In *Patriotic Gore* he traces the development of this kind of clear prose to the Civil War: "What was it, then, that led Grant and Lincoln to express themselves with equal concision? It was undoubtedly the decisiveness with which they had to speak. They had no time in which to waste words. ... This is the language of responsibility" (*PG* 650).

In Wilson's view, the function of the classical position, as embodied in the skeptical, informed, lucid student of history, is to bring order out of experience in both the historical and the literary sphere. As he says in "The Historical Interpretation of Literature":

All our intellectual activity, in whatever field it takes place, is an attempt to give a meaning to our experience—that is, to make life more practicable; for by understanding things we make it easier to survive and get around among them. ... [The original writer] must always find expression for something which has never yet been expressed, must master a new set of phenomena which has never yet been mastered. With each such victory of the human intellect, whether in history, in philosophy or in poetry, we experience a deep satisfaction: we have been cured of some ache of disorder, relieved of some oppressive burden of uncomprehended events. This relief that brings the sense of power, and, with the sense of power, joy is the positive emotion which tells us that we have encountered a first-rate piece of literature. [*TT* 269-70]

For Wilson, the function of literature is the same as the function of the mind; it is to save us, not be retreating from history as in Symbolism, or by transcending history as in religion, or such quasi-religions as Marxism, or even the faith of Lincoln, which saved the Union. Wilson's salvation is that of the Enlightenment man, to see things clearly and to exert one's mind to make sense of them in order to transform reality with imagination.

The meaning of Wilson's later persona and criticism is then basically cultural, not literary, in that he proposes his views as a way to save the Republic. The unique twist of Wilson's later position is that he proposes to save America not by a new or Futurist ideal, as do most avant-gardists and as he did earlier, but by the older ideal of the American professional class to which Wilson's family had traditionally belonged. Wilson opposes to the new vulgar America not a newer, more vulgar America, but a true ideal America, one which would transform America and make it new by recalling it to the ideas of the secular Enlightenment on which it was founded, and beyond that to the ideals of the classical civilization of Greece and Rome wherever they appear. In a memoir of his teacher at Hill School, Mr. Rolfe, he says: "As I write this memoir, it seems to me that the stream he was following flowed out of a past that is now remote: from Emerson with his self-dependence, and *The Wonderful One-Hoss Shay* with its satire on the too-perfect Calvinist system; from the days when people went to Germany to hear Wagner and study Greek; from Matthew Arnold, from Bernard Shaw—now almost an old-fashioned classic like Arnold. And I am glad to renew my sense of Alfred Rolfe's contribution to it, as I realize that I myself have been trying to follow and feed it at a time when it has been running low" (*TT* 255-56). America is thus to be redeemed by its classical and Puritan heritage, and this tradition originates with the Jew, is "a Gentile imitation of Judaism." In Wilson's words, "Our conception itself of America as a country with a mission in the world comes down to us from our Mosaic ancestors" (*PM* 90). In *Patriotic Gore* Wilson develops this idea of "the persistence through the nineteenth century of the New Englander's deep-rooted conviction that the Jews are a special people selected for a unique role by God, and that New England somehow shares this destiny" (*PM* 90; see also *BT* 98). He thus identifies himself with what he calls America's republican sense, with the ideal of his father's class of men and the ideal opposed to the commercial side of America, the ideal of Lincoln, Theodore Roosevelt, Woodrow Wilson, Franklin Roosevelt. Such Americans believe they "have a stake in the success of our system, that they share the responsibility to carry on its institutions, to find expression for its new point of view, to give it dignity, to make it work" (*PM* 25).

They have a sense of a special role for America and they identify their own interests with those of the American Republic, as did Oliver Wendell Holmes, Jr. For Edmund Wilson, "Americanism" means the ideal of the Teddy Roosevelt who challenged the trusts of his day, "the ideal of disinterested public service for the benefit of the American community" (*BT* 71; see also *PM* 32-34).

Contemplating Wilson contemplating himself as Justice Holmes saving America may evoke a slight smile at the pretentiousness of such an aspiration to permanent greatness, but to think on greatness as measured by Holmes, not by appearances on the Johnny Carson Show or the cover of *Time*, is in itself so novel a conception for the sixties as to qualify as startlingly original. Certainly Wilson found himself at odds with the America of his last decade, and his reputation may have suffered unfairly because of it. A more lasting, because less pretentious and more literary, standard of judgment may result from a comparison of Wilson not with Holmes but with his literary coevals T. S. Eliot and R. P. Blackmur. Wilson, like Eliot, comes from old American stock, establishes his authority early in his career, and becomes the father figure for a considerable literary movement. Unlike Eliot, however, he does not have the authority of the creative artist, of what he once called "carry-over value of literature" (*TT* 201). Hence his authority will fade with his movement, and one cannot say that he has attained the eponymous status of Eliot. Like Blackmur, Wilson is one of the first commentators on the modernist movement in literature. Wilson on novelists like Proust and Joyce seems the equal of Blackmur on poets like Pound, Yeats, or Stevens; and Wilson's extended lives—*lives* in Dr. Johnson's sense of analysis of works, biography, and character of the author—of Dickens, Kipling, and Shaw seem as valuable as Blackmur's close analyses of poets. Whether Wilson's persona of the old Roman will seem any more appealing to future critics than Eliot's pose of authoritative humility, or Blackmur's crabbed prophecies, or for that matter Saintsbury's connoisseurship or Tate's polemical advocacy, is problematic, but like all these men, Wilson has created for his time and ours a response to literature which is both personal and public. In her sardonic "Portrait of the Intellectual as a Yale Man" Mary McCarthy describes the figure of Jim Barnett, who is thought to be modeled on Wilson:

Jim also stood in awe of himself ... What he reverenced in himself was his intelligent mediocrity. He knew that he was the Average Thinking Man to whom in the end all appeals are addressed. He was the man that Uncle Sam points his finger at in the recruiting posters. ... He was a walking Gallup Poll, and he had only to leaf over his feelings to discover what America was thinking. ... His mind and character appeared to him as a kind of sacred trust that he must preserve inviolate. It was as if he were the standard gold dollar against which the currency is measured. ... Jim's function, as he saw it, was to ring the new ideas against himself, and let the world hear how they sounded. It was his duty, therefore, to "be himself."[61]

To this duty Wilson has been faithful, and since, unlike "New York" Intellectuals Rahv, Trilling, Howe, or Kazin, he did not have to learn about America through literature,[62] but had it in his bones, he can and does serve as our gold standard for journalistic criticism in the Republic of Letters.

Notes

All bibliographical notes are selective. I have tried to include all books and articles notable for substance, bibliography, wit, or the fame of the author, and have intentionally allowed much commentary that seemed neither original nor influential to sink quietly in the seas of scholarship. I have arranged sources historically, to show the development of interest in topics and the changes in critical reputations, rather than as alphabetical reading lists. Notes should be current through 1977, and I have added whatever has come to my attention since then.

Chapter 1. The Development of Literary Charters
  1. "The New Criticism Pro and Contra," *Critical Inquiry* 4 (1978): 611.
  2. "Literary Criticism and Its Discontents," *Ibid.* 3 (1976): 204-5, 216.
  3. "Beyond Interpretation: The Prospects of Contemporary Criticism," *Comparative Literature* 28 (1976): 253-54.
  4. Page references in the text are to the second edition, enlarged (Chicago: University of Chicago Press, 1970), which contains a postscript by Kuhn. The first edition was published in 1962. Important later essays by Kuhn include "Logic of Discovery or Psychology of Research?" and "Reflections on My Critics," both of which appear in *Criticism and the Growth of Knowledge,* ed. Imre Lakatos and Alan Musgrave (Cambridge: Cambridge University Press, 1970), pp. 1-23 and 231-78; this volume, which also contains a number of essays debating the positions of Kuhn and Sir Karl Popper, will be cited throughout as Lakatos and Musgrave. See also Kuhn's "Second Thoughts on Paradigms," with a number of comments, in *The Structure of Scientific Theories,* ed. Frederick Suppe (Urbana: University of Illinois Press, 1974), pp. 459-517. Most of the above and a number of other essays are printed in Kuhn's *The Essential Tension: Selected Studies in Scientific Tradition and Change* (Chicago: University of Chicago Press, 1977), which also contains an interesting autobiographical preface describing the development of his ideas.
  5. For articles on Kuhn's influence in various disciplines, see: Michael T. Ghiselin, "The Individual in the Darwinian Revolution," *New Literary History* 3 (1971): 113-34; and John C. Greene, "The Kuhnian Paradigm and the Darwinian Revolution in Natural History," in *Perspectives in the History of Science and*

Technology, ed. Duane H. D. Roller (Norman: University of Oklahoma Press, 1971), pp. 3-37. M. D. King applies Kuhn to the sociology of knowledge in "Reason, Tradition, and the Progressiveness of Science," *History and Theory* 10 (1971): 3-32; see also Herminio Martins, "The Kuhnian 'Revolution' and Its Implications for Sociology," in *Imagination and Precision in the Social Sciences,* ed. T. J. Nossiter, A. H. Hanson, and Stein Rokkan (London: Faber & Faber, 1972), pp. 13-58; and John Urry, "Thomas S. Kuhn as Sociologist of Knowledge," *British Journal of Sociology* 24 (1973): 462-73. Arend Lijphart, "The Structure of the Theoretical Revolution in International Relations," *International Studies Quarterly* 18 (1974): 41-74, applies Kuhn to international relations. For an application of Kuhn to political science, see Sheldon S. Wolin, "Paradigms and Political Theories," in *Politics and Experience,* ed. Preston King and B. C. Parekh (Cambridge: Cambridge University Press, 1968), pp. 125-52, and J.G.A. Pocock, *Politics, Language, and Time* (New York: Atheneum, 1971). David A. Hollinger, "T. S. Kuhn's Theory of Science and Its Implications for History," *American Historical Review* 78 (1973): 370-93, is a good survey of Kuhn's influence; see also Gene Wise, *American Historical Explanations* (Homewood, Ill.: Dorsey, 1973). Ian G. Barbour, *Myths, Models, and Paradigms* (New York: Harper & Row, 1974), applies Kuhn to religion. David Bleich, "The Subjective Paradigm in Science, Psychology, and Criticism," *New Literary History* 7 (1976): 315-34, uses Kuhn's terms but argues that knowledge is subjective; see also the commentary by Norman N. Holland in the same issue. For applications of Kuhn's theory to the history of linguistics, see *Studies in the History of Linguistics: Traditions and Paradigms,* ed. Dell Hymes (Bloomington: Indiana University Press, 1974); and W. Keith Percival, "The Applicability of Kuhn's Paradigms to the History of Linguistics," *Language* 52 (1976): 285-94.

For a good overview of the current state of study of the social history of science, the scientific research community, and other related topics, see *Science, Technology, and Society: A Cross-Disciplinary Perspective,* ed. Ina Spiegel-Rösing and Derek de Solla Price (London: Sage, 1977). See also Stephen Toulmin, "From Form to Function: Philosophy and History of Science in the 1950s and Now," *Daedalus* 106 (1977): 143-62.

6. "Logic of Discovery or Psychology of Research?" in Lakatos and Musgrave, p. 21.

7. "The Problem of Literary Evaluation," *Problems of Literary Evaluation,* ed. Joseph Strelka (University Park: Pennsylvania State University Press, 1969), pp. 8-9.

8. Preface to *Selected Essays* (New York: Random House, 1954), p. xiii.

9. (New York: Henry Regnery, 1952).

10. (Englewood Cliffs, N.J.: Prentice-Hall, 1963).

11. (New York: Modern Language Association, 1967).

12. The theoretical guide that first simplified the methodological approach for introductory students was David Daiches's *Critical Approaches to Literature* (1956), which discusses practical criticism (largely Formalist criticism), and criticism in relation to psychology, sociology, scholarship, and culture. This attempt to survey the possible approaches to criticism in some systematic way has been continued in most of the anthologies of modern criticism: Hyman's *The Critical Performance*

(1956), Danziger and Johnson's *An Introduction to Literary Criticism* (1961), Sutton and Foster's *Modern Criticism: Theory and Practice* (1963), Levich's *Aesthetics and the Philosophy of Criticism* (1963), and Zintner, Kissane, and Liberman's *The Practice of Criticism* (1966). Greater systematization and agreement on the main schools of criticism have resulted. Scott's *Five Approaches of Literary Criticism* (1962) settles on the importance of the formal, psychological, mythic, sociological, and moral approaches; Goldberg and Goldberg's *The Modern Critical Spectrum* (1962) adopts these five (calling morality Humanism) and adds sections on the use of biography, tradition, and scholarship. *A Handbook of Critical Approaches to Literature*, by Guerin *et al.* (1966), treats the formal, psychological, mythic, and "exponential" approaches at greatest length, while mentioning others briefly. Sheldon Grebstein's *Perspectives in Contemporary Criticism* (1968) divides critical essays from the fifties and sixties into historical, Formalist, sociocultural, psychological, and mythopoeic categories; and Handy and Westbrook's *Twentieth Century Criticism: The Major Statements* (1974) categorizes essays from the entire century as Formalist, genre, archetypal, historical, and interdisciplinary criticism.

13. "The Antitheses of Criticism: Reflections on the Yale Colloquium," *Modern Language Notes* 81 (1966): 557.

14. Such anthologies include *The Structuralists from Marx to Levi-Strauss*, ed. Richard and Fernande DeGeorge (1972); *Sociology of Literature and Drama*, ed. Elizabeth and Tom Burns (1973); *European Literary Theory and Practice from Existential Phenomenology to Structuralism*, ed. Vernon W. Gras (1973); *Issues in Contemporary Literary Criticism*, ed. Gregory T. Polletta (1973); and *Velocities of Change: Critical Essays from MLN*, ed. Richard Macksey (1974).

15. "The Function of Dogma in Scientific Research," in *Scientific Change*, ed. A. C. Crombie (New York: Basic Books, 1963), p. 363.

16. "The Nature of a Paradigm," in Lakatos and Musgrave, pp. 59–89.

17. "T. S. Kuhn's Theory of Science and Its Implications for History," p. 390. M. D. King makes the same point in "Reason, Tradition, and the Progressiveness of Science," p. 24.

18. "Roads Taken and Not Taken in Contemporary Criticism," *Contemporary Literature* 17 (1976): 331.

19. "The Idea of Authority in the West," *American Historical Review* 82 (1977): 258.

20. "Reason, Tradition, and the Progressiveness of Science," pp. 20, 19.

21. "Reflections on My Critics," p. 244.

22. *Scientific Knowledge and Its Problems* (Oxford: Clarendon Press, 1971), p. 246.

23. Ibid., p. 247.

24. (London: Kegan Paul, 1929), pp. 301, 302.

25. (New York: Vintage Books, 1958), p. 5.

26. "Rationality and Imagination in Cultural History: A Reply to Wayne Booth," *Critical Inquiry* 2 (1975): 462–63.

27. I use the terms "gestalt" and "gestalt switch" not in the technical sense employed by gestalt psychologists, but in a general sense to mean a configuration of literary works, ideas, and values that appears in different relationships as these works, ideas, and values are seen in terms of different literary charters.

28. "What's the Use of Theorizing about the Arts?" in *In Search of Literary Theory*, ed. Morton W. Bloomfield (Ithaca: Cornell University Press, 1972), p. 34.

29. *Magic, Science, and Religion and Other Essays* (Glencoe: Free Press, 1948), pp. 93, 102.

30. "The New Criticism," *American Scholar* 20 (1950/51): 98.

31. "Second Thoughts on Paradigms," p. 460; see also "Reflections on My Critics," p. 253; *Structure of Scientific Revolutions*, p. 10

32. "Second Thoughts on Paradigms," p. 461.

33. Ibid., p. 463.

34. *Collected Poems*, ed. Edward Mendelson (New York: Random House, 1976), p. 262.

35. Robert Boyers, "An Interview with Howard Nemerov," *Salmagundi*, no. 31/32 (Fall 1975/Winter 1976), pp. 116-17.

36. *Scientific Knowledge and Its Problems*, p. 252.

37. Ibid., p. 259.

38. The most complete work on critical quarterlies is G.A.M. Janssens, *The American Literary Review: A Critical History* (The Hague: Mouton, 1968). Accounts and lists of both little magazines and critical quarterlies can be found in *The Little Magazine*, by F. J. Hoffman, Charles Allen, and Carolyn F. Ulrich, rev. ed. (Princeton: Princeton University Press, 1947). This is the standard account. A list of critical quarterlies and scholarly magazines is found in Donna Gerstenberger and George Hendrick, *Fourth Directory of Periodicals Publishing Articles in English and American Literature and Language* (Chicago: Swallow Press, 1974). Morton D. Zabel lists "American Magazines Publishing Criticism" in *Literary Opinion in America*, 3rd ed., 2 vols. (New York: Harper & Row, 1962), 2: 812-21. See also: Eliseo Vivas, "Criticism and the Little Mags," *Western Review* 16 (Autumn 1951): 9-19; Philip Blair Rice, "The Intellectual Quarterly in a Non-Intellectual Society," *KR* 16 (1954): 420-39; Monroe K. Spears, "The Present Function of the Literary Quarterlies," *Texas Quarterly* 3 (Spring 1960): 33-50; Reed Whittemore, *Little Magazines* (Minneapolis: University of Minnesota Press, 1963); Felix Pollak, "Landing in Little Magazines—Capturing (?) a Trend," *Arizona Quarterly* 19 (1963): 101-15; "Concerning the Little Magazines: Something Like a Symposium," *Carleton Miscellany* 7, no. 2 (1966): 3-79; *The Little Magazine and Contemporary Literature* (New York: Modern Language Association, 1966); Beverly Gross, "Culture and Anarchy: What Ever Happened to Lit Magazines?" *Antioch Review* 29 (1969/70): 43-56; and "The Little Magazine in America: A Modern Documentary History," *TriQuarterly*, no 43 (Fall 1978) (a special issue that contains a large number of essays by magazine editors and publishers and an annotated bibliography of eighty-four important magazines of the postwar period).

39. "The Present Function of the Literary Quarterlies," pp. 49-50.

40. *The Little Magazine and Contemporary Literature*, p. 50.

41. Ibid., p. 31.

42. See the conclusion by Janssens, *The American Literary Review*, p. 18: "They did not believe in the 'common reader'; they addressed themselves to a highbrow audience. ... It is therefore nostalgic rather than helpful to regard the early nineteenth century English reviews, like the *Edinburgh Review* or *Blackwoods Maga-*

zine, as the direct precursors of the twentieth century reviews." See also Lionel Trilling, *LI* 89-92. This error is made by D. W. Brogan in "The Intellectual Review," *Encounter* 21 (November 1963): 7-15.

43. In "Concerning the Little Magazines," p. 64.

44. Ibid., p. 75.

45. "These Little Magazines," *American Scholar* 15 (1945/46): 551.

46. Editor's introduction to *Scholars and Their Publishers,* ed. Weldon A. Kefauver (New York: Modern Language Association, 1977), p. 4.

47. The process of making a tradition is in some ways parallel to the process of "Canon-formation in the Church" described by Ernst Robert Curtius in *European Literature and the Latin Middle Ages* (New York: Bollingen/Pantheon, 1953), pp. 256-72. I am indebted for this reference to Frank Kermode, whose "Institutional Control of Interpretation," *Salmagundi,* no. 43 (Winter 1979), pp. 72-86, deals with many of the same problems of "authority, hierarchy, canon, initiation, and differential readings" that I address here. Professor Kermode's suggestive essay appeared, alas, too late to be of use to me. For a detailed account of religious canon-formation, see Richard McKeon, "Canonic Books and Prohibited Books: Orthodoxy and Heresy in Religion and Culture," *Critical Inquiry* 2 (1976): 781-806.

48. *Poetry and the Age* (New York: Vintage Books, 1955), pp. 70-73.

49. *The New Republic,* November 29, 1975, p. 24.

50. "A Note on Wittgenstein and Literary Criticism," *ELH* 41 (1974): 552.

51. *Modern Philology* 64 (1966): 72.

52. For speculations about the relationship of the critic to criticism and about the conventions critics use, see Cary Nelson, "The Paradox of Critical Language: A Polemical Speculation," *Modern Language Notes* 89 (1974): 1003-16: idem, "Reading Criticism," *PMLA* 91 (1976): 801-15; Grant Webster, "A Potter's Field of Critical Rhetoric," *College English* 27 (1966): 320-22; and Thomas Postlewait, "Saving the Humanities—Or, A Call for Triple Speak," *College English* 40 (1978): 390-96.

53. *Collected Essays of Leslie Fiedler,* 2 vols. (New York: Stein & Day, 1971), 1: 537.

54. *Fugitives' Reunion,* ed. Rob Roy Purdy (Nashville: Vanderbilt University Press, 1959), pp. 180-81.

55. "The Myth of Relevancy and the Traditional Disciplines," *ADE Bulletin, Special Issue, The Ph.D. in English and Foreign Languages: A Conference Report,* June 1973, p. 35.

56. "The Literary Criticism of Frank Raymond Leavis," *Literary Views,* ed. Carroll Camden (Chicago: University of Chicago Press, 1964), p. 190. Wellek also observes of the New Humanists that "More and Babbitt had reached the age of forty in 1904 and 1905, respectively, and by that time most people's minds are made up, solidified and set in a mold" "Irving Babbitt, Paul More, and Transcendentalism," in *Transcendentalism and Its Legacy,* ed. Myron Simon and Thornton Parsons [Ann Arbor: University of Michigan Press, 1966], p. 188). Because of his consistent recognition of the historical limitations of other critics, it must be regarded as a failure of self-recognition rather than of theory that he cannot see that the Kantian aesthetic and Prague Structuralism fashionable in Central Europe in *his* youth are no less limited.

57. *The Twenties,* rev. ed. (New York: Free Press, 1962), p. 354.

58. Wellek says further: "The work of art, I have argued, can be conceived as a stratified structure of signs and meanings which is totally distinct from the mental processes of the author at the time of composition and hence of the influences which may have formed his mind" (*CC* 293).

59. Quoted in John Brooke, "Namier and Namierism," *History and Theory* 3 (1963/64): 333. So far as I have been able to discover, Namier wrote no systematic or theoretical exposition of his method. See also Lawrence Stone, "Prosopography," *Daedalus* 100 (1971): 46-79.

The genre of biography itself has been the object of some critical attention, and the principles enunciated by Richard D. Altick in his study of English and American literary biography apply also to critics: "The basic postulate of modern literary biography is that there is an essential connection between person and artist, that the personality of the writer and the events of his life have a demonstrable relevance to the psychic forces, however defined, that produce his art. Individual traits and circumstances, in other words, are the key to art" (*Lives and Letters* [New York: Knopf, 1969], p. 11). For an anthology and bibliography of statements on biography, see *Biography as an Art: Selected Criticism, 1560-1960,* ed. James L. Clifford (New York: Galaxy Books, 1962).

60. "April Inventory," *Heart's Needle* (New York: Knopf, 1969), p. 38.

61. "In Search of a Vocation," *Michigan Quarterly Review* 11 (1972): 246.

62. John Lavell, "Facts of Journal Publishing, IV," *PMLA* 81, no. 6 (1966): 3-12; see also William Pell, "Facts of Scholarly Publishing," ibid. 88 (1973): 639-70.

63. "Radical Styles," *PR* 36 (1969): 389.

64. *Views of a Nearsighted Cannoneer,* new ed. (New York: Dutton, 1968), p. 23.

65. *T. S. Eliot: A Bibliography,* rev. ed. (New York: Harcourt, 1969).

66. "Priorities in Scientific Discovery: A Chapter in the Sociology of Science," *American Sociological Review* 22 (1957): 654-55.

67. "The World and the Jug," *Shadow and Act* (New York: New American Library, 1966), p. 143. Howe's conflated essay was published as an article in *Dissent* (Autumn 1963) and has been reprinted in *The Decline of the New* (1970).

68. *The Rise and Fall of the Man of Letters* (New York: Macmillan, 1969), p. xiii. The phrase stems from Thomas Carlyle's essay "The Hero as Man of Letters" and was used by Allen Tate (*CE* 379-93).

69. *Essays in Critical Dissent* (London: Longmans, 1972), p. 234.

70. "Age, Aging, and Age Structure in Science," in *The Sociology of Science: Theoretical and Empirical Investigations,* ed. Norman W. Storer (Chicago: University of Chicago Press, 1973), pp. 531, 530.

71. Ibid., pp. 510, 515.

72. Ibid., p. 514.

73. Ibid., p. 558. Lewis S. Feuer points out a similar contrast between generations in the context of philosophy in "Arthur O. Lovejoy," *American Scholar* 46 (1976/77): 360: "Probably the most memorable meeting, however, was the great debate at Baltimore three years later (1935) between Lovejoy and Rudolf Carnap. . . . [In Lovejoy's paper] we were witnessing the last stand of classical American philosophy.

And for the next generation, metaphysics, apart from some existentialist outcroppings, was to suffer a desuetude. Carnap patently did not take seriously the objections of the metaphysicians. . . . He totally ignored Morris R. Cohen's reproach that his message was the old one they had heard from Ernst Mach, 'the high priest of positivism.' . . . Carnap still, however, refused to acknowledge metaphysics as having meaning, and annoyed some of his listeners by saying that it ought to be explained psychologically."

74. "Eliot's Weary Gestures of Dismissal," *Massachusetts Review* 7 (1966): 589.

75. *Principles of Literary Criticism* (New York: Harcourt, n.d.), p. 37.

76. "Logic of Discovery or Psychology of Research?" p. 7.

77. "Rationality and Imagination in Cultural History," p. 464.

78. "Reflections on My Critics," p. 252.

79. "Second Thoughts on Paradigms," pp. 461–62.

80. "What's the Use?" pp. 51–52.

81. May 23, 1976, "Arts and Leisure," p. 1.

82. *New Literary History* 2 (1971): 534.

83. *Scientific Knowledge and Its Problems,* pp. 401–2.

84. "Comment," *Comparative Studies in Society and History* 11 (1969): 407.

85. For a detailed analysis of the fluctuating reputations and prices in the art world, see Gerald Reitlinger, *The Economics of Taste: The Rise and Fall of the Picture Market, 1760–1960* (New York: Holt, 1961): and idem, *The Economics of Taste: The Rise and Fall of the Objets d'Art Market since 1750* (New York: Holt, 1963). For an analysis of changing literary reputations, see Jay B. Hubbell, *Who Are the Major American Writers? A Study of the Changing Literary Canon* (Durham: Duke University Press, 1972).

86. "The Sense of Verification: Pragmatic Commonplaces about Literary Criticism," *Daedalus* 101 (Winter 1972): 212.

87. "The Myth of Relevancy and the Traditional Disciplines," p. 37. On this point see also Robert Marsh, "Historical Interpretation and the History of Criticism," in *Literary Criticism and Historical Understanding,* ed. Phillip Damon (New York: Columbia University Press, 1964), pp. 20–24.

88. "What's the Use?" p. 25.

89. "Comment," p. 410.

90. "Priorities in Scientific Discovery," pp. 642–43. A recent attempt of this kind to reorder literary rankings retrospectively is found in Hugh Kenner's *The Pound Era* (Berkeley: University of California Press, 1971), where the author by his title claims the chief modernist figure to be Pound (not Eliot).

91. Foreword to *Problems of Literary Evaluation,* p. x.

Chapter 2. A Preliminary Theory of Literary Charters

1. "The Kuhnian 'Revolution' and Its Implications for Sociology," in *Imagination and Precision in the Social Sciences*, ed. T. J. Nossiter, A. H. Hanson, and Stein Rokkan (London: Faber & Faber, 1972), p. 22.

2. "What's the Use of Theorizing about the Arts?" in *In Search of Literary Theory*, ed. Morton W. Bloomfield (Ithaca: Cornell University Press, 1972), p. 34.

3. "T. S. Kuhn's Theory of Science and Its Implications for History," *American Historical Review* 78 (1973): 391, 392.

4. "Comment," *Comparative Studies in Society and History* 11 (1969): 411.

5. "Falsification and the Methodology of Scientific Research Programmes," in Lakatos and Musgrave, p. 92.

6. "Objectivity, Value Judgment, and Theory Choice," *The Essential Tension: Selected Studies in Scientific Tradition and Change* (Chicago: University of Chicago Press, 1977), p. 322.

7. See Gombrich's *Art and Illusion: A Study of the Psychology of Pictorial Representation* (Princeton: Princeton University Press, 1961); and Whorf's *Language, Thought, and Reality,* ed. John B. Carroll (Cambridge: M.I.T. Press, 1956).

8. "Meaning and Understanding in the History of Ideas," *History and Theory* 8 (1969): 52.

9. Introduction to *Literature as System: Essays toward the Theory of Literary History* (Princeton: Princeton University Press, 1971), p. 6.

10. "History and Literature," *Essays on History and Literature*, ed. Robert H. Bremner (Columbus: Ohio State University Press, 1966), p. 154.

11. "Privileged Criteria in Evaluation," *The Aims of Interpretation* (Chicago: University of Chicago Press, 1976), p. 122.

12. "Logic of Discovery or Psychology of Research?" in Lakatos and Musgrave, p. 12.

13. "Faulty Perspectives," *Essays in Criticism* 25 (1975): 161–63, 162, 166, 167.

14. "What's the Use?" p. 25.

15. "Historical Interpretation and the Theory of Criticism," in *Literary Criticism and Historical Understanding,* ed. Phillip Damon (New York: Columbia University Press, 1964), p. 21.

16. "The History of Ideas, Intellectual History, and the History of Philosophy," *History and Theory* 5, suppl. (1965): 51.

17. *Literature as System*, p. 464.

18. "Reflections on My Critics," in Lakatos and Musgrave, pp. 237–38; see p. 253 for an extended definition of the community of scientists.

19. Imre Lakatos, "Falsification and the Methodology of Scientific Research Programmes," in Lakatos and Musgrave, p. 178; see also p. 140, n. 3. For Kuhn's reply, see "Reflections," p. 263.

20. "Reason, Tradition, and the Progressiveness of Science," *History and Theory* 10 (1971): 30.

21. "Behaviorism and Deconstruction ... ," *Critical Inquiry* 4 (1977): 182.

22. Ibid., p. 191.

23. "The Republic of Science," *Minerva* 1 (1962/63): 59–60.

24. Harriet Zuckerman and Robert K. Merton, "Patterns of Evaluation in Science: Institutionalisation, Structure, and Functions of the Referee System," in *The Sociology of Science: Theoretical and Empirical Investigations*, ed. Norman W. Storer (Chicago: University of Chicago Press, 1973), p. 72.

25. Ibid., p. 74.

26. "The Decision to Publish: Scholarly Standards," in *Scholars and Their Publishers*, ed. Weldon A. Kefauver (New York: Modern Language Association, 1977), pp. 6–7.

27. "Patterns of Evaluation in Science," p. 77.

28. "The Decision to Publish," p. 13.

29. "A Note on Wittgenstein and Literary Criticism," *ELH* 41 (1974): 552, 553.

30. See Richard D. Altick, *The Art of Literary Research,* rev. ed. (New York: Norton, 1975), pp. 72–130.

Chapter 3. T. S. Eliot and the Tory Charter

1. In addition to many parenthetical comments by the New Critics themselves, the following works have been written about the New Criticism. William Elton, "A Glossary of the New Criticism," *Poetry* 73 (1947/48): 151–62, 232–45, 296–307, tries to work out from the various, often conflicting, statements made by the New Critics themselves a consistent terminology with which to talk about poetry. *The Critic's Notebook*, ed. Robert Wooster Stallman (Minneapolis: University of Minnesota Press, 1950), gathers *loci classici* by all the New Critics on the subjects of poetic form and meaning, life and art, the "objective correlative," the problem of belief, the personal element in poetry, and intention. Stallman also includes extensive bibliographies on each of these subjects. Murray Krieger, *The New Apologists for Poetry* (Minneapolis: University of Minnesota Press, 1956), studies New Criticism from the point of view of the aesthetician (concentrating on Hulme, Eliot, and Richards) and tries to formulate an adequate "contextualist" theory as a defense for the unique aesthetic experience he believes is provided by poetry. Richard Foster, *The New Romantics: A Reappraisal of the New Criticism* (Bloomington: Indiana University Press, 1962), discusses the New Critics, particularly Richards, Eliseo Vivas, Blackmur, and Tate, in terms of their hidden tendencies toward Romanticism. C. E. Pulos, *The New Critics and the Language of Poetry*, University of Nebraska Studies, n.s. (Lincoln: University of Nebraska Press, 1958), studies the relationship of Eliot, Richards, Empson, and Brooks to Imagists Ford Madox Ford and T. E. Hulme. Pulos feels that the New Critics' absolute separation of the language of poetry from that of science is untenable. Richard P. Blackmur, *New Criticism in the United States* (Tokyo: Kenkyusha, 1959), summarizes Blackmur's opinions on the movement. William J. Handy, *Kant and the Southern New Critics* (Austin: University of Texas Press, 1963), discusses the idealistic metaphysical assumptions of the New Criticism. Lee T. Lemon, *The Partial Critics* (New York: Oxford University Press, 1965), assumes that evaluation is the central activity of the critic and attempts to work out a systematic approach to literary evaluation through a long refutation of the closed form of the poem the New Critics support; he favors a view which unites the structure of the poem and the response of the reader to find the meaning of the poem.

General texts on the New Criticism also include Gerald Graff, *Poetic Statement and Critical Dogma* (Evanston: Northwestern University Press, 1970); and Wesley Morris, *Toward a New Historicism* (Princeton: Princeton University Press, 1972). Graff argues that the organicist, antipropositional theories of poetry held by critics like Cleanth Brooks, I. A. Richards, and Northrop Frye, which emphasize the truth of coherence of a poem and its dramatic unity, are contradictory and confused, and must be supplemented by a theory, such as that of Yvor Winters, which recognizes the truth of correspondence, propositional assertion, and expository argument as important semantic and structural principles of poetry.

The following articles have been written about Formalism, or the New Criticism: Arthur Mizener, "Recent Criticism," *SoR* 5 (1940): 376–400; H. J. Muller, "The New Criticism in Poetry," ibid. 6 (1941): 811–39; Walter J. Ong, "The Meaning of the 'New Criticism,' " *Modern Schoolman* 20 (1942/43): 192-209; Darrel Abel, "Intellectual Criticism," *American Scholar* 12 (1942/43): 414-28; Cleanth Brooks, "The New Criticism: A Brief for The Defense," *American Scholar* 13 (1943/44): 285-95 (a reply to Abel); Hoyt Trowbridge, "Aristotle and the 'New Criticism,' " *SR* 52 (1944): 536-55; Sgt. William Van O'Conner, "This Alexandrian Criticism," *American Scholar* 14 (1944/45): 357-61; Richard H. Fogle, "Romantic Bards and Metaphysical Reviewers," *ELH* 12 (1945): 221-50 (claims that Formalists misvalue Romantic poets); R. S. Crane, "The Critical Monism of Cleanth Brooks," *Modern Philology* 45 (1948): 226-45; Robert Wooster Stallman, "The New Criticism and the Southern Critics," in *A Southern Vanguard*, ed. Allen Tate (Englewood Cliffs, N.J.: Prentice-Hall, 1947), pp. 28-51, revised and reprinted as "The New Critics" in *Critiques and Essays in Criticism: 1920-1948*, ed. R. W. Stallman (New York: Ronald Press, 1949), pp. 488-506; Eric Bentley, "A Note on the New Criticism," *Virginia Quarterly Review* 24 (1948): 418-34; Roy Harvey Pearce, " 'Pure' Criticism and the History of Ideas," *Journal of Aesthetics and Art Criticism* 7 (1948/49): 122-32; William Van O'Connor, "A Short View of the New, Criticism" *College English* 11 (1949/50): 63-71; David Daiches, "The New Criticism: Some Qualifications," ibid., pp. 243-50; Douglas Bush, "The New Criticism: Some Old-Fashioned Queries," *PMLA* 64, suppl. pt. 2 (March 1949): 13-21; Robert Gorham Davis, "The New Criticism and the Democratic Tradition," *American Scholar* 19 (1949/50): 9-19 (maintains that the New Criticism is indebted to French reactionary clerics, and is un-American); "The New Criticism," ibid. 20 (1950-51): 86-104, 218-31 (an *"American Scholar* Forum" tape-recorded discussion on New Criticism by William Barrett, Kenneth Burke, Malcolm Cowley, Robert Gorham Davis, Allen Tate, and Hiram Haydn); John Holloway, "The Critical Intimidation," *HR* 5 (1952/53): 474-95; Frederick A. Pottle, "The New Critics and the Historical Method," *Yale Review* 43 September 1953): 14-23; Walter J. Ong, S.J., "The Jinnee in the Well Wrought Urn," *Essays in Criticism* 4 (1954): 304-20; Philip Rahv, "Fiction and the Criticism of Fiction," *KR* 18 (1956): 276-99 (maintains that New Critical methods distort novels); William J. Handy, "The Ontological Theory of the Ransom Critics," *Texas Studies in English* 35 (1956): 32-50; Roy Harvey Pearce, "Historicism Once More," *KR* 20 (1958): 554-91; John Henry Raleigh, "The New Criticism as an Historical Phenomenon," *Comparative Literature* 11 (1959): 21-28; Hyatt H. Waggoner, "The Current Revolt against the New Criticism," *Criticism* 1 (1959): 211-25; Walter J. Ong, S.J., "The Vernacular Matrix of the New Criticism," in *The Critical Matrix*, ed. Paul Sullivan (Washington, D.C.: Georgetown University Press, 1960); Mark Spilka, "The Necessary Stylist: A New Critical Revision," in *Modern Criticism: Theory and Practice*, ed. Walter Sutton and Richard Foster (New York: Odyssey Press, 1963), pp. 328-34; Murray Krieger, "After the New Criticism," *Massachusetts Review* 4 (1962): 183-205; Sister Mary Janet, S.C.L., "Poetry as Knowledge in the New Criticism," *Western Humanities Review* 16 (1962): 199-210; Douglas Day, "The Background of the New Criticism," *Journal of Aesthetics and Art Criticism* 24 (1965/66): 429-40; Alexander Karanikas, "The New Criticism," *Tillers of a Myth* (Madison: University of Wisconsin Press, 1966), pp. 189-210; "A Symposium on Formalist Criticism," *Texas Quarterly* 9 (Fall 1966): 185-268 (papers by Ransom, Elder Olson, Eliseo Vivas, and Kenneth Burke); Edgar Lohner,

"The Intrinsic Method: Some Reconsiderations," in *The Disciplines of Criticism*, ed. Peter Demetz, Thomas Greene, and Lowry Nelson, Jr. (New Haven; Yale University Press, 1968), pp. 147–72; Monroe K. Spears, 'The Newer Criticism," *Dionysius and the City* (New York: Oxford University Press, 1970), pp. 197–228; Paul de Man, "Form and Intent in the American New Criticism," *Blindness and Insight* (New York: Oxford University Press, 1971), pp. 20–35; H. M. Richmond, "The Dead Albatross: 'New Criticism as a Humanist Fallacy,' " *College English* 33 (1972): 515–31; Keith Cohen, "Le *New Criticism* aux États-Unis (1935–1950)," *Poètique*, No. 10 (1972), pp. 217–43; John Fekete, "The New Criticism: Ideological Evolution of the Right Opposition," *Telos*, no. 21 (Summer 1974), pp. 2–51; Gerald Graff, "What Was New Criticism?" *Salmagundi*, no. 27 (Summer/Fall 1974), pp. 72–93; Richard Strier, "The Poetics of Surrender: An Exposition and Critique of New Critical Poetics," *Critical Inquiry* 2 (1975): 171–89; Ralph Cohen, "On A Shift in the Concept of Interpretation," in *The New Criticism and After*, ed. Thomas Daniel Young (Charlottesville: University Press of Virginia, 1976), pp. 61–79; Richard Ohmann, "Teaching and Studying Literature at the End of Ideology," *English in America: A Radical View of the Profession* (New York: Oxford University Press, 1976), pp. 66–91.

2. On the surface, Richard Foster's assertion in *The New Romantics* (Bloomington: Indiana University Press, 1962) that a "romanticism of viewpoint or sensibility ... most truly constitutes, in my view, the 'real' identity of the New Criticism as a literary movement" (p. 21) would seem to be directly contradictory to my view of the Formalists. Actually, the difference in view is not total, since Foster also stresses the "essentially spiritual or religious motif [*sic*—motive?] of their seeking" (p. 42), and their doctrine of poetry as knowledge. There is a difference in actual subject, however, for Foster unaccountably makes Leslie Fiedler a New Critic and emphasizes the work of Vivas, Tate, and Blackmur, who he considers "the most important of the New Critics" (p. 201), rather than Eliot, Ransom, and Brooks, who I consider to be much more influential. Foster's "romanticism" seems to exist only as a thesis which has little to do with his actual analysis, since he gives no rigorous definition of what he means by *romanticism*, but incorporates almost everything under that rubric, including the "humanities" (pp. 28, 44) and philosophical idealism (p. 137). He asserts arbitrarily, often at the end of chapters, that what he has been saying illustrates the New Critics' "romanticism," when it does not in fact do so (pp. 87, 94, 124, 134, 150, 188, 197, 207). The best part of the book, his analysis of the rhetoric of the New Critics, has little to do with his thesis. There are, of course, elements of Romanticism in the Formalists, but it seems to me closer to the truth to say that they are governed by their Tory sensibilities and desires. Foster slights in particular the emphasis of Romantic criticism on the author, whom the Formalists ignore (see M. H. Abrams, *The Mirror and the Lamp* [New York: Oxford University Press, 1953]), and oversimplifies the history of New Criticism by seeing it as a unity, not a developmental process.

3. *The Muse Unchained* (London: Bowes & Bowes, 1958), p. 98; cf. "Comment," *The Dial* 70 (1921): 336; 73 (1922): 686; and 75 (1923): 402–3.

4. *Cambridge and Other Memories, 1920–1953* (New York: Norton, 1968), p. 26.

5. On *The Criterion* see Delmore Schwartz, "The Criterion, 1922–1939," *KR* 1 (1939): 437–49; Malcolm Bradbury, "*The Criterion*: A Literary Review in Retrospect," *London Magazine* 5, no. 2 (1958): 41–54; John Peter, "Eliot and the *Criterion*," in *Eliot in Perspective*, ed. Graham Martin (New York: Humanities Press, 1970), pp. 252–66; *TLS*, April 25, 1968, p. 130; Denis Donoghue, "Eliot and the *Criterion*," in *The Literary Criticism of T. S. Eliot*, ed. David Newton-de Molina (London: Athlone Press, 1977), pp. 20–41; and John D. Margolis, *T. S. Eliot's Intellectual Development, 1922–39* (Chicago: University of Chicago Press, 1972), *passim.* Considering that Margolis's book is generally sensible, it is hard to understand why he concludes that after 1939 Eliot's "future commitment would be different from that in the past—that he would be writing more as a man of faith than as a man of letters" (p. 205). Nearly all of Eliot's prose after 1948 is purely literary.

6. *Collected Poems,* ed. Edward Mendelson (New York: Random House, 1976), p. 98.

7. See Delmore Schwartz, "The Literary Dictatorship of T. S. Eliot," *PR* 16 (1949): 119–37.

8. "The Triumph of T. S. Eliot," *Critical Quarterly* 7 (1965): 337.

9. John M. Bradbury, *The Fugitives: A Critical Account* (Chapel Hill: University of North Carolina Press, 1958), p. 53.

10. *The Conservative Mind* (New York: Regnery, 1953), pp. 7–8. Kirk's later book, *Eliot and His Age* (New York: Random House, 1971), purports to demonstrate Eliot's relation to the Tory moral imagination of the Burkean tradition, but it is actually a chronological account of Eliot's career, with some elementary literary analysis. Roger Kojecký, in *T. S. Eliot's Social Criticism* (London: Faber & Faber, 1971), gives a more perceptive and analytical account of Eliot's Tory social views.

11. "Deliberate Exiles: Social Sources of Agrarian Poetics," in *Aspects of American Poetry*, ed. Richard M. Ludwig (Columbus: Ohio State University Press, 1962), pp. 283, 299.

12. In *Allen Tate and His Work: Critical Evaluations*, ed. Radcliffe Squires (Minneapolis: University of Minnesota Press, 1972), p. 44.

13. "The American Foreground of T. S. Eliot," *New England Quarterly* 45 (1972): 368–69.

14. "Mr. Bentley's Bad Boys: 'Reactionaries,' " *SR* 53 (1945): 116.

15. For a discussion of Baudelaire and Eliot, see Ronald Schuchard, " 'First-Rate Blasphemy': Baudelaire and the Revised Christian Idiom of T. S. Eliot's Moral Criticism," *ELH* 42 (1975): 276–95.

16. "Mr. Bentley's Bad Boys," p. 108.

17. "The Relative and the Absolute," *SR* 57 (1949): 375.

18. *The Conservative Tradition in America* (New York: Oxford University Press, 1967), p. 156; see also *AV* 70, 83.

19. "Eliot: The Expatriate as Fugitive," *Georgia Review* 13 (Spring 1959): 15, 16.

20. See Lyndall Gordon, *Eliot's Early Years* (Oxford: Oxford University Press, 1977).

21. "Last Words," *The Criterion* 18 (1939): 274.

22. *Tillers of a Myth: The Southern Agrarians as Social and Literary Critics* (Madison: University of Wisconsin Press, 1966), p. 188.

23. In *A Southern Vanguard,* ed. Allen Tate (New York: Prentice-Hall, 1947), p. 28. The history of the Fugitives and the Agrarian movement has been discussed at such length that it seems unnecessary to repeat it here. See John M. Bradbury, *The Fugitives: A Critical Account* (Chapel Hill: University of North Carolina Press, 1958), which has good bibliographies of the Fugitives; Louise Cowan, *The Fugitive Group: A Literary History* (Baton Rouge: Louisana State University Press, 1959), which covers 1920-28 only; John L. Stewart, *The Burden of Time* (Princeton: Princeton University Press, 1965), the best general survey; Karanikas, *Tillers of a Myth;* Richard Gray, "The Nashville Agrarians," *The Literature of Memory* (Baltimore: Johns Hopkins University Press, 1972), pp. 40-105, a historical treatment; and Louis D. Rubin, Jr., *Four Poets and the South* (Baton Rouge: Louisiana State University Press, 1978).

24. "The New Criticism," *American Scholar* 20 (1950/51): 227.

25. *The Little Magazines* (Minneapolis: University of Minnesota Press, 1963), p. 25. See also Tate's essay "The Man of Letters in the Modern World" (*CE* 379-93) and Brooks's later statement in "Telling It Like It Is in the Tower of Babel": "Our task is to try to listen to God, to reestablish the divinely ordained community which is the Church, and to restore an honest language on which any such community must be based" (*SR* 79 (1971): 155).

26. See "Science and Poetry," in *The Great Critics,* ed. James H. Smith and Edd W. Parks (New York: Norton, 1951), p. 747. See also René Wellek's conclusion in "On Rereading I. A. Richards": "Poetry in Richards is radically cut off from philosophy, ideology, doctrine, and knowledge of any kind" (*SoR*, n. s. 3 [1967]: 540).

27. For comment on the Formalists' attitude toward science, see H. J. Muller, "Recent Pathways in Criticism," *SoR* 6 (1940/41): 825; idem, *Science and Criticism* (New Haven: Yale University Press, 1943); Brooks's reply in *WWU* 223-26; and Stallman, *A Southern Vanguard,* pp. 38-41. John Holloway, in "The Critical Intimidation," *HR* 5 (1952/53): 474-95, argues that the Formalists were secretly influenced by science in that they accepted without question that scientific prose is the human norm (which it is not), tried to make poetry like science in complexity, and accepted the claim that only science is useful (which is not true). Holloway concludes that the explicatory method is tainted by these scientific ideals, and that it should be more itself by concentrating on poetry without regard to false scientific ideals.

28. Stewart, *The Burden of Time,* pp. 289-95.

29. For an account of Richards's intellectual progress, see Sister Mary Janet, S.C.L., "Poetry as Knowledge in the New Criticism," *Western Humanities Review* 16 (1952): 199-202.

30. See Stewart, *The Burden of Time,* pp. 114-19; and Karanikas, *Tillers of a Myth,* pp. 23-26. A more historically remote source for the Formalists' dislike of the abstraction of scientific language has been proposed by Wallace W. Douglas, in "Deliberate Exiles," pp. 293-94: "Perhaps no Northerner can ever understand all the reasons for the enormous quantity of negative affect that the notion of 'abstraction' evokes from Southern intellectuals like the Agrarians. ... William Lloyd Garrison and the Abolitionists may be more responsible for the peculiar attitude than Bergson, Whitehead, or Burtt. ... Garrison and the Abolitionists were radi-

cals who were committed to action in the name of abstract human rights and moral principles. Southerners, on the other hand, were realists, and they appealed to the realities of Southern environment, history, tradition, and social system. . . . Thus the slavery controversy and the Civil War itself were simply the results of the clash between the theoretical radicalism of the North and the historical realism or expediency of the South."

31. See also Ransom, "The Inorganic Muses," *KR* 5 (1943): 280-85.

32. See also Darrel Mansell, Jr., "Is Paraphrase Heretical," *Modern Language Journal* 50 (1966): 193-96.

33. (London: Oxford University Press, 1939).

34. *The Disciplines of Criticism,* ed. Peter Demetz, Thomas Greene, and Lowry Nelson, Jr., (New Haven: Yale University Press, 1968), pp. 193-225. A collection of excerpts on intention and a bibliography on the subject are found in *The Critic's Notebook,* ed. R. W. Stallman (Minneapolis: University of Minnesota Press, 1950), pp. 207-54, 289-93. See also the following: Leslie Fiedler, "Archetype and Signature: A Study of the Relationship Between Biography and Poetry," *SR* 60 (1952): 253-73; Walter J. Ong, S.J., "The Jinnee in the Well Wrought Urn," *Essays in Criticism* 4 (1954): 304-20; Monroe C. Beardsley, *Aesthetics: Problems in the Philosophy of Criticism* (New York: Harcourt, 1958); Patrick Cruttwell, "Makers and Persons," *HR* 12 (1959/60): 487-507; Wayne Booth, *The Rhetoric of Fiction* (Chicago: University of Chicago Press, 1961); Monroe C. Beardsley, "On the Creation of Art," *Journal of Aesthetics and Art Criticism* 23 (1965): 291-306; Emilio Roma III, "The Scope of the Intentional Fallacy," *The Monist* 50 (1966): 250-66; Albert Prior Fell, "Intention and the Interpretation of Works of Art," *University of Toronto Quarterly* 36 (1966): 12-23; A. D. Nuttall, "Did Meursault Mean to Kill the Arab?—The Intentional Fallacy Fallacy," *Critical Quarterly* 10 (1968): 95-106; E. D. Hirsch, Jr., *Validity in Interpretation* (New Haven: Yale University Press, 1967), who argues that only the author's meaning of a text is universally valid; cf. "Symposium on E. D. Hirsch's *Validity in Interpretation,*" *Genre* 1 (1968): 169-255; Rosemarie Maier, "'The Intentional Fallacy' and the Logic of Criticism," *College English* 32 (1970): 135-45; Paul de Man, "Form and Intent in the American New Criticism," *Blindness and Insight* (New York: Oxford University Press, 1971), pp. 20-35; Quentin Skinner, "Motives, Intentions, and the Interpretation of Texts," *New Literary History* 3 (1972): 393-408; Michael Hancher, "Three Kinds of Intention," *Modern Language Notes* 87 (1972): 827-51; Richard Harland, "Intention and Critical Judgment," *Essays in Criticism* 25 (1975): 215-25; Ralph Freedman, "Intentionality and the Literary Object," *Contemporary Literature* 17 (1976): 430-52; G. Thomas Tanselle, "The Editorial Problem of Final Authorial Intention," *Studies in Bibliography* 25 (1976): 167-211.

35. Stallman, *The Critic's Notebook,* contains a collection of excerpts on the problem of belief in poetry (pp. 177-203) and a bibliography on the subject (pp. 284-89); see also *Literature and Belief: English Institute Essays, 1957,* ed. M. H. Abrams (New York: Columbia University Press, 1958), which contains essays by Abrams, Cleanth Brooks, Walter J. Ong, S. J., Nathan A. Scott, Jr., and Louis L. Martz, and additional bibliographical information; Mark Spilka and John V. Hagopian, "The Affective Fallacy Revisited," *Southern Review of Australia* 1, no. 3

(1965): 57–79; and Wellek, "On Rereading I. A. Richards," pp. 540–43. For more recent studies on the relationship between the work of art and its audience, see Norman N. Holland, *The Dynamics of Literary Response* (New York: Oxford University Press, 1968); Walter J. Slatoff, *With Respect to Readers: Dimensions of Literary Response* (Ithaca: Cornell University Press, 1970); Stanley Fish, "Literature in the Reader: Affective Stylistics," *New Literary History* 2 (1970): 123–62; Gerald E. Graff, *Poetic Statement and Critical Dogma* (Evanston: Northwestern University Press, 1970), p. 160 *et passim*; Wolfgang Iser, "Indeterminacy and the Reader's Response," in *Aspects of Narrative,* ed. J. Hillis Miller (New York: Columbia University Press, 1971), pp. 1–45; idem, "The Reading Process: A Phenomenological Approach," *New Literary History,* 3 (1972): 279–99; Norman Holland, *5 Readers Reading* (New Haven: Yale University Press, 1975); idem, "Unity, Identity, Text, Self," *PMLA* 90 (1975): 813–22; idem, "Transactive Criticism: Re-creation through Identity," *Criticism* 18 (1976): 334–52; idem, "The New Paradigm: Subjective or Transactive," *New Literary History* 7 (1976): 335–46; Steven Mailloux, "Reader-Response Criticism?" *Genre* 10 (1977): 413–31.

36. "The Formalist Critics," *KR* 13 (1951): 75–76. See also *LC* 547; and Robert De Maria, Jr., "The Ideal Reader: A Critical Fiction," *PMLA* 93 (1978): 463–74.

37. Cf. Hirsch, *Validity in Interpretation,* p. 13. Even in scientific circles the concept of the ideal mind is suspect. Thomas S. Kuhn says of a critic that he "would like to reject those characteristics of even normal scientific minds which make them the minds of human beings. Apparently he sees no other way to retain the methodology of an ideal science in explaining the observed success of actual science. But his way will not do if he hopes to explain an enterprise practiced by people. There are no ideal minds, and the 'psychology of this ideal mind' is therefore unavailable as a basis for explanation" ("Reflections on My Critics," in Lakatos and Musgrave, p. 240).

38. "Implications of an Organic Theory of Poetry," *Literature and Belief,* p. 70.

39. "The Necessary Stylist: A New Critical Revision," in *Modern Criticism: Theory and Practice,* ed. Walter Sutton and Richard Foster (New York: Odyssey Press, 1963), pp. 332–33; cf. Hirsch, *Validity in Interpretation,* p. 3.

40. *The Mirror and the Lamp,* pp. 26, 28.

41. *The Conservative Tradition in America,* p. 157.

42. *Literature and Belief,* p. 68.

43. Quoted in Stallman, *The Critic's Notebook,* p. 178. Cf. Johan Huizinga's comments on the seriousness with which a game can be played, in *Homo Ludens* (Boston: Beacon Press, 1955), p. 8.

44. On the objective correlative, see the readings and bibliography in Stallman, *The Critic's Notebook,* pp. 117–58, 277–79.

45. "Criticism as Pure Speculation," in *The Intent of the Critic,* ed. Donald A. Stauffer (Princeton: Princeton University Press, 1941), p. 110. Cf. *NAP* 82–87, 143–47; Janet, "Poetry as Knowledge," pp. 202–10; and Francis X. Roellinger, Jr., "Two Theories of Poetry as Knowledge," *SoR* 7 (1942): 690–705. In his article "Concepts of Form and Structure in Twentieth-Century Criticism," René Wellek distinguishes between Eliot, Richards, and Leavis, who ignore form as a concept; Burke and Blackmur, who find form in the response of the reader; Ransom,

Winters, and Tate, who hold a dualistic conception of form and content; and Brooks and Wimsatt, who reconcile form and content in the organic unity of the poem (*D* 58-63). It seems to me that, in the ways I have shown, all these critics are trying to reconcile dualistic struggles in a new unity.

46. "Reflections on the Death of John Crowe Ransom," *SR* 82 (1974): 547. See also Cleanth Brooks, "I. A. Richards and the Concept of Tension," in *I. A. Richards: Essays in His Honor,* ed. R. Brower et al. (New York: Oxford University Press, 1973), pp. 135-56.

47. *Coleridge on Imagination* (Bloomington: Indiana University Press, 1960), p. 163.

48. Compare Ransom's statement in "Poetry: The Formal Analysis," *KR* 9 (1947): 437: "[Brooks] is seriously attempting now to see poems as wholes, and to conceive that difficult object, the unitary poem. But how will he reassemble and integrate the meanings when he has made it his first duty to dissipate them? I can scarcely think he succeeds in the new role [in *WWU*], and for me that is good evidence of its exceeding difficulty."

49. "The Formalist Critics," p. 72. See also James Benziger, "Organic Unity: Leibniz to Coleridge," *PMLA* 66 (1951): 24-48; D. C. Phillips, "Organicism in the Late Nineteenth and Early Twentieth Centuries," *Journal of the History of Ideas* 31 (1970): 413-32; and M. H. Abrams, *The Mirror and the Lamp, passim.*

50. *Literature and Belief,* p. 64.

51. For a comprehensive bibliography on metaphor, see Warren A. Shibles, *Metaphor: An annotated bibliography and history* (Whitewater, Wis.: Language Press, 1971). See also the special issue on metaphor, *Critical Inquiry* 5, no. 1 (1978).

52. See "The Inorganic Muses," p. 289.

53. "Metaphor and the Function of Criticism," in *Spiritual Problems in Contemporary Literature,* ed. Stanley Romaine Hopper (New York: Harper Torchbooks, 1957), p. 134.

54. The antitemporal dimension of modern poetry and novels and culture is described by Joseph Frank in a well-known essay, "Spatial Form in Modern Literature," first published in the *Sewanee Review* in 1945 and reprinted in Frank's *The Widening Gyre* (New Brunswick: Rutgers University Press, 1963). In "Spatial Form: An Answer to Critics," *Critical Inquiry* 4 (1977): 231-52, Frank surveys the comments on his article. See also Eric S. Rabkin, "Spatial Form and Plot," ibid., pp. 253-70; and William Holtz, "Spatial Form in Modern Literature: A Reconsideration," ibid., pp. 271-83.

55. *KR* 14 (1952): 178-88; see also Mario Praz, "T. S. Eliot and Dante," *The Flaming Heart* (Garden City, N.Y.: Anchor Books, 1958), pp. 348-74.

56. *Christianity and Culture* (New York: Harvest Books, n.d.), pp. 198, 200.

57. See "The Aesthetic of Regionalism," *American Review* 2 (1933/34): 290-310.

58. "Southern Literature: The Wellsprings of Its Vitality," *Georgia Review* 16 (1962): 239.

59. "Anglican Eliot," in *Eliot in His Time,* ed. A. Walton Litz (Princeton: Princeton University Press, 1973), p. 182.

60. "Regionalism in American Literature," *Journal of Southern History* 26 (1968): 41, 39; see also Marshall McLuhan, "The Southern Quality," in *A Southern Vanguard,* p. 114. For a black writer's description of the Southern critical tradi-

tion, one in which New Criticism is called the "Plantation School" and is traced to the Greeks, and which in general is polemical, heart-felt, and inaccurate, see Addison Gayle, Jr., *The Black Situation* (New York: Horizon Press, 1970), pp. 176–85.

61. "Southern Literature: The Wellsprings of Its Vitality," pp. 240–41.

62. "Mostly Nurtured from England," *SR* 82 (1974): 581.

63. "Dissociation of Sensibility," *KR* 19 (1957): 191, 193. On this concept see also *TCC* 19; *NC* 179ff.; F. W. Bateson, "Contributions to a Dictionary of Critical Terms," *Essays in Criticism* 1 (1951): 302–12; Harold W. Smith, "'The Dissociation of Sensibility,'" *Scrutiny* 18 (1951/52): 175–88; F. M. Kuna, "T. S. Eliot's Dissociation of Sensibility," *Essays in Criticism* 13 (1963): 241–52.

64. "John Donne," *Nation and Athenaeum,* June 9, 1923, pp. 331–32. For a scholarly demonstration that he was right, see Joseph E. Duncan, "The Revival of Metaphysical Poetry, 1872–1912," *PMLA* 68 (1953): 658–71.

65. See "Rudyard Kipling," *OPP* 265–94, and Eliot's appreciative remarks on Shelley in "A Talk on Dante," *KR* 14 (1952): 178–88.

66. "Interview," *Grantite Review* 24 (1962): 16.

67. For some attacks on Formalism by scholars of Romanticism, see Richard H. Fogle, "Romantic Bards and Metaphysical Reviewers," *ELH* 12 (1945): 221–50; Newell F. Ford, "Paradox and Irony in Shelley's Poetry," *Studies in Philology* 57 (1960): 648–62; and Emerson R. Marks, "T. S. Eliot and the Ghost of S.T.C.," *SR* 72 (1964): 262–80.

68. *Spiritual Problems in Contemporary Literature,* p. 134; see also "The Formalist Critics."

69. Quoted in Michael Millgate, "An Interview With Allen Tate," *Shenandoah* 12, no. 3 (1961): 31.

70. "Agrarianism in Exile," *SR* 58 (1950): 589–90.

71. *Spiritual Problems,* pp. 131–32.

72. "The Christianity of Modernism," *American Review* 6 (1935/36): 438, 439, 442. In this essay Brooks even goes so far as to judge religion by his critical principles. He says that "a religion which lacks the element of art is hardly a religion at all," and that "the fundamental point is this: religionists who can be satisfied with poor religious poetry can hardly have a very rich and complex worship."

73. "Cleanth Brooks, Critic of Critics," *SoR* 10 (1974): 152.

Chapter 4. The Age of the Explicators, 1938–1948

1. *Tillers of a Myth* (Madison: University of Wisconsin Press, 1966), p. 188.

2. Ibid., p. 192.

3. "The New Criticism," *American Scholar* 20 (1950/51): 88.

4. For a discussion of French *explication,* see the introduction and bibliography in W. D. Howarth and C. L. Walton, *Explications: The Technique of French Literary Appreciation* (London: Oxford University Press, 1971).

5. *Southern Writers in the Modern World* (Athens: University of Georgia Press, 1958), pp. 21–22.

6. "The Poem as Organism," *English Institute Annual, 1940,* ed. Rudolph Kirk (New York: Columbia University Press, 1941), p. 40; see also *NC* 301–2.

7. The connection between *A Survey of Modernist Poetry* and *Seven Types of Ambiguity* is acknowledged by Empson in his preface and is analyzed by Stanley Hyman in *AV* 261-65 and by George Watson in *The Literary Critics* (Baltimore: Penguin Books, 1962), pp. 202-8. In addition, Hyman discusses Empson's effect on Brooks (*AV* 265-70). See also James Jensen, "The Construction of *Seven Types of Ambiguity*," *Modern Language Quarterly* 27 (1966): 243-55. In response to this article, Graves claims: "I was, I believe, responsible for most of the detailed examination of poems in *A Survey of Modernist Poetry*—for example showing the complex implications of Sonnet 129 before its eighteenth-century repunctuation; Laura Riding certainly for the general principles quoted on p. 5" (ibid., p. 256). Empson says: "Robert Graves had used the method of analysis by recognizing ambiguity in a previous book, not collaborating with anyone; I ran into an irrelevant difficulty merely by quoting the wrong book" (ibid., p. 258). And Laura (Riding) Jackson notes: "Mr. Empson's book applied a method original to that work, [*A Survey of Modernist Poetry*] and originating with myself" ("Some Autobiographical Corrections of Literary History," *Denver Quarterly* 8, no. 4 [1974]: 12). As yet, no clear decision has been reached in this classic argument about priority.

To my knowledge, no one has made the connection between Fugitive *critical practice*, *A Survey of Modernist Poetry*, and *Seven Types of Ambiguity*. The point is not causally certain: Louise Cowan says in *The Fugitive Group* ([Baton Rouge: Louisiana State University Press, 1959], p. 184) that Miss Riding was not really influenced by the Fugitives' approach to poetry, but this seems to refer to her poetry rather than her critical technique. It is certain, however, that *A Survey of Modernist Poetry* had influenced R. P. Blackmur by 1931 (see his note in *FV* 291) and Allen Tate by 1937 (see his review of modern poetry, *SoR* 3 [1937/38]: 184).

8. "The Achievement of Cleanth Brooks," *Hopkins Review* 6 (1953): 161.

9. "The Mysterious Urn," *Western Review* 12 (1947/48): 54.

10. "The Achievement of Cleanth Brooks," p. 151.

11. "Irony as a Principle of Structure," in *Literary Opinion in America*, ed. Morton D. Zabel, 3rd ed. rev., 2 vols. (New York: Harper Torchbooks, 1962), 2: 732. Cf. *MPT* 41, *WWU* 255, and Brooks's "Irony and 'Ironic' Poetry," *College English* 9 (1948): 231-37. R. S. Crane criticizes Brooks for making irony, or paradox, "the One in which the Many in his theory ... are included as parts, the single source of all his predicates, the unique cause from which he generates all effects" (*C&C* 84). Crane goes on to point out that the irony Brooks posits as the unique quality of poetry is in fact found in all discourse, including science (*C&C* 100-105).

12. "Irony as a Principle of Structure," p. 738; cf. *WWU* 210. For a summary of Ransom's contrary view of irony, see *LC* 621-23. Geoffrey Hartman criticizes the lack of historical consciousness in Brooks's conception of irony: "What Brooks calls irony or paradox is not an independent structural principle but is mediated by literary traditions developing in contradistinction to each other. I would not be so naive as to equate formalism with an understanding of the history of style, but I do not see ... how it can do without this understanding" ("Beyond Formalism," *Modern Language Notes* 81 [1966]: 548-49).

13. "Irony as a Principle of Structure," pp. 730, 731; see also *WWU* 204-7, *MPT* 218, and *VI* xiv-xvi.

14. On Brooks' relation to Empson, see Cleanth Brooks, "Empson's Criticism," *Accent* 4 (1944): 208; and William Empson, "Thy Darling in an Urn," *SR* 55 (1947): 691-99, which has a postscript by Brooks. It is hard to believe that Brooks, who was a Rhodes Scholar in England from 1929 to 1932, did not read Empson earlier than 1938. See also Ransom's essay "Mr. Empson's Muddles," *SoR* 4 (1938/ 39): 322-39. Blackmur sees Brooks and Warren as Empson's "pupils" (*NCUS* 13).

15. "Hits and Misses," *KR* 14 (1952): 671.

16. "The State of Criticism: A Sampling," *SR* 65 (1957): 490.

17. "Metaphor, Paradox, and Stereotype," *British Journal of Aesthetics* 5 (1965): 320-22; cf. *WWU* 9-10.

18. "Milton and the New Criticism," *SR* 59 (1951): 3; cf. his remarks on Wordsworth in *WWU* 124-26.

19. "Poetry since *The Waste Land*," *SoR*, n.s. 1 (1965): 499.

20. "Milton and the New Criticism," pp. 14-15.

21. "The Achievement of Cleanth Brooks," p. 161.

22. Ibid., p. 156.

23. *Poems and Essays* (New York: Vintage Books, 1955), p. 149.

24. "In Search of a Vocation," *Michigan Quarterly Review* 11 (1972): 240.

25. "History of Ideas versus Reading of Poetry" *SoR* 6 (1940/41): 603.

26. *Validity in Interpretation* (New Haven: Yale University Press, 1967), p. 145; cf. *VI* 269.

27. Quoted in G.A.M. Janssens, *The American Literary Review: A Critical History, 1920-1950* (The Hague: Mouton, 1968), p. 253. See also Ronda Tentarelli, "The Life and Times of the *Southern Review*," *Southern Studies* 16 (1977): 129-51.

28. *SoR* 5 (1939/40): 511-23 and 6 (1940/41): 584-609.

29. The three essays published by Brooks in *SoR* in 1935, "Metaphor and the Tradition," "Wit and High Seriousness," and "Metaphysical Poetry and the Ivory Tower," form the first three chapters of *Modern Poetry and the Tradition* (1939).

30. Stewart's remarks are printed in the "Tribute to Ransom" issue of *Kenyon Collegian*, ed. D. David Long and Michael Burr, 90, no. 7, suppl. (1964): 9.

31. For Mizener's tribute, see ibid., p. 14; Crane's statement appears on p. 30 and Blackmur's remark is on p. 17. But compare Edmund Wilson's opinion, expressed in a letter to Allen Tate in 1943: "I would not write anything whatever at the request of *The Kenyon Review*. The dullness and sterility and pretentiousness of the *Kenyon*, under the editorship of Ransom, has really been a literary crime in this period when the market for serious work has been so limited. Mary [McCarthy] and I have both sent Ransom some of the best things we have written of recent years, and he has declined to print any of them—invariably keeping them for months and usually not sending them back till we wrote him or wired him. Of Mary's book he published a stupid and impudent review apparently composed by the office boy; my books he has not reviewed at all. I should be glad to have you send him this letter" (*Letters*, p. 399).

32. Janssens, *The American Literary Review*, p. 266.

33. The first encounter of Formalists and New York Intellectuals seems to have been at a meeting of the Modern Language Association in New Orleans in December 1939. According to James Atlas's account: "The 'liberals' thought of the Fugitives as 'Protofascists,' while the Fugitives considered the 'liberals' Communists. ... The two groups, initially so suspicious of each other, recognized 'with almost

ludicrous rapidity,' [Arthur] Mizener recalled, 'that they were very close together indeed in literary matters and felt alike on an astonishing number of social issues'" (*Delmore Schwartz: The Life of an American Poet* [New York: Farrar, 1977], pp. 157-58).

34. "*The Kenyon Review*, 1939-1970," *TriQuarterly*, no. 43 (Fall 1978), pp. 73-74.

35. *KR* 12 (1950): 561-601 and 13 (1951): 72-110, 207-30.

36. *John Crowe Ransom* (Minneapolis: University of Minnesota Press, 1962), p. 46.

37. "The Concrete Universal," *KR* 16 (1954): 559-60.

38. "The Fugitive Particular," in *John Crowe Ransom: Critical Essays and a Bibliography*, ed. Thomas D. Young (Baton Rouge: Louisiana State University Press, 1968), p. 112. Elder Olson also comments wittily on Ransom's critical metaphors: "The good critic [in Ransom's opinion] finds the 'ontology' of the poem, and it is the same as the poet's; it is a 'simple' ontology, of which perhaps a child might intuit the principles. It is apparently too simple to be put into words; for Mr. Ransom [in "Criticism as Pure Speculation"] does not state it except in terms of politics, houses, and puddings. Perhaps a poem *is* like a house or a pudding; it is also backed like a weasel, or like a whale—very like a whale for analogies may be made between all things; but there is little justification for making them unless they are significant ones" ("Recent Literary Criticism," *Modern Philology* 40 [1943]: 276).

In "John Crowe Ransom's Theory of Poetry," in *Literary Theory and Structure*, ed. Frank Brady et al. (New Haven: Yale University Press, 1973), René Wellek finds that Ransom's central insight is a defense of the particularity of things against abstractions. During a somewhat labored attempt to discover theoretical sources and coherence in Ransom, he notes that Ransom has invented one of his central terms, *Dinglichkeit* (p. 181), makes naturalistic statements that are unreconcilable with religious ones (p. 187), and holds to an ultimate dualism, though he makes gestures toward organicism and the Concrete Universal.

39. See William S. Knickerbocker, "The Dilemma of the Fugitives," *Contempo* 2 (May 25, 1932); or idem, "The Fugitives of Nashville," *SR* 35 (1927): 154-74; or Thomas Pressly, "Agrarianism: An Autopsy," ibid. 49 (1941): 145-63; or Knickerbocker's "Wam for Maw: Dogma versus Discursiveness in Criticism," ibid., pp. 520-36, for examples of the attitude of the magazine during Knickerbocker's editorship.

40. "The Sewanee Review," *SR* 40 (1932): 271; other facts about the early history of the magazine are found in the appreciations by Miss Turner and Gorham Munson on pp. 1-4, 129-39, and 257-75. For a general account of the magazine, see Janssens, *The American Literary Review*, pp. 275-84.

41. "The State of Letters," *SR* 52 (1944): 608-14.

42. "Editorial," ibid. 54 (1946): 733.

43. "Editorial," ibid. 60 (1952): 746-48.

44. "The State of Letters," ibid. 69 (1961): 711-12.

45. "The State of Letters," ibid. 75 (1967): 550-51.

46. "Editorial," ibid. 82 (1974): 191.

47. *The Muse Unchained* (London: Bowes & Bowes, 1958), pp. 82-83.

48. Jerome Schiller implicitly agrees with this estimate of Richards's influence. As he says: "Here, then, is the average critic's I. A. Richards: 'Richards may be important as one of the founders of the New Criticism. This can be due only to his conviction that poetry is important and to his technique for studying it. His theory of poetry is absurd: he claims that the only way to study poetry is through psychology; he maintains that poetry does not say anything, so it has nothing to do with our beliefs. No wonder he lost interest in poetry years ago and started worrying about Basic English and general education'" (*I. A. Richards' Theory of Literature* [New Haven: Yale University Press, 1969], pp. 3–4). The point of Schiller's book is, of course, to refute this estimate, but whether or not he proves that Richards's statements, properly considered, form a viable aesthetic theory (in my opinion he does not), he agrees that Richards's actual influence still stems from *Practical Criticism*.

49. "The New Criticism: Some Old-Fashioned Queries," *PMLA* 64, suppl., pt. 2 (March 1949): 13.

50. "Modern Criticism and the Teaching of Poetry in the Schools," in *The Teacher and American Literature*, ed. Lewis Leary (Champaign, Ill.: National Council of Teachers of English, 1965), p. 60; cf. Stewart, *The Burden of Time*, p. 453. For the immense effect the explicatory method ultimately had on the teaching and criticism of literature, see the files of the *Explicator* (1942–); *Poetry Explication: A Checklist of Interpretation since 1925 of British and American Poems Past and Present*, ed. J. Kuntz, rev. ed. (Denver: Swallow Press, 1962); and *The Explicator Cyclopedia*, ed. Charles Walcutt and J. Edwin Whitesell, 2 vols. (Chicago: Quadrangle Books, 1966–68).

51. "Mr. Kazin's America," *SR* 51 (1943): 59.

52. *Twentieth Century Authors: First Supplement*, ed. Stanley Kunitz (New York: H. W. Wilson, 1955), p. 679.

53. On the relationship of scholarship to criticism, see the discussions from 1904 to 1941 cited in René Wellek's excellent annotated bibliography in *Literary Scholarship: Its Aims and Methods* (Chapel Hill: University of North Carolina Press, 1941), pp. 239–55; "The Study of Literature in the Graduate School," in Wellek and Warren's *Theory of Literature* (1949 ed. only); the quotations collected by R. W. Stallman in *The Critic's Notebook* (Minneapolis: University of Minnesota Press, 1950), pp. 23–32 (and his list of further readings on pp. 261–66); the defenses of scholarship listed in Richard Altick's *The Art of Literary Research*, rev. ed. (New York: Norton, 1975), pp. 235–46; R. S. Crane, "Criticism as Inquiry ... ," *The Idea of the Humanities*, 2 vols. (Chicago: University of Chicago Press, 1967), 2: 25–44; Robert B. Heilman, "Historian and Critic: Notes on Attitudes," *SR* 73 (1965): 426–44; and idem, "History and Criticism: Psychological and Pedagogical Notes," *College English* 27 (1965): 32–38.

54. Essays by Brooks, Mizener, Sidney Cox, Hade Saunders, and Trilling appear in *KR* 2 (1940): 403–42; essays by Ransom, Tate, Joe Horrell, Wright Thomas, and Harry Levin appear in *SoR* 6 (1940/41): 225–69; see also Robert B. Heilman, "Footnotes on Literary History," ibid., pp. 759–70.

55. Rev. ed. (Bloomington: Indiana University Press, 1963); see also Brooks's reply, *WWU* 227–37.

56. *Yale Review* 43 (1953): 14–23.

57. "Past Significance and Present Meaning in Literary History," *New Literary History* 1 (1969): 91-109. Cf. Robert Heilman, "Historian and Critic: Notes on Attitudes," p. 443. Heilman contrasts neutrally what he had opposed polemically in past years: "But to leave polemics behind and look at the situation with neutral analytic eye: there is indeed a kinship between modes of literary study and general ways of conceiving reality. The non-historical, integrative sensibility in criticism has some affinity with what, in an attempt to find a single term of wide suggestive value, I will call the religious sensibility: the sense of the organic, and of the reality which lies outside time; the impulse to identify constants, the over-arching truth, the enduring integer, and so to attribute, to change and progress, a large measure of the illusive. On the other hand, the historical, differentiating temper in literary study has an affinity with the inclusive vision of truth as pluralistic, relative, non-hierarchical, successive in time, variable in space. I am describing two extremes which, presumably, ought to modify each other and be brought together in an ideal fusion."

58. On A. O. Lovejoy and the "history of ideas," see A. O. Lovejoy et al., *A Documentary History of Primitivism and Related Ideas in Antiquity* (Baltimore: Johns Hopkins Press, 1935), pp. ix-xiii, 1-22; A. O. Lovejoy, "Introduction: The Study of the History of Ideas," *The Great Chain of Being* (Cambridge, Mass.: Harvard University Press, 1936), pp. 1-23; idem, "The Historiography of Ideas," *Proceedings of the American Philosophical Society* 78 (1938): 529-43 (reprinted in *Essays in the History of Ideas* [1948]); idem, "Present Standpoints and Past History," *Journal of Philosophy* 36 (1939): 477-89; idem, "Reflections on the History of Ideas," *Journal of the History of Ideas* 1 (1940): 3-23; idem, "Reply to Professor Spitzer," *Journal of the History of Ideas* 5 (1944): 204-19; and idem, *Essays in the History of Ideas* (Baltimore: Johns Hopkins Press, 1948), which contains Lovejoy's more important essays and a bibliography of his works.

For essays influenced by, or critical of, Lovejoy, see Marjorie Nicolson, "The History of Ideas and the History of Thought," in *English Institute Annual, 1939* (New York: Columbia University Press, 1940); Leo Spitzer, "History of Ideas vs. Reading of Poetry," *SoR* 6 (1941): 584-609; Harold Taylor, "Further Reflections on the History of Ideas," *Journal of Philosophy* 40 (1943): 281-99; "Arthur O. Lovejoy at Seventy-Five: Reason at Work," *Journal of the History of Ideas* 9 (1948): 403-46 (tribute containing essays by George Boas, Maurice Mandelbaum, William P. Montague, Marjorie Nicolson, and Theodore Spencer); George Boas, "Some Problems of Intellectual History," in *Studies in Intellectual History,* ed. George Boas et al. (Baltimore: Johns Hopkins Press, 1953), pp. 3-21; R. S. Crane, "Literature, Philosophy, and the History of Ideas," *Modern Philology* 52 (1954): 73-83; P. P. Wiener, "Some Problems and Methods in the History of Ideas," *Journal of the History of Ideas* 22 (1961): 531-48; *Ideas in Cultural Perspective,* ed. P. P. Weiner and A. Noland (New Brunswick: Rutgers University Press, 1962); Paul Oskar Kristeller, "History of Philosophy and History of Ideas," *Journal of the History of Philosophy* 2 (1964): 1-14; Maurice Mandelbaum, "The History of Ideas, Intellectual History, and the History of Philosophy," *History and Theory* 4, suppl. 5 (1965): 33-66; Quentin Skinner, "Meaning and Understanding in the History of Ideas," ibid. 8 (1969): 3-53; Joseph Anthony Mazzeo, "Some Interpretations of the History of Ideas," *Journal of the History of Ideas* 33 (1972): 379-94; Leonard Krieger, "The Autonomy of Intellectual History," ibid. 34 (1973): 499-516; *Dictionary of the History of Ideas: Studies on Selected Pivotal Ideas,* ed. Philip P. Wiener, 4 vols. (New York: Scribner's 1973); Thomas Bredsdorff, "Love-jovianism—Or the Ideological Mechanism," *Orbis Litterarum* 30 (1975): 1-27; Albert William Levi, *"De Interpretatione*: Cognition and Context in the History of Ideas," *Critical Inquiry* 3 (1976): 153-78; Thomas Bredsdorff, "Lovejoy's Idea of "Idea,'" *New Literary History* 8 (1977): 195-212; *The History of Ideas: A Bibliographical Introduction,* 2 vols. (Santa Barbara, Calif.: American Bibliographical Center, 1977); and Lewis S. Feuer, "Arthur O. Lovejoy," *American Scholar* 46 (1976/77): 358-66.

59. These quotations are from Lovejoy's "Introduction: The Study of the History of Ideas," *The Great Chain of Being,* pp. 1-23.

60. *Kenyon Collegium,* pp. 22-23.

61. "Reflections on the History of Ideas," p. 14; cf. Marjorie Nicolson, "The History of Literature and the History of Thought," pp. 58-79.

62. "History of Ideas vs. Reading of Poetry," pp. 603, 588, 591, 595-96.

63. Lionel Trilling criticizes Lovejoy for thinking of poetry as "philosophical ideas in dilution" (*LI* 184) in "The Sense of the Past." R. S. Crane attacks Lovejoy's assumption that ideas are discrete compounds that can be considered without regard to their end in discourse, and his confusion of philosophical and literary forms, in "Literature, Philosophy, and the History of Ideas." See also Wimsatt's "History and Criticism: A Problematic Relationship" (*VI* 253-65).

64. *Journal of Aesthetics and Art Criticism* 7 (1948/49): 122-32.

65. *KR* 20 (1958): 554-91; see also "Literature, History, and Humanism," *College English* 24 (1963): 364-72.

66. "After the New Criticism," Massachusetts Review 4 (1962/63): 197-205. See also Wesley Morris, *Toward a New Historicism* (Princeton: Princeton University Press, 1972). Morris means by "new historicism" the "contextualism" of one of his mentors, Murray Krieger.

67. "The History of Ideas, Intellectual History, and the History of Philosophy," p. 41.

68. For discussion of the "Chicago School," see Kenneth Burke, "The Problem of the Intrinsic," *Accent* 3 (Winter 1942/43): 80-94; Hoyt Trowbridge, "Aristotle and the 'New Criticism,' " *SR* 52 (1944): 537-55 (a defense of the Aristotelian approach); John Crowe Ransom, "The Bases of Criticism," ibid., pp. 556-71 (a reply to Trowbridge); Murray Krieger, "Creative Criticism: A Broader View of Symbolism," ibid. 58 (1950): 36-51; John Crowe Ransom, "Humanism at Chicago," *KR* 14 (1952): 647-59; Eliseo Vivas, "The Neo-Aristotelians of Chicago," *SR* 61 (1953): 136-49; S. F. Johnson and R. S. Crane, " 'Critics and Criticism': A Discussion," *Journal of Aesthetics and Art Criticism* 12 (1953): 248-67; W. K. Wimsatt, "The Chicago Critics: The Fallacy of the Neo-Classic Species," *Comparative Literature* 5 (1953) (reprinted in *VI* 41-65); William Earle, "The Chicago School of Critics," *Western Review* 17 (1953): 150-55; Heinrich Straumann, "Cross Currents in Contemporary American Criticism," *English Studies* 35 (1954): 1-10; Northrop Frye, "Content with the Form," *University of Toronto Quarterly* 24

(1954/55): 92-97; C. Hugh Holman, "The Defense of Art: Criticism since 1930," in *The Development of American Literary Criticism*, ed. Floyd Stovall (Chapel Hill: University of North Carolina Press, 1955), pp. 242-44; Murray Krieger, *New Apologists for Poetry* (Minneapolis: University of Minnesota Press, 1956), pp. 93-98, 148-55; John Holloway, "The New and the Newer Critics," *The Charted Mirror* (London: Routledge, 1960), pp. 187-203; Walter Sutton, *Modern American Criticism* (Englewood Cliffs, N.J.: Prentice-Hall, 1963), pp. 152-74; Lawrence Lipking, "Review Article: R. S. Crane and *The Idea of the Humanities*," *Philological Quarterly* 47 (1968): 445-71; Robert D. Denham, "R. S. Crane's Critical Method and Theory of Poetic Form," *Connecticut Review* 5, no. 2 (1972): 46-56; and James L. Battersby, "Elder Olson: Critic, Pluralist, and Humanist," *Chicago Review* 28, no. 3 (1977): 172-86.

69. In "History vs. Criticism in the University Study of Literature," *English Journal* 24 (1935): 645-67.

70. *Eighteenth Century Studies* 3 (1970): 398.

71. "Privileged Criteria in Literary Evaluation," *Problems of Literary Evaluation*, ed. Joseph Strelka (University Park: Pennsylvania State University Press, 1969), p. 25.

72. "Content with the Form," p. 94.

73. *Modern American Criticism*, p. 173.

74. "The Bases of Criticism," p. 570.

75. Eliseo Vivas, "The Neo-Aristotelians of Chicago," pp. 137-38; see also *VI* 43-45.

76. "Communications," *HR* 12 (1959/60): 474.

77. *Texas Quarterly* 9 (Fall 1966): 202-30. Olson has collected his literary essays in *On Value Judgments in the Arts and Other Essays* (Chicago: University of Chicago Press, 1976).

78. See Booth's own account, *"The Rhetoric of Fiction* and the Poetics of Fictions," *Novel* 1 (1968): 105-17; and John Ross Baker, "From Imitation to Rhetoric: The Chicago Critics, Wayne C. Booth, and *Tom Jones*," ibid. 6 (1972/73): 197-217.

79. The other Fellows were Leonie Adams, Conrad Aiken, W. H. Auden, Louise Bogan, Katherine Chapin, Robert Lowell, Archibald MacLeish, Katherine Anne Porter, Karl Shapiro, Willard Thorp, and William Carlos Williams. Most of the relevant documents are found in *The Case against the "Saturday Review of Literature"* (Chicago: Poetry, 1949). See also the discussion in *PR* 16 (1949): 344-47, 512-22; and Archibald MacLeish, *Poetry and Opinion* (Urbana: University of Illinois Press, 1950). For a summary of the incident, see Robert A. Corrigan, "Ezra Pound and the Bollingen Prize Controversy," in *The Forties*, ed. Warren French (Deland, Fla.: Everett/Edwards, 1969), pp. 287-95; Beverly J. G. Loftus, "Ezra Pound and the Bollingen Prize: The Controversy in Periodicals," *Journalism Quarterly* 39 (1962): 347-54; and James P. Dougherty, "The Aesthetic and the Intellectual Analyses of Literature," *Journal of Aesthetics and Art Criticism* 22 (1963/64): 315-24.

80. "Ezra Pound and the Bollingen Prize Controversy," p. 294.

81. "Treason's Strange Fruit," *Saturday Review of Literature*, June 11, 1949, p. 11.

82. "Poetry's New Priesthood," ibid., June 18, 1949, pp. 7, 8, 38.

83. *KR* 12 (1950): 561–75.

84. *In Defense of Ignorance* (New York: Vintage Books, 1965), p. 41.

85. *Poetry and the Age* (New York: Vintage Books, 1955), p. 65.

86. *OPP* 131. Compare Wellek's remarks on Eliot, Shapiro, and Jarrell in *D* 262–68 and *CC* 342–43; and Wimsatt in *VI* 28–31 and *HCo* xv–xvi.

87. *William Faulkner: The Yoknapatawpha Country* (New Haven: Yale University Press, 1963).

88. Brooks discusses his ideal of community at length in "The Modern Writer and His Community," *A Shaping Joy: Studies in the Writer's Craft* (London: Metheun, 1971), pp. 17–36. He traces the strength of Yeats, Faulkner, Frost, and others to their search for community, and argues that the Negro and Jewish communities of New York are the source for the rise of these new schools of writing (p. 34). Much the same point is made in Brooks's "The Current State of American Literature," *SoR* 9 (1973): 273–87.

89. *The Disciplines of Criticism*, ed. Peter Demetz et al. (New Haven: Yale University Press, 1968), pp. 17–41.

90. *KR* 26 (1964): 188–89.

91. (New York: Harcourt, 1930), p. ix.

92. "A Symposium on Formalist Criticism," *Texas Quarterly* 9 (Fall 1966): 193.

93. Ibid., p. 199.

Chapter 5. The Formalist Men of Letters

1. This is perhaps the place to examine the charge, often repeated, that Eliot is anti-Semitic; the evidence for the charge is drawn from Eliot's middle period, particularly from *After Strange Gods*, when the High Church deacon does sometimes overwhelm the literary man. In this view, expressed in books like Kathleen Nott's *The Emperor's Clothes* (1954) and Rossell Hope Robbins's *The T. S. Eliot Myth* (1951), Eliot is damned totally for his anti-Semitic, sterile, fascistic opinions about culture and religion. It is true that Eliot (at his worst) did say in *After Strange Gods* that "reasons of race and religion combine to make any large number of free-thinking Jews undesirable [in the ideal society]" (*ASG* 20). But this, while offensive, is much less so than many things said by the above critics about Eliot, and unlike him they show no signs of regret.

In an interview published posthumously in *Mademoiselle* (May 1965, p. 68), Eliot says: "I might more easily regret some statements that I've made [than any poem]. There is one small book of lectures, *After Strange Gods*, which I let go out of print." He also says, while pleading for Pound's release from prison in *Books and Art* (1 [1958]: 59): "I have no sympathy with Pound's racial prejudices, and among the people of my acquaintance who wish, as I do, that he might be released, I know no one who shares those views." See also the "Letters" column of *TLS* for August 9, 1957 (p. 483), August 23, 1957 (p. 507), and September 13, 1957 (p. 547); and Morris Freedman, "The Meaning of T. S. Eliot's Jew," *South Atlantic Quarterly* 55 (1956): 198–206.

The like charge, that Eliot is a "fascist," also can be made only by ignoring the historical context. See Eliot's "The Literature of Fascism," *The Criterion* 8 (1928): 280–90; "*The Action Française*, M. Maurras, and M. Ward," ibid. 7 (1928):

195-203; and "Mr. Barnes and Mr. Rowse," ibid. 8 (1929): 682-91. According to William M. Chace (*The Political Identities of Ezra Pound and T. S. Eliot* [Stanford: Stanford University Press, 1975], p. 137), "To posit any direct link between Eliot and National Socialism is simply to ignore the facts." See also Denis Donoghue, "Literary Fascism," *Commentary*, August 1967, p. 82; James Torrens, S. J., "Charles Maurras and Eliot's 'New Life,'" *PMLA* 89 (1974): 312-22; Robert Alter, "Eliot, Lawrence, and the Jews, "*Commentary*, October 1970, pp. 83-84.

2. "Author against Critics," *TLS*, May 6, 1955, p. 237.

3. In his own analysis of this question, Eliot divides his career into three phases: the first is that of his *Egoist* essays before 1918; the second, his reviewing for *Athenaeum* and the *Times Literary Supplement* in the twenties; and the third, his lectures (*TCC* 17-18). His division, however, considers only his specifically literary criticism.

4. Ronald Schuchard, in "T. S. Eliot as an Extension Lecturer, 1916-1919" (*Review of English Studies*, n.s. 25, no. 99 [1974]), notes that "the necessities that forced him to give lectures from 1916 to 1919 also forced him into a three-year period of broad intensive reading" and that "his preparations refined the obvious erudition that he brought to his first critical efforts, and they provided a personal storehouse of allusions for his highly allusive poetic style" (pp. 302-3).

5. Ronald Schuchard claims, in "Eliot and Hulme in 1916: Toward a Revaluation of Eliot's Critical and Spiritual Development," *PMLA* 88 (1973): 1083-94, that "Eliot was deeply indebted to Hulme in and after 1916, to the extent that Hulme finally begins to emerge as the chief figure among those who stand behind the formulation of Eliot's moral and aesthetic canon" (p. 1092). Despite the full description of occasions on which Ezra Pound or Bertrand Russell *may have* introduced the two men, there is no evidence that they ever in fact met, and on Schuchard's own account Eliot denied that he knew Hulme or his works before 1924 to F. O. Matthiessen in 1935 and to S. E. Hynes in 1954, when there is no reason why he should have concealed the influence (pp. 1083, 1090). There is no question that Hulme was influential on Eliot after the publication of *Speculations* in 1924, and if Eliot had been influenced by Hulme before this, why did he not acknowledge it in his "Commentary," *The Criterion* 2 (1924): 231-32? Instead, he calls Hulme, quite correctly, a man who, on his death in 1917, was "known to a few people as a brilliant talker, a brilliant amateur of metaphysics, and the author of two or three of the most beautiful short poems in the language," but next to thinkers like Charles Maurras or Albert Sorel, "immature and unsubstantial." The new evidence Schuchard introduces from Eliot's "Syllabus of a Course of Six Lectures on Modern French Literature"—that Eliot used Hulme's translations of Henri Bergson and Georges Sorel—is again unconvincing because they were the only texts available in English. Though there are some interesting parallels of phrase between Hulme's essays and Eliot's syllabus, the descendant of Salem witch-burners and student of Babbitt did not need Hulme to tell him of the failures of Romanticism or of original sin. Schuchard's case for the influence of Hulme's poetry on Eliot before 1920 is, however, convincing, and to it may be added Lyndall Gordon's account in *Eliot's Early Years* (New York: Oxford University Press, 1977), p. 62, of the connection between Eliot's early poem "The Death of Saint Narcissus" and Hulme's "Conversion." In this connection it is interesting to speculate whether the tale Hulme told John Gould

Fletcher—that "his chief pleasure in life lay in reading Immanuel Kant's *Critique of Pure Reason* while lying prone, at full length, in a wellfilled, warm bathtub"—may not have inspired Eliot's picture of Apeneck Sweeney in the bath, "controversial, polymath," since Hulme was a huge man and a notorious bully. This story is quoted in the preface to *Further Speculations by T. E. Hulme*, ed. Sam Hynes (Minneapolis: University of Minnesota Press, 1955), pp. x, xxx. In sum, though there are many interesting parallels between Eliot and Hulme before 1924, there is no evidence of causal influence on Eliot's thought by Hulme before *Speculations*.

6. Quoted in R. P. Blackmur, "In the Hope of Straightening Things Out" (*LH* 166). Auden's essay was originally published in *The New Yorker*, April 23, 1949. Edmund Wilson also discusses Eliot's personae at length in " 'Miss Buttle' and 'Mr. Eliot,' " ibid., May 24, 1958 (reprinted in *BT* 364-402). Wilson describes six roles that Eliot plays: the Anglican clergyman, the formidable professor, Dr. Johnson, the genteel Bostonian, Old Possum, and the oracle.

7. "A Note on *Monstre Gai*," *HR* 7 (1954/55): 526.

8. *The Invisible Poet: T. S. Eliot* (New York: McDowell, 1959), p. 99.

9. *OPP* 113. For other examples of this rhetorical amnesia, see *OPP* 256, 259, 299, and Eliot's letter in *TLS*, August 9, 1957, p. 483. In "To Criticize the Critic," Eliot finally confesses to rereading his essays and says: "I am happy to say that I did not find quite so much to be ashamed of as I had feared. ... There are errors of judgment, and, what I regret more, there are errors of tone. ... Yet I must acknowledge my relationship to the man who made those statements" (*TCC* 14).

10. "Mr. Read and Mr. Fernandez," *The Criterion* 4 (1926): 753.

11. See E. P. Bollier, "T. S. Eliot and F. H. Bradley: A Question of Influence," *Tulane Studies in English* 12 (1962): 87-111; Eric Thompson, *T. S. Eliot: The Metaphysical Perspective* (Carbondale: Southern Illinois University Press, 1963); J. Hillis Miller, *Poets of Reality* (Cambridge: Harvard University Press, 1965), pp. 131-89; Kristian Smidt, *Poetry and Belief in the Work of T. S. Eliot* (London: Routledge, 1961), pp. 158-63; George Whiteside, "T. S. Eliot's Dissertation," *ELH* 34 (1967): 400-424; John J. Soldo, "Knowledge and Experience in the Criticism of T. S. Eliot," ibid. 35 (1968): 284-308; Richard Wollheim, "Eliot and F. H. Bradley: An Account," in *Eliot in Perspective: A Symposium*, ed. Graham Martin (New York: Humanities Press, 1970), pp. 148-93.

12. "Literature, Science, and Dogma," *The Dial* 82 (1927): 239.

13. "Ezra Pound's Influence on Literary Criticism," *Modern Language Quarterly* 29 (1968): 438, 425. For a detailed account of the Pound-Eliot relationship, see Donald Gallup, "T. S. Eliot and Ezra Pound: Collaborators in Letters," *Atlantic Monthly*, January 1970, pp. 49-62.

14. See the introduction to *Charles Olson and Ezra Pound*, ed. Catherine Seelye (New York: Grossman, 1975).

15. For a good account of the status of Eliot's letters and biography as of 1972, see Richard M. Ludwig, "T. S. Eliot," in *Sixteen Modern American Authors*, ed. Jackson R. Bryer (Durham: North Carolina University Press, 1974), pp. 184-90, 216-18. Lyndall Gordon has written a competent, factual biography in *Eliot's Early Years* (New York: Oxford University Press, 1977), but the dramatic reappraisal of Eliot and such concepts as "the impersonal poet" will come only with the release of

such manuscript material as the 2,000 letters from Eliot's early American love, Emily Hale (see p. 55). Alas, they will be sequestered until 2030.

16. "The Other T. S. Eliot," *Atlantic Monthly*, May 1965, pp. 61, 64.

17. On the Fugitive and Agrarian movements, see John M. Bradbury, *The Fugitives: A Critical Account* (Chapel Hill: University of North Carolina Press, 1958), which has bibliographies of all the Fugitives; Louise Cowan, *The Fugitive Group: A Literary History* (Baton Rouge: Louisiana State University Press, 1959), which concentrates on the years 1920–28; John L. Stewart, *The Burden of Time* (Princeton: Princeton University Press, 1965), the best general survey; and Alexander Karanikas, *Tillers of a Myth: The Southern Agrarians as Social and Literary Critics* (Madison: University of Wisconsin Press, 1966), which has a lengthy bibliography.

The best previous considerations of Tate's literary criticism are those of Monroe Spears, "The Criticism of Allen Tate," *SR* 57 (1949): 317–34; Richard Foster, "Allen Tate: From the Old South to Catholic Orthodoxy," in *The New Romantics* (Bloomington: Indiana University Press, 1962); and R. K. Meiners, *The Last Alternatives* (Denver: Swallow Press, 1963), chaps. 1–3.

Much useful information about Tate is also found in "A Symposium: The Agrarians Today," *Shenandoah* 3 (1952): 28–29; *Fugitives' Reunion: Conversations at Vanderbilt May 3–5, 1956*, ed. Rob Roy Purdy (Nashville: Vanderbilt University Press, 1959); "Homage to Allen Tate" issue of *SR* 67 (1959); and Michael Millgate, "An Interview with Allen Tate," *Shenandoah* 12, no. 3 (1961): 27–34.

18. "William Faulkner," *SR* 71 (1963): 160.

19. See Cowan, *The Fugitive Group*, pp. 123–25.

20. Sidney Hook, "The Late Mr. Tate," *SoR* 6 (1941): 840–41, 843. See also Alfred Kazin (*ONG* 440–44) and Eric Bentley, "Romanticism—A Re-evaluation," *Antioch Review* 4 (March 1944): 6–20.

21. "For John Ransom at Seventy Five," *Shenandoah* 14, no. 3 (1963): 8.

22. In his reminiscences, however, Tate sometimes becomes almost genial. Although the adjectives still flow freely in his essays, introductions, and letters— "mere secularization," "servile-mass society"—while reminiscing he seems able to accept reality and his place in it in a way he is otherwise unable to do. When he reminisces to an audience, the rhetoric and courtesy of his Southern heritage add to his charm, and like Eliot or Frost, he sometimes poses as the Grand Old Man of Letters. Like them, he indulges in the parables, the anecdotes, the mock-modest references to his own work, the apt allusions, the mystic summing-up, which make his reminiscences among the most enjoyable of all his writings. See, for example, "The Fugitive, 1922–25," *Princeton University Library Chronicle* 3 (1942): 75–84; "Random Thoughts on the 1920's," *Minnesota Review* 1 (1961): 46–56; "The Battle of Gettysburg," *Carleton Miscellany* 4, no. 3 (1963): 32–45.

23. "Poetry and the Absolute," *SR* 35 (1927): 49. On this point compare Bradbury. *The Fugitives*, pp. 55–58; Meiners, *The Last Alternatives*, pp. 29–30, 33; and Spears, "The Criticism of Allen Tate," *passim*.

24. "Southern Style," August 5, 1960, p. 496.

25. *The Literary Correspondence of Donald Davidson and Allen Tate*, ed. John Tyree Fain and Thomas Daniel Young (Athens: University of Georgia Press, 1974), p. 370.

26. Quoted in Millgate, "An Interview with Allen Tate," p. 32.

27. "Visiting the Tates," *SR* 67 (1959): 557–58.

28. Stewart, *The Burden of Time*, p. 313.

29. Bradbury, *The Fugitives*, pp. 115–16.

30. See "A Symposium: The Agrarians Today," pp. 28–29.

31. See Karanikas, *Tillers of a Myth*, p. 171.

32. Radcliffe Squires dates the conversion to December 22, 1950, in *Allen Tate: A Literary Biography* (New York: Pegasus, 1971), p. 188. Edmund Wilson writes to Malcolm Cowley of the conversion on January 5, 1951: "I yesterday had a letter from Allen announcing his conversion. ... It is strange to see habitually waspish people like Allen and Evelyn Waugh trying to cultivate the Christian spirit. ... I hope, though, that conviction will soften Allen, who has lately been excessively venomous about his literary contemporaries. He never could forgive any kind of success: when *The Cocktail Party* was a box-office smash, he even threw over Eliot—so I suppose that after that there was nothing for it but Christ" (*Letters* 496).

33. "In Amicitia," *SR* 67 (1959): 538–39.

34. "A Symposium: The Agrarians Today," p. 29.

35. "Christ and the Unicorn," *SR* 63 (1955): 179.

36. Foster, "Allen Tate," p. 129.

37. Purdy, ed., *Fugitives' Reunion*, p. 180.

38. Spears, "The Criticism of Allen Tate," p. 333; see also Meiners, *The Last Alternatives*, p. 17.

39. (Chicago: Swallow Press, 1975), p. 17.

40. For Tate's view of science, see *CE* 21, 43, 155; see also Stewart, *The Burden of Time*, pp. 289–91.

41. "Poetry in the Laboratory," *The New Republic,* December 18, 1929, p. 113.

42. "The Shame of the Graduate Schools" (letter), *Harpers,* May 1966, p. 82.

43. "The Unliteral Imagination; or, I, Too, Dislike It," *SoR*, n.s. 1 (1965): 530.

44. See Spears, "The Criticism of Allen Tate," pp. 326–27; Foster, "Allen Tate," pp. 119–21.

45. See Bentley, "Romanticism," p. 16.

46. See Stewart, *The Burden of Time*, p. 126.

47. Bradbury, *The Fugitives,* p. 113.

48. "The Unliteral Imagination," p. 531.

49. Purdy, ed., *Fugitives' Reunion,* pp. 192–93.

50. See Stewart, *The Burden of Time,* p. 176.

51. "The Unliteral Imagination," p. 531.

52. On Tate's use of "Platonism," for example, see Douglas Bush, "The New Criticism: Some Old Fashioned Queries," *PMLA* 64, suppl., pt. 2 (1949): 16–17. See also William Elton's remarks in *A Glossary of New Criticism* (Chicago: Poetry, 1948), s.v. "tension."

53. *SR* 64 (1956): 61–62.

54. See "Postscript by the Guest Editor" (special T. S. Eliot issue), *SR* 74 (1966): 383–87.

55. "In Amicitia," p. 536.

56. "Mr. Tate and Mr. Adams," *SR* 67 (1959): 583.

57. "R. P. Blackmur Re-Examined," *SoR*, n.s. 7 (1971): 839. This dislike of Blackmur's later style is shared by Hugh Kenner, but more vehemently, in "Inside the Featherbed," *Gnomon* (New York: McDowell, 1958), pp. 242–48; and by Cleanth Brooks, who tries rather heavy-footedly to explicate Blackmur's aphorisms in a review (*SR* 65 [1957]: 491–94).

58. "R. P. Blackmur Re-Examined," p. 844.

59. He says of Eliot that his "approach is invariably technical; I mean the matters touched on are always to some degree generalized characteristics of the work in hand" ("T. S. Eliot," *Hound and Horn* 1 [1928]: 294).

60. Joseph Frank suggests that, "faced with the [Marxist] attempt to appropriate literature for purely social and propagandistic purposes, it was only natural for the New Critics, defending the autonomy and integrity of art, to exaggerate and overemphasize its purity and independence from immediate social and political concerns. The concentration of criticism on 'form' was a natural result" ("R. P. Blackmur: The Later Phase," *The Widening Gyre* [Bloomington: Indiana University Press, 1968], p. 230).

61. *The Expense of Greatness* (orig. pub. 1940; Gloucester, Mass.: Peter Smith, 1958), p. 303.

62. "A Feather-Bed for Critics," *The Expense of Greatness,* p. 297.

63. *SoR* 5 (1939/40): 198.

64. "R. P. Blackmur," p. 238.

65. "Language as Gesture," *Language as Gesture* (New York: Harcourt, 1952), p. 11.

66. Ibid., pp. 16–17.

67. Ibid., p. 16.

68. "A Feather-Bed for Critics," p. 305.

69. "R. P. Blackmur Re-Examined," p. 841.

70. Joseph Frank says of *Anni mirabiles*: "It may be defined as criticism by aphoristic assertion rather than by explanation. ... This is criticism that itself has the gnomic quality of the great, late works of art and literature—works in which the artist focuses the compacted essence of his vision in its purest form" ("R. P. Blackmur," p. 247).

71. "The Scholar and the Critic: An Essay in Mediation," *University of Toronto Quarterly* 6 (1936/37): 267–77.

72. "St. Peter's School Theory and Practice," *SR* 82 (1974): 481.

73. "The 'New Humanism' Twenty Years After," *Modern Age* 3 (1958/59): 81.

74. "In Search of a Vocation," *Michigan Quarterly Review* 11 (1972): 246.

75. Ibid., p. 247.

76. "The 'New Humanism,'" p. 85. Warren's old friend Wallace Fowlie says that when Warren was offered a job at Norman Foerster's New Humanist School of Letters at the University of Iowa in 1940, "He responded to this 'call' in true Yankee fashion. He knew that Iowa City would be a necessary proving ground and a validation of his intellectual and moral parts" ("On Austin Warren: From the Personal Journal of Wallace Fowlie," *SR* 76 (1968): 670).

77. "The Marvels of M. R. James," *Connections* (Ann Arbor: University of Michigan Press, 1970), p. 99.

78. "On Austin Warren," p. 665.
79. (Ann Arbor: University of Michigan Press, 1966), p. 27.
80. (Ann Arbor: University of Michigan Press, 1956), p. 25.
81. *The New England Conscience*, p. 105.
82. Ibid., p. 193.
83. *Connections*, pp. 91-92.
84. See ibid., pp. 86-128.
85. The only extended commentary on Warren's work in recent decades has been George A. Panichas's "Austin Warren: Man of Letters," *The Reverent Discipline: Essays in Literary Criticism and Culture* (Knoxville: University of Tennessee Press, 1974), pp. 394-407.
86. "Continuity and Coherence in the Criticism of T. S. Eliot," *Connections*, p. 174.
87. "Grandfather Mather and His Wonder Book," *SR* 72 (1964): 115.
88. Ibid., p. 102.
89. Ibid., p. 103.
90. See Stanford's obituary, "Yvor Winters: 1900-1968," *SoR* n.s. 4 (1968): 861-63, and his attempt to create a new "classical" tradition based on the poetry of Winters, Robert Bridges, E. A. Robinson, and J. V. Cunningham: "Classicism and the Modern Poet," ibid., n.s. 5 (1969): 475-500.
91. See John Fraser's "Leavis and Winters: Professional Manners," *Cambridge Quarterly* 5, no. 1 (1970): 41-71; "Yvor Winters: The Perils of Mind," *Centennial Review* 14 (1970): 396-420; "Leavis, Winters, and 'Tradition,'" *SoR*, n.s. 7 (1971): 963-85; "Leavis, Winters, and Poetry," *Southern Review of Australia* 5 (1972): 179-96; "Leavis and Winters: A Question of Reputation," *Western Humanities Review* 26 (1972): 1-16; and "Evaluation and English Studies," *College English* 35 (1973): 1-16.
92. "Leavis, Winters, and 'Tradition,'" pp. 983-84.
93. *The Complex of Yvor Winters' Criticism* (The Hague: Mouton, 1973).
94. On Winters's failings as a theorist, see Stanley Edgar Hyman, *AV* 43-45; William Barrett, "Temptations of St. Ivor," *KR* 9 (1947): 532-51; John Holloway, "The Critical Theory of Yvor Winters," *Critical Quarterly* 7 (1965): 54-68.
95. "A Note on Yvor Winters," *Poetry* 57 (1940/41): 145.
96. "Yvor Winters and the Antimimetic Prejudice," *New Literary History* 2 (1971): 440.
97. Delmore Schwartz says: "Mr. Winters indulges himself in excess and exaggeration, displays prejudices which are wholly arbitrary, and is guilty either of misconstruction or ignorance. ... Each of these charges can be clearly demonstrated" ("Primitivism and Decadence," *SoR* 3 [1937/38]: 598). The most sustained polemic against Winters is T. Weiss's "The Nonsense of Winters' *Anatomy*," *Quarterly Review of Literature* 1 (1944): 212-34, 300-318; cf. Winters's reply, ibid. 2 (1945): 133-41. See also W. W. Robson, "Yvor Winters: Counter-Romantic," *Essays in Criticism* 25 (1975): 169-77.
98. Winters articulates a view of morality in re Henry Adams which is logically compatible with his nonbelieving Puritanism when he labels Calvinism a voluntaristic or fideistic faith in which "good works were good, not because of their intrinsic

worth but because God [Winters] had arbitrarily termed them so; good works were the fruits of faith" (*DR* 378). Or as he says later of his own beliefs: "A morality which preserves one from this loss of balance [of madness] is defensible beyond argument by virtue simply of the fact that it so preserves one" (*DR* 401). Such a voluntaristic faith seems to be as necessary for belief in Winters's critical standards, as he finds it to be for belief in Irving Babbitt's (*DR* 385). Winters thinks of himself, I believe, as being in the Aristotelian tradition of Babbitt's early works, where "morality is a fair subject in philosophical and psychological investigation, and ... its principles can be discovered in a large measure through the use of natural reason in the study of nature" (*DR* 387; cf. *DR* 395). Winters's "reason" seems to most to be arbitrary and allegorical (see note 97 above), and there is no principle or historical reality in his criticism to protect him from this charge.

99. For a more balanced defense of Cunningham as an epigrammatist, see Hayden Carruth, "A Location of J. V. Cunningham," *Michigan Quarterly Review* 11 (Spring 1972): 75-83.

100. James Laughlin says that "New Directions also had a Stanford connection through Yvor Winters. One of the earliest books we did was called 'Twelve Poets of the Pacific,' an an'/.ology edited by Winters of all his disciples. But when I didn't continue doing all the books by all the poets in his coterie, he wrote me off as a poor risk" (Linda Kuehl, "Talk with James Laughlin: New and Old Directions," *NYTBR*, February 25, 1973, p. 47).

101. "The Discovery of Form," *Michigan Quarterly Review* 12 (1973): 237, 240-41.

102. "Leavis, Winters, and 'Tradition,'" p. 964.

103. William Barrett finds him a peculiarly American type of crank: "In its wrongheadedness, idiosyncrasies, rancorous eccentricities, and provincialism, it [Winters's criticism] takes its place in the long line of that pathetic and peculiarly American phenomenon: the wandering off of superior gifts into private byways" ("Temptations of St. Yvor," p. 551).

104. "Kenneth Burke and Literary Criticism," *SR* 79 (1971): 186-87. Compare R. P. Blackmur's earlier statement: "The methodology is a wonderful machine that creates its own image out of everything fed into it: nobody means what he says but only the contribution of what he says to the methodology. ... Mr. Burke is only a literary critic in unguarded moments, when rhetoric nods. As a regular thing, Mr. Burke does not give an account of literature; he substitutes his account for the literature, with a general air that the account does well what the literature did badly" (*LH* 194, 195).

105. "As I Was Saying," *Michigan Quarterly Review* 11 (1972): 20. Burke's insistence on the necessity of translating things into his own terms is consistent; he makes exactly the same riposte to Sidney Hook thirty-four years earlier. See *PR* 4 (1938): 40-44.

106. Wayne Booth quotes Burke as posing the question of why we should choose his terms over all others and says: "Though all other philosophies would have a right, in Burke's view, to begin with exactly the same kind of unproved and circular beginnings, they could not hope to deal with *his* problem—the conflict of symbolic actions—unless they employed the terms of dramatism" ("Kenneth Burke's Way

of Knowing," *Critical Inquiry* 1 [1974]: 19). But this is begging the question. Burke's system is explicable only in its own terms, but no reason is given for adopting them, over, say, "Jabberwocky." For Burke, and for Booth, the reflexivity of a "self-proving, self-validating system" (ibid., p. 22) is not a fault, but most readers seem to demand that the truth of coherence be supplemented by the truth of correspondence to some other reality than that of Burke's mind.

107. (Minneapolis: University of Minnesota Press, 1969), p. 63.

108. "Symbolic Action in a Poem by Keats," *Accent* 6 (Autumn 1945): 7–12.

109. See "The Structural Study of Myth," *Structural Anthropology* (Garden City, N.Y.: Anchor Books, 1967), pp. 202–28.

110. "Abraham Cowley," *Lives of the English Poets* (London: Everyman, n.d.), 1: 12, 13.

111. For the reaction of the public to Burke, see Rueckert's summary notes in his *Critical Responses to Kenneth Burke,* pp. 297, 420; for the reaction of scholars, see ibid., pp. 187, 245, 293; for philosophical criticism, see the articles by Sidney Hook and Max Black, ibid., pp. 89–101 and 166–69; for the negative reaction of Europeans, see the article by Armin Frank, ibid., pp. 424–43.

112. Burke seems to have considerable influence among teachers of rhetoric and speech; see W. Ross Winterowd, *Rhetoric and Writing* (1965), and the files of *Today's Speech* and *Quarterly Journal of Speech.* For a critical argument that Burke unjustifiably broadens the scope of traditional rhetoric, see Wilbur Samuel Howell, "Rhetoric and Poetics: A Plea for the Recognition of the Two Literatures," *Poetics, Rhetoric, and Logic: Studies in the Basic Disciplines of Criticism* (Ithaca: Cornell University Press, 1975).

113. "The Symbolic Inference; or, Kenneth Burke and Ideological Analysis," *Critical Inquiry* 4 (1978): 523, 508.

Chapter 6. The Age of the Theorists, 1949–1978

1. Foreword to *Critiques and Essays in Criticism, 1920–1948,* ed. R. W. Stallman (New York: Ronald Press, 1949), pp. xv–xvi, xxi.

2. "The Relative and the Absolute," *SR* 57 (1949): 377, 376; see also "Hits and Misses," *KR* 14 (1952): 675, where Brooks advises Empson to read Wellek and Warren.

3. Wellek, Wimsatt, and Krieger are the most closely related, and have conducted a vigorous internecine argument over the last fifteen years. See Krieger's "Critical Dogma and the New Critical Historians," a review of Wimsatt and Brooks's *Literary Criticism: A Short History,* and his reprinting in dialogue form of several passages from his debate with Wimsatt: "Platonism, Manichaeism, and the Resolution of Tension: A Dialogue," in *PP* 177–218. See also Wimsatt's review of Krieger's *A Window to Criticism* in *Philological Quarterly* 64, no. 1 (1966): 71–74; and Krieger's review of Wellek's *A History of Modern Criticism,* "Critical Theory, History, and Sensibility," *Western Review* 21 (1956/57): 153–59.

4. (New York: Harcourt, 1949). Despite its historical importance as the first major work of Formalist theory, *Theory of Literature* does not seem to have received much attention at the time. The best review of the book is by Eliseo Vivas, who criticizes Wellek and Warren for not having a coherent aesthetic theory: "The

writers have not clearly worked out, at the theoretical level, how it is possible for a poem both to embody values and ideas of any kind whatever and yet, *at the same time,* to function as a non-referential aesthetic object" (*KR* 12 [1950]: 164).

5. "Some Principles of Criticism," *The Critical Moment* (New York: McGraw-Hill, 1964), p. 40.

6. "René Wellek's History," *HR* 19 (1966/67): 325.

7. For a survey of Kantian philosophy as it relates to modern literary criticism, see Kevin Kerrane, "Nineteenth-Century Backgrounds of Modern Aesthetic Criticism," in *The Quest for Imagination,* ed. O. B. Hardison, Jr. (Cleveland: Case Western Reserve University Press, 1971), pp. 3–25. Frank Lentricchia relates Cleanth Brooks's criticism to Kant in "The Place of Cleanth Brooks," *Journal of Aesthetics and Art Criticism* 29 (1970/71): 235–51.

8. Compare Brooks's statements in *The Well Wrought Urn:* "Any attempt to view it [poetry] *sub specie aeternitatis,* we feel, must result in illusion. Perhaps it must. Yet, if poetry exists as poetry in any meaningful sense, the attempt must be made" (pp. x–xi). "The studies of particular poems which fill up the earlier chapters of this book take as their assumption that there is such a thing as poetry ... and that there are general criteria against which the poems may be measured. ... The judgments are rendered, not in terms of some former historical period and not merely in terms of our own: the judgments are very frankly treated as if they were universal judgments" (p. 217).

9. *SR* 64 (1956): 427.

10. Ibid., p. 400.

11. "The Literary Criticism of Frank Raymond Leavis," in *Literary Views,* ed. Carroll Camden (Chicago: University of Chicago Press, 1964), pp. 175–93; "On Rereading I. A. Richards," *SoR* n.s. 3 (1967): 533–54.

12. "Contextualism Reconsidered," *Journal of Aesthetics and Art Criticism* 18 (1959/60): 237.

13. "The Fall of Literary History," in *Geschichte: Ereignis und Erzählung,* ed. Reinhart Koselleck and Wolf-Dieter Stempel (Munich: Wilhelm Fink, 1973), pp. 438–40.

14. The response to *A Short History* does much to prove the critical rule that bad reviews cannot kill large books. Helen Gardner says of it: "As a history the book is, in my judgment, worthless and dangerous." She says that it should be called "Rhapsody on Intimations of Brooks and Wimsatt in Early Criticism" and suggests that it is "messianic history, which treats all events as pointing forward to one final divine event, and all discourse as prophetic, only significant in its adumbration of a final revelation. As I do not think that the literary theory of the authors has the self-authenticating character of revelation, I cannot accept their claim to have written a 'true' history" (*Review of English Studies,* n.s. 12 [1961]: 224, 221).

Harry Levin suggests that it ought to be called "*A Historical Introduction to the New Criticism,*" criticizes its bias against the historical method and myth criticism and its Anglo-Saxon provinciality, and notes that "as a chronological apologia, the *Short History* uncomfortably resembles *The Education of Henry Adams.* After a long retrospect of distinguished failures, the departing class is advised to do better: *Nunc age*" (*Modern Language Notes* 73 [1958]: 159).

Stanley Edgar Hyman comes to the same point more sympathetically. After noting the inadequate treatment of Marxist and myth and ritual criticism, Hyman concludes that "the contemporary movement that really engages the authors' sympathies is the Roman Catholic literary counterreformation of the last decade. ... literary discussion is seen in the image of orthodoxy engaged in the refutation of heresy" (*KR* 19 [1957]: 657).

And in the most detailed review the book received, Chicago Critic Robert Marsh makes much the same point in a more philosophical way, accusing Wimsatt and Brooks of "the 'fallacy' of universal intention." He says: "I suggest it is impossible to prove ... that, whatever their own conscious intentions might have been, all the critics discussed in this book were 'actually' engaged in a common effort to solve the problem [of the cognitive value of poetry] by which our authors' narrative argument is controlled. And ... this argument is in itself fallacious ... since the authors simply assume what they desire to prove: the primacy and pervasive universality not only of a given critical problem but also of their own very special solution." Marsh concludes that "the book is actually an elaborate myth, a dialectical pattern with an element of chronology, exerted with considerable force upon historical materials. ... The result is a real poem—'a tensional union,' in Wimsatt's words, 'of making with seeing and saying,' whose 'truth' is primarily that of 'coherence' rather than 'correspondence'" (*Modern Philology* 55 [1957/58]: 265, 275).

15. "Abraham Cowley," *Lives of the English Poets* (London: Everyman, n.d.), 1: 11-12.

16. "Poetics *R*econstructed: The Presence vs. the Absence of the Word," *New Literary History* 7 (1976): 350.

17. "Literary Analysis and Evaluation—and the Ambidextrous Critic," *Contemporary Literature* 9 (1968): 308.

18. Ibid., p. 301.

19. Ibid., pp. 301-2.

20. See also Krieger's survey of Formalism, *TV* 228-41.

21. (Princeton: Princeton University Press, 1964), p. 3.

22. Krieger confusingly speaks of the "face" of reality as Manichaean, which would make the poet order a dualism within the further dualism of the poem. What he means, I think, is that the construction of reality is Manichaean, so that the poet orders things, the reality of the body, the chaos, by universals of language, into a new reality that reflects this dualism of form and content organically united.

23. "The Existential Basis of Contextual Criticism," *Criticism* 8 (1966): 313; see also *TV* 241-57.

24. "Critical Historicism: The Poetic Context and the Existential Context," *Orbis Litterarum* 21-22 (1966-67): 55.

25. "The Existential Basis," p. 317.

26. "Literary Analysis and Evaluation," p. 294; see also *PP* 142-46 and *TC* 14-15.

27. "Literary Analysis and Evaluation," p. 301.

28. Ibid., p. 309.

29. *SSR* 111.

30. "After the New Criticism," *Massachusetts Review* 4 (1962): 187, 184, 185.

31. "The Critic as Person and Persona," in *The Personality of the Critic,* ed.

Joseph Strelka (University Park: Pennsylvania State University Press, 1973), p. 72.

32. "Mediation, Language, and Vision in the Reading of Literature," in *Interpretation: Theory and Practice,* ed. Charles S. Singleton (Baltimore: Johns Hopkins Press, 1969), p. 211. See also "Theories about Theories about *Theory of Criticism,*" *Bulletin of the Midwest Modern Language Association* 11 (Spring 1978): 30-42.

33. A conspicuous exception is Wimsatt's brilliant demolition of Frye, "Northrop Frye: Criticism as Myth," in *Northrop Frye in Modern Criticism,* ed. Murray Krieger (New York: Columbia University Press, 1966), pp. 75-108.

34. *The Day of the Leopards* (New Haven: Yale University Press, 1976), p. 14.

35. *NYTBR,* December 10, 1972, pp. 5ff.

36. *American Scholar* 42 (1972/73): 41, 42.

37. *The Day of the Leopards,* pp. 8-9.

38. Ibid., p. xii.

39. *Structuralist Poetics* (Ithaca: Cornell University Press, 1975), p. 163.

40. "Some Aims of Criticism," *The Aims of Interpretation* (Chicago: University of Chicago Press, 1976), p. 127.

41. "Cleanth Brooks and the New Criticism," *British Journal of Aesthetics* 9 (1969): 285. Pole says, for example, that Brooks "consciously theorizes—among writers in the field a relatively rare and welcome merit" (p. 285); he credits Wimsatt, not Tate, with developing "tension" as a critical term (p. 289). The essay, with its rehearsal of thirty-year-old arguments between Brooks and Herbert Mueller, Krieger, Wimsatt, and others, reminds one of a discussion of Neville Chamberlain as a promising politician.

42. *Poétique,* no. 10 (1972), pp. 217-43.

43. *The Village Voice,* January 11, 1968, p. 8.

Chapter 7. The Essential Dialectic: Reality versus Imagination

1. Among the reviews of *Making It* (New York: Random House, 1967), see Norman Mailer, "Up the Family Tree," *PR* 35 (1968): 234-52; Edward Z. Friedenberg, *NYR,* February 1, 1968, p. 10; Wilfred Sheed, *Atlantic Monthly,* April 1968, pp. 97ff. Podhoretz's career since *Making It* has been marked by continued publicity about his personality and his shift to a militant conservatism. On the former, see Merle Miller, "Why Norman and Jason [Epstein] Aren't Talking," *New York Times Magazine,* March 26, 1972, pp. 34ff. On the latter, see Podhoretz's "Making the World Safe for Communism," *Commentary,* April 1976, pp. 31-41; and Joseph Epstein, "The New Conservatives: Intellectuals in Retreat," *Dissent* 20 (1973): 151-62.

2. *PR* 44 (1977); 176. The attempt to equate Jews with Intellectuals has also been made with even less evidence than Podhoretz, Kazin, and Howe offer, by Ernest van den Haag, *The Jewish Mystique* (New York: Stein & Day, 1969), pp. 128-46; and Nathan Glazer, "The Role of the Intellectuals," *Commentary,* February 1971, pp. 55-61.

3. "The Jew as Modern Writer," *Commentary,* April 1966, pp. 40-41.

4. "The Situation of the Jewish Writer," *An Age of Enormity* (Cleveland: World, 1962), pp. 67-68.

5. Allen Guttmann asks: "Can marginality lead to creativity for Jews and not for Gentiles when both feel equally marginal (or equally at home)? It does not seem likely" (*The Jewish Writer in America: Assimilation and the Crisis of Identity* [New

York: Oxford University Press, 1971], p. 226). Guttmann also describes the origin of the concept of marginality in Veblen and in Robert E. Parks's essay "Human Migration and the Marginal Man," *American Journal of Sociology* 33 (1928); see *The Jewish Writer,* pp. 136-37.

    6. "Under Forty: A Symposium on American Literature and the Younger Generation of American Jews," *Contemporary Jewish Record* 7 (1944): 15. The simple-mindedness of the equation of Intellectual with Jew may be seen in the variously intelligent comments in "The Jewish Writer and the English Literary Tradition: A Symposium" (*Commentary* 8 [1949]: 209-19, 361-70), which includes responses from Jewish writers to the anti-Semitic element in English literature, specifically their comments on a typical Fiedler article that reduces Jews in English literature to an "original nightmare of the circumcisor, ritual blade in hand": "What Can We Do about Fagin?" *Commentary* 7 (1949): 411-18.

    For further studies of the Jewish-American literary renaissance, see the checklist by Jackson R. Bryer in *Contemporary American-Jewish Literature: Critical Essays,* ed. Irving Malin (Bloomington: Indiana University Press, 1973), pp. 270-300, and, among others, Irving Malin, *Jews and Americans* (Carbondale: Southern Illinois University Press, 1965); Richard Kostelanetz, "Militant Minorities," *HR* 18 (1965): 472-80; William Freedman, "American-Jewish Fiction," *Chicago Review* 19 (1966): 90-107; Max F. Schulz, *Radical Sophistication* (Athens: Ohio University Press, 1969); the works of Leslie Fiedler, *passim,* particularly *The Jew in the American Novel* (New York: Herzel Institute, 1959) and *Waiting for the End* (New York: Stein & Day, 1964), pp. 65-103; Robert Alter, *After the Tradition: Essays on Modern Jewish Writing* (New York: Dutton, 1969).

    7. "A Memoir of the Thirties," *Steady Work* (New York: Harcourt, 1966), p. 350. Dwight Macdonald describes the scene as follows: "In the late thirties the *avant-garde* political spectrum looked like this, reading from right to left: *Communists* (who had moved overnight, on orders from Moscow, from the far left to the extreme right, becoming 'critical supporters' of the New Deal and later not-at-all-critical supporters of the war), *Social Democrats* (a small but well-heeled group of aging right-wing Socialists centering around the Rand School and the weekly *New Leader*), *Socialists* (led by Eugene Debs in World War One and now by Norman Thomas), *'Lovestoneites'* (called after their leader, Jay Lovestone, whom Stalin had deposed from the leadership of the American Communist Party in 1929 because Lovestone was an adherent of Bukharin; all groups to the left of the Lovestoneites sneered at them as 'centrists,' a fighting word, because they tried to steer a middle course between reform and revolution), *Socialist Workers Party* (*Trotskyites,* led by James P. Cannon and Max Shachtman, former Communists who had founded the party when Trotsky was exiled by Stalin in 1929 and who still lead it—or rather each leads one of the halves into which it split in 1940), *Socialist Labor Party* (followers—or, as we called them, 'epigones,' another fighting word—of Daniel De Leon, a turn-of-the-century theoretician whom Lenin had called the only American to have made a contribution to Marxian theory, an accolade about equal to a K.C.B. ... and a whole brigade of 'ites'" (*Memoirs of a Revolutionist* [New York: Meridian Books, 1958], pp. 15-16).

    8. A first-rate account of the influence of Marxism in America before 1940 can be found in Daniel Aaron's *Writers on the Left: Episodes in American Literary Communism* (New York: Harcourt, 1961). See also Philip Rahv, "Two Years of

Progress—from Waldo Frank to Donald Ogden Stewart," *PR* 4 (1938): 22-30. Aaron's account of the characteristics that caused Communism to satisfy Jewish radicals in the thirties is paralleled almost exactly by Poggioli's account of avant-gardism: "In Communism they find a composite answer to pressing social, psychological, and intellectual needs: (1) a company of associates with whom they can relax and be themselves without fear of social discrimination. ('They really meant "solidarity forever",' an ex-Communist of Catholic origin has commented, 'especially second generation Jews who were cut off from their Yiddish speaking parents and the outside world in general.'); (2) the promise of a classless world where Christian and Jew are brothers and in which they might escape from gentile snubs—particularly in the highly stratified and snobbish college and university campuses; (3) a doctrine that appeals to their latent religiosity, to their humanitarianism, and to their rationality, and one that offers a future when the Egyptians will be humbled and the righteous assume their rightful places; (4) a Party that provides opportunities for the Talmudic theoreticians (the lay rabbis contemptuous of business and consecrated to higher speculations) to refine and resolve the ambiguties of the Marxist scriptures; (5) a cause that enables the ambitiously gifted to acquire reputations and power; (6) a movement that offers a cloak of anonymity to people whose origins and background bar them from the gentile community" ("Communism and the Jewish Writer," *Salmagundi*, no. 1 [Fall 1965], p. 28).

9. Daniel Aaron also uses as his authority this key quote from Fitzgerald. In *Writers on the Left*, pp. 393-94, he says: "[Leftist writers] impoverished themselves not because they were disgusted with capitalism or because they damned social iniquity, but because they were unable or forbidden to enter into the world of their adversaries and retain what F. Scott Fitzgerald called the 'double vision,' the ability to hold two opposed ideas in the mind, at the same time, and still retain the ability to function."

10. "A Rejoinder to Mr. Barrett," *PR* 16 (1949): 656.

11. "Whatever Happened to Criticism," *Commentary*, February 1970, p. 60.

12. There has been no extended treatment of these Intellectuals as a group, but Paul Levine's "American Bards and Liberal Reviewers," *HR* 15 (1962/63): 91-109, is a good brief survey. For their conception of themselves I rely on *Making It*; Irving Howe's "The New York Intellectuals," *Commentary*, October 1968, pp. 29-51 (reprinted in *The Decline of the New*); and the discussion by Howe, Morris Dickstein, and Hilton Kramer, "New York in the National Culture," *PR* 44 (1977): 173-208. See also S. A. Longstaff, "The New York Family," *Queens Quarterly* 83 (1976): 556-73; and idem, "*Partisan Review* and the Second World War," *Salmagundi*, no. 43 (Winter 1979), pp. 108-29.

For further readings on the Intellectuals as a class, see J. F. Wolpert, "Notes on the American Intelligentsia," *PR* 14 (1947): 472-85; Merle Curti, "Intellectuals and Other People," *American Historical Review* 60 (1955): 259-82; Seymour M. Lipset, "American Intellectuals: Their Politics and Status," *Daedalus* 88 (1959): 460-86; *The Intellectuals: A Controversial Portrait*, ed. George B. de Huszar (Glencoe, Ill.: Free Press, 1960); Thomas Molnar, *The Decline of the Intellectual* (Cleveland: World, 1961); Richard Hofstadter, *Anti-Intellectualism in American Life* (New York: Knopf, 1963); Christopher Lasch, *The New Radicalism in America, 1889-1963*; *The Intellectual as a Social Type* (New York: Knopf, 1965); Lewis Coser,

Men of Ideas: A Sociologist's View (New York: Free Press, 1965); T. R. Fyvel, *Intellectuals Today: Problems in a Changing Society* (New York: Schocken Books, 1968); *On Intellectuals: Theoretical Case Studies,* ed. Philip Rieff (Garden City, N.Y.: Doubleday, 1969); Edward A. Shils, *"The Intellectuals and the Powers" and Other Essays* (Chicago: University of Chicago Press, 1972); special issues of *Daedalus* 101 (Spring and Summer 1972); and Charles Kadushin, *The American Intellectual Elite* (Boston: Little, Brown, 1974).

13. For a good survey of the journalistic scene, see Walter Goodman, "On the (N.Y.) Literary Left," *Antioch Review* 29 (1969/70): 67–75.

14. "The New York Family," p. 561. An able account of the development of *PR* to 1952 is found in James Burkhart Gilbert, *Writers and Partisans: A History of Literary Radicalism in America* (New York: Wiley, 1968), which includes a bibliographical essay. G.A.M. Janssens studies *PR* as a critical quarterly in *The American Literary Review: A Critical History* (The Hague: Mouton, 1968), pp. 284–307; and Daniel Aaron gives an account of its relation to Marxism in *Writers on the Left*, pp. 297–303. See also Reed Whittemore, *Little Magazines* (Minneapolis: University of Minnesota Press, 1963), pp. 16–22; William Arrowsmith, "Partisan Review and American Writing," *HR* 1 (1948/49): 526–36; Leslie Fiedler, "Partisan Review: Phoenix or Dodo?" *Perspectives U.S.A.*, no. 15 (1956), pp. 82–97; Irving Howe's review of *The Partisan Review Anthology, NYR*, August 20, 1963, p. 20; Lionel Trilling's "Introduction" and Philip Rahv and William Phillips's "In Retrospect," in *The Partisan Reader* (New York: Dial Press, 1946); "A Foreword by the Editors," *The New Partisan Reader, 1945–1953* (New York: Harcourt, 1953); William Barrett, "The Truants: 'Partisan Review' in the 40's," *Commentary*, June 1974, pp. 48–57; and William Phillips, "How 'Partisan Review' Began," *Commentary*, December 1976, pp. 42–46.

15. *PR* (1934): 2

16. "In Retrospect," p. 682.

17. "A Memoir of the Thirties," p. 354. Milton M. Gordon notes that even as immigrants the Jews were inescapably middle-class: "The traditional stress and high evaluation placed upon Talmudic learning was easily transferred under new conditions to a desire for secular education. ... The restrictions of Jewish occupational choice in medieval and post-medieval Europe had placed them in the traditional role of traders, self-employed artisans, and scholars. Thus the Jews arrived in America with the middle-class values of thrift, sobriety, ambition, desire for education, ability to postpone immediate gratifications for the sake of long-range goals, and aversion to violence already internalized" (*Assimilation in American Life* [New York: Oxford University Press, 1964], p. 186).

18. "In Retrospect," p. 682.

19. Janssens, *The American Literary Review,* p. 296.

20. *PR* 4 (December 1937): 3; see also Philip Rahv, "Proletarian Literature: A Political Autopsy, *SoR* 4 (1938/39): 616–28.

21. "In Retrospect," p. 683.

22. "The New York Family," p. 564.

23. *PR* 20 (1953): 797.

24. See especially ibid. 16 (1949): 649–65.

25. Foreword to *The New Partisan Reader,* pp. vi–vii.

26. "New York and the National Culture," p. 191.

27. (Cambridge: Harvard University Press, 1968). For further information about the avant-garde, see Clement Greenberg, "Avant-Garde and Kitsch," *PR* 6 (1939): 34-49; Harold Rosenberg, "The Herd of Independent Minds," *Commentary* 6 (1948): 244-52; Paul Goodman, "Advance-Guard Writing, 1900-1950," *KR* 13 (1951): 357-80; Richard Chase, "The Fate of the Avant-Garde," *PR* 24 (1957): 363-75; "The Changing Guard," *TLS*, August 6, 1964; "Any Advance," ibid., September 3, 1964; Leonard B. Meyer, "The End of the Renaissance: Notes on the Radical Empiricism of the Avant-Garde," *HR* 16 (1963): 169-86; William C. Seitz, "The Rise and Dissolution of the Avant-Garde," *Vogue*, September 1, 1963, pp. 182ff.; Hans M. Enzensberger, "The Aporias of the Avant-Garde," in *Modern Occasions*, ed. Philip Rahv (New York: Farrar, 1966), pp. 72-101; Donald D. Egbert, "The Idea of 'Avant-Garde' in Art and Politics," *American Historical Review* 73 (1967): 339-66; Norman Birnbaum, "The Making of a Vanguard," *PR* 36 (1969): 220-32; John Weightman, "The Concept of the Avant-Garde," *Encounter*, July 1969, pp. 5-16; Charles Millard, "Dada, Surrealism, and the Academy of the Avant-Garde," *HR* 22 (1969/70): 111-17; Roger Shattuck, "After the Avant-Garde," *NYR*, March 12, 1970, pp. 41-47; Vytautas Kavolis, "The Social Psychology of Avant-Garde Cultures," *Studies in the Twentieth Century*, no. 6 (1970), pp. 13-34; the special issue "Modernism and Postmodernism," *New Literary History* 3 (Autumn 1971); Clement Greenberg, "Counter Avant-Garde," *Art International*, May 1971, pp. 16-19; the symposium "Art, Culture, and Conservatism," *PR* 39 (1972): 382-453; Hilton Kramer, *The Age of the Avant-Garde* (New York: Farrar, 1973); Robert W. Corrigan, "The Transformation of the Avant-Garde," *Michigan Quarterly Review* 13 (1974): 31-48; Matei Calinescu, "The Idea of the Avant-Garde," *Faces of Modernity: Avant-Garde, Decadence, Kitsch* (Bloomington: Indiana University Press, 1977), pp. 95-148. The articles before Poggioli are of historical interest but are much less useful than his systematic treatise. Of the later writers Weightman is the most interesting; he finds the avant-garde to be basically a part of the larger Enlightenment move toward evolutionary thinking involving a stress on the reality of time, and hence a part of scientific thought.

28. It is hard not to accuse Irving Howe of a *suppressio veri*, since he cites Poggioli's book at the beginning of "The New York Intellectuals" but drops it midway through his article because Poggioli's conclusion that avant-gardes must change directly contradicts Howe's desire to call the Intellectuals to battle once more for the good old cause; see Howe's last paragraph. Howe's slipperiness here is particularly annoying because of his self-righteousness in accusing other writers (probably justly) of failure to "master the ethic of intellectual obligation." See his "The Middle-Class Mind of Kate Millett," *Harper's*, December 1970, p. 110. A similar failure of acknowledgment occurs in Richard Gilman's "The Idea of the Avant-Garde," *PR* 39 (1972): 382-96, where Gilman cites Poggioli's "useful if somewhat schematic study" in the marginal matter of defining the intelligentsia, but ignores Poggioli's systematic exposition of his central point, that the great modernist vision of art as creating an ideal adversary culture has been replaced by a nihilistic, postmodern culture of the French "new novel," pornographic art, the Theatre of the Absurd, etc.

29. Podhoretz is quoted in Philip Nobile, "A Review of the New York Review of Books," *Esquire*, April 1972, p. 120.

30. *PR* 14 (1947): 206.

31. Ibid. 12 (1945): 276.

32. Edmund Wilson's article "The Fruits of the MLA" was published in *NYR*, September 26 and October 10, 1968. The MLA replied in *Professional Standards and American Editions: A Response to Edmund Wilson* (New York: Modern Language Association, 1969).

33. Krim, *Views of a Nearsighted Cannoneer*, rev. ed. (New York: Dutton, 1968), p. 25. In *The Red Hot Vacuum* (New York: Atheneum, 1970), pp. 29–30, Theodore Solataroff says: "I share his [Krim's] point of view in almost every essay. . . . we both tried to become writers during a period when the conditions of the higher literary apprenticeship were as grueling and distorting as Krim says they were."

34. See Macdonald's review and a reply by James Sledd in *Dictionaries and That Dictionary*, ed. James Sledd and W. Ebbitt (New York: Scott, Foresman, 1962), pp. 166–90, 256–74.

35. For further readings in mass culture, see the bibliography of Leo Lowenthal's "Literature and Sociology," in *Relations of Literary Study*, ed. James Thorpe (New York: Modern Language Association, 1967), pp. 89–110, particularly the anthology *Mass Culture: The Popular Arts in America*, ed. Bernard Rosenberg and David M. White (Glencoe, Ill.: Free Press, 1957).

36. *PR* 6 (Fall 1939): 34–49.

37. "Masscult and Midcult," *Against the American Grain* (New York: Vintage Books, 1962), p. 50. For an intelligent analysis of Macdonald's thesis, see D. W. Brogan, "The Problem of High Culture and Mass Culture," *Diogenes*, no. 5 (Winter 1954), pp. 1–13. Edward Shils argues in "Daydreams and Nightmares: Reflections on the Criticism of Mass Culture," *SR* 65 (1957): 587–608, that the criticism of mass culture of Intellectuals like Macdonald, Lowenthal, and others is basically projected Marxism; they transfer their criticism of capitalist society to capitalist culture and are offended that the masses have embraced mass culture instead of the high culture Socialist theorists had destined for them. Their interpretation, according to Shils, rests on a Romantic conception of preindustrial peasant life, which derives from Hegel, Simmel, and other German sociologists.

38. On alienation, see Lowenthal "Literature and Sociology," pp. 92–93; Solomon Fishman, *The Disinherited of Art* (Berkeley and Los Angeles: University of California Press, 1953); and the anthology *Man Alone: Alienation in Modern Society*, ed. E. and M. Josephson (New York: Dell, 1962).

39. *PR* 21 (1954): 7–33.

40. For studies of the community of Intellectuals, see note 12 above.

41. *PR* 31 (1964): 329–51.

42. "A Remembrance of the Red Romance," *Esquire*, April 1964, p. 81. See also George P. Elliott, "Who is We?" *A Piece of Lettuce* (New York: Random House, 1964), pp. 206–20; and W. K. Wimsatt, "We, Teiresias," *Yale Review* 62 (1974): 431–38.

43. "The Herd of Independent Minds," pp. 248–49.

44. (Boston: Beacon Press, 1955), p. vii.

45. *E. M. Forster* (orig. pub. 1943; New York: New Directions, 1964), p. 124.

46. Karl Shapiro also discusses the Intellectuals' antipoetic bias in *Randall Jarrell, 1914–1965* (New York: Noonday Press, 1967), p. 226. For an extended demonstration of the use of the technique of close reading in the study of fiction, see Cleanth Brooks, "The Criticism of Fiction: The Role of Close Analysis," *A Shaping Joy* (London: Methuen, 1971), pp. 143–65; and *LC* 683–86.

47. *NYTBR*, March 25, 1973, p. 1. Emil Capouya says of Howe's essay on Céline: "If you do not read him [Céline] in his own language, and do not catch his tone of voice, then it is ten to one that you will not know with whom you are dealing and will not understand what he is up to. It is no shame to Mr. Howe that he is in such case; but why did he imagine that he had pierced to the heart of Céline's mystery?" ("Howe Now," *Studies on the Left* 4 [1964]: 67).

48. *The Literary Situation* (New York: Compass Books, 1958), p. 140. William Barrett recalls that "[Delmore Schwartz] once joked to me about the laboriousness with which Philip Rahv carved out his essays: 'You've got to remember that English is still a foreign language for Philip' " ("Delmore: A 30's Friendship and Beyond," *Commentary*, September 1974, p. 52).

49. (New York: Meridian Books, 1957), p. 19.

50. In *Literary Modernism*, ed. I. Howe (Greenwich, Conn.: Fawcett Books, 1967), pp. 11–40 (reprinted in *DN* 3–33).

51. (New York: Macmillan, 1967), pp. 134–35.

52. "New York and the National Culture," pp. 175, 176, 206.

53. The political nature of the Intellectuals' enthusiasm for James is seen in the latest turn of the screw by Philip Rahv, who recants his earlier praise when the more activist politics of the New Left becomes fashionable. See "Henry James and His Cult," *NYR*, February 10, 1972, pp. 18–22.

54. "The Native Critic," *PR* 10 (1943): 196.

55. "The Age of Criticism," *Poetry and the Age* (New York: Vintage Books, 1955), pp. 70–72.

56. *Views*, p. 25.

57. *Writers and Partisans*, p. 147.

58. *E. M. Forster*, pp. 3–4.

59. "A Speech on Robert Frost: A Cultural Episode," *PR* 26 (1959): 445–52. In the light of the long-established "paleface-redskin" contrast, Leslie Fiedler's attempt to restate it in geographical terms as the "eastern" and the "western" (in *Return of the Vanishing American* [New York: Stein & Day, 1968]) seems rather belated.

60. (New York: Anchor Books, 1957), pp. x, xii, 244.

61. See Kingsley Widmer, "The Academic Comedy," *PR* 27 (1960): 526–35; and Frederic I. Carpenter, "Fiction and the American College," *American Quarterly* 12 (1960): 443–55.

62. "Intellectuals at War," *Commentary*, October 1972, p. 6.

63. "The Editor [Philip Rahv] Interviews Mary McCarthy," *Modern Occasions* 1 (1970/71): 22.

64. *PR* 39 (1972): pp. 397, 419; cf. Norman Podhoretz, "Intellectuals at War," pp. 4–8.

65. *Steady Work*, p. 108.

66. In answer to assertions that *PR* received CIA money, William Phillips says: "The *fact* is that the American Committee for Cultural Freedom never to my knowledge received any money from the CIA or the Congress for Cultural Freedom while *Partisan Review* was published by it. ... The truth is that *Partisan Review* never received any money from the American Committee. The American Committee simply met *Partisan Review*'s need at the time to attach itself to a 'publisher.' However, it was always understood that the magazine was strictly on its own financially and editorially and subject to no controls by the American Committee" ("Editorial Notes," *Critical Inquiry* 3 (1977): 820). Phillips's antagonists, Carol and Richard Ohmann, conclude that, whatever the exact facts, "the whole history can give little pleasure to any of us on the left" (ibid., p. 818).

67. *The Agony of the American Left* (New York: Knopf, 1969), p. 94.

68. *Atlantic Monthly*, April 1968, p. 101. For further accounts of the cooptation of Intellectuals, see Jason Epstein, "The CIA and the Intellectuals," *NYR*, April 20, 1967, pp. 16–21; and Stephen Spender's account of the suborning of *Encounter* in *The Review* no. 23 (September–November 1970), pp. 29–31.

69. "On the Role of the Writer and the Little Magazine," *The Chicago Review Anthology*, ed. D. Ray (Chicago: University of Chicago Press, 1959), pp. 6, 9.

70. Quoted in Gilbert, *Writers and Partisans,* pp. 188–89.

71. *Steady Work,* p. 345.

72. *PR* 41 (1974): 503–5.

73. For other accounts of the entry of the Intellectuals into the bourgeoisie, see Alfred Kazin, "The President and the Intellectuals," *C* 447–65; and the interviews A. Alvarez made for the BBC and collected in *Under Pressure* (Baltimore: Penquin Books, 1965), pp. 99–189.

74. *Commentary,* September 1967, p. 63.

75. "A Memoir of the Thirties," p. 364.

76. *Commentary,* January 1969, p. 16. For other accounts of the politics of the whole intellectual class in the fifties and sixties, see Daniel Bell, *The End of Ideology* (Glencoe, Ill.: Free Press, 1960); Christopher Lasch, *The New Radicalism in America* (1965) and *The Agony of the American Left* (1969); and Morris Dickstein, *Gates of Eden: American Culture in the Sixties* (New York: Basic Books, 1977).

77. *The Sense of the Present* (New York: Chilmark Press, 1968), pp. 27–28.

78. *Writers and Partisans,* pp. 193–94.

79. "The Truants," p. 51.

80. "The Perils and Paucities of Democratic Radicalism," *Salmagundi*, no. 2 (Spring 1967), pp. 51–52.

81. *PR* 26 (1959): 214–30.

82. *A World More Attractive* (New York: Horizon Press, 1963), pp. 95–96.

83. Compare Rahv's own avowal of his campaign against "the latter-day nihilism, commercialized to the core, which finds it opportune to masquerade in the vestments of the classic avant-garde—and ... against a variety of empty spiritualizations of the world that finally and inexorably change nothing at all, leaving the world exactly as it is" (Foreword to *Literature and the Sixth Sense* [Boston: Houghton Mifflin, 1969, p. viii).

84. *The Sense of the Present*, p. 52.

85. *Under Pressure*, p. 176.

86. *PR* 32 (1965): 291; see also Diana Trilling, "Norman Mailer," *Encounter*, November 1962, pp. 45-56.

87. See Dickstein, *Gates of Eden*, p. 54.

88. *The Sense of the Present*, pp. 5, 6.

89. *Steady Work*, p. xv.

90. See Howe's articles on James Farrell, "The Critic Calcified," *PR* 14 (1947): 545-52; on Stanley Hyman's *The Armed Vision*, "The Critic as Stuffed Head," *Nation*, July 3, 1948, pp. 22-24; "The Sentimental Fellow-Travelling of F. O. Matthiessen," *PR* 15 (1948): 125-29; and on Malcolm Cowley's *The Literary Situation*, "The Expense of Shrewdness," ibid. 22 (1955): 272-74.

91. *PR* 36 (1969): 324; cf. Sitwell's letter, ibid. 26 (1959): 667-68.

92. "A Review of the New York Review of Books," p. 206.

93. In "The Social Psychology of Avant-Garde Cultures," p. 28, Kavolis notes that "there is a strong movement in the avant-garde culture engaged in transforming the Satanic mode (Melville, Nietzsche) into the Dionysian (Mailer, Ginsberg)."

94. The Howe quotation is from *PR* 16 (1949); 423; the Chase quotation is from ibid. 24 (1957): 373.

95. *Against the American Grain*, p. 74.

96. *A World More Attractive*, pp. 256-60.

Chapter 8. The Intellectual Men of Letters

1. Introduction, to Robert Warshow's *The Immediate Experience* (Garden City, N.Y.: Doubleday, 1962), p. 14.

2. See Chase, "Dissent on Billy Budd," *PR* 15 (1948): 1212-18; idem, "The Progressive Hawthorne," ibid. 16 (1949): 96-99; and the discussion "The Liberal Mind," by Chase, Trilling, and Barrett, ibid., pp. 649-65.

3. This point is also central to the thinking of Philip Rahv; see *II*, 83, 144, 154; and *MP* 96.

4. "Eugene O'Neill," *The New Republic*, September 23, 1936, p. 177.

5. *E. M. Forster* (orig. pub. 1943; New York: New Directions, 1964), p. 18; cf. *BC* 13.

6. See David H. Hirch, "Reality, Manners, and Mr. Trilling," *SR* 72 (1964): 420-32, for a criticism of Trilling's ambiguous use of reality.

7. "A Rejoinder to Mr. Barrett," *PR* 16 (1949): 658.

8. *New York Jew* (New York: Knopf, 1978), p. 193.

9. *E. M. Forster*, p. 14.

10. "Willa Cather," *The New Republic*, February 10, 1937, pp. 10, 12.

11. "Whatever Happened to Criticism?" *Commentary*, February 1970, p. 60.

12. *Mind in the Modern World* (New York: Viking Press, 1972), p. 18. Since Trilling got a $10,000 award for giving this thirty-eight-page lecture, it may be (at $268 a page) the most expensive literary criticism ever produced.

13. *Sincerity and Authenticity* (Cambridge: Harvard University Press, 1972), p. 159.

14. *NYTBR*, July 4, 1976, p. 3.

15. *The Critical Point* (New York: Horizon Press, 1975), p. 31.

16. *NYTBR*, January 6, 1974, p. 7.

17. "A Review of the New York Review of Books," *Esquire*, April 1972, p. 114.

18. *NYTBR*, February 17, 1974, p. 1.

19. "Cultural Malaise and Ultimate Culpability," *Modern Occasions* 1 (1970/71): 463–64.

20. "Henry James and His Cult," *NYR*, February 10, 1972, pp. 18–22.

21. "Philip Rahv, 1908–1973," *NYTBR*, February 17, 1974, p. 1.

22. Quoted in *NYTBR*, November 28, 1971, p. 20.

23. *The Critical Point*, p. 11.

24. Ibid.

25. "The Education of Alfred Kazin," *Commentary*, June 1978, pp. 47, 46.

26. "Notes on Some Problems in the Humanities Today," *PR* 41 (1974): 512.

27. (New York: Clarion Books, 1968), p. 48.

28. *Representations: Essays on Literature and Society* (New York: Random House, 1975), pp. xiii, xiv.

29. *Engels, Manchester, and the Working Class* (New York: Random House, 1974), p. ix.

30. (New York: Bantam Books, 1967), p. 17; see also pp. 152, 217, 246, 266.

31. *Engels*, p. 254.

32. "Some Problems in the Humanities," p. 515.

33. See Saul Bellow's memoir of Rosenfeld in *PR* 23 (1956): 565–67.

34. See *Selected Essays of Delmore Schwartz*, ed. Donald A. Dike and David H. Zucker (Chicago: University of Chicago Press, 1970), which contains a bibliography of Schwartz's writings; and James Atlas, *Delmore Schwartz: The Life of an American Poet* (New York: Farrar, 1977); see also William Barrett, "Delmore: A 30's Friendship and Beyond," *Commentary*, September 1974, pp. 41–54.

35. See Diana Trilling's *Claremont Essays* (New York: Harcourt, 1964) and *We Must March My Darlings* (New York: Harcourt, 1977); Elizabeth Hardwick's *A View of My Own: Essays in Literature and Society* (New York: Farrar, 1962) and *Seduction and Betrayal: Women and Literature* (New York, Farrar, 1974); and Mary McCarthy's *On the Contrary* (New York: Farrar, 1961), *Theatre Chronicles, 1937–1962* (New York: Farrar, 1963), and *"The Writing on the Wall" and Other Literary Essays* (New York: Harcourt, 1970).

36. His specifically autobiographical essays include: "The Case of the Author," *The American Jitters* (New York: Scribner's, 1932), pp. 297–313; "The Old Stone House," *The American Earthquake* (Garden City, N.Y.: Anchor Books, 1964), pp. 496–510; "Thoughts on Being Bibliographed" (*CCo* 105–20); and "The Author at Sixty" (*PM* 205–32).

37. "Encounters with Edmund Wilson," *SoR* 11 (1975): 738.

38. In "Edmund Wilson and Translation in Criticism," *AV* 19–48. Hyman eliminated his severe attack on Wilson from his revised edition of 1955.

39. See Mildred Martin, *A Half-Century of Eliot Criticism* (Lewisburg, Pa.: Bucknell University Press, 1972).

40. See, for example, Charles H. Foster's review of *Patriotic Gore* in the *New England Quarterly* 35 (1962): 524–27.

41. "The Case of the Author," pp. 311, 312.

42. "Encounters with Edmund Wilson," p. 733. Cleanth Brooks says of Wilson: "He is the one reviewer and critic—only Lionel Trilling, and he only partially, can

challenge him in this regard—to whom the American intellectual can turn with full confidence that this is a man who will reflect the *general* world view which he himself possesses. If Wilson has been wrong on almost all the big issues in the past, so has the typical intellectual. Besides, the timing has been right: both Wilson and the intellectual have been wrong at about the same time. For example, Wilson now reveals an Americanism which in the 1920's he himself would have had to regard as vulgarly jingoistic. If Edmund Wilson's ideas on religion are jejune, so are the typical intellectual's" ("The State of Criticism: A Sampling," *SR* 65 [1957]: 485–86).

43. *To the Finland Station* (Garden City, N.Y.: Anchor Books, n.d.), pp. 483, 484.

44. See Daniel Aaron, *Writers on the Left* (New York: Harcourt, 1961), *passim.*

45. *PR* 20 (1953): 113.

46. Ibid. 18 (1951): 126.

47. Ibid. 4 (1938): 51.

48. "Edmund Wilson: The Critic and the Age," *The Inmost Leaf* (New York: Noonday Press, 1959), p. 96.

49. Pp. 65, 66.

50. "Edmund Wilson vs. America," *Commentary,* January 1978, p. 34.

51. "The Intransigence of Edmund Wilson," *Antioch Review* 6 (1946): 558.

52. See Louis Fraiberg, *Psychoanalysis and American Literary Criticism* (Detroit: Wayne State University Press, 1960), pp. 161–82.

53. Rev. ed. (New York: Farrar, 1967), pp. 125–26. On this point compare Trilling (*LI* 160).

54. See Richard Gilman, "Edmund Wilson, Then and Now," *The New Republic,* July 2, 1966, p. 24.

55. *New York Jew,* p. 245.

56. (New York: Farrar, 1975), pp. 116, 118.

57. *The Devils and Canon Barham* (New York: Farrar, 1973), p. 165. See also *Letters* 689.

58. *To the Finland Station,* p. 14.

59. Norman Podhoretz is essentially right, but overstates the case when he says of Wilson's earlier portraits of Americans in *A Piece of My Mind*: "The real purpose of these essays is not an impersonal investigation of the particular subjects under discussion so much as his attempt to contruct [*sic*] an image of the American character that will show him to be the truest living representative of its most fundamental qualities and its deepest aspirations" (*DU* 48).

60. *New York Jew,* p. 245.

61. *The Company She Keeps* (New York: Harcourt, 1942), pp. 173–74.

62. See, for example, Robert Alter's comment on Kazin. "By acquiring a sure control of three continuous generations of American literary culture, he was taking possession, in a disciplined act of the imagination, of the America that has till then eluded him" ("The Education of Alfred Kazin," p. 45).

Profiles: The Lives
and Works of Selected American
Men of Letters

R. P. Blackmur

Richard Palmer Blackmur was born in Springfield, Massachusetts, on January 21, 1904. He was educated in the Boston public schools and attended lectures at Harvard, but had no formal higher education. During the late twenties and thirties he worked in bookstores in Cambridge and existed as a free-lance poet and critic. In 1929 he became associate editor of the *Hound and Horn*, which was published in Cambridge from 1927 to 1930. He married Helen Dickson in 1930 and was divorced in 1951. He received Guggenheim grants in 1937 and 1938.

In 1940 Blackmur went to Princeton as part of its Creative Arts Program, with which he remained affiliated until his death. He was successively a staff member of the Institute of Advanced Study in 1944-45, a Resident Fellow in Creative Arts from 1946 to 1948, an associate professor of English from 1948 to 1951, and in 1951 was appointed a professor of English. At Princeton he organized the Christian Gauss Seminars in Criticism, which brought leading critics to the campus for a series of lectures.

In 1958 Blackmur received a Litt.D. degree from Rutgers, and in 1961-62 he was appointed Pitt Professor of American History and Institutions at Cambridge, where he was made a Fellow of Christ's Church and given an honorary M.A. degree. He was a member of the National Institute of Arts and Letters and the American Academy of Arts and Sciences. A Library of Congress Fellow in American Letters from 1952 to 1964, he was also a Fellow of the Indiana School of Letters. He died on February 2, 1965.

The Double Agent (New York: Arrow Editions, 1935) contains twelve essays, including "A Critic's Job of Work," "The Dangers of Authorship," "The Critical Prefaces of Henry James," and individual studies of Cummings, Pound, Stevens, Lawrence, Hart Crane, Moore, Samuel Butler, and T. S. Eliot.

The Expense of Greatness (New York: Arrow Editions, 1940) contains "A Feather-bed for Critics," the title essay on Henry Adams, some omnibus reviews, and individual studies of T. E. Lawrence, Hardy's poetry, the later poetry of Yeats, Dickinson, Melville, Eliot, and Yvor Winters.

Language as Gesture (New York: Harcourt, 1952) includes reprints of eight essays from *The Double Agent,* four from *The Expense of Greatness,* and has nine new essays, including the title essay and studies of Yeats, Pound, Eliot, Stevens, and St. Augustine.

The Lion and the Honeycomb (New York: Harcourt, 1955) is the most theoretical of Blackmur's collections; it contains four reprinted essays, reviews of the criticism of Eliot, Trilling, and Babbitt, "Toward a Modus Vivendi," "A Burden for Critics," "Between the Numen and the Moha," and several other essays.

Anni mirabiles, 1921-25: Reason in the Madness of Letters (Washington, D.C.: Library of Congress, Reference Department, 1956) is the Library of Congress Lectures for 1956.

Form and Value in Modern Poetry (Garden City, N.Y.: Doubleday, 1957) is a reprinting of seventeen essays, largely practical studies of modern poets.

New Criticism in the United States (Tokyo: Kenkyusha, 1959) contains a summary of Blackmur's views on New Criticism, "My Critical Perspective," Frost, Henry Adams, and Henry James and is especially clear because he is trying to explain his positions to a foreign audience.

Eleven Essays in the European Novel (New York: Harcourt, 1964) contains "early entries in a Common-place Book of the Novel," six essays on Dostoevsky, two on Mann, and others on *Anna Karenina, Ulysses,* and *Madame Bovary.*

A Primer of Ignorance, ed. Joseph Frank (New York: Harcourt, 1967), is a posthumous volume that attempts to embody a plan Blackmur had for a book about the American cultural situation vis-à-vis Europe. In it are a reprinting of *Anni mirabiles, 1921-25,* a new essay "The Logos in the Catacomb: The Role of the Intellectual," and essays on Toynbee and Allen Tate, travel pieces on Rome and Zurich, three essays on Henry Adams, and one on Henry James.

Particularly in the thirties, Blackmur was as much a poet as a critic; he published three volumes of poetry, *From Jordan's Delight* (1937), *The Second World* (1942), and *"The Good European" and Other Poems* (1947). He has also edited or introduced several books, including James's *The Golden Bough* (1952), *Washington Square* (1959), and *The American* (1960), the *Prefaces* to his novels (1934), *American Short Novels* (1960), and *Collected Novels of Conrad Aiken* (1960). *The Poems of R. P. Blackmur* were collected and published in 1977.

There is a bibliography of Blackmur's early work in Carlos Baker, "R. P. Black- mur: A Checklist," *Princeton University Library Chronicle* 3 (1942): 99-106. Gerald J. Pannick, "R. P. Blackmur: A Bibliography," *Bulletin of Bibliography* 31 (1974): 165-69, concentrates on Blackmur's criticism but is inaccurate.

On R. P. Blackmur's criticism see Delmore Schwartz, "The Critical Method of R. P. Blackmur," *Poetry* 53 (1938): 28-39; John Crowe Ransom, "Ubiquitous Moralists," *KR* 2 (1941): 95-100; Ray B. West, Jr., "R. P. Blackmur," *Rocky Mountain Review* 8 (1944): 139-45; Stanley Edgar Hyman, "R. P. Blackmur and the Expense of Criticism," *The Armed Vision* (New York: Knopf, 1948); R.W.B. Lewis, "Casella as Critic: A Note on R. P. Blackmur," *KR* 13 (1951): 458-74; John Crowe Ransom, "The Shores of Criticism," *PR* 20 (1953): 108-11; Richard Foster, "R. P. Blackmur: The Technical Critic as Romantic Agonist," *Western Review* 23 (1958/59): 259-70 (reprinted in *The New Romantics* [Bloomington: Indiana University Press, 1962]); Hugh Kenner, "Inside the Featherbed," *Gnomon*

(New York: McDowell, 1958), pp. 242-48; Joseph Frank, "R. P. Blackmur: The Later Phase," *The Widening Gyre* (New Brunswick, N.J.: Rutgers University Press, 1963), pp. 229-50; William H. Pritchard, "R. P. Blackmur and the Criticism of Poetry," *Massachusetts Review* 8 (1967): 633-49; A. Alvarez, "R. P. Blackmur (1904-1965)," *The Review,* no. 18 (April 1968), pp. 21-25; and René Wellek, "R. P. Blackmur Re-Examined," *SoR,* n.s. 7 (1971): 825-45.

Cleanth Brooks

Cleanth Brooks was born in Murray, Kentucky, on October 16, 1906, the son of a minister. He studied at Vanderbilt University with John Ransom just after the demise of the magazine *The Fugitive,* receiving a B.A. in 1928. He received a M.A. degree from Tulane in 1929 and from 1929 to 1932 studied at Oxford on a Rhodes Scholarship, receiving his B.A. in 1931 with honors and a Litt.B. degree in 1932. He married Edith Blanchard in 1934.

From 1932 to 1947 Brooks taught at Louisiana State University, and from 1935 to 1942 he edited the *Southern Review* with Robert Penn Warren. In 1947 he was appointed a professor of English at Yale, where he remained except for the period 1964-66, when he became American Cultural Attaché in London. He is now Gray Professor of Rhetoric Emeritus. He has received several honorary degrees. He was a Fellow of and Honorary Consultant in American Letters to the Library of Congress from 1952 to 1964 and has been a Fellow of the Indiana School of Letters, the American Academy of Arts and Sciences, the American Philosophical Society, and the National Institute of Arts and Letters.

Understanding Poetry (New York: Holt, 1938) is one of the few poetry textbooks of permanent importance. In it Brooks and coeditor Robert Penn Warren propose to replace paraphrase, study of biography and historical background, and inspirational and didactic interpretation of poems with study of the structure of the poem itself, particularly of its irony, paradox, and ambiguity. The book contains full analyses of many poems; it tends to be sympathetic to Metaphysical poetry and to show the faults of the Romantics. Brooks has also edited a number of other textbooks, including *Understanding Fiction* (with Warren, 1943), and *Understanding Drama* (with Robert Heilman, 1946).

Modern Poetry and the Tradition (Chapel Hill: University of North Carolina Press, 1939) contains a number of analyses of modern poets, particularly Brooks's friends Ransom, Tate, and Warren, and Eliot, Frost, and Yeats. Brooks maintains that modern poetry requires a new kind of criticism that can deal with its wit and difficulty, and in "Notes for a Revised History of English Poetry" he suggests that poetry must be seen in terms of a Metaphysical, not a Romantic, conception of metaphor. The book is much influenced by Eliot and Richards.

The Well Wrought Urn: Studies in the Structure of Poetry (New York: Reynal & Hitchcock, 1947) contains close readings of ten poems from *Macbeth* to the present, including Donne's "The Canonization," "The Rape of the Lock," Gray's "Elegy," Keats's "Ode on a Grecian Urn," and Yeats's "Among School Children." Brooks hopes to show that his method of formal analysis is applicable to all kinds of poetry. The book also contains theoretical discussions, "The Language of Paradox" and "The Heresy of Paraphrase," as well as appendices entitled "Criticism, History, and Critical Relativism" and "The Problem of Belief and the Problem of Cognition."

Brooks expresses his theoretical position more briefly in "My Credo: The Formalist Critic," *Kenyon Review* 13 (1951): 72-81.
Literary Criticism: A Short History, with W. K. Wimsatt, Jr. (New York: Knopf, 1957), is a 751-page "history of ideas about verbal art and about its elucidation and criticism." Brooks is mainly responsible for the modern essays in it. The authors believe that the multitude of critical debates, between one and many, real and social, mimetic and formal views, "is far more difficult to orient within any of the Platonic or Gnostic ideal world views, or within the Manichaean full dualism and strife of principles, than precisely within the vision of suffering, the optimism, the mystery which are embraced in the religious dogma of the Incarnation" (p. 746).

The Hidden God: Studies in Hemingway, Faulkner, Yeats, Eliot, and Warren (New Haven: Yale University Press, 1963) contains essays, originally lectures given at Trinity College, Hartford, in 1955, in which Brooks tries to show the relevance of these writers to the Christian conception of man, especially as they contrast with our dehumanized present time.

William Faulkner: The Yoknapatawpha Country (New Haven: Yale University Press, 1963) shows how Faulkner is a Formalist.

A Shaping Joy: Studies in the Writer's Craft (New York: Harcourt, 1971), a collection of Brooks's essays and lectures of the fifties and sixties, includes studies of the criticism of Yeats and Auden, "Milton and the New Criticism," "Poetry since *The Waste Land,*" "The Criticism of Fiction: The Role of Close Analysis," a number of essays on the Southern writers, and "The Southern Temper."

William Faulkner: Toward Yoknapatawpha and Beyond (New Haven: Yale University Press, 1978) is a study of Faulkner's early works and the later novels set outside Yoknapatawpha County.

Brooks has also published *The Relation of the Alabama-Georgia Dialect to the Provincial Dialects of Great Britain* (1935), is one of the general editors of *The Percy Letters,* and has edited (with John Hardy) *The Poems of Mr. John Milton, . . . with Essays in Analysis* (1951) and *Tragic Themes in Western Literature* (1955).

R. W. Stallman, "Cleanth Brooks: A Checklist of His Critical Writings," *University of Kansas City Review* 14 (1948): 317-24, lists Brooks's writings as well as critical works on Brooks.

On Brooks's criticism see Allen Tate, "Understanding Modern Poetry," *English Journal* 19 (1940): 263-74 (review of *Modern Poetry and the Tradition*); John Crowe Ransom, "Apologia for Modernism," *KR* 2 (1940): 247-51; idem, "Poetry: The Formal Analysis," ibid. 9 (1947): 436-56 (review of *The Well Wrought Urn*); William Empson, "Thy Darling in an Urn," *SR* 55 (1947): 691-99; Lionel Trilling, "The Sense of the Past," *PR* 9 (1942): 229-41; R. S. Crane, "Cleanth Brooks; or, The Bankruptcy of Critical Monism," *Modern Philology* 45 (1948): 226-45 (reprinted in *Critics and Criticism*); A. B. Strauss, "The Poetic Theory of Cleanth Brooks," *Centenary Review* 1 (1949): 10-22; Charles V. Hartung, "A 'Tough-Minded' Critic—Cleanth Brooks," *University of Kansas City Review* 18 (1952): 181-89; John E. Hardy, "The Achievement of Cleanth Brooks," *Hopkins Review* 6 (1953): 148-61; John M. Bradbury, "Brooks and Warren, Critics," *The Fugitives: A Critical Account* (Chapel Hill: University of North Carolina Press, 1958), pp. 231-55; David Pole, "Cleanth Brooks and the New Criticism," *British Journal of Aesthetics* 9 (1969): 285-97; Frank Lentriccia, "The Place of Cleanth Brooks," *Journal of Aesthetics and Art Criticism* 29 (1970/71): 235-51; Gerald Graff, "Cleanth Brooks: New Critical Organicism," *Poetic Statement and Critical Dogma* (Evanston, Ill.: Northwestern University Press, 1970), pp. 87-111; and René Wellek, "Cleanth Brooks, Critic of Critics," *SoR* 10 (1974): 125-52. *The Possibilities of Order: Cleanth Brooks and His Work*, ed. Lewis P. Simpson (Baton Rouge: Louisiana State University Press, 1976), contains a dialogue between Brooks and Warren, reminiscences by Tate and Robert Heilman, and articles on Brooks's criticism by Walter J. Ong, S.J., T. D. Young, Monroe K. Spears, and Wellek.

I have been speaking here of Brooks's criticism, but most of his influential pedagogical works are collaborations with Robert Penn Warren. Warren wrote only a small amount of criticism independently, which is collected in his *Selected Essays* (New York: Random House, 1958), so Brooks is the more important critic, but Warren's contribution may be unjustly minimized by referring only to Brooks. A long, somewhat stilted dialogue between Brooks and Warren about their criticism is found in *The Possibilities of Order*, pp. 1-124. The only accounts of the collaboration I have found are a pamphlet put out by Prentice-Hall, *Notes on an Approach to Literature, Fifth Edition, 1975* (1975), and a brief essay, "Brooks on Warren," *Four Quarters* 21 (1972): 19-22.

For a bibliography of Warren's works, and criticism of him, see *Robert Penn Warren: A Bibliography*, comp. Mary Nance Huff (New York: David Lewis, 1968), and L. Hugh Moore, Jr., *Robert Penn Warren and History* (*The Hague: Mouton*, 1970), pp. 183-201. On his criticism, see Frederick P. W. McDowell, "Robert Penn Warren's Criticism," *Accent* 15 (1955): 173-96; and John Hicks, "Exploration of Value: Warren's Criticism," *South Atlantic Quarterly* 62 (1963): 508-15.

Kenneth Burke

Kenneth Burke was born in Pittsburg, Pennsylvania on May 5, 1897. He attended The Ohio State University and Columbia University briefly, but received no degrees. He married Lily Batterham in 1919 and they have three daughters; after his divorce from Lily he married her sister Elizabeth (in 1939) and they have two sons.

After a brief fling at Greenwich Village life with Malcolm Cowley, Matthew Josephson, Slater Brown, Hart Crane, and Gorham Munson from 1918 to 1922, Burke settled on a farm in Andover, New Jersey, in 1922. From 1921 to 1929 he was on the editorial board of *The Dial*, and was its music critic from 1927 to 1929. He began publishing stories in the little magazines *Secession, Broom*, and *S 4 N* in 1922-24. From 1926 to 1927 he was a research worker for the Laura Spelman Rockefeller Foundation, and in 1929 he did editorial work for the Bureau of Social Hygiene.

In the thirties, Burke flirted with the Leftist movements of the period and delivered papers at the American Writers' Conferences in 1935 and 1937. He also continued his work as a music critic, writing for *The Nation* from 1933 to 1936. In 1937 he began lecturing at the New School for Social Research, and in 1938 taught summer school at the University of Chicago. In 1943 Burke formed a permanent academic connection with Bennington College, where he taught until 1963. Most of Burke's disciples—Stanley Edgar Hyman, Francis Fergusson, Howard Nemerov—have been colleagues of his at Bennington or his students, as was Hugh Dalziel Duncan, the sociologist.

Burke received the *Dial* award in 1928, a Guggenheim grant in 1935, was elected to the National Institute of Arts and Letters in 1946, was a member of the Princeton Institute for Advanced Studies in 1949, a Fellow of the Indiana School of Letters, and a Fellow of the Stanford Center for Advanced Study in the Behavioral Sciences in 1957–58, was Regents Professor at the University of California at Santa Barbara in 1964, received an honorary Ph.D. from Bennington College in 1966 and the Brandeis Award for Achievement in the Arts in 1967, was elected to the American Academy of Arts and Letters in 1967, and received its Gold Medal in 1975. In 1968 he received an NEA distinguished service grant for lifelong contributions to American letters. Since his retirement he has lectured widely and has received honorary degrees from several universities, including Rutgers, Dartmouth, Northwestern, and Rochester.

Counter-Statement (New York: Harcourt, 1931) contains "Lexicon Rhetoricae," the first formulation of Burke's "machine for criticism," and studies of Pater, De Gourmont, Flaubert, Mann, and Gide which illustrate the theory.

The Philosophy of Literary Form: Studies in Symbolic Action (Baton Rouge: Louisiana State University Press, 1941), a collection of essays and reviews from the thirties, includes the long title essay and pieces on Freud, *Mein Kampf*, and *Julius Caesar*.

A Grammar of Motives (New York: Prentice-Hall, 1945) works out Burke's "dramatistic" system by means of the key terms "act," "scene," "agent," "agency," "purpose"; considers the history of philosophy, as well as the nature of constitutions, in these terms; and includes appendixes on Marianne Moore and "Symbolic Action in a Poem by Keats."

A Rhetoric of Motives (New York: Prentice-Hall, 1950) is an analysis of the rhetorical elements in what are usually thought to be nonrhetorical contexts.

Language as Symbolic Action: Essays on Life, Literature, and Method (Berkeley: University of California Press, 1966) develops Burke's dramatistic theory further and applies it to Goethe, Shakespeare, the Oresteia, *Kubla Khan, A Passage to India*, Roethke, W. C. Williams, etc.

Burke has also published two books that are primarily sociological, *Permanence and Change* (1935) and *Attitudes toward History* (1937); a book on religion, *The Rhetoric of Religion: Studies in Logology* (1961); a collection of stories, *The White Oxen* (1924); as well as *Towards a Better Life: Being a Series of Epistles, or Declamations* (1932), *Collected Poems, 1915–1967* (1968) and *The Complete White Oxen: Collected Short Fiction* (1968).

The following books have been written about Burke: George Knox, *Critical Moments: Kenneth Burke's Categories and Critiques* (Seattle: University of Washington Press, 1957); Virginia L. Holland, *Counterpoint: Kenneth Burke and Aristotle's Theories of Rhetoric* (New York: Philosophical Library, 1959); William H. Rueckert, *Kenneth Burke and the Drama of Human Relations* (Minneapolis: University of Minnesota Press, 1963), which contains a valuable annotated bibliography of works about Burke; Armin Frank, *Kenneth Burke* (New York: Twayne, 1969); and *Critical Responses to Kenneth Burke, 1924–1966*, ed. William H. Rueckert (Minneapolis: University of Minnesota Press, 1969), which has a complete bibliography of works by Burke and representative selections of works about him, with valuable headnotes by Rueckert.

Of the essays about Burke see the following on criticism: Charles I. Glicksberg, "Kenneth Burke: The Critic's Critic," *South Atlantic Quarterly* 36 (1937): 74-84; Sidney Hook, "The Technique of Mystification," *PR* 4 (1937): 57-62; William S. Knickerbocker, "Wam for Maw: Dogma versus Discursiveness in Criticism," *SR* 49 (1941): 520-36 (compares Burke with Ransom's *The New Criticism*); John Crowe Ransom, "An Address to Kenneth Burke," *KR* 4 (1942): 218-37; Max Black, review of *A Grammar of Motives, Philosophical Review* 55 (1946): 487-90; Francis Fergusson, "Kenneth Burke's 'Grammar of Motives,'" *The Human Image in Dramatic Literature* (Garden City, Anchor Books, 1957) (article first published in 1946); Isaac Rosenfield, "Kenneth Burke's *A Grammar of Motives*," *An Age of Enormity* (Cleveland and New York: World, 1962), pp. 155-64 (article first published in *KR* in 1946); Stanley Edgar Hyman, "Kenneth Burke and the Criticism of Symbolic Action," *The Armed Vision* (New York: Knopf, 1948); Bernard I. Duffey, "Reality as Language: Kenneth Burke's Theory of Poetry," *Western Review* 12 (1948): 132-45; Marius Bewley, "Kenneth Burke as Literary Critic," *Scrutiny* 15 (1947/48): 254-77; Andor Gomme, *Attitudes to Criticism* (Carbondale: Southern Illinois University Press, 1960), pp. 38-65; Richard Chase, "Rhetoric of Rhetoric," *PR* 17 (1950): 736-39; Marie Hochmuth Nichols, "Kenneth Burke and the 'New Rhetoric,'" *The Quarterly Journal of Speech* 38 (1952): 133-44; Herbert Blau, "Kenneth Burke: Tradition and the Individual Critic," *American Quarterly* 6 (1954): 323-36; Benjamin DeMott, "The Little Red Discount House," *HR* 15 (1962/63): 551-64; Walter Sutton, *Modern American Criticism* (Englewood Cliffs, N.J.: Prentice-Hall, 1963) (see index for sections on Burke); Joseph Frank, "Symbols and Civilization," *SR* 72 (1964): 484-89; Armin Paul Frank, "Notes on the Reception of Kenneth Burke in Europe," in *Critical Responses to Kenneth Burke, 1924-1966*, ed. William H. Rueckert (Minneapolis: University of Minnesota Press, 1969), pp. 424-43; Merle E. Brown, *Kenneth Burke* (Minneapolis: University of Minnesota Pamphlets, 1969); William H. Rueckert, "Kenneth Burke and Structuralism," *Shenandoah* 21, no. 1 (1969): 19-28; Howard Nemerov, "Everything, Preferably All at Once: Coming to Terms with Kenneth Burke," *SR* 79 (1971): 189-201; René Wellek, "Kenneth Burke and Literary Criticism," ibid., pp. 171-88; Wayne C. Booth, "Kenneth Burke's Way of Knowing," *Critical Inquiry* 1 (1974): 1-22; and Fredric R. Jameson, "The Symbolic Inference; or, Kenneth Burke and Ideological Analysis," ibid. 4 (1978): 507-23.

Richard Chase

Richard Volney Chase was born in Lakeport, New Hampshire, on October 12, 1914. He graduated from Dartmouth College in 1937 and received his Ph.D. from Columbia University in 1946. Except for a brief period when he was at the Connecticut College for Women (1945-49), he taught at Columbia University from 1939 until his death in 1963. He received a National Institute of Arts and Letters Award in 1953.

Quest for Myth (Baton Rouge: Louisiana State University Press, 1949) is Chase's history of the various conceptions and ،'efinitions of myth from Voltaire and Vico to the present. Chase takes the position that myth derives not from historical events, or from ritual and religion, but from the folk tale, with its accompanying *mana* and practical use of magic. Basically, myth is a story: "The fundamental myth is the dramatic human tale" (p. 73).

Herman Melville: A Critical Study (New York: Macmillan, 1949) treats Melville in relation to American Folklore and myth; most of the book is devoted to a close reading and provocative interpretation of Melville's novels and stories. Chase's main concern is to present Melville as a critic of the progressive oversimplifications of his time and, by extension, of the liberals of 1949, who refuse to recognize the complexity of life. Chase finds the character of the *Confidence Man* to be a symbol of this type of simplistic thinking.

Emily Dickinson (New York: Sloane, 1951) is an introduction to Dickinson.

Walt Whitman Reconsidered (New York: Sloane, 1955) criticizes Whitman's transcendentalist idea of progress, his *Democratic Vistas,* as being too simple and placing too much faith in the ultimate rationality of democratic society. Chase sees Whitman as in part the alienated artist, and defends his poetry as ultimately arising "from the native energies and dilemmas of life and . . . committed to the radical literary and cultural values of its time" (p. 186). He does a close reading of "Song of Myself," which he feels links Whitman to the modernist tradition, but expresses the belief that ultimately Whitman should be seen as an American visionary.

The American Novel and Its Tradition (Garden City, N.Y.: Anchor Books, 1957) expresses Chase's conviction that the essential form of American literature and imagination is an unresolved dualism: "Like the New England Puritan mind itself, [the American imagination] seems less interested in redemption than in the melodrama of the eternal struggle of good and evil, less interested in incarnation and reconciliation than in alienation and disorder" (p. 11). Thus our central literary form is the romance, which expresses this tension of contraries, not the English type of novel, which tends toward reconciliation, catharsis, transfiguration. Chase discusses the romances of Brockden Brown, Cooper, Hawthorne, Melville, James, Twain, Norris, and Faulkner in terms of this pattern.

The Democratic Vista: A Dialogue on Life and Letters in Contemporary America (Garden City, N.Y.: Doubleday, 1958) includes a number of Chase's essays rewritten as a painfully intellectual country house dialogue involving Ralph, a liberal professor of English raised in the thirties who speaks for Chase; George, a conformist graduate student raised in the forties; and Maggie, a free spirit left over from the twenties. Ralph advocates a dialectic of highbrow and lowbrow elements in culture rather than a middlebrow compromise, since America has no focal point of culture; criticizes myth and symbol criticism as ignoring experience, history, and literary particularity; defends Whitman as a comic poet who expresses ironically contrasting opinions; and says that the central dialectic of American culture is between liberal ideas and conservative habits and feelings, and that this dialectic should be sustained, not resolved.

Chase also wrote *Walt Whitman* (Minneapolis: University of Minnesota Pamphlets, 1961) and edited *Melville: A Collection of Critical Essays* (Englewood Cliffs, N.J.: Prentice-Hall, 1962).

Chase published his credo as a critic in "Art, Nature, Politics," *KR* 12 (1950): 580-94. He derives his ideal of criticism from philosophical naturalism, and finds formal elements in literature meaningful only when they are resonant of the dramatic rhythms of nature and emotion; of ideas, especially political ones; and of ritual. On the basis of Naturalism, Chase rejects Humanism, myth criticism, and other religious doctrines as oversimplified. Like Trilling, he thinks the central task of the critic is to make liberal politics intellectually respectable by adding to it the more complex understanding of reality which literature provides.

R. S. Crane

Ronald Salmon Crane was born in Tecumseh, Michigan on January 5, 1886. He married Julia Fuller in 1917 and they had two children. He received his B.A. from the University of Michigan in 1908 and his Ph.D. from the University of Pennsylvania in 1911. He taught at Northwestern University from 1911 to 1924 and was a Professor of English at the University of Chicago from 1925 until his retirement in 1951. He was chairman of the English Department from 1935 to 1947, managing editor of *Modern Philology* from 1930 to 1952, and after his retirement was a visiting professor at Toronto, Indiana, Cornell, Carleton College, Oregon, Stanford, and NYU. He was a member of the American Academy of Arts and Sciences. He died in 1967.

Critics and Criticism (Chicago: University of Chicago Press, 1952) was edited by Crane, and his introduction is the "manifesto" of the Chicago Neo-Aristotelians. It includes fourteen old essays by Crane, Elder Olson, Richard McKeon, and others, as well as six new ones that attack formalistic "New Criticism," show the superiority of the Aristotelian method, and develop the importance of Aristotle for the history of criticism. The collection also includes a number of other historical essays.

The Languages of Criticism and the Structure of Poetry (Toronto: University of Toronto Press, 1953) is a revised version of the 1952 Alexander Lectures in which Crane continues to argue for the superiority of Neo-Aristotelianism against both Formalists and myth critics.

The Idea of the Humanities, 2 vol. (Chicago: University of Chicago Press, 1967), is a collection of Crane's scholarly and critical essays. Volume 1 contains a long historical definition of what is meant by the humanities, and some studies in the history of ideas in the eighteenth century, including a criticism of Lovejoy. Volume 2 contains essays on the relationship between criticism and literary history. Crane continues his criticism of formalistic assumptions and develops further his own ideas about dramatic criticism, the failures of the Robertsonian School of medieval critics, and literary history.

Crane also published a number of scholarly books, including *The Vogue of Guy of Warwick from the Close of the Middle Ages to the Romantic Revival* (1915) and *The Vogue of Medieval Chivalric Romance during the English Renaissance* (1919). He was the compiler (with F. B. Kaye and M. E. Prior) of *A Census of British Newspapers and Periodicals, 1620–1800* (1927) and edited the standard *Collection of English Poems, 1660–1800* (1932) and a number of anthologies.

T. S. Eliot

Thomas Stearns Eliot was born in St. Louis, Missouri, on September 26, 1888, the scion of a long and distinguished line of New England Unitarian ministers, educators, and merchants. His grandfather was a Unitarian preacher and founded

Washington University; his father was a brickmaker. He attended Milton Academy and Harvard (with Conrad Aiken, Walter Lippman, Heywood Broun, and Robert Benchley), where he finished his B.A. in three years (1906-9) and received an M.A. in 1910. While an undergraduate, he studied under George Santayana and Irving Babbitt, and published poems in the *Harvard Advocate,* which he edited in 1909-10.

In 1910-11 he studied for a year at the Sorbonne, and returned to Harvard to do graduate work in philosophy from October 1911 to June 1914. In 1914 he was awarded a Sheldon Traveling Fellowhsip to Germany, but spent the year at Merton College, Oxford, because of the outbreak of World War I. From October 1915 to April 1916 he taught at the High Wycombe and Highgate schools in London while writing his dissertation, which he completed but never defended. In June 1915 he married Vivienne Haigh-Wood, a London dancer.

In September 1914 Eliot met Ezra Pound, who helped him get "Prufrock" and other poems published in *Poetry* in 1915. He published a volume of verse in 1917. From 1917 to 1925 he worked in the Colonial and Foreign Department of Lloyds Bank, and from May 1917 to 1919 he was assistant editor of *The Egoist.* In 1921 he had a breakdown and from October to December rested in Margate and Switzerland, where he wrote *The Waste Land,* which was published in New York in October 1922 in *The Dial,* and in book form in December 1922; for it he received the 1922 $2,000 *Dial* Award.

In October 1922 Eliot began to edit *The Criterion,* a new literary magazine financed by Lady Rothermere; *The Waste Land* appeared in the first issue. In 1925 Eliot resigned from Lloyds to become a member of the board and literary editor of Faber & Gwyer, where he remained until his death in 1965. In 1927 he became a British subject, and in 1928 announced his conversion to Anglo-Catholicism.

In 1926 Eliot gave the Clark Lectures on Donne at Cambridge, which reinforced the influence his writing of *The Sacred Wood* had established in the English School among critics like I. A. Richards, William Empson, and F. R. Leavis. In 1932 he returned to America for the first time since 1914 to give the Charles Eliot Norton Lectures at Harvard (published as *The Use of Poetry and the Use of Criticism* in 1933), and the Page-Barbour Lectures at the University of Virginia (published as *After Strange Gods* in 1934). When he returned to England in June 1933, he separated from his wife, who had been suffering from increasingly severe hysteria and was finally confined, and lived for some with the bookman John Hayward.

During the twenties and thirties Eliot devoted much of his effort to running *The Criterion*; the weekly luncheons for regular contributors and visiting literary men (held from 1922 to 1929 at the Grove Tavern in South Kensington) attracted such regulars as Herbert Read, F. S. Flint, Frank Morley, and Bonamy Dobrée, while meetings at the Commercio Restaurant in Soho or above Harold Munro's Poetry Bookshop near the British Museum were more widely known and attended. Eliot was also involved with numerous cultural movements, including the effort to save the English churches of the City of London, the *New English Weekly* Social Credit group of A. R. Orage and Philip Mairet in the thirties, and many others. During these years he continued to publish his poems, including *Ash Wednesday* (1930), *Sweeney Agonistes* (1932), *The Four Quartets* (1943), and *Old Possum's Book of Practical Cats* (1939). He began his career as a dramatist with *Murder in the Cathedral* (1935) and *The Family Reunion* (1939).

After giving up *The Criterion* in 1939, Eliot focused most of his attention on social questions, publishing *The Idea of a Christian Society* in 1939 and *Notes Towards the Definition of Culture* in 1948. In the postwar period he entered the most public phase of his career. In 1948, at the age of sixty, he was awarded the Nobel Prize, and in 1949 he received the Order of Merit; he would eventually receive practically every other award for poetry in the English-speaking world. Fame of another kind came to Eliot with the Broadway success of *The Cocktail Party* in 1950, which was followed by *The Confidential Clerk* (1954) and *The Elder Statesman* (1959). Eliot's many lectures during these years were collected in *On Poetry and Poets* (1957) and *To Criticize the Critic* (1965).

The most important event of Eliot's later private life was his marriage in January 1957 to Miss Valerie Fletcher, his private secretary, who was some thirty-eight years his junior. By all accounts his last years were his happiest.

The personal characteristics Eliot's friends speak of consistently are his love of practical jokes and joking, his fondness for musicals and music halls, his delight in good wine and food (especially cheese), his hypochondria, his persistent kindness and encouragement to younger writers, and his continuing and deep involvement in religion, particularly the affairs of St. Stephens Church in Gloucester Road, Kensington, where he was a churchwarden for twenty-five years.

He died on January 4, 1965, and was buried in East Coker, Somerset.

Knowledge and Experience in the Philosophy of F. H. Bradley (London: Faber & Faber, 1964) is Eliot's Harvard dissertation; written in 1915 but never presented for the degree, it was first published in 1964. (Eliot returned to Harvard as Charles Eliot Norton Professor of Poetry in 1933.)

The Sacred Wood: Essays on Poetry and Criticism (London: Methuen, 1920) contains "Tradition and the Individual Talent," "The Perfect Critic," "Imperfect Critics," "Hamlet and His Problems," and nine other essays on Marlowe, Blake, Jonson, Dante, Swinburne, Massinger, and poetic drama.

For Lancelot Andrewes (London: Faber & Gwyer, 1928) contains essays on Andrewes, John Bramhall, Machiavelli, Crashaw, Baudelaire, Middleton, F. H. Bradley, and Irving Babbitt. The preface contains Eliot's famous avowal that his general point of view is "classicist in literature, royalist in politics, and anglo-catholic in religion."

Selected Essays, 1917-1932 (London: Faber & Faber; New York: Harcourt, 1932) contains most of *The Sacred Wood* and *For Lancelot Andrewes*; Eliot's pamphlets *Homage to John Dryden, Shakespeare and the Stoicism of Seneca, Dante, Thoughts after Lambeth,* and *Charles Whibley: A Memoir*; and "The Function of Criticism," "Arnold and Pater," and ten other essays. To the second edition (1950) have been added "Religion and Literature" and three other essays.

The Use of Poetry and the Use of Criticism: Studies in the Relation of Criticism to Poetry in England (London: Faber & Faber; Cambridge: Harvard University Press, 1933) contains the lectures Eliot gave as Charles Eliot Norton Professor of Poetry at Harvard from November 1932 to March 1933: "Apology for the Countess of Pembroke," "The Age of Dryden," "Wordsworth and Coleridge," "Shelley and Keats," "Matthew Arnold," "The Modern Mind."

After Strange Gods: A Primer of Modern Heresy (London: Faber & Faber, 1934) is a compilation of the University of Virginia Page-Barbour Lectures, which attack modern heresies such as liberalism, personality, and immortality from the point of view of tradition and orthodoxy. Eliot is particularly severe in his discussion of D. H. Lawrence.

Elizabethan Essays (London: Faber & Faber, 1934) is a reprinting of ten essays on Elizabethan dramatists and "John Marston."

Essays Ancient and Modern (London: Faber & Faber, 1936) contains five essays from *Lancelot Andrewes*, as well as "Religion and Literature," "In Memoriam," "Modern Education and the Classics," and two others on Pascal and Catholicism.

The Idea of a Christian Society (London: Faber & Faber, 1939) marks Eliot's attempt to impose his religion on social organization.

Notes Towards the Definition of Culture (London: Faber & Faber, 1948) is Eliot's discussion of the proper relationship of culture to class, region, sect, education, and politics.

On Poetry and Poets (London: Faber & Faber, 1957) contains sixteen previously uncollected essays, eleven of which were first given as lectures (including "The Frontiers of Criticism," "The Social Function of Poetry," "What is Minor Poetry?" "What is a Classic?" "Poetry and Drama," and "The Three Voices of Poetry"), and essays on Vergil, Milton, Johnson, Byron, Goethe, Kipling, and Yeats.

"To Criticize the Critic" and Other Writings (London: Faber & Faber, 1965) contains Eliot's valuable summing up of the meaning of his criticism in the title essay, as well as "From Poe to Valery," "American Literature and the American Language," "The Aims of Education," "What Dante Means to Me," "The Literature of Politics," "The Classics and the Man of Letters," and two early essays on Pound and *vers libre*.

The standard bibiliography of Eliot's writings is Donald Gallup, *T. S. Eliot, a Bibliography: A Revised and Extended Edition* (New York: Harcourt, 1969). A valuable help in coping with criticism of Eliot is Mildred Martin's *A Half-Century of Eliot Criticism: An Annotated Bibliography of Books and Articles in English, 1916-1965* (Lewisburg, Pa.: Bucknell University Press, 1972), which lists and describes 2,692 items about Eliot. The articles are too numerous to list here.

The books most valuable for studying Eliot's criticism include the following: F. O. Matthiessen, *The Achievement of T. S. Eliot* (New York: Houghton Mifflin, 1935, 1947); Hugh Kenner, *The Invisible Poet: T. S. Eliot* (New York: McDowell, Obolensky, 1959); Vincent Buckley, *Poetry and Morality: Studies in the Criticism of Matthew Arnold, T. S. Eliot, and F. R. Leavis* (London: Chatto & Windus, 1959); Sean Lucy, *T. S. Eliot and the Idea of Tradition* (London: Barnes & Noble, 1960); Kristian Smidt, *Poetry and Belief in the Work of T. S. Eliot* (London: Routledge, 1961); Northrop Frye, *T. S. Eliot* (New York: Grove Press, 1963); Herbert Howarth, *Notes on Some Figures behind T. S. Eliot* (Boston: Houghton Mifflin, 1964); *T. S. Eliot, 1888-1965*, ed. Allen Tate (New York: Delacorte, 1967) (collection of essays first published in *SR* 75 [1966]); John Margolis, *T. S. Eliot's Intellectual Development, 1922-1939* (Bloomington: Indiana University Press, 1971); Allen Austin, *T. S. Eliot: The Literary and Social Criticism* (Bloomington: Indiana University Press, 1971); Bernard Bergonzi, *T. S. Eliot* (New York: Macmillan, 1972); William M. Chace, *The Political Identities of Ezra Pound and T. S. Eliot* (Stanford: Stanford University Press, 1973); Lyndall Gordon, *Eliot's Early Years* (Oxford and New York: Oxford University Press, 1977); and *The Literary Criticism of T. S. Eliot*, ed. David Newton-De Molina (London: University of London Athlone Press, 1977).

Irving Howe

Irving Howe was born in the East Bronx, New York, in 1920, the son of poor Jewish immigrants. At the age of fourteen, he joined the Socialist youth movement, and through his teens and twenties "the Movement was my home and passion, the Movement as it ranged through the various left-wing anti-Communist groups." He attended CCNY from 1936 to 1940 (B.S., 1940) and attended graduate school briefly at Brooklyn College, but "found it appalling, and quit." He spent three and a half years in the army in Alaska during World War II. In 1947 he married Arien Hausknecht and they have two children.

After World War II Howe returned to New York City to become a writer; his first essays were published in *Commentary* and the *Partisan Review.* In 1953 he began the Socialist magazine *Dissent,* which he has continued to edit. His academic career began with occasional lectures at the Indiana School of Letters, the University of Vermont, and the University of Washington. In 1953 he became an associate professor of English at Brandeis and taught there until 1961. From 1961 to 1963 he taught at Stanford. He became a professor of English at Hunter College in 1963, and later was named a Distinguished Professor of English at CUNY. He was a *Kenyon Review* Fellow and gave the Gauss Lectures at Princeton in 1953; received a Bollingen Prize in 1959, a National Institute of Arts and Letters Award in 1960, and a Guggenheim Fellowship in 1964 and 1971. He was a Fellow of the Indiana School of Letters, and received a Brandeis University Creative Arts Award in 1976.

Sherwood Anderson: A Critical Biography (New York: Sloane, 1951) is a model of the short critical biography. Though it contains little original scholarship, Howe organizes biographical and critical materials into a convincing account of Anderson as a gifted writer impoverished by a constricting culture, a minor writer whose best work will endure as it evokes "those feelings of loneliness, yearning, and muted love" which lie beneath our culture (p.viii).

William Faulkner: A Critical Study, 3rd ed. (orig. pub. 1952; New York: Random House, 1975), serves as a good introduction to Faulkner's work.

Politics and the Novel (New York: Horizon Press, 1957) gathers together essays Howe wrote from 1953 to 1957 on Stendhal, Dostoevsky, Conrad, Turgenev, Henry James, Malraux, Silone, Koestler, Orwell, Hawthorne, and Henry Adams. In these essays, Howe studies the tension between the necessary concrete life of the novel and the abstractions of political ideology in its several forms. The general chapters are not especially profound, but the analysis of individual novels is excellent.

Modern Literary Criticism: An Anthology (New York: Grove Press, 1958) contains in its introduction Howe's longest formal statement about literary criticism. For him, the purpose of literary criticism is to interpret a difficult avant-garde sensibility to the masses, to defend the values of high art against the debasement of mass culture, and to provide a field of operation for the disinterested intellect. These three points have continued to be Howe's central preoccupations. Howe treats the history of modern criticism under the conventional headings—New Criticism, social criticism, and psychological criticism—and predicts that the future lies in the intelligent individual's using a combination of methods.

A World More Attractive: A View of Modern Literature and Politics (New York: Horizon Press, 1963) contains two important general essays, "This Age of Conformity" and "Images of Socialism," as well as "Mass Society and Post-Modern Fiction" and important essays on T. E. Lawrence, Edith Wharton, Mailer, Frost, Whitman, Stevens, and others. The essential form of the book is found in Howe's belief that "modern" writers have by definition suffered from a severe crisis of belief, and that this self-doubt has led to a search by writers like Lawrence or Hemingway for private values to sustain them, and to the general loss of values in mass culture. Hope for the future is found in the ideals of freedom and fraternity represented historically by Socialism and in the disinterested intellectual.

Steady Work: Essays in the Politics of Democratic Radicalism, 1953–1966 (New York: Harcourt, 1966) is a collection of sociological essays in which Howe attempts to describe and come to terms with a new generation of radicals, and to face the fact that Socialism, *his* Socialism, is dead. His solution is to form a coalition of Socialists, liberals, Negroes, and labor leaders to redeem the welfare state. See especially "Radical Criticism and the American Intellectual" and "New Styles in Leftism," where he criticizes the New Leftists for being apolitical and ineffective, and for ignoring history and old Socialists. Also included are an excellent personal memoir of the thirties and "This Age of Conformity" and "Images of Socialism."

Thomas Hardy (New York: Macmillan, 1967) is a competent, somewhat pedestrian, introduction to Hardy's work.

Decline of the New (New York: Harcourt, 1970) contains "The New York Intellectuals," "The Culture of Modernism," and a number of reprinted essays, introductions, and reviews.

The Critical Point (New York: Horizon Press, 1973) contains a couple of polemical pieces on the crisis of civilization, as well as "The Middle-Class Mind of Kate Millett" and essays on the city, Zola, Dostoevsky, Pound, Bellow, Roth, Plath, Erik Erikson, and others.

Celebrations and Attacks: Thirty Years of Literary and Cultural Commentary (New York: Horizon Press, 1979) is a collection of essays and reviews, some reprinted, on Lillian Hellman, Quentin Anderson, Leslie Fiedler, Trilling, Wilson, and others.

Howe has edited a number of books, including *A Treasury of Yiddish Stories* (1954), *A Treasury of Yiddish Poetry* (1969), and *Voices from the Yiddish* (1972), all with Eliezer Greenberg; *Edith Wharton: A Collection of Critical Essays* (1962); and *Literary Modernism* (1967). He has also edited a number of anthologies on political topics. His history of Jewish immigrants, *World of Our Fathers* (1976), was a best-seller. His most recent book is *Leon Trotsky* (1978).

On Howe's criticism see Richard Kostelanetz, "The Perils and Paucities of 'Democratic Radicalism,' " *Salmagundi* 2, no. 1 (1960): 44–60; and Emile Capouya, "Howe Now," *Studies on the Left* 4 (1964): 63–67.

Alfred Kazin

Alfred Kazin was born in Brooklyn, New York, on June 5, 1915, of Russian Jewish parents. He received a B.S. from CCNY in 1935 and an M.A. from Columbia in 1938. He has been married three times and has two children.

Kazin began his career as a reviewer while an undergraduate, writing for the *New York Times* and the *Herald-Tribune* book review sections and for *The New Republic.* From 1937 to 1942 he was a tutor and instructor in English at CCNY. A Guggenheim Fellowship in 1940 and a Carnegie grant in 1941 allowed him to work on his first book, *On Native Grounds* (1942). In 1942 and 1943 he was literary editor of *The New Republic,* and in 1943 and 1944, associate editor of *Fortune.* From 1943 to 1963 Kazin was a parapetetic academician, teaching and lecturing off and on at the New School for Social Research and at Black Mountain College (1944), Minnesota (1946 and 1950), Harvard (1953), as Neilson Professor at Smith (1954–55), at Amherst (1955–58), as Berg Professor at NYU (1957), at the University of Puerto Rico (1959), as Christian Gauss Lecturer at Princeton (1962), as Buell Gallagher Professor at CCNY (1962), and as Beckman Professor at Berkeley (1963). Since 1963 he has been a distinguished professor of English at the State University of New York at Stony Brook. Over the years, he continued to review books, mostly *for Atlantic Monthly, Harper's, American Scholar, The New Republic,* the *New York Times Book Review, Partisan Review,* and *Commentary.* He received a Rockefeller Fellowship in 1945, a National Institute of Arts and Letters grant in 1949, and a teaching Fulbright to Cambridge in 1952. He was a Fellow of the Indiana School of Letters, and is a member of the American Academy of Arts and Sciences and the National Institute of Arts and Letters. He received a Brandeis University Creative Arts Award in 1973, and an honorary degree from Adelphi University in 1965.

On Native Grounds (New York: Harcourt, 1942) presents Kazin's general thesis that American prose literature is a response to the crises of capitalism and industrialism in the 1880s and after, and that it is marked by a realistic absorption in the details of American life and an idealistic alienation from it because of a transcendental vision of life which American reality betrayed. For example, the author discusses the conflict between the "Muckrake and the Superman" (Upton Sinclair and Teddy Roosevelt), Parrington's view of history as a struggle between the capitalist Constitution and Jeffersonian freedom, Van Wyck Brooks's lowbrow and highbrow, and the struggle between liberals and New Humanists in the twenties and between Marxist and Formalist critics in the thirties. The book is not thesis-ridden, however, and most of the specifically literary chapters are appraisals of the realistic/naturalistic tradition of fiction—Dreiser and Wharton, Anderson and Lewis, Cather and Glasgow, Hemingway and Dos Passos, Faulkner and Wolfe. The book is written in a popular style, is unfootnoted, and is generally nonacademic in tone. Because of this, its hostility to Formalism, and its avoidance of myth criticism, it has had little influence on subsequent studies of American literature. Nevertheless, Kazin's judgments, especially those of nonfiction, are often valuable.

The Inmost Leaf: A Selection of Essays (New York: Harcourt, 1955) contains the long introduction to *The Portable Blake* and twenty-seven short essays, mostly on novelists. The essay on Edmund Wilson and "The Writer and the University" are of particular interest to the student of criticism.

Contemporaries (Boston: Little, Brown, 1962) consists of seventy-three brief reviews, mostly on the American novel from Melville to Mailer. In general, Kazin holds to the standard that good literature must have social meaning, or more accurately, must provide the imaginative vision that will provide ideas central to social policy and moral behavior. In "The Function of Criticism Today" Kazin discusses his views and the situation in modern criticism.

Bright Book of Life: American Novelists and Storytellers from Hemingway to Mailer (Boston: Little, Brown, 1973) is a survey, informed by Kazin's usual critical good sense, of the decline of the "modern" writers of the twenties and their uncomfortable confrontation with their successors.

Kazin has edited a large number of anthologies and editions, including *The Portable Blake* (1946), *F. Scott Fitzgerald: The Man and His Work* (1951), *The Stature of Theodore Dreiser* (with Charles Shapiro, 1955), *Moby Dick* (1956), *Ralph Waldo Emerson: A Modern Anthology* (with Daniel Aaron, 1959), *The Works of Anne Frank* (with Ann Birstein, 1959), and *The Open Form: Essays for Our Time* (1961).

He has also been at work for a number of years on his autobiography, including *A Walker in the City* (1951) and *Starting Out in the Thirties* (1965), which give a valuable picture of New York literary life in the thirties. A third volume, *New York Jew* (1978), carries his story from 1940 to the seventies and contains a number of interesting portraits of the literary celebrities Kazin has known.

For a view of Kazin as a moral critic see Sherman Paul, "Alfred Kazin," *Repossessing and Renewing* (Baton Rouge: Louisiana State University Press, 1976), pp. 236-94; George H. Douglas, "Alfred Kazin: American Critic," *Colorado Quarterly* 23 (1974): 44-51; and Robert Alter, "The Education of Alfred Kazin," *Commentary,* June 1978, pp. 44-51.

Murray Krieger

Murray Krieger was born in Newark, New Jersey, on November 27, 1923. He was educated at Rutgers University and the University of Chicago (M.A., 1948), at the Kenyon School of English (1948-49), and at The Ohio State University (Ph.D., 1952). He married Joan Stone in 1947 and they have two children.

Krieger served in the army from 1942 to 1946. He began teaching in 1948 at Kenyon College, continued at The Ohio State University, and was appointed an assistant professor at the University of Minnesota in 1952, where he remained until 1958, when he became a professor at the University of Illinois. From 1963 to 1966 he was Carpenter Professor of Literary Criticism at the University of Iowa, and he is now University Professor of English at the University of California at Irvine, where he is also director of the School of Criticism and Theory. He received a Guggenheim Fellowship in 1956 and 1961, an ACLS grant in 1966, and a NEH grant in 1971.

The New Apologists for Poetry (Minneapolis: University of Minnesota Press, 1956) is an able and subtle study of the theoretical difficulties of New Critical poetic theory from the point of view of the aesthetician. Krieger concentrates on Hulme, Eliot, and Richards in an effort to formulate an adequate "contextualist" theory as a defense for the unique aesthetic experience he believes is provided by poetry.

The Tragic Vision: Variations on a Theme in Literary Interpretation (New York: Holt, 1960) marks Krieger's attempt to broaden the "organic monism," the closed contextual system of New Critical theory, by proposing the discipline of "thematics": "the study of the experiential tensions which, dramatically entangled in the literary work, become an existential reflection of that work's aesthetic complexity" (p. 242). For Krieger, art embodies the Manichaean dualism of life, which cannot be reconciled metaphysically or reduced to propositions. In support of his thesis, Krieger examines the main writers of modern Europe: Gide, Lawrence, Malraux, Silone, Mann, Kafka, Camus, Conrad, Dostoevsky, and Melville.

A Window to Criticism: Shakespeare's Sonnets and Modern Poetics (Princeton: Princeton University Press, 1964) represents Krieger's attempt to move beyond

Formalism by positing a language for poetry which functions referentially as a window to the world, which functions in an enclosed, formal system like a maze of mirrors, and which functions "as this same set of mirrors that miraculously becomes window again" (p. 3). The literary work is thus at once monistic (formal) and dualistic (reflecting existential tensions). Krieger traces these ideas through modern criticism, applies them to Shakespeare's sonnets, and defends the "Power of Poetic Effigy."

The Play and Place of Criticism (Baltimore: Johns Hopkins Press, 1967), a collection of sixteen essays, includes three defending Krieger's "contextual" theory of criticism, two on his differences with W. K. Wimsatt and Cleanth Brooks, one on Frye, one on J. W. Beach, and two defenses of criticism. The practical essays are on Shakespeare's sonnets, *Richard III*, Pope, Arnold, Hawthorne, Conrad, and Lessing's *Laokoön*.

The Classic Vision: The Retreat from Extremity in Modern Literature (Baltimore: Johns Hopkins Press, 1971) surveys literature from the Renaissance to the present in a discussion of four kinds of retreat from extremity: the worship of bloodless abstractions, the embrace of the community of man, the acceptance of the human barnyard, and the search for an alternative to sainthood.

Theory of Criticism: A Tradition and Its System (Baltimore: Johns Hopkins University Press, 1976) repeats Krieger's earlier defenses of the poem as an aesthetic object and of the necessity of theory; reinterprets the history of criticism, largely Aristotle and Coleridge; and defends Krieger's theory of the reality of fictions against the new Structuralists and Frye.

Poetic Presence and Illusion: Essays in Critical History and Theory (Baltimore: Johns Hopkins University Press, 1979) is Krieger's latest work.

Krieger also helped his teacher Eliseo Vivas edit *The Problems of Aesthetics* (New York: Rinehart, 1953) and edited and contributed an introduction to *Northrop Frye in Modern Criticism: Selected Papers from the English Institute* (New York: Columbia University Press, 1966).

On Krieger see Donald M. Kartiganer, "The Criticism of Murray Krieger: The Expansions of Contextualism," *Boundary 2* 2 (1974): 584–607.

Philip Rahv

Philip Rahv was born on March 10, 1908, in the Ukraine and emigrated via Israel to Providence, Rhode Island, in 1922. There he went to high school. He later moved to New York, where he became active in the John Reed clubs, and in 1934 he was named one of the founding editors of the *Partisan Review*, which he continued to edit until 1969 (an unusually long tenure for a little-magazine editor). He married Nathalie Swan, an architect, in 1941.

As editor of *PR*, Rahv became the "Doctor Johnson of his small group of radical intellectuals"; he was appointed a Fellow of the Kenyon School of English in 1949, a Senior Fellow of the Indiana School of Letters in 1950, and was given a Guggenheim fellowship in 1950. Though he had no university education, he taught at the Adult Extension Division of NYU, and was appointed a professor of English at Brandeis in 1957. In 1970 he left the editorship of *PR* to found a new journal, *Modern Occasions*. He died on December 23, 1973.

Image and Idea: Fourteen Essays on Literary Themes (New York: New Directions, 1949, 1957) includes "Paleface and Redskin," which divides American literature into the patrician, allegorical, consciously highbrow tradition of James and Melville, and the frontier, realistic, lowbrow tradition of Whitman and Twain (the palefaces dominated our classic period, the redskins the modern); "The Cult of Experience in American Writing," which isolates the Strether-like search for experience as the basis of our literature and shows how both James and Whitman (and others, p. 19) seek it, though they define it in different ways; "The Dark Lady of Salem," which traces an archetype in Hawthorne, and "The Heiress of All the Ages," which a type-figure finds in James; and "Attitudes towards Henry James," which defends James against the Philistines. Rahv also includes essays on Tolstoi, Chekhov, and Gogol, two on Kafka, and his own contribution to the 1952 *PR* symposium, "Our Country and Our Culture," where he worries that the new accommodation the Intellectuals have made to America, the universities, money, and the mass media may destroy their alienation and tradition of dissent. There are also a number of brief reviews of Williams, Miller, Koestler, Melville, Hemingway, and Eliot, and a defense of Naturalism.

The Myth and the Powerhouse (New York: Farrar, 1965) is basically an attack on New Criticism, myth and symbol criticism, and the religious revival of the fifties from the point of view of the historical critic; Rahv notes in the foreword that it is in part already dated. The title essay discusses the romantic Neoprimitivism and fear of history which are at the base of myth criticism and defends the reality of time and history—Rahv's ultimate metaphysical position. "Criticism and the Imagination of Alternatives" defends the same position, but with more specific observations on Harry Levin and Cleanth Brooks, and defends criticism as an expression of the values of the critic, a kind of literature about literature. "Criticism and the Criticism of Fiction" argues that importing the search for symbols (Stallman), the concern with style (Ransom), and technism (Schorer) from the poetic criticism to novel criticism is unwise. "The Native Bias" discusses the contrast between the American dream and historical reality as a theme for our fiction. "Plain Critic and *Enfant Terrible*" discusses the good sense of George P. Elliott and the lack of it in Leslie Fiedler. There are two long essays on Dostoevsky and reviews of Geismar, Bellow, Mailer, and Miller.

Literature and the Sixth Sense (Boston: Houghton Mifflin, 1969) reprints Rahv's first two collections (with the exception of the two long essays on Dostoevsky) and contains fourteen previously uncollected essays, including eight from the sixties. The best of them are an attack on F. R. Leavis for his view of Lawrence, and a laudatory review of Eliot's *To Criticize the Critic*.

Rahv edited *The Great Short Novels of Henry James* (1944) and *The Bostonians* (1945), which were contributions to the James revival; *The Short Novels of Tolstoy* (1946), *Discovery of Europe: The Story of American Experience in the Old World* (1947), *Great Russian Short Novels* (1951), *Literature in America: An Anthology of Literary Criticism* (1957), *Modern Occasions* (1966), *Eight Great American Short Novels* (1963), and *Modern Occasions Two* (1974). He also edited (with William Phillips) *The Partisan Reader: Ten Years of Partisan Review, 1934-44* (1946), *The New Partisan Reader, 1945-53* (1953), *Stories in the Modern Manner* (1954), and *The Partisan Review Anthology* (1962).

On Rahv see Mary McCarthy, "Phillip Rahv, 1908-1973," *NYTBR,* February 17, 1974; and *Images and Ideas in American Culture: The Function of Criticism.*

Essays in Memory of Philip Rahv, ed. Arthur Edelstein (Boston: Brandeis University Press, 1978).

John Crowe Ransom

John Crowe Ransom was born in Pulaski, Tennessee, on April 30, 1888, the son of a Methodist minister. He received a B.A. in classics and philosophy from Vanderbilt University in 1909. He was awarded a Rhodes Scholarship to Christ's Church, Oxford, where he received a B.A. in 1913. In 1920 he married Robb Reavill and they have two sons and a daughter.

Except for his service in the American army in France from 1917 to 1919, Ransom spent the years 1914-1937 teaching English literature at Vanderbilt. In 1919 he published *Poems about God,* and his volumes of the 1920s, *Chills and Fever* (1924), *Grace after Meat* (1924), and *Two Gentlemen in Bonds* (1927), contain most of the ironic lyrics for which he is famous. From 1919 to 1925 he was associated with the discussions and publication of *The Fugitive,* and he taught Fugitives Allen Tate and Robert Penn Warren. From 1928 to about 1936, Ransom, with Tate and others, was a leader of the Agrarian movement in defense of the Old South, which resulted in the publication of *I'll Take My Stand . . . by Twelve Southerners* in 1930 and *Who Owns America?* in 1936. He studied in England on a Guggenheim grant in 1931-32.

In 1937 Ransom left the South for Kenyon College in Ohio, where he founded the *Kenyon Review* in 1938. Ransom's model editing of this magazine from 1938 to 1959 made him influential on a generation of readers, and his influence is carried on by a number of distinguished students: Tate, Warren, Andrew Lytle, Cleanth Brooks, George Marion O'Donnell, Randall Jarrell, Robert Lowell, Peter Taylor, and Robie Macaulay.

In 1948, with Lionel Trilling and F. O. Mattheissen, Ransom founded the Kenyon School of English, which became a well-known summer school for critics. In 1950 the school metamorphosed into the Indiana School of Letters, which flourished until 1972.

Ransom was a member of the National Institute of Arts and Letters and the American Academy of Arts and Letters. From 1950 to 1960 he was a Fellow of and Honorary Consultant in American Letters to the Library of Congress. He was a member of the American Academy of Arts and Sciences. He received a Guggenheim in 1931, a Bollingen Prize in 1951, a Brandeis University Creative Arts Award in 1958, an Academy of American Poets Fellowship in 1962, a National Book Award in 1964, a National Endowment for the Arts Award in 1966, the Emerson-Thoreau Medal in 1968, and the National Institute of Arts and Letters Gold Metal in 1973. He died on July 3, 1974.

The World's Body (New York: Scribner's, 1938) contains fifteen essays written in the thirties, including appraisals of Tate, Stevens, Eliot, Richards, Santayana, Millay, Tennyson, and "Lycidas." In "Poetry: A Note on Ontology" Ransom shows how Metaphysical poetry miraculously unites the images of "pure poetry" and the ideas of "Platonic poetry." In "Criticism, Inc." he argues that we should replace biographical and historical study of literature with technical study of the text itself. In "The Cathartic Principle" he defends the need for theoretical discussion of critical questions and argues for mimetic art. In "A Psychologist Looks at

Poetry" he condemns the early Richards for denying that poetry conveys knowledge, and asserts that the late Richards has been converted to Coleridgian idealism about the status of art.

The New Criticism (Norfolk, Conn.: New Directions, 1941) is known mainly for its eponymic importance. In it Ransom praises the capacity for close reading of the text of Blackmur and others and analyzes, in separate chapters and with lengthy quotations, "I. A. Richards, the Psychological Critic, and William Empson, His Pupil"; "T. S. Eliot: The Historical Critic"; and "Yvor Winters: The Logical Critic." In "Wanted: An Ontological Critic" he defends poetry as offering a unique kind of knowledge of both the abstraction and the concretion of the world, both "structure" and "texture." He also expresses many of these same ideas in "Criticism as Pure Speculation," which is part of a symposium volume on criticism, *The Intent of the Critic,* ed. D. A. Stauffer (Princeton: Princeton University Press, 1941).

Poems and Essays (New York: Vintage Books, 1955) contains eight uncollected essays, including a criticism of the "Chicago School" of Neo-Aristotelian criticism; praise of Blackmur's close reading in *Language as Gesture* and of Cleanth Brooks's *Poems of Mr. John Milton* ("Why Critics Don't Go Mad"); and essays on Hardy and Shakespeare.

Beating the Bushes: Selected Essays, 1941-70 (New York: New Directions, 1972) contains the last chapter of *The New Criticism,* some dated reviews of now-forgotten critical books, and an afterword relating "the concrete universal" to Hegelian thought.

Ransom has edited several texts and anthologies and is the author of *God without Thunder: An Unorthodox Defense of Orthodoxy* (1930), which Yvor Winters characterized as "Thunder without God."

John Crowe Ransom: Critical Essays and a Bibliography, ed. Thomas Daniel Young (Baton Rouge: Louisiana State University Press, 1968), contains sixteen classic essays on all aspects of Ransom's career and a complete, annotated bibliography of works by and about him. In addition, Young has published *Gentleman in a Dustcoat: A Biography of John Crowe Ransom* (Baton Rouge: Louisiana State University Press, 1976). See also "Art as Adventure in Form: Letters of John Crowe Ransom, 1923-1927" (letters to Allen Tate) ed. Thomas Daniel Young and George Core, *SoR* 12 (1976): 776-97.

On Ransom see Yvor Winters, "John Crowe Ransom, or Thunder without God," *The Anatomy of Nonsense* (New York: New Directions, 1943); Winifred Lynskey, "A Critic in Action: Mr. Ransom," *College English* 5 (1944): 239-49; Edwin Berry Burgum, "An Examination of Modern Critics: John Crowe Ransom," *Rocky Mountain Review* 8 (1944): 87-93; "Homage to John Crowe Ransom Issue," *SR* 56 (1948): 365-476; Morgan Blum, "The Fugitive Particular: John Crowe Ransom, Critic," *Western Review* 14 (1950): 85-102; John Bradbury, "Ransom as Critic," *The Fugitives: A Critical Account* (Chapel Hill: University of North Carolina Press, 1958), pp. 126-46; *John Crowe Ransom ... A Tribute from the Community of Letters,* ed. D. David Long and Michael R. Burr (Gambier, Ohio, 1964), supplement to vol. 90, no. 7, of *Kenyon Collegian* (contains valuable comments and reminiscences on Ransom by a number of critics and friends); John L. Stewart, "Ransom's Theories of Poetry and Criticism," *The Burden of Time* (Princeton: Princeton University Press, 1965), pp. 257-306; George Lannery, "Ransom as Editor," *John Crowe Ransom: Critical Essays and a Bibliography*, ed. Thomas Daniel Young (Baton Rouge: Louisiana State University Press, 1968), pp. 210-20; James E. Magner, Jr., *John Crowe Ransom: Critical Principles and Preoccupations* (The Hague: Mouton, 1971); René Wellek, "John Crowe Ransom's Theory of Poetry," in *Literary Theory and Structure*, ed. Frank Brady et al. (New Haven: Yale University Press, 1973), pp. 179-98; "Memorial Issue," *SR* 82 (1974): 545-638 (contains a tribute by Allen Tate, a biographical chapter by T. D. Young, an article on Ransom's poetry by Louis D. Rubin, Jr., and a defense of Ransom as a theoretical critic by George Core); *The New Criticism and After*, ed. Thomas Daniel Young (Charlottesville: University Press of Virginia, 1976), the 1975 Ransom Memorial Lectures at Kenyon College (contains articles on Ransom's criticism by T. D. Young, Louis D. Rubin, Jr., and Hugh Kenner, as well as other essays); and "Memorial Issue," *Mississippi Quarterly* 30 (1976/77) (contains an article on structure and texture by Thomas Daniel Young, a reminiscence of Ransom by his granddaughter, a bibliography for the years 1967-76, and other essays).

Allen Tate

John Orley Allen Tate was born in Winchester, Kentucky, on November 19, 1899, the son of an unsuccessful businessman and a Virginia gentlewoman. He grew up in Kentucky and Tennessee, attended the Cincinnati Conservatory of Music briefly, and received his college education at Vanderbilt University (1918-23), where he was a pupil of John Crowe Ransom, a roommate of Robert Penn Warren, and a member of the group of poets which founded the magazine *The Fugitive*. He received his B.A. in 1923. He published several poems in little magazines, and was praised by T. S. Eliot and Hart Crane. In 1924 he visited New York, where he met Crane, Gorham Munson, Slater Brown, Edmund Wilson, Louise Bogan, and other Greenwich Village Bohemians. That summer he visited Warren in Guthrie, Tennessee. Tate married the writer Caroline Gordon on November 24, 1924, and they went to live in New York, where they stayed from 1924-1928, supporting themselves with editorial hack work and as reviewers for *The Nation, The New Republic,* and other journals. During these years the Tates associated with the Surrealist group around Crane, and with Mark Van Doren, Malcolm Cowley, Kenneth Burke, and others. They spent the winter of 1925 in a farmhouse in Patterson, New York, with Crane. In 1928 and 1929 Tate produced popular biographies of *Stonewall Jackson* and *Jefferson Davis.* His daughter, Nancy, was born in 1925.

In 1928 Tate was awarded a Guggenheim Fellowship and went to Europe, chiefly to London (where he met Eliot, Herbert Read, and Leonie Adams) and to Paris (where he met Hemingway, Fitzgerald, Gertrude Stein, Sylvia Beach, Ford Madox Ford, and John Peale Bishop). The family returned to America in 1930 to a farm ("Benfolly") Tate's brother Benjamin bought for him near Clarksville, Tennessee, where they stayed until 1938. During these years Tate was active in the Agrarian movement and contributed to its manifestoes *I'll Take My Stand* (1930) and *Who Owns America?* (which he coedited with Herbert Agar in 1936). In 1932 the Tates returned to France on a Guggenheim grant given to Caroline Tate and lived on the Riviera and in Paris. Tate taught at the Southwestern University in Memphis, from 1934 to 1936, at the Woman's College of the University of North Carolina at Greensboro in 1938 and 1939, and in 1939 became poet-in-residence in the Creative Arts Program at Princeton. In the spring of 1942 the Tates left Princeton for the summer resort Monteagle, Tennessee, where Robert Lowell and his wife Jean Stafford joined them for a literary winter. In September 1943 Tate moved to Washington to become Consultant in Poetry to the Library of Congress, in July 1944 he went to Sewanee, Tennessee, to become editor of the *Sewanee Review,* and in October 1945 he resigned and moved to New York, in part because of his divorce from and remarriage to Caroline Tate in late 1945 and early 1946. From 1946 to 1948 he was Editor of Belles Lettres for Henry Holt & Company, in the summer of 1948 he taught at the Kenyon School of English, and from 1948 to 1951 he lectured at NYU while living largely at Princeton. In December 1950 he converted to Catholicism. In 1951 Tate found a permanent home as a professor of English at the University of Minnesota, where he remained until his retirement in 1968. In 1955 Tate again separated from his wife Caroline; from 1959 to 1966 he was married to the poet Isabella Gardner, and in 1966 he married Helen Heinz, a former student and Minneapolis nurse, who bore him twin sons in 1967 (one of whom died in a nursery accident) and another boy in 1969.

Tate's final working years were marked by public honors. In 1956 he hosted a T. S. Eliot reading at the University of Minnesota, was awarded the Bollingen Prize, and lectured in India. In 1958 and 1959 he lectured at Oxford and Leeds, and in the autumn of 1959 a special "Homage to Allen Tate" issue was published by the *Sewanee Review.* In 1961 he received the Brandeis Medal for Poetry, in 1962 the Gold Medal of the Dante Society of Florence, and in 1963 the Fellowship Award of the Academy of American Poets. He was elected to the National Institute of Arts and Letters in 1949, the American Academy of Arts and Letters in 1964, and the American Academy of Arts and Sciences in 1965. He died on February 9, 1979.

Reactionary Essays on Poetry and Ideas (New York: Scribner's, 1936) contains "The Profession of Letters in the South," "Humanism and Naturalism," and essays on Robinson, MacLeish, Eliot, Millay, Cummings, Donne, and others.

Reason in Madness: Critical Essays (New York: Putnam's, 1941) contains "The Present Function of Criticism," "Tension in Poetry," "Literature as Knowledge," "Miss Emily and the Bibliographer," "Narcissus as Narcissus," "The Function of the Critical Quarterly," "What is a Traditional Society?" and five other essays.

On the Limits of Poetry: Selected Essays, 1928–48 (New York: Swallow Press, 1948) reprints twenty-five essays from his previous collections plus "Yeats's Romanticism," "Techniques of Fiction," "The Hovering Fly," "A Reading of Keats," "Hardy's Philosophic Metaphors," and "The New Provincialism."

"The Hovering Fly" and Other Essays (Cummington, Mass.: Cummington Press, 1948) contains "The Hovering Fly," "The New Provincialism," "Techniques of Fiction," "A Reading of Keats," "Stephen Spender's *Poems,"* "An Exegesis on Dr. Swift," "Longinus," and "A Suppressed Preface to a Collection of Poems."

The Forlorn Demon: Didactic and Critical Essays (Chicago: Regnery, 1953) contains "The Man of Letters in the Modern World," "To Whom is the Poet Responsible?" "The Symbolic Imagination: The Mirrors of Dante," "The Angelic

Imagination: Poe as God," "Our Cousin, Mr. Poe," "Is Literary Criticism Possible?" "Johnson on the Metaphysical Poets," "Longinus and the 'New Criticism,' " and "A Miscellany."

The Man of Letters in the Modern World: Selected Essays, 1928-55 (New York: Meridian, 1955) reprints twenty-seven essays.

His other major works are *Collected Essays* (Denver: Swallow Press, 1959) and *Memories and Opinions, 1926-1974* (Chicago, Swallow Press, 1975).

In addition to the biographies *Stonewall Jackson* (1928) and *Jefferson Davis* (1929), Tate published a novel, *The Fathers* (1938), and eleven volumes of poetry. He has edited several books, including *Who Owns America?* (with 1936), *A Southern Vanguard: The John Peale Bishop Memorial Volume* (1947), *The Collected Poems of John Peale Bishop* (1948), *The House of Fiction: An Anthology of the Short Story* (with Caroline Gordon, 1951), and *Modern Verse in English, 1900-1950* (with David Cecil, 1958). A complete listing can be found in *Allen Tate: A Bibliography*, comp. Marshall Fallwell, Jr. (New York: Lewis, 1969).

Besides the numerous comments on Tate's writing found in books and articles on the Fugitives and on "New Criticism," the following works have been written specifically about Tate's criticism: Charles I. Glicksberg, "Allen Tate and Mother Earth," *SR* 5 (1937): 284-95; Clifford Amyx, "The Aesthetics of Allen Tate," *Western Review* 13, no. 3 (1949): 135-45; Monroe K. Spears, "The Criticism of Allen Tate," *SR* 57 (1949): 317-34; Northrop Frye, "Ministry of Angels," *HR* 6 (1953/54): 442-47; Eliseo Vivas, "Allen Tate as Man of Letters," *SR* 62 (1954): 131-43; "Special Issue: Homage to Allen Tate," ibid. 67 (1959) (contains articles about Tate by Ransom, Blackmur, Cowley, Eliot, Robert Lowell, Mizener, Vivas, and others); Richard Foster, "Allen Tate: From the Old South to Catholic Orthodoxy," *The New Romantics* (Bloomington: Indiana University Press, 1962); R. K. Meiners, *The Last Alternatives: A Study of the Works of Allen Tate* (Denver: Swallow Press, 1962); George Hemphill, *Allen Tate* (Minneapolis: University of Minnesota Press, 1964); Ferman Bishop, *Allen Tate* (New York: Twayne, 1967) (a survey); Austin Warren, "Homage to Allen Tate," *SoR* 9 (1973): 753-77; and "A Special Section on Allen Tate," ibid. 12 (1976): 685-97 (contains articles on Tate by Cleanth Brooks, George Core, Radcliffe Squires, and others).

Radcliffe Squires has written an informative book, *Allen Tate: A Literary Biography* (New York: Pegasus, 1971), and edited a collection, largely of reprinted essays, *Allen Tate and His Work: Critical Evaluation* (Minneapolis: University of Minnesota Press, 1972). See also *The Literary Correspondence of Donald Davidson and Allen Tate*, ed. John Tyree Fain and Thomas Daniel Young (Athens: University of Georgia Press, 1974).

Lionel Trilling

Lionel Trilling was born in New York City on July 4, 1905, the son of a businessman. He married Diana Rubin, a writer, on June 12, 1929, and they have one son.

Trilling was educated at Columbia University, where he received a B.A. in 1925, an M.A. in 1926, and a Ph.D. in English in 1938. He began his academic career as an instructor at the University of Wisconsin (1926-27) and at Hunter College (1927-30). Since 1930 he has taught at Columbia, where he rose through the ranks to become a University Professor in 1970. He was George Eastman Visiting Professor at Oxford in 1964/65, Norton Lecturer at Harvard in 1969/70, and a Visiting Fellow at All Souls, Oxford, in 1972/73.

Trilling wrote for the *Menorah Journal* in the late twenties and joined the Trotskyite faction of the radical movement. He wrote reviews for the *New York Evening Post* in the thirties and after that published in many of the major literary magazines, particularly the *Partisan Review*, the *Kenyon Review*, and *Nation*. He served as Senior Fellow of the Kenyon School of English (1948-50) and of the Indiana School of Letters. He was elected to the National Institute of Arts and Letters in 1951, to the American Academy of Arts and Letters in 1952, and received a number of fellowships and honorary degrees. He received a Brandeis University Creative Arts Award in 1967. He died on November 5, 1975.

Matthew Arnold (New York: Norton, 1939) is a model critical biography.

E. M. Forster (Norfolk, Conn.: New Directions, 1943) is a brief biographical and critical introduction in which Trilling opposes Forster's ironic imagination to American liberalism.

The Liberal Imagination: Essays on Literature and Society (New York: Viking Press, 1950), the classic statement of the necessity to combine the ideas of liberal politics with the imagination of literature, includes essays written in the forties on Fitzgerald, Freud, Parrington, Wordsworth's "Immortality Ode," and the *Partisan Review*, as well as "The Sense of the Past," and "Manners, Morals, and the Novel."

The Opposing Self (New York: Viking Press, 1955) is a collection of nine essays on the theme of the quarrel of the self with culture, of the imagination with the prisons of respectability. The essays, largely introductions to books, are on Keats's *Letters, Little Dorrit, Anna Karenina,* Howells, *The Bostonians,* Wordsworth, Orwell, Flaubert, and *Mansfield Park.*

A Gathering of Fugitives (Boston: Beacon Press, 1956) contains seventeen brief, informal essays, largely for a book club magazine.

Beyond Culture: Essays on Literature and Learning (New York: Viking Press, 1965) contains essays on the relationship of bourgeois culture, largely as represented by the university, to the "adversary culture." Trilling is here concerned with the failure of the adversary culture to maintain its independence since it has become so successful.

Sincerity and Authenticity (Cambridge: Harvard University Press, 1972) is a recasting of the dialectic of mind and reality in new terms within the context of Western culture since Elizabethan times.

Mind in the Modern World (New York: Viking Press, 1973), the first Jefferson Lecture in the Humanities, is dispirited and disappointing.

Trilling also wrote a novel about ex-Leftists, *The Middle of the Journey* (1947), in which he discusses the trials and tribulations of the thirties, and some short stores. He edited a number of editions and anthologies, including *The Letters of Keats* (1951), *The Portable Matthew Arnold* (1949), and *Literary Criticism: An Introductory Reader* (1970), and (with Steven Marcus) abridged Ernest Jones's *The Life and Works of Sigmund Freud* (1961).

Marianne Gilbert Barnaby has compiled "Lionel Trilling: A Bibliography," *Bulletin of Bibliography* 31 (1974): 37-44, which includes works by and about Trilling.

On Trilling's criticism see particularly W. V. O'Connor, "Lionel Trilling's Critical Realism," *SR* 58 (1950): 482-94; R. P. Blackmur, "The Politics of Human Power," *KR* 12 (1950): 663-73; Delmore Schwartz, "The Duchess' Red Shoes," *PR* 20 (1953): 55-73; Joseph Frank, "Lionel Trilling and the Conservative Imagination," *SR* 64 (1956): 296-309 (*also Salmagundi*, no. 41 [Spring 1978], pp. 46-54); David H. Hirsh, "Reality, Manners, and Mr. Trilling," *SR* 72 (1964): 420-32; Diana Trilling, "The Other Night at Columbia: A Report from the Academy," *PR* 26 (1959): 214-30 (on Lionel and Allen Ginsberg); *Art, Politics, and Will: Essays in Honor of Lionel Trilling*, ed. Quentin Anderson, Stephen Donadio, and Steven Marcus (New York: Basic Books, 1977) (contains a memoir by Marcus reprinted from *NYTBR* and a brief chronology of Trilling's life and works); Tom Samet, "The Modulated Vision: Lionel Trilling's 'Larger Naturalism,'" *Critical Inquiry* 4 (1978): 539-57; Phillip Lopate, "Remembering Lionel Trilling," *American Review*, no. 25 (October 1976), pp. 148-78 (a memoir by a student of Trilling's); *Salmagundi*, no. 41 (Spring 1978) (contains the transcript of a symposium attended by Trilling, Howe, and others; Mark Shechner's "Lionel Trilling: Psychoanalysis and Liberalism"; Robert Langbaum's "The Importance of *The Liberal Imagination*"; and other essays); Denis Donoghue, "Trilling, Mind, and Society," *SR* 86 (1978): 161-86; and William M. Chace, "Lionel Trilling: The Contrariness of Culture," *American Scholar* 48 (1978/79): 49-58.

Austin Warren

Austin Warren was born on July 4, 1899, in Waltham, Massachusetts. He received a B.A. degree from Wesleyan University in 1920. While at Harvard, from which he received an M.A. degree in 1922, he was influenced by the Humanism of Irving Babbitt. His Ph.D. was awarded by Princeton in 1926. He taught at the University of Kentucky in 1920/21, at the University of Minnesota from 1922 to 1924, at Boston University from 1926 to 1939, at the University of Iowa from 1939 to 1948, and as a professor of English at the University of Michigan from 1948 until his retirement in 1968. He married Eleanor Blake in 1941, was widowed, and married Antonia Keese in 1959. During the twenties and thirties he was the co-founder of a summer school, St. Peter's School of Liberal and Humane Studies, in Hebron, Connecticut (see *SR* 82 (1974): 481-94; and "In Search of a Vocation," *Michigan Quarterly Review* 11 (1972): 237-47). He was a good organist and at various periods a devout Swedenborgian and Anglican. He was a Fellow of the Kenyon School of English and Senior Fellow of the Indiana School of Letters. He received a Guggenheim in 1961, a literary award from the American Academy of Arts and Letters in 1973, a Litt.D. from Brown University in 1974, and was elected to the National Institute of Arts and Letters in 1975.

Theory of Literature, with René Wellek (New York: Harcourt, 1949), is a treatise on literary theory which defends the "intrinsic" approach (the study of meter, style, symbol, and genre in a literary work) against the "extrinsic" approach (the study of a work in relation to biography, psychology, society, or other ideas). This book is the most important statement of the theory of New Criticism, or Formalism.

Rage for Order: Essays in Criticism (Ann Arbor: University of Michigan Press, 1948) contains summary essays on Edward Taylor, George Herbert, Pope, Hopkins, Yeats, Hawthorne, Kafka, Forster, James.

New England Saints (Ann Arbor: University of Michigan Press, 1956) discusses nineteenth-century New England Men of Letters, including Alcott, Emerson, the elder Henry James, Charles Eliot Norton, Irving Babbitt, and John Brooks Wheelwright.

The New England Conscience (Ann Arbor: University of Michigan Press, 1966) presents case histories of struggles of conscience by New Englanders like Mather, Edwards, Thoreau, Hawthorne, James, and Adams.

Connections (Ann Arbor: University of Michigan Press, 1970) contains essays on Donne, Thomas Browne, Cotton Mather, Dickinson, Paul Elmer More, Eliot, and other Puritans.

Warren also published three scholarly books, *Alexander Pope as Critic and Humanist* (1929), *The Elder Henry James* (1934), and *Richard Crawshaw: A Study of Baroque Sensibility* (1939).

A tribute to Warren, *Teacher and Critic: Essays by and about Austin Warren,* ed. Myron Simon and Harvey Gross (Los Angeles: Plantin Press, 1976), contains a number of Warren's reminiscences, the thoughts of others about him, and a bibliography of his writings. On Warren's writings see also George A. Panichas, "Austin Warren: Man of Letters," *The Reverent Discipline* (Knoxville: University of Tennessee Press, 1974), pp. 394–407.

René Wellek

René Wellek was born on August 22, 1903, in Vienna, Austria, the son of an official in the Austrian, and later the Czechoslovakian, civil service. He attended a *gymnasium* in Prague and studied English and German philology at Charles University there, where in 1926 he was awarded a doctoral degree for his dissertation on Carlyle and Romanticism. He studied at Princeton on a Proctor Fellowship in 1927, then taught at Smith College, and in 1929/30 taught at Princeton. As a docent at Charles University from 1930 to 1935, he was in charge of the teaching of English literature. He married Olga Brodska on December 22, 1932, and they have one son. He was widowed in 1967 and married Nonna Dolodarenko in 1968. From 1935 to 1939 he lectured on the Czech language and Czech literature at the School of Slavonic Studies of the University of London.

After Czechoslovakia was taken over by Hitler, Wellek came to the United States, where from 1939 to 1946 he taught at the University of Iowa. In 1946 he went to Yale as Professor of Slavic and Comparative Literature and in 1952 was appointed Sterling Professor of Comparative Literature there. He was chairman of the Slavic Department from 1948 to 1959, and of the Comparative Literature Department from 1960 until he retired in 1972; he is now Professor Emeritus. Wellek has held many visiting professorships; received Guggenheim awards in 1951–52 and 1957; and was awarded a Fulbright Scholarship in 1959/60. He received the Marjorie Peabody Waite Award of the National Institute of Arts and Letters in 1976. He has received honorary degrees from Lawrence College, Harvard, Oxford, Columbia, Michigan, Maryland, Montreal, Munich, the University of Rome, and other universities; received a Bollingen Prize in 1963; is a member of the American Academy of Arts and Sciences, the American Philosophical Society, and of several foreign academies; and has held many visiting professorships and fellowships.

Wellek's first major work was *Immanuel Kant in England, 1793-1838* (Princeton: Princeton University Press, 1931).

The Rise of English Literary History (Chapel Hill: University of North Carolina Press, 1941; rev. ed., New York: McGraw-Hill, 1966) is a standard treatment of the topic; it extends through 1800.

Theory of Literature, with Austin Warren (New York: Harcourt, 1949), an epoch-making book which was the first systematic study in English of the assumptions on which literary study is conducted, combines the Formalist assumptions of Warren with Wellek's knowledge of continental literary theory: "We have sought to unite 'poetics' (or literary theory), and 'criticism' (evaluation of literature) with 'scholarship' ('research') and 'literary history' " (p. 7). The authors divide criticism into the "extrinsic approach" (the study of biography, psychology, society, ideas, and the other arts) and the "intrinsic approach" (the study of metrics, stylistics, symbols, narrative modes, and genres). They find the intrinsic approach better at analyzing the true nature of poetry, which is a "structure of norms" (p. 138).

A History of Modern Criticism, 1750-1950, 4 vols. to date (New Haven: Yale University Press, 1955-), Wellek's *magnum opus*, surveys criticism in the Western world (England, France, Germany, Italy, and after 1850, Spain, Russia, and the United States) and is an incredible feat of learning. Its subject is the poetics of all imaginative writing, which is conceived as a mean between aesthetics and the practical judgment of literature. Wellek terms its point of view "perspectivism," an attempt to see literature from all sides; its ultimate standard of value is the aesthetic theory of Kant and the German Romantics. Volume 1 is entitled *The Later Eighteenth Century* (1955); volume 2, *The Romantic Age* (1955); volume 3, *The Age of Transition* (1965); and volume 4, *The Later Nineteenth Century* (1965). Two more volumes, on English and American, and on continental, criticism in the twentieth century, are in preparation; several chapters have already appeared.

Essays on Czech Literature (The Hague: Mouton, 1963) contains the most important of Wellek's writings on Czech literature, a bibliography of Wellek's writings in Czech and on Czech or Slavic topics, and an introduction by Peter Demetz.

Concepts of Criticism, ed. Stephen G. Nichols, Jr. (New Haven: Yale University Press, 1963), a collection of Wellek's most important essays, also contains a valuable bibliography of his writings through 1962 (except those in Czech). The essays are surveys of various phrases of contemporary criticism and long, Spitzerian pieces on important topics in literary theory: evolution, Baroque, Realism, Romanticism, form and structure, literary criticism.

Confrontations: Studies in the Intellectual and Literary Relations between Germany, England, and the United States during the Nineteenth Century (Princeton: Princeton University Press, 1965) concentrates on Carlyle, De Quincey, and Emerson.

Discriminations: Further Concepts of Criticism (New Haven: Yale University Press, 1970) is a second collection of essays on such subjects as Classicism and Symbolism, the nature of comparative literature, Kant's aesthetics, the literary theory of the Prague School, stylistics, Dostoevsky criticism, and Leo Spitzer. It also contains a bibliography of Wellek's writings from 1963 to 1969.

The Disciplines of Criticism: Essays in Literary Theory, Interpretation, and History, ed. Peter Demetz, Thomas Greene, and Lowry Nelson, Jr. (New Haven: Yale University Press, 1968) is a Festschrift dedicated to Wellek.

Edmund Wilson

Edmund Wilson was born on May 8, 1895, in Red Bank, New Jersey. The son of a successful lawyer who became a neurotic because he was unable to face the America of the robber-barons, Wilson is more the scion of his mother's pioneer New York family, whose old stone house at Talcottville serves him as a symbol of the values of work, decency, and professionalism of an older America. Wilson was educated at Hill School and Princeton, from which he received a B.A. in 1916. At Princeton he was a contemporary of F. Scott Fitzgerald and John Peale Bishop, was nicknamed "Bunny," and was much influenced by his teacher of French and Italian, Christian Gauss.

Wilson was married four times: to the actress Mary Blair from 1923 to 1929; to Margaret Canby from 1930 to 1932; to Mary McCarthy from 1938 to 1945; and to Elena Thornton in 1946. He also had a romantic attachment to Edna St. Vincent Millay, from 1920 to 1923, which he describes in his memoir of her in *The Shores of Light*. He has three children.

Wilson was a reporter for the New York *Evening Sun* in 1916, served in an army hospital in France during World War I, and came to New York in 1919. There he was managing editor of the fashionable *Vanity Fair* from 1920 to 1923 and from 1921 to 1940 served as book review editor, an associate editor, and member of the board of editors of *The New Republic*. After the Sacco-Vanzetti trial in 1927, he became increasingly involved in Leftist causes, although he was never a Communist. From the fall of 1930 to the spring of 1934, he spent much time reporting political and industrial events, and in 1932 he traveled with Waldo Frank to the mines of Kentucky. In 1934 he began a serious study of Marxism and the Russian Revolution, and in 1935 and 1936 traveled to Russia (whose social system he then idealized) on a Guggenheim Fellowship. His reporting of this period, including *The American Jitters: A Year of the Slump* (1932), was collected in *The American Earthquake* (1958). In the late thirties he moved between New York, his home in Wellfleet, Massachusetts, and Talcottville, writing regularly but holding no job. He tried lecturing briefly at the University of Chicago, Columbia, Smith, and other universities, and served as a regular literary editor and reviewer for *The New Yorker* from 1943 to 1965. Wilson toured Europe in 1945, 1954, and 1963-1964; in 1955 he made a tour of Israel to examine the Dead Sea Scrolls. A number of books resulted from these travels, including *Travels in Two Democracies* (1936), a comparison of Russia and the United States; *Europe without Baedeker: Sketches among the Ruins of Italy, Greece, and England* (1947); *The Scrolls from the Dead Sea* (1955); and *The Dead Sea Scrolls, 1947-1969* (1969). Wilson has written of travels nearer home in *The Boys in the Back Room: Notes on California Novelists* (1941) and *O Canada: An American's Notes on Canadian Culture* (1965). Some sections from the above titles and some scholarly studies are collected in *Red, Black, Blond, and Olive: Studies in Four Civilizations: Zuni, Haiti, Soviet Russia, Israel* (1956). His writings on Russian subjects are gathered in *A Window on Russia* (1972). Although he is not usually classed as a travel writer, these books contain some of his best work, and as an intellectual reporter giving honest (if sometimes opinionated) views of foreign countries and their literary cultures, he ranks as one of the masters of this genre.

Another facet of Wilson's literary achievement is his creative writing. His quasi-autobiographical fictions, *I Thought of Daisy* (1929) and *Memoirs of Hecate County* (1946), give disguised portrayals of literary New York intellectual life in the twenties and thirties. The latter also received much publicity because it was briefly suppressed as being obscene. Wilson also wrote some poetry, collected in *Night Thoughts* (1961); plays, collected in *Five Plays* (1954) and *"The Duke of Palermo" and Other Plays* (1969); and several late volumes of reminiscences: *A Piece of My Mind: Reflections at Sixty* (1956), *Apologies to the Iroquois* (1960), *The Cold War and the Income Tax: A Protest* (1963), and *Upstate* (1971). His notebooks, which he kept from his youth, are being edited for publication by Leon Edel; *A Prelude* (1967), and *The Twenties* (1975) have appeared. Wilson received the National Medal for Literature in 1966, the Aspen Award in 1966, and many other awards. He died on June 12, 1972.

Wilson's literary criticism can be divided empirically into two classes: the volumes containing his short (5-20 page) essays and reviews; and his longer essays and books on a single subject.

The Shores of Light: A Literary Chronicle of the Twenties and Thirties (New York: Farrar, 1952) includes particularly valuable surveys of criticism, "The All-Star Literary Vaudeville" and "American Critics, Left and Right." The prologue and epilogue contain reminiscences of Wilson's teacher Christian Gauss and of Edna St. Vincent Millay.

Classics and Commercials: A Literary Chronicle of the Forties (New York: Farrar, 1950) contains essays on George Saintsbury, Van Wyck Brooks, and the music critic Paul Rosenfeld, as well as Wilson's survey of his career and the critical scene in "Thoughts on Being Bibliographed." Selections from this book and from *Shores of Light* were published in the paperback *A Literary Chronicle, 1900-1950* in 1956.

The Bit Between My Teeth: A Literary Chronicle of 1950-1965 (New York: Farrar, 1965) reprints Wilson's memoir of John Peale Bishop, long essays on Swinburne, Cabell, Beerbohm, dictionaries, and the Marquis de Sade, " 'Miss Buttle' and 'Mr. Eliot,' " "An Interview with Edmund Wilson," and a number of reviews from *The Nation, The New Yorker,* and the *New York Review of Books.*

The Devils and Canon Barham (New York: Farrar, 1973), a final collection, includes Wilson's attack on MLA editions of American authors, a review of *The Waste Land* manuscript, and eight other pieces.

Wilson's more substantial works have reflected a concern with four subjects: symbolism, Marxism, Freud, and American literature.

Axel's Castle: A Study in the Imaginative Literature of 1870-1930 (New York: Scribner's, 1931) is Wilson's first, and perhaps best, book of criticism. Here he announces his credo "of what literary criticism ought to be—a history of man's ideas and imaginings in the setting of the conditions which have shaped them." In this pioneering study, Wilson defines Symbolism as an international literary movement and discusses six Symbolists: Yeats, Valéry, Eliot, Proust, Joyce, and Gertrude Stein.

The Triple Thinkers: Ten Essays on Literature (New York: Harcourt, 1938; rev. ed., New York: Oxford University Press, 1948) contains an account of Wilson's conversation with P. E. More, "Is Verse a Dying Technique?" "Marxism and Literature," "The Politics of Flaubert," "The Ambiguity of Henry James," "Bernard

Shaw at Eighty," and essays on John Jay Chapman, Pushkin, and Housman. In the revised edition Wilson adds an essay on Ben Johnson, a memoir of his prep school teacher Mr. Rolfe, and "The Historical Interpretation of Literature."

To the Finland Station: A Study in the Writing and Acting of History (New York: Harcourt, 1940) is a historical, not a literary, study of the origins of Socialism and Marxism. Useful for the literary critic as background for social criticism, this book embodies Wilson's preoccupations with Marxism and the intellectual as an actor in history during the thirties.

The Wound and the Bow: Seven Studies in Literature (Boston: Houghton Mifflin, 1941) contains a long essay on the social meaning of Dickens's novels and briefer studies of Kipling, Casanova, Wharton, Hemingway, *Finnegans Wake*, and Sophocles' *Philoctetes*.

Patriotic Gore: Studies in the Literature of the American Civil War (New York: Oxford University Press, 1962) is a study of post-Civil War American literature.

Wilson edited a collection of literary documents about American literature, *The Shock of Recognition: The Development of Literature in the United States Recorded by the Men Who Made It* (1943), which contains the reactions of writers on other writers; *The Collected Essays of John Peale Bishop* (1948); and Fitzgerald's *The Last Tycoon* (1941) and *The Crack-Up* (1945).

Richard D. Ramsay has compiled the standard bibliography of works by and about Wilson, *Edmund Wilson: A Bibliography* (New York: Lewis, 1971). A number of letters from Wilson to Christian Gauss are printed in *The Papers of Christian Gauss*, ed. K. G. Jackson and H. Haydn (New York: Random House, 1957), and Wilson's *Letters on Literature and Politics, 1912-1972*, ed. Elena Wilson (New York: Farrar, 1977), collects many other letters. Other volumes of Wilson's letters are forthcoming.

On Wilson see Allen Tate, review of *Axel's Castle, Hound and Horn* 4 (1931): 619-24; Charles I. Glicksberg, "Edmund Wilson: Radicalism at the Cross Roads," *South Atlantic Quarterly* 36 (1937): 466-77; F. W. Dupee, "Edmund Wilson's Criticism" (review of *The Triple Thinkers*), *PR* 4 (1938): 48-51; R. P. Blackmur, review of *The Triple Thinkers, Virginia Quarterly Review* 14 (1938): 445-50; Edward Fiess, "Edmund Wilson: Art and Ideas," *Antioch Review* 1 (1941): 356-67; Delmore Schwartz, "The Writing of Edmund Wilson," *Accent* 2 (1941/42): 177-86; Alfred Kazin, *On Native Grounds* (New York: Reynal & Hitchcock, 1942); George Snell, "Edmund Wilson: The Historical Critic," *Rocky Mountain Review* 8 (1944): 36-44; Granville Hicks, "The Intransigence of Edmund Wilson," *Antioch Review* 6 (1946): 550-62; Robert B. Heilman, "The Freudian Reading of *The Turn of the Screw*," *Modern Language Notes* 62 (1947): 433-45; Robert M. Adams, "Masks and Delays: Edmund Wilson as Critic," *SR* 56 (1948): 272-86; Stanley Edgar Hyman, "Edmund Wilson and Translation in Criticism," *The Armed Vision* (New York: Knopf, 1948), pp. 19-48; Norman Podhoretz, "Edmund Wilson: The Last Patrician, I," *The Reporter*, December 25, 1958, pp. 32-35; idem, "Edmund Wilson: The Last Patrician, II," ibid., January 8, 1959, pp. 25-28; R. J. Kaufman, "The Critic as Custodian of Sanity," *Critical Quarterly* 1 (1959): 85-98; Louis B. Fraiberg, "Edmund Wilson and Psychoanalysis in Historical Criticism," *Psychoanalysis and American Literary Criticism* (Detroit: Wayne State University Press, 1960), pp. 161-82; John Henry Raleigh, "America Revisited" (review of *Patriotic*

Gore), PR 29 (1962): 425-36; Daniel Aaron, "Edmund Wilson's War" (review of Patriotic Gore), *Massachusetts Review* 3 (1962): 555-70; Charles H. Foster, review of *Patriotic Gore, New England Quarterly* 35 (1962): 524-26; Marius Bewley, "Northern Saints and Southern Knights," *HR* 15 (1962): 431-39; Keith Botsford, "The American Plutarch, The Last Roman, or Plain Mr. Wilson," *Texas Quarterly* 6, no. 3 (1963): 129-40; Eleanor Perenyi, "Wilson," *Esquire,* July 1963, pp. 80 ff.; Louis D. Rubin, "Edmund Wilson and the Despot's Heel" (review of *Patriotic Gore*), *SR* 71 (1963): 109-15; Irving Howe, "Edmund Wilson and the Sea Slugs," *A World More Attractive* (New York: Horizon Press, 1963), pp. 300-307; Alfred Kazin, "The Imagination of a Man of Letters," *American Scholar* 34 (1964/65): 19-27; Sherman Paul, *Edmund Wilson: A Study of Literary Vocation in Our Time* (Urbana: University of Illinois Press, 1965); Vladimir Nabokov, "Nabokov's Reply," *Encounter,* February 1966, pp. 80-89; Frank Kermode, "Edmund Wilson's Achievement," ibid., May 1966, pp. 61-70; Richard Gilman, "Edmund Wilson, Then and Now," *The New Republic,* July 2, 1966, pp. 25-28; Werner Berthoff, *Edmund Wilson* (Minneapolis: University of Minnesota Pamphlets, 1968); Arthur Mizener, "Edmund Wilson's New Republic," *The New Republic,* May 9, 1970, pp. 28-30; Charles P. Frank, *Edmund Wilson* (New York: Twayne, 1970); Leonard Kriegel, *Edmund Wilson* (Carbondale: Southern Illinois University Press, 1971); Werner Berthoff, "Edmund Wilson and His Civil War," *Fictions and Events* (New York: Dutton, 1971), pp. 264-87; Haim Genizi, "Edmund Wilson and *The Modern Monthly,* 1934-5: A Phase in Wilson's Radicalism," *Journal of American Studies* 7 (1973): 301-19; George H. Douglas, "Edmund Wilson: The Critic as Artist," *Texas Quarterly* 17, no. 4 (1974): 58-72; Matthew Josephson, "Encounters with Edmund Wilson," *SoR* n.s. 11 (1975): 731-65; Pearl K. Bell, "Edmund Wilson's *Axel's Castle,"* *Daedalus* 105, no. 1 (1976): 115-25; and Robert Alter, "Edmund Wilson vs. America," *Commentary,* January 1978, pp. 29-35.

W. K. Wimsatt

William Kurtz Wimsatt was born in Washington, D.C., on November 17, 1907. He received a B.A. from Georgetown University in 1928, an M.A. in 1929, and his Ph.D. from Yale University in 1939. He married Margaret Hecht in 1944 and they have two children. He was a Roman Catholic.

From 1930 to 1935 Wimsatt was head of the English Department of Portsmouth Priory School in Rhode Island, and in 1935/36 was an assistant professor at the Catholic University of America. In 1939 he began teaching at Yale, where he was promoted to professor in 1955 and Sterling Professor in 1975. He received several honorary degrees and was awarded a Guggenheim in 1947. He died in 1975.

The Verbal Icon: Studies in the Meaning of Poetry (Lexington: University of Kentucky Press, 1954) collects Wimsatt's early essays, including the famous "The Intentional Fallacy" and "The Affective Fallacy" (written with Monroe Beardsley). The other essays, also largely theoretical arguments for Formalist criticism, include "The Concrete Universal," "Explication as Criticism," "History and Criticism: A Problematic Relationship," and "Poetry and Christian Thinking."

Literary Criticism: A Short History (New York: Knopf, 1957) was written with

Cleanth Brooks, but Wimsatt claims responsibility mainly for the historical chapters. (See also under Brooks.)

Hateful Contraries: Studies in Literature and Criticism (Lexington: University of Kentucky Press, 1965) collects Wimsatt's later essays. He inveighs in the introduction against the "new amateurism" and in "Horses of Wrath: Recent Critical Lessons" states his own support for a "tensional" view of criticism, which reconciles genetic, affective, formal, and didactic views of criticism in a way that is more sympathetic to the religious mind. The book also contains "The Criticism of Comedy," "The Augustan Mode in English Poetry," and studies of Aristotle, Boswell, and T. S. Eliot.

Day of the Leopards: Essays in Defense of Poems (New Haven: Yale University Press, 1976), a miscellaneous collection of essays, repeats old themes, including four on the eighteenth century, and discussions of genesis, mimesis, Frye, Richards, organic form, etc.

Wimsatt published three scholarly books on the eighteenth century: *The Prose Style of Samuel Johnson* (1941), *Philosophic Words: A Study of Style and Meaning in the Rambler and Dictionary of Samual Johnson* (1948), and *The Portraits of Alexander Pope* (1965). He edited part of the Yale edition of the Boswell Papers with F. A. Pottle, *Boswell for the Defence, 1769-74* (New York: McGraw-Hill, 1959); the English Institute volumes of *English Stage Comedy* (1955); and *Explication as Criticism* (1963), *Literary Criticism: Idea and Act* (1974), and other works.

The best article on Wimsatt's criticism is Eliseo Vivas, "Mr. Wimsatt on the Theory of Literature," *Comparative Literature* 7 (1955): 344-61. See also René Wellek, "The Literary Theory of William K. Wimsatt," *Yale Review* 66 (1977): 178-92.

A Festschrift published in Wimsatt's honor, *Literary Theory and Structure*, ed. Frank Brady, John Palmer, and Martin Price (New Haven: Yale University Press, 1973), contains a selected bibliography of his writings.

Yvor Winters

Arthur Yvor Winters was born in Chicago on October 17, 1900, and grew up in Chicago and various West Coast cities. He attended the University of Chicago and the University of Colorado, where he received a B.A. (1925) and an M.A. in romance languages. He was hospitalized for tuberculosis near Sante Fe from 1918 to 1921. He taught for two years at the University of Idaho and in 1927 returned to graduate school at Stanford University, where he received his Ph.D. in English literature in 1934 and remained for the rest of his career, becoming a professor in 1949. He married the writer Janet Lewis, and they have two children. Winters was a Fellow of the Indiana School of Letters and the American Academy of Arts and Sciences. He received a Guggenheim in 1961 and several awards for his poetry, including a National Institute of Arts and Letters Award in 1952, a Bollingen Prize in 1960, and a Brandeis University Creative Arts Award in 1963. He died on January 25, 1968.

Primitivism and Decadence: A Study of American Experimental Poetry (New York: Arrow Editions, 1937) considers "the forms of unconscious and of conscious obscurantism which are the ultimate development of Romantic aesthetic principles"

(*DR* 53) and discusses the relationship of meter and convention to good poetry in Williams, Pound, Eliot, Stevens, and others.

Maule's Curse: Seven Studies in the History of American Obscurantism (Norfolk, Conn.: New Directions, 1938) contains studies of Hawthorne, Cooper, Melville, Emerson, Poe, Dickinson, Henry James, and Jones Very.

The Anatomy of Nonsense (Norfolk, Conn.: New Directions, 1943) includes studies of Henry Adams, Wallace Stevens, T. S. Eliot, and John Crowe Ransom, whom Winters attacks for liberalism, obscurity, hedonism, determinism, nominalism, and other Romantic sins.

Edwin Arlington Robinson (New York: New Directions, 1946) serves as an introduction to Robinson.

In Defense of Reason (Denver: Swallow Press, 1947) reprints *Primitivism and Decadence, Maule's Curse,* and *Anatomy of Nonsense,* and includes a new essay on Hart Crane.

The Function of Criticism (Denver: Swallow Press, 1957) collects essays on Hopkins, Frost, and sixteenth-century English literature, "The Audible Reading of Poetry," and "Problems for the Modern Critic."

On Modern Poets (New York: World, 1957) reprints essays on Stevens, Eliot, Ransom, Crane, Hopkins, and Frost.

Forms of Discovery (Denver: Swallow Press, 1967) marks Winters's effort "to define what seems to me the most important forms that poetry has taken in modern English, that is, from about 1500 to our time" (p. xxii). Winters emphasizes sixteenth-century verse, Charles Churchill, and poetry after 1900; and dismisses most poetry of the eighteenth and nineteenth centuries as "sentimental-romantic decadence" (p. 147).

Yvor Winters: Uncollected Essays and Reviews (Chicago: Swallow Press, 1973) is edited and introduced by Francis Murphy.

Winters also published several volumes of poetry, beginning with *The Immobile Wind* in 1921. His *Collected Poems* was published in 1952. He edited *Twelve Poets of the Pacific* (1937), and *Twelve Poets of the Pacific: Second Series* (1949).

On Winters see Kenneth A. Lohf and Eugene P. Sheehy, *Yvor Winters: A Bibliography* (Denver: Swallow Press, 1959); G. Stone, "Poetry and Morals," *American Review* 9 (1937): 58–79; Delmore Schwartz, "Primitivism and Decadence," *SoR* 3 (1938): 597–614; Randall Jarrell, "The Morality of Mr. Winters," *KR* 1 (1939): 211–15; R. P. Blackmur, "A Note on Yvor Winters," *Poetry* 57 (1940/41): 144–52; John Crowe Ransom, "Yvor Winters: The Logical Critic," *The New Criticism* (Norfolk, Conn.: New Directions, 1941), pp. 211–75. Alan Swallow, "An Examination of Modern Critics: 6. Yvor Winters," *Western Review* 9 (1944): 31–37; T. Weiss, "The Nonsense of Winters' *Anatomy,*" *Quarterly Review of Literature* 1 (1944): 212–34, 300–318, (cf. Winters's reply, ibid. 2 (1945): 133–41); William Barrett, "Temptations of St. Yvor," *KR* 9 (1947): 532–51; Stanley Edgar Hyman, "Yvor Winters and Evaluation in Criticism," *The Armed Vision* (New York: Knopf, 1948); Marshall Van Deusen, "In Defense of Yvor Winters," *Thought* 32 (1957): 409–36; Keith F. McKean, *The Moral Measure of Literature* (Denver: Swallow Press, 1961); Robert Kimbrough, "Discipline of Saving Grace: Winters' Critical Position," *Renascence* 15 (1963): 62–67; John Holloway, "The Critical Theory of Yvor Winters," *Critical Quarterly* 7 (1965): 54–68; Paul Ramsay, "Yvor Winters:

Some Abstractions against Abstraction," *SR* 71 (1965): 451-64; Miller Williams, "Yvor Winters . . . ," in *Nine Essays*, ed. Donald Stanford (Baton Rouge: Louisiana State University Press, 1965), pp. 159-79; Leonard Greenbaum, "Yvor Winters and the Pacific Writers," *The Hound and Horn: The History of a Literary Quarterly* (The Hague: Mouton, 1966), pp. 160-88; Donald E. Stanford, "Yvor Winters, 1900-1968," *SoR* n. s. 4 (1968): 861-63; John Fraser, articles cited in note 91 of Chapter 5; Jonas A. Barish, "Yvor Winters and Antimimetic Prejudice," *New Literary History* 2 (1971): 419-44; Philip Hobsbaum, "The Discovery of Form," *Michigan Quarterly Review* 12 (1973): 235-42; Richard Sexton, *The Complex of Yvor Winters' Criticism* (The Hague: Mouton, 1974); René Wellek, "Yvor Winters Rehearsed and Reconsidered," *Denver Quarterly* 10, no. 3 (1975): 1-27; Grosvenor E. Powell, "Being, Poetry, and Yvor Winters' Criticism," ibid., pp. 54-66; W. W. Robson, "Yvor Winters: Counter-Romantic," *Essays in Criticism* 25 (1975): 169-77; Thomas Parkinson, "Hart Crane and Yvor Winters: A Meeting of Minds," *SoR*, n.s. 11 (1975): 491-512; and Gerald Graff, "Yvor Winters of Stanford," *American Scholar* 44 (1975): 291-98.

Index

The Johns Hopkins University Press

*This book was composed in Compugraphic English Times text and
display type by Action Comp. Co., Inc., from a design by Susan Bishop.
It was printed on 50-lb. Number 66 Eggshell Offset paper and bound in
Joanna Arrestox cloth by Universal Lithographers, Inc.*

Library of Congress Cataloging in Publication Data

Webster, Grant.
  The republic of letters.

  Includes bibliographical references and index.
  1. Criticism—United States—History. I. Title.
PS78.W4   801'.95   79-4951
ISBN 0-8018-2175-4